BEA WebLogic
Server™ Bible

2nd Edition

BEA WebLogic Server™ Bible

2nd Edition

Joe Zuffoletto and Lou Miranda

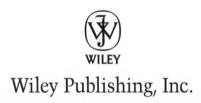

Wiley Publishing, Inc.

BEA WebLogic Server™ Bible, 2nd Edition

Published by
Wiley Publishing, Inc.
10475 Crosspoint Boulevard
Indianapolis, IN 46256
www.wiley.com

Library of Congress Control Number: 2003101898

ISBN: 0-7645-2602-2

Manufactured in the United States of America

10 9 8 7 6 5 4 3 2 1

2B/RQ/QW/QT/IN

About the Authors

Lou Miranda is a consultant specializing in J2EE technologies and Web services. He is owner and lead consultant for MirandaCorp.com, Inc., and has worked at major insurance, medical device, and manufacturing corporations. He has also worked through large consulting companies such as PricewaterhouseCoopers and KPMG Consulting. His Java and WebLogic experience has included architecting membership, payment, production line, and insurance systems, as well as a Web services proof of concept. Other writing assignments have included a stint as a Contributing Editor at *PC World* magazine, and articles for several programming magazines. He also holds a Masters degree in Molecular Biology.

Lou recently started a series of WebLogic training videos on DVD (`www.GeekSpeakPress.com`).

Joe Zuffoletto is a system architect specializing in application servers and their integration with other host systems. After receiving a computer science degree from Princeton in 1987, he began working with application servers in 1990, when he wrote a number of them for clients in the financial services and technology industries. These servers were based on a C++ framework he developed and enhanced over a five-year span, and they provided server-side execution of business logic, as well as access to embedded and separate relational database systems.

Joe has since left the hard work of writing application servers to others, such as BEA and Sun. He is currently president and co-owner of ZeeWare, Inc. (`www.zeeware.com`), a systems integration firm focused on building J2EE solutions with WebLogic Server. He lives with his wife in Sausalito, California.

Credits

Acquisitions Editor
Jim Minatel

Project Editor
Chandani Thapa

Technical Editor
Kunal Mittal

Copy Editor
Nancy Sixsmith

Editorial Manager
Mary Beth Wakefield

**Vice President & Executive
Group Publisher**
Richard Swadley

**Vice President and Executive
Publisher**
Bob Ipsen

Vice President and Publisher
Joseph B. Wikert

Executive Editorial Director
Mary Bednarek

Project Coordinator
Kristie Rees

Graphics and Production Specialists
Amanda Carter
Jennifer Click
Sean Decker
Joyce Haughey
Stephanie D. Jumper
Mary Gillot Virgin

Quality Control Technician
Laura Albert

Proofreading and Indexing
TECHBOOKS Production Services

*To my father, Joe Sr., who
gave me the courage to start
and the discipline to finish.*

Joe Zuffoletto

*In memory of my father, who
instilled in me the quest for the
new and the quest for the best.*

Lou Miranda

Foreword

The computer industry innovates at an unprecedented pace producing multiple technological revolutions — involving changes so dramatic they shift the entire industry — within a relatively short time period. Thirty years ago, computers were enormous, complex, and expensive, making them only economically feasible to large corporations, universities, and government. With the personal computer revolution, that same technology has arrived in schools, homes, and nearly every business. Application software such as Microsoft's Office and its predecessors rode this revolution and dramatically increased productivity in almost every industry. More recently, we've experienced the network revolution. Instead of computers exchanging information via floppy disks and isolated private networks, we've built a worldwide distributed network bridging disparate systems via common protocols such as TCP/IP and HTTP. Just as word processors and spreadsheets became vital office tools, computer networking both in the office and across the Internet has transformed how we work and live.

Each major revolution inspires many smaller technological changes, producing a drastically different computing landscape. During the Internet revolution, Sun Microsystems released its Java programming language to a world of eager programmers. Until this time, most systems programming was done in C or C++, and every programmer endured countless hours debugging memory problems or porting to different architectures. Java rode the sweeping Internet changes and brought garbage collection, safe programming, and multi-platform support into widespread use. Along with Sun's J2EE APIs, BEA WebLogic Server brought the ideas of Java to server-side enterprise computing. Instead of writing low-level system code or dealing with proprietary interfaces and programming languages, WebLogic Server provided the platform for developing these new Java-based enterprise applications.

Many in the software industry believe we are at the forefront of another major revolution. Traditionally large enterprises use a variety of different architectures and vital corporate data lives in separate and incompatible systems. Connecting and sharing information between these systems requires expensive custom programming and gives only limited functionality. With the advent of XML and Web services, a new platform for enterprise integration has arrived. Instead of exchanging proprietary binary information over custom interfaces, Web services and XML provide structured data integration over standard, Internet protocols. With BEA WebLogic Server 7.0, you have the tools to embrace and ride this integration revolution.

The software industry continues to innovate at a rapid pace so it is vital to have guides like the *BEA WebLogic Server Bible* to lead you into this new world. This book provides you with the foundation to build these next-generation applications on the WebLogic platform. With the WebLogic Server tools and guidance from this book, I hope you are able to inspire the next technological revolution and bring us all to a new world.

Rob Woollen

Staff Software Engineer

BEA WebLogic Server

Preface

Welcome to *BEA WebLogic Serve Bible,* 2nd Edition, a book designed to help you understand and apply the power of BEA WebLogic Server to help solve your organization's most complex distributed computing problems. This book is written for developers who have a decent knowledge of Java and the Java 2 Platform, Enterprise Edition (J2EE), but are either working with WebLogic Server for the first time or further honing their existing WebLogic skills. In other words, this book assumes you have experience with Java and J2EE, but not necessarily with WebLogic.

Why Do You Need This Book?

Perhaps you're thinking of buying this book because you've just downloaded and installed the trial version of WebLogic Server and have no idea what to do next. Or maybe you've become lost in the lush forest of WebLogic documentation on BEA's Web site and you're looking for a trail map. Or perhaps you've been programming WebLogic since the good old Tengah days and you're looking for additional insights on some of the newer features. Whatever your reasons for picking up this book, if you're looking for broad and fairly deep coverage of WebLogic Server, with a healthy balance between theory and hands-on learning, then this book is for you.

WebLogic Server is a large, complex product whose feature set can be positively overwhelming to newcomers. WebLogic's documentation, although excellent, is equally overwhelming, consisting of over 40 manuals and dozens of tutorials and samples. To the uninitiated, just figuring out how to learn WebLogic is a difficult job. This book is designed to take some of the pain out of that endeavor.

Although WebLogic Server is based on the Java 2 Platform, Enterprise Edition (J2EE), and although this book covers many of J2EE's features, this book will not teach you J2EE programming. In-depth coverage of that topic can be found on Sun's Web site (at http://java.sun.com/j2ee/tutorial/1_3-fcs/index.html), or in a number of other books, such as the *Java 2 Enterprise Edition Bible*.

Like all software products, WebLogic Server and the J2EE are constantly changing and evolving. This book is based on WebLogic Server 7.0 and the J2EE SDK version 1.3.

Cross-Reference — Be sure to visit the WebLogic Bible Web site (www.wiley.com/compbooks/zuffoletto), where you will find the complete source code listings for the book, along with updates, errata, and more!

How This Book Is Organized

Most computer scientists are familiar with the "divide-and-conquer" approach to programming, where programmers divide large programming problems into smaller ones that are more easily understood and solved. The same approach works well for learning WebLogic Server, and the organization of this book reflects that.

There is no required order for reading the chapters in this book. In fact, it's so comprehensive, you'd have a hard time reading it from cover to cover. Start wherever your immediate interest lies, and then jump to whichever chapters you need for background material. If you do read it from cover to cover, rest assured that the chapters do build upon each other. For example, chapters on writing EJBs come after chapters explaining JDBC, JNDI, and RMI, all technologies relevant to EJBs.

Note Whichever order you choose, we highly recommend you at least skim through Appendix B before doing any serious coding, building, or deploying. This appendix explains the basics about setting up a command line build environment. It can be very frustrating to get classpath and other build errors; Appendix B steers you through the requirements for getting productive right away. It's well worth the read if for no other reason than all the examples use Ant to build and run them, and Ant basics are explained in this appendix.

Part I: Preparing Your Enterprise for WebLogic

The book begins by explaining what WebLogic Server is and what its capabilities are. It goes on to explain how to assemble a WebLogic development team and how to design good WebLogic applications. It closes by showing you how to construct an efficient WebLogic development environment on your network. This part of the book is completely non-technical, directed not only at prospective WebLogic developers, but also to managers who are thinking of adopting WebLogic Server and want to understand the impact it will have on their organization.

Part II: WebLogic and the J2EE APIs

This section begins the technical portion of the book. Its chapters explain, in depth, how WebLogic implements each of the J2EE APIs, including JDBC (database access), JTA (transaction processing), RMI (distributed applications), JNDI (network and directory lookups), JMS (messaging), and JavaMail (electronic mail processing). The approach of each chapter is to explain the background and architecture of each API, show how to write and deploy a simple package in WebLogic Server using the API, and then move on with more advanced examples. Unlike the WebLogic documentation, which often segregates development and administrative information into different manuals, our approach is to put all this information in one place, for easy reference by the developer.

Part III: Developing Web Components

Virtually everyone who buys WebLogic Server uses it to write Web components, which include Java servlets, Java Server Pages (JSPs), and tag libraries. This important part of the book shows how to build, deploy, and manage these key components in the WebLogic environment. Servlets were the first successful server-side Java Web technology. They solved problems with older non-Java server-side technologies, such as CGI, because servlets are multithreaded. Servlets often use many of the APIs that were discussed in Part II, such as JDBC for database access and JNDI for looking up resources. We discuss how to create servlets, including how to store information in a session object, and how to implement security via a login process. JSPs build upon servlets by factoring out commonality and separating design from content, thus making them easier to program and maintain. We explain how to set up WebLogic for easy development and debugging of JSPs, how to handle errors, and how to use JSPs with servlets in an instance of a common design pattern. Tag Libraries expand on JSPs by allowing you to write tags — much like HTML tags — in which you can define and program their specific functionality. These are reusable, so you can keep tag libraries in different applications.

Part IV: Developing EJB Components

This part of the book builds on Part II, which covered the J2EE APIs. This section covers EJBs, which allow you to create easy to maintain, scalable, secure, transaction-aware code. It also builds on Part III, since EJBs are often the back end for a system fronted by Web applications. We start off with a broad overview of EJBs, since there are several types and subtypes. EJBs are powerful, and with that power comes significant complexity. Each of the following three chapters covers one of the major types of EJBs: session, entity, and message-driven. Session beans come in two flavors — stateless and stateful — and we discuss the similarities and differences. Then we explain how to code session beans with an example of each type. Even stateful session beans are only meant to store their information for a limited time; they're not considered persistent as are entity EJBs. Entity beans also come in two types: those with container-managed persistence (CMP) and those with bean-managed persistence (BMP). We discuss the pros and cons of choosing CMP or BMP, as well as some of the recent improvements to CMP in the EJB 2.0 specification. We go through an example of each type, including the deployment descriptors that are especially important in CMP. Message-driven EJBs are the newest type of enterprise bean, and we discuss their evolution from JMS. We contrast message-driven beans with using JMS, and then show an example of how to go about creating this kind of EJB.

Part V: Deploying and Testing Enterprise Applications

Designing, writing, and building WebLogic applications is important, but what happens when you're ready to go to production? Deploying applications on a local copy of WebLogic is easy, but complexities arise when packaging for deployment on test and production servers. We cover how WARs, JARs, and EARs are packaged, and some of the things to watch out for when packaging them. Classloading is a particularly thorny issue, and we give it a once-over along with an evaluation of different ways of attacking the problem. Once deployed, your application needs to be tested. Does it work? Is it fast enough? We cover the basics of performance tuning, and how to use WebLogic Server features to monitor the performance of your applications. Then we cover tuning WebLogic itself, along with JVM and application tuning. We conclude with an example of how you might go about tuning a real application.

Part VI: Implementing Security

WebLogic Server 7.0 introduces a completely new and robust security infrastructure that can stand on its own or integrate with outside security architectures. This part of the book explains some of the theory behind securing enterprise computing systems, and then explains WebLogic's new security architecture. It closes by showing how to secure WebLogic resources using a variety of approaches and methods.

Part VII: WebLogic Server Administration

This part of the book introduces you to WebLogic's administration tools and shows you how to use them to manage WebLogic domains, servers, clusters, and security. WebLogic Server 7.0 introduces new features for clustering and a completely new security architecture, and these chapters will get you up and running right away.

Part VIII: Enterprise Application Integration

Web Services and SOAP are two of the newest additions to the enterprise developer's toolkit, and WebLogic Server supports them both. You can code them by hand or use the newly introduced WebLogic Workshop to automate much of the drudgery of designing, developing, testing, and deploying Web services. This part of the book shows you how to work with these emerging technologies in the context of WebLogic Server and Workshop, and it also shows how WebLogic can be used in conjunction with the J2EE Connector Architecture to integrate with existing corporate systems.

Appendixes

The first appendix explains the major differences between WebLogic 7.0 and earlier versions and gives tips for migrating older WebLogic applications to the newest version. New to this second edition of the book, Appendix B explains many of the bundled tools and how they can make your development and deployment easier and faster. It even includes a jumpstart for Ant, the build tool that will undoubtedly become your best friend.

What You'll Need

To gain the most benefit from this book, you'll need a workstation loaded up with the following software:

✦ BEA WebLogic Server 7.0 (a free, fully functional trial version is available for download at `http://www.bea.com`).

✦ Sun's J2EE SDK, version 1.3 (a copy of this is included with the WebLogic Server trial version).

Optional items include the following:

✦ A relational database, such as Microsoft SQL Server or Oracle. (WebLogic Server ships with a demo version of PointBase relational database, but if your organization uses one of the other two then you should figure out how to work with it right away.)

✦ An integrated development environment (IDE) for Java, such as Borland JBuilder (`http://www.borland.com`).

✦ An SMTP-compliant mail server, if you plan to write applications that will process incoming or outgoing electronic mail.

Conventions Used in This Book

As you go through this book, you will find a few unique elements in nearly every chapter, such as source code listings and special icons that draw your attention to important tidbits of information.

Source Code

Any time you encounter source code, it will be in a special font; this applies to code listings as well as code fragments. This way, it's easy to identify code throughout the book. Whether in a fragment or a numbered listing, code in the text appears in the following style:

```
package bible.servlets;
import javax.servlet.*;
import javax.servlet.http.*;
import java.io.*;
import java.util.*;

public class MyServlet extends HttpServlet {
  public void service(HttpServletRequest request,
                      HttpServletResponse response)
    throws IOException {
    String servletName = this.getServletName();
    response.setContentType("text/html");
    PrintWriter out = response.getWriter();
    out.println("<html>");
    out.println("<head><title>" + servletName +
                "</title></head>");
    out.println("<body>");
    out.println("<p>Welcome to the servlet called " +
                servletName + ".</p>");
    out.println("</body></html>");
  }
}
```

Code elements that appear in the running text, such as the names of objects, classes, variables, methods, and so on, are also shown in the code font — for example, the MyServlet class or the service() method — as are file and folder names and Web URLs.

Command-line Entries

Any time a command-line entry appears in the book, it will reside on its own line and in the code style to distinguish it from the rest of the text. Command-line entries are "generic;" they don't appear in a certain format such as DOS or Unix. This is because most of the entries will work on either platform, as long as you follow the conventions for the platform you are using.

Icons

A number of special icons appear throughout the book to call your attention to topics of special relevance and interest.

The Note icon is used to bring your attention to things you might otherwise be tempted to highlight with a fluorescent marker.

The Tip icon is used to point out a tip or technique that will save you time, effort, money, or all three!

The Caution icon is used to alert you to potential problems that might wreak havoc in your WebLogic environment. Throughout the text, this icon pinpoints bugs, errors, oversights, gaffes, and anything else that may spoil your WebLogic experience.

The Cross-Reference icon refers you to other sections and chapters in the book, as well as to the book's Web site (www.wiley.com/compbooks/zuffoletto), and other Web sites that contain additional coverage of the topic being discussed. Often these sites are provided to give you information that can't be squeezed into this book, such as articles, API documentation, source code, or other resources that we hope you'll find valuable in your quest to become a WebLogic expert.

Contacting the Authors

We welcome your questions, comments, and constructive criticism regarding the book. Please do not submit questions about WebLogic Server or code you're trying to debug. You can contact Joe at joe@zeeware.com and Lou at Lou@MirandaCorp.com.

Acknowledgments

If you've ever thought of writing a book "for fun," please check your fantasy at the door.

That being said, writing this book has been a very rewarding experience. It's a great feeling knowing that you are writing something in a simple manner so your readers will not encounter the trials and tribulations that you have endured. It helps a lot that I'm standing on the shoulders of giants — Joe Zuffoletto and the other contributors to the first edition. I also ended up working with a great set of folks along the way.

I am indebted to Diana Reid of BEA who put me in touch with the fine folks at Wiley, and directed my technical inquiries to the right people at BEA. Thanks, too, to all the people at BEA who produce such awesome products.

Jim Minatel, an acquisitions editor at Wiley, stewarded me through the change from my being a contributor to the second edition to being the author. Updating an 1100+ page Bible is a daunting task that Jim's patience and good humor made much easier. My perfectionist tendencies (thanks, Dad!) caused untold grief for James Russell, development editor, and Chandani Thapa, project editor. They have more patience than I thought humanly possible. James, along with Nancy Sixsmith, did a wonderful job of finessing and clarifying my writing. I can only hope that their grief is paid back by you, the reader, getting the best book possible and spreading the word. Thanks, too, to Kunal for his technical reviewing skills.

Thanks also to my overworked and underappreciated wife, Karen, who never once said, "What? You've been home all day and you haven't cooked dinner?" even though I'm sure she was thinking it. Karen, you are truly the light of my life. My mother and siblings provided moral support and understanding, especially during an abbreviated Christmas and New Year's.

My contribution to this book would not have been possible without the critiques and camaraderie of the people I've worked with over the years. Thanks to Roy, Eswar, & Wes; Jeremy, Teddy, & Sharon; Suzie, Son, Mike, Heather, Chris, Jason, & Arum; and Norbert, Karen, Joe, & Dan. Unfortunately, there are others too numerous to mention.

Finally, two things transformed the day-to-day work on this book from the ordinary to the joyful. First, kudos to the architect of our 100-year-old house, whose appreciation of the natural world and the seasons produced a wonderful writing environment. The large, south-facing windows made the most of the feeble Minnesota sun, brightening and warming a house subject to many sub-zero days and nights. This is in stark contrast to a windowless, joyless, bland cubicle where, in 1984-esque fashion, our every phone call, e-mail, Web surfing, and physical comings and goings are tracked, stored, tabulated, and reported on. (What have we in the software field wrought upon ourselves?) The other joy was my Apple iBook running Unix (Macintosh OS X). This gave me a cool and ultraportable Unix box that allowed me to write and test the text and sample code for this book, all the while grooving to Internet radio (CelticMelt on Live365.com) on iTunes.

Lou Miranda

Saint Paul, MN

Contents at a Glance

Contents

Part II: WebLogic and the J2EE APIs   81

Part IV: Developing EJB Components 417

Part VIII: Enterprise Application Integration   777

Chapter 26: Web Services with WebLogic Server 779

Chapter 27: Web Services with WebLogic Workshop 807

Chapter 28: Working with WebLogic and the J2EE Connector
Architecture 841

Preparing Your Enterprise for WebLogic

A Quick Tour of WebLogic Server

In this chapter, we take you on a quick tour of WebLogic Server (often referred to simply as "WebLogic"). We introduce you to WebLogic and fire it up to show you what it looks like. After showing how some of WebLogic's capabilities are used in real-world Web sites, we'll show you some of WebLogic's components in more detail and discuss how they fit into its overall architecture. The chapter closes with a few questions that you can ask yourself to determine whether WebLogic is right for *your* projects.

Introducing WebLogic Server

WebLogic Server is an industrial-strength application server developed and marketed by BEA Systems, Inc. of San Jose, California. WebLogic is a pure-Java implementation of the *Java 2 Platform, Enterprise Edition*, more commonly known as *J2EE*. J2EE represents Sun's serious effort to make Java a powerful platform for developing enterprise applications. It defines a set of runtime architectures, network services, and application programming interfaces (APIs) that make it easy for developers to write distributed network-aware software components and applications. WebLogic has long been recognized as one of the best (if not *the* best (J2EE implementations on the market.

Note Although this book is not intended to be a tutorial on J2EE, WebLogic and J2EE are so tightly bound that you will inevitably learn a great deal about J2EE from this book. For the most part, however, we assume that you are already familiar with J2EE.

The shipping version of WebLogic Server at the time of this writing is 7.0. Version 7.0 has a lot in common with its immediate predecessors, especially versions 5.1, 6.0, and 6.1, but there are also significant differences. Therefore, instead of trying to cover multiple versions of WebLogic Server, this book focuses on version 7.0.

Like a database or mail server, WebLogic runs almost invisibly on a computer and provides services to clients that connect to it. The most common use of WebLogic is to deliver secure data-driven applications to Web clients over corporate intranets or the Internet. But WebLogic can also be used as a general-purpose application server for non-Web clients such as wireless devices and desktop applications. Basically, if you can design it with J2EE, you can build it and run it with WebLogic.

The WebLogic Server family consists of two products:

✦ WebLogic Server: the focus of this book.

✦ WebLogic Express: WebLogic Server without EJBs, RMI, and CORBA, used for building Web applications only. It comes in basic (no clustering) and premium (clustering support built in) editions.

WebLogic Server is part of BEA's WebLogic Platform family of technologies. This product line contains several products that run on top of WebLogic Server. Although some of these products are beyond the scope of this book, you may want to explore them further on your own. The following list briefly describes these products:

✦ WebLogic Portal: for managing access to Web-based information by customers, employees, and partners

✦ WebLogic Integration: for managing business processes, application integration using JCA, and B2B integration

✦ WebLogic Workshop: for simplifying the creation of Web services that run on WebLogic Server

These products provide many common capabilities that you may not want to write yourself. You can find more information about them at the following URL:

```
http://bea.com/products/weblogic/platform/index.shtml
```

The WebLogic product line runs on all of today's popular enterprise computing platforms, including Windows NT/2000, Sun Solaris, HP/UX, IBM AS/400, and Linux. Because WebLogic is a pure Java product, it is installed, configured, and managed almost identically on all platforms.

Companies around the world use WebLogic Server to build large-scale, industrial-strength Web applications for both internal and external use. They choose WebLogic because of its performance, reliability, cross-platform capability, versatility, and strong support for the J2EE standard. With WebLogic Server, you can do the following:

✦ Host Web sites for one or more Internet domains on one computer with one IP address, on multiple computers bundled together in a cluster, or on multiple computers managed by a proxy server

✦ Deploy server-side Java code written to the J2EE standard, including servlets, JavaServer Pages (JSPs), JavaBeans, and Enterprise JavaBeans (EJBs)

✦ Deploy Web services based on the SOAP, WSDL, and UDDI specifications

✦ Integrate disparate computing systems using J2EE's extensive network services, including JDBC for database connectivity, JMS for messaging, JNDI for network directory access, JTA for distributed transactions, and JavaMail for electronic mail

✦ Deploy Java-only distributed applications by using Remote Method Invocation (RMI)

✦ Deploy CORBA-accessible distributed applications by using RMI over Internet Inter-ORB Protocol (RMI-IIOP)

✦ Implement robust security by using Secure Sockets Layer (SSL) and WebLogic's built-in support for user authentication and authorization

✦ Provide high availability, load balancing, and failover by combining multiple WebLogic servers into a cluster

✦ Take advantage of Java's cross-platform capabilities by deploying WebLogic servers on Windows NT/2000, Sun Solaris, HP/UX, and other operating systems supported by WebLogic

✦ Easily manage one or more WebLogic servers on your network, regardless of platform, by using WebLogic's intuitive, Web-based management and monitoring tools

Now that you have some idea of what WebLogic is, let's take it for a spin on a Windows 2000 machine and see what it looks like.

Taking WebLogic for a Spin

WebLogic Server runs either as an application or service on Windows 2000. In this section, you're going to start WebLogic as an application and have a look under the hood by using the WebLogic Administration Console.

Cross-Reference   We discuss the various options for starting WebLogic Server in Chapter 4.

To start WebLogic on Windows 2000, choose User Projects ⇨ mydomain ⇨ Start Server from the BEA WebLogic Platform 7.0 program group. Enter the server's administration username and password (defined during the installation process) and the server starts. Figure 1-1 shows the console output from starting WebLogic Server.

Figure 1-1: WebLogic Server 7.0 started and ready for connections

Caution   After you start the server, you must either leave this window open or minimize it. Closing it shuts down the server!

The simple output in the command-line window belies the complexity of the engine running beneath. You can gain a better appreciation by looking at the server through the lens of the Administration Console. From the BEA WebLogic Platform 7.0 program group, choose WebLogic Server 7.0 ⇨ Server Tour and Examples ⇨ Start Admin Console. After entering the administrative username and password for your server, you'll see a Console display in your Web browser, similar to Figure 1-2.

Now it's beginning to look like you got your money's worth. On the left side of the screen is the *domain tree* showing the contents of the WebLogic domain (mydomain) to which this Console is pointed.

Figure 1-2: WebLogic Server Administration Console start screen

Note   A WebLogic domain is a collection of one or more WebLogic servers logically bundled together for administrative purposes and possibly also for clustering. Every WebLogic server belongs to one and only one domain. `mydomain` and `myserver` are default names set by WebLogic's installer. You can change your domain and server names to anything you want when you install your own servers.

On the right side of the screen is the *entity table* for the last item you clicked in the domain tree. You just started the Console and haven't clicked any items, so the entity table displayed is actually the Console home page, which is just a task- and service-oriented view of the domain tree.

You'll see a lot more of the Administration Console as you work through this book. For now, let's take a quick look at the status of the server started earlier. In the domain tree, expand the Servers node; then click `myserver`.

The entity table for `myserver` is shown in Figure 1-3. It shows basic information about your server, including its name, the machine, the TCP/IP port it's listening on, and so on.

This is only one of several sections of data about the server. Notice the tabs across the top for Configuration, Connections, Monitoring, and so on. Clicking one of them takes you to a different section of the entity table. Below these are subsections of the selected section. You're now looking at the General subsection of the Configuration section. (The selected tab of the top-level tabs has white text on a green background; the selected tab of the second-level tabs has black text on a white background.)

Figure 1-3: The Administration Console's view of your WebLogic Server

To get information about WebLogic Console itself, click Console at the top of the domain tree. The Preferences tab, shown in Figure 1-4, allows you to change the Console's defaults, including which language you want for on-screen displays, refresh intervals, and so on.

Figure 1-4: The Preferences tab of the Console Preferences page

The Console's Versions tab, shown in Figure 1-5, displays the product versions of the Console and the WebLogic Server to which it is pinned.

As you can see, the WebLogic Administration Console is an excellent tool for visualizing the innards of your server and understanding how it works. It is also an essential tool for managing your server and keeping it healthy. We explore these topics in greater depth throughout this book.

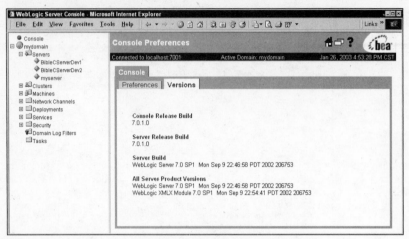

Figure 1-5: The Versions tab of the Console Preferences page

Surveying WebLogic's Features, Services, and Architecture

Now that we know the things WebLogic can do, let's examine the components of its architecture to gain a clearer understanding of how it does them.

HTTP server

If you think of WebLogic Server as a big house in which your Web applications live, its HTTP server is the front door. All requests made to your applications from Web browsers must pass through it.

WebLogic's integrated HTTP server allows you to host Web sites that contain HTML/XML pages only or HTML/XML pages plus JSPs and servlets. For applications requiring secure connections, WebLogic supports the HTTP-Secure (HTTPS) protocol, which requires you to purchase a certificate for your server from a certifying authority. If your environment requires you to deploy WebLogic behind Apache, Microsoft, or Sun ONE (formerly Netscape Enterprise Server) Web servers, you can do so using WebLogic's proxy plug-ins for those servers.

Note   WebLogic 7.0 supports *virtual hosting,* which allows you to map multiple Web sites to a single WebLogic server. For sites upgrading from earlier WebLogic versions, this may eliminate the need to proxy requests to WebLogic servers from other Web servers if the only reason for doing so is to support virtual hosting.

J2EE containers

WebLogic Server implements a Web container and an EJB container, which are the two server-side containers mandated by the J2EE standard. These containers give your applications a runtime environment and access to the J2EE APIs. The containers are an integral part of WebLogic Server and are available for use after the server is started.

Web container

WebLogic's Web container hosts servlets and JSPs. These application components are used to service requests originating from Web browsers.

Note   The first time JSPs are invoked, they are automatically compiled into servlets, and the servlet executes instead of the JSP itself. WebLogic manages this process invisibly and automatically, as required by the J2EE specification.

EJB container

As you might expect, WebLogic's EJB container hosts EJBs, including session beans, entity beans, and message beans. These application components are used to implement business logic, data access, and asynchronous messaging. They service requests from non-Web clients, such as client applications written in Java, or from Java code living in a servlet or JSP. They generally cannot be accessed directly from Web browsers unless there is an applet embedded in the page. WebLogic Server 7.0 includes J2EE 1.3 and supports the EJB 2.0 and 1.1 specifications.

Gateway to the J2EE APIs

WebLogic Server provides your Java applications with runtime access to the J2EE APIs, which are JDBC, JMS, JNDI, JTA, RMI, and JavaMail. As mentioned earlier, WebLogic Server includes J2EE 1.3.

Figure 1-6 shows the relationships among WebLogic's HTTP server, J2EE containers, the J2EE APIs, and external systems.

Web Services

WebLogic Server 7.0 supports current standards for implementing and deploying *Web Services*. Web Services is an exciting new technology that allows the construction and deployment of self-describing, modular, and reusable application components that can be made available to any other application running on a corporate intranet or the global Internet. WebLogic Server supports Web Services Description Language (WSDL) version 1.1 and Simple Object Access Protocol (SOAP) version 1.1, which are the enabling technologies behind Web Services.

Cross-Reference   WebLogic's support for Web Services, WSDL, and SOAP is covered in Chapters 26 and 27.

J2EE Connector Architecture

WebLogic Server 7.0 supports the J2EE Connector Architecture version 1.0, which defines a portable, open standard for integrating with back-end systems such as Enterprise Resource Planning (ERP) systems, Customer Relationship Management (CRM) systems, and other enterprise-class software and database systems.

Cross-Reference   WebLogic's support for the J2EE Connector Architecture is covered in Chapter 28.

Figure 1-6: WebLogic's J2EE architecture and its relationship to external systems

CORBA support

Many large corporations use CORBA (Common Object Request Broker Architecture) to implement distributed applications on their corporate networks. CORBA provides a means by which software objects can find and call each other remotely over a network. The communication protocol used for this process is IIOP, or Internet Inter-ORB Protocol, which sits on top of TCP/IP.

CORBA is a separate standard that predates J2EE and was indeed the inspiration for RMI, J2EE's remote object protocol. Unlike RMI, however, CORBA provides support for objects written in many languages, not just Java.

WebLogic Server includes CORBA support in the form of RMI over IIOP. RMI uses a communication protocol that is incompatible with CORBA; RMI/IIOP converts the RMI protocol into IIOP, and vice-versa, so RMI objects can coexist with CORBA objects on a network.

Security services

WebLogic provides a platform for three levels of application security: encryption, user authentication, and user authorization.

Encryption

Data transmitted to and from WebLogic Server can be encrypted by using Secure Sockets Layer (SSL). SSL, created by Netscape Communications (now a subsidiary of AOL Time Warner), is implemented for Web applications via HTTP-Secure (HTTPS) and is used in native form over RMI connections.

To use SSL, you must purchase a certificate for your server from a certificate vendor such as VeriSign. When clients request secure connections, the server sends the certificate to the client for validation. Once validated, the client and server exchange encrypted keys and establish the secure connection. WebLogic Server also supports mutual authentication, in which the client and server both exchange certificates before establishing a secure connection.

User authentication and authorization

User authentication is the process of ensuring that a user has the proper credentials to gain access to an application. *User authorization* is the process of mapping authenticated users to individual application services, usually at the group level. Sales managers, for example, have access to commission reports in a CRM application, whereas sales representatives do not.

Applications usually authenticate users by prompting them for a login name and password, and then validating these against a database. After the user is authenticated, authorization is performed by matching the user's group membership against a list of resources available to that group. This list is called an Access Control List (ACL).

Cross-Reference   See Chapters 20, 21, 22, and 25 for more information on WebLogic's comprehensive security implementation.

Clustering services

Clustering is the process of combining two or more WebLogic servers on a network into one logical entity for the purpose of increasing an application's *scalability* and *availability*. Scalability is increased because the more CPUs and memory you add to a system, the more users you can support. Availability is increased because if one server crashes, you have other servers available in the cluster to absorb the load.

WebLogic's clustering services are quite flexible and provide many benefits, including the following:

✦ Any number of servers can participate, so your site's scalability and availability are limited only by your hardware budget.

✦ Clustering is totally transparent to developers and users because the cluster looks like a single WebLogic server on the network.

✦ New servers can be added to a cluster dynamically without having to bring the site down.

✦ Allocation of resources in the cluster can be controlled by DNS and/or proxy servers, giving administrators tremendous flexibility for handling load balancing and failover.

Clustering is one of WebLogic's best features and a major reason for its popularity in large enterprises.

Management and monitoring tools

You can manage and monitor the servers in your WebLogic installation remotely by using tools supplied by BEA and third-party vendors. Third-party tools allow you to manage WebLogic Server in the context of your entire network installation, leveraging WebLogic's SNMP support to do so.

Tools provided by BEA

As we discussed earlier in this chapter, WebLogic Server includes command-line and browser-based tools for managing and monitoring the WebLogic Servers on your network. These tools make it easy for administrators to configure servers and clusters, delegate services across servers and clusters, configure security, deploy applications, and troubleshoot problems when they occur.

WebLogic Servers, whether running independently or as part of a cluster, are grouped into logical units called *domains*. In a domain containing multiple servers, one server is the administration server, and the others are managed servers. WebLogic's command-line and browser-based administration tools execute against the administration server, which propagates configuration settings to the managed servers. You decide which servers are which when you construct the domain.

Cross-Reference

Chapter 4 explains how to construct domains containing administration and managed servers.

WebLogic's browser-based administration tool is called the *Administration Console*. It provides an Explorer-like graphical interface to the WebLogic services available in its domain. As such, it's a great tool for beginners to get a clear mental picture of how a WebLogic installation works, especially if multiple servers are involved. Figures 1-3 and 1-4 show examples of Administration Console screens.

SNMP support

WebLogic Server 7.0 can communicate with management systems by using the *Simple Network Management Protocol,* or *SNMP.* This gives network administrators the ability to manage WebLogic installations within the framework of their overall hardware and software infrastructure.

Understanding WebLogic's Role in the Enterprise

WebLogic's long list of features and capabilities make it a powerful and versatile asset in any company's computing arsenal. Unlike mail and database servers, which fill well-defined and narrow roles in an enterprise's computing infrastructure, WebLogic Server can be made to solve an endless variety of computing problems. Here is a partial list of what you can do with WebLogic:

✦ Provide a robust, secure, and scalable platform for building intelligent, dynamic Web sites.

✦ Build enterprise applications that allow Web and non-Web (including wireless) clients to access the same business logic and data stores, reducing development costs.

✦ Build e-commerce systems that manage customers, product catalogs, orders, payments, order fulfillment, customer service, and electronic marketing via Web or e-mail.

✦ Build Web services that seamlessly interact with other Web services at your company or other companies over the Internet.

✦ Give programmers and users secure, friendly access to data locked away in legacy systems.

✦ Seamlessly display and manipulate data drawn from multiple back-end sources.

✦ Manage the real-time or batch movement of information from one data store to another, regardless of the types of the data stores or the platforms they run on.

✦ Build Web interfaces to non-Web applications, such as client/server or mainframe applications.

An investment in WebLogic Server can pay dividends throughout your enterprise in ways you may not yet have imagined. If your business demands big reliable systems, or if you need to integrate disparate computing systems on multiple platforms, you're likely to see a quick return on your WebLogic investment.

Is WebLogic Right for Your Project?

To determine whether WebLogic and the J2EE platform are a good fit for your project, ask yourself the following questions:

✦ Do I need fast, reliable access to my corporate databases from the Web? Are JDBC drivers available for these databases?

✦ Do I need to build dynamic, data-driven Web applications for large user populations that expect 24×7 availability?

✦ Do I need to automate e-mail or wireless communications with my partners, vendors, employees, or customers?

✦ Do I need to implement complex business logic and make it available to all my developers, so they don't have to constantly reinvent the wheel?

✦ Do I need to implement message-driven workflows that are tightly bound to database operations?

✦ Do I need to provide robust user authentication and authorization for Web resources and other services?

✦ Do I need to write applications (Web-based or otherwise) that seamlessly integrate data from disparate sources on multiple platforms?

✦ Do I need to execute distributed transactions across multiple data stores?

If you answered "yes" to any of the preceding questions and if your developers understand object-oriented technology and Java, WebLogic is probably a good fit for your project.

Summary

WebLogic Server is an industrial-strength implementation of the J2EE platform suitable for developing high-volume, dynamic Web sites and enterprise applications. It gives developers unmatched flexibility in how they design, implement, and deploy these systems on their corporate networks.

WebLogic provides exhaustive support for all aspects of the J2EE standard, making it easy to build Web and enterprise applications that connect to databases, mail systems, messaging systems, CORBA-based systems, and legacy systems on a variety of platforms. Extensive security features are built into WebLogic so you can tightly control access to applications, Web sites, and resources contained within them.

You can cluster WebLogic Server if you need to deploy highly scalable and reliable applications. WebLogic clusters, like the rest of WebLogic, can be easily managed by using command-line tools or the browser-based Administration Console application.

Companies around the world use WebLogic to solve a surprising array of difficult computing problems. WebLogic and the J2EE platform make it remarkably easy to build applications that seamlessly integrate data and computing resources from all corners of your organization.

✦   ✦   ✦

Assembling and Managing a WebLogic Development Team

✦ ✦ ✦ ✦

In This Chapter

What WebLogic
developers need
to know

Project team roles
and responsibilities

Project management
strategies

✦ ✦ ✦ ✦

For most enterprise developers, the glory days of writing mono-lithic applications for one operating system and hardware plat-form are over. Web applications have muscled their way into the enterprise, bringing with them a long list of development and deploy-ment advantages (and an equally long list of challenges.

WebLogic Server is a powerful tool for Web application development, but WebLogic developers are not immune to the challenges that all Web developers face. This chapter explores the demands WebLogic places on developers and identifies the roles and responsibilities that must be filled by an effective WebLogic development team. It closes by offering some project management strategies you may find useful as you launch your WebLogic projects.

What WebLogic Developers Need to Know

Becoming a knowledgeable, well-rounded WebLogic developer is a formidable task because WebLogic, like enterprise Web programming itself, covers a lot of technological ground. Being a good WebLogic developer requires a solid understanding of the following:

- ✦ The J2EE platform

- ✦ The enhancements and nuances WebLogic brings to J2EE

- ✦ The systems within your enterprise to which WebLogic will connect

Whew! That's a lot of stuff to know!

WebLogic Server's more than 40 manuals contain over 3000 pages of information, most of which assumes some level of knowledge about such diverse topics as networking, databases, e-mail systems, wire-less systems, distributed transactions, security, clustering, object-oriented programming, and Java. Sun's library for J2EE occupies a comparable number of pages on its Web site. This is a lot of information for the time-strapped enterprise developer to absorb.

Of course, enterprise developers seldom work alone these days, precisely because there is too much out there for any one person to know and too little time to learn it. Assuming, then, that WebLogic development is a team effort, what do the members of a WebLogic team need to know? The following sections give you the scoop.

Object-oriented programming in Java

First and foremost, developing WebLogic applications requires a solid understanding of object-oriented programming in Java. J2EE is written in Java, all J2EE applications are written in Java, and WebLogic itself is written in Java. Therefore, you must know Java.

This book assumes that you have a solid understanding of Java and know how to use its many features. Nevertheless, we want to emphasize that mastery of the following particular Java language features and concepts will save you a lot of time and frustration while working with WebLogic and J2EE:

✦ Packages

✦ Interfaces

✦ Serializable objects

✦ Classloaders and classpaths

✦ .jar files, .war files, .ear files, and J2EE application deployment concepts

Cross-Reference
This book does not contain a tutorial on Java, but J2EE application deployment concepts are covered in Chapter 18. In addition, background on using Ant is included in Appendix B. Ant is an open source, XML-based build tool that will greatly simplify creating and deploying WebLogic applications.

This book will help you learn more about these topics as they apply to WebLogic and J2EE programming.

J2EE

After you know Java, you need to understand J2EE. J2EE is a component-based architecture and you create J2EE applications by building and assembling J2EE components. Therefore, the more you understand the components and their intended use, the better your applications will be.

Understanding J2EE also makes clear the division of labor between J2EE, WebLogic, and your developers. If, for example, your WebLogic developers are writing complex code to handle user session tracking or database transactions, they may not realize that WebLogic and J2EE provide these features for them. Be sure that every member of your team has at least a basic understanding of J2EE before starting your project. You'll save time and build better applications.

Cross-Reference
Chapter 3 provides an in-depth discussion of J2EE, component software development, and the relationship of these items to WebLogic development.

Object-oriented analysis and design

To design a robust J2EE application that makes effective use of Java and J2EE, your team needs to know *object-oriented analysis and design* (OOAD). OOAD is the art of translating complex business requirements into elegant software designs based on reusable objects.

Applying good OOAD techniques to J2EE systems is quite challenging when compared to client/server or desktop systems. When designing client/server and desktop systems, first you model your business logic, and then your data, and then your user interactions; then you're done. But with J2EE, you must also map your design to J2EE's component architecture, deciding what pieces should be implemented as servlets, entity beans, session beans, and so on. Good OOAD for J2EE must also take into account the class frameworks provided by Java and J2EE, so you don't reinvent the wheel with your designs. This is hard work, but a good design more than pays for itself when it comes time to build, maintain, and extend your applications.

Most practitioners of OOAD express their designs using the *Unified Modeling Language,* or *UML.* UML provides a rich visual vocabulary for diagramming complex systems and it allows you to model them from multiple points of view. Most important, UML provides a convenient way to share the design with everyone on the team so it can be understood, improved, and implemented. You can learn more about UML by visiting Rational Software Corporation's UML Resource Center at the following site:

```
http://www.rational.com/uml/index.jsp
```

Note   Most UML tools on the market today, such as Embarcadero Technologies' Describe, Rational Software's Rational Rose, and Borland's (formerly TogetherSoft's) Together Control Center, provide built-in support for Java and J2EE projects.

Cross-Reference   Chapter 3 discusses some useful ways to incorporate UML into your WebLogic application designs.

HTML and JavaScript

No matter how much magic you perform on the server side with your JSPs, servlets, beans, and EJBs, you'll probably be pumping out HTML and JavaScript to the Web browser. Most successful Web sites are rendered with little more (with good reason. HTML and JavaScript are the most compatible and widely supported browser languages on the planet, and a good HTML/JavaScript programmer can build some nice front ends if your users are using Netscape/IE 4.0 or higher.

HTML, of course, renders all your static and dynamic data, including text, tables, graphics, hyperlinks, and so on. JavaScript is useful for performing client-side validation of data entry, and also for accomplishing certain GUI tricks. Just be certain that your users' browsers support the versions of HTML and JavaScript you use.

XML

XML is widely used in WebLogic 7.0 for creating properties files, configuration files, and deployment descriptors. WebLogic provides samples and templates for these types of files, so you don't need to be much of an XML expert to create and maintain them.

But XML is being used increasingly for data interchange, especially in domains such as financial services and applied science, because of its extensibility and capability to represent self-describing data. For these more-sophisticated applications of XML, your team will need at least one XML expert who also understands document type definitions (DTDs), the Simple API for XML (SAX), and Document Object Models (DOMs).

HTML experts are good candidates for learning XML, given that XML and HTML share syntactical attributes. But database experts should also be involved in the design of custom tags for data interchange.

TCP/IP networking and distributed systems

WebLogic and J2EE applications are almost always distributed systems (they're implemented on multiple computers that communicate with each other over a TCP/IP network. Therefore, having some knowledge of TCP/IP networking and distributed systems on your team is a big plus, if not a requirement.

Helpful TCP/IP knowledge includes the following:

✦ TCP/IP addresses, sockets, and ports

✦ IP multicasts (used by WebLogic clusters)

✦ DNS (used for name resolution and load balancing)

Helpful distributed systems knowledge includes the following:

✦ An understanding of clients, servers, and peer-to-peer systems

✦ Distributed database transactions and two-phase commit

✦ Messaging, e-mail, and wireless protocols

✦ Remote Method Invocation (RMI — used by Java clients and EJBs)

✦ CORBA (if you plan to use it)

✦ Programming with stubs, skeletons, and Interface Definition Languages (IDLs) — structures used in RMI and CORBA

Relational databases and SQL

Almost all Web applications connect with relational databases. The most popular flavors these days seem to be Oracle, IBM DB2, Microsoft SQL Server, and MySQL. There's also Pointbase, a pure-Java relational database that ships in a demo version with WebLogic. Some shops also use the CloudScape object-relational database, a demo version of which used to ship with WebLogic Server; it is now an IBM product.

Data is selected, inserted, updated, and deleted in a relational database by issuing commands in *Structured Query Language,* or *SQL.* Java's two SQL packages (`java.sql` and `javax.sql`) provide excellent wrappers for performing common database functions with SQL in a vendor-neutral way.

We want to emphasize that if an SQL-compliant database is a big part of your Web application's design, your project's ultimate success will hinge on your team's understanding of that database and SQL. Badly designed and programmed databases are the leading cause of poor performance in Web applications.

If you want to avoid database-related performance problems, make sure that your team includes or has access to gurus in your database platform of choice. These people should understand all the intricacies of SQL, your database's query optimizer, indexes, table partitions, caching, and all the other features that make databases sing. Otherwise, you'll be crying the blues later.

Legacy systems

If your WebLogic application will connect with legacy systems, such as a mainframe or a dBase III database running on a noisy old PC/AT, you'll need some creative people to help you wire them together.

Virtually all access to legacy systems is driven by the need to get to data residing on those systems. Therefore, those who are charged with doing this should know multiple methods of data access for the system at hand and have the capability to devise creative workarounds when things aren't going well.

Joe once saw a good example of such creativity at a client site: A WebLogic developer was building an application to process data residing on an AS/400. His WebLogic instance was running under Solaris, and he was using JDBC to move data from DB2 on an AS/400 to Oracle on a Sun machine for processing. But he ran into trouble because of the huge data volumes involved: the millions of rows he was moving were choking the network and his application. After some thought, he realized that he could install a WebLogic instance on the AS/400, do the processing there, and ship only the few thousand rows of results to the Sun machine. In doing so, he reduced the execution time of the job from over an hour to less than a minute. He also did a good job of exploiting the cross-platform capabilities of WebLogic and J2EE.

Collaborative discipline

If a group of people is to work together as a team, they must develop structured, predictable methods for capturing, storing, and sharing their accumulated knowledge and work products. Otherwise, chaos rules the day, valuable information is lost, and productivity goes into the tank. We call this orderly, cooperative behavior among team members *collaborative discipline* because establishing and enforcing consistent team development standards requires discipline, especially in the fast-paced world of Web development.

Collaborative discipline is especially important in WebLogic development because WebLogic applications consist of dozens of components assembled by multiple team members that must fit together like pieces of a jigsaw puzzle — or the application won't work.

Achieving the collaborative discipline required for WebLogic and J2EE development requires, at a minimum, three ingredients: effective content management, continuously updated "living" documentation, and open lines of communication among all team members. These three ingredients are discussed in the following sections.

Content management

Although you may try, you will eventually find that you cannot successfully execute a WebLogic project of appreciable size without an effective content management system.

Content management is important because it:

✦ Clearly defines where all the materials for a project are stored

✦ Prevents file modification conflicts among multiple users

✦ Allows the input of descriptive comments to help document the system

✦ Provides backups, revision histories, and version control

What is content? For WebLogic application, content usually includes the following:

✦ Static Web documents, such as HTML files, XML files, and stylesheets

✦ Graphics files, such as JPGs, GIFs, and PNGs; and also their source files, such as Adobe Illustrator AI files or PhotoShop PSD files

✦ Java source code files for servlets, beans, EJBs, and helper classes

✦ JSP files

✦ XML descriptors for applications and components

✦ Relational database scripts written in SQL

✦ Downloadable files such as Adobe Acrobat PDF files and software installers

✦ Multimedia files

A content management system stores these elements into a repository, regulates access to them by multiple users, and provides some level of version control.

The type of content management system you choose depends on the size and scope of your project, and the types of users who will be creating and updating the content. Some projects are "pure programming" projects, in which software developers are creating a Web-based application with no day-to-day involvement by non-programmers. In that case a source code control system, such as PVCS, Microsoft Visual SourceSafe, or CVS may adequately meet your content management needs. For larger projects involving developers *and* users, such as large corporate intranets or external Web sites, you may need a dedicated content management system, such as those marketed by Interwoven, Documentum, and others, to manage non-code resources such as brochures, photographs, illustrations, catalog copy, and so on. In between these two extremes is Rational ClearCase, which is a popular configuration management tool for large teams or enterprise-wide deployments.

Regardless of the product you use, features for check-in/check-out and version control are essential, as is the capability to deploy the content to multiple locations for development, testing, and production.

Living documentation

Web development is an iterative process, and although iterative development has been around since the beginning of programming, Web development raises it to a new level. There are two main reasons for this. First, because Web development requires the assembly of multiple, disparate, and often independent components, the traditional compile-edit-test-debug cycle doesn't apply to the development of a Web site as a whole. Instead, smaller changes are made to pieces of a site and tested independently of the rest. Second, Web sites by their very nature change on a daily, hourly, or even continuous basis. Web sites are indeed "living" systems, always changing and growing, and living systems require living documentation that always changes and grows with them.

Living documentation has three important characteristics:

✦ Software developers are the primary authors.

✦ It's easy for developers to create and update while they're programming.

✦ Changes and updates are easily propagated to the rest of the team.

During the development of Java, Sun was quick to recognize the importance of living documentation and added support for it in the form of JavaDoc. JavaDoc is a flexible documentation tool that addresses the three characteristics of living documentation. First, it recognizes that software developers are the primary authors by being implemented as a code-commenting tool for Java. Second, developers can easily create and update documentation while they're programming by inserting JavaDoc-readable comments directly into their source code. Third, JavaDoc makes it easy to propagate changes to the rest of the team by incorporating a tool that publishes JavaDoc comments to an internal Web site that organizes the documentation the way the code itself is organized. Developers can easily surf and search this Web site to find the information they need.

JavaDoc is a powerful tool for WebLogic developers because it allows them to follow a single documentation standard that easily captures their knowledge and makes it available to the rest of the team.

Information about JavaDoc is available at the following URL:

```
http://java.sun.com/j2se/javadoc/index.html
```

An excellent example of a JavaDoc-generated Web site is Sun's documentation site for J2EE, which can be found at the following site:

```
http://java.sun.com/j2ee/sdk_1.3/techdocs/api/index.html
```

Open lines of communication

Multiple developers working together in a highly iterative fashion must be capable of naturally approaching each other without fear or hesitation to share information and discuss issues that arise during the life of a project. They should be equally comfortable approaching the non-developer members of their team (including management), and vice-versa. Communications may occur in person, via e-mail, or via telephone, and all team members must be conditioned to respond promptly, because time is always of the essence on Web projects.

Web development teams are not the place for those who are unwilling to share information or ask for help when needed. If you can't avoid including one or two of these characters on your team, you'll have to find a way to make them cooperative and approachable. Available methods for doing so are beyond the scope of this book!

Project Team Roles and Responsibilities

The members of a WebLogic development team will be called upon to wear many hats. Several different types of work must be done; sometimes by only a handful of people. Therefore, the best WebLogic teams are composed of experienced, resourceful people who possess the discipline to work well together, to do the job right, and to deliver complex systems that won't break under heavy loads.

Although details vary from project to project, the key roles described in the following sections need to be filled on almost every project.

Project manager

Every project needs a leader who can keep the team on track and assume responsibility for timely delivery of the project. A strong project manager is good at breaking enormous tasks into bite-sized pieces, delegating responsibility for the delivery of those pieces, assigning due dates, and enforcing the project schedule. This person must also be good at communicating with people outside the team, including outside technical resources, corporate management, and members of business units whose interests are at stake.

But there is more to good project management than Gantt charts, delegation, and deadlines. A good project manager can be compared to a good athletics coach. The best coaches know how to

✦ Size up their teams and combine their players' talents for the best possible outcome.

✦ Maximize each player's strengths while minimizing their weaknesses.

✦ Keep the team focused and motivated, even in the face of adversity.

✦ Keep the team playing as a *team,* not as a collection of individuals pulling in separate directions.

When a good coach pulls all of this together, the team usually wins — and the same goes for software project managers.

Application architect

A project has a much greater chance for success if it has a strong technical leader responsible for the overall architecture of the solution. A veteran with a history of architecting, developing, and implementing distributed systems is invaluable; if that person knows J2EE, so much the better.

The architect's role is to see the "big picture" of the project and map out the solution to the technologies and the surrounding environment. This person must be able to synthesize high-level considerations such as high availability, application and database performance, application and network security, and integration with existing client/server applications or a variety of specialized third-party subsystems. A good architect understands the trade-offs that must be made and chooses the right ones.

To be successful at this role, the application architect must

✦ Possess the knowledge of both leading edge and proven technologies suitable for developing application solutions.

✦ Understand several technologies, including relational databases, hardware and operating system platforms, the latest enterprise technologies such as J2EE, and the tools and vendor products available to implement solutions.

✦ Have object-oriented design capabilities and know how to express his designs in UML.

✦ Draw his designs from a sophisticated awareness of design patterns, including generic object-oriented patterns and patterns specific to J2EE.

✦ Be able to "stir up the pot;" forcing a project's developers to consider approaches they may have overlooked, or may not favor.

✦ Encourage developers to take calculated risks, seek innovative solutions to problems, and create software systems that exceed users' expectations.

Your organization may have such a person in a management position serving as technical advisor on a variety of projects. Or perhaps this person is someone who has the development lead role, serving as a technical mentor to other team members. Either way, a knowledgeable, opinionated application architect is a vital part of helping your project team achieve success.

Database designer/database administrator

After you gather requirements for your project and select an application architecture, the first person to actually design and build something is usually the database designer. This is because in systems that depend on databases, you must first have a database before you can write code to manipulate it.

A good database begins with a good data model. Data modeling is an art, not a science because there are several "correct" ways to do it wrong. A relational database design, for example, may conform to all the rules of normalization, but it may not perform well because common queries require too many table joins. Denormalizing the database solves the performance problem but compromises the purity of the design. Good database designers know that these trade-offs are normal (so to speak) and necessary and they know how to make wise decisions while designing the system, not after putting it into production.

Good database designers work with users to determine *what* data will be used. Based on this information, they sketch out an initial design that meets project requirements and some level of normalization rules. The best database designers work with users *and* programmers to understand precisely *how* the data will be used. This information is used to bring the model in line with expected data storage and retrieval patterns for maximum throughput and performance. Just as you wouldn't design an interstate highway with hairpin curves because of the wrecks that would surely result, you wouldn't build a database in fifth normal form for a high-volume, online transaction processing system because processing an insert or update would take a prohibitively long time.

In keeping with the trend toward smaller project teams, your database designer may also function as your database administrator. This can work well during development, but usually doesn't fly after a system goes into production. Why? Although these jobs seem similar, they're quite different. Database administrators are tasked with keeping databases alive, healthy, and recoverable in case of disasters. The variables that go into meeting these requirements vary tremendously, depending on the database product being used, the size and structure of the database, the database's usage patterns, and even the operating system it is running on. The reservoir of required knowledge is so huge and the value of experience so great, that people build careers around being Oracle, Sybase, or MS SQL Server DBAs. Being a proficient, responsive DBA is generally not something you can do well on a part-time basis, especially for larger systems.

User Interface (UI) designer

Great UI designers combine artistic ability with technological awareness to create attractive, efficient UIs for Web applications. It's a difficult job for a number of reasons, and good designers are hard to find.

Creating a good-looking site that is easy to use and simplifies the task at hand is no accident. It requires a lot of knowledge, communication, hard work, experimentation, and rework to get it right. The best UI designers know how to work with users *and* developers to create the best possible design. Users provide insight on workflows, daily usage patterns, functionality, and the friendliness of a system, whereas developers provide feedback on what can actually be built with available technology.

UI design for Web applications is especially challenging — and frustrating. Anyone who has been involved with software development for more than five years knows that Web browsers and HTML are a big step backward for human-computer interaction. Web UI designers are often asked to render stunning landscapes with the software equivalent of a hammer and chisel. Great designers can actually pull it off to some extent, but the shortcomings and compromises imposed by the environment are many.

From a practical standpoint, the UI designer on your team should

✦ Be an expert in HTML and, increasingly, XML.

✦ Know how to write JavaServer pages that incorporate JavaBeans and custom tag libraries.

✦ Know JavaScript and how to use it in a browser-neutral manner to perform client-side validations.

✦ Understand HTML forms processing and know how to effectively weave animations and multimedia into a design.

✦ Be able to envision and create the artwork necessary to bring a design to life.

Java/J2EE developer

Java developers are the core of a WebLogic team because the bulk of WebLogic applications are built in Java.

WebLogic development is, by definition, server-side development. Experienced desktop developers, such as those with backgrounds in Visual Basic or client-side Java development, find they have to shift their focus away from UI coding in favor of more "faceless" tasks such as session management and efficient manipulation of back-end data. UI design and implementation is still very important in WebLogic applications, but these tasks are usually assigned to HTML and JSP developers.

Good Java and J2EE developers

✦ Have a passion for issues involving system architecture and design.

✦ Combine their expert knowledge of Java with a deep understanding of object-oriented design.

✦ Read, absorb, and apply design patterns.

✦ Recognize the many design patterns employed by J2EE itself (some of which are discussed in the next chapter).

✦ Enjoy combining these patterns into tangible solutions, using UML to create, refine, and share their designs.

The best Java and J2EE developers can

✦ Quickly translate well-designed models into working code, taking advantage of the power and flexibility that Java, J2EE, and WebLogic have to offer.

✦ Be willing to try multiple approaches to solving problems.

✦ Be willing to keep plodding away when things don't work right the first time.

✦ Know enough about databases to write reliable efficient code by using JDBC (although Java developers are not necessarily database experts); this implies at least a fair knowledge of SQL, which is really a requirement for all server-side developers today.

✦ Be great team players that collaborate effectively with their fellow server-side developers, with the database team, and with the UI design team to deliver rich, functional solutions in compressed timeframes.

Quality Assurance (QA) team

If your organization has a dedicated QA team, consider yourself lucky and try to take full advantage of their unique capabilities and talents.

Good QA engineers derive a unique, almost perverse satisfaction from breaking software. Whereas developers test under the assumption that previously coded sections still work, QA engineers test under the assumption that nothing *ever* works. Developers test applications as they are designed to be used, but QA engineers test applications as they are designed *not* to be used. Developers are under pressure to build software, whereas QA engineers are under pressure to *break* it. That's why it's best to separate the roles of developers and QA engineers if you can; developers make the application and QA engineers try to break it.

Another reason why a dedicated QA team is a major asset is that team members can devote time to building test scripts and otherwise automating the testing process to maximize productivity and shorten testing cycles. A number of third-party tools exist for testing the functionality and load-bearing capacity of Web applications. None of these tools is easy to learn or use. Having one or more people available full-time to learn and apply these products can be a major boon to your project.

Smaller shops that don't have access to dedicated QA teams almost always task their developers with testing. Getting end users involved can also help in these situations, to help mitigate the previously mentioned developer bias. If your shop falls into this category, you may want to schedule occasional testing events in which employees throughout your organization log on to the system at a predetermined time and try to break it. You may want to provide a script for people to follow, or you may want to just turn them loose on your application to see what breaks when users start poking around. It's important, however, to carefully record what goes wrong so that problems can be relayed back to the development team. A couple of observers can walk around and do this or you can have users record their experiences on feedback forms. The bottom line is that any kind of structured testing approach is better than no testing at all, and if you can dedicate a team of pros to the effort, your software will benefit tremendously.

Documentation team

In these days of rapid development and extreme programming, documentation is one of those parts of software development that invariably gets little to no attention at all. Why? For the following reasons:

   ✦ Writing and maintaining accurate system documentation is exceedingly difficult, especially when the system is frequently changing.

   ✦ Unlike other aspects of a project, the documentation is not required for the software to function.

A fairly painless way to solve part of the problem is to take advantage of the JavaDoc facility to ensure that at a minimum, your source code documentation is well organized and available to the team. Of course, this requires that developers do a good job of embedding JavaDoc comments in their code. Enforcing at least this much discipline is a huge improvement over not documenting the system at all, especially when you consider the disruption that can occur when developers are assigned to other projects or leave the organization entirely.

 Tip   On Joe's company's projects, the developers create scripts that automatically run JavaDoc against the company's development servers on a nightly basis. This process provides developers and project managers with a central, up-to-date internal Web site with the latest documentation for all code the company has written.

Most large software-development organizations have dedicated technical writers who work with development teams to create robust documentation. Some of the documentation is aimed at system administrators that need to install and configure the software, and some is aimed at end users that use the software on a day-to-day basis.

Documentation for IT administrators usually includes a brief description of the project and its business purpose, a high-level architecture and network topology, detailed installation instructions of all the key software components, troubleshooting and maintenance instructions, and support escalation paths with contact numbers. Such documentation is usually posted in a secure central location, such as a dedicated intranet site.

Tip   User documentation should be minimal but informative. A quick reference guide (published as a laminated, 8-1/2 " × 11 " card), context-sensitive online help, or a site navigation map are tools that actually get used. Thick user manuals usually wind up on the shelf, never to be read by anyone!

WebLogic administrator

The WebLogic administrator is the person who deploys applications on your WebLogic Server and keeps the server online and properly tuned. This person could be a Unix or Windows NT/2000 system administrator, or one of the more technical developers.

The WebLogic administrator must have a medium-to-advanced level of understanding of the operating system upon which you'll be deploying WebLogic Server. This is because the proper installation and tuning of WebLogic differs slightly from platform to platform, and it is also affected by the nature of the applications deployed to the server.

A competent WebLogic administrator should

✦ Be familiar with loading and configuring the hardware, the operating system, and system patches.

✦ Know how to tune the operating system and its usage of available hardware for maximum performance.

✦ Should know basic Java concepts such as classpath and how to run a Java program.

✦ Remember that WebLogic is written in Java, and a lot of the administration problems encountered when running WebLogic can be more easily solved when the administrator knows Java.

✦ Know how to install and configure WebLogic Server (including multiple server instances and clusters), JDBC drivers, ODBC and native database drivers (if necessary), and messaging and mail interfaces.

✦ Understand and be able to deploy the various types of application packages, including JAR, WAR, and EAR files.

Project Management Strategies

In this section, we share some of the in-the-trenches wisdom that we've accumulated in our collective experience managing large, enterprise-class software projects. If you're a senior developer, team leader, or project manager, you've likely gathered some pearls of your own over the years. But if you're like us, you're always willing to share ideas with other experienced people in the industry. So for what they're worth, here are some thoughts on how to effectively manage nontrivial software projects.

Note

We don't believe in some of the more extreme methods of project management, nor do we believe in an exhaustive, by-the-book approach. Our approach is not based upon any textbook or project management seminar, it's simply that what we've discovered has worked well for us in the real world of management, users, developers, technology, and deadlines.

In a nutshell, we believe the following:

✦ Proper due diligence in gathering requirements and a well-thought-out design is a necessity to architecting a good enterprise solution.

✦ Documentation should be concise but complete, providing the design and development teams with the critical information they need, but no more.

✦ Project management documents during development should also be kept simple but up-to-date; this way, at a moment's notice you can identify tasks completed or in-progress, those responsible for their completion, and what their priorities are.

✦ You should be able to communicate with management and end users with the same documents without having to reformat the content to suit them.

✦ Throughout all the project stages, documents should be formatted in a way that minimizes the need for maintenance as the project progresses. Let's break these points down into more specifics.

Gathering requirements

The requirements-gathering stage is a necessary evil. Most software project managers hate it, but good work done here pays huge dividends later on.

You and management should have some preliminary agreement about project scope, including budgetary constraints, the definition of the user community, and the business problem to be solved. There should likewise be a clear definition of who and what are *not* part of the scope.

A thorough set of interviews should be conducted with users to gather information about existing systems and proposed solutions. These interviews should cover existing source documents, workflows, demos of existing systems, and a complete understanding of what they desire the solution to be. If you have any preconceived ideas of the solution, run them by the users to get their feedback. But don't make any promises!

Keep notes during these interviews, jot down ideas as they come to you, and highlight issues and questions that come up through these conversations. Start a project binder and include your notes in this. For example, Joe likes to type his notes in a Word document to allow him to review the discussion and add more detail as he types because he typically thinks of more issues and questions while he types.

When you believe you have a good picture of what needs to be done, you'll inevitably need to prepare a Requirements document and present it to management and users. Your organization may have a template for you to use; otherwise, you'll need to deliver the information in a logical order. The document should include a summary description of the project, including the nature of the problem and current workflows. Characteristics of a solution should be discussed, including the identification of roles, requirements by role, and proposed phasing. A couple of well-thought-out diagrams make it easier to help people see the big picture that you've drawn in your head during the requirements gathering process. If everything goes well, you should get sign-off to proceed with a design after one or two rounds of discussions.

Designing the solution

Your organization may require that you complete Design Specifications and Functional Specifications documents, or there may be just one document, or you'll need to make up your own. It doesn't really matter — what does matter is that you do it. A good design enables you to see how the big picture will be accomplished. It also allows you to drill down into the sub-processes that make up the complete system, which is essential for the ensuing software design meetings.

The entire development team should participate in the design. Ultimately, a high-level design will show the servers, software components, other interfacing systems, databases, high-level workflows, and so on. From here, you can break down processes and components into detailed workflows, interface designs, report layouts, validation rules, error conditions and user error messages, database diagrams, and Java class diagrams.

Tip   Learn UML. Use entity-relationship diagrams to design the data model and Java structures. Use activity diagrams to document workflows, validations, and exception handling. Use sequence diagrams to map your system to J2EE components.

Cross-Reference   Chapter 3 walks through an example of applying UML as described in the preceding Tip.

Meanwhile, the UI designer should be creating mock-up pages in HTML and reports in whatever media are appropriate. Effective UI design is an iterative process that involves meeting with users, making modifications based upon feedback, and reviewing changes with the development team.

The format of the documents created during this phase is not important, as long as they present the design as the developer would like to receive it. Another important aspect is that they should deliver enough information, but not too much. Keep it as simple as possible while still getting the information delivered. Maintain these documents only as necessary, such as a major requirements or design change. Don't worry so much about the small things; no design document is ever perfect, nor does any design document typically ever match the final product exactly.

Managing development

During the development phase, the intensity of project management activities dies down a little. But a few basic components should be in place, as described in the following sections.

Source code control

Source control should be implemented and used by all members of the teams at all times — *no exceptions*. Many products are available to provide source control and, as a result, a few different definitions of source control exist. Here's ours: The purpose of source control is to keep track of who currently "owns" any given source document. If someone needs the source, they check it out, thereby preventing anyone else from changing it until that first person has coded it, tested it, and checked it back in. Throughout the course of the project, all the source documents are in one place — another important aspect of source code control systems.

Periodically, preferably each evening, rebuild your development staging server from the latest version of the source in your source control system. This will provide you with an up-to-date, functioning version of the software (even if it's missing a lot of features). It will also reinforce to the team that this is the master copy of the source.

Task list

You should maintain a simple task list to track completed, in-progress, and outstanding tasks. More importantly, it should become a natural means of communication within the team. Each task should be described at a fairly detailed level, enough so that a developer considers it a single component of work. This typically represents something that can be completed in a week or less. Information about completed tasks should include who did the work and when, along with any important comments. Tasks in progress should describe who is working on what. Anything outstanding should have some sort of priority rating that is understood by the project team.

You can use an elaborate, expensive project-tracking tool, or you can use something as simple as a Microsoft Excel document or even an intranet-hosted Web page. Whatever product you use, all members of the team should be able to add tasks to the list as they think of them. The project manager should occasionally meet with the team to discuss outstanding tasks, make assignments, and assign priorities.

Project plan

The task list is a great tool for communicating low-level programming issues among technical team members. But to communicate with management and users, you'll need a higher-level document, often called the *project plan.*

The dreaded project plan isn't so bad if you make it a useful management tool. Too often, project managers create excessively detailed plans that are difficult to maintain. Such detailed plans are hardly ever correct, so they become an exercise in futility. Keep the project plan simple and make it work for you. If the project plan is a tool that you can actually use to *manage* your project, it will become your friend.

The project plan should accomplish two things: It should show concurrent activities and document project progress versus milestones. You don't need multiple levels of detail. If a project is broken down into phases, and those phases have requirements, design, coding, QA, and user acceptance stages, all you need is one line item for each. If it's important that you track things by team member, break it down one more level. Or, if you want to track development by major processes, break down just the development stages one more level. Include only the levels of detail in your plan that you need and no more.

As a result, you will have a usable, easily maintainable document. You won't mind keeping it up-to-date because you'll find that doing so is an easy way to track the progress of your project. An added bonus is that the plan is at a level that managers and users can understand, so you can discuss it with them without reformatting. You no longer need to reserve the day before a status meeting to update the plan.

Planning the rollout

The rollout phase of a project can almost become a project in itself. To plan the rollout, the entire project team should get together well before the rollout date to discuss the necessary tasks. All aspects of the rollout should be discussed, including hardware, software installations and configurations, database implementation, application server and components, users and roles, application training, initial application support, and support turnover to administrators.

To document and manage this, you may want to create a separate project plan focused only on the rollout. Or you can simply add rollout tasks to your existing project plan if that works better for you and your team.

Keeping morale high

An important part of managing a project is managing your manager and the users. Frequent and regular updates, at least once every week or two, can help boost morale by making everyone feel that requirements are being met and progress is being made. In the IT community, in which enterprise projects cost big bucks, no news is *not* good news! Keeping management and users up-to-date is your opportunity to keep them interested, involved, and supportive of your efforts. You can even assign them tasks from time to time!

One form of communication to managers and end users is the status report. A status report should

✦ Relay the status of the major project activities.

✦ Divide the project or project phases into major components and present these components in an organized, tabular format.

✦ For each component, provide percentage complete, resource assignments, and a descriptive comment.

✦ List accomplishments since the last report.

✦ List items to be completed before the next report, along with a date for that report.

✦ List outstanding issues, including what they are and what is needed to address them.

A quick note about outstanding issues: They should remain on your status reports until they are completely resolved. After they are resolved, continue to report them for at least one additional cycle to document the resolution and when it was closed.

Throughout the project, whether casually or formally, touch base with managers and end users to let them know your progress and next steps. Typically, status reports and project plans are reviewed at periodic status meetings. Very often, however, these meetings lose audience members over time and therefore don't really do a good job of getting the word out about your project's status. We're not saying don't have meetings, but we do suggest that you e-mail everyone a copy of your status report after the meeting is completed. Go a step further by seeking out the people that matter and having a quick, five-minute conversation with them about the project. This could be the most fruitful five minutes of your day.

During development, conduct occasional demos. As components of the application are completed, show them off and gather feedback. The input you receive will be valuable, but more importantly, demonstrating progress gives managers and users ownership of the system, a stake in seeing it through successfully, and the warm, fuzzy feeling that those mysterious WebLogic developers in the corner are actually getting something done.

Summary

WebLogic development is challenging and demanding. WebLogic development teams must possess multiple talents and skill sets, and they must work hard to work well together. But working on a WebLogic development team is rewarding and enjoyable for developers and project managers alike. After all, solving tough technical problems and delivering complex systems that work well are what being a competent IT professional is all about.

Managing WebLogic projects isn't much different than managing other types of software projects, except that the need to foster teamwork and collaboration, and the need to weave disparate skill sets into a productive whole, is greater. Aside from these differences, WebLogic project management doesn't require any special techniques, documentation, or tricks. It just requires common sense, persistence, and discipline . . . the same ingredients that make any project successful.

✦   ✦   ✦

Designing WebLogic Applications

In this chapter, we present some background and ideas that should be helpful to you in your quest to become a good J2EE and WebLogic application designer.

J2EE is designed for the construction of distributed applications and is based on the Model-View-Controller (MVC) paradigm, a proven approach for designing multitier, enterprise applications that are scalable and maintainable. A good understanding of MVC and how it relates to J2EE and WebLogic will definitely make you more proficient at designing WebLogic applications.

After explaining the relationship between MVC and J2EE, we'll demonstrate some application design and modeling techniques that may help you shorten your time-to-market. Included is a brief tutorial on how to use Unified Modeling Language (UML) to construct *understandable* and *helpful* models of your J2EE designs, a topic we have found to be conspicuously absent from today's programming literature.

Although this chapter does not contain a lot of WebLogic-specific information, it does contain a wealth of relevant background information and real-world techniques that will help you maximize the return on your WebLogic investment.

Understanding Multitier Applications

A *multitier application* is an application whose code is distributed across multiple logical and physical tiers of execution. Each tier is tied to a specific application function and communicates with the others in well-defined, predictable ways. The application gets its work done by moving signals and data from tier to tier in response to user and program inputs.

J2EE is designed expressly for building multitier applications. In this section, you will learn how J2EE's architects accomplished this feat in the context of multitier thinking and design patterns that have been around for more than 20 years.

How J2EE separates applications into tiers

Although it may sound complicated, the good news is that the J2EE design is based on only three tiers:

✦ **Client:** This part of the application is seen and manipulated by the user. It can live in a Web browser or be a standalone application.

✦ **Middle:** This part of the application contains business logic that controls the flow of information between users and corporate data. In J2EE, the middle tier consists of two subtiers: the Web tier, which handles communications with the client tier, and the Enterprise JavaBeans (EJB) tier, which manages business logic and access to corporate data.

✦ **Enterprise Information System (EIS):** This part of the application provides access to various corporate data stores, such as relational databases, e-mail systems, messaging systems, legacy systems, and so on. All such access is accomplished through the use of standard APIs.

The J2EE designers had very good reasons to build their platform around a multitier model. J2EE is designed primarily to build Web systems, and Web systems are inherently multitier. The Web is a world of browsers, Web servers, and database back ends. In other words, it's a world of clients, middles, and enterprise information systems. This is the world that J2EE was created to tame.

The Model-View-Controller design pattern

When the J2EE designers looked at the Web, they saw an environment whose widely distributed nature gave it remarkable power. But the distributed nature of the Web also made it difficult to build Web applications. One of the major challenges was trying to figure out where the code for Web applications should live. Should it live in the browser or should it live on the Web server? Should pieces of it live in both places? Or should the code live somewhere completely different? There were no clear answers.

Whatever the solution was, it seemed reasonable that the code should be divided up somehow. One sensible approach was to put code for interacting with the user near the user, code for interacting with other systems (such as databases) near those systems, and code for tying the two ends together somewhere in-between. This approach reminded the J2EE engineers of a popular, proven, 20-year-old application design pattern that they thought might help them bring order to the chaos. That design pattern is called *Model-View-Controller.*

Model-View-Controller (MVC) is a widely used and highly successful design pattern for building maintainable applications. Introduced by Xerox researchers in 1980, MVC is especially useful for designing multitier applications, so the architects of J2EE designed the platform with MVC in mind.

MVC revolves around the concept that application logic can be clearly divided into three layers:

✦ **Model:** This layer of application logic deals with core business entities and their associated business logic. In real-world applications, model objects usually map to rows in database tables and also consist of code for the proper manipulation of that data. Model objects are implemented as a stable set of reusable business objects that are available to developers across the enterprise for use in multiple applications.

✦ **View:** This layer deals with the presentation of application data and commands to the user. In other words, it is the user's view of the system. View objects can be HTML pages rendered in a browser or the graphical user interface rendered by a Java client application. They are usually application-specific.

✦ **Controller:** This layer sits between the View and Model layers and implements business logic and workflows. A command initiated by a user in the View layer typically triggers code in the Controller layer, which manipulates one or more objects in the Model layer to complete the command. Controller objects are usually application-specific, but can also be designed for use by multiple applications.

Note the resemblance to the J2EE EIS, Client, and Middle layers.

Over the past 20 years, MVC has proven itself to be a resilient, productive model for building distributed applications of all kinds. As you shall see, it turns out to be especially useful for designing Web applications, which is why it became the cornerstone of the J2EE platform.

Model-View-Controller in action: An ATM machine

A simple example of MVC in action is a bank customer interacting with an ATM machine. Figure 3-1 shows how the various components of this system map to MVC.

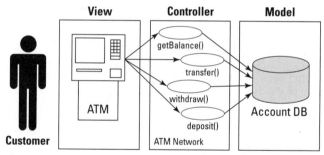

Figure 3-1: An ATM mapped to MVC

Note Although the paradigm is called Model-View-Controller, we prefer to diagram it from left-to-right as View-Controller-Model, which shows the usual flow of information from user to middle tier to back end. This is exactly what Sun's team does when it draws Client-Middle-EIS diagrams for J2EE.

Model-View-Controller as a methodology for designing multitier applications

MVC is a powerful model because it cleanly divides code based on its functionality, so changes made in one layer of an application need not affect the other layers. Separating code by functionality, a concept that is known as *decoupling*, is especially useful in the View layer, which is by far the most changeable layer of an application. For example, consider your favorite Web sites; their appearances often change to keep up with current fashion and browser technology, but the underlying data remains relatively unchanged. Multitier development organized around MVC is what makes this possible.

Decoupling View code from Controller and Model code pays big dividends over the lifetime of an application because frequent changes can be made to the GUI without rewriting the guts of the application. Some of the dividends accrue in the form of increased developer productivity, because developers can focus on what really needs to be changed without having to worry about the ripple effect their changes have on the rest of the system. This leads in turn to reduced development costs. Additional dividends accrue in the form of reduced time to market (and therefore, reduced time to revenue) for the Web site or application.

The decoupling concept is what makes MVC useful for designing multitier applications. In a networked environment, decoupling makes it theoretically possible to deploy different parts of an application on different machines. While code in the Client layer, for example, is executing on a user's workstation, code in the Controller and Model layers can be executing on powerful servers, in which it can be made easily accessible to all clients and physically close to corporate data stores for increased performance. If you combine this with the cross-platform capabilities of Java, you create an incredibly flexible environment in which code can be deployed to the best combinations of hardware *and* operating systems for a given application.

Another strong motivator for MVC is that it cleanly divides development teams by skill set, so GUI design experts can work in the View layer, domain experts can work in the Controller layer, and database experts can work in the Model layer. This clean division of labor capitalizes on the team members' strengths while increasing the productivity of the team as a whole.

Returning to the ATM example, you can see that ATMs are a perfect application for MVC because of their distributed nature and the need for code in each layer to be almost completely independent of the others. Imagine the chaos that would ensue if every little change made to the network required reprogramming all the machines! Thanks to MVC, this is not the case. The guts of the network are completely isolated from the machines, except for the well-defined commands that move between them. Therefore, major changes can be made to the network (such as optimizing the code or moving it to faster computers) without affecting the machines in any way, as long as the structure of the commands doesn't change. Likewise, banks can upgrade their machines (perhaps by installing graphical operating systems so they can display color advertisements) without affecting the network. And your account data, regardless of the bank in which it resides, is available to every machine on the network — even the ones owned by other banks — because the data formats are also well-defined. ATMs, as simple as they seem, are one of the best examples of MVC in practice.

Note   An excellent example of MVC at work in the world of personal computers is Microsoft Outlook. Its View layer (the Outlook application) has gone through three revisions since 1997, but all three versions use the same Controller (the MAPI interface) to talk to the same model (Exchange Server). Because of this, all three versions of Outlook can simultaneously connect to the same Exchange Server with no problems.

Building Multitier Applications with J2EE: Containers and Components

After the J2EE designers decided to embrace MVC as the model for their architecture, the next step was to figure out how to implement it. Their elegant solution was to map a small set of software *components* to the MVC model and then define specifications for containers that would host those components. The container specifications would be made public, so any application vendor interested in building and marketing J2EE containers could do so. And although vendors would be free to add their own differentiating features to the containers, they would have to meet a strict set of compatibility requirements before their containers would be certified by Sun. This certification process would ensure that components written to the base J2EE standard would run within *any* vendor's container.

As mentioned earlier, J2EE was designed not only with MVC in mind, but also with the idea that most people would use it to build general-purpose, distributed, enterprise applications. Furthermore, J2EE's designers assumed that most of these applications would run on the Web: either on the Internet, on private corporate intranets, or both. These design principles are readily apparent when you look at how containers and components are defined in J2EE.

Containers

Containers provide runtime support for the types of components they support. J2EE defines four types of containers:

✦ A *Web container,* for hosting Web components

✦ An *EJB container,* for hosting EJB components

✦ An *applet container,* for hosting client-side applets that run within Web browsers

✦ An *application client container,* for hosting client-side Java applications that run outside of Web browsers

Furthermore, each container must provide support for the following three items:

✦ Access to container-specific APIs and services (the servlet API for servlets, the EJB API for EJBs, security and transaction services for EJBs, and so on). These services also include lifecycle support for the components themselves; in most cases, the container automatically manages the creation and destruction of components in response to user demands on the system.

✦ Access to the J2EE APIs for interfacing with other systems and components (JDBC, JMS, JNDI, JTA, JavaMail, and RMI).

✦ Support for runtime configuration of contained components through deployment descriptors, which are implemented as XML files. This allows those who are assembling applications from J2EE components to modify the runtime behavior of those components simply by adjusting entries in the XML files. You may, for example, point an entity EJB to a different database server or specify that only certain users may invoke a servlet. With deployment descriptors, you can do so without recompiling the component's code or even having access to the code.

Note   WebLogic Server, being a server-side product, includes Web and EJB containers, but not applet or application client containers.

Components

Components are chunks of application functionality you write that run inside containers. For your components to work, you must follow the specifications and APIs for the types of components you are writing. You must also create default deployment descriptors for your components. This is easy, however, because WebLogic and third-party development tools provide automated support for the creation of deployment descriptors.

J2EE components come in four types:

✦ *Web components* (JSPs and servlets), which run in the Web container

✦ *EJB components* (session beans, message beans, and entity beans), which run in the EJB container

✦ *Applet components* (miniature client-side applications written in Java), which run in an applet container (usually a Web browser)

✦ *Client Application components* (full-featured, client-side applications written in Java), which run in the client application container (usually a Java Virtual Machine on a client computer)

Furthermore, J2EE components share the following characteristics:

✦ They are developed according to the specifications and APIs of their containers.

✦ They perform well-defined roles within an application (the rest of this chapter spells these roles out in detail).

Note   WebLogic Server supports deployment of Web and EJB components only.

Organizing Components into Applications

J2EE's creators designed each J2EE component to fill certain roles in the MVC architecture. Therefore, a good recipe for designing an application's components is to do the following:

1. Map the application to the MVC model.

2. Decide which J2EE components you need to build and what functionality they need to provide.

This sounds easy, but it's not. As many project teams have discovered, some MVC roles can be filled by more than one type of J2EE component. This means that you don't need every type of J2EE component to build perfectly functional J2EE applications. In fact, it's sometimes preferable to omit certain types of components, especially for smaller projects, to reduce application complexity, development time, and costs.

Although it may sound like cheating, Sun's own documentation for J2EE endorses this approach. According to *Designing Enterprise Applications with the Java 2 Platform, Enterprise Edition* (Sun Microsystems, Inc., 2000):

"The J2EE specifications and technologies can, by definition, make few assumptions about how precisely the APIs are going to be used to deliver application-level functionality. . . . The J2EE programming model needs to embrace application scenarios that treat the Web container, and the EJB container, as optional logical entities."

The upshot of all this is that Step 2 is more difficult than it sounds, and the exercise of mapping application functionality to J2EE components often generates lively debate among a project's team members.

As a starting point, most J2EE developers accept the following guidelines:

✦ *Entity EJBs* typically occupy the *Model* layer.

✦ *JSPs* typically occupy the *View* layer.

✦ *Servlets, Session EJBs,* and *Message EJBs* typically occupy the *Controller* layer.

What causes debate is when designers and developers "color outside the lines" to solve certain problems under certain circumstances. Nothing in the J2EE specification, for example, prevents you from using a servlet in the View layer or a session EJB in the Model layer. No technical barriers prevent you from doing so, either. It generally boils down to questions of preference and taste, with no right or wrong answers.

In an attempt to bring consistency to the process, the Sun Java Center recently published a set of application design guidelines known as the *Sun Java Center J2EE Patterns.* These patterns, first released to the public in March 2001, are the most comprehensive guidance available for J2EE application designers. They help designers identify common recurring problems in J2EE application design, for which they recommend specific solutions by using various combinations of J2EE components. Written by J2EE experts in Sun's consulting division, the patterns represent three years of wisdom accumulated while executing projects for the likes of Ford Motor Company and E*Trade.

The patterns are not "the law," and are themselves open to interpretation and modification. Your team should study the patterns, experiment with them, make appropriate modifications to suit your circumstances, and move on. If the patterns work for you — great. If not, invent your own. But whatever approach you choose, you'll be more productive if you try to apply it consistently from project to project.

The following sections describe commonly used patterns in each layer of MVC. These are just a few of the many patterns available, but they give you a good idea of what the patterns are all about. You can find the full catalog of patterns at the following URL:

```
http://developer.java.sun.com/developer/technicalArticles/J2EE/patterns/
```

Model tier patterns

Model tier patterns are designed to facilitate the exchange of data between an application and its data stores. This section describes data access objects and value objects, two of the most commonly used patterns in this tier.

Data Access Object (DAO)

Data Access Objects (often called DAOs) provide interfaces to persistent data stores, such as relational databases, network directories, messaging systems, e-mail systems, and so on. DAOs encapsulate access to their underlying stores, hiding the details from the rest of the application.

A DAO that connects to a relational database, for example, would handle all the details of connecting to the database server, submitting SQL queries, retrieving results, and returning results to callers. Callers would be presented with a high-level interface to the data that requires no knowledge of the database system or the mechanisms used to manipulate it.

Note   DAOs are an example of a J2EE *helper class.* A helper class supports the processing needs of an application, but is not a formal J2EE component itself. A JavaBean is another example of a helper class.

A common approach is to insert a DAO between an entity EJB and the database, as shown in Figure 3-2.

Figure 3-2: DAO managing database access for an entity EJB

By using a DAO this way, you insulate the entity EJB from changes in database platforms or changes in the mechanisms used to access the database. Such changes would impact the DAO but would be hidden from the entity EJB as long as the DAO's public interface didn't change.

Value object

A *value object* is a helper class that gives components in the View and Controller layers more efficient access to components in the Model layer (usually entity EJBs).

An entity EJB is usually mapped to a row in a database, with getter and setter methods defined for each column in the row. Imagine writing a JSP to display the row of data represented by an entity EJB. The JSP must call every getter method to retrieve the complete row. This means that the JSP must have knowledge of the entity EJB's structure. Furthermore, each getter call is a remote method invocation, so the network overhead created by this arrangement is very high.

Value objects are designed to overcome these problems. When a value object is incorporated into the design, the JSP calls a special method in the entity EJB that creates a value object, populates it with the full row of data, and returns it to the JSP. This reduces the number of remote method calls to one and eliminates the need for the JSP to know the structure of the entity EJB. Figure 3-3 illustrates this arrangement.

 Note   In this context, the value object is usually implemented as a JavaBean, allowing the JSP developer to take advantage of the programming linkages between JSPs and JavaBeans.

Figure 3-3: Value object providing a JSP with efficient access to an entity EJB

You can write value objects that are *updateable.* In this scenario, the client makes changes to the data in the value object and then sends the value object back to the entity EJB to be copied to the database. Note, however, that if other clients are holding copies of the same data in value objects of their own, their data will now be stale, so you may need to devise a strategy for dealing with this. Updateable value objects also increase the potential for the old client/server problem of *lost updates.* These occur when user A and user B both get copies of the same data. User A saves changes first, followed by user B. User B's changes overwrite user A's, resulting in user A's updates being lost.

> **Note**   In the diagrams, J2EE components are represented with heavy outlines and helper classes with regular outlines.

View tier patterns

View tier patterns are designed to support presentation logic and user navigation through an application. The most common such pattern is the *view helper,* which is a class that performs low-level processing for a View component. This pattern is used to enforce the separation of presentation logic from business logic in J2EE.

View helpers are most often used in conjunction with JSPs to prevent the mixing of too much Java code (embedded in scriptlets) with HTML or XML markup code. J2EE provides two types of view helpers for this purpose: JavaBeans (available in JSP 1.0 and higher) and JSP tag libraries (available in JSP 1.1 and higher). Figure 3-4 shows view helpers mapped to MVC.

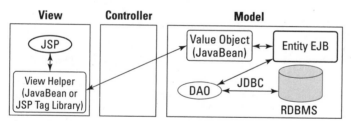

Figure 3-4: JSP with a view helper, implemented as a JavaBean or JSP tag library

Figure 3-4 shows the view helper accessing a database, but this need not be the case. View helpers can perform any kind of low-level processing that you want to isolate from your JSPs.

View helpers provide many benefits. They help separate the View layer from other layers of the application, making the application as a whole more amenable to change. They also provide significant opportunities for code reuse. A well-written JSP tag library, for example, could provide useful functionality for hundreds of JSPs written far into the future. Another benefit of view helpers is that they support a clear division of labor between View developers (working in HTML or XML) and Controller or Model developers (working in Java).

Controller tier patterns

Controller tier patterns support processing that occurs between the View and Model layers. In this section, you will learn about front controllers, dispatchers, and session façades, which manage an application's flow-of-control and access to system resources.

Front controllers and dispatchers

In this pattern, processing initiated by JSPs passes through a *front controller* (implemented as a servlet) that controls access to other system resources via helpers. The servlet also contains code that dispatches requests to other JSPs in the View layer for navigation purposes. This part of the servlet is called a *dispatcher*. Figure 3-5 illustrates this pattern.

Figure 3-5: Front controller with helpers and an embedded dispatcher

The front controller is usually written as a servlet because Java code is necessary to implement the required flow-of-control, and the servlet API provides routines designed for this purpose.

The benefit of the front controller pattern is that it centralizes navigation and access to server-side resources. This eliminates code duplication (caused by copying and pasting identical navigation code into multiple JSPs) and allows JSPs in the View layer to focus on presentation.

Session facades

A *session facade* provides clients with uniform controlled access to business objects in the Controller and Model layers of an application. These business objects are usually implemented as session EJBs, entity EJBs, DAOs, or other types of helpers.

In the absence of a session façade, clients access business objects directly to do their work. This situation is illustrated in Figure 3-6.

Figure 3-6: Client application accessing business objects directly

This configuration suffers from three major drawbacks:

✦ Because the client application manipulates the business objects directly, it is tightly coupled to them. If changes are made to the business objects or if the rules for using them change, the client application could fail.

✦ Business objects implemented as EJBs are accessed via remote method calls, which incur high network overhead. As the number of client applications increases, the number of remote calls increases, and overall system performance suffers.

✦ Assume that a business process requires the use of three business objects. One client application might invoke the objects in one order, whereas another client application might invoke them in a different order. Additionally, two or more clients might try to execute their versions of the business process simultaneously. This combination of factors could lead to data synchronization errors and other unanticipated consequences.

Session facades are designed to overcome these drawbacks. A *facade*, normally implemented as a session EJB, stands between the client applications and business objects and ensures that access to the business objects takes place in an efficient, predictable manner. Figure 3-7 shows the previous application after introducing a session facade:

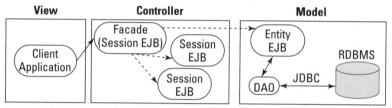

Figure 3-7: Client application accessing business objects through a session facade

The session facade overcomes the drawbacks mentioned earlier as follows:

✦ Now that the client calls the facade, it's no longer tightly coupled to the business objects. Changes made to business objects can be absorbed by the facade, decreasing or eliminating the likelihood of breaking the clients.

✦ Encapsulating calls to multiple business objects within the facade reduces the high network overhead of remote method calls. The client makes only one remote method call to the facade, which in turn remotely calls the business objects. If the facade and business objects reside in the same EJB container, the network overhead of the calls between them drops to nearly zero.

✦ The coding of business processes that require the participation of multiple business objects can be centrally captured in the facade. Any client that wants to execute a business process executes the code for it in the facade. This reduces the likelihood of synchronization errors and other problems because every client executes the business process identically.

A session facade can be implemented either as a stateful or stateless session EJB, depending on the need to maintain conversational state between the user and the business objects during calls to the facade.

Deploying Components in WebLogic's Containers

Remember that WebLogic Server consists of a Web container and an EJB container. These containers host the Web components and EJB components of an application, as defined in the J2EE component model.

Before WebLogic's containers can do any work, they must have content deployed to them. Figure 3-8 shows how Web components and EJB components are assembled for deployment in WebLogic Server. The boxes enclosing the various objects and components represent special deployment files (known as *archive* files) that contain those items. The boundaries of these boxes are superimposed on the MVC model to show how a complete, deployed J2EE application maps to MVC.

The archive files are copied to deployment directories on your WebLogic Server. WebLogic's containers access the contents of these files at runtime to provide your application's functionality.

Note   Archive files are created with the Java `jar` utility. These files, referred to as JAR files, are nothing more than slightly modified WinZip files. The `jar` utility creates files with the extension `.jar`, which you can simply rename to obtain the extensions described in this section. Detailed instructions for creating these archive files appear in later chapters of this book.

Figure 3-8: WebLogic application components bundled for deployment and mapped to MVC

The Web Archive (`.war`) file contains the J2EE components (servlets and JSPs) and non-J2EE components that make up a Web application. At runtime, WebLogic's Web container manages the contents of this file.

The Java Archive (`.jar`) file contains the J2EE components (EJBs) that comprise the EJB portion of an enterprise application. WebLogic's EJB container manages the contents of this file.

The Enterprise Archive (`.ear`) file is simply an archive file containing the WAR and JAR files.

The Resource Adapter Archive (`.rar`) file contains classes for interfacing with other enterprise information systems, via the J2EE connector architecture.

 Cross-Reference   Chapter 18 covers the creation and deployment of JAR, WAR, and EAR files. Chapter 27 covers the J2EE Connector Architecture and the creation of RAR files.

WebLogic, being a server-side product, does not provide deployment support for client applications and applets. WebLogic does, however, allow you to deploy HTML, XML, graphics, multimedia, and downloadable files with your Web components in the WAR file.

The various archive files are a tremendous convenience when it comes to deploying your application or moving it from one server to another. Instead of having to copy an entire directory structure containing hundreds of files to your server, you simply copy a single archive file, register it with WebLogic Server, and your application is ready to run.

Designing an Example Application: J2EE Online Brokerage

Now it's time to put theory into practice by designing a WebLogic application. Your application is the J2EE Online Brokerage (JOB), a simplified online stock brokerage system. JOB is a Web application that will be used by a fictitious brokerage firm's customers and employees. Although it will not be as powerful as a real brokerage site, JOB will have enough features to demonstrate the various aspects of designing and building J2EE applications with WebLogic.

Identifying requirements

JOB supports a retail brokerage, one that provides services for individual investors like you and me, as opposed to institutional investors such as mutual funds and pension plans. Each investor's account consists of a mix of cash and securities. To keep the example manageable, you will make a few simplifying assumptions:

✦ First, you will only support trading of common stocks on Nasdaq and the New York Stock Exchange (NYSE)—no options, warrants, or derivatives, and no trading on commodities exchanges or foreign exchanges.

✦ Second, you will only support cash purchases of securities on the expectation that their prices will rise; stocks cannot be bought on margin or sold short.

✦ Third, each customer can have only one brokerage account.

Before diving into the design of the application, it's helpful to understand who will be using it. The brokerage's clients, the individual investors, are certainly one group of users, but why stop with them? Customers interact with a company's employees, so it might be worthwhile to make the site useful to the employees as well. After all, J2EE and WebLogic give you the power to build much more than a pretty Web site—you can build a full-featured *application* disguised as a Web site that serves an entire community of users.

With this in mind, you will design JOB to serve five different types of users:

✦ *Customers:* The individual investors who form the brokerage's client base. These are the only users who are not brokerage employees.

✦ *Brokers:* Registered stockbrokers who manage one or more customer accounts.

✦ *Managers:* The stockbrokers' bosses. Each broker reports to one manager and each manager supervises one or more brokers. Managers do not directly manage customer accounts.

+ *Research Analysts:* These people examine promising companies and industry trends and write reports about their findings. The reports are made available to customers to help them make intelligent stock purchase decisions.

+ *System Administrators:* These people are charged with managing the brokerage's Web site, including the JOB application.

Next, you need to decide in broad terms what functionality you want to deliver to your users. You do this by imagining what options should appear in the application's main menu. The options for JOB are the following:

+ *Portfolio tracking:* Where users can see how much cash they have and how much their securities are worth based on current prices.

+ *Real-time quotes:* Where users can enter a ticker symbol for a stock and get back its current price.

+ *Online trading:* Where users buy and sell stocks.

+ *Investor's Library:* A searchable database of useful documents for investors.

+ *Report Center:* Where employees can run reports on client trading activity, account status, and sales commissions.

+ *User Profile Editor:* Where users of all types can securely update their mailing address, e-mail address, password, and other personal information.

A good online brokerage not only supports the mechanics of trading, but also provides timely information to guide investors' trading decisions. Trading activity often regulates access to such information; the more you trade, the more information you can obtain. This common feature would be interesting to implement in your example, so you will invent a scheme to partition the contents of the Investor's Library into tiers of increasing value. JOB's Investor's Library contains the following types of documents, arranged in order from lowest value to highest:

+ *Annual Reports:* Detailed reports of business activity and financial results for the past year, filed by publicly traded companies. These are posted to the library as they become available.

+ *Industry Outlook Reports:* In-depth studies of entire industry segments (such as semiconductors or health care), written by the brokerage'sresearch analysts. These reports are posted to the library on a quarterly basis.

+ *Research Reports:* In-depth studies of publicly traded companies, written by the brokerage's research analysts. These reports are posted to the library on a weekly basis.

+ *Morning Meeting Notes:* Late-breaking news stories and a daily assessment of market conditions, written by the brokerage's research analysts. These are posted to the Investor's Library every weekday morning before the stock markets open.

To govern access to material in the Investor's Library, each JOB user shall be granted varying access privileges, based on his or her recent trading activity:

+ *Bronze:* The default level, granted to all customers regardless of trading activity. Bronze customers can access annual reports and industry outlook reports.

+ *Silver:* A higher level, granted to customers who made at least five trades in the preceding month. Silver customers can access annual reports, research reports, and industry outlook reports.

✦ *Gold:* The highest level, granted to customers who made at least ten trades in the preceding month. Gold customers can access annual reports, research reports, industry outlook reports, and morning meeting notes. Brokerage employees have Gold level access to all areas of the site, regardless of their trading activity.

You now have enough background information about your online brokerage to proceed with a detailed design.

Organizing requirements by user role

JOB's development team has interviewed management and customers to discover what features they want to see in an online brokerage system. They have also surveyed the competitive landscape to see what services other online brokerages provide. The result of these efforts is the following list of high-level site requirements, broken down by the type of site user.

Customer

Customer privileges include the following:

✦ View portfolio (cash and stocks)

✦ Make a trade (buy or sell shares of a stock)

✦ Get real-time quotes

✦ Browse, search, and download content in the Investor's Library, subject to access privileges (Gold, Silver, or Bronze)

✦ Edit personal profile

System administrator

Customer privileges, plus the following:

✦ Enable/disable Web access for all users

✦ Run reports on system activity

Research analyst

Customer privileges, plus the following:

✦ Post annual reports, industry outlook reports, research reports, and morning meeting notes to the Investor's Library

✦ Delete previously published information from the Investor's Library

Broker

Customer privileges, plus the following:

✦ View portfolios of their customers

✦ Make trades for their customers

✦ Edit personal profiles of their customers

✦ Run commission reports for themselves

At JOB, each customer trade generates a $10 commission for the customer's broker, unless the trade is made online, in which case the trade generates a $5 commission for the "house account."

Manager

Broker privileges, plus the following:

✦ View portfolios of all customers

✦ Make trades for all customers

✦ Edit personal profiles of all customers and brokers

✦ Run commission reports for all brokers

Expressing requirements in use case diagrams

The Unified Modeling Language (UML) provides a number of ways to express various aspects of system designs visually. A useful tool for visualizing system requirements is the UML use case diagram. Use case diagrams show, at a high level, who the users of a system are and what functionality they have available to them. Figure 3-9 is a use case diagram that illustrates the system requirements for JOB.

Note   A detailed discussion of UML is beyond the scope of this book, but UML diagrams are used occasionally throughout the book. A number of resources are available for learning UML. A good place to start is *UML Weekend Crash Course* by Thomas A. Pender, 2002 (Wiley Publishing).

This use case diagram shows functionality available to the Customer as a series of ovals (Log in, View portfolio, Make a trade, and so on). Arrows pointing from other users to the Customer show that those users inherit the Customer's functionality (but not the other way around), whereas separate use cases attached to the other users show the functionality available only to them. A Research Analyst, for example, can do everything a Customer can do, plus post reports to the Investor's Library.

The value of use case diagrams is that they provide concise, visual representations of textual requirements that are easy to read and share. They also serve as a starting point for more detailed UML diagrams of various types.

Exploding use cases into activity diagrams

One such detailed diagram is an activity diagram, which illustrates a workflow. Figure 3-10 is a high-level activity diagram for the Log In use case. We say "high-level" because the diagram captures the essential aspects of the workflow, but omits most of the details, which will be filled in later.

The workflow begins with the solid black dot in the upper-left corner, which leads to the Display Log In Page activity state. The user presumably supplies a username and password. If the user hits Cancel, he returns to the home page and the workflow ends (as indicated by the solid black dot with the circle around it). If the user hits Submit, the workflow proceeds to the diamond-shaped decision point, where you check to see if the user has ever signed in before (the diagram does not specify how). If so, you authenticate him against the user database, update his sign-in information, take him to the main screen, and the workflow ends. If not, you set up his Web account. No details are given about this process; it's probably a good candidate for a separate activity diagram. During the course of setting up the user's account, you will authenticate him. Afterwards, you update his sign-in information, take him to the main screen, and the workflow ends.

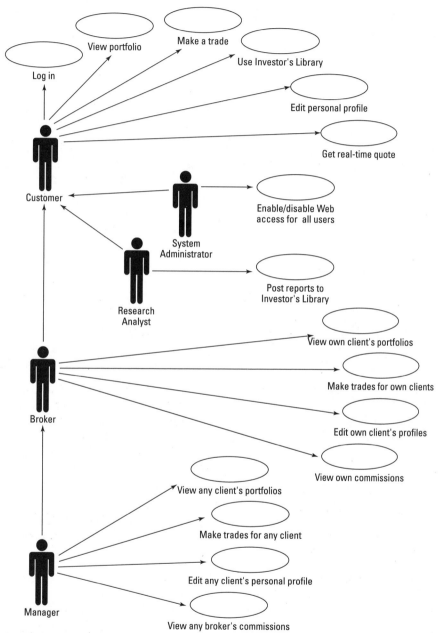

Figure 3-9: UML use case diagram for the J2EE online brokerage system

Figure 3-10: Activity diagram for the Log In use case

High-level activity diagrams are a valuable tool for modeling workflows in Web applications. But they don't provide enough detail to determine what components a system needs. Adding more detail to the diagram — say, by expanding each activity into multiple subactivities — doesn't help either because then you simply have more information about the workflows with no additional insight on how to build them.

Mapping functionality to MVC with swimlanes

The key to unlocking this puzzle is to remember that J2EE applications are Model-View-Controller applications. Is it possible to draw an activity diagram of your system mapped to MVC?

The answer is yes. UML defines a refinement to activity diagrams called *swimlanes* that will do the trick. Swimlanes divide a workflow into multiple roles of responsibility. A vertical column running down the page depicts each role and the role's name appears on top. Activities are drawn in the columns that have responsibility for them, and arrows link activities as before. Activity diagrams with swimlanes show the clear division of labor among the various participants in a workflow.

For the purpose of designing J2EE applications, we like to create an activity diagram with three swimlanes: View, Controller, and Model. This forces us to map the system's workflows to MVC, which we try to do in more detail than in the high-level diagram. Figure 3-11 shows an expanded activity diagram for the Log In use case with MVC swimlanes added.

Note As mentioned earlier, we prefer to diagram MVC from left-to-right as View-Controller-Model, and we do so in our swimlane diagrams as well.

Here are some tips for drawing MVC swimlane activity diagrams:

✦ The View layer should contain only activities initiated by users and pages displayed to users.

✦ The Model layer should contain only atomic actions against data stores, such as selects, inserts, updates, deletes for databases, and posts and retrieves for message queues.

✦ If you're modeling activities triggered by users, all begin and end states should appear in the View layer. The *begin* state shows that the user initiated the process. The *end* state, which usually appears immediately after a concluding page is displayed, shows that the user knows the process has ended.

✦ In the View layer, use actions that correspond to button presses or menu selections to label state transitions. In UML, leading forward slashes (/) denote actions. Examples in Figure 3-11 include /Submit and /Cancel, which indicate what happens when the user clicks these buttons in their Web browser.

✦ Choose verbs for activity states that are appropriate to the layer. In the View layer, we use *display* to indicate the display of a page to the user. In the Controller layer, we use *redirect* to indicate a page transition; and for data manipulations we use verbs such as *read, compare, increment, decrement,* and *set.* In the Model layer, we use the SQL verbs *select, insert, update,* and *delete* to generically describe database operations.

Selecting appropriate J2EE components and modeling their interactions

If you study the diagram in Figure 3-11 with the J2EE design patterns in mind, you should be able to see possible ways to implement the login process with J2EE components. One option is to use a front controller with a JavaBean helper and an embedded dispatcher. In this scenario, you see from the View swimlane that you need five JSPs: a login page, a home page, a contact your broker page, a setup your Web account page, and a main menu page. You see from the Model swimlane that you need one database table: Customer. At a minimum, the Customer table must contain columns for the customer's tax ID, password, total number of logins, and last login date. The Controller swimlane shows that you need code to process requests, manipulate data from the Customer table, and display different JSPs depending on the results. You can use a servlet controller to handle requests and dispatching to the JSPs, and a JavaBean DAO to front-end the Customer table. Figure 3-12 is a class diagram showing the required entities, including the Customer relational database table.

Figure 3-11: Activity diagram for the Log In use case, with MVC swimlanes added

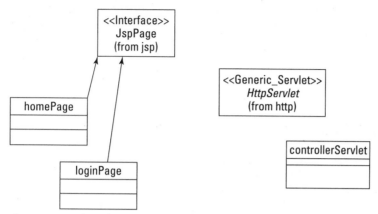

Figure 3-12: Class diagram showing components to implement the Log In use case

The class diagram provides a static view of the application; it shows what pieces must be built. To get a better idea of what the pieces of a system must do, UML defines a *sequence diagram*. A sequence diagram is similar to an activity diagram, but it shows workflows expressed in terms of actual system components, not generic activities.

Figure 3-13 is a sequence diagram that shows how the components in the class diagram work together to accomplish the Log In use case.

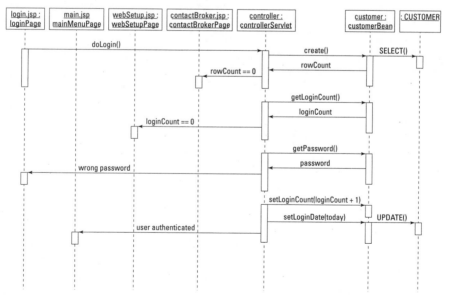

Figure 3-13: Sequence diagram showing component interactions for the Log In use case

Notice the structural similarities between Figures 3-5, 3-11, and 3-13. They are three completely different views of the system, but they are remarkably consistent. Figure 3-5 is the J2EE design pattern used to model the Log In use case, molded around MVC. Figure 3-11 is an activity diagram of the Log In use case, also molded around MVC. What's remarkable is that Figure 3-13, the sequence diagram showing the J2EE component interactions, is *not* explicitly molded around MVC, yet the same overall structure shines through. This diagram makes it strikingly obvious that J2EE was designed with MVC in mind.

Other considerations

Besides pure J2EE issues, there are other issues to consider when designing WebLogic applications that will have an impact on how you design your applications.

Databases

One of the most important non-J2EE considerations is the database (or multitude of databases) with which your WebLogic applications will interact. If you are using a modern RDBMS such as Oracle or Microsoft SQL Server, remember that these products are powerful servers in their own right. Don't assume that all the advances made in RDBMS technology over the past 15 years should be thrown out the window in favor of the wanton use of session or entity EJBs. On the contrary, such a design approach is likely a recipe for disaster. In almost every case, you will achieve maximum performance if you leave database processing to the database.

Operations on large sets of data

Take advantage of stored procedures, packages, views, and other RDBMS features that specialize in bulk operations on sets of data. A stored procedure that uses SQL to apply a formula to a set of rows, for example, will execute orders of magnitude faster than a session EJB that reads the rows out of the database, applies the formula in memory, and then writes the rows back.

Operations embedded in transactions

Likewise, a business rule that makes small changes to multiple database tables runs faster and more reliably if it is coded into a stored procedure, especially if the entire process is embedded in a transaction.

We believe that database transactions against a single data source should never be started or stopped outside of the database engine, even if the external code resides on the same machine as the RDBMS. The penalty for failures is simply too high. If the code crashes in the middle of a transaction or if the network connection between the code and the database is lost, operations against the database may block until the transaction is somehow forced to complete—usually by rolling it back and losing the changes.

The absolute worst offense is to have user input determine the boundaries of a transaction. Imagine a JSP that begins a transaction when the user puts a record into Edit mode in their browser. If the user saves changes, the transaction is committed; otherwise, it is rolled back. What if the user hits the Back button on their browser or goes home for the night without saving? The affected database tables will be locked until the transaction is somehow completed. This sounds like a ridiculous case, but it does happen. Beware!

The only exception to our "transactions-stay-inside-the-database" rule are operations involving two-phase commit (transactions spanning multiple databases). It is obviously impossible for such transactions to stay inside any single database.

See Chapter 6 for a complete discussion of transactions.

Security

The log-in scenario explored in this chapter is based on a simple design where usernames and passwords are transmitted across the network and validated against a database. Thousands of such systems exist in production today. In many cases, the usernames and passwords are transmitted in clear text (no encryption), and the passwords are stored unencrypted in a relational database. Such a "security" system is hardly secure! Fortunately, a number of better options are available.

WebLogic Server's comprehensive security is described in more detail in Chapters 20, 21, 22, and 25.

WebLogic startup and shutdown classes

WebLogic allows you to deploy Java classes that execute when WebLogic Server starts up and shuts down. Such classes can perform housekeeping tasks for any or all J2EE applications deployed on your server, such as verifying connections to databases, file servers, message queues, credit card processing services, and so on.

Startup and shutdown classes fall outside the realm of normal J2EE design, but they are useful tools you should keep in mind as you design your applications.

Summary

This chapter has covered a lot of background material that should give you a much clearer understanding of J2EE and how to design multitier, component-based applications for the J2EE platform. Because WebLogic applications are in fact J2EE applications, you are now a more informed WebLogic application designer as well!

J2EE is heavily predicated on the Model-View-Controller (MVC) application design pattern. Quite simply, if you understand MVC and thoroughly embrace it during your application's design phase, you will save valuable time. You will also design a much better application that takes advantage of all the power J2EE has to offer.

The Unified Modeling Language (UML) can be a powerful ally in helping you chart out your application's design. Unfortunately, today's programming literature contains very little information on how to use UML effectively when designing J2EE applications. We have tried to remedy this situation somewhat by showing how to combine use cases, activity diagrams, swimlanes, class diagrams, and sequence diagrams into a concise package of J2EE design documents that clearly show you *what* to build, *why* to build it, and *how* to hook it together.

This chapter concludes the discussion of how to prepare your enterprise for WebLogic. Now, whether you think you're ready or not, it's time to dive into WebLogic!

✦   ✦   ✦

Setting Up a WebLogic Environment

Our goal in this part of the book has been to introduce you to WebLogic Server's many capabilities and to help you understand how to field a team that can effectively take advantage of them. We've also given you some ideas on how to design J2EE applications that can be deployed with WebLogic.

The rest of this book is hands-on, showing you in great detail how to configure WebLogic's features, how to write code that uses those features, and how to deploy and test that code. To derive the most benefit from this book, you need to install WebLogic Server and create a WebLogic environment to play in. This chapter shows you how to do so.

We start off by showing you how to install the simplest possible WebLogic development environment on a computer and verify that it is working correctly. We then show you how to connect WebLogic to two popular relational database systems, Oracle and Microsoft SQL Server, so that you can write and test database code. Finally, we give you some tips and techniques on how to create a WebLogic development environment that supports a complete application development workflow, from development to testing to final deployment.

We want to make this chapter concrete without making it too long, so we limit our discussion to WebLogic Server 7.0 running on the Windows 2000 Server operating system. WebLogic runs on a multitude of platforms, including several flavors of Unix, but showing how to install and configure WebLogic on each platform would take too much space. Many developers, especially individual developers, start with Windows 2000 anyway, so we think the greatest number of readers will benefit if we focus on that platform. Knowledgeable Unix developers can easily adapt the instructions we give here to the version of Unix that they are using. The steps to install WebLogic on those platforms are fairly similar and well-documented in the WebLogic manuals.

After you have finished reading this chapter, you will have a fully functional copy of WebLogic Server running on your machine, and you'll be ready to conquer the material in the rest of this book. So let's get to work!

Configuring a Computer for WebLogic Development

WebLogic Server's published hardware requirements are modest and sufficient for one developer working with one computer. The minimum requirements for an Intel-based, Windows system are the following:

✦ Hardware: Pentium 200MHz or faster, 236MB free disk space (plus 170MB for temporary installation files), 256MB RAM

✦ Operating System: Microsoft Windows NT 4.0 or Microsoft Windows 2000

Obviously, the more capable your computer, the more productive you will be. For example, Lou runs WebLogic on a desktop running Windows 2000 Professional (this is certified only for development; Windows 2000 Server is certified for production). This machine has a 733MHz Pentium III chip, a 40GB hard drive, and 640MB of RAM. In addition to WebLogic Server, it comfortably supports his Oracle 8i installation, so he can develop and test database code.

Note that the stated minimums are not at all sufficient for large production systems. Requirements for them will vary, depending on user traffic, application complexity, clustering configurations, and so on.

In addition to the hardware and software requirements, WebLogic Server 7.0 requires the following to be installed on the computer running WebLogic Server:

✦ Java Development Kit (JDK) 1.3. As of this writing, JDK 1.3.1_03 is bundled with WebLogic 7.0 and is automatically installed by WebLogic's installer.

✦ Netscape 4.7.*x* and 6.2 are supported on all platforms (Windows and Unix). Microsoft Internet Explorer 5.*x* or 6.0 are supported on Windows. You need one of these Web browsers to run the WebLogic Console application (used to administer WebLogic).

Note   Having a supported browser for the WebLogic console mainly has to do with the Java applet tree on the left. Using this applet is optional in WebLogic 7.0 — you can configure the console to display only the Web pages (no Java applet) in the main console window instead. For example, you can use any browser on Mac OS X (which is BSD Unix under the covers) and have no trouble administering WebLogic servers through the console.

Obtaining a Copy of WebLogic Server

The quickest way to get a copy of WebLogic Server is to download it from the BEA Web site. BEA provides complete, fully functional copies of all its products on its Web site. The download URL for WebLogic Server 7.0 is

```
http://commerce.bea.com/downloads/weblogic_server.jsp
```

Note   Beware — the download for the Windows 2000 version of WebLogic Server is more than 150MB.

In addition to the product itself, you need a valid license file with which to run WebLogic Server. BEA controls the distribution of WebLogic Server through the use of XML license files. These files contain encrypted keys that enable the product to varying degrees, depending on the type of license you purchase. The free download of WebLogic Server includes a license key for a 30-day evaluation that allows up to five simultaneous connections to the server. This is sufficient for most evaluations and is certainly sufficient for use with this book.

All WebLogic Server downloads include the jDriver for Oracle, the jDriver for Microsoft SQL Server, and the jDriver for Informix. You can, therefore, connect to any of these databases after installing WebLogic Server. The drivers include 30-day evaluation licenses that support up to two simultaneous database connections each. In addition, BEA bundles various versions of the Oracle Thin Driver and Sybase jConnect Type 4 JDBC drivers.

Finally, you may want to download your own copy of the WebLogic documentation set, which is available in PDF format at the following URL:

```
http://edocs.bea.com/wls/docs70/pdf.html
```

Installing WebLogic Server

This section walks you through the procedure for installing WebLogic Server 7.0 on a computer running the Windows 2000 operating system. The steps for installing on Windows NT 4.0 are exactly the same. Before continuing, you may also want to read the *BEA WebLogic Server Installation Guide*, which is included with the WebLogic documentation set.

> **Note** Windows XP is not officially supported by BEA. As a client operating system, XP would never be used in production. However it's perfectly reasonable to use it for developers. You might want to contact BEA Support before configuring developer machines with an operating system.

This section shows you how to perform what BEA calls a GUI-mode installation; in other words, we show you how to interactively install WebLogic by using its GUI-based installer program rather than perform a script-based or silent installation.

> **Note** Script-based and unattended modes for installing WebLogic Server are available for use by system administrators. See the *WebLogic Server Installation Guide* for details.

There are two options for the GUI installer: You have the choice of downloading the Package Installer or just the WebLogic Platform Net Installer, as shown in Figure 4-1. The Net Installer is a much smaller download, and it allows you to pick and choose which features to download and install. If you don't need documentation or examples, or you want to add other products from the WebLogic Platform, it could save you time in downloading. We'll show you the installation process using the Net Installer, since that's what BEA recommends and it's usually the logical choice.

Running the Installer

Downloading the WebLogic Platform Net Installer places a file called net_platform701_win32.exe on your computer. This executable is the installer program. To begin the installation, run this program. After a few moments, the installation screen appears, as shown in Figure 4-2.

Figure 4-1: Choosing between the Net Installer and the Package Installer

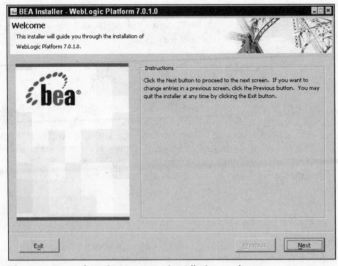

Figure 4-2: WebLogic Server 7.0 installation welcome screen

Click the Next button to start the installation wizard. The installer walks you through a series of screens in which you can set your installation options. Your first task is to read and accept the license agreement, as shown in Figure 4-3.

Figure 4-3: Accepting the license agreement

'The next step is to choose or define a BEA home directory, as shown in Figure 4-4. If you have never installed any BEA WebLogic Platform applications on your computer before, your only option is to create a new BEA home directory, which is where information about the installation and configuration of your installed BEA products is kept.

Figure 4-4: Creating a new BEA home directory

You can install *one* copy of each *different* version of every BEA product in the BEA home directory. You can, for example, install WebLogic 6.1 *and* WebLogic 7.0 in the same BEA home directory without any ill effects. As such, BEA recommends that you create only one BEA home directory per computer.

Note   Don't confuse the BEA home directory with the product directory or the domain location. The BEA home directory contains information shared across multiple BEA products, such as JDKs, pointers to product location, and licensing information. Later on, you'll specify the product directory, which is where WebLogic Server itself is installed. Still later, you'll specify the domain location, which is where your specific applications and server configuration(s) are installed.

Note   The BEA home directory is passed to WebLogic Server in startup scripts as `bea.home`.

Enter a directory path for your BEA home directory (it can reside on any drive that has enough room) and click Next. From Figure 4-4, you can see that we elected to specify `D:\bea` as the BEA home directory.

Now it's time to choose an installation type, either Typical or Custom, as shown in Figure 4-5. Choosing Typical Installation will download and install all products and examples included in the entire WebLogic Platform, not just WebLogic Server. Because we don't want absolutely everything, we chose Custom Installation and clicked Next.

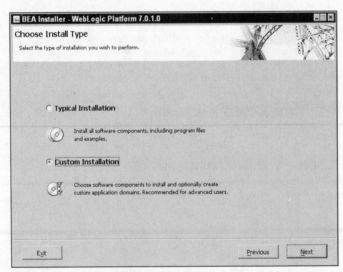

Figure 4-5: Choose Custom Installation to fine-tune what gets downloaded and installed.

Because we chose Custom Installation, the window in Figure 4-6 appears. Here, you can choose which applications — and which components of those applications — to download and install.

The four major components you can choose are:

✦ *WebLogic Server*: To get the most out of this book, install this and all its subcompo-nents. You must install the Server component or you won't be able to do anything in this book. The Workshop component is necessary to complete Chapter 27 which cov-ers WebLogic Workshop. If you're tight on space or have a slow connection and you're not (yet!) interested in Web Services, you can leave this unchecked. We don't cover the Server Examples in this book, but if you need this book chances are you'll want the examples so leave this checked.

✦ *WebLogic Integration*: WebLogic Integration is used to communicate with back end corporate systems. It's a powerful and robust system, but it's beyond the scope of this book. So while it's not necessary to download it, you might want to download and evaluate it. More information is available at BEA's Web site (`http://www.bea.com/framework.jsp?CNT=index.htm&FP=/content/products/integrate`).

✦ *WebLogic Portal*: This is another powerful BEA tool that runs on top of WebLogic Server. If you're interested in using and configuring a portal as a front end to your Web sites, take a look at this product. We don't cover it in this book, though, so it's not absolutely necessary to install these components.

✦ *Platform Samples and Utilities*: The three products we just described — WebLogic Server, Integration, and Portal — are marketed together by BEA as an all-in-one suite named BEA WebLogic Platform. They integrate well together now, and you can expect further tight integration in the future. If you're curious to see how the pieces fit together, the QuickStart and Platform Tour will get you up to speed quickly.

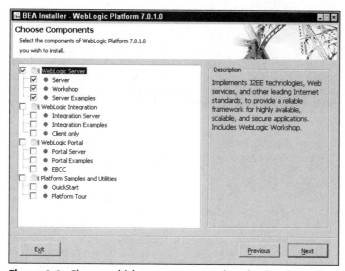

Figure 4-6: Choose which components to download and install.

After clicking Next, the installer needs to know where to download the installation files. This and other options are specified in the download options window, as shown in Figure 4-7. The *storage directory* is where the downloaded files are placed. We chose a generic directory named `ftp` that we use to download things from the Web. If you select the Remove downloaded files when installer exits checkbox, the storage directory will function as a temp directory, and the installation files will be deleted when installation finishes. If you plan on doing multiple similar installations, leave this box unchecked. If your network is configured with an HTTP proxy, select the checkbox and fill in the host name and port number. Click Next to continue.

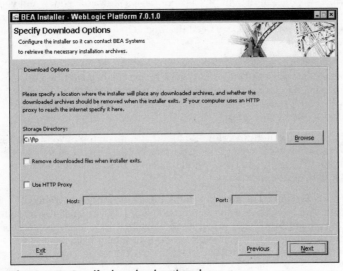

Figure 4-7: Specify download options here.

Now it's time to take a break and go for pizza (or whatever) because this is where the downloading takes place. A progress dialog box, shown in Figure 4-8, displays the current status as it downloads the various components you've chosen. Depending on your Internet connection speed, this can take anywhere from minutes to hours. Leave the Automatically continue installation after completion checkbox selected so that the installer will automatically start the installation when the download is finished, unless you plan on installing it later or on another machine.

Tip   Thankfully, this is a smart downloader and so the dialog box sports a Pause button with which you can pause the download and continue it at another time if necessary (such as if you need to disconnect your Internet connection). This is especially helpful on a dialup line— if you need to use the phone, for example.

The next step is to choose a directory into which the WebLogic Server product will be installed. In the installer, this is referred to as the *product directory*, but in various runtime scripts and developer documentation, this directory is referred to by a system variable named WL_HOME. This directory need not be a subdirectory of the BEA home directory, but the default option is to put it there in a directory called weblogic700, as shown in Figure 4-9. Choosing this option is fine for now.

Figure 4-8: Status of the download; this is when you go for your pizza.

Figure 4-9: Choosing a product directory for WebLogic Server

Now the installer asks if you want to configure a domain and server, as shown in Figure 4-10. You'll eventually have to do it anyway, so just select Yes and click Next.

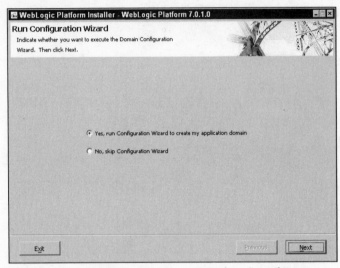

Figure 4-10: Select Yes to create your own domain and server.

Now it's time to choose what kind of domain to create. You have several options of template domains here, shown in Figure 4-11, and if you install other parts of the WebLogic Platform, you'll have even more to choose from.

Figure 4-11: Select a template domain from which to create your new domain.

A *WebLogic domain* is a collection of one or more WebLogic servers (or clusters) grouped for administrative purposes and sharing common configuration parameters. The servers in a domain are managed as a group by using the WebLogic Console administrative application.

Note

> WebLogic domains are completely independent of Windows NT, Windows 2000, and Internet domains. They exist only to facilitate the management of multiple WebLogic Server instances.

Select WLS Domain, which is a domain with a single server with no applications, and accept the default name of mydomain.

WebLogic Server has several ways of setting up servers, including a standalone server, administration server, managed server, and clusters. The next step in the wizard, shown in Figure 4-12, asks you to select which type of server you want to set up. For the purposes of this book, select Single Server and click Next.

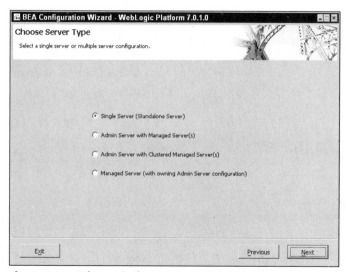

Figure 4-12: Select a single server to create in the domain.

Now it's time to choose where to set up the domain. Version 7.0 is the first version of WebLogic Server to automate the creation of a domain in a directory separate from the WebLogic Server binaries. It's always a good idea to keep your domains and applications separate from WebLogic itself, just as you keep your source code separate from your Java editor's binaries. In Figure 4-13, you can see that we've installed our domain on a separate drive in a separate directory structure: H:\WebLogicUserDomains\mydomain.

Administration Servers versus Managed Servers

WebLogic Server contains an implementation of the Java Management Extension (JMX) standard called the *Administration Service*. Management of a WebLogic domain's configuration occurs through the Administration Service, and the WebLogic Console is your window into its features.

WebLogic is designed so that only one WebLogic Server in a domain can run the Administration Service. This server is called the *administration server*. All other servers in the domain are managed by the administration server and obtain their runtime configuration from it. These servers are called *managed servers*.

The administration server is the single point of control for the entire domain, and it must be running for you to make changes to the configurations of any of the managed servers running beneath it. If you run only one server for development purposes, you must run it as an administration server or you can't configure it.

By default, when you execute the class `weblogic.Server` to create a server instance, the server starts up as an administration server. To start a server as a managed server, you must specify its administration server by using the `-Dweblogic.management.server=URL` command-line option. In the absence of this option, the server starts as an administration server.

For more details about how to use administration servers and managed servers, see the *BEA WebLogic 7 Server Administration Guide*.

Figure 4-13: Select a directory for your new domain.

The next step is to specify a basic server configuration. Figure 4-14 shows the default options.

Figure 4-14: Default server configuration screen

The meanings of the entries on this screen are as follows:

✦ *Server Name*: The name of this WebLogic Server, which must be unique within its domain.

✦ *Server Listen Address*: The IP address on which you want this server to listen. You can leave this field blank, or if you have multiple network cards on your machine, you can specify one of their configured IP addresses.

✦ *Listen Port*: The TCP/IP port on which WebLogic's HTTP server listens for requests. The default port is 7001, but you can change it to any valid port. It is common to change this to port 80 if you plan to use WebLogic as your default HTTP server.

✦ *Secure (SSL) Listen Port*: The TCP/IP port on which WebLogic's HTTPS server listens for requests. The default is 7002, but you can change it to any valid port. You can change it to port 443, for example, if you plan to use WebLogic as your default HTTPS server.

A useful strategy for creating a WebLogic development environment is to create separate domains for development, testing, and production. This enables you to stage your applications on the appropriate servers as they move through the development life cycle. It also enables you to protect production code from experiments you may be conducting in the development area because each domain has its own distinct configuration. A full discussion of domains is available at http://e-docs.bea.com/wls/docs70/admin_domain/overview.html#1065083.

To create such an environment, define three domains: dev, test, and prod. Within each domain, create a server called admin, which is the default administrative server for that domain. Later, you can add additional servers to each domain with different names and purposes.

You can rerun the configuration wizard after you're done with the initial installation here. Using the wizard, you can create the additional domains and servers we just described.

The next step is to define a username and password for administering WebLogic, as shown in Figure 4-15. This username and password are required to start the server and also to log in to the server by using the WebLogic Console administrative application. Previous versions of WebLogic Server forced you to use a username of `system`, but now you are free to create your own name. Choose any username and a password (between 8 and 20 characters), enter it twice, and then click Next.

Figure 4-15: Defining a username and password for administering WebLogic

Next, the installer asks whether you want to install the server you just configured as a Windows service. For development purposes, it's usually better not to do this, so you can explicitly control the starting and stopping of your server. But in a production environment, installing WebLogic Server as a service provides two key benefits:

✦ WebLogic Server restarts automatically whenever the machine restarts.

✦ You can start and stop WebLogic Server from a remote machine by using the server management tools included with Windows 2000.

Cross-Reference

You do not need to install WebLogic Server as a Windows service to start and stop it remotely; you can use WebLogic's Node Manager to do that in an administration server, but that's beyond the scope of this chapter. Configuring the Node Manager is discussed in Chapter 23.

Because we are installing a development environment, we elect not to install WebLogic Server as a service.

Next, the wizard asks if you want to install a Windows Start Menu entry for this server. This can be handy, so we selected Yes. After clicking Next, the wizard displays a summary list of all the parameters you entered, as shown in Figure 4-16. If you notice any mistakes, click Previous to change your entries. Otherwise click Create to create your domain and server.

Figure 4-16: A summary of your new domain and server parameters

After a few moments, your domain and server are created. As shown in Figure 4-17, the wizard asks if you want to create another domain or server.

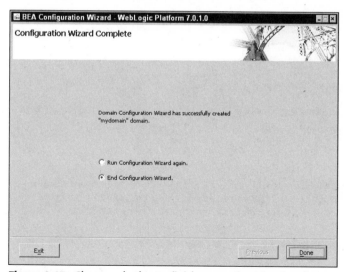

Figure 4-17: Choose whether to finish or run the wizard again.

When the installation is complete, your WebLogic Server is ready for use. You don't need to reboot the computer.

Starting WebLogic Server

The best way to tell whether the installation succeeded is to start WebLogic Server. To do so, choose Start ➪ Programs ➪ BEA WebLogic Platform 7.0 ➪ User Projects ➪ mydomain ➪ Start Server. A command window opens and the startup sequence begins. You are prompted to enter a username to boot WebLogic Server; enter the username you defined during the installation process and then press Enter. Then, type in the password you defined. After a few moments, WebLogic Server starts and is ready to go. The command window looks something like Figure 4-18.

Tip   If for some reason the server will not start, you can go to BEA's excellent developer portal at http://dev2dev.bea.com where you'll find FAQs and newsgroups dedicated to WebLogic Server installation.

Figure 4-18: WebLogic Server, up and running

Running the WebLogic Console

After the server is up and running, start the WebLogic Console by choosing Start ➪ Programs ➪ BEA WebLogic Platform 7.0 ➪ WebLogic Server 7.0 ➪ Server Tour and Examples ➪ Start Admin Console. You are prompted for a username and password. Enter the username and password you defined during installation. After a few moments, the Console's main screen appears, as shown in Figure 4-19.

The WebLogic Console is simply a Web application deployed on WebLogic Server. It presents its user interface by using the default Web browser on your computer. You can exit the WebLogic Console by closing its browser window, but leave it open for now.

Shutting down WebLogic Server

To perform an orderly shutdown of WebLogic Server, right-click the server's entry in the domain tree of the WebLogic Console and then choose Start/stop this server..., as shown in Figure 4-20.

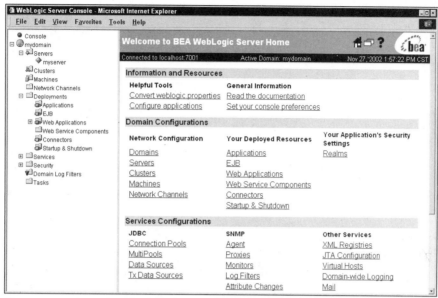

Figure 4-19: The WebLogic Console

Figure 4-20: Stopping a WebLogic Server from the WebLogic Console

This brings you to a console page in which you can start or stop the server, as shown in Figure 4-21. Select Shutdown this server... to shut it down.

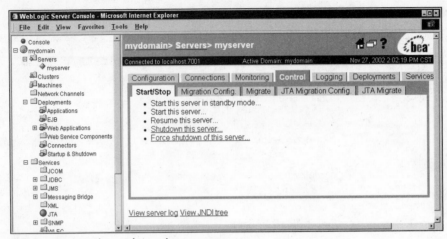

Figure 4-21: Starting and stopping a server

After the server is shut down, console commands against it no longer work; you need to restart the server, as described earlier in this chapter, before you can execute console commands against it.

Optimizing the WebLogic Server startup process for development

Because you will likely be starting and stopping your development WebLogic Server frequently, you may want to perform the steps described in the following sections to optimize your development environment.

Add the password to the startup script

Having to enter a username and password every time you start WebLogic Server becomes tedious after awhile. You can short-circuit this process by storing the administrative username and password in WebLogic's startup script. Then the server starts without prompting for the username and password.

Note   This shortcut exposes your password in plain text to anyone who has access to the startup script. For one developer working on one computer, this isn't usually a problem (especially if you choose an innocuous password), but larger shops with several developers sharing machines in a lab may not want to do this.

To add the password to the startup script, edit the server startup script in the following location:

    <user domain path>\<domain name>\startWebLogic.cmd

So, using the directories we specified in the installation, the startup script file's location is

    H:\WebLogicUserDomains\mydomain\startWebLogic.cmd

Open this file in a text editor. If your username is *wlsadmin* and your password is *password*, for example, add it to the indicated line, as follows:

```
@rem Set WLS_USER equal to your system username and WLS_PW equal
@rem to your system password for no username and password prompt
@rem during server startup.  Both are required to bypass the startup
@rem prompt.  This is not recommended for a production environment.
set WLS_USER=wlsadmin
set WLS_PW=password
```

Start the server in development mode

While you have startWebLogic.cmd open, let's make a few more changes. The first is to change WebLogic Server's startup mode to development mode.

By default (if you don't start WebLogic with the -Dweblogic.ProductionModeEnabled option), WebLogic Server starts in development mode, which enables the autodeployment feature. With autodeployment enabled, WebLogic polls the /applications subdirectory of the active domain to detect changes in deployed applications. This is a useful feature during development because it means you don't have to restart WebLogic Server every time you make changes to your code. But the feature incurs additional overhead that you probably want to avoid in production systems, which should not change except in rare and controlled circumstances.

To change the startup mode to development mode, change the indicated line in startWebLogic.cmd as follows:

```
@rem Set Production Mode.  When this is set to true, the server starts up in
@rem production mode.  When set to false, the server starts up in development
@rem mode.  If it is not set, it will default to false.
set STARTMODE=false
```

Disable the discovery of managed servers

Recall that WebLogic Server can run either as an administration server for a domain or as a managed server within the domain. If you are running only one WebLogic instance for development purposes, you always run it as an administration server and it has no managed servers running beneath it.

By default, when WebLogic Server is started as an administration server, it attempts to discover which, if any, of its managed servers are running. It does so by consulting a file called running-managed-servers.xml, which is a list of the managed servers that the administration server knows about. This file is created on-the-fly when you run an administration server and start another instance with the startManagedWebLogic command. The file is stored in the configuration directory for the domain.

When you set -Dweblogic.management.discover=false, you disable the capability of the administration server to detect the presence of managed servers that may be running. You may want to do this to save a little time at startup if you know you will be running an administration server, but no managed servers, in your domain. To do so, open startWebLogic.cmd and change the Java options as shown:

```
@rem Set JAVA_OPTIONS to the java flags you want to pass to the vm. i.e.:
@rem set JAVA_OPTIONS=-Dweblogic.attribute=value -Djava.attribute=value
set JAVA_OPTIONS=-
Dweblogic.security.SSL.trustedCAKeyStore=D:\p\bea\weblogic700\server\lib\
cacerts  -Dweblogic.management.discover=false
```

Examining the WebLogic environment

Figure 4-22 shows the directory structure of the WebLogic installation we just performed. At the top level of this structure is the `bea` directory, which is our BEA home directory. Within this directory are directories containing JDK 1.3.1, installation logs, and Java utilities. The contents of these directories are shared by all BEA products installed to this BEA home directory.

Our BEA home directory also contains a directory called `wlserver6.1`, which is the product directory for WebLogic Server 7.0. Although we elected to install WebLogic Server inside our BEA home directory, we could have installed it anywhere on our computer. The installer would have linked it to our home directory via classpath settings and the installation log file.

Figure 4-22: WebLogic directory structure

Inside the `weblogic700` directory are several subdirectories. Table 4-1 explains their contents.

Table 4-1: WebLogic Platform 7.0 Directory Structure

Directory	Contents
/common	Utilities shared among WebLogic Platform applications, such as the Configuration Wizard.
/samples	Sample code and resources. The samples directory has a `server` subdirectory that contains the following subdirectories: `config\examples` A collection of simple applications that demonstrate WebLogic's features. `config\petStore` The WebLogic Server Pet Store application, which is a full-blown e-commerce application based on the Sun Microsystems, Inc., J2EE Blueprint example. The J2EE Blueprint example has been slightly modified to demonstrate WebLogic's features and capabilities.

Directory	Contents
	`eval` An evaluation copy of the Pointbase relational database management system (RDBMS), which is included so that you can run the examples and Pet Store applications with a live database.
	`src` The source code to the examples and PetStore samples in the `config` directory.
	Staging. A staging directory in which the source code is built and compiled in jars, wars, and ears.
`/server`	Where WebLogic Server 7.0 is installed. See Table 4-2 for more information.
`/uninstall`	Code required to uninstall WebLogic Platform applications, including WebLogic Server 7.0.
`/workshop`	Executables and JDK 1.4 for running WebLogic Workshop.

WebLogic Server itself is located inside the `server` directory, and its subdirectories are described in Table 4-2.

Table 4-2: WebLogic Server Directory Structure

Directory	Contents
`/bin`	Executable programs, plus Windows libraries to support JDBC drivers, jCom, Apache plug-ins, Internet Information Server (IIS) API plug-ins, Netscape Server (NS) API plug-ins, and other native code packages.
`/builder`	WebLogic Builder help files.
`/ext`	JDBC Type 4 drivers for Oracle and Sybase, WebLogic JSP tag libraries, and XML JAR files.
`/lib`	The JAR files to run WebLogic Server, plus Unix libraries to support JDBC drivers, Apache plug-ins, Internet Information Server (IIS) API plug-ins, Netscape Server (NS) API plug-ins, and other native code packages.

Your domains are located in the user domains directory. For example, the `mydomain` domain we created has the contents shown in Figure 4-23. This directory contains the scripts to set the Java environment for compiling and running applications and has the subdirectories described in Table 4-3.

Additional directories related to service packs may be present if you have installed WebLogic Server service packs. Service packs contain bug fixes and improvements to WebLogic Server and become available from time to time. At this writing, there is one service pack for WebLogic Server 7.0.

Figure 4-23: User domain directory listing

Table 4-3: WebLogic User Domain Directory Structure

Directory	Contents
/applications	The deployed applications for the domain. They can either be compressed as jars, wars, and ears; or they can be exploded in physical directories.
/logs	Log files for the domain.
/<servername> (e.g., myserver)	LDAP configuration and log files for the server.
/userConfig	Security information persisted from a management bean (MBean).

Note   BEA has recently instituted a new policy where you need to be a customer to get service packs separately from WebLogic Server itself. If you're evaluating WebLogic and a new service pack comes out, you'll need to redownload the entire server with the service pack. If you're a customer, contact BEA support for information on how to get a service pack.

Adding domains for testing and production

We mentioned earlier that a useful strategy for creating a WebLogic development environment is to create separate domains for development, testing, and production so that you can isolate the effects of your development from code that is being tested or is already in production. Thankfully, creating domains is vastly simplified in WebLogic Server 7.0. There is now a utility called Domain Configuration Wizard that creates domains for you, as shown in Figure 4-24. It's the same utility that you used during installation of WebLogic Server, so we won't take you step-by-step through it. You can run that utility to create new domains called dev, test, and prod. To start the wizard, choose Start ➪ Programs ➪ BEA WebLogic Platform 7.0 ➪ Domain Configuration Wizard.

Figure 4-24: The Domain Configuration Wizard

Some important things to keep in mind when creating new domains:

✦ If you want to run multiple domains (say, dev, test, and prod) on the same machine at the same time, remember to assign different ports to each server. A server won't start if a port that it's trying to listen on is already taken.

✦ Remember to create all your domains under a single parent directory (the user domains directory) for ease of administration.

✦ In the Configuration Wizard, the WLS Domain template creates an empty domain — this is what you'd want to use for creating a domain for production. The WLS Examples template creates a domain with all the example applications. The WLS Petstore template creates a domain with Sun's Pet Store application. The WebLogic Workshop template creates a new domain for use with a WebLogic Workshop project, which we'll discuss in Chapter 27.

Installing JDBC Drivers

One of the most common uses of WebLogic Server is to Web-enable data residing in relational database management systems (RDBMSs) such as Oracle, Microsoft SQL Server, Cloudscape, and others. Access to such data is enabled through the Java Database Connectivity (JDBC) API, which is part of J2EE.

JDBC is covered in detail in Chapter 5.

JDBC is implemented with drivers provided by BEA, database vendors, and others. As mentioned earlier, WebLogic Server is bundled with the jDriver for Oracle, jDriver for Microsoft SQL Server, and jDriver for Informix.

The correct installation and configuration of JDBC drivers depends on the database you are using, the drivers you are using, and how your database and network are configured. You can find detailed instructions for installing the BEA-provided drivers in the following locations:

✦ *Configuring and Using WebLogic jDriver for Oracle*, available at `http://edocs.bea.com/wls/docs70/oracle/index.html`

✦ *Configuring and Using WebLogic jDriver for Microsoft SQL Server (Deprecated)*, available at `http://edocs.bea.com/wls/docs70/mssqlserver4/index.html`

✦ *Using Third-Party Drivers with WebLogic Server*, available at `http://e-docs.bea.com/wls/docs70/jdbc/thirdparty.html`

Selecting an IDE to Use with WebLogic Server

Many developers today use an *integrated development environment* (IDE) to facilitate the rapid prototyping, development, and deployment of applications. These environments contain a number of labor-saving features that automate redundant tasks, such as generating EJB templates, XML deployment descriptors, and so on. They also provide source code management and build support, which can further increase developer productivity.

One of the most popular IDE products on the market today is Borland JBuilder. JBuilder contains hooks for integrating with WebLogic Server that may increase the productivity of your team. Togethersoft recently bought the remains of WebGain's WebGain Studio, and Borland subsequently bought Togethersoft. Combining JBuilder's outstanding IDE with Togethersoft's outstanding UML modeling will produce a best-of-class suite. If you don't use JBuilder already, we recommend that you evaluate it to see whether it has a place in your shop.

You can find more information about Borland JBuilder at `http://www.borland.com/jbuilder`.

Lately, open source tools have matured quite a bit, and you may want to take a look at NetBeans (`http://www.netbeans.org`) or Eclipse (`http://www.eclipse.org`).

Summary

Installing and configuring WebLogic Server is relatively easy, considering the complexity of the product. In this chapter, we showed you how to download, install, and configure a flexible WebLogic development environment. We also pointed you to additional steps you may want to take, such as installing JDBC drivers and using an IDE with WebLogic to make your development environment as complete and productive as possible.

The rest of this book is spent playing in the sandbox you have just created. So grab your pail and shovel and prepare to dive in!

✦   ✦   ✦

WebLogic and the J2EE APIs

✦   ✦   ✦   ✦

Working with WebLogic JDBC

Java Database Connectivity, or JDBC, is the standard API used by
Java programs to communicate with database systems. JDBC provides a uniform programming interface to any JDBC-compliant
database system and provides powerful features for solving
enterprise-level database-management tasks.

WebLogic provides excellent support for JDBC and contains a number of features that allow you to write portable, maintainable, available, and efficient JDBC code.

This chapter begins with an overview of JDBC, introducing you to
important JDBC concepts and terms. It then dives into WebLogic's
JDBC features, showing you in great detail how to configure and program them.

Note that it is not our intent to provide a comprehensive JDBC tutorial in this chapter. Plenty of other resources are available for this
purpose, including Sun's JDBC tutorial at the following URL:

```
http://java.sun.com/docs/books/tutorial/jdbc/
index.html
```

Our goal in this chapter is to show you how to use JDBC in the
WebLogic environment, with a focus on how to configure and use
WebLogic's drivers, connection pools, data sources, and transaction
support. When you are finished with this chapter, you will have a
solid understanding of how to combine WebLogic with today's leading database engines to build fast, reliable, data-driven applications.

Understanding JDBC

This section explains "generic" JDBC architecture, focusing on issues
independent of vendor implementations (including BEAs). A clear
understanding of these concepts helps you to take firm control of
database-access issues in your applications and to take better advantage of WebLogic's excellent support for JDBC.

JDBC versions and packages

WebLogic 7.0 runs on top of JDK 1.3, which contains JDBC version 2.0. JDBC 2.0 consists of two sets of calls: the JDBC 2.0 Core API and the JDBC 2.0 Standard Extension API. The Core API includes all the functionality of JDBC 1.0, plus enhancements for handling query results, batch updates, Java object persistence, and advanced SQL data types. The Standard Extension API includes additional enterprise features, such as support for connection pools, distributed transactions, and sophisticated result set handling.

JDBC is implemented in two packages:

- ✦ `java.sql`, the Core API
- ✦ `javax.sql`, the Optional Package API

To work with JDBC in your WebLogic applications, simply import these packages into your code. You don't need to import special WebLogic packages because the JDBC API simply routes calls to whatever JDBC driver is in use.

JDBC architecture

The JDBC API encapsulates relational database access into a hierarchy of Java classes and interfaces. JDBC is a fairly low-level API; in other words, it doesn't magically make a relational database look like a set of Java objects, but it gives you the tools to do so yourself if you wish. After explaining JDBC drivers, which contain database-specific implementations of the API, this section explains the major components of the API and how they are related.

Drivers and driver types

JDBC *drivers* manage data interchange between Java applications and relational database management systems (RDBMSs). To understand how these drivers work, it's helpful to know how databases exchange data with outside systems in general.

All major databases, such as Oracle, Sybase Adaptive Server, Microsoft SQL Server, and others, ship with *network libraries* that are used to communicate with the database over a network. Network libraries typically consist of a client-side component that communicates with applications running on a client machine, and a server-side component that communicates with the database server itself. The client-side and server-side components in turn communicate with each other over the network. Figure 5-1 shows database access through a typical network library.

Network libraries expose their functionality through APIs that are callable from C, C++, and other programming languages. On the Windows platform, network libraries usually ship as dynamic link libraries (DLLs). Examples of network libraries include the Oracle Call Interface (OCI), Sybase Open Client, and DBLibrary—a legacy network library used both by Sybase and Microsoft SQL Server.

Note   BEA has licensed OCI for distribution with WebLogic Server. On Windows machines, you can find the OCI DLLs in the `WL_HOME\server\bin\oci817_8` and `oci901_8` directories.

Figure 5-2 shows an application accessing databases from different vendors through their respective network libraries.

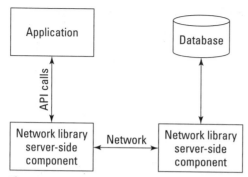

Figure 5-1: Accessing a database through its network library

Figure 5-2: An application accessing multiple databases through their native network libraries

Because they're written to exploit the special features of a vendor's database and because their programmers have intimate knowledge of that database's inner workings, network libraries offer the best performance of any type of remote database access. But every network library API is different, so code written to one vendor's API will not work with any other vendor's database, and vice versa. This makes it difficult and time-consuming to write applications that support multiple databases.

To solve this problem, several vendors came up with the idea of abstracting network library functionality into a high-level API that sits on top of the various network libraries. Developers write to the high-level API, which makes calls to network libraries behind the scenes. At the same time, database vendors make sure that their network libraries provide support for the calls in the high-level API. Through this mechanism, access to vendor-specific functionality is possibly reduced, but this is offset by the developer's ability to write one set of code to access any database.

The most well-known solution of this type is Microsoft's Open Database Connectivity (ODBC) API. Over a period of several years, ODBC has become the de facto standard for accessing databases from applications running on the Microsoft Windows platform, and other platforms as well. As a result, virtually all major database vendors offer ODBC drivers for their products. Figure 5-3 shows an application accessing different vendors' databases through ODBC.

Figure 5-3: An application accessing multiple databases through ODBC

JDBC is an ODBC-like solution designed for Java developers. But unlike ODBC, which supports applications written in multiple programming languages, JDBC is designed exclusively for Java and supports applications written only in Java.

Sun has divided JDBC drivers into four different types, based on how they're implemented. The following sections discuss these four types of JDBC drivers.

Type 1 drivers

A type 1 JDBC driver provides a bridge between Java applications and ODBC drivers, as shown in Figure 5-4 (in fact, this type of driver is called a *JDBC-ODBC bridge*). Type 1 drivers are acceptable for development purposes, but their performance is generally not sufficient for production systems because of the multiple driver layers involved.

Figure 5-4: An application accessing a database through a type 1 JDBC driver

Type 2 drivers

Type 2 JDBC drivers link applications directly to network libraries, as shown in Figure 5-5. Because of this, you must install the network libraries on computers that use the drivers, such as the one hosting WebLogic Server. Most database vendors provide type 2 drivers for their products. Type 2 drivers provide better performance than type 1 drivers because they bypass the ODBC layer. As a result, they are commonly used in both development and production systems. The WebLogic jDriver for Oracle is an example of a type 2 JDBC driver.

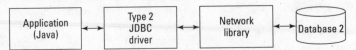

Figure 5-5: An application accessing a database through a type 2 JDBC driver

Type 3 drivers

Type 3 JDBC drivers link applications to middleware servers that allow easy client connections to multiple database back ends (see Figure 5-6). To achieve this, the middleware server maps the application's JDBC calls to appropriate drivers, which are installed on the middleware server, not on the client. The advantage of this approach is that it removes the necessity to install network libraries on client machines. The WebLogic Pool driver is an example of a type 3 JDBC driver, as is the WebLogic RMI driver.

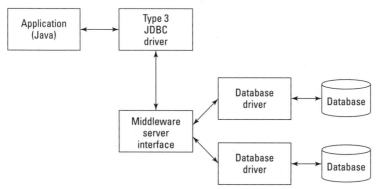

Figure 5-6: An application accessing a database through a type 3 JDBC driver

Type 4 drivers

The type 4 JDBC driver is implemented completely in Java and requires no additional drivers or client-side network libraries to function (in fact, the client-side network libraries are incorporated into this type of driver). Figure 5-7 shows a type 4 driver. Type 4 drivers, like network libraries, are vendor- and database-specific. As such, they provide maximum optimal access to the vendor's database features, but cannot be used with databases from any other vendor. The Sybase jConnect driver is an example of a type 4 JDBC driver.

Figure 5-7: An application accessing a database through a type 4 JDBC driver

Choosing which type of driver to use

Choosing the right driver for your application is a complex decision that depends on several factors, including the following:

✦ The version of JDBC you plan to use (1.0 versus 2.0)

✦ Database features supported in the driver (such as WebLogic 7.0's support for ARRAYs, STRUCTs, and REFs only within the Oracle Thin Driver)

✦ The desired application performance

✦ Requirements for transaction support

✦ Software licensing issues for the JDBC driver and database

✦ The overall topology of your application

✦ Your application's expected patterns of database access

You may find it advantageous to test several candidate drivers and topologies before arriving at a final decision. You may even find that your final design should use different drivers for different tasks.

Sun maintains a directory of JDBC drivers on the Internet that currently contains more than 150 different drivers. You can find the directory at the following URL:

```
http://industry.java.sun.com/products/jdbc/drivers
```

Connections

A *connection* is a communication link between client-side Java code and the database server, established via the JDBC driver. It forms the context for all calls made against that database server. Before working with a database in your code, you must open a connection (unless you're using RowSets, but more on that later in this chapter).

In JDBC, connections are represented by the `java.sql.Connection` interface. Connections are obtained by calling the driver's `connect` method. After a connection is created, you can call its methods to get and set connection options, manage transactions, and create statement objects.

There are two major types of connections: *direct connections* and *pooled connections*.

Direct connections

Direct connections are opened and maintained directly in code, against a type 1, 2, or 4 JDBC driver that physically exists in the calling code's classpath. Code that opens direct connections is fully responsible for managing those connections, and must remember to close them when it's finished using them. Otherwise, the database server's connection limit may be exceeded or the overall performance of the system may suffer due to too many open connections.

Pooled connections

Pooled connections are opened and maintained by J2EE servers, against one or more type 1, 2, or 4 JDBC drivers that physically exist in the server's classpath. Pooled connections are a fixed number of direct connections that are available to potentially any code running within the J2EE server's containers. Connection sharing is managed by a *pool driver,* which is a type 3 JDBC driver used to obtain pooled connections (pooled connections follow the access scheme shown in Figure 5-6).

At startup, the J2EE server is configured to open some number of pooled connections (five for this example). This becomes the pool's minimum size; the pool will always maintain at least five open connections to the database.

When a software module needs a connection, it requests it from the pool driver instead of from a two-tier JDBC driver. The pool driver returns a connection that is not being used and marks that connection as busy. If all pooled connections are busy, the pool driver opens additional connections, the number of which is determined by its configuration parameters. When the caller is finished with a connection, it is marked as unused by the pool driver and returned to the pool for use by other callers.

If a large number of pooled connections remains unused for a configurable period and if the pool size is greater than the minimum, the pool can be configured to shrink itself in predetermined increments by physically closing connections. The pool, however, never shrinks below its minimum size.

Using connection pools is generally preferable to direct connections because they improve performance while conserving precious resources (such as database connections). In most applications, database connections are typically opened, used briefly (usually within the scope of a method), and then closed. This kind of usage pattern makes the idea of sharing connections a good one. Opening a database connection is a CPU- and network-intensive task. Repeatedly opening direct connections during the lifetime of an application is therefore a performance killer. Pooled connections are opened only once at server startup, eliminating this performance problem. Connections can be effectively shared because they're used only for short periods. And privileged information about connection parameters, such as database usernames and passwords, is available only to the pool driver, increasing system security and manageability.

Statements

A *statement* is used to issue a command to a database for the manipulation of data. Statements (also known as *queries*) are almost always written in Structured Query Language, or SQL. SQL is an industry-standard language for database commands that is supported by all leading database products. SQL includes commands for retrieving, adding, modifying, and deleting data from a database.

Relational databases store data in *tables*. A table is a collection of zero or more rows of data, each with identical structure. Each row contains one or more columns that define the structure of the table. Oracle, for example, defines an example table called EMP (for employee) that contains the columns EMPNO, ENAME, JOB, and HIREDATE, among others. The table contains one row of data for each employee, as shown in Figure 5-8.

EMP			
EMPNO	**ENAME**	**JOB**	**HIREDATE**
7369	SMITH	CLERK	12/17/1980
7499	ALLEN	SALESMAN	02/20/1981
7521	WARD	SALESMAN	02/22/1981
7566	JONES	MANAGER	04/02/1981
7654	MARTIN	SALESMAN	09/28/1981

Figure 5-8: Oracle's EMP database table

SQL statements operate on database tables. SQL commands that retrieve data return some number of rows, depending on the query. For example, the following SQL statement returns all five rows of the EMP table:

```
SELECT * FROM EMP
```

Whereas the following SQL statement returns only the last row:

```
SELECT * FROM EMP WHERE ENAME = "MARTIN"
```

SQL statements are represented in JDBC by the java.sql.Statement, java.sql.CallableStatement, and java.sql.PreparedStatement interfaces. Statement objects are created by requesting them from an open connection. After creating a statement, you call its methods to define the SQL command, execute the command, and retrieve the results (if any).

A Statement object is used to execute simple SQL commands. A PreparedStatement can be precompiled (or prepared) for increased performance (statement preparation is performed by the database). A PreparedStatement can also be defined to accept runtime parameters, and the PreparedStatement interface includes methods for setting the values of these parameters. A CallableStatement is used to execute stored procedures that are defined within the database. Stored procedures are blocks of SQL code that perform repetitive, well-defined tasks. They execute more quickly than equivalent SQL generated on-the-fly because the database stores them in a compiled, optimized format.

ResultSets

After a statement executes, its results are available in a *ResultSet,* which is represented in JDBC by the java.sql.ResultSet interface. If, for example, you execute a statement to retrieve all employees in your employee database, you use the ResultSet to retrieve the results for use within your Java program.

A ResultSet contains all rows returned by an SQL statement. To retrieve the information in each row, you traverse the ResultSet using a while loop. In JDBC 1.0, a ResultSet can be traversed only once from beginning to end. JDBC 2.0 introduces scrollable ResultSets, which can be traversed any number of times and in any order.

The following code shows how to obtain a connection, a statement, and a ResultSet, and how to traverse the ResultSet to display its data:

```
// Create a connection
Connection conn = DriverManager.getConnection(connectionURL);

// Create a statement
Statement statement = conn.createStatment();

// Execute a query
ResultSet resultSet =
    statement.executeQuery("SELECT * FROM EMPLOYEE");

while (resultSet.next()) {
  // Output the results in last name, first name format
  System.out.println(resultSet.getString("LAST_NAME") +
    ", " + resultSet.getString("FIRST_NAME");
}

// Close the statement and the connection
statement.close();
conn.close();
```

RowSets

A RowSet is a JDBC 2.0 feature that combines connections, statements, and ResultSets into one interface. RowSets extend the java.sql.ResultSet interface and are represented in JDBC by the javax.sql.RowSet interface. Note that javax.sql.RowSet is an abstract interface that cannot be used directly; you must use a vendor's implementation of this interface.

The most distinctive feature of RowSets is that they are JavaBean-compliant, so they can be used by tools or components that rely on the JavaBean's specification to do their job.

The best way to illustrate the difference between ResultSets and RowSets is to rewrite the preceding example using a RowSet. In this example, we use Sun's reference implementation of the RowSet interface, which you can find in the `sun.jdbc.rowset` package:

```
// Create a RowSet
JdbcRowSet rowSet = new JdbcRowSet();

// Do the rest
rowSet.setUrl(connectionURL);
rowSet.setCommand("SELECT * FROM EMPLOYEE");
rowSet.setUserName("sa");
rowSet.setPassword("password");
rowSet.execute();

while (rowSet.next()) {
  // Output the results in last name, first name format
  System.out.println(rowSet.getString("LAST_NAME") +
    ", " + rowSet.getString("FIRST_NAME");
}

rowset.close();
```

In contrast with the previous example, you can now do all the work with a single interface, the RowSet. Some developers may find this easier.

Because RowSets extend ResultSets, you lose no functionality by using RowSets. The choice of which interface to use boils down to personal preference unless the capability to use RowSets as JavaBeans is a big win for your project.

Transactions

Transactions provide a means of encapsulating multiple related database operations into one logical unit of work. If all the operations succeed, the transaction succeeds, and the effects of the operations are stored in the database. If any of the operations fail, the transaction fails and no changes are written to the database.

 Cross-Reference   WebLogic and its JDBC drivers provide comprehensive support for transactions. Chapter 6 is devoted to this large and complex topic.

Understanding WebLogic JDBC

Now that you understand the basics of JDBC, it should be much easier for you to understand WebLogic's implementation of it, which is the focus of this section.

WebLogic and third-party drivers

WebLogic provides a number of JDBC drivers for use by developers. Some are strictly for database connectivity, while others provide support for transactions, database access via RMI, and pooled connections.

WebLogic two-tier drivers (types 2 and 4)

The drivers discussed in this section are two-tier drivers. This means that you can use them to make direct database connections from any Java application. For the type 2 drivers, you must also have the appropriate client-side libraries installed.

The most common use of the drivers is to make direct connections from code running within WebLogic Server or to use them in conjunction with WebLogic's three-tier driver (discussed in the next section) to create connection pools usable from within WebLogic Server.

These drivers are included with WebLogic Server and do not require separate installation. But they do require separate software license agreements with their respective vendors.

WebLogic jDriver for Oracle

The WebLogic jDriver for Oracle is a type 2 driver for connecting to Oracle databases. As such, it requires Oracle's client-side network libraries to be installed on the computer that will connect to the Oracle database. The driver supports JDBC 2.0.

Proper installation and configuration of the jDriver for Oracle depends on your Oracle installation. For detailed installation instructions, see *Installing and Using WebLogic jDriver for Oracle,* available at the following URL:

```
http://edocs.bea.com/wls/docs70/oracle/index.html
```

WebLogic jDriver for Microsoft SQL Server

The WebLogic jDriver for Microsoft SQL Server is a pure Java, type 4 driver for connecting to Microsoft SQL Server. Two separate versions of the driver exist. One is for connecting to SQL Server versions 6 and 6.5, and the other is for versions 7.0 and 2000. Both versions support JDBC 2.0.

Proper installation and configuration of the jDriver for Microsoft SQL Server depends on your SQL Server installation. For detailed installation instructions, see *Installing and Using WebLogic jDriver for Microsoft SQL Server,* available at the following URL:

```
http://edocs.bea.com/wls/docs70/mssqlserver4/index.html
```

Note   The WebLogic jDriver for Microsoft SQL Server is deprecated as of WebLogic Server version 7.0. You should now use the SQL Server 2000 Driver for JDBC from Microsoft, which supports a subset of JDBC 2.0 Optional Package. See *Installing and Using the SQL Server 2000 Driver for JDBC from Microsoft* at the following URL:

```
http://edocs.bea.com/wls/docs70/jdbc/thirdparty.html#sqlserver
```

WebLogic jDriver for Informix

This driver is also a pure Java, type 4 driver for connecting to Informix databases. It supports JDBC 2.0.

WebLogic multitier drivers (type 3)

WebLogic provides a number of multitier drivers that sit on top of their two-tier drivers, increasing their reach and functionality. These multitier drivers are discussed in the following sections.

WebLogic pool driver

The WebLogic pool driver enables container-managed connection pooling as specified in the JDBC 2.0 Optional API, and as described in the "Pooled connections" section earlier in this chapter.

The pool driver is a "pass-through" driver; it receives JDBC calls from clients and passes them directly through to the drivers used to create the pooled connections. Therefore, the pool driver's level of JDBC compliance is the same as the underlying driver(s) it uses.

The pool driver can be used in conjunction with any WebLogic or third-party JDBC driver that is certified to work with WebLogic Server (the precise meaning of this is discussed in the "Third-party drivers" section, a bit later in this chapter).

Connection pools are configured by using the WebLogic console and become active when WebLogic Server starts up.

WebLogic RMI driver

The WebLogic RMI driver allows Java client applications to connect to a database via RMI. Like the pool driver, the RMI driver uses a separate JDBC driver to connect WebLogic Server to the database. But all client-to-server communication takes place via RMI.

Additionally, WebLogic uses the RMI driver for clustered JDBC, allowing JDBC connections to be shared among the participants in a WebLogic cluster.

The RMI driver replaces the deprecated T3 database driver, which used the proprietary WebLogic T3 protocol for communication.

You can access RMI drivers by looking up their associated `DataSource` object in the JNDI tree. This is discussed further in the "DataSources" section, later in this chapter.

Transaction-aware drivers

WebLogic and other vendors provide a number of drivers that are transaction-aware — that is, they support the execution of transactions across one or more data stores. You can find details about these drivers and their usage in Chapter 6.

Third-party drivers

In addition to the drivers provided by BEA, you can use JDBC drivers written by database vendors and other third parties. When evaluating such drivers, be sure they meet the following criteria, or they won't work with WebLogic:

- ✦ They must be thread-safe.
- ✦ They must be EJB-accessible (they support JDBC transaction calls).

To get the most out of WebLogic and your JDBC driver, you should consider two additional criteria for selecting third-party JDBC drivers:

- ✦ Drivers you use should preferably support JDBC 2.0. The advanced transaction and DataSet features of JDBC 2.0 are indispensable for serious database applications.

- ✦ If possible, you should use drivers that support JNDI lookups via the `DataSource` interface. This allows you to completely decouple your database connection parameters from your Java code, resulting in applications that are more portable and easier to maintain.

For more information about WebLogic Server's support for third-party JDBC drivers, visit the following URL:

```
http://e-docs.bea.com/wls/docs70/jdbc/thirdparty.html
```

MultiPools

MultiPools allow single-server WebLogic configurations to create pools of pools, for one of two reasons:

- ✦ To provide redundancy in case of database-connectivity failures. This type of pool is called a *backup* or *high-availability* pool.

- ✦ To provide database load balancing for heavy usage scenarios. This type of pool is called a *load balancing* pool.

The type of pool to use is determined when the pool is configured in the WebLogic console. Like connection pools, MultiPools become active when WebLogic Server starts.

High-availability pools

Database connection redundancy is achieved through the use of a *high-availability pool*. A high-availability pool consists of an ordered list of connection pools. When a database connection request is made, the first pool in the list serves the request. If the connection fails for some reason — perhaps the server is down or the network connection is broken — the connection request is passed to the next pool on the list (called by some a *failover event*). This sequence continues until the connection is successfully made.

Note   Simply exceeding the capacity of a connection pool does not trigger a failover event in a backup pool. Failover events in backup pools are triggered only by database connectivity failures or by manually disabling the pool.

An example of an application that would benefit from a high-availability pool is an online catalog that uses a read-only product database. Assume that the product database consists of a primary instance and a backup, configured for one-way replication from the primary to the backup. Assume also that the primary database is updated once per day. During the update, which is disk-intensive, the DBA brings down the primary database. Thanks to the high-availability pool, catalog users are automatically redirected to the backup database when connections to the primary database fail. After the primary database is returned to service, catalog users once again get connections to the primary database, giving them access to the latest information. Meanwhile, replication from the primary to the backup occurs in the background, so by the time tomorrow's update occurs, the backup database once again mirrors the primary.

Load balancing pools

Load balancing pools distribute connection requests evenly to every pool in the list, using a simple "round-robin" algorithm. Each successive connection request goes to the next pool in the list, with the rotation going back to the first pool after the last pool is used.

Using the online catalog example from before, assume that site traffic is heavy, and therefore multiple instances of the read-only product database are put into service to handle demand. A load balancing pool is configured to round-robin requests among all the instances.

However, the algorithm will behave like the high-availability algorithm—if one of the pools goes down, it will switch to the next pool.

DataSources

DataSources are new in JDBC 2.0 and are fully supported in WebLogic 7.0. The `javax.sql.DataSource` interface is a factory for `java.sql.Connection` objects and can be registered with a JNDI service. This allows information about database connections to be completely separated from your Java code, making the code more portable and the database connections more secure and manageable.

In WebLogic, DataSources are fully integrated with the WebLogic pool driver, the WebLogic RMI driver, and the WebLogic JTS driver. `DataSource` objects are configured by using the WebLogic console.

Clustered JDBC

Clustered JDBC provides a means for JDBC connections to be shared among participants in a WebLogic cluster. One important feature is that it allows clients to restore database connections that are lost when a participating server in a WebLogic cluster fails. Clustered JDBC requires the use of DataSources and WebLogic RMI.

Configuring WebLogic JDBC

Now that you have a good grasp of JDBC concepts and WebLogic's implementation of JDBC, it's time to learn how to configure WebLogic's JDBC features.

Configuring connection pools

Almost all JDBC code you write for deployment on WebLogic Server will use connection pools. Therefore, understanding how to configure a connection pool is essential. It's easy to do, assuming that you've properly installed WebLogic, the JDBC drivers you plan to use, and the database systems to which you plan to connect.

Creating a new pool

The following example shows how to create a connection pool by using the Oracle Thin Driver. This pool will open connections to an Oracle instance running on a different machine from WebLogic Server.

 Note It is now easier to substitute Type 4 drivers because as of version 7.0, WebLogic Server no longer bundles the driver jars directly in the `weblogic.jar` file. Instead, `weblogic.jar` loads driver jars listed in its manifest file. So using a new or updated driver jar is simply a matter of copying the driver jar to `WL_HOME\server\lib` (where `weblogic.jar` lives) and updating the manifest file in `weblogic.jar`.

1. Start WebLogic Server and open the WebLogic Console. In the domain tree, choose Services ➪ JDBC ➪ Connection Pools. This displays a list of previously created connection pools (if any) as well as a link to create new ones, as shown in Figure 5-9.

Figure 5-9: The JDBC Connection Pools page in the WebLogic console

2. Click Configure a New JDBC Connection Pool. The screen to create a pool appears, as shown in Figure 5-10.

3. In the Name box, type **OraclePool** (you can use any name you want, as long as it's not being used by any other connection pool in the domain).

Caution

Choose the connection pool name carefully because you will not be able to change it later on. All fields except for the name can be changed later. If for some reason you need to change the name later, you can clone the connection pool and use the new name for the clone. Then you can safely remove the original pool. See "Cloning a connection pool" later in this chapter.

4. In the URL box, type **jdbc:oracle:thin:@<server name or ip address>:<port number>:<instance name>,** where `server name or ip address` is the database server's network name or IP (internet protocol) address; `port number` is the TCP/IP port number that the database server is listening on; and `instance name` is the name of the Oracle instance running on the database server. On my network, I'm running Oracle on the machine at address 192.168.0.3, on port 1521 (the default for Oracle), and the Oracle instance is called `LOU`. The URL tells the pool driver where to find your database on the network.

Figure 5-10: JDBC Connection Pool configuration screen

Tip   For whatever driver you are using, supply the same URL that you would use in code to open a direct connection with that driver yourself. To use the WebLogic jDriver for Oracle, set the URL to `jdbc:weblogic:oracle:<serverName>`. To use the jDriver for Microsoft SQL Server, set the URL to `jdbc:weblogic:mssqlserver4`. To use the jDriver for Informix, set the URL to `jdbc:weblogic:informix4`. To use a third-party driver, set the URL according to the vendor's instructions.

5. In the Driver Classname box, type **oracle.jdbc.driver.OracleDriver**. This instructs the pool driver to use the Oracle Thin Driver to create its connections.

Tip   For whatever driver you are using, supply the same Driver Classname that you would use in code to open a direct connection with that driver yourself. To use the WebLogic jDriver for Oracle, set the Driver Classname to `weblogic.jdbc.oci.Driver`. To use the jDriver for Microsoft SQL Server, set the Driver Classname to `weblogic.jdbc.mssqlserver4.Driver`. To use the jDriver for Informix, set the Driver Classname to `weblogic.jdbc.informix4.Driver`. To use a third-party driver, set the Driver Classname to the full class name of whatever type 2 or type 4 driver you are using. Whichever driver you use, be sure the driver is in the Java classpath used to run WebLogic.

6. In the Properties text box, type **user=SCOTT**. This instructs the jDriver to connect to Oracle's sample schema (the database owned by SCOTT, the sample user).

Note

When using the WebLogic jDriver for Oracle, you can also specify the property server= <serverName>, where serverName is the name of the desired Oracle instance, as defined in TNSNAMES.ORA. But when you stop and restart WebLogic Server to initialize the pool, you will find that WebLogic appends serverName to the URL, as described in Step 4, and removes it from the properties. Therefore, you can just append it to the URL.

Tip

You can separate the properties by using semicolons or carriage returns. Joe prefers carriage returns because it makes the property entries more readable.

7. Enter the password. Oracle's default password for SCOTT is tiger.

8. Your fully filled out form should appear as shown in Figure 5-11. Click Create to create the pool.

9. Your browser should now look similar to Figure 5-12. Verify that your settings are correct.

10. Click the Connections tab to configure the pool driver's connection parameters. Set the parameters as shown in Figure 5-13 and then click Apply.

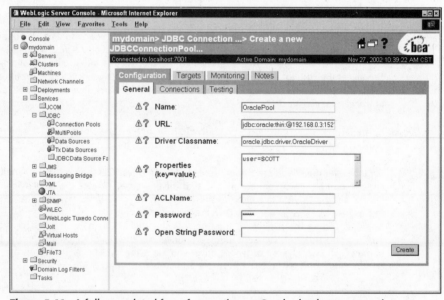

Figure 5-11: A fully populated form for creating an Oracle database connection

Figure 5-12: Once created, a connection pool's name cannot be modified.

Figure 5-13: Connection parameters for the Oracle connection pool

The parameters have the following meanings:

- *Initial Capacity:* The number of connections to Oracle the pool will create at startup. You can enter any number that's within the maximum supported by your WebLogic jDriver for Oracle license and/or your Oracle server.

- *Maximum Capacity:* The maximum number of Oracle connections the pool will open, regardless of client demand.

- *Capacity Increment:* If a new connection is requested and all open connections are busy, the pool will add this number of new connections to the pool, subject to the limits imposed by your license and the Maximum Capacity. Because opening a database connection is time-consuming, it's wise to open connections in bunches.

- *Login Delay Seconds:* The amount of time the pool driver waits between opening each new connection at startup.

- *Refresh Period:* Open connections are closed and reopened at this interval unless they're in use, either to ensure that the database is still available or to restore lost connections in case the database is shut down and then restarted again.

- *Supports Local Transaction:* This attribute applies to XA connection pools only and is ignored for non-XA drivers. Check it if you're using an XA driver that supports SQL with no global transaction. For this example, however, leave it unchecked because you're not using the Oracle XA driver.

- *Allow Shrinking and Shrink Period:* If the size of the pool is greater than its initial capacity and if any of the connections are idle for the duration of the shrink period, the idle connections will be closed at the end of the shrink period.

- *Prepared Statement Cache Size:* The number of prepared statements that will be cached. This can speed performance as long as your schema does not change at runtime.

11. Click the Testing tab. In the Test Table Name box, type **dual**, which is the name of Oracle's built-in test table. You can leave the other testing parameters unchecked, as shown in Figure 5-14. Click Apply.

Caution   If you leave the Test Table Name box blank, the connection pool will not work—only if you do testing. I have also found this to be true for connections to Microsoft SQL Server, which doesn't even have a test table like Oracle does. I found by trial-and-error that entering dual for the Test Table Name works for both Oracle and Microsoft SQL Server.

The other parameters on this screen have the following meanings:

- *Test Reserved Connections:* Checking this option instructs WebLogic Server to briefly test a connection every time a client requests (or *reserves*) one from the pool. This test incurs a slight performance hit every time a connection is requested.

- *Test Released Connections:* Checking this option instructs WebLogic Server to test a connection every time a client releases it back to the pool.

Figure 5-14: Testing parameters for the Oracle connection pool

12. Now that you have configured the connection pool, you must pin it to a WebLogic server. Click the Targets tab and specify the WebLogic Server under which the pool will run, as shown in Figure 5-15. Click Apply.

Figure 5-15: Pinning the connection pool to a WebLogic Server instance

As soon as you click Apply, WebLogic Server activates the connection pool by creating the initial number of Oracle connections you specified. If all goes well, you will see an indication in the WebLogic server log that the Oracle Thin Driver was used to create four connections, as shown in Figure 5-16.

Figure 5-16: WebLogic Server's server log after successful initialization of the connection pool

13. You can further verify the pool's health in the WebLogic console. In the domain tree, choose Services ➪ JDBC ➪ Connection Pools. The list should contain the pool you just created. Click the name of the pool to go to the monitoring page and then click Monitor All Instances of OraclePool. You should see a screen similar to Figure 5-17.

Figure 5-17: Verifying the connection pool's health in the WebLogic console

The connection pool is now ready to accept connection requests. We show you how to obtain a connection to this pool from within your Java code in the "Obtaining pooled connections from the WebLogic pool driver" section later in this chapter.

Cloning a connection pool

In this section, we show you how to clone the pool you just created so that you have two pools available for your MultiPool example later. To clone a pool, follow these steps:

1. In the domain tree, choose Services ➪ JDBC ➪ Connection Pools to display the list of available connection pools (see Figure 5-17).

2. Click the Clone Pool icon, which appears on the right side of the screen, to the left of the trash can. The pool-cloning screen appears, as shown in Figure 5-18.

Figure 5-18: Cloning a connection pool

3. You can give the clone any name you like, as long as it's unique within your WebLogic domain. The default cloned pool name, Clone of OraclePool, is fine for this example. Click Clone.

Caution If you try to change the password before clicking Clone, a bug in the WebLogic Console takes you to the password-configuration screen for OraclePool. Therefore, you must clone the pool first and then change the password.

4. You must stop and restart WebLogic Server to activate the cloned pool connections. Alternatively, you can unassign and reassign the cloned pool to your server, remembering to click Apply after each step.

Configuring MultiPools

Creating a MultiPool is very similar to creating a connection pool. In this example, you'll create a MultiPool containing the two Oracle connection pools you created in the previous sections.

1. In the domain tree, choose Services ⇨ JDBC ⇨ MultiPools. The screen shown in Figure 5-19 appears.

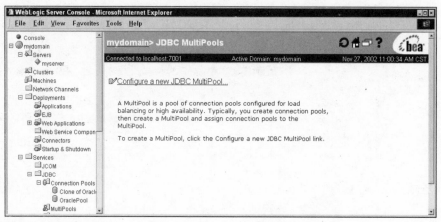

Figure 5-19: Preparing to configure a WebLogic MultiPool

2. Click Configure a New JDBC MultiPool and complete the MultiPool configuration screen, as shown in Figure 5-20 (for this example, you'll create a Load Balancing MultiPool). Click Create.

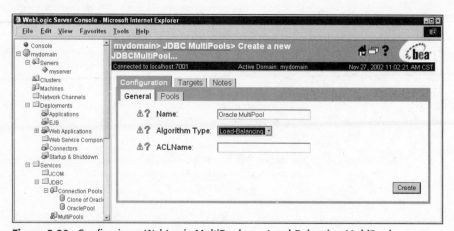

Figure 5-20: Configuring a WebLogic MultiPool as a Load-Balancing MultiPool

3. Click the Pools tab and move both Oracle connection pools into the Chosen list, as shown in Figure 5-21. Click Apply.

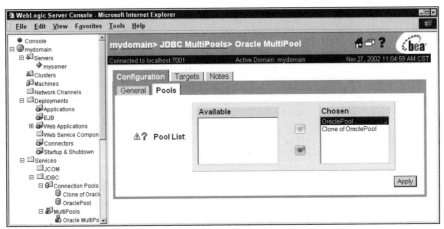

Figure 5-21: Choosing connection pools to include in the MultiPool

4. Click the Targets tab and move your instance of WebLogic Server into the Chosen list, as shown in Figure 5-22. Click Apply.

Figure 5-22: Assigning the MultiPool to a WebLogic Server instance

5. Confirm proper creation of the MultiPool by viewing it in the WebLogic console, as shown in Figure 5-23.

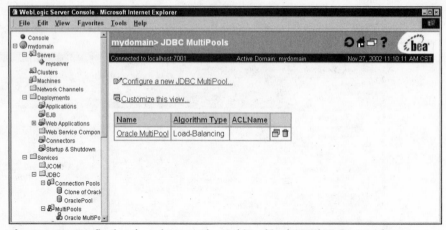

Figure 5-23: Confirming the existence of a MultiPool in the WebLogic console

Configuring DataSources

Now you will create a DataSource for the OraclePool connection pool, which enables your server applications to obtain connections by looking up the DataSource in WebLogic's JNDI tree.

1. In the domain tree, choose Services ➪ JDBC ➪ Data Sources. The screen shown in Figure 5-24 appears.

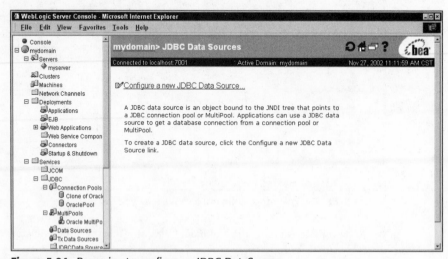

Figure 5-24: Preparing to configure a JDBC DataSource

2. Click Configure a New JDBC Data Source to display the DataSource configuration screen, as shown in Figure 5-25.

Figure 5-25: Configuring a JDBC DataSource for OraclePool

The entries on this page are as follows:

- *Name*: A name for the DataSource, which must be unique within the WebLogic Server domain. Type **DataSource for OraclePool** for this value.

- *JNDI Name:* The JNDI name for the DataSource, which must conform to the rules for Java identifiers and be unique within the WebLogic Server domain. Type **jdbc/ OraclePoolDataSource** for this value.

Note The JNDI Name should always begin with `jdbc/` so that it follows Sun's Java conventions.

- *Pool Name:* The name of the existing JDBC connection pool to which this DataSource is mapped. Type **OraclePool** for this value.

- *Row Prefetch Enabled:* Check this option if the JDBC DataSource will be used by external Java clients, such as RMI clients, that are not executing within WebLogic's JVM. It increases performance by automatically prefetching a given number of rows and sending them to the client when it opens a JDBC ResultSet, thereby reducing the number of network roundtrips between the client and WebLogic Server.

- *Row Prefetch Size:* The number of rows that will be automatically prefetched and sent to an external client when it opens a ResultSet. The optimal value for this parameter depends on your application and database.

- *Stream Chunk Size:* When multiple rows are prefetched from the server, the data is streamed to the client in chunks whose size is determined by this parameter. Generally speaking, larger values increase performance by reducing network roundtrips between the client and server.

3. After completing the configuration screen, click Create.

4. Click the Targets tab and move your WebLogic Server instance into the Chosen list, as shown in Figure 5-26. Click Apply.

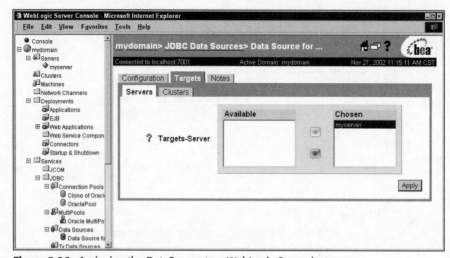

Figure 5-26: Assigning the DataSource to a WebLogic Server instance

5. Stop and restart WebLogic Server to activate the DataSource.

Configuring Tx DataSources

We discuss the configuration of Tx DataSources (Transactional DataSources) in Chapter 6.

Programming WebLogic JDBC

The rest of this chapter is devoted to code examples that show how to program WebLogic JDBC. Each example shows how to perform the same tasks by using Microsoft SQL Server and Oracle, which are the databases that most WebLogic programmers work with on a daily basis.

Because the RowSet interface is youthful and still evolving, the examples focus on the use of Connections, Statements, and ResultSets.

The local network you built for these examples is quite simple. It consists of only two machines, as shown in Figure 5-27.

Figure 5-27: The simple network used for the JDBC examples

Obtaining connections

This section shows how to obtain JDBC connections from a variety of sources, including type 2 and 4 JDBC drivers, the WebLogic pool driver, and DataSources (including Tx DataSources). Keep in mind that all connections are used the same way, regardless of how they are obtained.

Obtaining direct connections from type 2 or type 4 JDBC drivers

To obtain a direct connection from a type 2 or type 4 JDBC driver, follow these steps:

1. Obtain an instance of the JDBC driver you will be using. This is done with the following code:

```
import java.sql.*;

Driver myDriver =
   (Driver)Class.forName(driverName).newInstance();
```

where `driverName` is one of the following:

   `weblogic.jdbc.oci.Driver` for the WebLogic jDriver for Oracle

   `weblogic.jdbc.mssqlserver4.Driver` for the WebLogic jDriver for Microsoft SQL Server

   `weblogic.jdbc.informix4.Driver` for the WebLogic jDriver for Informix

or the full class name of whatever type 2 or type 4 driver you are using. Be sure the driver is in your WebLogic classpath.

2. Obtain a Connection by calling the driver's `connect` method, providing a username, password, server name, and other necessary parameters for accessing the database. These parameters are loaded into a `Properties` object and passed to the `connect` method, along with a URL to the database you're using. The URL is one of the following:

   `jdbc:weblogic:oracle` for the Oracle driver

   `jdbc:weblogic:mssqlserver4` for the Microsoft SQL Server driver

   `jdbc:weblogic:informix4` for the Informix driver

or the URL of whatever other type 2 or type 4 driver you are using. Note that the components of the URL are separated by colons, not periods.

The following code shows how to obtain a connection to an Oracle database using the WebLogic jDriver for Oracle:

```
import java.sql.*;
import java.util.*;

String driverURL = "weblogic:jdbc:oracle";
Properties myProperties = new Properties();

// The Oracle server name should match the entry in
// the tnsnames.ora file
myProperties.put("server", "ORADEV1.ZEEWARE.COM");

// The db property is not needed for Oracle connections,
// because the schema (i.e. "SCOTT") determines the
// database used. You can omit setting this property, or
// simply set it to an empty string as shown.
myProperties.put("db", "");
myProperties.put("user", "SCOTT");
myProperties.put("password", "tiger");

Connection myConnection =
  myDriver.connect(driverURL, myProperties);
```

Similarly, to obtain a connection to Microsoft SQL Server, use this code:

```
import java.sql.*;
import java.util.*;

String driverURL = "weblogic:jdbc:mssqlserver4";
Properties myProperties = new Properties();

// IP addresses work best for MS SQL Server. Simply
// provide the IP address of the SQL Server host.
// You can omit the port if SQL Server is running on
// its default port of 1433.
myProperties.put("server", "192.168.0.1");

// The db property is not needed for MS SQL Server or
// Sybase connections, but if you don't use it then
// you'll need to execute a "use database" statement
// elsewhere in your code. It's simpler to just use
// the property, as shown here.
myProperties.put("db", "pubs");
myProperties.put("user", "sa");
myProperties.put("password", "password");

Connection myConnection =
  myDriver.connect(driverURL, myProperties);
```

Note   You must provide hard-coded IP addresses for your SQL Server hosts, even if you have installed the SQL Server Client Network Utility on your WebLogic machine and defined SQL Server host names. The WebLogic jDriver for Microsoft SQL Server, being a type 4 driver, does not communicate with the Client Network Utility.

When specifying the IP address of an SQL Server host, you can omit the port number if SQL Server is running on its default port of 1433. Otherwise, specify the port by adding a colon and the port number to the IP address, as in 192.168.0.1:7005.

Obtaining pooled connections from the WebLogic pool driver

To obtain a pooled connection from the WebLogic pool driver, follow these steps:

1. Obtain an instance of the WebLogic pool driver with the following code:

```
import java.sql.*;

String driverName = "weblogic.jdbc.pool.Driver";
Driver myDriver =
  (Driver)Class.forName(driverName).newInstance();
```

   Note that this is always the driver name used for pooled connections, regardless of whether the underlying database is Oracle, Sybase, Informix, or something else.

2. Obtain a connection by calling the driver's connect method and providing the name of the pool from which you want a connection. You don't need to provide a username, password, or database name, because these details are handled by the pool when it creates its connections.

   You can either pass the pool name in a Properties object or append it to the URL. To pass it in a Properties object, use the following code:

```
import java.sql.*;
import java.util.*;

String driverURL = "jdbc:weblogic:pool";
Properties myProperties = new Properties();
myProperties.put("connectionPoolID", "OraclePool");

Connection myConnection =
  myDriver.connect(driverURL, myProperties);
```

   The preceding code obtains a connection from OraclePool, the pool you configured in the WebLogic console earlier in this chapter.

   To do the same thing by appending the pool name to the URL, use the following code:

```
import java.sql.*;

String driverURL = "jdbc:weblogic:pool:OraclePool";

Connection myConnection =
  myDriver.connect(driverURL, null);
```

   Neither method is better than the other — the one you choose is a matter of personal preference.

Obtaining pooled connections from predefined DataSources or Tx DataSources

To obtain a pooled connection from a predefined DataSource or Tx DataSource, follow these steps:

1. Obtain an instance of the DataSource by performing a JNDI lookup on it, passing the full JNDI name of the DataSource as defined in the WebLogic console. To obtain, for example, an instance of jdbc/OraclePoolDataSource, the DataSource defined in the earlier example, write the following code:

```
import javax.naming.*;
import java.sql.*

javax.sql.DataSource myDataSource = null;

try {
  Context myContext = new InitialContext();
  myDataSource =
    (javax.sql.DataSource)
    myContext.lookup("jdbc/OraclePoolDataSource");
}
catch (NamingException e) {
}
```

2. Obtain a connection by calling the DataSource's getConnection method:

```
try {
  myConnection = myDataSource.getConnection();
}
catch (SQLException e) {
}
```

Using connections to execute statements and process results

After you obtain a connection to a database, you make the same standard JDBC calls against it, no matter which method you used to get the connection. In other words, a connection is a connection is a connection—whether it's direct, pooled, obtained via a driver, or obtained via a DataSource. The only caveat is that the underlying source of the connection (the JDBC driver that physically connects to the database) must support whatever version of JDBC calls you plan to make.

To illustrate this, consider the following method to select and display all rows of the EMP table in the Oracle schema SCOTT:

```
public static void getData(Connection theConnection) {
  try {
    Statement myStatement = theConnection.createStatement();
    ResultSet rs =
      myStatement.executeQuery("SELECT * FROM EMP");
    while (rs.next()) {
      System.out.println(rs.getInt("EMPNO") +
```

```
         "     " + rs.getString("ENAME") +
         "     " + rs.getString("JOB"));
      }
    }
    catch (SQLException e) {
    }
}
```

You can pass this method any valid database connection, regardless of how the connection was obtained. In fact, the connection doesn't even have to be to an Oracle database, as long as getData's SQL is valid for the database described by the connection.

Incidentally, when executed against the SCOTT schema in Oracle, the output from getData is the following:

```
7369    SMITH    CLERK
7499    ALLEN    SALESMAN
7521    WARD     SALESMAN
7566    JONES    MANAGER
7654    MARTIN   SALESMAN
7698    BLAKE    MANAGER
7782    CLARK    MANAGER
7788    SCOTT    ANALYST
7839    KING     PRESIDENT
7844    TURNER   SALESMAN
7876    ADAMS    CLERK
7900    JAMES    CLERK
7902    FORD     ANALYST
7934    MILLER   CLERK
```

Note   You can obviously do much more with JDBC than open connections and select data from tables, but providing demonstrations of generic JDBC programming techniques is beyond the scope of this book. In addition to the many books written on the subject, a great way to learn more is to take Sun's online JDBC tutorial, which you can find at the following URL:

```
http://java.sun.com/docs/books/tutorial/jdbc/index.html
```

Closing connections

After using a connection, it's imperative to close it to release unused database resources. The code to close a connection is the same regardless of how the connection is obtained. The following code closes a connection:

```
public static void closeConnection(Connection theConnection) {
  try {
    theConnection.close();
  }
  catch (SQLException e) {
    System.out.println("A SQLException occurred: " +
                       e.getMessage());
    e.printStackTrace();
  }
}
```

If you pass this method a direct connection, the connection's driver physically closes the connection, rendering the connection unusable. If you pass a pooled connection, the WebLogic pool driver does not physically close the connection. Instead, it marks the connection as unused and returns it to the pool of available connections.

Summary

This chapter provided you with a thorough understanding of how WebLogic implements JDBC. JDBC is a complex API sitting on top of an even more complex architecture. This chapter showed how the pieces of this architecture fit together and how to properly configure and use them in the WebLogic environment. Specifically, you learned about the various types of JDBC drivers, how to use them directly or in WebLogic connection pools, and how to extend their functionality by accessing them through data sources.

Chapter 6 digs deeper into the Java Transaction API (JTA), showing you how to program user transactions by using J2EE and transaction-aware database drivers.

Understanding Transactions and Working with WebLogic JTA

Transactions provide an "all-or-nothing" method of making permanent changes to data residing in one or more data stores, such as
relational databases and messaging systems. Transactions are an
essential component of enterprise computing because they help
enforce data integrity. This feature becomes even more important in
the context of distributed systems, in which network failures, server
outages, and a host of other unexpected problems can wreak havoc
on your business logic.

The *Java Transaction API,* or *JTA,* gives Java developers the ability to
control transactions easily and reliably from within Java code by using
a simple set of transaction-oriented commands. Such transactions
can include EJB method calls, JDBC database operations, JMS
messaging operations, and operations against any other computing
source that provides transaction support. WebLogic, working in con-
cert with transaction-enabled drivers for the participating datasources, handles the considerable load of back-end processing that
transactions require.

This chapter introduces you to essential transaction concepts. We
then explain JTA and show you how to properly configure and program it in the WebLogic environment.

Understanding Transactions

In a networked computing environment, in which enterprise systems
consist of multiple application servers, databases, messaging systems, and other resources working together, the concept of transactions is essential because of the possibility that components might
fail in the overall system. If unexpected errors occur, for example, in a
database that is participating in a complex sequence of business
logic, developers must have a reliable way to reverse all the other
effects of the business logic. This not only allows them to ensure that
the system as a whole remains consistent, but it also gives them the
ability to retry the entire sequence of operations later, after the
offending system has been repaired or brought back online.

As we mentioned in the chapter's introduction, transactions are a critical part of the enterprise computing equation. Unfortunately, transactions are difficult to program correctly, and are even more difficult to troubleshoot when something goes wrong. A solid understanding of the theory behind transactions will help you become a more effective transactions programmer.

What is a transaction?

A *transaction* is a means of encapsulating multiple related operations against one or more data stores into one logical unit of work. If all the operations succeed, the transaction succeeds, and the effects of the operations are permanently written to the data stores. If any of the operations fail, the transaction fails, and the effects of the operations on the data stores are reversed.

The first step in transaction processing is notifying the data stores that you wish to begin a transaction. This tells the data stores to batch subsequent commands into the transaction until you either *commit* the transaction (indicating success) or *roll back* the transaction (indicating failure).

Performing a funds transfer at an ATM is a good example of a transaction. Suppose that you step up to an ATM and try to transfer $1,000 from your savings account to your checking account. It's one button for you, but in the background a program must first remove $1,000 from your savings account (that's one operation) and then update your checking account by adding $1,000 (that's another operation). Let's say the first operation occurs, but then a rolling blackout hits and prevents completion of the second operation. You now have $1,000 floating around in electronic limbo! But when power is restored, the database will automatically roll back the incomplete transaction, restoring $1,000 to your savings account. Without transactions, that money would be gone forever.

Transactions and the ACID test

For a logical unit of work comprising a transaction to be considered transactional, it must meet the ACID test. *ACID* is an acronym describing the essential characteristics of a transaction; its letters stand for *atomic, consistent, isolated,* and *durable.*

✦ *Atomic* means that the operations comprising the unit of work succeed or fail as a group. In other words, a transaction is an "all-or-nothing" operation.

✦ *Consistent* means that all data stores affected by a transaction are left in a state consistent with the business logic of the system, whether the transaction succeeds or fails.

✦ *Isolated* means that multiple transactions occurring simultaneously against the data stores will not interfere with each other or get tangled up in each other's effects. If two transactions, for example, each successfully deposit $1,000 into a bank account at the same time, the account balance must increase by $2,000, not $1,000.

✦ *Durable* means that if a transaction succeeds, its effects will be permanently and reliably written to the data stores. In practical terms, this means that all database changes are flushed to disk.

Resources and resource managers

Each participant in a transaction is called a *resource*. A resource can be a database system, persistent messaging store, or any other transaction-enabled entity.

For a resource to be transaction-enabled, it must have a transaction-aware *resource manager,* which coordinates communications between the resource and the transaction manager (transaction managers are defined in the next section). Resource managers can be implemented as drivers, as is the case with transaction-aware JDBC drivers; or they can be integrated with the resource they control, as is the case with WebLogic JMS (see Chapter 9 for more on JMS).

Local and distributed transactions

Transactions can be *local* or *distributed.* A local transaction is confined to one resource, whereas a distributed transaction spans multiple resources, including resources of different types (such as databases and messaging systems), possibly provided by multiple vendors.

Local transactions

A *local transaction* is the simplest type of transaction. It involves a single resource and resource manager. Multiple inserts into a single database, for example, could be contained within a local transaction, as could multiple messaging operations against a JMS queue.

> **Note** Most relational database systems have the capability to manage local transactions themselves, without involving an external resource manager. Sybase's Transact-SQL language and Oracle's PL/SQL language, for example, both contain commands to manage local transactions. These commands execute more quickly and potentially with greater reliability than those issued from external resource managers. They also support additional features such as transaction nesting, which is not available in WebLogic's transaction manager. For these reasons, it's better in almost every case to control local transactions from within the databases themselves, rather than from Java code.

Distributed transactions

A *distributed transaction* involves multiple resources and resource managers. A transaction spanning inserts into a database followed by messages being written to a JMS queue, for example, would be contained within a distributed transaction. Distributed transactions are managed by a *transaction monitor,* which runs outside the participating databases and coordinates transactions among them.

Transaction isolation levels

As mentioned earlier in the chapter, one of the ACID properties of transactions is isolation — that is, the effects of simultaneously occurring transactions are isolated from one another. But maintaining perfect transaction isolation can be costly in terms of application performance. Additionally, certain real-world situations don't require perfect isolation in order to function acceptably. To accommodate these realities, many transactional resource managers support *isolation levels* that give developers some degree of control over how strictly perfect isolation is enforced.

In J2EE, developers set transaction isolation levels by using the `java.sql.Connection` interface. This interface provides getter and setter methods for the connection's isolation level:

```
int getTransactionIsolation() throws SQLException;
void setTransactionIsolation(int level) throws SQLException;
```

Additionally, the `java.sql.DatabaseMetaData` interface provides methods to discover the level of isolation level support provided by a data store. An instance of an object that implements this interface is obtained by calling `Connection.getMetaData()`, and the methods relevant to transaction isolation levels are

```
int getDefaultTransactionIsolation() throws SQLException;
boolean supportsTransactionIsolationLevel(int level)
  throws SQLException;
```

The `java.sql.Connection` interface defines the following five integer constants for transaction isolation levels:

✦ `TRANSACTION_READ_UNCOMMITTED`

✦ `TRANSACTION_READ_COMMITTED`

✦ `TRANSACTION_REPEATABLE_READ`

✦ `TRANSACTION_SERIALIZABLE`

✦ `TRANSACTION_NONE`

These isolation levels are designed to address specific data-inconsistency scenarios defined by the ANSI/ISO 92 standard. The following sections explore these scenarios in more detail.

Dirty read

A *dirty read* occurs when a transaction is allowed to read data affected by another transaction before the other transaction commits. Suppose, for example, that transaction 1 (T1) updates a row in the database. Immediately afterward, transaction 2 (T2) reads the row, retrieving the change made by T1. If T1 then issues a rollback, the data previously read by T2 becomes inconsistent with the state of the database.

Non-repeatable read

A *non-repeatable read* occurs when a transaction attempts to select the same row twice, but a second transaction has modified or deleted the row in the interim. This situation may lead to unpredictable or incorrect results in the first transaction.

Phantom read

A *phantom read* occurs when a transaction reads all rows that meet certain criteria, but then a second transaction inserts a new row that meets the same criteria. If the first transaction rereads the rows, the new phantom row appears in the results.

Table 6-1 shows JTA's transaction isolation levels across the top and data inconsistency scenarios on the left. Checkmarks indicate that the given isolation level prevents the given inconsistency scenario.

Table 6-1: JTA Transaction Isolation and Data Inconsistency

	Uncommitted	Committed	Repeatable	Serializable
Dirty read		✓	✓	✓
NR read			✓	✓
Phantom read				✓

As you can see, `TRANSACTION_READ_UNCOMMITTED` is the most lenient of the isolation levels (it essentially does nothing), and therefore performs the best. The remaining isolation levels are listed in ascending order of strictness, with `TRANSACTION_SERIALIZABLE` providing "perfect" isolation. Which isolation level you choose will depend on your databases (because different databases support different levels), your system's data integrity requirements, and your performance requirements.

> **Note** Some databases do not support the `TRANSACTION_SERIALIZABLE` attribute. Oracle, for example, throws an exception if you try to commit a transaction this way. Consult the WebLogic Server documentation and the documentation for your database to learn how you can work around this limitation.

Keep in mind that a distributed transaction operating against multiple stores must execute at the same isolation level across all stores, or unpredictable results may occur. Consult the documentation for your databases and drivers for more information.

Transaction demarcation

Transaction demarcation is the process of specifying when a transaction is started, suspended, resumed, committed, and rolled back. With J2EE, transactions can be manually demarcated in code by using calls to the JTA, or they can be automatically demarcated by using declarative rules stored in XML deployment descriptors.

Automatically demarcated transactions, called *container-managed transactions,* are available for session, message-driven, and entity EJBs (Enterprise JavaBeans). The EJB container reads the declarative rules in the deployment descriptors and executes the affected methods in the appropriate transaction context.

When writing servlets, RMI applications, and Enterprise JavaBeans, you must manually demarcate transactions by using the JTA. You can also manually demarcate transactions in session and message-driven EJBs called *bean-managed transactions.* The EJB 2.0 specification, however, prohibits the use of bean-managed transactions in entity EJBs; entity EJBs must always use container-managed transactions.

Container-managed transaction demarcation attributes

The EJB specification defines several attributes for container-managed transactions that control how EJB methods participate in transactions. EJB developers must specify these attributes in the deployment descriptors of EJBs that use container-managed transactions. This section summarizes how the EJB 2.0 specification defines the container's behavior for each attribute, but you should consult the EJB 2.0 specification for more details (available at `www.java.sun.com`).

NotSupported

This attribute applies to EJB methods that do not support transactions. The container invokes the EJB method with an unspecified transaction context. If the caller has a transaction in progress when such a method is invoked, the container suspends the transaction before invoking the method and then resumes it when the method completes.

Required

The container must establish a valid transaction context before invoking an EJB method with this attribute. If a transaction is already under way, the container will associate the method with that transaction. If not, the container will start a new transaction, invoke the method, and then commit the transaction when the method completes.

Note, however, that message-driven EJB methods never execute within the context of an existing transaction, so the container always creates a new transaction context for them prior to executing the `onMessage()` method. After `onMessage()` completes, the container commits the transaction. If the container rolls back the transaction, the message is marked for redelivery in accordance with the JMS specification.

Supports
This attribute is a cross between `NotSupported` and `Required`. If the EJB method is invoked with a transaction in progress, the container proceeds as in the `Required` case. If not, the container proceeds as in the `NotSupported` case.

RequiresNew
This attribute always forces the new container to start a new transaction for the EJB method and to commit that transaction when the method completes. If the caller has a transaction under way, that transaction is suspended until the method completes and then is resumed again.

Mandatory
The caller is required to have a transaction under way before calling EJB methods with this attribute set, and the container executes the methods within the context of the caller's transaction. If no transaction is under way, the container throws an exception.

Never
This attribute is the opposite of `Mandatory`. The caller must invoke the EJB method with no transaction under way. If a transaction is under way, the container throws an exception; otherwise, it proceeds as in the `NotSupported` case.

Two-phase commit and the XA interface

Two-phase commit is a protocol used to control distributed transactions. It specifies a series of states and commands that travel between the transaction manager and resource managers during the course of a transaction.

In the first phase of the two-phase commit process, updates that will be written to the resources are sent to those resources and saved in a transaction log file. Each resource is then asked if it can guarantee the successful completion of its portion of the transaction. The second phase of the process depends on the results of the first. If all resources answer yes, the transaction manager notifies all resource managers to commit, and the effects of the transaction are permanently saved to all participating resources. If one or more resources answers no, the transaction manager notifies all resource managers to roll back, and the effects of the transaction are reversed.

The WebLogic transaction manager uses the Open Group's XA interface to implement two-phase commit. The *XA interface* is simply a realization of the XA specification, which is a standard for distributed transaction protocols that was developed by the Open Group. This standard has been adopted by many database vendors. The XA specification is available at the following URL:

    http://www.opengroup.org/products/publications/catalog/c193.htm

If a resource manager is XA-compliant, WebLogic will issue XA commands to it directly. If not, WebLogic automatically maps XA commands to the resource manager's native commands as the transaction proceeds.

Understanding JTA

Although the JavaSoft implementation of JTA gives Java developers programmatic control over transactions, the WebLogic JTA gives developers access to WebLogic's robust transaction manager. The WebLogic transaction manager fully supports local and distributed transactions, transaction isolation levels, two-phase commit via the XA interface, and complete monitoring, diagnostics, and logging to facilitate performance tuning and troubleshooting.

JTA versions and packages

WebLogic 7.0 supports version 1.0.1a of the JTA specification. JTA is implemented in the following packages:

- ✦ `javax.transaction`, which contains the API for managing local transactions

- ✦ `javax.transaction.xa`, which contains the API for managing distributed transactions by using the X/Open XA interface

- ✦ `weblogic.transaction`, which contains WebLogic extensions to some of the classes and interfaces defined in `javax.transaction` and `javax.transaction.xa`

You can download the JTA 1.0.1a specification from the Sun Web site at the following URL:

```
http://java.sun.com/products/jta/
```

JTA architecture

The JTA architecture follows the familiar layered pattern common to most J2EE APIs. Figure 6-1 shows the major components of the architecture.

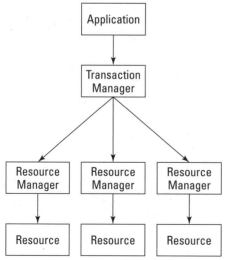

Figure 6-1: Components of the JTA architecture

The top layer of the architecture is the *application,* which can be implemented as a servlet, JSP, RMI application, EJB, or standalone Java application. The application makes calls to the *transaction manager,* which manages communications between the application and the transaction's resource managers. WebLogic Server has embedded within it a transaction manager that is fully J2EE-compliant.

Transaction-aware resource managers

WebLogic Server works in tandem with a number of transaction-aware resource managers, including JDBC drivers provided by BEA and others, and the WebLogic built-in messaging broker, which serves as the resource manager for WebLogic's Java Message Service (JMS) implementation.

Cross-Reference For more information about JDBC drivers, see Chapter 5. For more information about JMS, see Chapter 9.

WebLogic Java Transaction Services (JTS) driver

The WebLogic JTS driver is a special-purpose, type 3 JDBC driver that supports local transactions spanning one or more blocks of server-side code. Transactions are controlled by using the `javax.Transaction.UserTransaction` interface.

A transaction can be initiated, for example, by a servlet running on WebLogic server A, continued by an RMI server running on WebLogic server B, and concluded by a session EJB running back on server A. The only requirement is that all three code modules execute in the same thread and draw their database connections from the same connection pool.

Under the covers, the JTS driver does some fancy bookkeeping to make things work. After a thread initiates a transaction against a pooled connection, the JTS driver ensures that the *same connection* is delivered to that thread for all subsequent connection requests made against the *same pool,* until the transaction is either committed or rolled back. Only then does it return the connection to the pool.

Therefore, to program with JTS, you simply ensure that all code participating in a transaction executes in the same thread and requests connections from the same connection pool. JTS handles the rest.

Distributed transactions using XA and non-XA drivers

Distributed transactions require *XA drivers* that implement the X/Open XA interface for distributed transactions. The Oracle driver referenced by `weblogic.jdbc.oci.xa.XADataSource` is an example of such a driver. This driver is included with WebLogic.

You can also use a non-XA driver (such as the WebLogic jDriver for Oracle) in conjunction with a TxDataSource to perform distributed transactions. For this combination to work, however, the TxDataSource must be configured with two-phase commit enabled. This essentially wraps stubbed-out XA calls around the non-XA driver. Don't worry if you accidentally enable two-phase commit for an XA driver — the Tx DataSource is smart enough to ignore this setting if the underlying driver is XA. We demonstrate how to configure TxDataSources later in the chapter.

Caution

Although WebLogic can manage both local and distributed transactions, local transactions are best handled within the databases themselves, using their embedded transaction management commands. The reason for this is simple: suppose that Java code running on WebLogic begins a local transaction against a database located elsewhere on the network. If the transaction updates a table, it will gain a lock on that table, which prevents other users from using that table until the transaction completes. Now suppose that the network link goes down or a bug in the Java code crashes WebLogic Server. The transaction is now in limbo, the table remains locked indefinitely, and other users are blocked until a DBA steps in and kills the suspended transaction. By confining local transactions to the database server, you eliminate the possibility of database disruption due to unanticipated network or programming errors.

Note that distributed transactions must *always* be managed from outside the affected databases because a separate transaction monitor (in this case, WebLogic Server) is required to coordinate transaction processing among all involved datasources.

Configuring WebLogic JTA

Configuring WebLogic JTA is quite simple—all you need to do is define transaction-aware DataSources mapped to existing JDBC connection pools. In this section, you'll see how to create a TxDataSource (Transactional DataSource) for the `OraclePool` connection pool created in the preceding chapter. This is the type of datasource that must be used for applications wishing to perform distributed transactions.

Like DataSources, TxDataSources are bound to the JNDI tree, in which calling applications can look them up by using the `javax.naming` interface.

Here are the required steps to define a TxDataSource against the `OraclePool` connection pool:

1. In the domain tree, choose Services ➪ JDBC ➪ TxDataSources. The screen shown in Figure 6-2 appears.

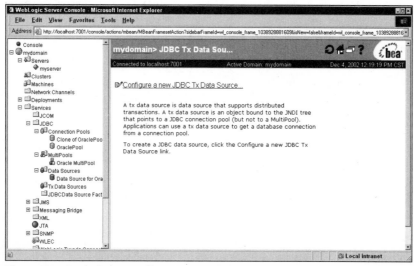

Figure 6-2: Preparing to configure a JDBC TxDataSource

2. Click Configure a New JDBC TxDataSource to display the DataSource configuration screen. Fill out the fields on the screen, as shown in Figure 6-3; then click Create.

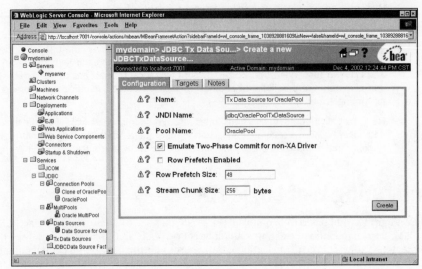

Figure 6-3: Configuring a JDBC TxDataSource for OraclePool

Note

Check the Emulate Two-Phase Commit for non-XA Driver box only if the JDBC driver used by the underlying connection pool is not XA, which is the case for the following drivers:

```
weblogic.jdbc.oci.Driver
weblogic.jdbc.mssqlserver4.Driver
weblogic.jdbc.informix4.Driver
```

Do not check the box if the underlying pool was created with any of the following XA drivers:

```
weblogic.jdbc.oci.xa.XADataSource
oracle.jdbc.xa.client.OracleXADataSource
COM.cloudscape.core.XADataSource
```

If you are using a third-party driver that does not appear in these lists, check your driver's documentation to determine whether or not it is XA, and check the box accordingly.

3. Click the Targets tab and move your WebLogic Server instance into the Chosen list, as shown in Figure 6-4. Click Apply.

Figure 6-4: Assigning the TxDataSource to a WebLogic Server instance

4. Stop and restart WebLogic Server to activate the TxDataSource.

Programming WebLogic JTA

This section provides two examples of how to manually program transaction demarcation by using the Java Transaction API.

Programming a local transaction with the WebLogic JTS driver

In Chapter 5, we mentioned that the WebLogic JTS driver is a special-purpose, type 3 JDBC driver that supports local transactions spanning one or more blocks of server-side code. In this example, you'll see how to use the JTS driver in a single block of server code to control multiple inserts into a table of a single Oracle database. We use the EMP table described in Chapter 5.

First, write two utility methods to perform important tasks. The first task is to obtain a reference to an object that implements the javax.transaction.UserTransaction interface. WebLogic provides this object as part of its runtime environment. Calling the begin method of this object tells it to associate a transaction with your thread and begin controlling it. Note that the UserTransaction object does not represent a single transaction in memory. Rather, it's a service class that might be controlling several transactions running in multiple threads of execution.

The UserTransaction object reference is obtained via a JNDI lookup. The following method performs the lookup and returns a reference to the object:

```
public static UserTransaction getUserTransaction() {
  Context ctx = null;
  Hashtable env = new Hashtable();
  UserTransaction tx = null;

  try {
    // Get the context of the WebLogic runtime environment.
    env.put(Context.INITIAL_CONTEXT_FACTORY,
            "weblogic.jndi.WLInitialContextFactory");
    env.put(Context.PROVIDER_URL, "t3://localhost:7001");
    env.put(Context.SECURITY_PRINCIPAL, "wlsadmin");
    env.put(Context.SECURITY_CREDENTIALS, "password");
    ctx = new InitialContext(env);

    // Obtain a reference to its UserTransaction class.
    tx = (UserTransaction)
            ctx.lookup("javax.transaction.UserTransaction");
  }
  catch (Exception e) {
    e.printStackTrace();
  }
  finally {
    // Return the UserTransaction reference to the caller.
    return tx;
  }
}
```

The second task is to get a JTS connection bound to the connection pool you want to use. This is accomplished by using the following method:

```
public static Connection getJTSConnection(String poolName) {
  Connection myConnection = null;

  try {
    Driver myDriver =
     (Driver)
     Class.forName("weblogic.jdbc.jts.Driver").newInstance();

    myConnection = myDriver.connect("jdbc:weblogic:jts:" +
      poolName, null);
  }
  catch (Exception e) {
    e.printStackTrace();
  }
  finally {
    return myConnection;
  }
}
```

After incorporating the utility methods into a class, add another method to the class, demoJTS, which demonstrates how to perform a transaction with JTS by using OraclePool, the connection pool to Oracle defined earlier:

```
public static void demoJTS(String demoMode) {
  Connection myConnection = null;
  UserTransaction tx = null;
  Driver myDriver = null;

  try {
    // Get a reference to the UserTransaction class
    // and associate a new transaction with our thread.
    tx = getUserTransaction();
    tx.begin();

    // Obtain a JTS-enabled connection.
    myConnection = getJTSConnection("jdbc/OraclePoolTxDataSource");

    // Insert new employees into the SCOTT.EMP table.
    insertEmp(8000, "ZUFFOLETTO", "WRITER");
    insertEmp(8001, "WELLS", "MANAGER");
    insertEmp(8002, "TUCKER", "ENGINEER");
    insertEmp(8003, "GILL", "ENGINEER");
    insertEmp(8004, "SEKANDER", "SALES");
    insertEmp(8005, "SCHNEIDER", "ENGINEER");
    insertEmp(8006, "MIRANDA", "DVDTrain");

    // Commit the transaction
    tx.commit();
  }
  catch (Exception e) {
    // Something went wrong - roll back the transaction.
    // In this case, no employees will be inserted.
    tx.rollback();
    e.printStackTrace();
  }
  finally {
    try {
      // Close the database connection, returning it
      // to the pool.
      myConnection.close();
    }
    catch (Exception e) {
      e.printStackTrace();
    }
  }
}
```

As you can see, coding a JTS transaction is pretty straightforward. First, you get a UserTransaction reference and then you get a transaction-enabled connection from the JTS driver. Next, you perform your data manipulations. If no exceptions occur, you commit the transaction. Otherwise, you roll it back.

The code that makes JTS interesting appears in the insertEmp method, shown here:

```
public static void insertEmp(int empNo,
                             String empName,
                             String empJob)
                             throws SQLException {

    // Obtain a JTS-enabled connection from OraclePool
    Connection myConnection = getJTSConnection("OraclePool");

    // Define a SQL statement to insert an employee into EMP
    String sql = "INSERT INTO EMP (EMPNO, ENAME, JOB) " +
                 "VALUES (?, ?, ?)";

    // Bind the SQL statement to a PreparedStatement
    PreparedStatement myStatement =
      theConnection.prepareStatement(sql);

    // Load the input variables into the INSERT statement
    myStatement.setInt(1, empNo);
    myStatement.setString(2, empName);
    myStatement.setString(3, empJob);

    // Perform the INSERT
    if (myStatement.executeUpdate() == 1) {
      System.out.println("Employee inserted.");
    } else {
      System.out.println("Employee not inserted.");
    }
    myStatement.close();
}
```

Notice that `insertEmp` does not receive a JTS-enabled connection as an input parameter. Instead, it seemingly obtains its own JTS-enabled connection to `OraclePool` by calling `getJTSConnection` just as `demoJTS` did. How can this possibly work?

The answer lies in the way the JTS driver works. Recall that after a thread initiates a transaction against a pooled connection, the JTS driver ensures that the *same connection* is delivered to that thread for all subsequent connection requests made against the *same pool,* until the transaction is either committed or rolled back. Only then does it return the connection to the pool. The preceding code shows this feature of the JTS driver at work.

Nevertheless, if you prefer, you can pass a JTS-enabled connection as a parameter to `insertEmp` and simply use that connection instead of calling `getJTSConnection`. The results will be the same.

Note that `insertEmp` could have been a method residing in a JavaBean, EJB, RMI server, or any other component callable by `demoJTS`. As long as `insertEmp` executes in the same thread as `demoJTS` and uses the same connection pool, it will correctly participate in the transaction.

Caution   If you rely on the Java exception handling mechanism to either commit or roll back transactions (as we have in these examples), be sure any methods you call that participate in the transaction throw exceptions to the calling method. In this example, `insertEmp` throws an SQLException rather than catching it itself. If `insertEmp` caught its own SQLExceptions, the caller would never know about them, and transaction processing would continue, possibly terminating with a bogus commit.

Programming a distributed transaction with the Oracle XA driver

This example implements a "brute force" database replication engine that inserts identical data into the EMP tables of two different Oracle databases. It does so by performing a distributed transaction across the two databases by using the Oracle XA driver.

Getting distributed transactions to work is tricky business, so we'll walk you through the complete configuration and programming steps required to make it work.

Say you have two Oracle instances on your network: ORADEV1.ZEEWARE.COM (residing in Denver, CO) and JOEVAIO.ZEEWARE.COM (residing in Sausalito, CA). Both are standard Oracle 8.1.6 installations.

The first step is to create connection pools to each of these databases by using the Oracle XA driver. These are the specifications of the two pools:

```
Configuration of pool 1
  Pool Name = DenverPool
  URL = jdbc:weblogic:oracle:ORADEV1.ZEEWARE.COM
  Driver Classname = weblogic.jdbc.oci.xa.XADataSource
  Properties
    user=SCOTT
    password=tiger
    dataSourceName=DenverPool
    serverName=ORADEV1.ZEEWARE.COM

Configuration of pool 2
  Pool Name = SausalitoPool
  URL = jdbc:weblogic:oracle:JOEVAIO.ZEEWARE.COM
  Driver Classname = weblogic.jdbc.oci.xa.XADataSource
  Properties
    user=SCOTT
    password=tiger
    dataSourceName=SausalitoPool
    serverName=JOEVAIO.ZEEWARE.COM
```

Both pools have the following additional settings:

```
Connections
  Initial Capacity = 4
  Maximum Capacity = 10
  Capacity Increment = 2
  Login Delay Seconds = 0
  Refresh Period = 15 minutes
  Allow Shrinking = true
  Shrink Period = 15 minutes

Testing
  Test Table Name = dual
  Test Reserved Connections = false
  Test Released Connections = false

Targets
  Chosen = myserver
```

The next step is to create a TxDataSource for each pool. These are the specifications for the datasources:

```
Configuration of Tx Data Source 1
   Name = DenverTxDS
   JNDI Name = DenverTxDS
   Pool Name = DenverPool
   Enable Two-Phase Commit = false

Configuration of Tx Data Source 2
   Name = SausalitoTxDS
   JNDI Name = SausalitoTxDS
   Pool Name = SausalitoPool
   Enable Two-Phase Commit = false

Targets (both pools)
   Chosen = myserver
```

Note that you do not enable two-phase commit because you are using an XA-enabled driver.

The code that uses these datasources and does the distributed transaction is fairly simple. We enclosed it in a method called demoXA:

```java
public static void demoXA() {
   javax.sql.DataSource ds1 = null;
   javax.sql.DataSource ds2 = null;
   Connection conn1 = null;
   Connection conn2 = null;
   InitialContext ctx = null;
   UserTransaction tx = null;
   Driver myDriver = null;

   try {
      // Get a reference to the UserTransaction class
      // and associate a new transaction with our thread.
      tx = getUserTransaction();
      tx.begin();

      // Get a context for making JNDI calls.
      ctx = new InitialContext();

      // Use JNDI to lookup references to the two data sources.
      ds1 = (javax.sql.DataSource)ctx.lookup("DenverTxDS");
      ds2 = (javax.sql.DataSource)ctx.lookup("SausalitoTxDS");

      // Obtain database connections from the data sources.
      conn1 = ds1.getConnection();
      conn2 = ds2.getConnection();

      // Insert employee records into the Denver database.
      insertEmp(conn1, 8000, "ZUFFOLETTO", "WRITER");
      insertEmp(conn1, 8001, "WELLS", "MANAGER");
```

```
        insertEmp(conn1, 8002, "TUCKER", "ENGINEER");
        insertEmp(conn1, 8003, "GILL", "ENGINEER");
        insertEmp(conn1, 8004, "SEKANDER", "SALES");
        insertEmp(conn1, 8005, "SCHNEIDER", "ENGINEER");

        // Insert identical records into the Sausalito database.
        insertEmp(conn2, 8000, "ZUFFOLETTO", "WRITER");
        insertEmp(conn2, 8001, "WELLS", "MANAGER");
        insertEmp(conn2, 8002, "TUCKER", "ENGINEER");
        insertEmp(conn2, 8003, "GILL", "ENGINEER");
        insertEmp(conn2, 8004, "SEKANDER", "SALES");
        insertEmp(conn2, 8005, " SCHNEIDER ", "ENGINEER");

        // All's well and the databases are in sync, so commit
        // the transaction. This causes the data to be
        // permanently written to each database.
        tx.commit();
    }
    catch (Exception e) {
        try {
            // Something went wrong - roll back the transaction.
            // In this case, no employees are inserted into either
            // database.
            tx.rollback();
            e.printStackTrace();
        }
        catch (Exception ex) {
            ex.printStackTrace();
        }
    }
    finally {
        try {
            // Close the database connections, returning them
            // to the pool.
            conn1.close();
            conn2.close();
        }
        catch (Exception e) {
            e.printStackTrace();
        }
    }
}
```

After getting a `UserTransaction` reference (using the same `getTransaction` method as in the previous example), it begins the transaction. Then it gets references to the datasource instances by performing JNDI lookups on `DenverTxDS` and `SausalitoTxDS`, the datasources defined in the console. The transaction uses these datasources to get transaction-enabled connections to the databases and then passes these connections to a version of `insertEmp` that accepts a connection as a parameter. After performing identical calls to `insertEmp` for each database, it commits the transaction. But if `insertEmp` throws an exception or if any of the other code throws an exception, the transaction is rolled back. The following is the code for this new version of `insertEmp`:

```
public static void insertEmp(Connection theConnection,
                             int empNo,
                             String empName,
                             String empJob)
                             throws SQLException {

// Define a SQL statement to insert an employee into EMP
String sql = "INSERT INTO EMP (EMPNO, ENAME, JOB) " +
             "VALUES (?, ?, ?)";

// Bind the SQL statement to a PreparedStatement
PreparedStatement myStatement =
  theConnection.prepareStatement(sql);

// Load the input variables into the INSERT statement
myStatement.setInt(1, empNo);
myStatement.setString(2, empName);
myStatement.setString(3, empJob);

// Perform the INSERT
if (myStatement.executeUpdate() == 1) {
  System.out.println("Employee inserted.");
} else {
  System.out.println("Employee not inserted.");
}
myStatement.close();
}
```

This concludes the discussion of database transaction programming with WebLogic. If you're a relative newcomer to database programming, you probably don't fully appreciate the wonder of what these examples have accomplished. Joe has been programming databases for nearly 15 years, and he considers the distributed transaction support provided by Sun, WebLogic, and the database vendors to be just slightly short of miraculous. The simplicity of the transaction calls belies a monstrous amount of very difficult work that is going on behind the scenes.

Summary

Transactions are an essential tool for maintaining data integrity in distributed computing systems. WebLogic's implementation of JTA gives Java programmers access to a robust transaction manager that supports manual or automatic transaction management in accordance with the J2EE specification. The WebLogic transaction manager also fully supports the EJB 2.0 specification, including container-managed transaction semantics for session, message-driven, and entity EJBs.

Transactions can be local (spanning one data store) or distributed (spanning multiple data stores). Out of the box, WebLogic supports distributed transactions that can span operations against multiple relational databases and/or Java Message Service stores.

Considering their underlying complexity, programming transactions with JTA is quite simple, requiring the use of only a handful of methods in the `javax.Transaction.User-Transaction` interface. Configuring transactions in WebLogic Server is equally easy, requiring only the configuration of transaction-enabled datasources that are mapped to existing database connection pools.

If you're interested in transactions, chances are you're writing database code for servlets or EJBs. The next logical step in your learning is JNDI, which is useful for accessing JDBC datasources and looking up EJB remote interfaces, among many other uses. We cover JNDI in the next chapter.

✦　　✦　　✦

Working with WebLogic JNDI

T he *Java Naming and Directory Interface,* or *JNDI,* provides a mechanism for linking Java programs to external naming and directory
services, such as file systems, network resources, and corporate
directories. JNDI enables Java programmers to find objects and data
registered in these services, and to register their own objects and
data for use by others.

In this chapter, an overview of JNDI is provided, as well as details on
how JNDI is used in WebLogic. You will learn how to register and
look up objects in the WebLogic JNDI tree, which is a simple, JNDI-
accessible naming service built into WebLogic. You will also learn
how to use JNDI to access an external directory based on the
Lightweight Directory Access Protocol (LDAP).

Understanding JNDI

To use JNDI effectively, you need to understand its package structure,
architecture, and a few key concepts. JNDI is easy to understand and
use, especially if you use it only to access WebLogic's JNDI tree. Keep
in mind, however, that you can use JNDI to access other directory
structures as well.

JNDI versions and packages

WebLogic 7.0 runs on top of JDK 1.3.1, and supports JNDI version
1.2.1. JNDI is implemented in the following packages:

+ `javax.naming`, which contains classes and interfaces for
  accessing naming services, such as the WebLogic JNDI tree

+ `javax.naming.directory`, which contains classes and interfaces for accessing directories such as LDAP directories

+ `javax.naming.ldap`, which contains classes and interfaces
  that extend those in `javax.naming.directory` and support
  LDAP v3 extensions

+ `javax.naming.event`, which contains classes and interfaces
  for event notification in naming and directory services

You can find complete documentation for these packages on Sun's FTP site at the following FTP site:

```
ftp://ftp.javasoft.com/docs/j2se1.3/jndi.pdf
```

In addition to the core JNDI packages, Sun provides the package `javax.naming.spi` for those implementing service provider interfaces (SPIs). We discuss the role of SPIs in the next section. You can find complete documentation for this package at the following FTP site:

```
ftp://ftp.javasoft.com/docs/j2se1.3/jndispi.pdf
```

JNDI architecture

Figure 7-1 shows the layers of the JNDI architecture. At the top is Java application code, implemented as a servlet, EJB, or other component, which makes calls to the JNDI API. These calls are routed by the naming and directory manager (in your case, WebLogic Server) to the appropriate JNDI service provider interface (SPI), which translates the JNDI calls into native commands for the naming or directory resource being accessed. This resource can be the JNDI tree built into WebLogic, an external LDAP directory, an RMI registry, a file system, or virtually any other resource for which an appropriate JNDI SPI can be written.

Figure 7-1: JNDI architecture

JNDI service providers are similar in concept to JDBC drivers: They convert JNDI API calls into protocol-specific commands for underlying services. An LDAP service provider, for example, converts JNDI calls into LDAP calls; whereas a file system service provider converts JNDI calls to local file system calls, and so on.

A full understanding of JNDI requires an understanding of a few key concepts, which we cover in the next section.

Naming services

Naming services enable Java programmers to assign meaningful names to computing resources of various types, and thus to perform lookups on those resources by name. Names are easier for humans to deal with, and they insulate programmers from changes that might be made to the resources associated with the name. As long as the name doesn't change, the programmer will always get the correct resource when finding it by name.

The most ubiquitous naming service on Earth is the Internet's Domain Name System, or DNS, which associates network host names (such as `www.zeeware.com`) with IP addresses (such as `204.56.46.11`). Thanks to DNS, you can surf the Internet by using easily remembered names such as `www.yahoo.com`, `www.cnn.com`, and `www.bea.com`. Your browser performs lookups on these names by using DNS and then uses the IP addresses that DNS returns to communicate with the Web sites. Imagine how difficult surfing the Internet would be if you had to remember the IP addresses yourself! Worse, suppose that Yahoo reorganized its network, causing its IP addresses to change. You wouldn't be able to find Yahoo at all, unless you knew the new IP addresses. DNS insulates you from this problem because it always returns the correct address if you provide the correct name (assuming Yahoo correctly updates its DNS records, of course).

The WebLogic JNDI tree is another naming service. It enables programmers to publish Java classes into the tree (such as RMI stubs, JDBC connection pools, JDBC data sources, or any other class that implements the `java.io.Serializable` interface) and then retrieve instances of them by name for use in their programs. This makes it easy for developers to create a server-side code repository available to code running on the server and also to any authorized user accessing the naming service over the network.

Directory services

Directory services are like naming services, but they also allow additional attributes beyond names to be associated with objects and allow object lookups based on any combination of the attributes.

A common directory example is that of an e-mail directory that allows lookups by a person's name and returns the name along with one or more e-mail addresses for that person. Such directories may also include information about the person's address, telephone numbers, corporate department, and so on.

LDAP is a standard protocol for accessing directories and performing lookups on their contents. Industry support for LDAP is steadily increasing, making LDAP a preferred method for communicating with directory services. The Windows 2000 Active Directory, for example, which replaces Windows NT domains and integrates with Microsoft Exchange's e-mail directory, is fully LDAP-compliant.

Service providers

A *service provider* is simply the underlying service being accessed via JNDI. It can be a naming service, directory service, native file system, RMI registry, LDAP-compliant directory, or any other service for which a JNDI-compliant SPI exists.

Note   Sun's Web site contains service provider interfaces for accessing LDAP directories, CORBA naming services, the Windows registry, native file systems, Novell directory services, DNS, and more. You can find it at the following URL:

> `http://java.sun.com/products/jndi/serviceproviders.html`

Contexts

Contexts provide the programmatic link between your Java code and the JNDI service provider you want to use. A JNDI context is analogous to a JDBC connection — it's the pipe through which your code's commands to the naming or directory service flow and through which data from the service provider is received.

When obtaining a context, your code passes properties to JNDI that specify which *context factory* to use. This determines, in turn, which SPI to use. You must also provide a URL that specifies the location of the naming or directory resource to be used. Optional parameters include a username, password, and various configuration parameters, as shown in Table 7-1.

Table 7-1: Properties for Creating JNDI Contexts

Property	Comments
INITIAL_CONTEXT_FACTORY	The fully qualified name of the class used to create the JNDI context. Example: `weblogic.jndi.WLInitial ContextFactory`.
PROVIDER_URL	The protocol, host, and port used to connect to the naming or directory service provider. Example: `t3://localhost:7001`.
SECURITY_PRINCIPAL	The identity of the user in the WebLogic security realm with whom to associate the context. Defaults to the WebLogic `guest` account, unless the current thread is already associated with a different user.
SECURITY_CREDENTIALS	The password of the user defined by the `SECURITY_PRINCIPAL` property or an object that implements the `weblogic.security.acl.UserInfo` interface. Defaults to the password of the WebLogic `guest` account unless the current thread is already associated with a different user.
SECURITY_PROTOCOL	Specifies which security protocol to use, such as SSL.
SECURITY_AUTHENTICATION	Specifies the level of authentication to use. Values include `none`, `simple`, `strong`, or a provider-specific string.
AUTHORITATIVE	If `true`, the naming or directory service being accessed is deemed the ultimate authority for JNDI lookups, and lookups will bypass any caches or replicas that may exist.
REFERRAL	A value of `follow` specifies that the service provider should automatically follow referrals generated by the naming or directory service. A value of `ignore` means the service provider should not follow referrals.
OBJECT_FACTORIES	A colon-separated list of class names that specifies which object factories to use.
STATE_FACTORIES	A colon-separated list of class names that specifies which state factories to use.
CONTROL_FACTORIES	A colon-separated list of class names of response control factory classes to use.
URL_PKG_PREFIXES	A colon-separated list of package prefixes to use when loading URL context factories.
DNS_URL	Specifies the DNS host to use for looking up addresses associated with JNDI URLs.

Property	Comments
BATCHSIZE	Specifies the size of the buffer the service provider should use to return data. If a lookup generates more data than BATCHSIZE accommodates, the data will be returned in multiple chunks, each the size of BATCHSIZE.
LANGUAGE	A colon-separated list of languages to use with the service provider. Acceptable values are the tags defined by RFC 1766, such as en-US, fr, and ja-JP-kanji.
APPLET	An instance of java.applet.Applet to use to obtain the values of some environment properties. Almost never used with WebLogic.
REPLICATE_BINDINGS	If true, replicate this bound object to all JNDI trees in a cluster. Otherwise, bind it only to its home server. This property is WebLogic-specific and available only when using the WebLogic context factory to bind objects to the WebLogic JNDI Tree.

Programming WebLogic JNDI

When you write JNDI code, it is to perform one or more of the following tasks:

✦ Obtain a reference to WebLogic server's context

✦ Bind objects to WebLogic's JNDI tree

✦ Look up objects already bound to WebLogic's JNDI tree

✦ Perform binds and lookups against other JNDI-compliant resources, such as LDAP servers

In this section, you learn how to write Java code to do all these things.

Obtaining a reference to WebLogic's context

Before making any JNDI calls, you must obtain a reference to WebLogic Server's context. You can do this in one of two ways:

✦ Use the javax.naming.InitialContext class, which is the portable, J2EE way of doing it

✦ Use the weblogic.jndi.Environment class, which is the non-portable, WebLogic-specific way of doing it

To obtain a context using javax.naming.InitialContext, you must provide values for the properties INITIAL_CONTEXT_FACTORY and PROVIDER_URL. You may optionally provide values for SECURITY_PRINCIPAL and SECURITY_CREDENTIALS, but if you don't, the context will be obtained by using the WebLogic guest account. Listing 7-1 shows how to obtain a WebLogic context by using the WebLogic system account:

Listing 7-1: Obtaining a WebLogic Context by Using the `javax.naming.InitialContext` Class

```
import javax.naming.*;
import weblogic.jndi.*;
import java.util.*;

Context ctx = null;
Hashtable ht = new Hashtable();

ht.put(Context.INITIAL_CONTEXT_FACTORY,
       "weblogic.jndi.WLInitialContextFactory");
ht.put(Context.PROVIDER_URL, "t3://localhost:7001");
ht.put(Context.SECURITY_PRINCIPAL, "wlsadmin");
ht.put(Context.SECURITY_CREDENTIALS, "password");

try {
  ctx = new InitialContext(ht);
  // do something with the context
}
catch (NamingException e) {
}
finally {
  try {
    // close the context when finished with it
    ctx.close();
  }
  catch (Exception e) {
  }
}
```

Note   BEA recommends using the Java Authentication and Authorization Service (JAAS) instead of JNDI to associate a user with a security context. Nevertheless, the preceding example shows how to do it with JNDI, and is provided as a reference.

The WebLogic-specific way to obtain a context is to use the `weblogic.jndi.Environment` interface. This interface provides defaults for the context's properties that reduce the amount of code you need to write, especially if the code is running within WebLogic Server. With this interface, `INITIAL_CONTEXT_FACTORY` defaults to `weblogic.jndi.WLInitialContext Factory`, `PROVIDER_URL` defaults to `t3://localhost:7001`, `SECURITY_PRINCIPAL` defaults to WebLogic's `guest` account, and `SECURITY_CREDENTIALS` defaults to the `guest` account's password.

If you want to set the context properties to different values, the `Environment` interface provides `set` methods for this purpose. The code in Listing 7-2 reimplements the preceding example by using the `Environment` interface and two of its `set` methods to change the security context to the `system` account.

Listing 7-2: Obtaining a WebLogic Context by Using the
`weblogic.jndi.Environment` **Interface**

```
import javax.naming.*;
import weblogic.jndi.*;
import java.util.*;

Context ctx = null;
Environment env = new Environment();

env.setSecurityPrincipal("wlsadmin");
env.setSecurityCredentials("password");

try {
  ctx = env.getInitialContext();
  // do something with the context
}
catch (NamingException e) {
}
finally {
  try {
    // close the context when finished with it
    ctx.close();
  }
  catch (Exception e) {
  }
}
```

Binding objects to the WebLogic JNDI tree

After you obtain a context, you can use it to bind objects to the WebLogic JNDI Tree. The following code snippet shows how to bind an instance of a hypothetical Person class to the JNDI Tree under the logical name Person Object:

```
try {
  ctx = env.getInitialContext();
  Person myPerson = new Person();
  ctx.bind("Person Object", myPerson);
}
catch (NamingException e) {
}
```

Note that if an object is already bound to the tree with this name, the call to Initial-Context.bind() will throw a NamingException. If you don't want an exception thrown in this case, call InitialContext.rebind() instead, which overwrites any previous bindings with the new one:

```
try {
  ctx = env.getInitialContext();
  Person myPerson = new Person();
```

```
        ctx.rebind("Person Object", myPerson);
    }
    catch (NamingException e) {
    }
```

You can use the WebLogic console to view bound objects in the JNDI Tree. Expand the
Servers node in the domain tree and then right-click myserver (or whatever server you are
using). From the pop-up menu of server-related operations, select View JNDI Tree. The JNDI
Tree appears in a new browser window, as shown in Figure 7-2.

Figure 7-2: A Person object bound to the WebLogic JNDI Tree

Using subcontexts to organize the JNDI tree

Notice that the Person object was bound to the root level of the JNDI Tree. If you are binding
a lot of objects or if you want to organize your bound objects by application, you may want to
bind your objects into *subcontexts,* which are simply folders in the JNDI Tree. In Figure 7-2,
there are subcontexts called javax, jdbc, and weblogic. Subcontexts can nest to any number of levels, similar to directories in a file system, and are case-sensitive.

The following example shows how to create a subcontext called JNDI Chapter and bind a
Person object into it:

```
    try {
        ctx = env.getInitialContext();
        Context subctx = ctx.createSubContext("JNDI Chapter");
        Person myPerson = new Person();
        subctx.bind("Person Object", myPerson);
    }
    catch (NamingException e) {
    }
```

Figure 7-3 shows the result of this binding in the WebLogic JNDI Tree.

Figure 7-3: A `Person` object bound to a subcontext in the WebLogic JNDI Tree

Performing lookups on objects bound to the WebLogic JNDI tree

After you bind objects to the WebLogic JNDI Tree, you can obtain references to them by performing lookups. You accomplish this by calling the `Context.lookup()` method, which returns a Java `Object`, and casting the result to the proper object type. The following code shows how to obtain a reference to the `Person` object you stored in the preceding example:

```
try {
  ctx = env.getInitialContext();
  Person myPerson =
    (Person) ctx.lookup("JNDI Chapter/Person Object");
  // You can now call myPerson's methods
}
catch (NamingException e) {
}
```

Note   Classes used in this manner (`Person`) must implement the `java.io.Serializable` interface.

Another shortcut is to call `Environment.getContext()` instead of `Environment.get-InitialContext()`, passing the name of the subcontext you want to use for the lookup. `getInitialContext()` always returns a reference to the root context, whereas `getContext()` returns a reference to any valid subcontext:

```
try {
  ctx = env.getContext("JNDI Chapter");
  Person myPerson = (Person) ctx.lookup("Person Object");
  // You can now call myPerson's methods
}
catch (NamingException e) {
}
```

Performing lookups against an LDAP directory

In this section, we show you how to use JNDI to obtain a context to an external LDAP directory and then perform simple lookups on its contents. Before proceeding with the example, however, we give you a brief overview of LDAP. LDAP directories are hierarchical, usually organized from the top down using geographical or organizational divisions. The design of an LDAP directory (the way it's organized and the items it tracks) is called its *schema;* LDAP schemas are completely user-definable. To find an entry in the directory, you provide a *distinguished name* (DN), which consists of one or more *relative distinguished names* (RDNs) that fully specify the entry. Table 7-2 lists the standard LDAP RDNs found in all LDAP directories.

Table 7-2: Standard LDAP RDNs

RDN Type	Description
C	Country name
ST	State or province name
L	Locality or city name
STREET	Street address
O	Organization name
OU	Organizational unit name
CN	Common name

To perform a lookup in an LDAP directory, you construct a DN from one or more RDNs. The more RDNs you supply, the more specific the query becomes. Here is an example of a DN constructed from the RDNs in Table 7-2:

```
CN=Joe Zuffoletto, OU=Management, O=ZeeWare, L=Sausalito,
ST=California, C=US
```

When passed as a query to an LDAP server, the preceding DN, which specifies a person, will probably return only one entry. You can pass less-specific DNs to retrieve multiple entries; for example, the following DN retrieves the entries for all members of management at ZeeWare's offices in California:

```
OU=Management, O=ZeeWare, ST=California, C=US.
```

You now have enough background to understand the examples. For these examples, we installed Sun ONE (formerly iPlanet) Directory Server v5.1 on the same Windows 2000 machine as our WebLogic Server (you can download Sun ONE Directory Server, along with installation instructions, from `http://wwws.sun.com/software/download/5279.html`). After downloading, we expanded the zip file and ran the default setup. The installer created a directory instance with a root suffix of `dc=JMZ,dc=local` (derived from our Windows 2000 domain name).

After completing the installation, we used the iPlanet Console to add sample organizational units and users to the directory tree, organized as follows:

```
dc=JMZ (root)
  ou=Management
    uid=GWells
    uid=JZuffoletto
  ou=Developers
    uid=BGill
    uid=GSchneider
    uid=BTucker
  ou=Clients
    uid=SJohnson
    uid=MJones
    uid=DMiller
    uid=NSmith
```

Figure 7-4 shows the iPlanet Console after we added this information.

Figure 7-4: iPlanet Console showing sample organizational units and users

Obtaining a directory context

Now that the directory is up and running, the first programming step is to write a method that obtains the LDAP directory's context. But rather than obtaining an instance of `javax.naming.Context`, you need to obtain an instance of `javax.naming.directory.DirContext`. A `DirContext` contains methods that enable you to access the attributes of entries in the directory, which is essential when working with LDAP.

The following method returns a `DirContext` to the LDAP directory specified by `providerUrl`:

```
public static DirContext getLDAPContext(String providerUrl)
throws javax.naming.NamingException {
  DirContext ctx = null;
  Hashtable ht = new Hashtable();

  ht.put(Context.INITIAL_CONTEXT_FACTORY,
         "com.sun.jndi.ldap.LdapCtxFactory");
  ht.put(Context.PROVIDER_URL, providerUrl);

  ctx = new InitialDirContext(ht);
  return ctx;
}
```

Notice that you're using a different `INITIAL_CONTEXT_FACTORY` — Sun's default LDAP context factory, contained in the factory class `com.sun.jndi.ldap.LdapCtxFactory`. This class should already be in your Java/WebLogic classpath, so there's no need to install it. Note also that you're creating a new `InitialDirContext`, which returns a `DirContext`, rather than `InitialContext`, which returns a regular `Context`.

The following call obtains a context to the local iPlanet directory we installed:

```
try {
  DirContext ctx = getLDAPContext("ldap://localhost:389");
}
catch (NamingException e) {
}
```

Authenticating a user

After you have obtained the LDAP directory's context, you can do some useful work with the directory. One common task is to authenticate users by comparing a given name and password (such as those keyed into a login page) against the entries in the directory. The following code performs this task:

```
Properties p = new Properties();
p.put(Context.INITIAL_CONTEXT_FACTORY,
  "com.sun.jndi.ldap.LdapCtxFactory");
p.put(Context.PROVIDER_URL, LdapURL);
p.put(Context.SECURITY_AUTHENTICATION, "simple");
p.put(Context.SECURITY_PRINCIPAL, "cn=" + strUserName);
p.put(Context.SECURITY_CREDENTIALS, strPassword);
```

```
try {
  DirContext ctx = new InitialDirContext(p);
} catch (Exception e) {
  System.out.println("Login failed.");
}
```

Retrieving user attributes

Another important task is to retrieve attributes for selected users, perhaps to support a system administrator's ability to manage the user list. The following code retrieves a list of all users in the organizational unit Clients; then iterates through the list to print the full name of each user:

```
Attributes match = new BasicAttributes();
match.put("cn", username);
try {
  NamingEnumeration list = dctx.search("ou=Clients", match);
  if ((list != null) && (list.hasMore())) {
    SearchResult sr = (SearchResult) list.next();
    Attributes attrs = sr.getAttributes();
    if (attrs != null) {
      System.out.println("Full Name: " +
        attrs.get("cn")).get());
      System.out.println("E-mail: " +
        attrs.get("mail")).get());
      System.out.println("");
    }
  } else {
    System.out.println("No clients found.");
  }
} catch (NamingException ne) {
  System.out.println("Error finding clients.");
}
```

Here is what the output might look like:

```
Full Name: David Miller
E-mail: dmiller@somecompany.com

Full Name: Melissa Jones
E-mail: mjones@someothercompany.com

Full Name: Nancy Smith
E-mail: nsmith@another.com

Full Name: Scott Johnson
E-mail: sjohnson@yetanother.com
```

Accessing Microsoft's Active Directory

One popular topic on the newsgroups these days is how to use JNDI to access Microsoft's Active Directory. Active Directory is Microsoft's LDAP-compliant replacement for Windows NT domains that ships with Windows 2000 servers. Being able to access the Windows 2000 directory from Java is a major boon for many enterprise programmers. The question is this: How do you do it?

It turns out to be fairly easy if Active Directory and DNS are properly configured for your Windows 2000 domain. Assuming they are, the following code snippet gets you a `DirContext` to Active Directory:

```
DirContext ctx = null;
Hashtable ht = new Hashtable();

ht.put(Context.INITIAL_CONTEXT_FACTORY,
       "com.sun.jndi.ldap.LdapCtxFactory");

ht.put(Context.PROVIDER_URL, "ldap://pdc.mycompany.com:389");
ht.put(Context.SECURITY_AUTHENTICATION, "simple");
ht.put(Context.SECURITY_PRINCIPAL, "MYCOMPANY\\Administrator");
ht.put(Context.SECURITY_CREDENTIALS, "password");

ctx = new InitialDirContext(ht);
```

In this example, `PROVIDER_URL` contains the DNS host name of the Active Directory server (pdc.mycompany.com), plus the (optional) port of 389. You must specify a `SECURITY_AUTHENTICATION` of simple, or Active Directory will expect Windows 2000 authentication, which Java does not support. The `SECURITY_PRINCIPAL` can be the Windows Administrator account (shown), or any other account with access to the directory. To make your code location-independent, include the Windows 2000 domain name before the account name, using the usual Windows 2000 syntax, as in `MYCOMPANY\\Administrator`. The `SECURITY_CREDENTIALS` simply contain the password for the account given by `SECURITY_PRINCIPAL`.

After you obtain a `DirContext` to Active Directory, you can use it like any other LDAP directory. The following code dumps all the `Person Objects` in the directory:

```
SearchControls cons = new SearchControls();
cons.setSearchScope(SearchControls.SUBTREE_SCOPE);
NamingEnumeration results = ctx.search("dc=zeeware,dc=com",
                                       "objectclass=person",
                                       cons);
while (results.hasMore()) {
  System.out.println("\n\n");
  SearchResult result = (SearchResult) results.next();
  Attributes rAttrs = result.getAttributes();
  for (NamingEnumeration ne = rAttrs.getAll(); ne.hasMore();) {
    Attribute nAttr = (Attribute) ne.next();
    String sID = nAttr.getID();
    for (Enumeration vals = nAttr.getAll();
         vals.hasMoreElements();) {
      System.out.println(sID + ": " + vals.nextElement());
```

```
        }
      }
    }
```

Beware! Active Directory contains a lot of administrative information, so you will need to experiment and tune your queries so they return only the information you need.

Using WebLogic JNDI to Deploy Objects in a Clustered Environment

Because of the way WebLogic JNDI works in a clustered environment, additional planning is required when designing and deploying resources that will be bound to the JNDI Tree of a cluster. This section explains how JNDI works in a WebLogic cluster and then provides a set of strategies you can choose from to make your design and deployment decisions.

By default, when a WebLogic Server instance joins a cluster, the contents of its JNDI Tree are merged with the contents of the cluster's tree, and the resulting tree is replicated to every server in the cluster. Figure 7-5 shows the effects of this process.

As you might imagine, the two-way replication that takes place among all participants in a cluster to synchronize the JNDI Tree generates a potentially large amount of network traffic. Fortunately, BEA recognized this problem and designed two features into WebLogic to help programmers cope with it.

First, BEA designed WebLogic RMI so that WebLogic RMI stubs are incredibly compact. Therefore, replicating RMI stubs across a cluster generates relatively little network traffic.

Second, the BEA JNDI context factory, `weblogic.jndi.WLInitialContextFactory`, supports the use of an additional property, `REPLICATE_BINDINGS`, which allows the programmer to decide which objects will be replicated to the cluster tree and which ones will not. This reduces network overhead during JNDI Tree replications at the cost of reduced load-balancing and failover capability for nonreplicated objects.

Non-RMI, custom objects (such as the `Person` object implemented earlier) are the ones that require the most attention when binding to a cluster-wide JNDI tree. This is because custom objects can be potentially large and are replicated in their entirety across the cluster. If you have created a large custom object and want to minimize network traffic when deploying it to a cluster, you can choose from a number of strategies to do so; these strategies are discussed in the following sections.

Write an RMI proxy for the custom object

The first strategy is to write an RMI proxy for the object, creating stubs for the methods you want to be made available across the cluster. Then, you bind the custom object to the JNDI tree with `REPLICATE_BINDINGS = false`. During JNDI tree replication, only the stubs will be replicated, and they will all point back to a single instance of the custom object.

The shortcoming of this strategy is that you give up a certain amount of availability for the object. If the server hosting the custom object goes down, none of the stubs will work, and the object will be rendered completely unavailable.

```
                               Cluster
 ┌──────────────────────┐  ┌──────────────────────┐    ┌──────────────────────┐
 │ WebLogic Server A    │  │ WebLogic Server B    │    │ WebLogic Server C    │
 │                      │  │                      │    │                      │
 │ JNDI Tree            │  │ JNDI Tree            │    │ JNDI Tree            │
 │ JDBC                 │  │ JDBC                 │    │ JDBC                 │
 │   Pool A             │  │   Pool A             │    │   Pool A             │
 │   Pool B             │  │   Pool B             │    │   Pool C             │
 │ RMI                  │  │ RMI                  │    │ RMI                  │
 │   Stub A             │  │   Stub A             │    │   Stub C             │
 │   Stub B             │  │   Stub B             │    │ EJB                  │
 │ EJB                  │  │ EJB                  │    │   Bean B             │
 │   Bean A             │  │   Bean A             │    │   Bean C             │
 │ Custom               │  │ Custom               │    │ Custom               │
 │   Object A           │  │   Object A           │    │   Object B           │
 │   Object B           │  │   Object B           │    │   Object C           │
 └──────────────────────┘  └──────────────────────┘    └──────────────────────┘
```

Before adding server C to the cluster

```
                               Cluster
 ┌──────────────────────┐  ┌──────────────────────┐  ┌──────────────────────┐
 │ WebLogic Server A    │  │ WebLogic Server B    │  │ WebLogic Server C    │
 │                      │  │                      │  │                      │
 │ JNDI Tree            │  │ JNDI Tree            │  │ JNDI Tree            │
 │ JDBC                 │  │ JDBC                 │  │ JDBC                 │
 │   Pool A             │  │   Pool A             │  │   Pool A             │
 │   Pool B             │  │   Pool B             │  │   Pool B             │
 │   Pool C             │  │   Pool C             │  │   Pool C             │
 │ RMI                  │  │ RMI                  │  │ RMI                  │
 │   Stub A             │  │   Stub A             │  │   Stub A             │
 │   Stub B             │  │   Stub B             │  │   Stub B             │
 │   Stub C             │  │   Stub C             │  │   Stub C             │
 │ EJB                  │  │ EJB                  │  │ EJB                  │
 │   Bean A             │  │   Bean A             │  │   Bean A             │
 │   Bean B             │  │   Bean B             │  │   Bean B             │
 │   Bean C             │  │   Bean C             │  │   Bean C             │
 │ Custom               │  │ Custom               │  │ Custom               │
 │   Object A           │  │   Object A           │  │   Object A           │
 │   Object B           │  │   Object B           │  │   Object B           │
 │   Object C           │  │   Object C           │  │   Object C           │
 └──────────────────────┘  └──────────────────────┘  └──────────────────────┘
```

After adding server C to the cluster

Figure 7-5: Adding WebLogic Server C to a two-server cluster causes the combined JNDI Tree to be replicated to all three servers in the cluster.

To overcome this, you can deploy the object to more than one server in the cluster. In this case, WebLogic creates a replica-aware stub that knows how to locate all instances of the object that you have deployed to the cluster. If one of the servers goes down, the replica-aware stub traverses the remaining instances until it finds one that's available. During JNDI Tree replication, copies of the replica-aware stub are distributed to all participants in the cluster.

Pin the custom object to one server

In this strategy, you set `REPLICATE_BINDINGS=false` for the custom object, which causes it to appear only in the JNDI Tree of its home server. Then, whenever you call the object, you must explicitly specify its home server in the context's `PROVIDER_URL`, or you will get `javax.naming.NamingException` when you perform a lookup on the object.

The downside of this strategy is that you give up both failover and availability for the custom object. Failover doesn't exist because the object is only available via its home server. Availability is compromised because if the home server goes down, the custom object goes down with it.

Deploy the custom object separately to all servers

The final strategy is to manually deploy the custom object to all servers in the cluster, binding it to each server's JNDI tree with `REPLICATE_BINDINGS=false`. Then, each server will have a copy of the object, and it will not be replicated.

One problem with this strategy is that it creates a maintenance headache. Whenever the custom object is changed, programmers must remember to redeploy it to every server in the cluster. If the object cannot be hot-deployed, the entire cluster must be brought down while the object is copied around. Also, if additional servers are added to the cluster later on, someone must remember to copy the custom object to them. In a rapidly changing runtime environment, this is certain to cause problems.

Another weakness of this strategy is that you might sacrifice performance if the object caches data at runtime. If, for example, user A invokes the copy on server A during his first call, but then invokes the copy on server B on his next call, any performance gain he might have seen from the data cached with object A is lost because the data must be refetched by object B.

Summary

WebLogic JNDI is a convenient way to publish code resources for easy lookup and use across the distributed enterprise. Combined with a WebLogic cluster, WebLogic JNDI allows these code resources to be made available in a fault-tolerant way.

JNDI is easy to use and provides an extensible, vendor-independent way to access resources other than code, including corporate directories, file systems, e-mail systems, and even databases.

JNDI includes features that make it easy to interface with LDAP-compliant directory services. These features will become indispensable in the near future, especially for programmers who are integrating WebLogic with the Active Directory component of Microsoft Windows 2000.

✦ ✦ ✦

Working with WebLogic RMI

Remote Method Invocation, or RMI, is the standard Java facility for distributed, object-oriented computing over a network. RMI enables code in one Java virtual machine (JVM) to execute methods against objects in other JVMs as if those objects were available locally. This capability enables developers to write powerful, network-aware applications without writing complex networking code or designing bidirectional communications protocols.

RMI provides an efficient, Java-centric way to write distributed applications. Java client applications can use RMI to invoke methods residing in servers, and application servers can use RMI to invoke methods residing in other application servers. With WebLogic RMI, clients can even invoke methods in other clients, with the remote calls being routed through WebLogic Server.

Many Java developers find RMI intimidating, probably because it reminds them of the bad old days when network programming was exceedingly difficult. But RMI is really quite easy—after you figure it out. This chapter will make it much easier for you to do so.

RMI is a powerful weapon in the J2EE arsenal. Knowing it enables you to easily write applications you might have otherwise considered too difficult to attempt. Another good reason to learn and understand RMI is that RMI is used behind the scenes to call methods in EJBs.

Understanding RMI

To effectively use RMI within the WebLogic environment, you need to understand that Sun and WebLogic provide separate implementations of the RMI specification, with WebLogic's implementation being highly tuned for the WebLogic environment. You can use either vendor's implementation in your WebLogic applications. This section explains the class packages required for each implementation and then discusses RMI's architecture and the optimizations that have been coded into WebLogic's implementation.

RMI versions and packages

RMI is included with the Java 2 Platform, Standard Edition (J2SE) and also with J2EE. WebLogic's documentation refers to this as *JavaSoft's RMI*. WebLogic provides its own version of RMI as well, called *WebLogic RMI*. WebLogic RMI is implemented as a drop-in replacement for JavaSoft's RMI and is fully compatible with JavaSoft's RMI specification. But WebLogic RMI is optimized to take advantage of the WebLogic environment and provides some features and extensions not available in the standard implementation.

JavaSoft's RMI is implemented in seven packages:

- ✦ `java.rmi`, the core API
- ✦ `java.rmi.activation`, the API for activatable objects
- ✦ `java.rmi.dgc`, the API for the distributed garbage collector (DGC)
- ✦ `java.rmi.registry`, the API for RMI's network naming service
- ✦ `java.rmi.server`, the API for server-side operations
- ✦ `javax.rmi`, the core API for RMI over Internet Inter-Orb Protocol (RMI-IIOP)
- ✦ `javax.rmi.CORBA`, additional portability APIs for RMI-IIOP to provide a standard interface between the generated stubs and ties and the RMI-IIOP runtime

WebLogic RMI replaces five of the seven `java.rmi` packages with its own packages, as follows:

- ✦ `weblogic.rmi`
- ✦ `weblogic.rmi.activation`
- ✦ `weblogic.rmi.dgc`
- ✦ `weblogic.rmi.registry`
- ✦ `weblogic.rmi.server`

You can write WebLogic applications by using either RMI implementation. To switch implementations, you only need to switch Java import statements for RMI. To switch from JavaSoft's RMI to WebLogic's, for example, just replace all occurrences of

```
import java.rmi.<packageName>
```

with:

```
import weblogic.rmi.<packageName>
```

or vice versa. Of course, this works only if you adhere to the JavaSoft specification and do *not* use WebLogic's RMI extensions, which I explain later in this chapter.

Caution   You cannot mix and match the Java and WebLogic RMI packages in your application because of major differences in their low-level implementations.

Note   In WebLogic Server 7.0, `weblogic.rmi.Remote` and `weblogic.rmi.RemoteException` have been deprecated. Use the standard `java.rmi.Remote` and `java.rmi.Remote Exception` instead.

RMI architecture

RMI employs a layered architecture that makes use of the proxy design pattern and serialization to do its work.

Cross-Reference   Design patterns are introduced in Chapter 3.

Clients and servers

In an RMI system, code executing in one JVM (the RMI client) executes methods belonging to objects residing in a different JVM (the RMI server). The client need not be a client in the normal client/server sense. Code executing in one WebLogic server, for example, can act as an RMI client, invoking methods on a different WebLogic server (in this case, it is also the RMI server). In fact, the client can even make "remote" calls to objects running in its own JVM, as is usually the case when session EJBs invoke methods on entity EJBs.

Stubs and skeletons

To make the process of invoking server-side objects appear transparent to the client, RMI employs *stubs* on the client side; these stubs function as proxies for the server-side code. From the perspective of the client, the stubs look exactly like the server-side methods, with the same method names, parameter lists, and return values. Instead of containing the actual method code, however, the stubs contain code that transmits the client-side calls to the server, processes the results sent back from the server, and returns the results back to the client.

On the server side, proxies called *skeletons* are used to perform the inverse operations of receiving remote calls from clients, converting them into local calls on the server, making the local calls, and transmitting the results back to the clients.

Stubs and skeletons are automatically generated by an *RMI compiler*. This piece of software analyzes the server-side classes you write and creates the appropriate code fragments for the stubs and skeletons. You deploy these fragments along with your RMI server. Sun and BEA both provide RMI compilers for their implementations of the RMI specification.

Note   Be sure to use the correct compiler; if your code uses WebLogic RMI, you must use WebLogic's RMI compiler to generate your stubs and skeletons.

Figure 8-1 shows the layered architecture that makes up an RMI client and server.

Serialization, marshalling, and unmarshalling

The stubs and skeletons work their magic by using Java serialization. Stubs convert client-side calls of server methods into serialized byte streams; this process is called *marshalling*. During this process, each object is checked to see if it implements the `java.rmi.Remote` (or `weblogic.rmi.Remote`) interface. If so, its remote reference is added to the marshalled byte stream. If not, the object itself is serialized and added to the byte stream.

When an object is serialized, its fields (including arrays, collections, and references to other objects) are serialized recursively, assuming that all such nested objects themselves implement the `Serializable` interface. This is an important point to remember — if you don't watch the size of your objects and the objects they contain, you may find yourself generating far more network traffic than you want, impairing the performance of your application.

Figure 8-1: RMI's layered architecture

The stub forwards the marshalled calls to the Remote Reference Layer for transmission to the server. Skeletons receive these serialized byte streams from the Remote Reference Layer and convert them back into method calls. This is called *unmarshalling*. After the method calls complete on the server machine, the skeletons marshal the results and send them back to the stubs. The stubs unmarshal these results and return them to the calling thread on the client.

Note   Objects that will be marshalled by RMI must implement either the `java.rmi.Remote` or `java.io.Serializable` interface. This applies to objects embedded in the marshalled objects as well.

Tip   You can prevent certain fields in your objects from being serialized by marking them as `transient`. For example:

```
private transient boolean myBoolean;
public transient Connection myConnection;
```

This technique can be used to protect sensitive information in your objects or to suppress the transmission of unnecessary data, such as local network connections or file references.

Note that `static` fields will not be serialized and marshalled either. For example:

```
private static String serverName;
```

This is because `static` fields are class fields, and RMI is concerned with object instances, not classes.

Registries and naming

A client finds a server object on the network by using a naming service. WebLogic programmers have access to two RMI naming services: the default RMI registry, and the WebLogic RMI registry.

The default RMI registry

JavaSoft's RMI registry is a server process that returns remote references to objects that have been registered with it. This registry is started simply by executing the `rmiregistry` command on the command line, with an optional port number on which to listen for client lookups. If you don't specify a port, the registry listens on the default port of 1099.

> **Note**   You must explicitly start the default RMI registry before using it. You can find copies of `rmiregistry.exe` in either the `/bea/jdk131_03/bin` directory or the `/bea/jdk131_03/jre/bin` directory. You can also start a registry instance in code by calling `java.rmi.Registry.LocateRegistry.createRegistry(int port)`.

Remote references are mapped to unique logical names of type `String` and these mappings are stored in a hash table. Servers create entries in the registry by making calls to a running registry process. They can do so by using the `java.rmi.registry.Registry` interface, the `java.rmi.registry.LocateRegistry` class, or the `java.rmi.Naming` class. Clients look up entries in the registry by using the `java.rmi.Naming` class. Code examples that appear later in this chapter show you how to perform these operations.

The WebLogic RMI registry

The WebLogic RMI registry is a drop-in replacement for the default registry that runs automatically when WebLogic Server starts up. Registry and naming calls made to the `weblogic.rmi` packages operate against this registry. Unlike the default RMI registry, only one WebLogic RMI registry can run per WebLogic server. Calls to create additional registries, even on different ports, simply return references to the existing registry.

The WebLogic RMI registry is fully integrated with WebLogic JNDI. In fact, it makes calls to WebLogic JNDI methods when it registers and looks up remote references. BEA recommends that you use JNDI directly to do the same, bypassing the WebLogic RMI registry calls completely. This enables you to set up meaningful namespaces for your applications and also allows you to publish RMI objects to enterprise directories such as NDS or LDAP. We demonstrate how to take advantage of these features in the examples; the first example ("Your First WebLogic RMI Application") uses the RMI registry, while the remaining examples use the recommended JNDI method.

> **Cross-Reference**   Chapter 7 covers WebLogic JNDI in detail.

Comparing WebLogic RMI to JavaSoft RMI

Although WebLogic RMI and JavaSoft RMI are functionally identical, the WebLogic implementation has a number of advantages over the JavaSoft implementation. Most of these advantages boil down to ease-of-use for the programmer and application performance and scalability.

Ease-of-use

The WebLogic RMI is much easier to use than the JavaSoft RMI because there is less administrative overhead. When you start WebLogic Server, the supporting infrastructure for RMI starts up automatically, including the runtime environment, a security environment, and a JNDI-enabled RMI registry. This saves you from writing code to start RMI servers, manage security, and configure JNDI-enabled registries yourself.

From a coding standpoint, WebLogic's RMI runtime environment is set up so your remote classes aren't required to inherit from `UnicastRemoteObject`. This allows you to implement a proper class hierarchy instead of conforming to this arbitrary runtime requirement of the reference implementation that throws a wrench into your class tree.

Note   You can code around the requirement to extend `UnicastRemoteObject`, even if you're using the JavaSoft RMI. A discussion of the techniques for doing so is beyond the scope of this book, but you can learn more by reading *Mastering RMI*, by Rickard Öberg (Wiley Publishing, 2001).

Another handy WebLogic RMI feature is that remote methods need not declare `RemoteExceptions`. This gives developers additional flexibility in how they design their applications. With JavaSoft RMI, client calls to remote methods must be enclosed in try/catch blocks that handle the `RemoteExceptions`. This means that if the server crashes, can't marshal a call, or is simply down, an exception gets thrown to the client. In some cases, you may find that these events happen so infrequently that you don't want to deal with the possibility on every call. Or, you may simply want your code to handle all runtime exceptions the same way, regardless of their origin. WebLogic RMI gives you this flexibility.

After you deploy your RMI application, the WebLogic Console provides a graphical interface to the state of your RMI environment. You can easily see which remote implementations are deployed, where in the JNDI tree they're deployed, and how much usage they're experiencing. This information is a big help when you're trying to optimize or troubleshoot an installation.

With WebLogic 7.0, you don't even need to run the RMI compiler because WebLogic automatically generates stubs and skeletons at runtime. The only time you must run the RMI compiler yourself is when you are creating clusterable or Internet Inter-Orb Protocol (IIOP) clients; see the WebLogic documentation for more information.

Performance and scalability

WebLogic RMI incorporates a number of optimizations that increase performance and scalability, as discussed in the following sections.

Efficient network communications

One of WebLogic RMI's most significant optimizations is the way it handles network connections between RMI clients and WebLogic Server. JavaSoft RMI opens separate socket connections for communication between the client and the server, and also between the client and the RMI registry. WebLogic RMI, on the other hand, multiplexes all this network traffic over a single socket connection, which is also used for other client-to-server communications such as JDBC, JMS, and so on. Sockets are a relatively expensive and limited networking resource; by minimizing socket use, WebLogic makes it possible for more clients to communicate with the server. Figure 8-2 shows the difference in TCP/IP port usage between JavaSoft RMI and WebLogic RMI.

Figure 8-2: TCP/IP socket use by JavaSoft RMI (top) and WebLogic RMI (bottom)

Optimized remote method calls within the same JVM

Another important difference between WebLogic RMI and JavaSoft RMI is the way WebLogic handles remote method calls made within the same JVM. JavaSoft RMI makes no distinction in this regard; the full method invocation process always occurs, complete with the loading of stubs and skeletons, object serialization, marshalling and unmarshalling of parameter lists, and so on. WebLogic, however, short-circuits this process by directly calling remote methods that are resident in the same JVM. Figure 8-3 illustrates this concept.

WebLogic's approach yields significant performance improvements when RMI servers and EJBs are deployed on the same WebLogic server as the code that calls them. Keep this in mind when you're deploying facades, DAOs, and view helpers that access entity EJBs.

Note, however, that when WebLogic refers to objects in the same JVM, it does so by reference—not by value, as does the JavaSoft implementation. Although this subtle difference shouldn't matter in most cases, it's an important semantic difference of which you should be aware.

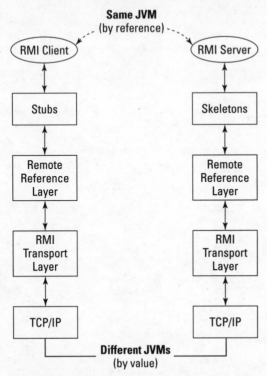

Figure 8-3: WebLogic remote method calls in the same versus different JVMs

Client-to-server, server-to-client, and client-to-client method invocation

Another unique feature of WebLogic RMI is its support for various remote method invocation schemes. WebLogic allows RMI clients to invoke remote methods not only on RMI servers, but also on other RMI clients that have published their remote interfaces to the WebLogic RMI registry. RMI servers hosted by WebLogic can invoke remote methods published by clients as well. This enables programmers to create flexible applications that support peer-to-peer processing schemes as well as bidirectional processing schemes between clients and servers. Because of the way WebLogic optimizes remote method calls made within the same JVM, clients incur no performance penalty for invoking their own methods.

Writing Your First WebLogic RMI Application

Now that you have a good understanding of the WebLogic RMI architecture, it's time to write and deploy a WebLogic RMI application. You'll start with a simple example that shows how to create the required software components, install them in WebLogic, verify the installation, and then test them out. Later in the chapter, you'll develop a more complex example.

This first example is an adaptation of the Hello sample that appears in the WebLogic documentation (`http://edocs.bea.com/wls/docs70/rmi/index.html`). You'll keep the coding to a minimum for now so that you can focus on the steps required to make the application work.

To write and deploy a WebLogic RMI application, follow these steps:

1. Write the remote interface, which exposes the methods on the server that are available to RMI clients. It must extend the `weblogic.rmi.Remote` interface, which contains no method signatures.

2. Write the server. The server is a class that implements the remote interface. The server may also contain additional methods, not exposed through the interface, for its internal operations and housekeeping. One such method is the `main` method (or a method called by `main`), which registers the server in the RMI registry.

3. Compile the remote interface and the server with the Java compiler.

4. (Optional) Compile the server with the WebLogic RMI compiler to generate the stub and skeleton classes. If you don't do it, WebLogic will do it for you at runtime, but you must do it yourself if you're writing clusterable or IIOP clients.

5. Write a client that makes remote calls to the server.

6. Compile the client with the Java compiler.

7. Run WebLogic Server and use the console to configure the RMI server class as a WebLogic startup class.

8. Stop and restart WebLogic Server so it executes the RMI server class at startup. This will cause the RMI server to register itself in the WebLogic RMI registry.

9. Use the WebLogic console to verify that the RMI server is correctly deployed and visible in the JNDI tree (remember that WebLogic RMI is integrated with WebLogic JNDI, so all RMI registrations are written to the JNDI tree).

10. Run the client and see if it works!

Cross-Reference These instructions assume that you are working with the default WebLogic Server (`myserver`), or a clone of it that has been configured to run these examples. Chapter 4 shows how to install and configure such a server.

Now that you know the steps to follow, you can get to work. You will write an RMI server with one remote method that returns the string `Hello, remote world!` Then you will write an RMI client that invokes the method and writes the returned string to standard output.

Write the remote interface

The remote interface exposes the methods on the server that are available to RMI clients. The interface may have any number of methods, but it must extend the `weblogic.rmi.Remote` interface. What follows is the remote interface for the simple example `HelloInterface.java`:

```
package com.wiley.wlsbible.rmi.example1;
import weblogic.rmi.*;   // as opposed to java.rmi.*

public interface HelloInterface extends weblogic.rmi.Remote {
```

```
   // This method is called by clients and is implemented
   // by the server class.
   public String sayHello() throws RemoteException;
}
```

This interface exposes only one method, `sayHello`, to RMI clients. Note that it extends the `weblogic.rmi.Remote` interface, as required.

Note   As mentioned earlier in this chapter, the `weblogic.rmi.Remote` interface has been deprecated. We use it here only so that we can show an example of using `weblogic.rmi.Naming.rebind()`. The remaining examples in this chapter all use JNDI for naming, and therefore use the `java.rmi.Remote` interface. This latter pattern is what you should use for all new code written for WebLogic.

Tip   After reading the next section on using JNDI, you might want to try modifying this code to use JNDI. We leave that as an exercise for the reader.

The interface and the method are both declared to be `public`, which they must be in order to be remotely accessible. You also defined the method to throw a `RemoteException`, which is required in JavaSoft RMI but not in WebLogic RMI — this ensures that your interface is compatible with both.

Write the server

The server is a class that provides the guts behind the method signatures in the remote interface. The server should also know how to install itself in the RMI registry. Here's the code for your server, `HelloServer.java`, which performs these functions.

```
package com.wiley.wlsbible.rmi.example1;
import weblogic.rmi.*;

public class HelloServer implements HelloInterface {

   // This method is called by remote clients.
   public String sayHello() throws RemoteException {
     // Write a status message to the server's console
     System.out.println("HelloServer.sayHello()" +
                         "has been remotely invoked.");

     // Return a message to the client
     return "Hello, remote world!!";
   }

   // The main() method registers our server in the
   // WebLogic RMI registry, which by default resides
   // in the WebLogic JNDI tree.
   public static void main(String[] argv) {
     try {
       // Create a remote object instance
       HelloServer obj = new HelloServer();
```

```
      // Register the server with the naming service
      Naming.rebind("HelloServer", obj);

      // Write a status message to the console
      System.out.println("HelloServer was created and " +
                          "bound in the registry " +
                          "to the name HelloServer");
    }
    catch (Exception e) {
      System.out.println("HelloServer error: " +
                          e.getMessage());
      e.printStackTrace();
    }
  }
}
```

This most basic server class implements only two methods: the sayHello method defined in the remote interface and a main method to register the server in the RMI registry. The sayHello method first writes a message to standard output, indicating that it has been invoked; this message will appear on the console of the JVM hosting the server. It then returns the Hello, remote world! message to the client.

A main method creates an instance of the remote object and then registers it with the naming service under the name HelloServer. In this example, you use the weblogic.rmi. Naming.rebind method to register the object. That way, if you need to stop and restart the RMI server for some reason, the new binding will overwrite the old one. If you had used weblogic.rmi.Naming.bind to register the object, the new binding would fail if a previous binding already existed by that name. Note also that it is the remote object's stub that is bound to the registry, not the remote object itself. This is convenient for clients doing registry lookups for the remote object because the stub is what they need.

Note   In JavaSoft RMI, you must perform the additional step of *exporting* the server object to the RMI implementation. Exporting creates a reference to the server object that is used by the stubs at runtime to forward calls to the server. One way to export a server object is to write a default constructor for the server class that simply calls super() on its parent class: UnicastRemoteObject. Another way is to call the static method java.rmi. server.UnicastRemoteObject.exportObject from the default constructor.

Neither step is required with WebLogic RMI — WebLogic Server automatically exports objects that implement the remote interface. But if you're porting existing RMI code to WebLogic or if you just want to write your WebLogic code to be compatible with JavaSoft RMI, you can export the object by using either technique with no ill effects.

Compile the remote interface and the server

The next step is to compile the Java classes for the remote interface and the server.

Cross-Reference   Appendix B shows you how to set up a WebLogic development environment for compiling and running the examples, including how to set up environment variables for classpath, compiler output directories, and so on.

The commands to build these classes are similar to the following:

```
> javac -classpath %classpath% -d %outputdir%
com.wiley.wlsbible.rmi.example1.HelloInterface

> javac -classpath %classpath% -d %outputdir%
com.wiley.wlsbible.rmi.example1.HelloServer
```

These commands result in `HelloInterface.class` and `HelloServer.class` being written to the output directory specified.

Generate stubs and skeletons for the server

To generate the RMI server's stubs and skeletons, run `weblogic.rmic`, WebLogic's RMI compiler, against the `HelloServer` class. As discussed earlier in this chapter, running `weblogic.rmic` is necessary only for clustering or using IIOP. If you do run the RMI compiler, it will output the generated classes to the same destination folder as before:

```
> java -classpath %classpath% weblogic.rmic
com.wiley.wlsbible.rmi.example1.HelloServer -d %outputdir%
```

Running WebLogic's RMI compiler causes two additional classes, `HelloInterface_WLStub.class` and `HelloInterface_WLSkel.class`, to be written to the output directory. The stub class is the one that is marshalled and sent to remote clients invoking the server. The skeleton class is the one used by the server to handle communications between the client stub and the server.

When the WebLogic RMI compiler runs, it generates intermediate Java source files for the stubs and skeletons, compiles those source files into classes, and then deletes the source files. If you want to examine the source files, you can instruct the WebLogic RMI compiler to keep them by using the `-keepgenerated` option, as shown in the following code:

```
> java -classpath %classpath% weblogic.rmic -keepgenerated
com.wiley.wlsbible.rmi.example1.HelloServer -d %outputdir%
```

Now when you look in the output directory, you see `HelloInterface_WLStub.java` and `HelloInterface_WLSkel.java`, in addition to the generated class files. A discussion of the contents of these files is beyond the scope of this book, but feel free to study them on your own.

Write a client that remotely calls the server

Now that the server, stubs, and skeletons are successfully built, you can build a simple client application that calls the server's remote method. Following is the code for such a client, `HelloClient.java`:

```
package com.wiley.wlsbible.rmi.example1;

import weblogic.rmi.*;
import weblogic.common.*;

public class HelloClient {

  public final static String SERVERNAME =
    "rmi://localhost:7001/HelloServer";
```

```
public static void main(String[] argv) {
  try {
    HelloInterface obj =
      (HelloInterface)Naming.lookup(SERVERNAME);
    System.out.println("Connected to HelloServer.");
    String message = obj.sayHello();
    System.out.println(message);
  }

  catch (Throwable t) {
    t.printStackTrace();
    System.exit(-1);
  }
 }
}
```

Compile the client

Assuming that your environment variables are set as explained in Chapter 4, compile HelloClient.java as follows:

```
> javac -classpath %classpath% -d %outputdir%
com.wiley.wlsbible.rmi.example1.HelloClient
```

This command results in HelloClient.class being written to the output directory, along with the server, stub, and skeleton classes built earlier.

Configure the RMI server as a WebLogic startup class

Start the WebLogic Server that will run the classes you've created. Then start the default WebLogic Console (recall from Chapter 1 that you do this by selecting Start Default Console from the WebLogic program group).

In the domain tree on the left side of the console, expand the Deployments node and click Startup and Shutdown. The console should look like Figure 8-4.

Figure 8-4: Configuring startup and shutdown classes in the WebLogic Console

Click Configure a New Startup Class to bring up the startup class configuration page, as shown in Figure 8-5.

Figure 8-5: Startup class configuration page with entries for your RMI server

Fill out the configuration page as shown. The name of the startup class is simply the name of the class that implements the RMI server — in this case, HelloServer. The ClassName is the fully qualified name of the class, including its package name. HelloServer takes no arguments, so leave that field blank. Also elect *not* to abort startup on failure for now. Click Create.

After the class is created, click the Targets tab. Figure 8-6 shows the resulting display.

Figure 8-6: Choosing a target WebLogic server for the RMI server

This page enables you to select any WebLogic server in your domain to host the startup class. Because only one server is available (myserver), that's the server you will choose. Click myserver in the Available list and then click the right-pointing arrow to move it into the Chosen list, as shown in Figure 8-7. Click Apply.

You should now be able to expand the Startup & Shutdown node in the domain tree; HelloServer deploys within that node, as shown in Figure 8-7 under the Startup and Shutdown folder in the tree in the left pane.

Figure 8-7: HelloServer has been deployed to the domain tree.

Now that you've deployed the startup class, exit the console.

At this point, you told WebLogic about the startup class, but WebLogic can't find it. Right now, it's just in whatever output directory you chose when you compiled it. Before continuing, you must place the remote interface (HelloInterface.class) and implementation class (HelloServer.class) on the WebLogic server's classpath.

Cross-Reference   See Appendix B for information on adding classes to the server's classpath.

Stop and restart WebLogic Server

Although you used the WebLogic Console to specify a startup class and pin it to a target server, the class will not deploy until you stop and restart WebLogic Server. Go ahead and do so. When WebLogic Server restarts, it will call the main method of your HelloServer class. It will also cause HelloServer to register itself in the WebLogic RMI registry.

Recall that you wrote your main method to write a startup message to standard output. When you start WebLogic Server, you should see the message HelloServer was created and bound in the registry to the name HelloServer appear while the server is starting, as shown in Figure 8-8.

Figure 8-8: The RMI server tells you that HelloServer has been created and bound.

Verify correct deployment of the RMI server

After WebLogic Server restarts, restart the console. In the domain tree, expand mydomain and then expand Servers. Right-click myserver to display a pop-up menu of server-related operations. From this pop-up menu, select View JNDI tree, as shown in Figure 8-9.

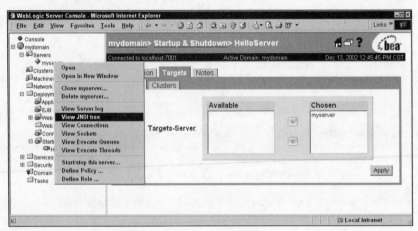

Figure 8-9: Viewing the WebLogic Server JNDI tree

A new browser window opens, displaying the JNDI tree. Expand the weblogic node and then expand the rmi node. HelloServer should appear within this node, as shown in Figure 8-10.

You can now feel reasonably confident that your RMI server is deployed correctly. The ultimate test is to call its remote method, which you will do next.

Run the client and test the server

On a new command line, run HelloClient.java. The command to do so resembles the following:

```
> java -classpath %classpath% com.wiley.wlsbible.rmi.example1.HelloClient
```

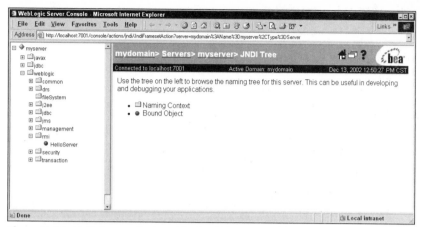

Figure 8-10: HelloServer displayed in the JNDI tree under `weblogic.rmi`

After a few seconds, you should see the following on your screen:

```
> Connected to HelloServer.
> Hello, remote world!!
```

Additionally, you should see the message `HelloServer.sayHello() has been remotely invoked` written to the WebLogic command window by the remote method on the server (see Figure 8-11).

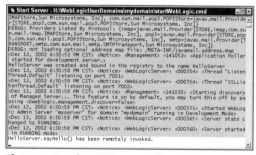

Figure 8-11: The RMI server tells you that `HelloServer` has been created and bound.

Congratulations! You've successfully written, deployed, and tested your first WebLogic RMI application. In the rest of this chapter, you'll explore additional features and coding techniques applicable to WebLogic RMI.

Using WebLogic RMI with JNDI and Multiple Clients

Now that you know how to write and deploy an RMI application, it's time to try some additional variations. The remaining examples in this chapter implement a simple stock-trading system while demonstrating important features of WebLogic RMI, including its integration with JNDI, support for client callbacks, and integration with EJBs.

Building a server

The first piece of software we'll build is an RMI server called `PriceServer`, which maintains a database of stock ticker symbols and prices (stored in memory as a Java `HashTable`) and provides methods to get and set stock prices for stocks with given symbols. `PriceServer` also provides a method to retrieve all stock symbols in the database. A remote interface that meets this specification is defined in `PriceServer.java`:

```java
package com.wiley.wlsbible.rmi.example2;

import weblogic.rmi.Remote;

public interface PriceServer extends weblogic.rmi.Remote {

    // Used to locate or register a PriceServer via RMI.
    public static final String PRICESERVERNAME = "priceserver";

    // Return the current price of the given security.
    public float getPrice(String symbol);

    // Set the price of the given security.
    public void setPrice(String symbol, float price);

    // Return all ticker symbols in this server's database.
    public String[] getSecurities();
}
```

Following the RMI programming methodology established in the preceding section, we next write the implementation of the remote interface. This class will be called `PriceServerImpl`. `PriceServerImpl` manages a `Hashtable` of securities and prices, so a good job for the default constructor is to initialize this `Hashtable`:

```java
// Declare a Hashtable for the stock price database.
private Hashtable stockTable = null;

// Default constructor - creates a stock price database
// with three stocks and their starting prices for the
// session.
public PriceServerImpl() {
    stockTable = new Hashtable();
    Float f = new Float(0);
    stockTable.put("SUNW", f.valueOf("20"));
    stockTable.put("INTC", f.valueOf("30"));
    stockTable.put("BEAS", f.valueOf("40"));
}
```

`getPrice` takes a stock ticker symbol (such as SUNW or BEAS) as input, finds the stock in the database, and returns the stock's price:

```
public float getPrice(String symbol) {
  Float f = (Float)stockTable.get(symbol);
  return f.floatValue();
}
```

`setPrice` takes a stock ticker symbol and price as input, finds the symbol in the database, and updates its price. Because the database is a `Hashtable`, a new entry is automatically created if the symbol does not exist in the database:

```
public void setPrice(String symbol, float price) {
  Float f = new Float(price);
  stockTable.put(symbol, f);
}
```

`getSecurities` returns a string array containing all the symbols in the database:

```
public String[] getSecurities() {
  if(stockTable.size() > 0) {
    String[] securities = new String[stockTable.size()];
    Enumeration enum = stockTable.keys();
    int i = 0;

    while(enum.hasMoreElements()) {
      securities[i] = (String)enum.nextElement();
      i++;
    }
    return securities;
  }
  return null;
}
```

With all the remote methods implemented, it's time to think about how to register the RMI server with WebLogic. Unlike our earlier example, which used the WebLogic RMI interface to register itself, `PriceServerImpl` will register itself using JNDI calls. This turns out to be quite simple, requiring only three lines of code:

```
PriceServerImpl server = new PriceServerImpl();
Context ctx = new InitialContext();
ctx.bind(PRICESERVERNAME, server);
```

This code binds a reference to the `PriceServerImpl` stubs to the root of the WebLogic JNDI tree. We'll put it in the `main` method of the `PriceServerImpl` class.

The advantage of using JNDI directly is that you can register your servers anywhere you want in WebLogic's JNDI tree, creating your own hierarchy of registrations (WebLogic RMI always registers classes in the `weblogic.rmi` node). These registrations might be organized by functionality, application, or some other criterion. Also, you can use JNDI to register RMI servers in other JNDI-accessible directories, such as LDAP directories or other external naming services.

Cross-Reference

This chapter presents the JNDI calls necessary for RMI registration and lookup, but does not explain them in great detail. See Chapter 7 for in-depth information about using WebLogic JNDI.

Listing 8-1 shows `PriceServerImpl.java`, the complete implementation of the `Price ServerImpl` class. The code has gained some minor enhancements to write status messages to the WebLogic Console and also to deal with exceptions.

Listing 8-1: PriceServerImpl.java, an RMI Server to Manage Securities Transactions

```
package com.wiley.wlsbible.rmi.example2;

import java.util.*;
import javax.naming.*;
import weblogic.rmi.*;

public class PriceServerImpl implements PriceServer {

  // Stock price database, implemented as a Hashtable.
  private Hashtable stockTable = null;

  // Default constructor - creates the stock price database.
  public PriceServerImpl() {
    stockTable = new Hashtable();
    Float f = new Float(0);
    stockTable.put("SUNW", f.valueOf("20"));
    stockTable.put("INTC", f.valueOf("30"));
    stockTable.put("BEAS", f.valueOf("40"));
  }

  // Return the price of the given security.
  public float getPrice(String symbol) {
    Float f = (Float)stockTable.get(symbol);
    System.out.println("PriceServer: Call to getPrice " +
                       "for symbol : " + symbol);
    return f.floatValue();
  }

  // Set the price of the given security.
  public void setPrice(String symbol, float price) {
    Float f = new Float(price);
    stockTable.put(symbol, f);
    System.out.println("PriceServer: Call to setPrice " +
                       "for " + symbol + " to " + price);
  }

  // Return all ticker symbols in this server's database.
  public String[] getSecurities() {
    if(stockTable.size() > 0) {
      String[] securities = new String[stockTable.size()];
```

```
      Enumeration enum = stockTable.keys();
      int i = 0;

      while(enum.hasMoreElements()) {
        securities[i] = (String)enum.nextElement();
        i++;
      }
      return securities;
    }
    return null;
  }

  // Main method - registers the RMI server using JNDI.
  public static void main (String [] args) {
    try {
      PriceServerImpl server = new PriceServerImpl();
      Context ctx = new InitialContext();
      ctx.bind(PRICESERVERNAME, server);
      System.out.println("PriceServer was created and bound " +
                         "in the registry " +
                         "to the name " + PRICESERVERNAME);
    }
    catch(Exception e) {
      e.printStackTrace();
      System.exit(1);
    }
  }
}
```

This completes the coding of the server. The next step is to write some clients that call its methods.

Building the clients

Instead of writing just one client to call `PriceServer`'s remote methods, we'll write two. One, called `MarketMakerClient`, will be responsible for updating securities prices on a periodic basis; it simulates (in a very rudimentary way) a pricing feed from an exchange such as Nasdaq. The other, called `QuoteClient`, retrieves the latest prices of stocks on a periodic basis; it simulates (also in a very rudimentary way) a stock portfolio tracking system.

Using WebLogic JNDI to find the RMI server

Both clients find `PriceServer` by making JNDI calls. To support this functionality, we'll create a class called `Environment` that stores the server access paths and makes the JNDI call to return the server's context to the clients. The advantage of this approach is that if the server ever moves, only the `Environment` class needs to be changed.

Listing 8-2 contains `Environment.java`, the code to implement the `Environment` class.

Listing 8-2: Environment.java, a WebLogic JNDI Lookup Class

```java
package com.wiley.wlsbible.rmi.example2;

import javax.naming.*;
import java.util.*;

public class Environment {

  // Specify that we'll be using WebLogic JNDI
  public final static String JNDI_FACTORY =
    "weblogic.jndi.WLInitialContextFactory";

  // Specify the location of our WebLogic server
  public final static String WEBLOGIC_URL =
    "t3://localhost:7001";

  public static InitialContext getInitialContext()
   throws NamingException {

    // Load a Hashtable with the factory and URL information,
    // then use it to retrieve the WebLogic server's context.
    Hashtable env = new Hashtable();
    env.put(Context.INITIAL_CONTEXT_FACTORY, JNDI_FACTORY);
    env.put(Context.PROVIDER_URL, WEBLOGIC_URL);
    return new InitialContext(env);
  }
}
```

Chapter 7 contains a more detailed explanation of JNDI, but notice that `Environment.get-InitialContext` is implemented as a static method. This is done as a convenience for clients; it allows them to invoke the method without creating an instance of the class, as in the following:

```java
InitialContext ctx = Environment.getInitialContext();
```

After the client retrieves the `InitialContext`, only one additional call is required to obtain a reference to the RMI server we wrote earlier:

```java
PriceServer server =
  (PriceServer) ctx.lookup(PriceServer.PRICESERVERNAME);
```

where `PriceServer.PRICESERVERNAME` is the name under which the RMI server registered itself, defined as a `public static final String` in the `PriceServer` interface.

As you can see, using JNDI to register and look up RMI servers is quite simple, and gives you more control over how registrations are organized. Using JNDI gives you access to the full capabilities of your naming service, whether it's WebLogic Server or an LDAP directory such as Sun ONE Directory Server. This allows you to partition your RMI namespaces in meaningful ways to ease the administration and use of a large server.

Implementing MarketMakerClient

The `MarketMakerClient` generates random price fluctuations for the securities tracked by `PriceServer` and posts these to `PriceServer` every few seconds. To accomplish this, `MarketMakerClient` extends `java.util.TimerTask` and is scheduled for periodic execution using `java.util.Timer`.

After retrieving a remote reference to `PriceServer`, `MarketMakerClient` invokes the server's `setPrice` method for each of the three securities, adjusting their prices in random increments. The code to do this appears in the `MarketMakerClient.run` method, which is invoked every five seconds by the timer:

```
InitialContext ctx = Environment.getInitialContext();
PriceServer server =
  (PriceServer)ctx.lookup(PriceServer.PRICESERVERNAME);

// Remote call to get securities tracked by server
securities = server.getSecurities();
for(int i = 0; i < securities.length; i++) {
  // Randomly increase or decrease each security's
  // price by 0, 0.25, or 0.5
  boolean increase = rand.nextBoolean();
  Float amount = new Float(0.25 * rand.nextInt(2));
  if (increase) {
    server.setPrice(securities[i],
    server.getPrice(securities[i]) + amount.floatValue());
  } else {
    server.setPrice(securities[i],
    server.getPrice(securities[i]) - amount.floatValue());
  }
}
```

In the `main` method of `MarketMakerClient`, we simply create a timer and schedule the periodic execution of the security price updating code:

```
Timer t = new Timer();
MarketMakerClient client = new MarketMakerClient();

//Starting in 5 secs, update prices every 5 seconds.
t.schedule(client, 5000, 5000);
```

Listing 8-3 contains the complete implementation of `MarketMakerClient`. In addition to the code discussed previously, it contains code to write status messages to standard output, close the JNDI contexts we open, and handle exceptions.

Listing 8-3: **MarketMakerClient.java**

```
package com.wiley.wlsbible.rmi.example2;

import weblogic.rmi.*;
import java.util.*;
import javax.naming.*;
```

Continued

Listing 8-3 *(continued)*

```java
public class MarketMakerClient
    extends TimerTask
    implements Runnable {

    private Random rand = new Random();
    private String[] securities = null;

    // Get a reference to PriceServer, get its list of
    // securities, and adjust their prices.
    public void run() {
        // Write a status message to standard output
        System.out.println("MarketMakerClient setting prices.");
        System.out.println(" Time: "
                           + new Date(System.currentTimeMillis()));

        InitialContext ctx = null;
        try {
            // Obtain a reference to the RMI server using JNDI
            ctx = Environment.getInitialContext();
            PriceServer server =
             (PriceServer) ctx.lookup(PriceServer.PRICESERVERNAME);

            // Remote call to get securities tracked by server
            securities = server.getSecurities();
            for(int i = 0; i < securities.length; i++) {
                // Randomly increase or decrease each security's
                // price by 0, 0.25, or 0.5
                boolean increase = rand.nextBoolean();
                Float amount = new Float(0.25 * rand.nextInt(2));
                if (increase) {
                    server.setPrice(securities[i],
                        server.getPrice(securities[i]) +
                        amount.floatValue());
                } else {
                    server.setPrice(securities[i],
                        server.getPrice(securities[i]) -
                        amount.floatValue());
                }
            }
        }
        catch (Exception e) {
            e.printStackTrace();
        }
        finally {
            try {
                ctx.close();
            }
            catch (Exception e) {
```

```
            e.printStackTrace();
        }
    }
}

// Create a new client and schedule it to
// execute periodically.
public static void main(String [] args) {
    Timer t = new Timer();
    MarketMakerClient client = new MarketMakerClient();

    //Starting in 5 secs, update prices every 5 seconds.
    t.schedule(client, 5000, 5000);
    }
}
```

Note   There is one nonoptimal aspect of this design that is worth discussing. Rather than calling `server.setPrice` repeatedly for each individual security, which generates a lot of excess network traffic for the RMI calls, it is more efficient to transmit an entire data structure of symbols and prices to the server by using only one remote method call. We won't redesign our example code for this, but you should keep these kinds of issues in mind when you design your own RMI systems.

Implementing QuoteClient

QuoteClient is even simpler than MarketMakerClient. Like MarketMakerClient, it extends java.util.TimerTask and executes on a periodic basis — every 20 seconds. Every time it runs, it retrieves a list of securities being tracked by PriceServer and then retrieves the prices of those securities. And, of course, it performs these queries using remote method calls to PriceServer.getSecurities and PriceServer.getPrice, respectively. The code for QuoteClient, much of which is identical to MarketMakerClient, appears in Listing 8-4.

Listing 8-4: **QuoteClient.java**

```
package com.wiley.wlsbible.rmi.example2;

import weblogic.rmi.*;
import java.util.*;
import javax.naming.*;

// Periodically ask PriceServer for prices
// of all securities.
public class QuoteClient
    extends TimerTask
    implements Runnable {
```

Continued

Listing 8-4 *(continued)*

```
// Get a reference to PriceServer, get a list of securities,
// and display prices.
public void run() {
  System.out.println("QuoteClient getting quotes.");
  System.out.println("Quote time: " +
                     new Date(System.currentTimeMillis()));

  try {
    // Get the remote stub for the Price server via JNDI.
    InitialContext ctx = Environment.getInitialContext();
    PriceServer server =
      (PriceServer) ctx.lookup(PriceServer.PRICESERVERNAME);

    // Remote call to get the list of securities
    String securities[] = server.getSecurities();

    if(securities != null) {
      for(int i = 0; i < securities.length; i++) {
        // Remote call to get each security's price
        System.out.println("Security: " + securities[i] +
            " Price: " + server.getPrice(securities[i]));
      }
    }
    else {
      System.out.println("No securities registered " +
                         "with the server at this time.");
    }
  }
  catch(Exception e) {
    e.printStackTrace();
  }
  finally {
    try {
      ctx.close();
    }
    catch (Exception e) {
      e.printStackTrace();
    }
  }
}

// Create a new client and schedule it to
// execute periodically.
public static void main(String [] args) {
  Timer t = new Timer();
  QuoteClient client = new QuoteClient();
  System.out.println("QuoteClient started.");
```

```
        //Starting in 10 secs, get prices every 20 seconds.
        t.schedule(client, 10000, 20000);
    }
}
```

Building and deploying the example

Follow the instructions in the first example to build and deploy this RMI application. You need to compile the Java source files first:

```
> javac -classpath %classpath% -d %outputdir%
com.wiley.wlsbible.rmi.example2.PriceServer

> javac -classpath %classpath% -d %outputdir%
com.wiley.wlsbible.rmi.example2.PriceServerImpl

> javac -classpath %classpath% -d %outputdir%
com.wiley.wlsbible.rmi.example2.Environment

> javac -classpath %classpath% -d %outputdir%
com.wiley.wlsbible.rmi.example2.MarketMakerClient

> javac -classpath %classpath% -d %outputdir%
com.wiley.wlsbible.rmi.example1.QuoteClient
```

Next, you need to run the RMI compiler on `PriceServerImpl`:

```
> java -classpath %classpath% weblogic.rmic
com.wiley.wlsbible.rmi.example2.PriceServerImpl -d %outputdir%
```

Deploy `PriceServerImpl` as a WebLogic startup class. As explained earlier in this chapter, you need to define a new `Startup` class in the console and add the remote interface and implementation class to the WebLogic server's classpath.

Tip See the book's Web site (`http://www.wiley.com/compbooks/zuffoletto/`) for all the source code, along with Ant build files that automate much of the process.

You can run the clients against your new startup class in their own JVMs by executing the following commands:

```
> java -classpath %classpath% com.wiley.wlsbible.rmi.example2.MarketMakerClient
```

```
> java -classpath %classpath% com.wiley.wlsbible.rmi.example2.QuoteClient
```

The output from `MarketMakerClient` will look something like the following:

```
> MarketMakerClient setting prices.
>  Time: Mon Apr 30 13:33:29 PDT 2001

> MarketMakerClient setting prices.
>  Time: Mon Apr 30 13:33:59 PDT 2001
```

The output from `QuoteClient` will look something like this:

```
QuoteClient started.
QuoteClient getting quotes.
Quote time: Mon Apr 30 13:33:44 PDT 2001
Security: SUNW Price: 20.25
Security: INTC Price: 30.5
Security: BEAS Price: 39.75
QuoteClient getting quotes.
Quote time: Mon Apr 30 13:34:04 PDT 2001
Security: SUNW Price: 20.5
Security: INTC Price: 30.25
Security: BEAS Price: 40
```

Meanwhile, the output from `PriceServerImpl`, displayed in the WebLogic Server command window, will look something like this:

```
PriceServer: Call to setPrice for SUNW to 20.25
PriceServer: Call to setPrice for INTC to 30.5
PriceServer: Call to setPrice for BEAS to 39.75
PriceServer: Call to getPrice for symbol : SUNW
PriceServer: Call to getPrice for symbol : INTC
PriceServer: Call to getPrice for symbol : BEAS
PriceServer: Call to setPrice for SUNW to 20.5
PriceServer: Call to setPrice for INTC to 30.25
PriceServer: Call to setPrice for BEAS to 40
PriceServer: Call to getPrice for symbol : SUNW
PriceServer: Call to getPrice for symbol : INTC
PriceServer: Call to getPrice for symbol : BEAS
```

Invoking Client Methods from RMI Servers

Now that we have our stock market up and running, let's make a further enhancement that demonstrates WebLogic RMI's support for server-to-client remote method invocation.

Consider the code we have already written. `PriceServerImpl`, the RMI server, simultaneously services requests from `MarketMakerClient` and `QuoteClient`. However, these communications occur in only one direction, from the clients to the server, as shown in Figure 8-12.

This architecture works well most of the time, but it has weaknesses for some designs. For example, what happens if a client invokes a long-running method on the server? If the call is made synchronously, the invoking client thread will be blocked until the server method returns. If the call is made asynchronously, the client has no way of knowing when the server method completes. This creates a problem if subsequent client processing depends on the server method's results, or if the client wants to be notified when the server has finished.

WebLogic RMI provides a solution for this problem. It allows clients to register remote interfaces of their own with WebLogic Server. These methods can then be invoked by server-side code, or even by code running on other clients, just as if it resided on the server.

To illustrate the usefulness of this feature, we will create another client for our securities system called `TradingClient`. `TradingClient` will asynchronously place market orders for stocks with `PriceServerImpl` (a *market order* is an order to purchase stock at the prevailing market price). After an artificial delay, `PriceServerImpl` will execute the orders; then notify `TradingClient` of the executions. This requires two-way communications between `PriceServerImpl` and `TradingClient`, as shown in Figure 8-13.

Figure 8-12: One-way communications from the clients to the server

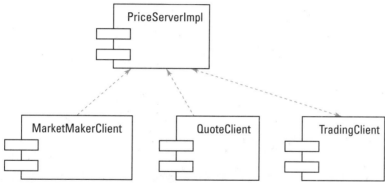

Figure 8-13: Two-way communications between PriceServerImpl and TradingClient

To facilitate these communications, we will create two new classes: Order and Execution. These nearly identical classes will transmit information concerning the security being purchased, the number of shares, and the price. Because we plan to transmit instances of them across the wire via RMI, they must implement the java.io.Serializable interface. These class definitions appear as follows (the methods have been omitted to save space):

```
public class Order implements java.io.Serializable {
  private int number;      // unique order number
  private String symbol;   // ticker symbol
  private int shares;      // number of shares to purchase
  // plus method definitions
}

public class Execution implements java.io.Serializable {
  private int number;      // copied from order number
  private String symbol;   // ticker symbol
  private int shares;      // number of shares purchased
  private float price;     // price per share at execution
  // plus method definitions
}
```

Much of the code in `TradingClient` is the same as the code in our other clients. `Trading-Client` extends `java.util.TimerTask` and submits a new order every 30 seconds. When submitting an order, `TradingClient` uses JNDI to get a remote reference to `PriceServer`. Then it calls `PriceServer.getSecurities` to get the list of securities `PriceServer` knows about:

```
// Get the list of securities managed by the server.
String securities[] = server.getSecurities();
```

Next, `TradingClient` creates a new `Order` instance and populates it with the order specifications. The order number (an integer class field) is incremented, so each order has a unique number that enables us to match the returning executions against the orders. The security to be purchased is chosen at random from those available, and the number of shares to purchase is randomly chosen as well. Finally, a remote call is made to `PriceServerImpl.enter-MarketOrder` to place the order. The interesting aspect of this call is that `TradingClient` passes a reference to itself (`this`) that the server uses to call it back. Here is the code to implement these steps:

```
// Create a new Order instance
Order order = new Order();
Random rand = new Random();

// Increment the order number
order.setNumber(++orderNumber);

// Choose one of the available securities at random
order.setSymbol(securities[rand.nextInt(securities.length)]);

// Choose a random number of shares
order.setShares(rand.nextInt(1000) + 1);

// Enter the order via a remote call to the server.
// Pass a reference to ourselves so the server can call back.
server.enterMarketOrder(order, this);
```

On the server side, `PriceServerImpl.enterMarketOrder` accepts two input parameters: the order being submitted by the client and the client's reference to itself. This reference is of type `ExecutionAlert`, which is the remote interface that the client implements.

`enterMarketOrder` does its work asynchronously by spawning a separate thread to handle the execution of the order. It passes the order and the client reference to the new thread; then returns control to the caller, which is `TradingClient`. Here is the code for `enterMarketOrder`:

```
public void enterMarketOrder(Order order,
                             ExecutionAlert clientRef) {
    // Receives an order from a client, and also a
    // reference to the client. Spawns a new thread
    // to execute the trade (which may take some time),
    // then returns.
    System.out.println("A client has placed an order!");
    System.out.println("Time: " + new Date());
    System.out.println(order + "\n");
```

```
DoExecution exec = new DoExecution(order, clientRef);
new Thread(exec).start();
}
```

`DoExecution` is implemented as an inner class. Its default constructor copies the `Order` and `ExecutionAlert` references to instance fields, and its `run` method executes the order. To do this, the `run` method first sleeps for 10 seconds (this simulates the time it might take for the order to be filled). Upon awakening, the code creates an `Execution` instance and copies the relevant data from the incoming order to it. Then it gets the current price of the requested security by calling `PriceServerImpl.getPrice`. This is the price at which the order is filled. Finally, it calls the `notifyOfExecution` method of the `ExecutionAlert` remote interface, using the incoming client reference to do so. This causes the notification code to execute remotely on the client that submitted the order.

Listing 8-5 shows the complete implementation of `PriceServerImpl.enterMarketOrder`.

Listing 8-5: **PriceServerImpl.enterMarketOrder**

```
public void enterMarketOrder(Order order,
                             ExecutionAlert clientRef) {
  // Receives an order from a client, and also a
  // reference to the client. Spawns a new thread
  // to execute the trade (which may take some time),
  // then returns.
  System.out.println("A client has placed an order!");
  System.out.println("Time: " + new Date());
  System.out.println(order + "\n");
  DoExecution exec = new DoExecution(order, clientRef);
  new Thread(exec).start();
}

// Inner class to handle order executions.
private class DoExecution implements Runnable {
  private Order order;
  private ExecutionAlert client;

  public DoExecution(Order ord, ExecutionAlert clientRef) {
    order = ord;
    client = clientRef;
  }

  public void run() {
    try {
      // Wait 10 seconds to simulate submission of the order
      // to a stock exchange.
      Thread.currentThread().sleep(10000);
      // Create an Execution instance and execute the order.
      Execution execution = new Execution();
      // Copy order data into the execution.
      execution.setNumber(order.getNumber());
```

Continued

Listing 8-5 *(continued)*

```
        execution.setSymbol(order.getSymbol());
        execution.setShares(order.getShares());
        // Execute at the stock's current price and write a
        // status message to standard output.
        execution.setPrice(getPrice(order.getSymbol()));
        System.out.println("An order has been executed!");
        System.out.println("Time: " + new Date());
        System.out.println(execution + "\n");
        // Make a remote call to the client to notify them
        // of the execution.
        client.notifyOfExecution(execution);
      } catch (Exception e) {
        e.printStackTrace();
      }
    }
  }
```

`TradingClient.notifyOfExecution` is a simple method; it merely writes a status message to standard output, along with the execution data:

```
public void notifyOfExecution(Execution exec) {
  System.out.println("An order has been executed!");
  System.out.println("Time: " + new Date());
  System.out.println(exec + "\n");
}
```

To recap: `TradingClient` creates an order and transmits it to `PriceServer` by invoking a remote method on `PriceServer`. `PriceServer`'s remote method receives the order, hands it off to a new server thread for execution, and then exits. As soon as the order is executed, `PriceServer` transmits the execution data back to `TradingClient` by invoking a remote method on `TradingClient`. This remote method receives the execution data, displays it onscreen for the user, and exits.

Keep in mind that `TradingClient` could have just as easily invoked a remote method in a different client or vice versa. All that's required is that the clients implement interfaces that extend `weblogic.rmi.remote` and that stubs are available in WebLogic's classpath for the clients' remote methods. To create these stubs, simply run the WebLogic RMI compiler on the client classes.

You might be wondering why there is no code to register the `TradingClient` class in the RMI registry, or at least the `TradingClient.notifyOfExecution` method. Instead of doing a registry lookup to find this code, we simply use the client reference passed to us by the client to do it, which enables us to ensure that the correct client gets notified of the execution. This being the case, how does WebLogic know that a remote call must be made and therefore that the stub must be used? It knows because the client reference is of type `ExecutionAlert`, which extends `weblogic.rmi.remote`. Recall that `WebLogic` always uses a remote reference (stub) to call methods that extend this interface, unless they live in the same JVM. If the stub is not available, the method call will fail with a `ClassDefNotFound` exception for the stub.

You can, however, register `TradingClient` (or any other client) in the RMI registry and look it up in the usual way from the server or another client. To register `TradingClient` in WebLogic Server's RMI registry, write this code in `TradingClient`:

```
TradingClient client = new TradingClient();
Context ctx = Environment.getInitialContext();
ctx.bind("TradingClient", client);
System.out.println("TradingClient was started and bound " +
                   "in the registry to the name " +
                   "TradingClient");
```

This causes a remote reference to `TradingClient` to appear in the WebLogic JNDI tree, alongside `PriceServer`. Take careful note of the second line, in which we obtain a `Context`. Recall that in `PriceServer` we did this as follows:

```
Context ctx = new InitialContext();
```

In `TradingClient`, we must use the `Environment` class to get the `Context` because `TradingClient`'s code is not executing in WebLogic's JVM. Therefore, we must explicitly specify the JNDI factory and provider URL for WebLogic Server, which the `Environment` class does for us (we use the `Environment` class for the same reason when clients look up remote references registered on WebLogic Server).

To invoke a remote method in `TradingClient` from another client, you write the following code:

```
InitialContext ctx = Environment.getInitialContext();
ExecutionAlert tc = (ExecutionAlert)
  ctx.lookup("TradingClient");
Execution exec = new Execution();
tc.notifyOfExecution(exec);
```

Notice that this is no different from invoking remote methods on the server. The remote reference lookup and the method call are routed through WebLogic Server, but the invoked method executes in `TradingClient`'s JVM—not WebLogic's.

Build and deploy the example as you did for the first PriceServer example, as described in "Building and deploying the example" after Listing 8-4. Again, you need to register the startup class in the WebLogic Console and add the remote interface and implementation classes to the server's classpath. So as not to conflict with the first PriceServer's JNDI name, we renamed this example's JNDI lookup name as `priceserver2`.

Calling EJBs from RMI Servers

Our final example introduces a session EJB into the design. It shows how to invoke the EJB's remote methods from the RMI server and how to invoke the RMI server's and RMI client's remote methods from the EJB. EJBs are essentially RMI servers, but because they live in the EJB container and support a great deal of additional functionality (such as pooling and transaction support), they are used somewhat differently. This example highlights the differences and allows you to leverage your newly acquired RMI knowledge to better understand EJBs.

Cross-Reference   Part IV covers EJBs in detail. The intent of this section is to show you how RMI and EJBs are related.

The change we will make in the application is to move the execution code out of
PriceServerImpl and into a session bean called ExecuteTrade. We will modify
PriceServerImpl.enterMarketOrder so it invokes the bean method, as shown following:

```
public void enterMarketOrder(Order order,
                                ExecutionAlert client) {
  // The ExecuteTrade bean returns immediately and calls back
  // the client when the trade has been executed.
  try {
    // Create a context with which to lookup the bean
    Hashtable ht = new Hashtable();
    ht.put(Context.INITIAL_CONTEXT_FACTORY,
           Environment.JNDI_FACTORY);
    ht.put(Context.PROVIDER_URL, Environment.WEBLOGIC_URL);
    Context ctx2 = new InitialContext(ht);
    // Get a reference to the bean object
    Object objref = ctx2.lookup("ExecuteTrade");
    // Get a reference to the bean's home interface
    ExecuteTradeHome home = (ExecuteTradeHome)
      javax.rmi.PortableRemoteObject.narrow(objref,
      ExecuteTradeHome.class);
    // Get a reference to the bean's remote interface
    ExecuteTradeRemote executionBean = home.create();
    // Invoke the bean's remote method to execute the trade
    executionBean.executeTrade(order, client);
  } catch (Exception e) {
    e.printStackTrace();
  }
}
```

Notice the differences in the way remote references are obtained for EJBs as opposed to RMI
servers. A JNDI lookup is used to get a reference to the session EJB's *object*, not its remote
references:

```
Object objref = ctx2.lookup("ExecuteTrade");
```

This object reference is cast to an instance of the EJB's home interface:

```
ExecuteTradeHome home = (ExecuteTradeHome)
  javax.rmi.PortableRemoteObject.narrow(objref,
  ExecuteTradeHome.class);
```

Finally, a remote reference to the bean is obtained by calling the home interface's create
method:

```
ExecuteTradeRemote executionBean = home.create();
```

At this point, we are finally able to invoke one of the bean's methods.

The reasons for these differences are due to the architecture of the EJB container and the EJB
API. Although the EJB is an RMI server, the EJB API must do a lot more work behind the scenes
beyond simply dealing with RMI issues. We'll explore this further later in the book when we
learn about EJBs, but for now it's interesting to see the coding differences side by side.

The `ExecuteTrade` session bean exposes the following remote interface. Note we could have put the bean in a separate package, which would likely be the case in a real application:

```
package com.wiley.wlsbible.rmi.example4;

import java.rmi.*;
import javax.ejb.*;

// Remote interface for the ExecuteTrade Session EJB.
public interface ExecuteTradeRemote extends EJBObject {

   // Execute an order and alert the client of the execution.
   public void executeTrade(Order order, ExecutionAlert alert)
      throws RemoteException;
}
```

The bean's `executeTrade` method looks like this:

```
public void executeTrade(Order order, ExecutionAlert alert)
    throws RemoteException {
  DoExecution exec = new DoExecution(order, alert);
  new Thread(exec).start();
}

private class DoExecution implements Runnable {
  private Order order;
  private ExecutionAlert client;

  public DoExecution(Order ord, ExecutionAlert alert) {
    order = ord;
    client = alert;
  }

  public void run() {
    try {
      Thread.currentThread().sleep(15000); //sleep 15 seconds.

      // Get a remote reference to the PriceServer RMI
      // server so we can invoke its getPrice() method
      // to get the latest price for the security
      InitialContext ctx = Environment.getInitialContext();
      PriceServer server = (PriceServer)
        ctx.lookup(PriceServer.PRICESERVERNAME);

      // Create and populate an Execution instance
      Execution execution = new Execution();
      execution.setNumber(order.getNumber());
      // Remote method call to the server to get the price
      execution.setPrice(server.getPrice(order.getSymbol()));
      execution.setShares(order.getShares());
      execution.setSymbol(order.getSymbol());
      System.out.println("An order has been executed!");
```

```
            System.out.println("Time: " + new Date());
            System.out.println(execution + "\n");
            // Remote method call to the calling instance of
            // TradingClient to notify it of the execution
            client.notifyOfExecution(execution);
        } catch (Exception e) {
            e.printStackTrace();
        }
    }
}
```

This code is almost identical to `PriceServer`'s `executeTrade` code shown in Listing 8-5. The only difference is that our bean must invoke `PriceServer.getPrice()` remotely, whereas `PriceServer` was able to call its own method locally.

Summary

You should now have a strong understanding of RMI, and the advantages of WebLogic RMI over the JavaSoft implementation. You have learned, step-by-step, how to write, deploy, and test WebLogic RMI applications, and you have seen the various ways in which RMI servers and clients can work together in a WebLogic-hosted environment to solve difficult distributed computing problems. Finally, you have seen a glimpse of how RMI and EJBs work together, which should give you a better understanding of the way EJBs work.

Working with WebLogic JMS

CHAPTER

9

✦ ✦ ✦ ✦

In This Chapter

Understanding JMS

Configuring
WebLogic JMS

Programming
WebLogic JMS

Working with
transactions

✦ ✦ ✦ ✦

The *Java Message Service,* or *JMS,* provides a mechanism for Java processes to send synchronous or asynchronous messages to each other. These processes can run in the same or different JVMs and can run on the same or different computers on a network or on the Internet.

In this chapter, we provide an overview of the JMS architecture and show you how to configure WebLogic JMS, a process that involves a large number of important interrelated steps. After you configure a working JMS infrastructure, we provide several code examples that show you how to use the many powerful JMS features. We conclude by showing you how to build reliable, fault-tolerant applications by using JMS, JDBC, and the Java Transaction API (JTA).

Understanding JMS

This section introduces you to the organization, architecture, and features of JMS, as well as configuring and programming JMS in the WebLogic environment.

JMS versions and packages

WebLogic 7.0 runs on top of JDK 1.3.1 and supports JMS version 1.0.2b. JMS is implemented in a multitude of packages; the following list shows the packages you will most commonly import:

- ✦ `javax.jms`, which contains the JMS API

- ✦ `weblogic.jms.ServerSessionPoolFactory`, which contains WebLogic extensions for server-side JMS session pools

- ✦ `weblogic.jms.extensions`, which includes WebLogic extensions for creating XML messages, dynamically creating message queues and topics, creating session exception listeners, managing message multicasting, and converting between WebLogic 7.0 and pre-6.0 JMS message ID formats

You can download the latest JMS specification from the Sun Web site at the following URL:

```
http://java.sun.com/products/jms/docs.html
```

JMS architecture

Like JNDI, JMS has a multilayered architecture, as shown in Figure 9-1. A Java application (or application component) accesses a JMS-enabled message server through the JMS API. References to the message server are obtained via JNDI lookups. WebLogic Server contains a complete, feature-rich message server of its own; third-party message servers that run outside of WebLogic Server (such as IBM MQSeries) can also be used if their vendors provide JMS API implementations for them.

WebLogic JMS interfaces with WebLogic JTA to transaction-enable the delivery of messages, and it interfaces with the file system and/or JDBC to provide persistent storage of messages when desired by the developer.

 Cross-Reference   Chapter 6 discusses WebLogic JTA.

Application
JMS API
JNDI
Message Server (WebLogic)

Transaction Services (via JTA)	Persistent Message Store (file or JDBC)

Figure 9-1: JMS architecture

A full understanding of JMS requires an understanding of a few key concepts, which we cover in the next section.

Messages

A *message* is an object containing information that is being sent from one application (or part of an application) to another. JMS provides the `Message` interface as the base interface for all messages in JMS. Five distinct JMS message types, plus one type specific to WebLogic, extend this interface (as shown in Figure 9-2).

A message consists of a fixed set of header fields, a user-configurable set of optional properties fields, and a message body that carries the content of the message (see Figure 9-3).

Message producers and consumers

A *message producer* is a Java application or component that creates and sends messages. A *message consumer* is a Java application or component that receives messages. Between them lives the *message server*, which manages the delivery of messages between the two.

Point-to-point (PTP) messaging

Point-to-point messaging occurs when a message producer sends a message to exactly one message consumer. Point-to-point messaging is managed by JMS message *queues*. The message producer is called a *queue sender*, and the message consumer is a *queue receiver*. Any number of message producers may send to a queue, and any number of consumers may listen to a queue, but only one can be the queue receiver, as shown in Figure 9-4. JMS selects the listener who has been listening the longest to be the receiver. JMS removes incoming messages from queues as soon as the receiver has received them.

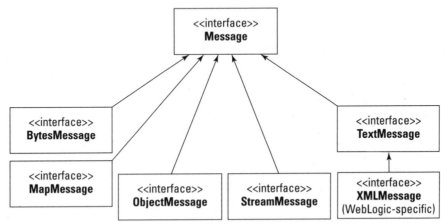

Figure 9-2: The JMS Message interface hierarchy

Figure 9-3: The structure of a JMS message

Figure 9-4: Point-to-point messaging using queues

Publish-and-subscribe (Pub/Sub) messaging

Publish-and-subscribe messaging occurs when a message producer sends a message to multiple message consumers. Publish-and-subscribe messaging is managed by JMS message *topics*. The message producer is called a *topic publisher*, and the message consumer is a *topic subscriber*. Any number of message producers can publish to a topic, and any number of consumers can subscribe to a topic. JMS delivers published messages to all topic subscribers and removes incoming messages from topics only after *all* subscribers have received them. Figure 9-5 illustrates publish-and-subscribe messaging.

Figure 9-5: Publish-and-subscribe messaging using topics

Message persistence

A message is classified as being either *persistent* or *non-persistent*. A persistent message is guaranteed to be delivered at least once. It is considered to be delivered after it has been successfully written to a persistent message data store, which in WebLogic is either a disk file or JDBC-enabled database. A non-persistent message is also guaranteed to be delivered at least once, but messages may be lost if there is a system failure. Non-persistent messages are considered to be delivered when a recipient acknowledges their receipt.

Connection factories

A *connection factory* is a class that spawns JMS connections for a given message server and system configuration. Connection factories are the developer's first line of interaction with JMS. After the developer obtains a reference to a connection factory (via JNDI lookup), he can use that reference to obtain a connection, from there a reference to a queue, to a topic, and so on.

In WebLogic, system administrators use the WebLogic Console to define connection factories with predefined characteristics. Developers can also create connection factories in code if they prefer to define connection factory characteristics at runtime.

Connections

A *connection* is an application's communication link with JMS. Connections are obtained from connection factories and they create the client-side and server-side resources necessary to manage messaging interactions. User authentication may also be embedded in connections, so applications can be sure that only authorized users are sending and receiving messages.

Connections can be *started*, *stopped*, or *closed* by calling `Connection.start()`, `Connection.stop()`, and `Connection.close()`, respectively. Connections are in stopped mode when they are first created. Messages can be sent or received only through started connections, so you must call `Connection.start()` before using the connection. Calling `Connection.stop()` pauses message delivery for that connection without releasing the connection's system resources. To completely tear down a connection and release its system resources, call `Connection.close()`.

Separate Connection subclasses exist for each type of messaging. A `QueueConnection` is used for point-to-point messaging, and a `TopicConnection` is used for publish-and-subscribe messaging.

Sessions

Sessions handle the actual production and consumption of messages by applications and application components. After creating a message, a Java application uses a session to send it. Similarly, an application listening for messages retrieves them through a session.

Separate session subclasses exist for each type of messaging and are created by the corresponding `Connection` classes. A `QueueSession` is used to send and receive point-to-point messages, and a `TopicSession` is used to send and receive publish-and-subscribe messages.

Configuring WebLogic JMS

Before writing code to send or receive messages, you must configure WebLogic JMS by using the WebLogic Console. Configuring JMS involves performing a series of interrelated steps. This section shows you how to perform the required steps in the correct order, and helps you understand the meanings and implications of your configuration choices.

Here is the list of configuration steps that you should perform in the following order:

1. Create a connection factory and assign it a JNDI name.

2. Define *backing stores* for your messages (optional). Backing stores are disk files or JDBC-accessible databases that provide persistent storage for messages. You need to create backing stores only if you want to support persistent messages or durable subscribers.

3. Define *destination keys* (optional). Destination keys are a WebLogic extension to JMS that allow you to control the order in which messages are delivered.

4. Define *templates* (optional). Templates are another WebLogic extension that allows you to group several destination keys together, giving you the ability to send messages that are sorted by multiple criteria.

5. Create a JMS server, which is a logical container for queues and topics, and which optionally maps queues and topics to backing stores.

6. Create one or more queues or topics and map them to the JMS server you created in step 5.

You can change certain configuration settings later. For example, you can define backing stores, destination keys, or templates at any time and assign them to existing JMS servers, queues, and topics. You can also create or delete queues and topics whenever you want.

Creating a connection factory

Start WebLogic Server and open the WebLogic Console. In the Services node of the domain tree, expand the JMS node and then click Connection Factories. At the top of the page, click Configure a New JMS Connection Factory. Figure 9-6 shows the connection factory configuration page with the data we provided for our factory.

Figure 9-6: Configuring a JMS connection factory in the WebLogic Console

The entries on this page are as follows:

✦ **Name:** A name for the connection factory, which must conform to the rules for Java identifiers and be unique within the WebLogic Server domain. Type **BibleJMSFactory** for this value.

✦ **JNDIName:** This name is used to look up instances of the connection factory with JNDI. It must be a valid Java identifier and be unique within the JNDI namespace of the server or cluster. Type **BibleJMSFactory** for this value as well.

✦ **Client ID:** Leave this blank unless you want to use the connection factory to support a durable subscriber for pub/sub messaging. Durable subscribers are explained in the "Creating durable subscribers to topics" section later in this chapter.

✦ **Default Priority:** When sending messages, you can assign them numeric priorities between zero (lowest) and nine (highest). Higher-priority messages are delivered first. The default priority defined here is automatically assigned by JMS to messages for which no priority is specified. WebLogic sets this value to 4 (medium) by default, which is fine for this example.

✦ **Default Time To Live:** This is the default maximum time (in milliseconds) that undelivered messages are allowed to exist in the system before being destroyed. The value applies only to messages for which the programmer did not assign a priority. A value of zero indicates that undelivered messages are allowed to exist indefinitely, which is fine for this example.

✦ **Default Time To Deliver:** This is the default time (in milliseconds) that elapses between the time that a message is delivered and the time it appears at its destination. A value of zero indicates that messages appear at their destinations immediately after being delivered, which is fine for this example.

✦ **Default Delivery Mode:** Allows you to choose between persistent and non-persistent message delivery, as described in the "Message persistence" section earlier in this chapter. If you select persistent, you must specify a backing store for the messages; we show how to do this shortly. Select Persistent.

✦ **Default Redelivery Delay:** Default time delay (in milliseconds) before rolled back or recovered messages are redelivered. A value of zero indicates that such messages are redelivered immediately, which is fine for this example.

✦ **Messages Maximum:** The maximum number of messages that can exist in an asynchronous session that have not been forwarded to a message listener. A value of -1 indicates there is no limit, in which case messages will be held on the server up to the limit of available virtual memory. If a positive value is specified and then exceeded at runtime, WebLogic handles the situation according to a complex set of rules that are discussed in the WebLogic Console help. Type **-1** for this example.

✦ **Overrun Policy:** Instructs WebLogic what to do for multicast messages if Messages Maximum is exceeded for this factory. If Keep Old is selected, then the newest messages (based on time of receipt) are discarded; if Keep New is selected, then the oldest messages are discarded as new ones come in. Select Keep Old for this example.

✦ **Allow Close in On Message:** Checking this box means that asynchronous message handlers are allowed to close the connection in their `onMessage()` methods, and an acknowledgment of message receipt will still be sent. Leave this box unchecked.

✦ **Acknowledge Policy:** This parameter was new in WebLogic 6.1 and is included as a workaround for a change that took place in the JMS specification between versions 6.0 and 6.1 of WebLogic. Setting the value to All causes all messages to be acknowledged, which is the behavior specified in the latest JMS specification. Setting the value to Previous causes all messages previously received to be acknowledged, which used to be the behavior specified by the JMS specification. You should set this value to All unless you need to provide backward compatibility with an application written to the old JMS specification.

✦ **Load Balancing Enabled:** This parameter is new in WebLogic 7.0; when it is checked, producers are load balanced on every call to send or publish. If it is not checked, what happens depends on whether the producer is anonymous or not. Anonymous producers (those that don't designate a destination when created) load balance only when switching destinations if this box is not checked. Non-anonymous producers load balance on the first send or publish, and continue to use that destination until they fail, at which point they are load balanced at the next send or publish call, when the box is not checked.

✦ **Server Affinity Enabled:** This parameter is new in WebLogic 7.0; it tells WebLogic to load balance across other physical destinations on the same WebLogic Server first.

After completing the configuration screen, click Create.

The next step is to attach the connection factory to a server or cluster. Click the Targets tab and then move the desired server into the Chosen list of the desired server or cluster. Click Apply. Figure 9-7 shows a connection factory attached to a local WebLogic Server instance.

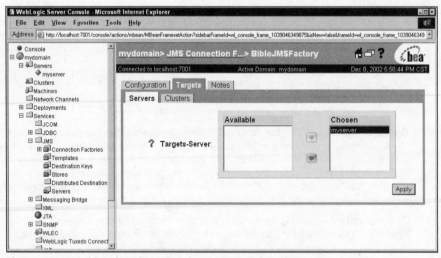

Figure 9-7: Attaching the connection factory to a WebLogic Server

This completes configuration of the connection factory. Next we show how to define backing stores.

Defining a file backing store

In the domain tree of the WebLogic Console, expand the JMS node and then click Stores. At the top of the page, click Configure a New JMSFile Store. Figure 9-8 shows the resulting configuration page.

Figure 9-8: Creating a JMS file store

The entries on this page are as follows:

✦ **Name:** A name for the file store, which must conform to the rules for Java identifiers and be unique within the WebLogic Server instance or its cluster. Type **BibleJMSFileStore** for this value.

✦ **Synchronous Write Policy:** This is new in WebLogic 7.0 and applies to JMS File Stores only. It can be used for tuning performance at the major expense of reliability, so choose wisely. **Disabled** means that WebLogic depends on the operating system and file system to do its caching; of course, if the server goes down, you risk getting missing or duplicated messages. **Cache-Flush** means that transactions are held up until all caches are flushed to the hard disk. This is very reliable, so we'll select this for our example. **Direct-Write** means no caching is involved, but has several operating system dependencies. Therefore, it's probably best to read the WebLogic caveats at the following URL before choosing this option:

```
http://edocs.bea.com/wls/docs70/adminguide/jms.html#sync_write_to_
filestore
```

✦ **Directory:** A pathname to a valid file system directory in which the store will be kept. This directory must exist on your system, so be sure to create it before completing this page.

After completing the configuration screen, click Create.

WebLogic creates the JMS file store automatically the first time that messages are sent to a queue or topic backed by the store. The structure of this file is private and undocumented.

Defining a JDBC backing store

In the domain tree of the WebLogic Console, expand the JMS node, and then click Stores. At the top of the page, click Configure a New JMSJDBCStore. Figure 9-9 shows the resulting configuration page.

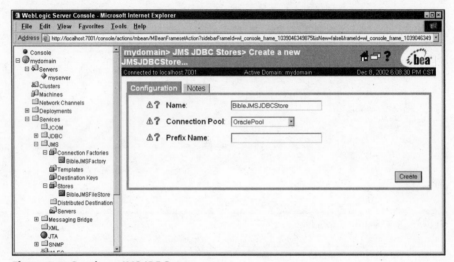

Figure 9-9: Creating a JMS JDBC store

The entries on this page are as follows:

✦ **Name:** A name for the JDBC store, which must conform to the rules for Java identifiers and be unique within the WebLogic Server domain. Type **BibleJMSJDBCStore** for this value.

✦ **Connection Pool:** A valid JDBC connection pool already defined on your server (the drop-down menu will be populated with available pool names). See Chapter 5 for instructions on how to configure JDBC connection pools.

Caution   The connection pool you specify must use a non-XA driver because the WebLogic classes that manage the JMS system tables are not XA-aware.

✦ **Prefix Name:** A string value that is prepended to all table names whenever JMS makes JDBC calls to the JDBC store. Enter a value if your RDBMS requires fully qualified table names. Some instances of SQL Server or Sybase, for example, require dbo to be prepended to all table names. Check with your database administrator if you have any doubts. If your instance does not, leave this attribute blank.

After completing the configuration screen, click Create.

When you restart WebLogic Server, it automatically adds two system tables to the database specified by your JMS connection pool if they don't already exist (note the contrast with file stores, which are not created until they are actually used). Each table contains one non-clustered index. The following code is the resulting DDL for Oracle. We created a schema called JMS to hold the tables, but you can put them in any schema you want:

```
CREATE TABLE JMS.JMSSTATE
(
    RECORDHANDLE      NUMBER      NULL,
    RECORDSTATE       NUMBER      NULL,
    RECORDGENERATION  NUMBER      NULL
);

CREATE INDEX JMS.JMSMSG_X
    ON SCOTT.JMSSTATE(RECORDHANDLE);

CREATE TABLE JMS.JMSSTORE
(
    RECORDHANDLE NUMBER       NULL,
    RECORDSTATE  NUMBER       NULL,
    RECORD       LONG RAW     NULL
);

CREATE INDEX JMS.JMSMSGQ_X
    ON SCOTT.JMSSTORE(RECORDHANDLE);
```

Next is the DDL for Microsoft SQL Server:

```
CREATE TABLE dbo.JMSState
(
    recordHandle      numeric(12,0) NULL,
    recordState       int           NULL,
    recordGeneration  int           NULL
)
go
CREATE NONCLUSTERED INDEX JMSMSG_X
    ON dbo.JMSState(recordHandle)
    ON [PRIMARY]
go
CREATE TABLE dbo.JMSStore
(
    recordHandle numeric(12,0) NULL,
    recordState  int           NULL,
    record       image         NULL
)
go
CREATE NONCLUSTERED INDEX JMSMSGQ_X
    ON dbo.JMSStore(recordHandle)
    ON [PRIMARY]
go
```

Although the structure of these tables is private and undocumented, it's worth noting that the table JMSStore contains persisted messages, which remain in this table until they are delivered. After delivery, the messages are automatically deleted from the table by WebLogic JMS.

Defining destination keys

Destination keys are a WebLogic-specific feature that control the order in which messages are delivered to a queue or topic. Destination keys operate on the user-definable properties that are stored in a message.

Suppose, for example, that an application sends error messages to an error queue. We can define an `int` property called `severity`, whose values range from 1 (least severe errors) to 10 (most severe errors), and attach it to our messages. By default, messages are delivered to destinations in the order in which they're sent. But if we want the most severe errors delivered first, we can define a destination key that delivers error messages in descending order by `severity`.

To create such a destination key, expand the JMS node in the WebLogic Console and then click Destination Keys. At the top of the page, click Configure a New JMS Destination Key. Figure 9-10 shows the resulting configuration page.

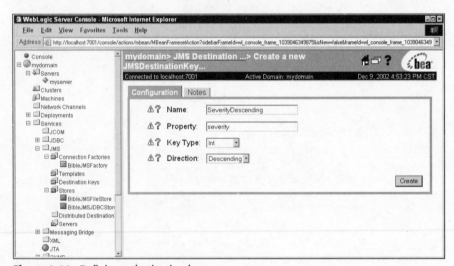

Figure 9-10: Defining a destination key

The entries on this page are as follows:

- ✦ **Name:** A name for the destination key, which must conform to the rules for Java identifiers and be unique within the WebLogic Server domain. Type **SeverityDescending** for this value.

- ✦ **Property:** The name of the message property to which the key applies. The name must match the property name you use in your Java code and is case-sensitive. Type **severity** for this value.

- ✦ **Key Type:** The Java type of the key (one of: `boolean`, `byte`, `short`, `int`, `long`, `float`, `double`, or `String`). Select `Int`.

- ✦ **Direction:** The sort direction of the key (`Ascending` or `Descending`). Select `Descending`.

After completing the configuration screen, click Create.

Defining templates

Templates are collections of one or more destination keys that can be applied to JMS servers, queues, or topics. Use templates to create a set of message delivery attributes once and apply it to multiple queues and topics. You also can use templates to deliver messages sorted by multiple criteria.

Returning to the application error log example, suppose that an error queue receives messages from every application in our company. Suppose that applications are prioritized by order of importance and are storing this attribute in an `int` property called `appPriority`, whose values are 1 (high), 2 (medium), and 3 (low). We create a destination key for `appPriority`, sorted in ascending order, and then we create a template containing the `severity` and `appPriority` keys. This template, when applied to our queue, will cause messages to be delivered in descending order by `severity` and in ascending order by `appPriority`.

To create a template, expand the JMS node in the WebLogic Console and then click Templates. At the top of the page, click Configure a New JMS Template. Figure 9-11 shows the resulting configuration page.

Figure 9-11: Defining a template

The entries on this page are as follows:

✦ **Name:** A name for the template, which must conform to the rules for Java identifiers and be unique within the WebLogic Server instance or its cluster. Type **AppErrors Template** for this value.

✦ **Destination Keys:** Available destination keys for the template. Even if you have already defined some keys, none will be shown until you create the template. Click Create to create the template with no keys; the available keys will appear. Move the desired keys from the Available list to the Chosen list and then click Apply. In our case, move `SeverityDescending`—that you just created—into this box.

Defining a JMS server

In the domain tree of the WebLogic Console, expand the JMS node and then click Servers. At the top of the page, click Configure a New JMS Server. Figure 9-12 shows the resulting configuration page.

The entries on this page are as follows:

✦ **Name:** A name for the JMS server, which must conform to the rules for Java identifiers and be unique within the WebLogic Server domain. Type **BibleJMSServer** for this value.

✦ **Store:** The name of an existing JMS file or JDBC store to use for this JMS server. Select `BibleJMSFileStore`, the file store you created earlier.

✦ **Paging Store:** This is a new feature in WebLogic 7.0 that has great potential benefits for very large enterprise installations because it allows you to specify a threshold of messages at which you page them to disk. It's complex enough to be beyond the scope of this book, so we suggest that you read the WebLogic documentation at the following URL:

`http://edocs.bea.com/wls/docs70/adminguide/jms.html#using_message_paging`

✦ **Temporary Template:** The name of the JMS template (if any) that will be applied to all temporary destinations created against this server. Select `(none)`.

After completing the configuration screen, click Create. Then click the Targets tab and select your server or cluster, and click Apply so it will be the target for the JMS server you just defined.

Figure 9-12: Defining a JMS server

Creating a message queue

Before you can use your JMS server, you must create message queues or topics for applications to use.

In the domain tree of the WebLogic Console, expand the JMS node and then click Servers. BibleJMSServer, the server you just created, should appear. Click BibleJMSServer to expand it; you will now see entries for Destinations and Session Pools. Click Destinations.

At the top of the page, click Configure a New JMSQueue. Figure 9-13 shows the resulting configuration page.

Figure 9-13: Configuring a JMS queue

The entries on this page are as follows:

✦ **Name:** A name for the JMS queue, which must conform to the rules for Java identifiers and be unique within the WebLogic Server domain. Type **BibleJMSQueue** for this value.

✦ **JNDIName:** Programs will use this name to perform JNDI lookups on the queue at runtime. The name must be unique within the server's or cluster's JNDI namespace. Type **BibleJMSQueue** for this value.

✦ **Enable Store:** If `true`, messages sent to the queue will be written to the backing store defined for the JMS server. If `false`, they will not. If `default` is selected, messages will be written to the backing store if one is defined; otherwise, they will not.

✦ **Template:** The JMS template that controls the order in which messages are delivered to the queue. Select `(none)`.

✦ **Destination Keys:** JMS destination keys that control the order in which messages are delivered to the queue. These can be chosen in lieu of or in addition to a template. Even if you have already defined some keys, none will be shown until you create the queue. Click Create to create the queue with no keys; the available keys will appear. Move the desired keys from the Available list to the Chosen list and then click Apply. In our example, add `SeverityDescending` to the Chosen list and click Apply.

Creating a message topic

In the domain tree of the WebLogic Console, expand the JMS node and then click Servers. BibleJMSServer, the server you just created, should appear. Click BibleJMSServer to expand it; you will now see entries for Destinations and Session Pools. Click Destinations.

At the top of the page, click Configure a New JMSTopic. Figure 9-14 shows the resulting configuration page.

Figure 9-14: Configuring a JMS topic

The entries on this page are as follows:

✦ **Name:** A name for the JMS topic, which must conform to the rules for Java identifiers and be unique within the WebLogic Server domain. Type **BibleJMSTopic** for this value.

✦ **JNDIName:** Programs use this name to perform JNDI lookups on the topic at runtime. The name must be unique within the server's or cluster's JNDI namespace. Type **BibleJMSTopic** for this value.

✦ **Enable Store:** If `true`, messages sent to the topic will be written to the backing store defined for the JMS server. If `false`, they will not. If `default` is selected, messages will be written to the backing store if one is defined; otherwise, they will not. `Enable Store` must be true if the topic will have durable subscribers. See the "Creating durable subscribers to topics" section later in this chapter for more details.

✦ **Template:** The JMS template that controls the order in which messages are delivered to the topic. Select `(none)`.

✦ **Destination Keys:** JMS destination keys that control the order in which messages are delivered to the topic. These can be chosen in lieu of or in addition to a template. Even if you have already defined some keys, none will be shown until you create the topic. Click Create to create the topic with no keys; the available keys will appear. Move the desired keys from the Available list to the Chosen list and then click Apply. In our example, move the `SeverityDescending` key to the Chosen list and click Apply.

In the domain tree of the WebLogic Console, expand the JMS node and then click Servers. BibleJMSServer, the server you just created, should appear. Click BibleJMSServer to expand it; you will now see entries for Destinations and Session Pools. Click Destinations.

At the top of the page, click Configure a New JMSQueue. Figure 9-13 shows the resulting configuration page.

Figure 9-13: Configuring a JMS queue

The entries on this page are as follows:

✦ **Name:** A name for the JMS queue, which must conform to the rules for Java identifiers and be unique within the WebLogic Server domain. Type **BibleJMSQueue** for this value.

✦ **JNDIName:** Programs will use this name to perform JNDI lookups on the queue at run-time. The name must be unique within the server's or cluster's JNDI namespace. Type **BibleJMSQueue** for this value.

✦ **Enable Store:** If `true`, messages sent to the queue will be written to the backing store defined for the JMS server. If `false`, they will not. If `default` is selected, messages will be written to the backing store if one is defined; otherwise, they will not.

✦ **Template:** The JMS template that controls the order in which messages are delivered to the queue. Select `(none)`.

✦ **Destination Keys:** JMS destination keys that control the order in which messages are delivered to the queue. These can be chosen in lieu of or in addition to a template. Even if you have already defined some keys, none will be shown until you create the queue. Click Create to create the queue with no keys; the available keys will appear. Move the desired keys from the Available list to the Chosen list and then click Apply. In our example, add `SeverityDescending` to the Chosen list and click Apply.

Creating a message topic

In the domain tree of the WebLogic Console, expand the JMS node and then click Servers. BibleJMSServer, the server you just created, should appear. Click BibleJMSServer to expand it; you will now see entries for Destinations and Session Pools. Click Destinations.

At the top of the page, click Configure a New JMSTopic. Figure 9-14 shows the resulting configuration page.

Figure 9-14: Configuring a JMS topic

The entries on this page are as follows:

✦ **Name:** A name for the JMS topic, which must conform to the rules for Java identifiers and be unique within the WebLogic Server domain. Type **BibleJMSTopic** for this value.

✦ **JNDIName:** Programs use this name to perform JNDI lookups on the topic at runtime. The name must be unique within the server's or cluster's JNDI namespace. Type **BibleJMSTopic** for this value.

✦ **Enable Store:** If `true`, messages sent to the topic will be written to the backing store defined for the JMS server. If `false`, they will not. If `default` is selected, messages will be written to the backing store if one is defined; otherwise, they will not. `Enable Store` must be true if the topic will have durable subscribers. See the "Creating durable subscribers to topics" section later in this chapter for more details.

✦ **Template:** The JMS template that controls the order in which messages are delivered to the topic. Select `(none)`.

✦ **Destination Keys:** JMS destination keys that control the order in which messages are delivered to the topic. These can be chosen in lieu of or in addition to a template. Even if you have already defined some keys, none will be shown until you create the topic. Click Create to create the topic with no keys; the available keys will appear. Move the desired keys from the Available list to the Chosen list and then click Apply. In our example, move the `SeverityDescending` key to the Chosen list and click Apply.

Programming WebLogic JMS

After you finish configuring JMS on your server, you can write Java code that uses your messaging infrastructure. This section shows you how to write code to send and receive messages, using both the point-to-point and publish-and-subscribe models, for the messaging infrastructure we created in the previous section.

Sending messages

Whether you're sending messages to a queue, or publishing them to a topic, the programming steps are the same. You use different classes, however, depending on whether you're working with queues or topics. Here is a summary of the steps:

1. Obtain a reference to WebLogic Server's context.

2. Use the context and JNDI to obtain a reference to a connection factory.

3. Use the connection factory to create a connection.

4. Use the connection to create a session.

5. Use the connection to create an instance of the type of message you want to send and then populate the message with data.

6. Use the connection to create a queue sender or topic publisher and then use the sender or publisher to send the message.

Obtaining a server context

Programming JMS requires the use of JNDI to look up connection factories and other resources. Therefore, the first step in any JMS session is to obtain the server context of the WebLogic Server in question.

Cross-Reference For more information about JNDI and obtaining server contexts, see Chapter 7.

The following code obtains the context of the local WebLogic Server:

```
import javax.naming.*;
import java.util.*;

Context ctx = null;
Hashtable ht = new Hashtable();

ht.put(Context.INITIAL_CONTEXT_FACTORY,
        "weblogic.jndi.WLInitialContextFactory";
ht.put(Context.PROVIDER_URL, "t3://localhost:7001");

try {
  ctx = new InitialContext(ht);
}
catch (NamingException e) {
  e.printStackTrace();
}
```

We refer to the Context you obtained, stored in the variable ctx, in subsequent code examples.

Sending messages to a queue

To send messages to a queue, follow these steps:

1. Use the server context to look up a reference to a connection factory that has been defined in the WebLogic Console. Cast this reference to the `QueueConnectionFactory` type. The following code obtains a reference to `BibleJMSFactory`, the factory you defined earlier in this chapter:

```
import javax.jms.*;

QueueConnectionFactory qConnectionFactory =
  (QueueConnectionFactory) ctx.lookup("BibleJMSFactory");
```

2. Use the `QueueConnectionFactory` to create a `QueueConnection` instance. You can call one of two methods to do this, depending on whether a username and password (both strings) are required for your application:

```
QueueConnection qConnection =
  qConnectionFactory.createQueueConnection();
```

or:

```
QueueConnection qConnection =
  qConnectionFactory.createQueueConnection(userName,
                                           password);
```

3. Use the `QueueConnection` to create a `QueueSession` instance:

```
QueueSession qSession =
  qConnection.createQueueSession(TRANSACT_MODE,
    ACKNOWLEDGE_MODE);
```

`TRANSACT_MODE` is a Boolean specifying whether or not the session will operate in transactional mode. If `true`, then you can bundle a series of messages into a JMS transaction and send them as an atomic unit. Committing the transaction sends all the messages; rolling it back sends none. Also, when `TRANSACT_MODE` is `true`, `ACKNOWLEDGE_MODE` is ignored.

Cross-Reference

We demonstrate how to manage JMS transactions in the "Working with transactions" section later in this chapter.

`ACKNOWLEDGE_MODE` is an `int` specifying how your application will acknowledge the receipt of messages for non-transacted sessions. Table 9-1 describes its different values and their meanings.

Table 9-1: JMS Non-transacted Acknowledge Modes

Mode	Description
AUTO_ACKNOWLEDGE	The `Session` object automatically acknowledges receipt of the message after the application processes it.

Mode	Description
CLIENT_ACKNOWLEDGE	The Session object relies on the application to explicitly call Message.acknowledge() from time to time to acknowledge one or more messages. Calling this method acknowledges all messages received since the last call, which allows applications to acknowledge large batches of messages with one call.
DUPS_OK_ACKNOWLEDGE	Similar to AUTO_ACKNOWLEDGE, except that the Session is notified that duplicate acknowledgments are allowed, so duplicate messages may be sent if the first attempt to send fails. Although this is the most efficient mode in terms of JMS resource overhead, use it only if your application can handle the receipt of duplicate messages.
NO_ACKNOWLEDGE	Notifies the Session that no acknowledgment is required. Messages sent this way are immediately deleted from the server on receipt. If receipt fails, the message is lost. Duplicate messages may be sent if the first attempt to send fails. Use this mode only if your application can cope with lost or duplicate messages.
MULTICAST_NO_ACKNOWLEDGE	This mode is the same as NO_ACKNOWLEDGE, but is used for WebLogic message multicasting.

4. Use the server context to look up a reference to the desired JMS Queue. To look up a reference to BibleJMSQueue, for example, write this code:

```
Queue q = (Queue) ctx.lookup("BibleJMSQueue");
```

5. Use the QueueSession object to create a QueueSender instance for the Queue:

```
QueueSender qSender = qSession.createSender(q);
```

6. Use QueueSession to create an instance of the desired Message type (BytesMessage, MapMessage, ObjectMessage, StreamMessage, TextMessage, or XMLMessage). To create a TextMessage, for example, write this code:

```
TextMessage textMsg = qSession.createTextMessage();
```

7. Populate the message with data. Set its header information and properties as well, if your application requires it. The following code sets a user-defined int property called severity to a known value and then populates the body of a TextMessage:

```
textMsg.clearBody();
textMsg.setIntProperty("severity", 1);
textMsg.setText("The mail server is down!");
```

8. Use the QueueSender object to send the following message:

```
qSender.send(textMsg);
```

When this call completes, the message was delivered to the queue.

The class BibleQueueSender, shown in Listing 9-1, illustrates the preceding steps. This class sends 10 messages, plus a "stop" message signaling that the transmission is complete.

Note   You are not required to send "stop" messages. We are doing it in the examples for demonstration purposes only.

Listing 9-1: **BibleQueueSender.java**

```java
package com.wiley.wlsbible.jms;

import javax.jms.*;
import javax.naming.*;
import java.util.*;

public class BibleQueueSender {

  public static void main(String[] args) {
    Context ctx = null;
    Hashtable ht = new Hashtable();
    QueueConnectionFactory qConnectionFactory = null;
    QueueConnection qConnection = null;
    QueueSession qSession = null;
    QueueSender qSender = null;
    Queue q = null;
    TextMessage textMsg = null;
    String msg;

    try {
      // Obtain references to JMS queue components.
      ht.put(Context.INITIAL_CONTEXT_FACTORY,
             "weblogic.jndi.WLInitialContextFactory");
      ht.put(Context.PROVIDER_URL, "t3://localhost:7001");
      ctx = new InitialContext(ht);
      qConnectionFactory =
        (QueueConnectionFactory)
        ctx.lookup("BibleJMSFactory");
      qConnection =
        qConnectionFactory.createQueueConnection();
      qSession = qConnection.createQueueSession(false,
        javax.jms.QueueSession.AUTO_ACKNOWLEDGE);
      q = (Queue) ctx.lookup("BibleJMSQueue");
      qSender = qSession.createSender(q);

      System.out.println("Sending messages to queue...");
      textMsg = qSession.createTextMessage();
      for (int i=1; i<=10; i++) {
        msg = "Message #" + i + " to queue";
        textMsg.clearBody();
        textMsg.setIntProperty("severity", i);
```

```
          textMsg.setText(msg);
          System.out.println("  Sending message: " + msg);
          qSender.send(textMsg);
        }
        msg = "Stop";
        textMsg.clearBody();
        textMsg.setIntProperty("severity", 0);
        textMsg.setText(msg);
        System.out.println("  Sending message: " + msg);
        qSender.send(textMsg);
      }
      catch (Exception e) {
        e.printStackTrace();
      }
      finally {
        try {
          // Release JMS resources.
          qSender.close();
          qSession.close();
          qConnection.close();
        }
        catch (Exception e) {
          e.printStackTrace();
        }
      }
    }
  }
```

After starting WebLogic Server, running `BibleQueueSender.main()` in its own JVM yields the following output:

```
Sending messages to queue...
  Sending message: Message #1 to queue
  Sending message: Message #2 to queue
  Sending message: Message #3 to queue
  Sending message: Message #4 to queue
  Sending message: Message #5 to queue
  Sending message: Message #6 to queue
  Sending message: Message #7 to queue
  Sending message: Message #8 to queue
  Sending message: Message #9 to queue
  Sending message: Message #10 to queue
  Sending message: Stop
```

The result is that the preceding 11 messages are waiting in `BibleJMSQueue`. The first queue receiver to read this queue will receive the messages.

Publishing messages to a topic

Publishing messages to a topic is analogous to sending messages to a queue — only the data types change. To publish a message to a topic, follow these steps:

1. Use the server context to look up a reference to a connection factory that has been defined in the WebLogic Console. Cast this reference to the `TopicConnectionFactory` type. The following code obtains a reference to `BibleJMSFactory`, the factory you defined earlier in this chapter:

```
import javax.jms.*;

TopicConnectionFactory tConnectionFactory =
  (TopicConnectionFactory) ctx.lookup("BibleJMSFactory");
```

2. Use the `TopicConnectionFactory` to create a `TopicConnection` instance. You can call one of two methods to do this, depending on whether a username and password (both strings) are required for your application:

```
TopicConnection tConnection =
  tConnectionFactory.createTopicConnection();
```

or:

```
TopicConnection tConnection =
  tConnectionFactory.createTopicConnection(userName,
                                           password);
```

3. Use `TopicConnection` to create a `TopicSession` instance:

```
TopicSession tSession =
  tConnection.createTopicSession(TRANSACT_MODE,
    ACKNOWLEDGE_MODE);
```

`TRANSACT_MODE` and `ACKNOWLEDGE_MODE` have the same meanings in `TopicSessions` as they do in `QueueSessions`. Refer to Table 9-1 for a list of valid acknowledge modes.

4. Use the server context to look up a reference to the desired JMS `Topic`. To look up a reference to `BibleJMSTopic`, for example, write the following code:

```
Topic t = (Topic) ctx.lookup("BibleJMSTopic");
```

5. Use the `TopicSession` object to create a `TopicPublisher` instance for the `Topic`:

```
TopicPublisher tPublisher = tSession.createPublisher(t);
```

6. Use `TopicSession` to create an instance of the desired `Message` type (`BytesMessage`, `MapMessage`, `ObjectMessage`, `StreamMessage`, `TextMessage`, or `XMLMessage`). To create a `TextMessage`, for example, write the following code:

```
TextMessage textMsg = tSession.createTextMessage();
```

7. Populate the message with data. Set its header information and properties as well, if your application requires it. The following code sets a user-defined `int` property called `priority` to a known value and then populates the body of a `TextMessage`:

```
textMsg.clearBody();
textMsg.setIntProperty("priority", 1);
textMsg.setText("The mail server is down!");
```

8. Use the `TopicPublisher` object to send the message:

```
tPublisher.publish(textMsg);
```

When this call completes, the message was published to the topic.

The class `BibleTopicPublisher`, shown in Listing 9-2, illustrates the preceding steps, again by publishing 10 messages plus a "stop" message.

Listing 9-2: BibleTopicPublisher.java

```
package com.wiley.wlsbible.jms;

import javax.jms.*;
import javax.naming.*;
import java.util.*;

public class BibleTopicPublisher {

  public static void main(String[] args) {
    Context ctx = null;
    Hashtable ht = new Hashtable();
    TopicConnectionFactory tConnectionFactory = null;
    TopicConnection tConnection = null;
    TopicSession tSession = null;
    TopicPublisher tPublisher = null;
    Topic t = null;
    TextMessage textMsg = null;
    String msg;

    try {
      // Obtain references to JMS Topic components.
      ht.put(Context.INITIAL_CONTEXT_FACTORY,
             "weblogic.jndi.WLInitialContextFactory");
      ht.put(Context.PROVIDER_URL, "t3://localhost:7001");
      ctx = new InitialContext(ht);
      tConnectionFactory =
        (TopicConnectionFactory)
        ctx.lookup("BibleJMSFactory");
      tConnection =
        tConnectionFactory.createTopicConnection();
      tSession = tConnection.createTopicSession(false,
        javax.jms.TopicSession.AUTO_ACKNOWLEDGE);
      t = (Topic) ctx.lookup("BibleJMSTopic");
      tPublisher = tSession.createPublisher(t);

      System.out.println("Publishing messages to topic...");
      textMsg = tSession.createTextMessage();
      for (int i=1; i<=10; i++) {
        msg = "Message #" + i " to topic";
        textMsg.clearBody();
        textMsg.setIntProperty("severity", i);
        textMsg.setText(msg);
        System.out.println("  Publishing message: " + msg);
        tPublisher.publish(textMsg);
      }
```

Continued

Listing 9-2 *(continued)*

```
        msg = "Stop";
        textMsg.clearBody();
        textMsg.setText(msg);
        textMsg.setIntProperty("severity", 0);
        System.out.println("  Sending message: " + msg);
        tPublisher.publish(textMsg);
      }
      catch (Exception e) {
        e.printStackTrace();
      }
      finally {
        try {
          // Release JMS resources.
          tPublisher.close();
          tSession.close();
          tConnection.close();
        }
        catch (Exception e) {
          e.printStackTrace();
        }
      }
    }
  }
```

After starting WebLogic Server, running `BibleTopicSender.main()` in its own JVM yields the following output:

```
Publishing messages to topic...
  Publishing message: Message #1 to topic
  Publishing message: Message #2 to topic
  Publishing message: Message #3 to topic
  Publishing message: Message #4 to topic
  Publishing message: Message #5 to topic
  Publishing message: Message #6 to topic
  Publishing message: Message #7 to topic
  Publishing message: Message #8 to topic
  Publishing message: Message #9 to topic
  Publishing message: Message #10 to topic
  Publishing message: Stop
```

The result is that the preceding 11 messages are published to `BibleJMSTopic`. But if no durable subscribers are registered with the topic, and if there are no active nondurable subscribers, the messages are immediately lost. We describe durable and nondurable subscribers in the "Creating durable subscribers to topics" section later in this chapter.

Receiving messages synchronously

Although receiving messages synchronously is sometimes useful, is usually the least efficient way to process incoming messages. Synchronous code spends most of its time in loops waiting for messages to arrive, consuming precious CPU cycles and server threads in the process.

On a busy server, large numbers of synchronous messaging threads can deadlock the entire server. Therefore, before writing synchronous code to receive messages, take a hard look at your application to make sure that an asynchronous approach isn't better.

Nevertheless, situations exist for which synchronous message processing makes sense, especially for queues — this section shows you how to do so.

Receiving messages synchronously from a queue

Receiving messages synchronously from a queue is useful for batch applications that connect to the queue on a periodic basis, download the queue's contents, and then disconnect until the next scheduled batch session. A log analyzer program, for example, could retrieve log entries from a queue on a nightly basis, add them to its database, perform statistical analysis on the day's entries, and e-mail the results to a system administrator. As a side effect of this operation, the queue is emptied in preparation for the next day's activity.

To receive messages synchronously from a queue, follow these steps:

1. Obtain `QueueConnectionFactory` and `QueueConnection` instances and then call `QueueConnection.start()` to start the connection.

2. Use the `QueueSession` to create a `QueueReceiver` instance for the `Queue`.

3. Use the `QueueReceiver` to retrieve messages from the queue.

4. After retrieving all desired messages, call `QueueConnection.stop()` to stop the connection.

5. Release JMS resources by calling the `close` method of `QueueReceiver`, `QueueSession`, and `QueueConnection`.

The class `SyncQueueReceiver`, shown in Listing 9-3, illustrates the preceding steps. The function of this class is to retrieve messages synchronously from a queue until the queue is empty.

Listing 9-3: **SyncQueueReceiver.java**

```
package com.wiley.wlsbible.jms;

import javax.jms.*;
import javax.naming.*;
import java.util.*;

public class SyncQueueReceiver {

  public static void main(String[] args) {
    Context ctx = null;
    Hashtable ht = new Hashtable();
    QueueConnectionFactory qConnectionFactory = null;
    QueueConnection qConnection = null;
    QueueSession qSession = null;
    QueueReceiver qReceiver = null;
    Queue q = null;
    TextMessage textMsg = null;
```

Continued

Listing 9-3 *(continued)*

```java
String msg;

try {
  // Obtain references to JMS queue components.
  ht.put(Context.INITIAL_CONTEXT_FACTORY,
         "weblogic.jndi.WLInitialContextFactory");
  ht.put(Context.PROVIDER_URL, "t3://localhost:7001");
  ctx = new InitialContext(ht);
  qConnectionFactory =
    (QueueConnectionFactory)
    ctx.lookup("BibleJMSFactory");
  qConnection =
    qConnectionFactory.createQueueConnection();
  qSession = qConnection.createQueueSession(false,
    javax.jms.QueueSession.AUTO_ACKNOWLEDGE);
  q = (Queue) ctx.lookup("BibleJMSQueue");
  qReceiver = qSession.createReceiver(q);

  // Start a connection to the queue, retrieve all
  // messages in the queue, then stop the connection.
  System.out.println("Receiving messages...");
  qConnection.start();
  textMsg = (TextMessage)qReceiver.receiveNoWait();
  while (textMsg != null) {
    System.out.println("  Receiving message: " +
                       textMsg.getText());
    textMsg = (TextMessage)qReceiver.receiveNoWait();
  }
  qConnection.stop();
}
catch (Exception e) {
  e.printStackTrace();
}
finally {
  try {
    // Release JMS resources.
    qReceiver.close();
    qSession.close();
    qConnection.close();
  }
  catch (Exception e) {
    e.printStackTrace();
  }
}
  }
}
```

After starting WebLogic Server and running `BibleQueueSender.main()`, running `SyncQueueReceiver.main()` in its own JVM yields the following output:

```
Receiving messages...
   Receiving message: Message #1 to queue
   Receiving message: Message #2 to queue
   Receiving message: Message #3 to queue
   Receiving message: Message #4 to queue
   Receiving message: Message #5 to queue
   Receiving message: Message #6 to queue
   Receiving message: Message #7 to queue
   Receiving message: Message #8 to queue
   Receiving message: Message #9 to queue
   Receiving message: Message #10 to queue
   Receiving message: Stop
```

Now the queue is empty.

The line of code that synchronously examines the queue is as follows:

```
textMsg = (TextMessage)qReceiver.receiveNoWait();
```

`QueueReceiver.receiveNoWait()` returns the next message in a queue or returns `null` if there are no messages. The call returns immediately; it does not wait for messages to arrive, nor does it wait for any predetermined period of time. Therefore, if you know a queue contains messages and you just want to grab them, `receiveNoWait()` is the way to go. In the example, we repeatedly call `receiveNoWait()` in a `while` loop until the queue is empty.

A variation of this call is `QueueReceiver.receive()`, which comes in two forms. Calling `receive()` with no arguments results in `receive()` waiting (and therefore blocking its thread) until a message arrives, at which time it returns the message. If a message never arrives, `receive()` blocks indefinitely. An alternative is to call `receive(long timeout)`, which causes `receive()` to wait the number of seconds given by `timeout` before returning, regardless of whether a message arrives. If no message arrives within the timeout period, `receive()` returns `null`; otherwise, it returns the message.

Receiving messages synchronously from a topic

Topic subscribers can synchronously retrieve messages published to a topic. But a topic subscriber will receive only those messages published *after* the subscriber registers with the topic. (Contrast this with queues: A queue receiver receives messages sent before *or* after the receiver reads the queue, as long as the messages published before are persistent, have a long enough time-to-live, and haven't been retrieved by any other receivers.)

To receive published messages synchronously, follow these steps:

1. Obtain `TopicConnectionFactory` and `TopicConnection` instances and then call `TopicConnection.start()` to start the connection.

2. Use `TopicSession` to create a `TopicSubscriber` instance for the `Topic`.

3. Use `TopicSubscriber` to retrieve messages from the topic.

4. After retrieving all desired messages, call `TopicConnection.stop()` to stop the connection.

5. Release JMS resources by calling the `close` method of `TopicSubscriber`, `TopicSession`, and `TopicConnection`.

The class SyncTopicSubscriber, shown in Listing 9-4, illustrates these steps. The function of this class is to receive messages synchronously from a topic until a "stop" message is received. Looking for a "stop" message is necessary because receiving a message from a topic doesn't necessarily remove it from the topic — if other subscribers exist, the message will remain until they receive it.

Listing 9-4: SyncTopicSubscriber.java

```java
package com.wiley.wlsbible.jms;

import javax.jms.*;
import javax.naming.*;
import java.util.*;

public class SyncTopicSubscriber {

  public static void main(String[] args) {
    Context ctx = null;
    Hashtable ht = new Hashtable();
    TopicConnectionFactory tConnectionFactory = null;
    TopicConnection tConnection = null;
    TopicSession tSession = null;
    TopicSubscriber tSubscriber = null;
    Topic t = null;
    TextMessage textMsg = null;
    String msg;

    try {
      // Obtain references to JMS Topic components.
      ht.put(Context.INITIAL_CONTEXT_FACTORY,
          "weblogic.jndi.WLInitialContextFactory");
      ht.put(Context.PROVIDER_URL, "t3://localhost:7001");
      ctx = new InitialContext(ht);
      tConnectionFactory =
        (TopicConnectionFactory)
        ctx.lookup("BibleJMSAsyncFactory");
      tConnection =
        tConnectionFactory.createTopicConnection();
      tSession = tConnection.createTopicSession(false,
        javax.jms.TopicSession.AUTO_ACKNOWLEDGE);
      t = (Topic) ctx.lookup("BibleJMSTopic");
      tSubscriber = tSession.createSubscriber(t);

      System.out.println("Receiving messages...");
      tConnection.start();
      textMsg =
        (TextMessage)tSubscriber.receive();
      while (true) {
        msg = textMsg.getText();
        System.out.println("  Receiving message: " + msg);
```

```
        if (msg.equals("Stop")) {
          break;
        }
        textMsg = (TextMessage) tSubscriber.receive();
      }
      tConnection.stop();
    }
    catch (Exception e) {
      e.printStackTrace();
    }
    finally {
      try {
        // Release JMS resources.
        tSubscriber.close();
        tSession.close();
        tConnection.close();
      }
      catch (Exception e) {
        e.printStackTrace();
      }
    }
  }
}
```

After starting WebLogic Server and running `SyncTopicSubscriber.main()`, running `BibleTopicPublisher.main()` causes messages to be published to the topic. The messages are immediately received by `BibleTopicSubscriber`, which displays the following output:

```
Receiving messages...
  Receiving message: Message #1 to topic
  Receiving message: Message #2 to topic
  Receiving message: Message #3 to topic
  Receiving message: Message #4 to topic
  Receiving message: Message #5 to topic
  Receiving message: Message #6 to topic
  Receiving message: Message #7 to topic
  Receiving message: Message #8 to topic
  Receiving message: Message #9 to topic
  Receiving message: Message #10 to topic
  Receiving message: Stop
```

The topic is now empty if no durable subscribers registered with the topic, or if there are no active, nondurable subscribers. Otherwise, the messages remain in the topic for delivery to other subscribers.

In this example, we call the blocking version of `receive()` to retrieve messages because a topic, by definition, is initially "empty" to a new subscriber; messages delivered to that topic before the new subscriber comes online are not available to that subscriber. Therefore, you must wait for a subsequent message to arrive before beginning message processing. For this reason, it's almost always better to write asynchronous topic subscribers, which we discuss in the next section.

Receiving messages asynchronously

Receiving messages asynchronously is almost always the preferred approach because it consumes fewer resources, doesn't block threads, and doesn't deadlock WebLogic Server. For this reason, JMS and WebLogic make it very easy to write asynchronous message listeners, and this section shows you how.

Receiving messages asynchronously from a queue

Receiving PTP messages asynchronously is useful for real-time applications that need to process incoming messages as they arrive. A stock-trading application, for example, might receive messages about a stock's price movements that can immediately trigger trades in that stock.

To receive PTP messages asynchronously, you must write a class that implements the javax.jms.MessageListener interface. This interface defines an onMessage() method that is automatically called when a message arrives in the subject queue. The code you write for onMessage() defines how you respond to messages arriving in that queue.

Another wrinkle is that the message listener cannot use the same JMS connection factory as code writing to the queue if both are connected to the queue at the same time *and* the connection factory has a nonblank Client ID. Doing so leads to a javax.jms. InvalidClientIDException, which results in the offending code being disconnected from the queue. To avoid this, either use a connection factory with a blank Client ID, or configure a second connection factory for use by the asynchronous queue receiver.

For our example, we'll configure a second connection factory. We start by cloning the JMS connection factory that we created earlier in the chapter, and we'll give it a client ID BibleJMSAsyncClient. We clone the BibleJMSFactory by going into the WebLogic Console, clicking on JMS, and then clicking on Connection Factories. In the pane on the right, you'll see a list of connection factories. Scroll all the way to the right and click the clone icon; it's just to the left of the delete (garbage can) icon. Then change the JNDI Name to BibleJMS-AsyncFactory and change the Client ID to BibleJMSAsyncClient, and click the Clone button. You may need to restart the server for the change to take effect.

Note   Client IDs are not used with queues anyway—they're designed to support durable subscribers to publish-and-subscribe topics. But we're alerting you to this issue because you may encounter it someday on a busy server, and it can be difficult to troubleshoot unless you know the reason.

The class we wrote to receive messages asynchronously is called bible.jms.AsyncQueue Receiver, which appears in Listing 9-5. Its main() method creates an instance of Async QueueReceiver and calls its init() method to initialize JMS structures and register it as a listener for the queue. Next, main() calls AsyncQueueReceiver.wait() (inherited from java.lang.Object) to suspend execution of its thread. This puts AsyncQueueReceiver into a state where it can wait for incoming messages.

Listing 9-5: **AsyncQueueReceiver.java**

```
package bible.jms;

import javax.jms.*;
import javax.naming.*;
import java.util.*;
```

```java
public class AsyncQueueReceiver implements MessageListener {

  // Instance variables.
  private boolean finished = false;
  private Context ctx = null;
  private Hashtable ht = null;
  private QueueConnectionFactory qConnectionFactory = null;
  private QueueConnection qConnection = null;
  private QueueSession qSession = null;
  private QueueReceiver qReceiver = null;
  private Queue q = null;

  public void init() {
    try {
      // Obtain references to JMS queue components.
      ht = new Hashtable();
      ht.put(Context.INITIAL_CONTEXT_FACTORY,
          "weblogic.jndi.WLInitialContextFactory");
      ht.put(Context.PROVIDER_URL, "t3://localhost:7001");
      ctx = new InitialContext(ht);
      qConnectionFactory = (QueueConnectionFactory)
        ctx.lookup("BibleJMSAsyncFactory");
      qConnection =
        qConnectionFactory.createQueueConnection();
      qSession = qConnection.createQueueSession(false,
        javax.jms.QueueSession.AUTO_ACKNOWLEDGE);
      q = (Queue) ctx.lookup("BibleJMSQueue");
      qReceiver = qSession.createReceiver(q);
      qReceiver.setMessageListener(this);
      // Must start the connection in order to listen.
      qConnection.start();
    }
    catch (Exception e) {
      e.printStackTrace();
    }
  }

  public void close()
      throws JMSException
  {
    try {
      // Release JMS resources.
      qReceiver.close();
      qSession.close();
      qConnection.close();
    }
    catch (Exception e) {
      e.printStackTrace();
    }
  }
```

Continued

Listing 9-5 *(continued)*

```java
public void onMessage(Message message) {
  if (message instanceof BytesMessage) {
    BytesMessage bytesMessage = (BytesMessage) message;
    //Process bytesMessage here
  }
  else {
    if (message instanceof MapMessage) {
      MapMessage mapMessage = (MapMessage) message;
      //Process mapMessage here
    }
    else {
      if (message instanceof ObjectMessage) {
        ObjectMessage objectMessage =
          (ObjectMessage) message;
        //Process objectMessage here
      }
      else {
        if (message instanceof StreamMessage) {
          StreamMessage streamMessage =
            (StreamMessage) message;
          //Process streamMessage here
        }
        else {
          if (message instanceof TextMessage) {
            try {
              TextMessage textMessage =
                (TextMessage) message;
              //Process textMessage here
              String msg = textMessage.getText();
              System.out.println("Received message: " +
                                 msg);
              if (msg.equals("Stop")) {
                synchronized(this) {
                  finished = true;
                  // Notify main thread to quit
                  this.notifyAll();
                }
              }
            }
            catch (Exception e) {
              e.printStackTrace();
            }
          }
        }
      }
    }
  }
}
```

```
public static void main(String[] args) {
  try {
    AsyncQueueReceiver qr = new AsyncQueueReceiver();
    qr.init();
    System.out.println("Ready to receive messages....");

    // Receive text messages until one is equal to "Stop"
    synchronized(qr) {
      while (!qr.finished) {
        try {
          qr.wait();
        } catch (InterruptedException ie) {}
      }
    }
    qr.close();
  }
  catch (Exception e) {
    e.printStackTrace();
  }
}
}
```

When a message arrives in `BibleJMSQueue`, JMS invokes `AsyncQueueReceiver.onMessage()`, which resumes execution in `AsyncQueueReceiver`'s thread until `onMessage()` completes. If a `TextMessage` is received whose contents are "Stop," `onMessage()` sets the instance variable `finished` to `true` and then calls `notifyAll()` to awaken the main thread, which closes all JMS connections and quits.

Notice that `onMessage()` is written to handle incoming messages of any type. It is good programming practice to check incoming message types so that your code will be less likely to break if you change your messaging protocols later.

Receiving messages asynchronously from a topic

The code for receiving pub/sub messages asynchronously is nearly identical to the code for receiving PTP messages asynchronously. The only difference is that topics are substituted for queues. In case you skipped the PTP section, I'll describe the process again.

To receive pub/sub messages asynchronously, you must write a class that implements the `javax.jms.MessageListener` interface. This interface defines an `onMessage()` method that is automatically called when a message is published to the topic. The code you write for `onMessage()` defines how you respond to messages published to the topic.

The class we wrote to receive messages asynchronously is called `bible.jms.AsyncTopicSubscriber`, which appears in Listing 9-6. Its `main()` method creates an instance of `AsyncTopicSubscriber` and calls its `init()` method to initialize JMS structures and register it as a subscriber to the topic. Next, `main()` calls `AsyncTopicSubscriber.wait()` (inherited from `java.lang.Object`) to suspend execution of its thread. This puts `AsyncTopicSubscriber` into a state where it can wait for incoming messages.

Listing 9-6: **AsyncTopicSubscriber.java**

```java
package com.wiley.wlsbible.jms;

import javax.jms.*;
import javax.naming.*;
import java.util.*;

public class AsyncTopicSubscriber
  implements MessageListener {

  // Instance variables.
  private boolean finished = false;
  private Context ctx = null;
  private Hashtable ht = null;
  private TopicConnectionFactory tConnectionFactory = null;
  private TopicConnection tConnection = null;
  private TopicSession tSession = null;
  private TopicSubscriber tSubscriber = null;
  private Topic t = null;

  public void init() {
    try {
      // Obtain references to JMS queue components.
      ht = new Hashtable();
      ht.put(Context.INITIAL_CONTEXT_FACTORY,
          "weblogic.jndi.WLInitialContextFactory");
      ht.put(Context.PROVIDER_URL, "t3://localhost:7001");
      ctx = new InitialContext(ht);
      tConnectionFactory =
        (TopicConnectionFactory)
        ctx.lookup("BibleJMSAsyncFactory");
      tConnection =
        tConnectionFactory.createTopicConnection();
      tSession = tConnection.createTopicSession(false,
        javax.jms.QueueSession.AUTO_ACKNOWLEDGE);
      t = (Topic) ctx.lookup("BibleJMSTopic");
      tSubscriber = tSession.createSubscriber(t);
      tSubscriber.setMessageListener(this);
      // Must start the connection in order to listen.
      tConnection.start();
    }
    catch (Exception e) {
      e.printStackTrace();
    }
  }

  public void close() throws JMSException {
    try {
      // Release JMS resources.
      tSubscriber.close();
      tSession.close();
      tConnection.close();
```

```
      }
    catch (Exception e) {
      e.printStackTrace();
    }
}

public void onMessage(Message message) {
  if (message instanceof BytesMessage) {
    BytesMessage bytesMessage = (BytesMessage) message;
    //Process bytesMessage here
  }
  else {
    if (message instanceof MapMessage) {
      MapMessage mapMessage = (MapMessage) message;
      //Process mapMessage here
    }
    else {
      if (message instanceof ObjectMessage) {
        ObjectMessage objectMessage =
          (ObjectMessage) message;
        //Process objectMessage here
      }
      else {
        if (message instanceof StreamMessage) {
          StreamMessage streamMessage =
            (StreamMessage) message;
          //Process streamMessage here
        }
        else {
          if (message instanceof TextMessage) {
            try {
              TextMessage textMessage =
                (TextMessage) message;
              //Process textMessage here
              String msg = textMessage.getText();
              System.out.println("Received message: " +
                                  msg);
              if (msg.equals("Stop")) {
                synchronized(this) {
                  finished = true;
                  // Notify main thread to quit
                  this.notifyAll();
                }
              }
            }
            catch (Exception e) {
              e.printStackTrace();
            }
          }
        }
      }
    }
  }
```

Continued

Listing 9-6 *(continued)*

```
        }
      }

    public static void main(String[] args) {
      try {
        AsyncTopicSubscriber ts = new AsyncTopicSubscriber();
        ts.init();
System.out.println("Ready to receive messages....");

        // Receive text messages until one is equal to "Stop"
        synchronized(ts) {
          while (!ts.finished) {
            try {
              ts.wait();
            } catch (InterruptedException ie) {}
          }
        }
        ts.close();
      }
      catch (Exception e) {
        e.printStackTrace();
      }
    }
  }
```

When a message is published to `BibleJMSTopic`, JMS invokes `AsyncTopicSubscriber.onMessage()`, which resumes execution in `AsyncTopicSubscriber`'s thread until `onMessage()` completes. If a `TextMessage` is received whose contents are "Stop," `onMessage()` sets the instance variable `finished` to true; it then calls `notifyAll()` to awaken the main thread, which closes all JMS connections and quits.

Notice that `onMessage()` is written to handle incoming messages of any type. It's good programming practice to check incoming message types, so your code will be less likely to break if you change your messaging protocols later.

Receiving from a topic using a multicast session

WebLogic's JMS implementation supports *multicasting*, in which messages are simultaneously delivered to multiple hosts and then forwarded by these hosts to subscribers. Multicasting provides increased messaging throughput at the expense of reliability because not all messages are guaranteed to be delivered to all hosts. This makes multicasting useful for applications where large numbers of messages must be delivered to large numbers of recipients, and where the negative impact of lost messages is minor. Multicasting can be used for publish-and-subscribe messaging only.

To receive messages from a topic that participates in a multicast session, simply change the call to create the `TopicSession` as follows:

```
tSession = tConnection.createTopicSession(false,
          WLSession.MULTICAST_NO_ACKNOWLEDGE);
```

Then create a topic subscriber as usual:

```
tSubscriber = tSession.createSubscriber(t);
```

Receiving messages concurrently using session pools

WebLogic session pools provide a convenient way to deploy asynchronous message listeners to WebLogic Server without having to set up and tear down the JMS infrastructure. For each session pool you create, WebLogic allocates a thread and JMS session for the message listener you provide.

Receiving messages by using session pools is identical to receiving messages asynchronously. Simply write a class that implements the `MessageListener` interface, implement the `onMessage()` method, deploy it to the server bound to a session pool, and you're in business. In fact, the `onMessage()` method is *all* you need to write—WebLogic handles the JMS infrastructure for you, so there's no need to obtain server contexts, connections, sessions, or any other JMS structures.

Before using session pools, consider the following caveats:

✦ Participants in a session pool consume messages concurrently, so message ordering is not guaranteed.

✦ There is no way to predict which participant in a pool will receive any given message, so session pools should be used only for "stateless" conversations, in which the identity of a message's recipient doesn't matter.

Listing 9-7 shows the code for `SessionPoolConsumer.java`, a class that can be used in conjunction with session pools to consume messages for queues or topics.

Listing 9-7: **SessionPoolConsumer.java**

```
package com.wiley.wlsbible.jms;

import javax.jms.*;

public class SessionPoolConsumer implements MessageListener {

  public void onMessage(Message message) {
    if (message instanceof BytesMessage) {
      BytesMessage bytesMessage = (BytesMessage) message;
      //Process bytesMessage here
    }
    else {
      if (message instanceof MapMessage) {
        MapMessage mapMessage = (MapMessage) message;
        //Process mapMessage here
      }
      else {
        if (message instanceof ObjectMessage) {
          ObjectMessage objectMessage =
            (ObjectMessage) message;
          //Process objectMessage here
```

Continued

Listing 9-7 *(continued)*

```
        }
      else {
        if (message instanceof StreamMessage) {
          StreamMessage streamMessage =
            (StreamMessage) message;
          //Process streamMessage here
        }
        else {
          if (message instanceof TextMessage) {
            try {
              TextMessage textMessage =
                (TextMessage) message;
              //Process textMessage here
              String msg = textMessage.getText();
              System.out.println("Received message: " +
                                  msg);
              if (msg.equals("Stop")) {
                synchronized(this) {
                  finished = true;
                  // Notify main thread to quit
                  this.notifyAll();
                }
              }
            }
            catch (Exception e) {
              e.printStackTrace();
            }
          }
        }
      }
    }
  }
}
```

Notice that SessionPoolConsumer is nothing more than the onMessage() method you implemented earlier in both the AsyncQueueReceiver and AsyncTopicSubscriber classes (Listings 9-5 and 9-6, respectively).

Because of issues with client IDs that we discussed earlier in the chapter, we need to clone the BibleJMSFactory in the WebLogic Console and give it a new JNDI Name of BibleJMS-ConsumerFactory and a Client ID of BibleJMSConsumerClient. Restart the server before continuing.

After deploying the SessionPoolConsumer class to your WebLogic classpath, the next step is to configure a session pool in the WebLogic Console to which you can bind SessionPool-Consumer. To do this, expand the Servers node under JMS in the domain tree and then expand the node for BibleJMSServer (the server created earlier in this chapter). Click Session Pools, and then click Configure a New JMS Session Pool. The session pool configuration screen appears, as shown in Figure 9-15.

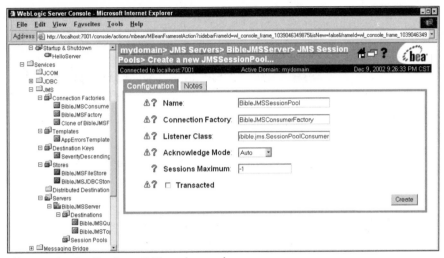

Figure 9-15: Configuring a JMS session pool

The entries on this page are as follows:

✦ **Name:** A name for the session pool, which must conform to the rules for Java identifiers and be unique within the WebLogic Server instance or its cluster. For this example, type **BibleJMSSessionPool**.

✦ **Connection Factory:** The name of a connection factory that has already been defined for the server or cluster. Type **BibleJMSFactory**, the factory you created earlier in this chapter.

✦ **Listener Class:** The fully qualified name of the class that provides the `onMessage()` method for listening on the session. For this example, type **com.wiley.wlsbible. jms.SessionPoolConsumer**, the class shown in Listing 9-7.

Caution You must correctly deploy the listener class to the WebLogic classpath, or else the creation of the session pool will fail.

✦ **Acknowledge Mode:** The mode you want the session pool to use to acknowledge messages, chosen from the list in Table 9-1. Choose Auto for this example.

✦ **Sessions Maximum:** The maximum number of sessions you want WebLogic to allocate to this session pool. A value of -1 means no limit, which is fine for this example.

✦ **Transacted:** Check this box if you want message processing in the session to occur in the context of JMS transactions. For this example, leave the box unchecked.

After completing the configuration screen, click Create.

After you create the session pool, you must create a consumer within that pool that binds the listener class to a queue or topic defined on the server. To do so, expand the pool you just created in the domain tree, and then click Consumers. Click Configure a New JMS Connection Consumer at the top of the page; the configuration screen shown in Figure 9-16 appears:

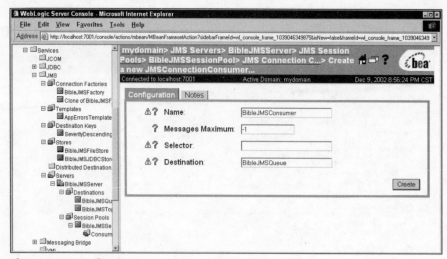

Figure 9-16: Configuring a connection consumer for a session pool

The entries on this page are as follows:

✦ **Name:** A name for the connection consumer, which must conform to the rules for Java identifiers and be unique within the WebLogic Server instance or its cluster. For the example, type **BibleJMSConsumer**.

✦ **Messages Maximum:** The maximum number of messages you want this consumer to manage. A value of -1 means no limit, which is fine for this example.

✦ **Selector:** A valid message selector statement used to filter messages. For more details, see the next section.

✦ **Destination:** The queue or topic, already defined on your WebLogic Server, to which the message listener should be bound. For this example, type **BibleJMSQueue**, the queue you defined earlier in this chapter.

After completing the configuration screen, click Create. You must stop and restart the server to use `BibleJMSQueue`. The session pool is now ready for use. In this example, sending messages to `BibleJMSQueue` with the `BibleQueueSender` class you wrote earlier (Listing 9-1) results in the session pool writing the following output to the WebLogic command window:

```
Receiving messages from queue...
  Receiving message: Message #1 to queue
  Receiving message: Message #2 to queue
  Receiving message: Message #3 to queue
  Receiving message: Message #4 to queue
  Receiving message: Message #5 to queue
  Receiving message: Message #6 to queue
  Receiving message: Message #7 to queue
  Receiving message: Message #8 to queue
  Receiving message: Message #9 to queue
  Receiving message: Message #10 to queue
  Receiving message: Stop
```

Note   After setting up and running this example, none of the other queue examples (receive, browse) will work because all messages are now being pulled off the queue by this session pool. So remember to delete the session pool before continuing with the other examples. Do this by clicking BibleJMSServer in the WebLogic Console, click Configure Session Pools, and then click the trash can icon next to this session pool.

Filtering incoming messages

By default, a queue receiver or a topic subscriber retrieves all incoming messages on a queue or topic. But you may want to filter messages based on various criteria to accomplish certain tasks. You may, for example, want to write an asynchronous queue receiver or topic subscriber that immediately acts on log messages with high severity, leaving the rest in the queue for overnight batch processing.

To activate a filter, you specify a *message selector* when you create the queue receiver or topic subscriber. A message selector is a conditional expression, written using SQL-92 syntax and stored in a `String` that JMS applies to incoming messages in the queue or topic. The message selector is compared against the properties of incoming messages. Therefore, to use message selectors, you must set the properties in your messages to known values.

To understand how message selectors work, recall the code from `BibleQueueSender` (Listing 9-1) that set an `int` property called `severity` for each message to the value of the `for` loop counter. The property is also set to zero for the "stop" message:

```
for (int i=1; i<=10; i++) {
  msg = "Message #" + i;
  textMsg.clearBody();
  textMsg.setIntProperty("severity", i);
  textMsg.setText(msg);
  System.out.println("  Sending message: " + msg);
  qSender.send(textMsg);
}
msg = "Stop";
textMsg.clearBody();
textMsg.setIntProperty("severity", 0);
textMsg.setText(msg);
System.out.println("  Sending message: " + msg);
qSender.send(textMsg);
```

You can filter this property by using a message selector. To include only messages with severity less than 5, for example, we can modify `SyncQueueReceiver` (Listing 9-3) by creating a queue receiver with the appropriate message selector attached:

```
qReceiver = qSession.createReceiver(q, "severity < 5");
```

This results in the following output from `SyncQueueReceiver`:

```
Receiving messages...
  Receiving message: Message #1
  Receiving message: Message #2
  Receiving message: Message #3
  Receiving message: Message #4
  Receiving message: Stop
```

Consider a few more examples of message selectors. To select messages whose severity is between 3 and 7 inclusive, write a message selector like this:

```
"severity >= 3 and severity <= 7"
```

Or, equivalently:

```
"severity between 3 and 7"
```

To select messages whose severity is equal to 7 or 9, write this:

```
"severity = 7 or severity = 9"
```

If you're filtering on String properties, note that strings are enclosed in single quotes and are case-sensitive, as in:

```
"strProperty = 'hello world'"
```

To select messages containing the string pattern #3, use the % character as a wildcard, like this:

```
"strProperty like '%#3%'"
```

Cross-Reference You can find additional message selector examples in the WebLogic manual, *Developing a WebLogic JMS Application,* which is part of the WebLogic documentation set.

Just as queue receivers can filter incoming messages on their queues, topic subscribers can filter incoming messages on their topics using the same mechanism. The only exception is that the filter is applied when creating the topic subscriber:

```
tSubscriber =
    tSession.createSubscriber(t, "severity < 5", true);
```

The variant of TopicSession.createSubscriber() used in this code also requires a Boolean value specifying whether to exclude locally generated messages from the topic (messages published to the topic by the subscriber). If noLocal is true, locally generated messages are excluded.

Browsing messages in a queue

When a QueueReceiver receives messages from a queue, it removes them from the queue. In some cases, however, it might be convenient to examine a queue's contents *before* receiving messages, perhaps to allow a user to interactively choose which messages to remove and when. JMS provides two methods in the QueueSession interface for this purpose:

```
public QueueBrowser createBrowser(Queue queue)
                        throws JMSException

public QueueBrowser createBrowser(Queue queue,
                        java.lang.String messageSelector)
                        throws JMSException
```

The first version of createBrowser takes a Queue as input and returns a java.util. Enumeration listing the messages in that queue, in the order in which they will be delivered. The second version takes a Queue and a String as input, allowing you to filter the browse results with a message selector. Both methods return a snapshot of the queue at the moment of the method call. If you think the queue has changed and you want to update the browse list, you must call createBrowser again. Neither method removes messages from the queue.

Listing 9-8 contains a simple class, BrowseQueue, to browse a queue. It provides no message selector, so it simply prints all messages in the queue to standard output.

Listing 9-8: **BrowseQueue.java**

```
package com.wiley.wlsbible.jms;

import javax.jms.*;
import javax.naming.*;
import java.util.*;

public class BrowseQueue {

  public static void main(String[] args) {
    Context ctx = null;
    Hashtable ht = new Hashtable();
    QueueConnectionFactory qConnectionFactory = null;
    QueueConnection qConnection = null;
    QueueSession qSession = null;
    QueueBrowser qBrowser = null;
    Queue q = null;
    TextMessage textMsg = null;
    String msg;

    try {
      // Obtain references to JMS queue components.
      ht.put(Context.INITIAL_CONTEXT_FACTORY,
             "weblogic.jndi.WLInitialContextFactory");
      ht.put(Context.PROVIDER_URL, "t3://localhost:7001");
      ctx = new InitialContext(ht);
      qConnectionFactory =
        (QueueConnectionFactory)
        ctx.lookup("BibleJMSFactory");
      qConnection =
        qConnectionFactory.createQueueConnection();
      qSession = qConnection.createQueueSession(false,
        javax.jms.QueueSession.AUTO_ACKNOWLEDGE);
      q = (Queue) ctx.lookup("BibleJMSQueue");
      qBrowser = qSession.createBrowser(q);

      System.out.println("Browsing messages...");
      Enumeration enum = qBrowser.getEnumeration();
      while (enum.hasMoreElements()) {
        textMsg = (TextMessage) enum.nextElement();
        System.out.println("    " + textMsg.getText());
      }
    }
    catch (Exception e) {
      e.printStackTrace();
    }
```

Continued

Listing 9-8 *(continued)*

```
      finally {
        try {
          // Release JMS resources.
          qBrowser.close();
          qSession.close();
          qConnection.close();
        }
        catch (Exception e) {
          e.printStackTrace();
        }
      }
    }
}
```

The resulting output is the following:

```
Browsing messages...
    Message #2
    Message #3
    Message #4
    Message #5
    Message #6
    Message #7
    Message #8
    Message #9
    Message #10
    Stop
```

To filter the results, simply modify the line that creates the QueueBrowser, as follows:

```
qBrowser = qSession.createBrowser(q, "severity > 8");
```

This modification changes the output to the following:

```
Browsing messages...
    Message #9
    Message #10
```

Note   Browsing is available only for queues. You cannot browse the contents of a publish-subscribe topic.

Creating durable subscribers to topics

Recall that messages are delivered to topic subscribers only when subscribers are actively listening for messages. If a subscriber quits and restarts later, messages published in the interim are never delivered to that subscriber. Such a subscriber is called a *nondurable subscriber*, and it is the default subscriber type in JMS.

You can, however, create a subscriber that receives all messages published to a topic, even if the subscriber is not actively listening when the messages are sent. Such a subscriber is called a *durable subscriber*. Durable subscribers receive all messages posted to a topic *after* the subscriber's initial registration with the topic.

The "preferred" way to support durable subscriptions is to configure WebLogic JMS as follows:

1. Specify a connection factory with a defined `Client ID` for each durable subscriber. The `Client ID`, a `String`, must be unique within the WebLogic Server or cluster in which it resides. For information on how to do this, see the section titled "Creating a connection factory," earlier in this chapter.

2. Define a file or JDBC backing store to hold undelivered messages. Instructions for doing so appear earlier in this chapter (in the sections titled "Defining a file backing store" and "Defining a JDBC backing store").

3. Define a JMS server that uses the backing store you create. Instructions for doing so appear in the section titled "Defining a JMS server," earlier in this chapter.

4. Define a message topic for which `Enable Store` is `true`. Instructions for doing so appear in the section titled "Creating a message topic," earlier in this chapter.

After you configure JMS for durable subscribers, call one of the following `TopicSession` methods to create a durable subscriber:

```
public TopicSubscriber createDurableSubscriber(
    Topic topic,
    String name) throws JMSException
```

```
public TopicSubscriber createDurableSubscriber)
    Topic topic,
    String name,
    String messageSelector,
    boolean noLocal) throws JMSException
```

where `myTopic` is a reference to the appropriate `Topic`, `myName` is a `String` that is unique for the given `Client ID`, `messageSelector` is a valid filter expression, and `noLocal` is true if the subscriber should not receive messages it publishes itself.

You also can support durable subscriptions by dynamically setting a `Client ID` for the subscriber in code without reconfiguring JMS. To do so, you must call the following `Topic-Connection` method immediately after creating a connection:

```
public void setClientID(String clientID) throws JMSException
```

Problems may arise if you specify a `Client ID` that is already in use or if two blocks of code are trying to specify the same `Client ID` at the same time. In the latter case, `setClientID` does not throw an exception, but the durable subscriber does not work. To avoid this, test for a duplicate `Client ID` by first calling `TopicConnection.getClientID()`:

```
public String getClientID() throws JMSException
```

Working with Transactions

Transactions enable you to send and receive messages in logical groups that represent units of work. Committing a group of messages results in all messages being sent or received, whereas rolling back a group of messages results in none of them being sent or received.

JMS sessions that manage transactions are called *JMS-transacted sessions*. WebLogic also supports transactions that span JMS and other components, such as EJBs. The Java Transaction API (JTA) manages these transactions.

 Cross-Reference   Chapter 6 covers JTA in detail.

Working with JMS-transacted sessions

When working with JMS-transacted sessions, the first step is to make sure that the connection factory you intend to use has a transaction timeout period long enough to support the expected maximum length of your transactions. This parameter is set in the WebLogic Console page for the connection factory under the `Transactions` tab, as shown in Figure 9-17:

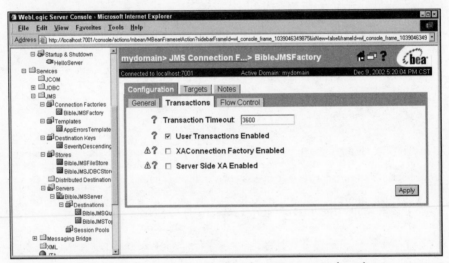

Figure 9-17: Configuring the transaction timeout for JMS-transacted sessions

By default, a connection factory's `Transaction Timeout` is set to 3600 seconds (one hour). This should be more than long enough for most applications. If a transaction is held open beyond the timeout period, JMS automatically rolls it back.

 Note   The User Transactions Enabled checkbox makes the connection factory JTA-aware. Leave it unchecked for now; we discuss JTA transactions in the next section.

To use a JMS-transacted session, set the `transacted` Boolean variable to `true` when you create a `QueueSession` or `TopicSession`:

```
qSession = qConnection.createQueueSession(true,
        javax.jms.QueueSession.AUTO_ACKNOWLEDGE);

tSession = tConnection.createTopicSession(true,
        javax.jms.TopicSession.AUTO_ACKNOWLEDGE);
```

Recall that `ACKNOWLEDGE_MODE` is ignored for transacted sessions, so the value you provide (in this case, `AUTO_ACKNOWLEDGE`) doesn't matter.

The following code snippet, adapted from `BibleQueueSender.java` (Listing 9-1), illustrates how to create a JMS-transacted session and how to commit and roll back transactions:

```
qSession = qConnection.createQueueSession(true,
        javax.jms.QueueSession.AUTO_ACKNOWLEDGE);
q = (Queue) ctx.lookup("BibleJMSQueue");
qSender = qSession.createSender(q);

System.out.println("Sending messages...");
textMsg = qSession.createTextMessage();
for (int i=1; i<=10; i++) {
  msg = "Message #" + i;
  textMsg.clearBody();
  textMsg.setIntProperty("severity", i);
  textMsg.setText(msg);
  System.out.println("  Sending message: " + msg);
  qSender.send(textMsg);
}
// Cancel the 10 messages sent so far.
qSession.rollback();
msg = "Stop";
textMsg.clearBody();
textMsg.setText(msg);
textMsg.setIntProperty("severity", 0);
System.out.println("  Sending message: " + msg);
qSender.send(textMsg);
// Commit the "Stop" message.
qSession.commit();
```

The result of this code is that the 10 messages sent in the `for` loop will not be sent, but the "stop" message will be sent. The output from running this program is therefore the following:

```
Receiving messages...
  Receiving message: Stop
```

Note that JMS transactions execute back-to-back; transaction boundaries are set by calls to `commit()` and `rollback()`. These calls also reset the transaction timeout counter for the active session. The first transaction in a program, however, is implicitly made active when the transacted session is created.

Working with JTA transactions

The Java Transaction API (JTA) supports transactions spanning multiple data sources. You can use JTA, for example, to manage a transaction that involves receiving a JMS message, writing a row to a JDBC database, invoking a method in an EJB, and then sending a different JMS message elsewhere. If all four operations succeed, the transaction is committed; otherwise, it is rolled back and the effects of the operations are reversed as if they never happened.

JTA and JMS transactions are independent of each other and do not cooperate in any way. The effects of JMS transactions are ignored by JTA and vice versa. Also, JTA transactions work only within the context of synchronous messaging; asynchronous message listeners cannot participate in JTA transactions unless they are implemented by using message-driven EJBs.

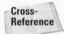

Cross-Reference   Chapter 17 covers using JTA with message-driven EJBs.

Consider an example in which an online brokerage client wants to purchase 1000 shares of BEA stock. The client enters his order on the brokerage's Web site, which causes a message to be written to an order queue. After the market closes, a Java application settles the transaction by performing these steps:

1. Initiates a JTA transaction.

2. Retrieves the client's purchase order synchronously from the queue.

3. Calculates the amount of cash required to purchase the stock.

4. Retrieves the client's cash account balance from an account database.

5. Deducts the amount required from the account database if the client has enough cash for the purchase. If not, it throws an insufficient funds exception.

6. Adds the shares purchased to the client's portfolio database. If this operation fails for any reason, it throws an exception.

7. If no exceptions were thrown, it commits the transaction. Otherwise, it rolls back the transaction, and the effects of all operations up to and including the step where the exception occurred are reversed.

Listing 9-9 is `ClientHandler.java`, an application that performs the preceding tasks. The `main()` method starts by loading `BibleJMSQueue` with a "test" trade. Then it initiates a JTA transaction, within which it removes the trade from the queue, updates the client's account data in Oracle, and updates the client's portfolio in Oracle. If all operations succeed, it commits the transaction. Otherwise, it rolls back the transaction, which has the following effects:

1. JMS returns the trade to the queue.

2. Oracle reverses the update to the account data.

3. Oracle reverses the update to the portfolio data.

Listing 9-9: **ClientHandler.java**

```java
package com.wiley.wlsbible.jms;

import java.util.*;
import java.sql.*;
import javax.jms.*;
import javax.naming.*;
import javax.transaction.UserTransaction;

public class ClientHandler {

  // Unique client ID for
  // database operations
  private String clientID = null;

  // Data structure describing a trade
  private class Trade {
    String clientID = null;
    String side = null;
    String ticker = null;
    int shares = 0;
    double sharePrice = 0.0;
  }

  public ClientHandler() {
  }

  public ClientHandler(String id) {
    clientID = id;
  }

  // Get the WebLogic server's context
  public Context getServerContext() {
    Context ctx = null;
    Hashtable ht = new Hashtable();
    ht.put(Context.INITIAL_CONTEXT_FACTORY,
      "weblogic.jndi.WLInitialContextFactory");
    ht.put(Context.PROVIDER_URL,
      "t3://localhost:7001");

    try {
      ctx = new InitialContext(ht);
    }
    catch (NamingException e) {
      e.printStackTrace();
    }
    finally {
      return ctx;
    }
```

Continued

Listing 9-9 *(continued)*

```java
}

// Load the queue with a single trade:
// BUY 1000 shares BEAS at $30/share
public void loadQueue() {
  Context ctx = null;
  QueueConnectionFactory qConnectionFactory = null;
  QueueConnection qConnection = null;
  QueueSession qSession = null;
  QueueSender qSender = null;
  Queue q = null;
  TextMessage textMsg = null;

  try {
    // Obtain references to JMS structures
    qConnectionFactory =
      (QueueConnectionFactory)
      getServerContext().lookup("BibleJMSFactory");
    qConnection =
      qConnectionFactory.createQueueConnection();
    qSession = qConnection.createQueueSession(false,
      javax.jms.QueueSession.AUTO_ACKNOWLEDGE);
    q = (Queue) getServerContext().lookup("BibleJMSQueue");
    qSender = qSession.createSender(q);
    textMsg = qSession.createTextMessage();

    // Pass a human-readable trade summary
    // in the message's body
    textMsg.clearBody();
    textMsg.setText("BUY 1000 BEAS 30.0");

    // Pass essential trade data in
    // user-defined message properties
    textMsg.setStringProperty("client_id", clientID);
    textMsg.setStringProperty("side", "BUY");
    textMsg.setStringProperty("ticker", "BEAS");
    textMsg.setIntProperty("shares", 1000);
    textMsg.setDoubleProperty("sharePrice", 30.0);

    // Send the message
    qSender.send(textMsg);
  }
  catch (Exception e) {
    e.printStackTrace();
  }
  finally {
    try {
      if (qSender != null) {
        qSender.close();
      }
      if (qSession != null) {
```

```
        qSession.close();
      }
      if (qConnection != null) {
        qConnection.close();
      }
    }
    catch (Exception e) {
    }
  }
}

// Synchronously read a single trade from
// the queue for the given client
public Trade getNextTrade() throws Exception {
  QueueConnectionFactory qConnectionFactory = null;
  QueueConnection qConnection = null;
  QueueSession qSession = null;
  QueueReceiver qReceiver = null;
  Queue q = null;
  Trade trade = null;

  try {
    // Obtain references to JMS structures
    qConnectionFactory =
      (QueueConnectionFactory)
      getServerContext().lookup("BibleJMSFactory");
    qConnection =
     qConnectionFactory.createQueueConnection();
    qSession = qConnection.createQueueSession(false,
      javax.jms.QueueSession.AUTO_ACKNOWLEDGE);
    q = (Queue) getServerContext().lookup("BibleJMSQueue");

    // Note the use of a message filter - we
    // only want the next trade for the client
    // represented by this ClientHandler instance
    qReceiver = qSession.createReceiver(q,
      "client_id = '" + clientID + "'");

    // Start the connection
    qConnection.start();

    // Grab the next trade, if there is one,
    // and copy its data from the message
    // properties to a Trade data structure
    TextMessage textMsg =
      (TextMessage) qReceiver.receiveNoWait();
    if (textMsg != null) {
      trade = new Trade();
      trade.clientID = clientID;
      trade.side = textMsg.getStringProperty("side");
      trade.ticker = textMsg.getStringProperty("ticker");
      trade.shares = textMsg.getIntProperty("shares");
```

Continued

Listing 9-9 *(continued)*

```
        trade.sharePrice =
          textMsg.getDoubleProperty("sharePrice");
      }

      // Stop the connection
      qConnection.stop();
    }
    catch (Exception e) {
      throw e;
    }
    finally {
      try {
        if (qReceiver != null) {
          qReceiver.close();
        }
        if (qSession != null) {
          qSession.close();
        }
        if (qConnection != null) {
          qConnection.close();
        }
      }
      catch (Exception e) {
      }
      return trade;
    }
  }

  // Update the cash balance remaining in
  // the client's account. Account data is
  // stored in an Oracle table. For simplicity,
  // this code handles BUY transactions only.
  public void updateAccountBalance(Trade trade)
  throws Exception {
    javax.sql.DataSource ds = null;
    java.sql.Connection conn = null;
    PreparedStatement statement1 = null;
    PreparedStatement statement2 = null;
    String sql = null;
    double balance = 0.0;

    try {
      // Obtain a JDBC connection from a transaction-enabled
      // DataSource. I'm using the Oracle thin driver
      // with two-phase commit enabled, rather than
      // the Oracle XA driver.
      ds = (javax.sql.DataSource)
        getServerContext().lookup("jdbc/OraclePoolTxDataSource");
      conn = ds.getConnection();

      // Execute a query to obtain the client's current
```

```
    // account balance from the database.
    sql = "SELECT BALANCE FROM ACCOUNT_BIBLE " +
          "WHERE CLIENT_ID = ?";
    statement1 = conn.prepareStatement(sql);
    statement1.setString(1, clientID);
    ResultSet resultSet = statement1.executeQuery();
    if (resultSet.next()) {
      balance = resultSet.getDouble(1);
    } else {
      Exception ex = new Exception("No such account");
      throw ex;
    }

    // Calculate the cash required to buy the stock
    double cost = trade.sharePrice * trade.shares;

    // If the client has enough money, deduct the
    // cost from their account balance and update
    // their account in the database.
    if (balance > cost) {
      balance -= cost;
      sql = "UPDATE ACCOUNT_BIBLE SET BALANCE = ? " +
            "WHERE CLIENT_ID = ?";
      statement2 = conn.prepareStatement(sql);
      statement2.setDouble(1, balance);
      statement2.setString(2, clientID);
      if (statement2.executeUpdate() != 1) {
        Exception ex =
          new Exception("Error updating account balance");
        throw ex;
      }
    } else {
      Exception ex = new Exception("Insufficient funds");
      throw ex;
    }

  }
  catch (Exception e) {
    e.printStackTrace();
    throw e;
  }
  finally {
    statement1.close();
    statement2.close();
    conn.close();
  }
}

// Add an entry for stock purchased to
// the client's portfolio, which is stored
// in an Oracle table.
public void updatePortfolio(Trade trade) throws Exception {
```

Continued

Listing 9-9 *(continued)*

```
    javax.sql.DataSource ds = null;
    java.sql.Connection conn = null;
    PreparedStatement statement = null;
    String sql = null;

    try {
      // Obtain a JDBC connection from a transaction-enabled
      // DataSource. I'm using the Oracle thin driver
      // with two-phase commit enabled, rather than
      // the Oracle XA driver.
      ds = (javax.sql.DataSource)
        getServerContext().lookup("jdbc/OraclePoolTxDataSource");
      conn = ds.getConnection();

      // Execute a query to insert the client's stock
      // purchase into the portfolio table.
      sql = "INSERT INTO PORTFOLIO " +
            "(CLIENT_ID, SIDE, TICKER, SHARES, PRICE) " +
            "VALUES (?, ?, ?, ?, ?)";
      statement = conn.prepareStatement(sql);
      statement.setString(1, clientID);
      statement.setString(2, trade.side);
      statement.setString(3, trade.ticker);
      statement.setInt(4, trade.shares);
      statement.setDouble(5, trade.sharePrice);
      if (statement.executeUpdate() != 1) {
        Exception ex =
          new Exception("Error updating client's portfolio");
        throw ex;
      }
    }
    catch (Exception e) {
      e.printStackTrace();
      throw e;
    }
    finally {
      statement.close();
      conn.close();
    }
  }

  // Method to test our example
  public static void main(String[] args) {

    UserTransaction tx = null;

    try {
      // Create a ClientHandler instance for fictitious
      // customer "joe." Load the queue with a hard-coded
      // trade for this client.
```

```
      ClientHandler ch = new ClientHandler("joe");
      ch.loadQueue();

      // Obtain a reference to WebLogic Server's context.
      // Use it to perform a JNDI lookup on the server's
      // UserTransaction object.
      Context ctx = ch.getServerContext();
      tx = (UserTransaction)
        ctx.lookup("javax.transaction.UserTransaction");

      // Begin the transaction
      tx.begin();
      // Grab the trade from the message queue
      Trade trade = ch.getNextTrade();
      // Update the client's account balance
      ch.updateAccountBalance(trade);
      // Update the client's portfolio
      ch.updatePortfolio(trade);
      // If no exceptions, commit the transaction
      tx.commit();
    }
  catch (Exception e) {
    try {
      // Something went wrong... roll back
      // the transaction
      tx.rollback();
    }
    catch (Exception ee) {
      ee.printStackTrace();
    }
  }
}
}
```

Listing 9-10 shows the simple tables we added to Oracle's SCOTT schema to support the example.

Listing 9-10: **Trading System Table Definitions**

```
CREATE TABLE SCOTT.ACCOUNT_BIBLE
(
    CLIENT_ID VARCHAR2(10) NOT NULL,
    BALANCE   NUMBER(10,2)     NULL
);

CREATE TABLE SCOTT.PORTFOLIO
(
    CLIENT_ID VARCHAR2(10) NOT NULL,
    SIDE      CHAR(4)          NULL,
```

Continued

Listing 9-10 *(continued)*

```
    TICKER     VARCHAR2(10)      NULL,
    SHARES     NUMBER(10)        NULL,
    PRICE      NUMBER(10,2)      NULL
);
```

Add one record to the `ACCOUNT_BIBLE` table, with a `CLIENT_ID` = joe and `BALANCE` = 50 000.00.

To connect to the database in a transaction-enabled mode, we used the JDBC connection pool we created in Chapter 5 named `OraclePool` and its corresponding TxDataSource with a JNDI name of `jdbc/OraclePoolTxDataSource`.

Cross-Reference See Chapter 5 for more information on configuring JDBC connection pools and transaction-enabled data sources.

Finally, we made sure that our JMS connection factory, `BibleJMSFactory`, was JTA-enabled. To do so, we edited the factory in the WebLogic Console. On the factory's Transaction tab (see Figure 9-17) is a checkbox, `User Transactions Enabled`, which we checked.

 Tip Study Listing 9-9 carefully. It's well commented, and gives a good, real-world example of JMS and JDBC in action in a transacted environment. Considering the incredible amount of work that is being done (messaging and database operations controlled by a transaction manager using two-phase commit), the amount of code required is very small, which is a testament to the power of WebLogic and J2EE.

Summary

WebLogic JMS is a powerful messaging system that enables you to build flexible communications into your distributed applications. WebLogic JMS supports two messaging models: point-to-point (using queues), and publish-subscribe (using topics). Within each mode, you can easily send many types of messages, as well as receive them either synchronously or asynchronously.

Although JMS code is easy to write, the WebLogic JMS infrastructure requires a fair amount of configuration before it can be used. Fortunately, the WebLogic Console provides an intuitive interface for performing the multitude of configuration tasks, which this chapter has shown you how to do in significant detail.

JMS derives a significant amount of its power from its integration with the rest of J2EE. Foremost in this regard is the capability of JMS to participate in transactions that incorporate messaging, database operations (using JDBC), and business logic (using EJBs). The JMS transactional capabilities, which result from its seamless integration with the Java Transaction API (JTA), enable developers to incorporate messaging into robust, fault-tolerant applications that work with a multitude of enterprise data sources.

✦   ✦   ✦

Working with WebLogic JavaMail

The JavaMail API provides interfaces and abstract classes that developers can use to write functionally complete mail clients by using a variety of mail transfer protocols. Sun and third-party vendors have extended the API to provide protocol-specific implementations.

Early in this chapter, we give you an overview of the JavaMail architecture and show you how to configure WebLogic JavaMail for various protocols. Later in the chapter, we provide several code examples that show you how to send mail via SMTP, navigate folders, and receive mail via IMAP or POP3.

Understanding JavaMail

This section gives you an introduction to JavaMail's organization, architecture, and features. A firm understanding of these concepts makes programming JavaMail much easier.

JavaMail versions and packages

WebLogic 7.0 runs on top of JDK 1.3.1, and `weblogic.jar` contains JavaMail version 1.1.3. But JavaMail 1.3 is the latest version supported by Sun. JavaMail 1.1.3 includes support for SMTP and IMAP (discussed later in this chapter), and JavaMail 1.3 adds support for POP3. You can download JavaMail 1.3 from the Sun Web site and then insert it into your classpath ahead of `weblogic.jar` to suppress the 1.1.3 API.

The intention of the Sun JavaMail specification is to describe a generic interface for mail network servers regardless of the mail protocol used by that server. The API is not a mail server application, but rather a Java interface to network mail servers that support SMTP, IMAP, and POP3.

JavaMail is implemented in the following packages:

✦ `javax.mail`, which contains the first part of the JavaMail API and provides abstract implementations of addresses, messages, parts, stores, transports, and related classes.

✦ `javax.mail.internet`, which contains the remainder of the JavaMail API and provides abstract implementations of Internet addresses and MIME messages and body parts.

✦ `javax.activation`, which contains the JavaBeans Activation Framework (JAF). Unlike earlier versions of WebLogic Server, version 7.0 now comes with the JAF. The function of JAF is to handle access to data based on data type and to facilitate the addition of data types and commands on those data types. The JavaMail API provides convenience functions to simplify these coding tasks.

You can find the JavaMail 1.3 specification, API, and tutorial on the Sun Web site at the following URL:

    http://java.sun.com/products/javamail/index.html

And you can find more information about the JAF here:

    http://java.sun.com/products/javabeans/glasgow/jaf.html

JavaMail architecture

JavaMail has a multilayered architecture, as shown in Figure 10-1.

Mail-handling functions are provided in the abstract layer interfaces, abstract, and concrete classes. You can extend mail-handling functions as necessary in order to support standard data types, and to interface with message access and message transport protocols.

RFC822 and MIME Internet standards are implemented as part of the abstract layer. The JAF is used to encapsulate message data and to handle commands intended to interact with message data.

Service providers implement the JavaMail API, which in turn is utilized by a JavaMail client. The layered design architecture enables clients to use the same JavaMail API calls to send, receive, and store a variety of messages by using different data types from different message stores and by using different message transport protocols.

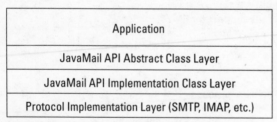

| Application |
| JavaMail API Abstract Class Layer |
| JavaMail API Implementation Class Layer |
| Protocol Implementation Layer (SMTP, IMAP, etc.) |

Figure 10-1: The JavaMail architecture

Mail protocols

Three major protocols are used to send mail messages around the Internet: SMTP, POP, and IMAP. Although other protocols exist, these three are the most commonly used and are therefore the focus of this chapter:

✦ *SMTP*, which stands for *Simple Mail Transfer Protocol*, is the protocol used by mail servers to send messages to each other. It is also used by mail clients to send messages to mail servers. When you send a mail message, it travels first from your mail client to your mail server. From there, it is sent to one or more destination mail servers, depending on the number of recipients and the configurations of the mail servers involved.

✦ *POP*, which stands for *Post Office Protocol,* is used by mail clients to retrieve incoming messages from mail servers. Two versions of POP exist. The first is POP2, which emerged in the mid-1980s and requires SMTP to function. The second is POP3, which became widespread in the 1990s and can function with or without SMTP. POP3 is used almost exclusively by POP clients today.

✦ *IMAP* means *Internet Message Access Protocol.* Like POP, IMAP is used by mail clients to retrieve messages from servers. The latest version, IMAP4, is similar to POP3, but it includes additional features that allow you to inspect messages on the server before downloading them to the client.

JavaMail services, transports, and stores

The JavaMail API represents mail protocols as services, transports, and stores. Classes representing these entities are used to send and receive messages. The abstract class `javax.mail.Service` is at the top of the hierarchy and is extended by `javax.mail.Transport` and `javax.mail.Store`.

The `javax.mail.Transport` class is used to send messages. The `Transport` class included in the Sun JavaMail distribution is a fully functional SMTP implementation, and it is the class you will almost always use to send messages.

The `javax.mail.Store` class is used to retrieve messages. JavaMail 1.1.3 contains a `Store` class that implements IMAP4, whereas JavaMail 1.3 contains a `Store` class that implements both IMAP4 and POP3.

Messages

Figure 10-2 shows the relationships among the classes and interfaces that comprise JavaMail messages.

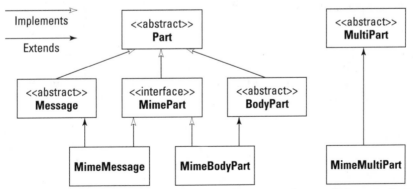

Figure 10-2: The relationships among JavaMail's Part Interfaces and Message classes

At the core of JavaMail are `Message`, `BodyPart`, and `Multipart` objects. `Message` objects can be simple, containing only header information and content; or they can be more complex, with a nested set of `Multipart` and `BodyPart` objects to support nested messages or multiple enclosures.

The `Message` class is an abstract class that implements the `Part` interface. It declares the content and attributes of a message. Subclasses of the `Message` class implement several standard message formats such as the `MimeMessage` class, which implements the RFC822 and MIME standards.

A `Message` object declares message content, addresses for the sender and the recipients, structural information about the message, and content type of the message body. `Message` objects also contain a set of flags that describe the state of the message within the folder. A `DataHandler` object contains the actual content data.

The `BodyPart` class is an abstract class that implements the `Part` interface. It is intended to be stored as part of a `Multipart` container; therefore, it declares only attributes and content. The class does not declare addressing header information as a `Message` object does. Because a `BodyPart` object is an instantiation of the `Part` interface, it can contain either a new `Multipart` object or a `DataHandler` object.

The `Multipart` class is an abstract class that extends `java.lang.Object`. A `Multipart` object is a container class that holds multiple `BodyPart` objects. It provides methods to retrieve and set its subparts.

The JavaMail API documentation has multiple examples of how to create messages implementing this structure. To understand one way, an example later in the chapter uses a `MimeMessage` object with a `MimeMultiPart` object as its content. The `MimeMultiPart` object will contain multiple `MimeBodyPart` objects — the first holding message text and the second holding an enclosure.

Folders

Folders are where mail messages are stored, either on the mail server or on the client's device. They are similar to file system directories in that they are hierarchical in structure. A folder can contain messages or other folders. The default folder is the parent folder in the structure. A special folder named INBOX exists as a child of the default folder and is the recipient of incoming messages. To read incoming mail, you establish a connection, get the store from the session, get the default folder from the store, and then get the INBOX folder from the default folder.

An IMAP mail server stores message folders directly on the mail server, including folders that contain incoming messages and archived messages. A POP3 mail server provides only a folder for incoming messages. It is the mail client's responsibility to retrieve the messages and transfer them to a message store via WebLogic Server, possibly using a database or file system to represent folders.

Figure 10-3 is a diagram showing the relationships among messages, protocols, mail servers, stores, and folders.

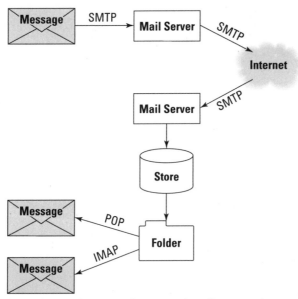

Figure 10-3: The JavaMail message handling process

Sessions and properties

The Session class is a concrete class that extends java.lang.Object. It acts as a factory for the installed Transport and Store implementations and is the way providers are associated with a particular set of user mail configuration settings. A Session also manages user authentication for the Transport and Store services.

WebLogic provides the facility for predefining various mail sessions for use by any of your WebLogic applications. They are associated with default session properties and named for easy accessibility via JNDI.

When a session is instantiated, it uses a Properties object to define the configuration information. The following list describes the properties that you can set, along with their default values. You should expect that at least the mail.store.protocol, mail.transport. protocol, mail.host, mail.user, and mail.from properties are set.

If necessary, you can override the properties in your Java code when establishing a session for connecting to a transport or a store. But it is recommended that you take full advantage of predefining your mail sessions in WebLogic and avoid hard-coding them in your application.

✦ mail.store.protocol: Name the protocol to use to retrieve mail. The Session. getStore() method returns a Store object that implements this protocol. Note that the JavaMail library bundled within the weblogic.jar has support for IMAP and POP3.

```
mail.store.protocol=imap
```

✦ `mail.transport.protocol`: Specify the protocol to use to send mail. The `Session.getTransport()` method returns a `Transport` object that implements this protocol. Note that the JavaMail library bundled within the `weblogic.jar` has support for SMTP.

```
mail.transport.protocol=smtp
```

✦ `mail.host`: Specify the name of the mail host machine. If not specified, the default is the local machine name.

```
mail.host=mail.mycompany.com
```

✦ `mail.user`: Specify the name of the user for retrieving mail. If not specified, the default is the `user.name` Java system property.

```
mail.user=userid
```

✦ `mail.protocol.host`: Specify the mail host for a specific protocol. This is useful if you are using multiple protocols to connect to multiple hosts. If not specified, the default is the value of the `mail.host` property.

```
mail.imap.host=mail.mycompany.com
mail.pop3.host=pop3.mycompany.com
```

✦ `mail.protocol.user`: Specify the protocol-specific default username for logging into a mail server. If not specified, the default is the value of the `mail.user` property.

```
mail.pop3.user=pop3userid
```

✦ `mail.from`: Specify the default return address. If not specified, the default is the value of the `mail.user` property.

```
mail.from=custserv@mycompany.com
```

✦ `mail.debug`: Specify `true` if you want to see debug information on the console and in the WebLogic system log. If not specified, the default is `false`.

```
mail.debug=true
```

Configuring WebLogic JavaMail

Before writing code to send or receive messages, you must configure WebLogic JavaMail by using the WebLogic Console. Configuring JavaMail for the first time is quite simple, requiring only a couple of steps. This section shows you how to perform the required steps, and helps you understand the meanings and implications of your configuration choices.

To configure a new mail session, start WebLogic Server and open the default console. In the domain tree, under the Services node, click Mail. At the top of the page, click Configure a New Mail Session. Figure 10-4 shows the mail session configuration page with the data we provided for this session.

Figure 10-4: Creating a mail session in WebLogic Console

The entries on this page are as follows:

✦ **Name:** This is where you enter a name for the mail session, which must conform to the rules for Java identifiers and be unique within the WebLogic Server domain. Type **BibleMailSession** for this value.

✦ **JNDIName:** You use this name to look up instances of the session with JNDI. The name must be a valid Java identifier and be unique within the JNDI namespace of the server or cluster. Type **BibleMailSession** for this value as well.

✦ **Properties:** This defines the properties that are used when WebLogic returns an instance of this mail session. For these examples, we define the protocols `mail.transport.protocol=smtp` and `mail.store.protocol=imap`; as well as the host and user, `mail.host=mail.mycompany.com` and `mail.user=userid`. We want to see debug messages on the console, so we define `mail.debug=true` for these examples only.

Note   The sample values for `mail.host` and `mail.user` are provided here for example only. For the examples in this chapter to work correctly, you must enter valid entries for all these examples.

Note   You can override these properties in your Java code, but it makes sense to define everything here. If multiple types of connections are needed to connect to multiple mail servers, define multiple mail sessions.

After completing the configuration screen, click Create.

The next step is to attach the mail session to a server or cluster. Click the Targets tab and then move the desired server into the Chosen list of the desired server or cluster. Click Apply. Figure 10-5 shows our mail session attached to our local WebLogic server instance.

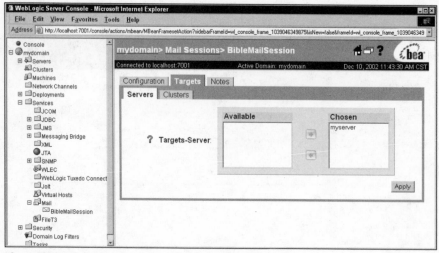

Figure 10-5: Targeting the mail service to a WebLogic Server

After you add the mail session to a WebLogic Server, you see debug messages regarding the providers being loaded. The messages should appear as shown in Figure 10-6 (note the inclusion of a POP3 provider):

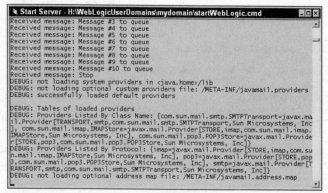

Figure 10-6: The WebLogic Server command display with JavaMail debug messages

We don't cover any of the debug messages in this chapter, but because you have the option turned on, watch the console during the execution of the examples. You'll find it interesting to see what's happening under the hood.

This completes the configuration of a mail session. The next section covers how to send messages with JavaMail.

Note   Contrary to WebLogic's own documentation, Sun's POP3 provider implementation is included, as well as those for IMAP and SMTP. No further configuration is necessary.

Sending Messages with WebLogic JavaMail

If you plan to use JavaMail in your application, you probably want to send outgoing mail messages, so we'll dive into that topic first.

Obtaining a mail session via JNDI

For the examples, you must import the packages for JavaMail, JAF, and JNDI. After that's done, the first step is to create a new `InitialContext` and use it to look up a mail session by its JNDI name.

 Cross-Reference   For more information about JNDI and contexts, see Chapter 7. Otherwise, just understand that successful execution of this code will result in your program having a handle to a JavaMail session.

The following code snippet is the minimum that you need to obtain a mail session. You can see the complete code in the `SendMailServlet.java` example code.

```
import javax.activation.*;
import javax.mail.*;
import javax.mail.internet.*;
import javax.naming.*;

try {
  InitialContext context = new InitialContext();
  Session session = (Session)
    context.lookup("BibleMailSession");
} catch (NamingException e) {}
```

Sending a simple message

The next step is to construct a message (we're using a `MimeMessage`) and set its attributes. Notice that we use the static `InternetAddress.parse()` convenience method to take a list of addresses, either separated by commas or spaces, and parse it into recipients of the message.

In the following example, taken from `SendMailServlet.java`, we use the static `Transport.send()` convenience method. First, it saves the changes to the message via the `Message.save-Changes()` method. Then it connects to the default transport, sends the message, and closes the transport via the `Transport.connect()`, `Transport.sendMessage()`, and `Transport.close()` methods, respectively.

```
try {
  Message msg = new MimeMessage(session);
  msg.setFrom();
  msg.setRecipients(Message.RecipientType.TO,
    InternetAddress.parse(to, false));
  msg.setSubject(subject);
  msg.setSentDate(new Date());
  msg.setText(messageText);
  Transport.send(msg);
} catch (AddressException e) {
} catch (MessagingException e) {}
```

Deployment descriptor for the examples

For all examples in this section, we're using servlets to keep things simple and to keep all the code for each example in one source file.

Cross-Reference   See Chapter 11 for more information about servlets and how to program them.

Of course, the example code works in whatever J2EE component you choose to use, whether it's servlets, JavaBeans, or EJBs. Listing 10-1, web.xml, defines the servlets and servlet mappings necessary to run all the examples in this chapter.

Listing 10-1: **web.xml**

```xml
<?xml version="1.0" ?>
<!DOCTYPE web-app PUBLIC "-//Sun Microsystems, Inc.//DTD Web Application
2.3//EN"
  "http://java.sun.com/dtd/web-app_2_3.dtd">
<web-app>
  <servlet>
    <servlet-name>SendMailServlet</servlet-name>
    <servlet-class>com.wiley.wlsbible.javamail.SendMailServlet</servlet-class>
  </servlet>
  <servlet>
    <servlet-name>SendMailServlet2</servlet-name>
    <servlet-class>com.wiley.wlsbible.javamail.SendMailServlet2</servlet-class>
  </servlet>
  <servlet>
    <servlet-name>DisplayFolders</servlet-name>
    <servlet-class>com.wiley.wlsbible.javamail.DisplayFolders</servlet-class>
  </servlet>
  <servlet>
    <servlet-name>DisplayMessages</servlet-name>
    <servlet-class>com.wiley.wlsbible.javamail.DisplayMessages</servlet-class>
  </servlet>
  <servlet>
    <servlet-name>DisplayMessage</servlet-name>
    <servlet-class>com.wiley.wlsbible.javamail.DisplayMessage</servlet-class>
  </servlet>
  <servlet-mapping>
    <servlet-name>SendMailServlet</servlet-name>
    <url-pattern>/sendmail</url-pattern>
  </servlet-mapping>
  <servlet-mapping>
    <servlet-name>SendMailServlet2</servlet-name>
    <url-pattern>/sendmail2</url-pattern>
  </servlet-mapping>
  <servlet-mapping>
    <servlet-name>DisplayFolders</servlet-name>
```

```
        <url-pattern>/folders</url-pattern>
    </servlet-mapping>
    <servlet-mapping>
        <servlet-name>DisplayMessages</servlet-name>
        <url-pattern>/messages</url-pattern>
    </servlet-mapping>
    <servlet-mapping>
        <servlet-name>DisplayMessage</servlet-name>
        <url-pattern>/message</url-pattern>
    </servlet-mapping>
</web-app>
```

Example: Send Mail servlet

Listing 10-2 contains the code for `SendMailServlet.java`, a servlet that supports the composing and sending of e-mail messages.

`SendMailServlet.java` is structured as follows:

1. Its `doGet()` method displays an HTML form in the user's browser, prompting for a message recipient's e-mail address, a message subject, and a message body. The form also contains a Submit button that, when clicked, posts the form's contents to the server. Figure 10-7 shows this form rendered in a Web browser.

2. Its `doPost()` method retrieves the user's input for the message recipient, subject, and body; then makes JavaMail calls to build and send the message using the messaging infrastructure we defined in the "Configuring WebLogic JavaMail" section earlier in this chapter.

Figure 10-7: Send Mail servlet: simple version

Listing 10-2: SendMailServlet.java

```java
package com.wiley.wlsbible.javamail;

import java.io.*;
import javax.servlet.*;
import javax.servlet.http.*;

import java.util.*;
import javax.activation.*;
import javax.mail.*;
import javax.mail.internet.*;
import javax.naming.*;

public class SendMailServlet extends HttpServlet {

  private String to = "";
  private String subject = "";
  private String messageText = "";
  private String successMessage = "";

  public void doGet(HttpServletRequest req, HttpServletResponse res)
  throws ServletException, IOException {

    PrintWriter pw = res.getWriter();
    res.setContentType("text/html");

    pw.println("<HTML><HEAD><TITLE>Send Mail - Simple</TITLE></HEAD>");
    pw.println("<BODY><H1>Send Mail - Simple</H1>");
    pw.println("<FORM ACTION='sendmail' METHOD=post><TABLE>");
    pw.println("<TR><TD>To:</TD><TD><INPUT NAME=to size=60></TD></TR>");
    pw.println("<TR><TD>Subject:</TD>" +
      "<TD><INPUT NAME=subject size=60></TD></TR>");
    pw.println("<TR><TD VALIGN>Message:</TD>");
    pw.println("<TD><TEXTAREA NAME=messageText rows=10 cols=60>" +
      "</TEXTAREA></TD></TR>");
    pw.println("<TR><TD>" +
      "<INPUT TYPE=SUBMIT NAME=Submit VALUE=Submit></TD></TR>");
    pw.println("</TABLE></FORM>");
    pw.println("<STRONG>" + successMessage + "</STRONG>");
    pw.println("</BODY></HTML>");
  }

  public void doPost(HttpServletRequest req, HttpServletResponse res)
  throws ServletException, IOException {

    to = req.getParameter("to");
    subject = req.getParameter("subject");
    messageText = req.getParameter("messageText");
    sendMessage();
```

```
      doGet(req, res);
  }

  public void sendMessage() {

    try {
      // lookup mail session in JNDI
      InitialContext context = new InitialContext();
      Session session = (Session) context.lookup("BibleMailSession");

      // set message with to, subject, and message text
      Message msg = new MimeMessage(session);

      // set message with to, subject, and message text
      msg.setFrom();
      msg.setRecipients(Message.RecipientType.TO,
                        InternetAddress.parse(to, false));
      msg.setSubject(subject);
      msg.setSentDate(new Date());
      msg.setText(messageText);

      // send message
      Transport.send(msg);
      successMessage = "Message sucessfully sent.";
      session = null;
    }
    catch (Exception e) {
      successMessage = e.getMessage();
    }
  }
}
```

Overriding mail session properties

You can override mail session properties in your Java code by creating a `Properties` object
that contains the properties you want to override. Then call the `Session.getInstance()`
method with your `Properties` to get a customized `Session`. The `getInstance()` method
also takes an `Authenticator` object to create an authenticated session (if your SMTP mail
server does not require authentication to send mail, specify `null` for the `Authenticator`
object). The following code snippet demonstrates the technique:

```
Properties mailProps = new Properties();
mailProps.put("mail.transport.protocol", "smtp");
mailProps.put("mail.host", "mail.mycompany.com");
mailProps.put("mail.user", "userid");
mailProps.put("mail.from", "custserv@mycompany.com");
mailProps.put("mail.debug", "true");
Session mySession = session.getInstance(mailProps, null);
```

Authenticating a mail session

If your SMTP mail server does require authentication to send mail, you'll need to pass an Authenticator object to the Session.getInstance() method to get an authenticated mail session.

To do this, you must first create your own MailAuthenticator class that extends Authenticator. Listing 10-3 shows a simple example of such a class. We're creating this as a class that gets instantiated and set by some other process, perhaps by prompting the user or retrieving user information from a database. The important part is that it must have a getPasswordAuthentication() method that returns a PasswordAuthentication object.

Here's how this works: the getInstance() method creates a new Session object and associates it with the Authenticator. The Session object has a package-level method it calls, which in turn calls the getPasswordAuthentication() method on the Authenticator. The result is that only the requestPasswordAuthentication() method can use the Authenticator to obtain an authenticated session.

Listing 10-3: **MailAuthenticator.java**

```
package com.wiley.wlsbible.javamail;

import javax.mail.*;

public class MailAuthenticator extends Authenticator {

  private String user;
  private String password;

  public void setUser(String s) {
    user = s;
  }
  public String getUser() {
    return user;
  }
  public void setPassword(String s) {
    password = s;
  }
  public String getPassword() {
    return password;
  }
  public PasswordAuthentication getPasswordAuthentication(){
    return new PasswordAuthentication(user, password);
  }
}
```

The next step is to specify that you're requesting SMTP authentication by setting the mail.smtp.auth property to true, as follows:

```
Properties mailProps = new Properties();
mailProps.put("mail.transport.protocol","smtp");
mailProps.put("mail.host","mail.mycompany.com");
mailProps.put("mail.user","userid");
mailProps.put("mail.from","custserv@mycompany.com");
mailProps.put("mail.debug","true");
mailProps.put("mail.smtp.auth","true");
```

Now create a new `MailAuthenticator` and set the values. Then we'll get an authenticated session by calling the `getInstance()` method with the `Properties` and `Authenticator` objects as parameters.

 Note

We set the user and password values here for this example only. In real life, you get the `Authenticator` object as a result of a user login or from accessing a database or descriptor.

```
MailAuthenticator mailAuth = new MailAuthenticator();
mailAuth.setUser("userid");
mailAuth.setPassword("password");
Session authSession = session.getInstance(mailProps,
  mailAuth);
```

You're almost done, but not quite. In the non-authenticated example (Listing 10-2: `SendMailServlet.java`), you called the static `Transport.send()` convenience method. For authenticated sessions, however, you must manually save the message changes, get a new transport from the authenticated session, connect, send the message, and disconnect, as shown below.

```
msg.saveChanges();

// get transport and send a message
Transport authTransport = authSession.getTransport();
authTransport.connect();
authTransport.sendMessage(msg, msg.getAllRecipients());
authTransport.close();
```

Sending an enclosure using a MimeMultipart

To send a message with attachments, a multipart message is used with multiple body parts. The first part contains the message text and the other parts contain the attachments. The multipart message is then set as the content of the message.

In the following example, we use a `MimeMultipart` with multiple `MimeBodyParts`. We only have one enclosure, which is set into the second `MimeBodyPart`. Additional enclosures can be set in multiple `MimeBodyParts` as necessary. The raw data from the `FileDataSource` is wrapped in a `DataHandler` object and stored in the `MimeBodyPart`. We also set the filename in the `MimeBodyPart`. Finally, we set the message content to the `MimeMultipart`.

```
// set with message text via a mime multipart
Multipart mp = new MimeMultipart();

MimeBodyPart mbp1 = new MimeBodyPart();
mbp1.setText(messageText);
mp.addBodyPart(mbp1);
```

```
MimeBodyPart mbp2 = new MimeBodyPart();
FileDataSource fds = new FileDataSource(filename);
mbp2.setDataHandler(new DataHandler(fds));
mbp2.setFileName(fds.getName());
mp.addBodyPart(mbp2);

msg.setContent(mp);
```

Example: Send Mail servlet 2

The second example, shown in Figure 10-8, expands upon the first servlet to send more complex messages. This example will prompt for the To, Cc, and Bcc addresses; Subject; filename
of an enclosure; message text; and an indication of whether the message text is HTML.

This example also demonstrates how to override the session's default properties, use an
authenticator to get an authenticated SMTP session, use a `MimeMultipart` to optionally
include an enclosure, optionally flag the message text as HTML, and manually execute the
steps to send the message through a transport obtained from the authenticated session.

Figure 10-8: Send Mail servlet: complex version

Note   In Listing 10-4, the Java code to store an enclosure in a message gets the file from the local
file system. Because our example is a servlet, the file must be in the local file system of the
server running WebLogic. You need to explore further if you wish to get the file from the
client's file system.

Listing 10-4: **SendMailServlet2.java**

```java
package com.wiley.wlsbible.javamail;

import java.io.*;
import javax.servlet.*;
import javax.servlet.http.*;

import java.util.*;
import javax.activation.*;
import javax.mail.*;
import javax.mail.internet.*;
import javax.naming.*;

public class SendMailServlet2 extends HttpServlet {

  private String to = "";
  private String cc = "";
  private String bcc = "";
  private String subject = "";
  private String filename = "";
  private String messageText = "";
  private boolean isHTML;
  private String successMessage = "";

  public void doGet(HttpServletRequest req, HttpServletResponse res)
  throws ServletException, IOException {

    PrintWriter pw = res.getWriter();
    res.setContentType("text/html");

    pw.println("<HTML><HEAD><TITLE>Send Mail - Complex</TITLE></HEAD>");
    pw.println("<BODY><H1>Send Mail - Complex</H1>");
    pw.println("<FORM ACTION='sendmail2' METHOD=post><TABLE>");
    pw.println("<TR><TD>To:</TD><TD><INPUT NAME=to size=60></TD></TR>");
    pw.println("<TR><TD>Cc:</TD><TD><INPUT NAME=cc size=60></TD></TR>");
    pw.println("<TR><TD>Bcc:</TD><TD><INPUT NAME=bcc size=60></TD></TR>");
    pw.println("<TR><TD>Subject:</TD><TD><INPUT NAME=subject size=60>" +
      "</TD></TR>");
    pw.println("<TR><TD>Enclosure:</TD><TD>" +
      "<INPUT NAME=filename size=60></TD></TR>");
    pw.println("<TR><TD VALIGN>Message:</TD>");
    pw.println("<TD><TEXTAREA NAME=messageText rows=10 cols=60>" +
      "</TEXTAREA></TD></TR>");
    pw.println("<TR><TD>HTML:</TD><TD><input type=checkbox NAME=isHTML>" +
      "</TD></TR>");
    pw.println("<TR><TD><INPUT TYPE=SUBMIT NAME=Submit VALUE=Submit>" +
      "</TD></TR>");
    pw.println("</TABLE></FORM>");
```

Continued

Listing 10-4 *(continued)*

```
    pw.println("<STRONG>" + successMessage + "</STRONG>");
    pw.println("</BODY></HTML>");
}

public void doPost(HttpServletRequest req, HttpServletResponse res)
throws ServletException, IOException {
  to = req.getParameter("to");
  cc = req.getParameter("cc");
  bcc = req.getParameter("bcc");
  subject = req.getParameter("subject");
  filename = req.getParameter("filename");
  messageText = req.getParameter("messageText");
  isHTML = "on".equals(req.getParameter("isHTML"));
  sendMessage();
  doGet(req, res);
}

public void sendMessage() {

  try {
    // lookup mail session in JNDI
    InitialContext context = new InitialContext();
    Session session = (Session) context.lookup("BibleMailSession");

    // override mail session properties
    Properties mailProps = new Properties();
    mailProps.put("mail.transport.protocol","smtp");
    mailProps.put("mail.host", "mail.mycompany.com");
    mailProps.put("mail.user", "userid");
    mailProps.put("mail.from", "userid@mycompany.com");
    mailProps.put("mail.debug", "true");
    mailProps.put("mail.smtp.auth", "true");

    // get an authenticated session
    MailAuthenticator mailAuth = new MailAuthenticator();
    // For testing, set the values here. The user should be prompted or
    // retrieved from a database or descriptor
    mailAuth.setUser("userid ");
    mailAuth.setPassword("password");
    Session authSession = session.getInstance(mailProps, mailAuth);

    // set message with to, subject, and message text
    Message msg = new MimeMessage(authSession);

    // set message with to, cc, bcc, and subject
    msg.setFrom();
    msg.setRecipients(Message.RecipientType.TO,
      InternetAddress.parse(to, false));
```

```
msg.setRecipients(Message.RecipientType.CC,
  InternetAddress.parse(cc, false));
msg.setRecipients(Message.RecipientType.BCC,
  InternetAddress.parse(bcc, false));
msg.setSubject(subject);
msg.setSentDate(new Date());

// set with message text via a mime multipart
Multipart mp = new MimeMultipart();

MimeBodyPart mbp1 = new MimeBodyPart();
if (isHTML) {
  mbp1.setContent(messageText, "text/html");
} else {
  mbp1.setText(messageText);
}
mp.addBodyPart(mbp1);

if (!filename.equals("")) {
  MimeBodyPart mbp2 = new MimeBodyPart();
  FileDataSource fds = new FileDataSource(filename);
  mbp2.setDataHandler(new DataHandler(fds));
  mbp2.setFileName(fds.getName());
  mp.addBodyPart(mbp2);
}

msg.setContent(mp);
msg.saveChanges();

// get transport and send message
Transport authTransport = authSession.getTransport();
authTransport.connect();
authTransport.sendMessage(msg, msg.getAllRecipients());
authTransport.close();
successMessage = "Message successfully sent.";
session = null;

} catch (Exception e) {
  successMessage = e.getMessage();
}
  }
}
```

Sending a message to multiple recipients (bulk mail)

JavaMail is commonly used to add automated e-mail notification to applications. The application typically sends an e-mail message to multiple recipients based upon a list of addresses retrieved from a database. Often, the e-mails are tailored to the recipient with name and other personal information. In this case, it's inefficient to repetitively connect to a transport, send, and disconnect because connecting is a time-consuming, network-intensive operation. A more efficient way is to connect, customize, and send multiple messages; then disconnect. The following code snippet demonstrates this technique:

```
Transport transport = session.getTransport();
transport.connect();

// personalize message and send
for (int i = 0; i < recipients.length, i++) {
  // personalize message here ...
  msg.saveChanges();
  transport.sendMessage(msg, recipients[i]);
}
transport.close();
```

Navigating stores

Most e-mail clients provide a mechanism for organizing messages into folders and browsing the folders. To provide this functionality with JavaMail, you must use the JavaMail Store object to drive the display of and interaction with the folder hierarchies your users define. The next four sections provide several examples of how to work with stores.

Obtaining a new mail session

Before working with stores, you must obtain a mail session via a JNDI lookup, just as you did when sending messages:

```
import javax.activation.*;
import javax.mail.*;
import javax.mail.internet.*;
import javax.naming.*;

try {
  InitialContext context = new InitialContext();
  Session session = (Session)
    context.lookup("BibleMailSession");
} catch (NamingException e) {}
```

Connecting to a store and the default folder

Next, you must connect to a store by using the protocol defined in the mail session (in this case, mail.store.protocol=imap) and get the default folder. As described earlier, the default folder is the root folder of a user's default folder hierarchy.

```
try {
  // get store and create an authenticated session
  Store store = session.getStore();
  store.connect("mail.mycompany.com", "userid", "password");
  defaultFolder = store.getDefaultFolder();
} catch (NoSuchProviderException e) {
} catch (MessagingException e) {}
```

Listing folders

After you have a reference to the default folder, you can retrieve the user's entire folder hierarchy and navigate through it. In this example, we specifically include only folders that hold messages and explicitly exclude the Public Folders folder. For each folder, we display its name and some information about it, such as the total number of messages, the number of new messages, and the number of unread messages. Several other folder attributes are available as well; see the J2EE documentation for a complete list of information available for a folder.

Note   Some implementations of certain folder methods may not return expected data if the folder is not opened first. In this example, the folder is opened and closed. If your implementation works without these steps, it's more efficient to omit them.

```
try {
  Folder[] allFolders = defaultFolder.list();
  for (int i = 0; i < allFolders.length; i++) {
    String name = allFolders[i].getName();
    if (allFolders[i].HOLDS_MESSAGES ==
        Folder.HOLDS_MESSAGES &&
        !name.equals("Public Folders")) {
      allFolders[i].open(Folder.READ_ONLY);
      System.out.print ("Name: " + allFolders[i].getName());
      System.out.print("  Messages: " +
        allFolders[i]. getMessageCount());
      System.out.print("  New: " +
        allFolders[i]. getNewMessageCount());
      System.out.println("  Unread: " +
        allFolders[i].getUnreadMessageCount());
      allFolders[i].close(false);
    }
  }
} catch (MessagingException e) {}
```

Example: Display folders

The next example displays a list of folders in the user's folder hierarchy. After obtaining a mail session via JNDI, the code establishes an authenticated connection to the store, opens the default folder, retrieves a list of folders, and displays the folders with some basic information about them.

Figure 10-9 shows a list of folders and their attributes retrieved by using the IMAP protocol.

Figure 10-10 shows a list of folders and their attributes retrieved by using the POP3 protocol. Notice that there is only one folder: the INBOX.

Figure 10-9: Displaying folders by using IMAP

Note   This is a prime example of how the JavaMail API provides a common interface for all proto-cols. POP3 doesn't actually support the concept of folders, but the JavaMail API ensures that the POP3 container for storing messages is presented as the INBOX within the default folder.

Figure 10-10: Displaying folders by using POP3

Listing 10-5 contains the code that generates Figures 10-9 and 10-10.

Listing 10-5: **DisplayFolders.java**

```java
package com.wiley.wlsbible.javamail;

import java.io.*;
import javax.servlet.*;
import javax.servlet.http.*;

import javax.activation.*;
import javax.mail.*;
import javax.mail.internet.*;
import javax.naming.*;

public class DisplayFolders extends HttpServlet {

  private PrintWriter pw;
  private Session session;
  private Store store;
  private Folder defaultFolder;

  public void doGet(HttpServletRequest req, HttpServletResponse res)
  throws ServletException, IOException {

    pw = res.getWriter();
    res.setContentType("text/html");

    pw.println("<HTML><HEAD><TITLE>Folders</TITLE></HEAD>");
    pw.println("<BODY><H1>Folders</H1>");

    try {
      getDefaultFolder();
      displayFolders();
      store.close();
    } catch (Exception e) {
      pw.println("<BR><BR><STRONG>" + e.getMessage() + "</STRONG>");
    }

    pw.println("</BODY></HTML>");
  }

  private void getDefaultFolder()
  throws NamingException, NoSuchProviderException, MessagingException {

    // lookup mail session in JNDI
    InitialContext context = new InitialContext();
    Session session = (Session) context.lookup("BibleMailSession");
```

Continued

Listing 10-5 *(continued)*

```
  // get store and create an authenticated session
  store = session.getStore();
  store.connect("mail.mycompany.com", "userid", "password");

  // get the default folder
  defaultFolder = store.getDefaultFolder();
}

private void displayFolders() throws MessagingException {
  Folder[] allFolders = defaultFolder.list();
  if (allFolders.length > 0) {

    pw.println("<TABLE width='100%'>");
    pw.println("<TR><TD><STRONG>Folder</STRONG></TD>");
    pw.println("<TD><STRONG>Messages</STRONG></TD>");
    pw.println("<TD><STRONG>New</STRONG></TD>");
    pw.println("<TD><STRONG>Unread</STRONG></TD></TR>");

    for (int i = 0; i < allFolders.length; i++) {
      String name = allFolders[i].getName();

      if (allFolders[i].HOLDS_MESSAGES == Folder.HOLDS_MESSAGES &&
          !name.equals("Public Folders")) {
        allFolders[i].open(Folder.READ_ONLY);
        pw.println("<TR><TD><A HREF='messages?folder=" + name +
          "'>" + name + "</A></TD></TD>");
        pw.println("<TD>" + allFolders[i].getMessageCount() + "</TD>");
        pw.println("<TD>" + allFolders[i].getNewMessageCount() +
          "</TD>");
        pw.println("<TD>" + allFolders[i].getUnreadMessageCount() +
          "</TD></TR>");
        allFolders[i].close(false);
      }
    }
    pw.println("</TABLE>");
  }
}
}
```

Retrieving and Displaying Messages with WebLogic JavaMail

If you plan to write the "Next Great J2EE E-mail Client," you need to know how to retrieve and display e-mail messages using JavaMail. This section shows you how to do it.

Listing messages

Before you can retrieve a list of messages from a folder, it must first be opened via the Folder.open() method. This method takes an integer as a parameter corresponding to the mode in which to open the folder. Two modes, READ_ONLY and READ_WRITE, are provided as public static final variables. For the following example, we use READ_ONLY because we're only retrieving information about the messages, not changing their state or their content.

To obtain a list of messages, simply call the getMessages() method against a folder and it will return an array of Messages. You can then loop through the messages and retrieve information about them or the data they contain.

Of course, if you're like us, you probably have a number of messages sitting on your mail server at any one time. Unconditionally getting all messages can be a time-consuming process. What we show uses the getMessageCount() and getMessages(x, y) methods. The former tells you how many messages there are, and the latter gets the messages numbered from x to y. Keep in mind that message numbers start at 1, not 0. Notice, too, that we bypass messages flagged as deleted further down in the code.

```
try {
  // open folder and get messages
  folder.open(Folder.READ_ONLY);
  Message[] messages;
  int msgCount = folder.getMessageCount();
  if (msgCount > 10)
  {
    messages = folder.getMessages(msgCount - 10, msgCount);
  }
  else
  {
    messages = folder.getMessages();
  }


  // loop through messages
  for (int i = 0; i < messages.length; i++) {
    // skip deleted messages
    if (!messages[i].isSet(Flags.Flag.DELETED)) {
    System.out.print ("MessageNumber: " +
      messages[i].getFrom());
    System.out.print ("From: " +
      messages[i].getFrom());
    System.out.print ("Subject: " +
      messages[i].getSubject());
    System.out.print ("Received: " +
      messages[i].getReceivedDate());
  }
  folder.close(false);
} catch (MessagingException e) {}
```

Another way to keep your mail client as efficient as possible is to use the Folder.fetch() method. Using fetch allows you to get header information without getting the entire message and attachments. Keep in mind, though, that you are limited in the amount of information you can get by prefetching the information this way. The lightweight Message object forces the downloading of the entire message if you access a property that is not prefetched by the fetch() method. See Sun's Javadoc for the JavaMail API at the following URL for more information on fetch() and the related FetchProfile class:

http://java.sun.com/products/javamail/1.3/docs/javadocs/index.html

Example: Display messages

A basic function of an e-mail client is to display a list of incoming messages. This display is done in JavaMail by opening a folder, retrieving the messages it contains, and writing their attributes to the screen. These attributes usually include the sender of the message, the subject of the message, the date and time the message was received, the size of the message in bytes, whether or not the message has an enclosure, and whether or not the message has been read. Figure 10-11 shows what such a display might look like. It is the result of retrieving a list of messages using the IMAP protocol.

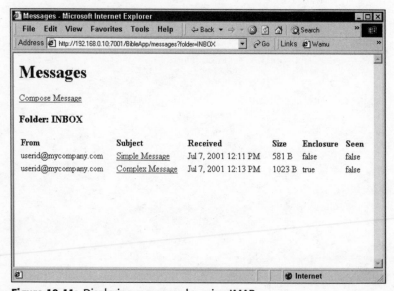

Figure 10-11: Displaying messages by using IMAP

Figure 10-12 shows the results of retrieving a list of messages and their attributes by using the POP3 protocol. Notice that there are a few differences in the output. First, there is no *received* date. Also, the size of each message is different from that in the IMAP execution because, according to the JavaMail API documentation, "the size may not be an exact measure of the content size and may or may not account for any transfer encoding of the content. The size is appropriate for display in a user interface to give the user a rough idea of the size of this part." In other words, don't count on Message.getSize() to return 100-percent accurate message sizes if you are using POP3 to retrieve messages.

Figure 10-12: Displaying messages by using POP3

Listing 10-6 shows the Java code used to generate Figures 10-11 and 10-12.

Listing 10-6: **DisplayMessages.java**

```java
package com.wiley.wlsbible.javamail;

import java.io.*;
import javax.servlet.*;
import javax.servlet.http.*;

import java.util.*;
import java.text.*;
import javax.activation.*;
import javax.mail.*;
import javax.mail.internet.*;
import javax.naming.*;

public class DisplayMessages extends HttpServlet {

  private PrintWriter pw;
  private Session session;
  private Store store;
  private Folder defaultFolder;
  private Folder folder;
  private String folderName;
  private Message message;

  public void doGet(HttpServletRequest req, HttpServletResponse res)
  throws ServletException, IOException {
```

Continued

Listing 10-6 *(continued)*

```
    pw = res.getWriter();
    res.setContentType("text/html");

    folderName = req.getParameter("folder");

    pw.println("<HTML><HEAD><TITLE>Messages</TITLE></HEAD>");
    pw.println("<BODY><H1>Messages</H1>");

    try {
      getDefaultFolder();
      displayMessages(folderName);
    } catch (Exception e) {
      e.printStackTrace(pw);
      pw.println("<BR><BR><STRONG>" + e.getMessage() + "</STRONG>");
    }

    pw.println("</BODY></HTML>");
}

private void getDefaultFolder()
throws NamingException, NoSuchProviderException, MessagingException {

    // lookup mail session in JNDI
    InitialContext context = new InitialContext();
    Session session = (Session) context.lookup("BibleMailSession");

    // get store and create an authenticated session
    store = session.getStore();
    store.connect("mail.mycompany.com", "userid", "password");

    // get the default folder
    defaultFolder = store.getDefaultFolder();
}

private void displayMessages (String folderName)
throws MessagingException, IOException {

    pw.println("<A HREF='sendmail2'>Compose Message</A><BR>");
    pw.println("<H3>Folder: " + folderName + "</H3>");

    folder = defaultFolder.getFolder(folderName);
    folder.open(Folder.READ_ONLY);

    Message[] messages;
    int msgCount = folder.getMessageCount();
    if (msgCount > 10)
    {
      messages = folder.getMessages(msgCount - 10, msgCount);
    }
```

```
    else
    {
      messages = folder.getMessages();
    }


    if (messages.length > 0) {
      pw.println("<TABLE width='100%'>");
      pw.println("<TR><TD><STRONG>From</STRONG></TD>");
      pw.println("<TD><STRONG>Subject</STRONG></TD>");
      pw.println("<TD><STRONG>Received</STRONG></TD>");
      pw.println("<TD><STRONG>Size</STRONG></TD>");
      pw.println("<TD><STRONG>Enclosure</STRONG></TD>");
      pw.println("<TD><STRONG>Seen</STRONG></TD></TR>");

      // loop through messages
      for (int i = 0; i < messages.length; i++) {

        // skip deleted messages
        if (!messages[i].isSet(Flags.Flag.DELETED)) {
          message = messages[i];
          pw.println("<TR><TD>" + getFrom() + "</TD>");
          String subject =
            ("".equals(getSubject()) ? "None" : getSubject());
          pw.println("<TD><A HREF='message?cmd=display&folder=" +
            folderName + "&msgid=" + getMessageNumber() + "'>" +
            subject + "</A></TD>");
          pw.println("<TD>" + getReceived() + "</TD>");
          pw.println("<TD>" + getSize() + "</TD>");
          pw.println("<TD>" + hasEnclosure() + "</TD>");
          pw.println("<TD>" + hasBeenSeen() + "</TD></TR>");
        }
      }
      pw.println("</TABLE>");
      folder.close(false);
      store.close();
    }
}

public String getFrom() throws MessagingException {
  Address[] addresses = message.getFrom();
  return addresses[0].toString();
}

public String getSubject() throws MessagingException {
  return message.getSubject();
}

public int getMessageNumber() throws MessagingException {
  return message.getMessageNumber();
}
```

Continued

Listing 10-6 *(continued)*

```
public String getReceived() throws MessagingException {
  String date = "";
  Date receivedDate = message.getReceivedDate();
  if (receivedDate != null) {
    date = DateFormat.getDateTimeInstance(DateFormat.MEDIUM,
          DateFormat.SHORT).format(receivedDate);
  }
  return date;
}

private String getSize() throws MessagingException {
  int size = message.getSize();
  String sizeDesc = size + " B";
  if (size >= 1024) {
    size /= 1024;
    sizeDesc = size + " KB";
    if (size >= 1024) {
      size /= 1024;
      sizeDesc = size + " MB";
    }
  }
  return sizeDesc;
}

private boolean hasEnclosure() throws MessagingException, IOException {
  boolean b = false;
  if (message.isMimeType("multipart/*")) {
    Multipart mp = (Multipart)message.getContent();
    int count = mp.getCount();
    for (int j = 0; j < count; j++) {
      BodyPart bp = mp.getBodyPart(j);
      if (bp.getFileName() != null) {
        b = true;
      }
    }
  }
  return b;
}

private boolean hasBeenSeen() throws MessagingException {
  boolean b = false;
  if (message.isSet(Flags.Flag.SEEN))
    b = true;
    return b;
  }
}
```

Analyzing message flags

Flags describe the state of a message within its containing folder. The `Message.getFlags()` method returns a `Flags` object that holds all the flags currently set for that message. Messages can contain multiple flags, both system and user-defined.

The system flags are defined as public static final fields in the public static final class `Flags.flag`. They include `ANSWERED`, `DELETED`, `DRAFT`, `FLAGGED`, `RECENT`, `SEEN`, and `USER`. The mail server can automatically set system flags as operations are executed against the message, or they can be manually set by your Java code. The `getPermanentFlags()` method in a folder returns a `Flags` object that contains all the system flags supported by that folder. Each mail server is not guaranteed to support all flags and may use them somewhat differently, so you will need to experiment to understand how your particular mail server behaves.

The presence of the special `USER` flag indicates that the client can set arbitrary user-definable flags on any message belonging to this folder.

The following code defines a method, `getFlags()`, that returns a `String` containing all of a message's flags:

```
private String getFlags() throws MessagingException {

  Flags flags = message.getFlags();
  StringBuffer sb = new StringBuffer();
  Flags.Flag[] sysFlags = flags.getSystemFlags();
  for (int i = 0; i < sysFlags.length; i++) {
    if (sysFlags[i] == Flags.Flag.ANSWERED)
      sb.append("Answered ");
    else if (sysFlags[i] == Flags.Flag.DELETED)
      sb.append("Deleted ");
    else if (sysFlags[i] == Flags.Flag.DRAFT)
      sb.append("Draft ");
    else if (sysFlags[i] == Flags.Flag.FLAGGED)
      sb.append("Flagged ");
    else if (sysFlags[i] == Flags.Flag.RECENT)
      sb.append("Recent ");
    else if (sysFlags[i] == Flags.Flag.SEEN)
      sb.append("Seen ");
    else if (sysFlags[i] == Flags.Flag.USER)
      sb.append("User ");
    else
      sb.append("Unknown ");
  }

  String[] userFlags = flags.getUserFlags();
  for (int i = 0; i < userFlags.length; i++) {
    sb.append(userFlags[i].toString() + " ");
  }
  return sb.toString();
}
```

Deleting a message

To delete a message, simply set its DELETED flag to true via the setFlag() method. The message is flagged as deleted, yet it still exists with its current message number. It can still be retrieved, displayed, and have its DELETED flag set back to false. It is not until the folder containing the messages is *expunged* that the messages are permanently deleted — we discuss the expunging of messages in the next section.

```
try {
  getMessage();
  message.setFlag(Flags.Flag.DELETED, true);
} catch (MessagingException e) {}
```

Expunging messages

As mentioned in the preceding section, messages flagged as DELETED still exist and maintain their message number. Expunging a folder permanently deletes all messages flagged as DELETED. Additionally, all remaining messages in the folder are assigned new message numbers.

You can expunge messages in one of two ways. The first is to call the expunge() method against the folder:

```
try {
  folder.expunge();
} catch (MessagingException e) {}
```

The other is to specify that the folder should be expunged when it is closed. To do so, you must pass true to the folder.close() method:

```
try {
  folder.close(true);
} catch (MessagingException e) {}
```

Displaying message details

In this section, we display the details of a message. The folder name and message number are passed as request parameters from the previous Display Messages servlet. We open the folder in READ_WRITE mode, retrieve the message by its message number, and display information about the message — including sent, received, reply to, to, cc, subject, size, flags, the message text, and the name of the enclosed file. A link appears that enables the user to delete the message.

Figure 10-13 shows the results of displaying a message's content and attributes by using the IMAP protocol.

Figure 10-14 shows the results of displaying a message's content and attributes by using the POP3 protocol. Again, notice the protocol differences by comparing the received date, size, and flags to the IMAP execution.

Figure 10-13: Displaying message details by using IMAP

Figure 10-14: Displaying message details by using POP3

Listing 10-7 contains the Java code for displaying message details that generated Figures 10-13 and 10-14.

Listing 10-7: **DisplayMessage.java**

```java
package com.wiley.wlsbible.javamail;

import java.io.*;
import javax.servlet.*;
import javax.servlet.http.*;

import java.util.*;
import java.text.*;
import javax.activation.*;
import javax.mail.*;
import javax.mail.internet.*;
import javax.naming.*;

public class DisplayMessage extends HttpServlet {

  private PrintWriter pw;
  private Session session;
  private Store store;
  private Folder defaultFolder;
  private Folder folder;
  private String folderName;
  private int msgid;
  private Message message;

  public void doGet(HttpServletRequest req, HttpServletResponse res)
  throws ServletException, IOException {

    pw = res.getWriter();
    res.setContentType("text/html");

    String cmd = req.getParameter("cmd");
    folderName = req.getParameter("folder");
    msgid = new Integer(req.getParameter("msgid")).intValue();

    // display message
    if (cmd.equals("display")) {
      displayMessage();

    // delete message
    } else if (cmd.equals("delete")) {
      deleteMessage();
      RequestDispatcher rd =
        getServletContext().getNamedDispatcher("DisplayMessages");
      rd.forward(req, res);
    }
  }
```

```
private void getDefaultFolder()
throws NamingException, NoSuchProviderException, MessagingException {

  // lookup mail session in JNDI
  InitialContext context = new InitialContext();
  session = (Session) context.lookup("BibleMailSession");

  // get store and create an authenticated session
  store = session.getStore();
  store.connect("mail.mycompany.com", "userid", "password");

  // get the default folder
  defaultFolder = store.getDefaultFolder();
}

private void getMessage() throws MessagingException, NamingException {

  // try to open folder read/write otherwise read-only
  getDefaultFolder();
  folder = defaultFolder.getFolder(folderName);
  try {
    folder.open(Folder.READ_WRITE);
  } catch (MessagingException ex) {
    folder.open(Folder.READ_ONLY);
  }

  // get message
  message = folder.getMessage(msgid);
}

private void displayMessage() {

  pw.println("<HTML><HEAD><TITLE>Message Detail</TITLE></HEAD>");
  pw.println("<BODY><H1>Message Detail</H1>");

  try {
    getMessage();

    // display the message
    pw.println("<TABLE width='100%'>");
    pw.println("<TR><TD>Sent:</TD><TD>" + getSent() + "</TD></TR>");
    pw.println("<TR><TD>Received:</TD><TD>" + getReceived() +
      "</TD></TR>");
    pw.println("<TR><TD>From:</TD><TD>" + getFrom() + "</TD></TR>");
    pw.println("<TR><TD>Reply to:</TD><TD>" + getReplyTo() +
      "</TD></TR>");
    pw.println("<TR><TD>To:</TD><TD>" + getTo() + "</TD></TR>");
    pw.println("<TR><TD>Cc:</TD><TD>" + getCc() + "</TD></TR>");
    pw.println("<TR><TD>Subject:</TD><TD>" + getSubject() +
      "</TD></TR>");
    pw.println("<TR><TD>Size:</TD><TD>" + getSize() + "</TD></TR>");
```

Continued

Listing 10-7 *(continued)*

```
    pw.println("<TR><TD>Flags:</TD><TD>" + getFlags() + "</TD></TR>");
    pw.println("<TR><TD VALIGN>Message:</TD><TD>" + getMessageText() +
      "</TD></TR>");
    String enclosure = getEnclosureName();
    pw.print("<TR><TD>Enclosure:</TD><TD>" + enclosure + "</TD></TR>");
    pw.print("<TR><TD><BR><A HREF='message?cmd=delete&folder=" +
      folderName + "&msgid=" + msgid + "'>Delete</A></TD></TR>");
    pw.println("</TABLE>");
    folder.close(false);
    store.close();
  } catch (Exception e) {
    pw.println("<BR><BR><STRONG>" + e.getMessage() + "</STRONG>");
  }

  pw.println("</BODY></HTML>");
}

private void deleteMessage() {
  try {
    getMessage();
    message.setFlag(Flags.Flag.DELETED, true);
  } catch (Exception e) {}
}

public String getSent() throws MessagingException {
  Date sentDate = message.getSentDate();
  return DateFormat.getDateTimeInstance(DateFormat.MEDIUM,
  DateFormat.SHORT).format(sentDate);
}

public String getReceived() throws MessagingException {
  String date = "";
  Date receivedDate = message.getReceivedDate();
  if (receivedDate != null) {
    date = DateFormat.getDateTimeInstance(DateFormat.MEDIUM,
    DateFormat.SHORT).format(receivedDate);
  }
  return date;
}

public String getFrom() throws MessagingException {
  Address[] addresses = message.getFrom();
  return addresses[0].toString();
}

public String getReplyTo() throws MessagingException {
  StringBuffer sb = new StringBuffer();
  Address[] addresses = message.getReplyTo();
```

```
  if (addresses != null) {
    for (int j = 0; j < addresses.length; j++) {
      sb.append(addresses[j].toString() + " ");
    }
  }
  return sb.toString();
}

public String getTo() throws MessagingException {
  StringBuffer sb = new StringBuffer();
  Address[] addresses = message.getRecipients(Message.RecipientType.TO);
  if (addresses != null) {
    for (int j = 0; j < addresses.length; j++) {
      sb.append(addresses[j].toString() + " ");
    }
  }
  return sb.toString();
}

public String getCc() throws MessagingException {
  StringBuffer sb = new StringBuffer();
  Address[] addresses = message.getRecipients(Message.RecipientType.CC);
  if (addresses != null) {
    for (int j = 0; j < addresses.length; j++) {
      sb.append(addresses[j].toString() + " ");
    }
  }
  return sb.toString();
}

public String getSubject() throws MessagingException {
  return message.getSubject();
}

private String getSize() throws MessagingException {
  int size = message.getSize();
  String sizeDesc = size + " B";
  if (size >= 1024) {
    size /= 1024;
    sizeDesc = size + " KB";
    if (size >= 1024) {
      size /= 1024;
      sizeDesc = size + " MB";
    }
  }
  return sizeDesc;
}

private String getFlags() throws MessagingException {
  Flags flags = message.getFlags();
  StringBuffer sb = new StringBuffer();
```

Continued

Listing 10-7 *(continued)*

```java
      Flags.Flag[] sysFlags = flags.getSystemFlags();
      for (int i = 0; i < sysFlags.length; i++) {
        if (sysFlags[i] == Flags.Flag.ANSWERED)
          sb.append("Answered ");
        else if (sysFlags[i] == Flags.Flag.DELETED)
          sb.append("Deleted ");
        else if (sysFlags[i] == Flags.Flag.DRAFT)
          sb.append("Draft ");
        else if (sysFlags[i] == Flags.Flag.FLAGGED)
          sb.append("Flagged ");
        else if (sysFlags[i] == Flags.Flag.RECENT)
          sb.append("Recent ");
        else if (sysFlags[i] == Flags.Flag.SEEN)
          sb.append("Seen ");
        else if (sysFlags[i] == Flags.Flag.USER)
          sb.append("User ");
        else
          sb.append("Unknown ");
      }

      String[] userFlags = flags.getUserFlags();
      for (int i = 0; i < userFlags.length; i++) {
        sb.append(userFlags[i].toString() + " ");
      }
      return sb.toString();
    }

    public String getMessageText() throws IOException, MessagingException {
      String text = "";
      if (message.isMimeType("text/plain")) {
        text = (String)message.getContent();
      } else if (message.isMimeType("multipart/*")) {
        Multipart mp = (Multipart) message.getContent();
        BodyPart bp = mp.getBodyPart(0);
        if (bp.isMimeType("text/plain") | bp.isMimeType("text/html")) {
          text = (String)bp.getContent();
        }
      }
      return text;
    }

    private String getEnclosureName()
    throws MessagingException, IOException {
      StringBuffer sb = new StringBuffer();
      if (message.isMimeType("multipart/*")) {
        Multipart mp = (Multipart)message.getContent();
        int count = mp.getCount();
        for (int i = 0; i < count; i++) {
```

```
        BodyPart bp = mp.getBodyPart(i);
        if (bp.getFileName() != null) {
          sb.append(bp.getFileName() + " ");
        }
      }
    }
  }
  return sb.toString();
  }
}
```

Summary

WebLogic Server and Sun's J2EE make adding electronic mail capabilities to your applications easy. The JavaMail API defines classes and interfaces that enable you to solve the simplest or most complex requirements in a protocol-independent manner. You can add a sendmail-like facility or create a complete, fully functional mail client.

This chapter covered the most commonly used JavaMail functionality, but a great deal more exists. The JavaMail API documentation covers the remainder in detail and gives examples of how to list providers, prefetch message headers, search for messages by using search terms, copy and move messages to other folders, and much more. Now that you have read this chapter, you should have no problem implementing the rest . . . have fun!

✦   ✦   ✦

Developing Web Components

Developing Servlets

Now that you have learned how to program the J2EE APIs, it's time to learn about how you are most likely to put them to use: by writing Web applications. This chapter (about servlets) and Chapter 12, which covers Java Server pages (JSPs), show you how to use two important J2EE technologies in conjunction with WebLogic Server to build and deploy dynamic, scalable Web applications.

In this chapter, we introduce you to the basics of servlets and show you how to write, deploy, and test a simple servlet for WebLogic Server. Then we cover a number of advanced servlet programming topics, including session tracking, database access, J2EE API access, security, clustering, and more.

What's a Web Application?

Quite simply, a *Web application* is a collection of pages, delivered to a Web browser, that provides useful functionality to a community of users. A Web application might be as simple as a personal photo album deployed on the World Wide Web or as complex as an employee benefits application running on a corporate intranet. You can write both kinds of applications with servlets and JSPs, but you are more likely to use these technologies to write the complex type; this requires effective security as well as the capability to handle substantial user input, to make decisions based on that input, and to interface with databases and other back-end systems to do "real" work.

Servlets are especially important because they bridge the gap between Web browsers and the power of J2EE. A *servlet* is a Java class that receives HTTP requests from a Web server, processes them, and then sends a response back to the HTTP server for transmission to the client's Web browser. In effect, a servlet is a seamless extension of a Web server that can perform any task you are capable of programming in Java.

In the case of WebLogic, a *servlet* is a seamless extension of a Web server that also has complete access to the power of J2EE. From within a WebLogic-hosted servlet, you can do the following:

+ Access databases by using JDBC and JTA

+ Make calls to RMI servers

+ Perform JNDI lookups

+ Send messages by using JMS

+ Process e-mail by using JavaMail

✦ Invoke Enterprise JavaBeans (EJBs)

✦ Dynamically generate HTML (or any other kind of client-side script) for transmission back to the client

✦ Use session tracking to conduct an extended conversation with a client

✦ Use security to authenticate users and control their access to content

✦ Transfer control to other servlets and JSPs

That's a lot of power!

Another reason servlets are important is because they are the foundation of JSPs. As you will see in Chapter 12, when a JSP is invoked for the first time, a J2EE-compliant Web container (such as WebLogic) automatically compiles the JSP into a servlet and then executes the servlet any time a request comes in for that JSP (unless the JSP is subsequently changed). Understanding servlets will give you a better understanding of JSPs. See the next section for more on servlets.

Understanding Servlets

To program servlets effectively, you need to understand the Servlet API, how servlets function within WebLogic's Web container, and how servlets interact with HTTP requests and responses.

The servlet API: Versions and packages

Servlets are Java classes written to the Java Servlet API. WebLogic Server 7.0 implements version 2.3 of the Servlet API, which was released in fall 2001. Version 2.2 of the Servlet API is in common use today, and WebLogic Server 7.0 fully supports this version as well. You can find copies of both versions of the specification at the following URL:

```
http://java.sun.com/products/servlet/download.html#specs
```

The Servlet API is implemented in two packages:

✦ `javax.servlet`, the generic package for servlets that respond to requests using any network protocol.

✦ `javax.servlet.http`, the package for servlets that respond to requests using the HTTP protocol. These are known as *HTTP Servlets* and are the only type of servlets supported by WebLogic Server. We focus on HTTP servlets for the remainder of this chapter.

The Sun JavaDocs for both packages are available at the following locations:

✦ `http://java.sun.com/products/servlet/2.2/javadoc/` (version 2.2)

✦ `http://java.sun.com/products/servlet/2.3/javadoc/` (version 2.3)

Every servlet must implement the `javax.servlet.Servlet` interface, and the servlet API contains a class called `javax.servlet.http.HttpServlet` that does so. This is the class you extend when you write HTTP servlets of your own, as in the following:

```
import javax.servlet.*;
import javax.servlet.http.*;

public class MyServlet extends HttpServlet {
   // your class implementation here
}
```

Before diving further into the code, let's examine how servlets are deployed within the WebLogic Web container and how they function in general.

The Web container and Web applications

Recall from Chapter 1 that servlets execute within the WebLogic Web container, as mandated by the J2EE standard. This container provides a runtime environment that includes lifecycle support, access to server resources (usually through JNDI lookups), and access to the J2EE APIs. Servlets can also access EJBs and RMI servers that are hosted by WebLogic or other servers, as long as the objects are J2EE-compliant and can be located on the network via JNDI lookups.

In WebLogic 7, a servlet exists within the context of a *Web application*. A Web application is a collection of resources that implements a desired functionality. These resources can include servlets, static HTML pages, images, movies, sounds, templates, and so on. The resources are organized into a predefined directory structure on disk, which is defined by the J2EE standard. The application must also contain one or more deployment descriptors, written in XML, that define various properties of the application, including the servlets it contains and the URL patterns required to access them. Web applications deployed in WebLogic Server require two deployment descriptors: web.xml, the descriptor required by J2EE, and weblogic.xml, a descriptor that provides WebLogic-specific deployment information.

Figure 11-1 shows the required directory structure for a Web application. The Application Root folder is usually located as a subfolder of the /<user domains folder>/<domain name>/applications folder, but can be located anywhere on the server computer.

With WebLogic 7.0's new flexibility in folder locations, this folder location can seem a little daunting at first. Let's examine a concrete example to make it a little easier to understand. When you install WebLogic (see Chapter 4), you are given the opportunity to create a new domain with the Domain Configuration Wizard. It asks you for a home for the user domains you create — we'll refer to that generically as <user domains folder> — but let's say you called that D:\WebLogicUserDomains. You're then prompted for a name for your domain — we'll call that <domain name>, generically — let's say you called it mydomain. And now let's say you want to create a servlet with an <application root> of bibleServlets. Generically, that would be represented as follows:

/<user domains folder>/<domain name>/applications/<application root>

Or, in this specific case, it would end up on your hard drive as follows:

D:\WebLogicUserDomains\mydomain\applications\bibleServlets where bibleServlets is the Application Root shown in Figure 11-1.

You can have any number of applications, each inside its own Application Root folder. You can name each Application Root folder anything you like, but we recommend using names that don't contain spaces.

Figure 11-1: Web application directory structure

Tip   Unless you're extraordinarily careful, it's not a good idea to put spaces in folder or filenames. If you use scripting or Java-based tools, you'll have to make sure to put quotes around names with spaces so they are not treated as parameters. And sometimes even GUI tools call shell scripts behind the scenes. This gets ugly very quickly so, please, don't go there!

When developing servlets, you must copy the compiled class files to the `/<user domains folder>/<domain name>/applications/<application root>/WEB-INF/classes` directory for your application or they won't work.

Note   To see an example of a deployed Web application, go to any WebLogic domain you have created and then go to `<domain-name>/applications/DefaultWebApp`. Inside this folder is the application that comes up when you point your Web browser to WebLogic Server (by typing **http://localhost:7001**).

To make Web applications more manageable and portable, you can bundle them into an archive, similar to a JAR file, and deploy the archive instead. The archive is called, fittingly enough, a *Web application archive* and is bundled into a WAR file — using the JAR utility, no less. We show you how to create and deploy WAR files later in this chapter.

During development, it's common to deploy to the full directory structure without creating a WAR file. This makes it easy to replace files with newer versions as development proceeds. When you're ready to go into production, you can create a WAR file that can be easily moved to a different box or deployed on multiple boxes in a cluster.

Note   Web applications deployed to a full directory structure will work only if WebLogic Server is running in Development mode. When WebLogic Server is running in Production mode, your Web applications must be deployed in WAR files.

How servlets work

Servlets bridge the gap between HTTP and J2EE. The Servlet API is designed to make it easy to work with HTTP requests and responses in a Java-friendly way. And because servlets are ordinary Java classes running within WebLogic, they have complete access to the power of J2EE. In this section, we'll explain how servlets interact with HTTP requests, how servlets are structured programmatically, and how they are managed by WebLogic Server.

HTTP requests

When a client requests data from an HTTP server, it does so by using an HTTP request method. The most commonly used methods are GET and POST. The GET method is used to retrieve information from the server (such as a Web page), whereas the POST method is used to transmit data to the server (such as the data required to complete a credit card transaction).

Even though the GET method is used to retrieve data, you can include parameters in your request that specify what to get. These parameters are appended to the request URL in the form of a *querystring*. The querystring is separated from the rest of the URL by a question mark, as in the following:

```
http://localhost:7001/myWebApp/myServlet?name=Joe+Zuffoletto
```

Parameters are passed as name=value pairs. Note that plus signs are used in place of spaces; URLs cannot contain spaces. Multiple parameters are separated by the ampersand (&) character.

Querystrings are visible to users (in the address boxes of their browsers), so make sure that they don't contain privileged information, such as passwords or other sensitive information that can be easily hacked. Also, you should use querystrings only for simple requests containing up to a handful of parameters because some Web servers truncate incoming URLs that exceed 240 characters or so. WebLogic doesn't do this, but if your querystrings contain 100 characters or more, you should consider using the POST method (discussed later in this section) to avoid shipping large URLs around.

Caution   Querystrings pose other hazards as well. URLs containing querystrings can be bookmarked; they can also be revisited by clicking the browser's Back button. Therefore, servlets that respond to these types of requests should be designed to perform read-only tasks, such as displaying an account activity or the contents of an electronic mailbox. Otherwise, you may cause users to inadvertently make multiple purchases or delete multiple records from a database, which in turn would reduce your marketability as a Java developer.

The `POST` method sends information to the server in a different way as part of its HTTP request body. This enables you to send long lists of parameters to the server or parameters of great length, such as graphics or long blocks of text. The data being posted is invisible to the user; it doesn't appear in the URL, so it's slightly more secure. Unlike `GET` requests, `POST` requests cannot be bookmarked, e-mailed, or re-sent with the Back button. Therefore, `POST` requests are better for transmitting sensitive data, such as the user's approval to purchase something, because there is less chance the user will erroneously duplicate the request.

Other request methods include `HEAD`, which the client sends when it only wants to see the headers of the response. The `PUT` method is used to copy documents to the server, and the `DELETE` method is used to remove documents. The `TRACE` method is a debugging tool that returns the exact contents of its request to the client, and the `OPTIONS` method is used to ask the server which methods it supports or what other types of options are available. All these methods are far less commonly used than `GET` and `POST`, so we don't cover them any further in this chapter.

How servlets are structured

An *HTTP servlet* is a Java class that extends `javax.servlet.http.HttpServlet`. It includes methods you can override that map to the various HTTP request methods. These methods are `doGet()`, `doPost()`, `doHead()`, `doPut()`, `doDelete()`, `doTrace()`, and `doOptions()`. Each of these methods accepts two input parameters. The first is an object of type `HttpServletRequest`, which contains the client's request data and methods to retrieve it. The second is an object of type `HttpServletResponse`, into which your response to the request is written. When your servlet finishes executing, WebLogic transmits the data contained in this object back to the client.

`HttpServlet` also contains a generic `service()` method that is invoked by the Web container whenever a request comes in for a servlet. This method also receives the `HttpServletRequest` and `HttpServletResponse` objects as parameters, and its default behavior is to simply turn around and call the appropriate `doXXX()` method, based on the HTTP request method received from the client.

When you write a servlet, you can structure your implementation in one of three ways:

   ✦ *Override the `service()` method.* This causes your servlet to respond to all requests in the same way. This is usually sufficient and is the path most WebLogic developers take.

   ✦ *Override one or more of the `doXXX()` methods.* This enables you to respond to different types of requests in different ways. But your servlet will return an error message if you receive a request type that you do not support.

   ✦ *Override the `service()` method and one or more `doXXX()` methods.* This technique enables you to respond to different types of requests in different ways while also performing processing common to all types. For this to work, you must call `super.service()` from your `service()` method, or the `doXXX()` methods will not be called.

How WebLogic Server invokes servlets

When WebLogic Server receives a request for a Web page, it examines the incoming URL to see if it maps to a Web application and/or servlet deployed on the server. It makes this determination by examining the `web.xml` file of all deployed applications. These deployment descriptors contain entries that map URL patterns to servlets and other resources.

If the URL maps to a servlet, WebLogic loads the HTTP request information into an `HttpServletRequest` object. It also creates an instance of an `HttpServletResponse` object. It then invokes the servlet's `service()` method, passing the `HttpServletRequest` and

`HttpServletResponse` objects as parameters. The servlet does its work, writing data to the `HttpServletResponse` object along the way, and then returns the `HttpServletResponse` object back to WebLogic Server for transmission back to the client. This object usually contains a stream of HTML data, so from the client's perspective, the server simply returned an HTML document. But instead of returning static HTML data from a disk file, the server returns HTML that was dynamically constructed by the servlet — usually in response to one or more input parameters sent by the client — and therein lies the power of servlets.

When to use servlets

When servlets first arrived on the scene, they were used not only to perform server-side processing in response to requests, but also to generate extensive amounts of markup language (usually HTML) for transmission back to the client. A common example is for a servlet to perform a database search based on the contents of its input parameters and then to render possibly hundreds of rows of results as an HTML table.

Although there is nothing technically wrong with this approach, it creates application maintenance headaches because it causes client-side markup code to be tightly bound with server-side Java code. If a change is desired in the client-side display, even something as simple as a font size or color, a server-side Java developer must be called upon to recode and recompile one or more servlets. This undermines the clean separation that J2EE strives to achieve between business and presentation logic.

The designers of J2EE responded to this problem by introducing JSPs. Since the advent of JSPs, the proper way to structure Web applications is to embed presentation logic in JSPs and business logic in servlets and/or JavaBeans. This allows client-side developers to focus on coding markup language into JSPs and server-side developers to focus on coding Java into servlets and JavaBeans.

Cross-Reference   JSPs are discussed in depth in Chapter 12.

The upshot of this is that the "proper" use of servlets these days is as server-side controllers and dispatchers that do not generate client-side markup. As a controller, a servlet is called upon to manage access to server-side resources, such as EJBs, JMS message queues, and so on in response to client-side requests. As a dispatcher, a servlet is called upon to forward requests to other servlets or JSPs based on the current state of the application; in other words, the servlet provides server-side support of client-side navigation and workflow.

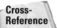

Cross-Reference   See Chapter 3 for a more detailed discussion about servlets as controllers and dispatchers.

The early examples in this chapter break the rules a bit and use servlets to generate markup so that you can see how it's done. The later examples, however, try to demonstrate the proper use of servlets as controllers and dispatchers.

The servlet lifecycle

A deployed servlet exists in one of five states, which comprise the servlet lifecycle:

✦ **Instantiation:** The Web container loads the servlet into memory and calls its default constructor. This happens once in the servlet's lifetime — either the first time a client invokes the servlet or at server startup (if the servlet is configured to load at server startup).

✦ **Initialization:** The Web container calls the servlet's init() method to perform initialization tasks. This also happens once: immediately after instantiation. Overriding the init() method is your opportunity to perform one-time initialization of data structures, database connections, class variables, and other infrastructure that will be used by the servlet during its lifetime.

✦ **Service:** A client invokes the servlet, resulting in the Web container calling its service() method. In HTTP servlets, the service() method automatically calls the appropriate doXXX() method, which is the method you override to make the servlet do its work.

✦ **Destruction:** The Web container is removing the servlet instance from memory. Before doing so, it calls the servlet's destroy() method. You can override this method to perform cleanup tasks, such as closing database connections and reversing tasks you performed in the initialization state.

✦ **Unavailable:** The servlet is destroyed and awaiting garbage collection.

After a servlet is loaded into the JVM, the same instance of the servlet is used to respond to all client requests for that servlet until either the servlet is modified or WebLogic Server restarts. When either of those events happens, WebLogic calls the servlet's destroy() method before unloading it from the JVM.

Note

The exception to this rule is when the servlet implements the javax.Servlet. SingleThreadModel interface. By default, each incoming request for a servlet spawns its own execution thread in the JVM, and multiple threads simultaneously execute the servlet if traffic is heavy. You can support heavy concurrent loads if you have your servlet implement the SingleThreadModel interface, in which case WebLogic Server spawns a pool of servlet instances, the size of which you specify in the WebLogic Console. WebLogic guarantees that only one thread executes each servlet instance at a time. For more information, see the "Threading Issues in HTTP Servlets" section of the BEA *Programming WebLogic HTTP Servlets* guide (http://e-docs.bea.com/wls/docs70/servlet/progtasks.html #129285).

To detect whether a servlet has been modified, WebLogic periodically compares the timestamp of the servlet instance loaded into memory with that of the servlet's class file on disk. If the timestamps are different, WebLogic assumes that the servlet has been modified. When this happens, WebLogic calls the destroy() method of the servlet loaded in memory before unloading that instance. Upon loading the modified version from disk, WebLogic calls its init() method.

Programming Servlets

To see how to program servlets and deploy them within Web applications, you're going to develop a simple Web application from the ground up that starts with a static HTML document and then adds a servlet. This will help you understand how Web applications are deployed in WebLogic and how servlets fit into the picture.

Note

For the rest of this chapter, we develop to the WebLogic domain called dev that we created in Chapter 4. You may want to create the same domain on your machine to follow along with the examples. Also, we work with WebLogic Server set to Development mode, as explained in Chapter 4.

Creating a simple Web application

Before writing a servlet, let's create and deploy the simplest possible Web application — one that contains a home page implemented as static HTML. This application will become the shell into which you deploy your servlets later.

1. Use your favorite file manager to navigate to the applications directory of your WebLogic domain. On our sample system, the path is h:\WebLogicUserDomains\dev\applications. Within this directory, create a directory called BibleApp. Then, within BibleApp, create an empty directory called WEB-INF (this directory name must be in all caps, include a hyphen in the middle, and contain no spaces); inside that directory, create two additional empty directories named classes and lib. In other words, create the directory structure shown in Figure 11-1, with the root directory called BibleApp.

2. Create a simple home page in HTML using your favorite text editor. Here's the code for ours:

```
<html>
<head>
<title>WebLogic 7 Bible Web App Home Page</title>
<meta http-equiv="Content-Type" content="text/html">
</head>
<body>
Hello, Bible reader!
</body>
</html>
```

Save this to the BibleApp directory as index.html.

3. Create a J2EE deployment descriptor, also in your favorite text editor, that matches the following:

```
<!DOCTYPE web-app PUBLIC "-//Sun Microsystems, Inc.//DTD Web
Application 2.3//EN" "http://java.sun.com/dtd/web-app_2_3.dtd">

<web-app>
  <welcome-file-list>
    <welcome-file>index.html</welcome-file>
  </welcome-file-list>
</web-app>
```

Save this file in the WEB-INF directory as web.xml. This file tells WebLogic that index.html is the welcome file for your Web application; if a user navigates to your Web application without specifying a file in the URL, index.html will be displayed.

Note   The web.xml deployment descriptor begins with a reference to the Sun DTD (Document Type Definition) for Web applications. Use the one shown if you want your Web applications to support the features of the Servlet 2.3 specification. If you want to support the Servlet 2.2 specification, use the following DTD instead:

```
<!DOCTYPE web-app PUBLIC "-//Sun Microsystems, Inc.//DTD Web
Application 2.2//EN" "http://java.sun.com/j2ee/dtds/web-
app_2.2.dtd">
```

4. Start WebLogic Server in Development mode. Open your Web browser and go to `http://localhost:7001/BibleApp`. The Web page created in Step 2 should appear, as shown in Figure 11-2.

Figure 11-2: BibleApp home page, implemented as HTML

Notice that although the full URL of the home page is `http://localhost:7001/BibleApp/index.html`, you don't need to specify the `index.html` part; it was previously defined in the deployment descriptor as the welcome page.

A peek inside the WebLogic Console shows how WebLogic automatically deployed the application in our domain, as shown in Figure 11-3.

Figure 11-3: The WebLogic Console view of the Web application

Writing a simple servlet

Next, you'll write a simple servlet called `HelloServlet` and add it to the application. This servlet accepts a username as an input parameter and then outputs that name as part of the HTML page that it creates on the fly. It also keeps count of how many times it has been called. Listing 11-1 shows the Java code for the servlet.

The code begins by importing the `javax.servlet` packages. You also import `java.io.*` so you can work with output streams. You declare an instance variable called `counter`, of type `int`, to keep track of how many times the servlet has been called.

This servlet includes a "do-nothing" default constructor that simply writes a message to the WebLogic command window by using `System.out.println()`. This enables you to follow the servlet's movement through its lifecycle when it is invoked. The `init()` method does the same thing, but it also initializes the hit counter by resetting it to zero. A `destroy()` method appears at the end of the listing that writes a message to the command window in support of your lifecycle tracking. Obviously, your production servlets wouldn't waste cycles with methods such as `HelloServlet()` and `destroy()` that simply write messages to WebLogic's command window — we included them only for instructional purposes.

The `service()` method does the servlet's work. Its input parameters enable you to work with the request and response objects associated with the servlet. The first step is to increment the servlet's hit counter and to then call the `getParameter()` method of the request object to find out what username was provided in the querystring. Recall that querystrings consist of name-value pairs, separated by the & character. When you pass one of the names in your querystring to `getParameter()`, it returns a string containing the corresponding value. The name of our parameter is `username`, so we get its value with this line:

```
String userName = request.getParameter("username");
```

The next step is to use the response object to construct an HTML response to the client's request. Begin by calling the response object's `setContentType()` method to tell it you will be returning text formatted as HTML. Then use the `getWriter()` method to obtain a reference to the response object's output stream. It's to this stream that you must send your properly formatted HTML, which you do with a series of `println()` calls. These calls construct, in the proper sequential order, the set of HTML tags that make up your response. Notice in particular the statements that read as follows:

```
out.println("<p>Hello, " + name + "!</p>");
out.println("This servlet has been invoked " +
    counter + " times.");
```

This is the *dynamic* portion of the servlet; these statements insert the name you received as an input parameter into the HTML, as well as the number of times the servlet has been invoked. Therefore, if the name changes, so does the HTML that is sent back to the client. The HTML also changes when the counter changes.

Note   Notice how cumbersome it is to generate HTML from within a servlet by using a succession of `PrintWriter.println()` calls. You can imagine the difficulty of maintaining this code for pages that are very complex. This is why JSPs were invented!

The `service()` method closes by writing a message to the WebLogic command window, indicating that the servlet was invoked.

Listing 11-1: **HelloServlet.java**

```
package com.wiley.wlsbible.servlets;

import javax.servlet.*;
import javax.servlet.http.*;
import java.io.*;
```

Continued

Listing 11-1 *(continued)*

```java
private int counter;

public class HelloServlet extends HttpServlet {

  public HelloServlet() {
    // Perform instantiation tasks here (rare).
    super();
    System.out.println("HelloServlet instantiated.");
  }

  public void init() throws ServletException {
    // Perform one-time initialization tasks here.
    counter = 0;
    System.out.println("HelloServlet initialized.");
  }

  public void service(HttpServletRequest request,
   HttpServletResponse response) throws IOException {
    // Do the servlet's work here.
    counter++;
    String userName = request.getParameter("username");
    response.setContentType("text/html");
    PrintWriter out = response.getWriter();
    out.println("<html>");
    out.println("<head><title>HelloServlet</title></head>");
    out.println("<body>");
    out.println("<p>Hello, " + userName + "!</p>");
    out.println("This servlet has been invoked " +
      counter + " times.");
    out.println("</body></html>");
    System.out.println("HelloServlet.doGet() invoked.");
  }

  public void destroy() {
    // Perform cleanup tasks here.
    System.out.println("HelloServlet destroyed.");
  }
}
```

Deploying and testing the servlet

To deploy this servlet, you must compile it (saving the class file to your application's WEB-INF/classes directory) and create an entry for it in your web.xml deployment descriptor.

Note   All the code for this chapter, along with Ant build scripts, is available at the book's Web site at http://www.wiley.com/compbooks/zuffoletto.

Compiling the servlet

A command similar to the following (depending on your classpath and system settings) compiles the servlet and copies the class file into the proper directory:

```
javac -d BibleApp/WEB-INF/classes BibleApp/HelloServlet.java
```

Adding the servlet to the web.xml deployment descriptor

Modify the web.xml deployment descriptor (as shown by the bolded text in the following code sample) to deploy the servlet:

```
<!DOCTYPE web-app PUBLIC "-//Sun Microsystems, Inc.//DTD Web Application
2.3//EN" "http://java.sun.com/j2ee/dtds/web-app_2.3.dtd">

<web-app>
  <welcome-file-list>
    <welcome-file>index.html</welcome-file>
  </welcome-file-list>

  <servlet>
    <servlet-name>HelloServlet</servlet-name>
    <servlet-class>com.wiley.wlsbible.servlets.HelloServlet</servlet-class>
  </servlet>

  <servlet-mapping>
    <servlet-name>HelloServlet</servlet-name>
    <url-pattern>/helloservlet</url-pattern>
  </servlet-mapping>
</web-app>
```

Studying this file, you can see that the `<welcome-file-list>` has not changed—it still points to index.html. But now you have added `<servlet>` and `<servlet-mapping>` tags that tell the Web container the name of the servlet, the class that implements it, and what incoming URL pattern should invoke it. Note that the string you give for `<url-pattern>` should *not* include the name of your Web application; the Web container handles this for you.

After compiling the servlet and updating web.xml, stop and restart WebLogic Server. It's best to restart WebLogic Server after changing a deployment descriptor.

Testing the servlet

To invoke a servlet, you provide a URL that matches the following pattern:

```
http://host:port/web-application-name/servlet-name?query-string
```

An example of a URL that invokes HelloServlet follows:

```
http://localhost:7001/BibleApp/helloservlet?username=Joe+Zuffoletto
```

Of course, you can provide any value for username you like (this is a good thing if your name is Joe Zuffoletto). The servlet simply retrieves the name provided as an input parameter and inserts it into the HTML it generates in response. Figure 11-4 shows a browser window after invoking the servlet with the preceding URL. If you call the servlet again, the counter will increase until either the servlet's class file changes on disk (causing WebLogic to destroy the in-memory version and load the new disk version) or WebLogic Server is restarted.

Figure 11-4: Output from HelloServlet

Advanced Servlet Programming Techniques

Now that you've mastered the basics of servlets, it's time to learn about advanced servlet programming techniques that make it possible to build useful applications. These techniques involve working with sessions, working with servlet context, dispatching requests to other application resources, and implementing servlet security.

Working with sessions

A *session* is a prolonged conversation between a server and a client, during which time the client's state is updated and used to drive the client's flow through the application.

As almost every Web developer knows, HTTP is a stateless protocol. Web servers receive requests from clients (usually Web browsers), fulfill those requests, and then move on, completely forgetting about the clients they have served and the requests they have fulfilled in the past.

In traditional client/server systems, clients establish network connections with servers that remain open from the time users start the application until the time they quit. This length of time, which can span from minutes to hours, corresponds to each user's session. During the course of a session, the server and the client can keep track of each other's state and pass that information back and forth at will. As a result, many complex applications have been built using the client/server model because it's easy to track a user's progress through the system.

Building such systems with HTTP is more difficult. The problem is that when you interact with a Web server, even for an extended period of time (such as when you're using an online shopping cart), there is no persistent network connection held open between you and the server. Every time you call up a new page, a new network connection is opened. After the page is delivered to you, the network connection is closed. Therefore, the user's concept of a single session with a Web application is actually a multitude of HTTP sessions that are completely independent of each other, and across which no state is maintained.

Note   The HTTP 1.1 specification introduces the notion of connections being held open to service multiple requests from the same client. But the purpose of this feature is strictly to improve performance. It has no impact on HTTP's inability to maintain state.

Fortunately, this limitation of HTTP is easily overcome. Think for a moment about how client/server applications work. When you start such an application, the first thing it does is prompt you for a username and password. This serves two purposes: It makes the system secure and it gives the server a token that it can use to identify you in order to establish a stateful session. To accomplish the latter, the server matches this token (your unique username) against

its user profile database and retrieves your profile for use during the session. This profile might include personal information (such as your name, address, and phone number) as well as application-specific information, such as your access privileges and search preferences. As you move through the application, your profile is updated as necessary. When you quit the application, your updated profile is saved back to the database so it can be reused during your next session.

The next day, you log in to the application again. This new session with the application is completely independent of the last, yet the server is able to restore your state, just as it did the day before, by matching your login token to your user profile.

This same technique is used to achieve the effect of a stateful session with HTTP. A token is created and exchanged between the Web browser and the Web server, uniquely identifying you as a user. The server uses this token to work with your profile on the server. The only differences are that the sessions are shorter and more numerous, and the token is created by the server instead of the client.

Session-tracking methods

Over the past few years, three methods for tracking sessions and state in Web applications have emerged:

✦ URL rewriting

✦ Cookies

✦ Hidden form fields

All three methods can be used to exchange one or more tokens of the developer's choosing between the Web server and the browser. The server can then use these tokens to retrieve, update, and save a session's state on the server.

URL rewriting

URL rewriting uses querystrings to pass tokens between the browser and server. After a user named John, for example, is identified by the server, the server can dynamically rewrite all URLs served to John so they include his name in the querystring

```
http://myBank.com/reports?type=creditReport&user=John
```

```
http://myBank.com/reports?type=accountSummary&user=John
```

and so on. Now whenever John clicks a link in the Web application, his name is transparently sent to the server, from which it can be retrieved with a `request.getParameter()` call.

The J2EE specification takes this one step further by requiring that the client-specific token be called `jsessionid` and that it be automatically generated by the server, as in

```
http://myBank.com/reports?jsessionid=3T78X90W225PQ46&type=creditReport
```

WebLogic Server generates long random `jsessionid`s. This increases security by reducing the chances a user will masquerade as someone by faking their `jsessionid`. Furthermore, you don't use `request.getParameter()` to manipulate `jsessionid`s yourself. Instead, you use other methods in the servlet API to work with the session. We explain these in the next section.

 Cross-Reference   Chapter 23 discusses configuring `jsessionid` length in the WebLogic Console.

Because rewritten URLs are different for each user, URL rewriting cannot be used in static HTML pages. The server must dynamically generate pages that include rewritten URLs, either by using servlets or JSPs. To specify that a URL is to be rewritten, use the `javax.servlet.http.HttpServletResponse.encodeURL()` method. The following statement in a servlet, for example, generates a non-encoded URL:

```
out.println("<a href=\"/reports?type=creditReport\">Credit Report</a>");
```

To encode the same URL, write the following:

```
out.println(<a href=\"" + response.encodeURL("/reports?type=creditReport) +
        "\">Credit Report</a>");
```

Cookies

Cookies are the most popular technology used for session tracking. A *cookie* is a token sent to a Web browser as part of an HTTP response header. The cookie is saved by the browser and then resubmitted to the server the next time the browser connects to that server.

A cookie consists of a name, a value, and optional attributes. The attributes include the following:

✦ The Internet domain to which the browser should present the cookie, and optionally a path within that domain. The default is the domain that issued the cookie.

✦ The cookie's lifetime, after which the cookie expires and is no longer valid

✦ A security setting that determines whether the cookie must be presented using a secure protocol, such as SSL

✦ The cookie's version

✦ A short comment stating the cookie's purpose

In J2EE, servlets and JSPs create and send cookies by using the `javax.servlet.http.Cookie` class. The following code shows how to do this.

```
// Create a new cookie, providing a name and value
// to its constructor.
Cookie cookie = new Cookie("userID", "John");

// Set the cookie's lifetime in seconds.
// This one expires in 2 hours.
cookie.setMaxAge(7200);

// Set the cookie's domain. Note the leading dot.
cookie.setDomain(".myBank.com");

// Set the cookie's path within the domain. The cookie
// is presented only to URLs in that path.
cookie.setPath("/myWebApp");

// Add the cookie to the HTTP response.
response.addCookie(cookie);
```

Corresponding methods exist to read the values and attributes of cookies.

You can learn more about cookies by reading RFC 2109, available at the following URL:

```
http://www.faqs.org/rfcs/rfc2109.html
```

The problem with cookies is that some users perceive them to be a security risk, so they disable cookies in their browser. Obviously, if a user has disabled cookies, you cannot use them to track sessions.

Hidden form fields

Hidden form fields are similar in concept to URL rewriting, except that tokens are embedded in HTML forms as hidden fields, as in the following:

```
<input type="hidden" name="userID" value="John">
```

The tokens are invisible to the user, but are posted to the server when the form is submitted. The server can then read the values of the hidden fields and act on them.

Like URL rewriting, this approach requires the affected pages to be dynamically generated by the server. But this approach is more restrictive than URL rewriting because it can be used only on pages that employ HTML forms.

How J2EE implements session tracking

J2EE implements session tracking through the servlet API by using a collection of methods that are intuitive and easy to use. Behind the scenes, the servlet API uses cookies and URL rewriting to implement the session-tracking calls. Hidden form fields are not used at all.

Creating a session

To enable session tracking in your Web application, you must first create a session, which is an instance of `javax.servlet.http.HttpSession`. To do so, you call `HttpServletRequest.getSession()`:

```
HttpSession session = request.getSession();
```

Sessions are bound to users. If a session already exists for the current user, `getSession()` returns the existing session. Otherwise, it creates a new one.

To create a session, `getSession()` transparently creates a cookie *and* rewrites your URLs. They are transmitted to the browser in the next response, at which time the browser may or may not join the session. If the browser accepts cookies, it sends the cookie back with the next request and is said to have *joined the session*. The servlet API detects this and automatically uses cookies for the remainder of the session. But if a cookie is not returned, the servlet API assumes that the browser has rejected the cookie, and it automatically uses URL rewriting instead. In this case, the browser has not joined the session, but if your application uses URL rewriting, you'll still be able to perform session tracking. Therefore, if you want your applications to work with or without cookies, you must use URL rewriting.

Working with session attributes

You can store any number of named attributes into a session and retrieve them later. Each attribute must have a unique name. The following code shows how to do this.

```
HttpSession session = request.getSession();
session.setAttribute("userID", "John");
session.setAttribute("accountNo", "1234-345-456");
session.setAttribute("phoneNo", "555-1212");
...
String userID = (String) session.getAttribute("userID");
String accountNo = (String) session.getAttribute("accountNo");
String phoneNo = (String) session.getAttribute("phoneNo");
```

`setAttribute()` creates the attribute if it doesn't exist; otherwise, it overwrites its value. `getAttribute()` returns null if the given attribute doesn't exist.

You can also permanently remove an attribute from a session with the following code:

```
session.removeAttribute("phoneNo");
```

By default, WebLogic caches session attributes in memory, so they don't persist across server restarts. You can, however, configure WebLogic to support persistent sessions by using either a disk file or JDBC data source as a backing store. For more information, see the "Making Sessions Persistent" section in the *Programming WebLogic HTTP Servlets* guide (http://e-docs.bea.com/wls/docs70/servlet/progtasks.html#163051).

Invalidating a session

When a user's session has ended, you can invalidate it, which removes all attributes bound to the session and effectively kills the session:

```
session.invalidate();
```

You normally call invalidate() when a user explicitly logs off your Web application or when you choose to log the user off.

If you don't explicitly invalidate a session, WebLogic automatically invalidates it after it expires. All sessions expire after a certain period of time, which you can configure in the WebLogic Console. The default is 60 minutes.

Working with the servlet context

Although sessions allow your application's servlets to maintain state with users, the *servlet context* enables your servlets and JSPs to maintain state with each other across the entire Web application. Every Web application has its own servlet context, which you can think of as a global storage area for the application.

You access an application's servlet context through the javax.servlet.ServletContext interface, which provides methods for storing and retrieving attributes, obtaining information about the servlet container and the servlet's runtime environment, logging events to the application log file, and more.

To obtain a reference to the servlet context, call ServletContext.getServletContext():

```
ServletContext ctx = this.getServletContext();
```

where this refers to your class that extends HttpServlet.

After you have a reference to the servlet context, you can set and get attributes much as you would with a session:

```
ctx.setAttribute("myAttribute", myObject);
myObject = (myObjectType) ctx.getAttribute("myAttribute");
```

setAttribute() takes a string containing a unique name for the attribute and an object containing the attribute's data. getAttribute() returns the object corresponding to the given name or null if no attribute by that name exists.

You can remove attributes with the removeAttribute() method:

```
ctx.removeAttribute("myAttribute");
```

ServletContext contains a number of other useful methods; see the JavaDocs for more information.

A Web application contains only one servlet context. The servlet context exists for the life-time of the application and cannot be invalidated or destroyed by the programmer.

Dispatching requests to other resources

One of the most important features of servlets is their capability to act as traffic cops for your application. Instead of responding to HTTP requests themselves, servlets can dispatch the requests to other servlets, JSPs, or even static HTML pages residing on the same server. Thus, servlets can manage the flow of control through the application based on decisions made in the business logic.

Two types of dispatching are available: *forwarding* and *redirecting*. Forwarding is achieved through the `javax.servlet.RequestDispatcher` interface and redirecting through the `javax.servlet.http.HttpServletResponse` interface.

When should you forward, and when should you redirect? Behind the scenes, the two func-tion quite differently. When you forward, the Web container makes a direct call to the target resource without the browser's knowledge. Therefore, the URL in the browser's address win-dow does not change. If users refresh the display or otherwise cause the page to reload (in some browsers, merely resizing the window will do it), they get the page you forwarded from, not the page you forwarded to.

Redirecting, on the other hand, forces the browser to issue a completely new request to the target page, as if users had requested it themselves.

To forward a request, you call `javax.servlet.RequestDispatcher.forward()`, passing the request and response objects as parameters. You obtain a reference to the `Request Dispatcher` interface either from the `ServletContext` or the `HttpServletRequest`. The fol-lowing code snippet shows how to obtain a `RequestDispatcher` from the `ServletContext` and then forward the request to a servlet called `registerServlet` located at the root of the servlet context (at the application root):

```
if (!user.isRegistered) {
  ServletContext ctx = this.getServletContext();
  RequestDispatcher dispatcher =
    ctx.getRequestDispatcher("/registerServlet");
  dispatcher.forward(request, response);
}
```

Note that you can also forward to a JSP by using its filename, such as `/register.jsp`.

The next snippet shows how to obtain a `RequestDispatcher` from the `HttpServletRequest` and then forward to the same servlet:

```
if (!user.isRegistered) {
  RequestDispatcher dispatcher =
    request.getRequestDispatcher("/registerServlet");
  dispatcher.forward(request, response);
}
```

These methods work identically in this example, but there is a key difference between them. In the `ServletContext` version, the path you provide for the `RequestDispatcher` must begin with a / and is always relative to the context root. In the `HttpServletRequest` version, you can omit the leading /, in which case the path is interpreted to be relative to the servlet doing the forwarding.

The next code snippet shows how to redirect. In this example, users indicate that they want to log off of your application, so you invalidate their session and redirect them to your home page:

```
if (request.getParameter("action").equals("logoff")) {
  session.invalidate();
  response.sendRedirect("/myApp/home.html");
}
```

The rules for URL rewriting apply for both versions of `forward()` and `redirect()`, so be sure to encode your target URLs in case cookies are turned off, as in

```
response.sendRedirect(response.encodeURL("/myApp/home.html"));
```

Dynamically retrieving your application's URL

As much as possible, you want to avoid hard-coding URLs in your code. Let's say you want to embed a link to the current servlet in its output, or you want to embed a link to a GIF or JPEG file. After deployment descriptors can be changed without recompiling the source code; this is a good idea because you don't always know the URL your application will be deployed at. You can retrieve the Web App's context URL and the current servlet's URL from the incoming request. To do so, use the following

```
request.getContextPath();
```

to get the Web application's URL, and the following

```
request.getServletPath();
```

to get the servlet's URL. So, if your servlet is deployed at `http://localhost:7001/Bible App/myServlet`, then your context path is `/BibleApp` and your servlet path is `/myServlet`.

Securing your application

Security is an essential part of many Web applications, as it is often necessary to restrict access to a site to authorized users or to provide different levels of access to different groups of users. WebLogic supports a number of basic security mechanisms that you can incorporate into your Web applications. You can also roll your own security by using J2EE facilities such as the Java Authentication and Authorization Service (JAAS). The following sections focus on the basic security mechanisms available to WebLogic Web applications. JAAS and other advanced security topics are covered in Part VI.

Application security consists of two elements: *authentication* and *authorization*. Authentication is the process of verifying a user's identity, usually by prompting for a username and password, or perhaps a digital certificate, and checking that against a user database. Authorization is the process of granting a user access to various parts of an application based on that person's level of access privileges. The WebLogic Web security mechanisms support both authentication and authorization.

To secure a Web application, perform the following steps:

1. Use the WebLogic Console to define the users and groups that will have access to your application.

2. Select an authentication method. WebLogic supports three methods, which we explain in the next section. Each Web application uses only one of these methods. You specify your method in the application's deployment descriptor, `web.xml`.

3. Define one or more security constraints, also in `web.xml`. Each security constraint protects a set of resources (HTML pages, servlets, JSPs, and so on) that share a common URL pattern. The presence of a security constraint on a resource automatically triggers the authentication method you selected whenever a user tries to access that resource.

4. Define one or more security roles in `web.xml` and map them to your security constraints. Security roles define the different types of users who use the application. You can define any number of roles (such as administrator, manager, and normal user) and map any number of them to each security constraint. You can, for example, specify that administrative screens be available only to administrators; reporting screens only to managers; and everything else to administrators, managers, and normal users.

5. Create security role assignments, which map the users and groups you defined in Step 1 to the security roles you defined in Step 4. These mappings go into the `weblogic.xml` file, which is the WebLogic-specific deployment descriptor for Web applications. You must create `weblogic.xml` in a text editor (if it doesn't exist already) and put it into your application's `WEB-INF` folder.

We demonstrate these five steps later in this chapter when we show you how to create and deploy a secured Web application. See the section titled "Building the application" later in this chapter.

WebLogic supports three methods of authentication for Web applications: *basic, form-based,* and *client certificates.* You can also devise your own authentication mechanism, but that's beyond the scope of this chapter.

Basic authentication

Basic authentication is the oldest form of Web authentication. In this scheme, the Web browser displays a pop-up window prompting for a username and password whenever the user encounters a protected resource. This is the method employed by the WebLogic Console, as shown in Figure 11-5.

Figure 11-5: Pop-up window that appears in a Web browser for applications that employ basic authentication

To specify basic authentication as the method to use in your application, make the following entries to `web.xml`:

```
<web-app>
   ...
   <login-config>
```

```
        <auth-method>BASIC</auth-method>
        <realm-name>default</realm-name>
      </login-config>
      ...
    </web-app>
```

The realm-name entry specifies that the WebLogic default realm is to be used for authenticating users.

Cross-
Reference   Security realms, including the default realm, are covered in Part VI of this book.

Form-based authentication

With form-based authentication, you provide an HTML page, JSP, or servlet that renders a login screen. Additionally, you provide an error screen to which the user is redirected if the login fails. This gives you complete control over the appearance and navigation on these screens, so you can make them fit into the rest of your application.

The login screen you provide must follow certain rules so that the container can accurately retrieve its data to perform authentication. The form should prompt only for a username and password, and must return them in form elements named j_username and j_password, respectively. Additionally, the form action attribute must be called j_security_check.

The following HTML renders the simplest possible login form:

```
<html>
  <head>
    <title>My Web Application</title>
  </head>
  <body>
    <p>Welcome to my Web application! Please log in.</p>
    <form method="POST" action="j_security_check">
      <p>User name: <input type="text" name="j_username"></p>
      <p>Password: <input type="password" name="j_password"></p>
      <p><input type="submit" name="Submit" value="Login"></p>
    </form>
  </body>
</html>
```

Figure 11-6 shows the form as it appears in a Web browser.

Figure 11-6: Login screen for form-based authentication

The error page has no design requirements; you can design it any way you want.

The following entries in `web.xml` demonstrate how to specify static HTML pages as the login and error pages:

```
<web-app>
  ...
  <login-config>
    <auth-method>FORM</auth-method>
    <realm-name>default</realm-name>
    <form-login-config>
      <form-login-page>login.html</form-login-page>
      <form-error-page>loginError.html</form-error-page>
    </form-login-config>
  </login-config>
  ...
</web-app>
```

Note that you can use servlets and/or JSPs for the login and error pages, as long as they render the login form according to the rules described earlier.

Authenticating with client certificates

Client certificates enable you to authenticate users in a highly secure manner by using digital certificates and Secure Sockets Layers (SSLs). Configuring WebLogic to support client certificates is a complex, multistep process that is beyond the scope of this chapter. You can find more information about it in the WebLogic documentation, under "Configuring the SSL Protocol." This information is available on the Internet at the following URL:

```
http://e-docs.bea.com/wls/docs70/secmanage/ssl.html#1127954
```

 Cross-Reference You can also refer to Part VI of this book for more information about securing Web applications with client certificates.

Building an Advanced Application with Servlets

In this section, we'll show you how to build a Web application that uses the advanced features discussed in earlier sections, including sessions, the servlet context, request dispatching, and security. In the process, we demonstrate how to properly configure and deploy such an application in WebLogic Server, and how to configure a simple security scheme by using the WebLogic Console and the application's deployment descriptors.

Gathering the requirements

The application, called `BibleServlets`, has two entry points: one for normal users and one for administrators. The application's home page welcomes users to the application and provides hyperlinks to the two entry points.

Clicking either entry point brings up the login form, in which the user is prompted for a name and password. An error page is displayed if the login is invalid; otherwise, the user gains entry to their chosen entry point.

The normal user area is a simple succession of five Web pages that the user can traverse in forward or reverse. Each page displays the user's name and the number of the page they are on (1 through 5), as well as hyperlinks to the previous and next pages. Each page also contains a hyperlink to log off, which returns the user to the home page.

The administrator area is a Web page that lists the names of all users who are navigating through the normal user area, along with what page numbers they are on. If no one is logged on, the page indicates that as well. The page also provides a hyperlink to log off.

Note   After users have logged into the application, they cannot log in again from a different Web browser. If they attempt to do so, their login attempt is rejected.

Finally, the application must work even if cookies are turned off in the client's browser.

Figure 11-7 shows a flow diagram for the application.

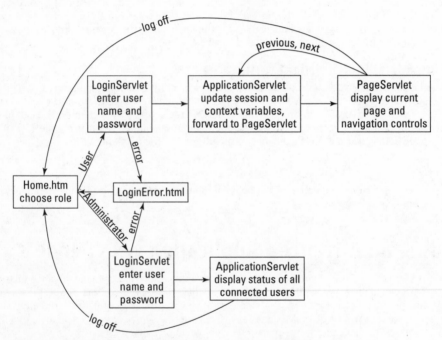

Figure 11-7: Flow diagram for the advanced servlet application

Brainstorming a design

You will implement the meat of the application with two servlets: one to manage the normal user pages, and one for the administrator page. Call the first servlet `ApplicationServlet` and the second `AdminServlet`.

If you think about it for a moment, you can see that `ApplicationServlet` is a dispatcher. It sends users to one of five pages based on the page they're on and the direction in which they want to go (forward or backward). Therefore, you need to keep track of who each user is and which page they're on. This is the perfect kind of information to store in the session. You also need to know the direction in which the user wants to go. This is a good job for a parameter passed as a querystring, so you'll design `ApplicationServlet` to accept and act on such a parameter.

The five application pages themselves must be dynamically generated if they are to display the user's name and current page, and also if they are to support URL rewriting to meet the cookies/no cookies requirement. Therefore, you will implement these pages as servlets.

Note   In a real-world application, you would implement these pages as JSPs because they consist mostly of markup language. But JSPs are the topic of the next chapter, so we'll stick with discussing servlets in this chapter.

Closer study of the requirements reveals that the five application pages are identical except for the page number displayed. Therefore, you can easily write a single servlet, which you will call `PageServlet`, to generate these pages. After updating the application's business logic, `ApplicationServlet` will forward to `PageServlet`, which will render the appropriate page. This process gives a nice demonstration of request dispatching.

Now let's turn to `AdminServlet`. Its purpose is to display the current state of all active sessions. Somehow it must be able to communicate with all instances of `ApplicationServlet` to discover what pages the users are on. This is a job for the servlet context. You'll add code to `ApplicationServlet` to store each user's name and page number into the servlet context, and code `AdminServlet` to retrieve this information and render it as HTML in the browser.

The home page will be implemented as static HTML with links to the two servlets.

You will use form-based authentication to control access to the application, and you will define security roles to differentiate between administrators and normal users. Only administrators are allowed to execute `AdminServlet`, and all authenticated users are allowed to execute `ApplicationServlet`. For the sake of illustration, you will implement the login page as a servlet called `LoginServlet`. The login error page, however, will be straight HTML.

Wow! You gathered your requirements and documented your design. Now you can start coding!

Building the application

In this section, we'll show you how to build the advanced servlet application, step by step.

Creating the directory structure and home page

The first thing you need to do is set up a directory structure for your application in the WebLogic domain. Create a directory in the domain's `applications` directory called `BibleServlets` and create another directory within that called `WEB-INF`. Then populate `WEB-INF` with directories called `classes` and `lib`, as discussed earlier in this chapter.

Next create a static HTML home page for your application. Listing 11-2 shows the code.

Listing 11-2: **Home.html, the home page for BibleServlets**

```
<html>
<head>
<title>WebLogic7 Server Bible</title>
<meta http-equiv="Content-Type" c ontent="text/html">
```

Continued

Listing 11-2 *(continued)*

```
</head>

<body>
<p>Welcome to BibleServlets! Please choose your role:</p>
<p><a href="appServlet">User</a></p>
<p><a href="adminServlet">Administrator</a></p>
</body>
</html>
```

This code contains instructions for the user and hyperlinks to the servlets. Notice that the links do not need to be fully qualified; they are relative to the current Web application.

Save the home page into the `BibleServlets` directory, where it is available to all users. Also create a `web.xml` file, add a `<welcome-file>` tag that points to `Home.html`, and save it into the `WEB-INF` directory. Here are the initial contents of `web.xml`:

```
<!DOCTYPE web-app PUBLIC "-//Sun Microsystems, Inc.//DTD Web Application
2.3//EN" "http://java.sun.com/j2ee/dtds/web-app_2.3.dtd">

<web-app>
  <welcome-file-list>
    <welcome-file>Home.html</welcome-file>
  </welcome-file-list>
</web-app>
```

Now you can start WebLogic Server and test your application by navigating to `http://localhost:7001/BibleServlets`. Figure 11-8 shows the resulting display in a Web browser.

Figure 11-8: The home page for the BibleServlets application

Implementing form-based authentication

Now you're going to create the pages to implement form-based authentication. The first is `LoginServlet`, which generates an HTML form that follows the rules for accepting a username and password (as discussed earlier in this chapter). Listing 11-3 shows the code for `LoginServlet`.

Listing 11-3: **LoginServlet**

```java
package com.wiley.wlsbible.servlets.example;

import javax.servlet.*;
import javax.servlet.http.*;
import java.io.*;
import java.util.*;

public class LoginServlet extends HttpServlet {

  public void service(HttpServletRequest request,
                      HttpServletResponse response)
  throws IOException {

    ServletContext ctx = this.getServletContext();
    HttpSession session = request.getSession();
    String servletName = this.getServletName();

    response.setContentType("text/html");
    PrintWriter out = response.getWriter();
    out.println("<html>");
    out.println("<head><title>BibleServlets</title></head>");
    out.println("<body>");
    out.println("<p>Welcome to BibleServlets!</p>");
    out.println("<p>Please log in.</p>");
    out.println("<form method=\"POST\" action=\"" +
                response.encodeURL("j_security_check") + "\">");
    out.print("<p>User name: ");
    out.println("<input type=\"text\" name=\"j_username\"></p>");
    out.print("<p>Password: ");
    out.println("<input type=\"password\" name=\"j_password\"></p>");
    out.print("<p><input type=\"submit\" ");
    out.println("name=\"Submit\" value=\"Login\"></p>");
    out.println("</form>");
    out.println("<p></p><p><b>Servlet name:</b> " + servletName + "<br>");
    out.println("<b>Servlet deployed at URL:</b> " +
                request.getServletPath() + "<br>");
    out.println("<b>Web App deployed at URL:</b> " +
                request.getContextPath() + "</p>");
    out.println("</body></html>");
  }
}
```

If you refer to the HTML code for a simple login page shown previously, you'll notice that LoginServlet does little more than spit out that code. The only difference is that you rewrite the URL for the j_security_check page by using response.encodeURL(). This ensures that the login page will function with cookies turned off and is also the reason you implemented the page as a servlet.

After compiling this servlet to the `WEB-INF/classes` directory, create the login error page called `LoginError.html`. The HTML for this page appears in Listing 11-4. This page notifies users of a problem with their login and includes a button that returns them to `Home.html`.

Listing 11-4: **LoginError.html**

```html
<html>
<head>
<title>BibleServlets Login Error</title>
<meta http-equiv="Content-Type" content="text/html">
</head>

<body>
<p>An error occurred trying to log you in. Please double-check your user name
and password.</p>
<form method="POST" action="Home.html">
<input type="submit" name="submit" value="Start Over">
</form>
</body>
</html>
```

The next piece of the login puzzle is to add a `<login-config>` tag to `web.xml`, which tells the Web container that you're using the form-based authentication method. It also specifies which security realm to use for authentication and which resources to use for the login page and error page. The security realm is `default`, which corresponds to the WebLogic default realm.

Cross-Reference   Chapters 20 and 21 explain the various types of security realms supported by WebLogicß.

```
<login-config>
   <auth-method>FORM</auth-method>
   <realm-name>default</realm-name>
   <form-login-config>
      <form-login-page>loginServlet</form-login-page>
      <form-error-page>LoginError.html</form-error-page>
   </form-login-config>
</login-config>
```

Defining users in the WebLogic Default realm

Because your application requires authentication, you need to define a set of authorized users. The place to do it is in the WebLogic Console. Create users in the default realm named `Joe`, `Lou`, and `Karen`. To do so, expand the Security node in the domain tree, expand `Realms`, expand `myrealm`, and then click Users. This presents you with the page to add a new user. Enter a name, a description, and a password of eight or more characters. Figure 11-9 shows the Users page after you enter the information for `Lou`.

Click Create, and `Lou` is added to the list of existing users you'll see when you click on the `Users` tree node. Figure 11-10 shows the state of your realm after adding all three users.

Figure 11-9: Adding a new user to the realm

Figure 11-10: The state of your user list after adding Lou, Joe, and Karen

This is all the work you need to do in the WebLogic Console. The remainder of the security setup takes place in the application's deployment descriptors. We'll come back to that later in the chapter.

Writing the dispatcher servlet

The next step is to write `ApplicationServlet`, your application's dispatcher.

Creating the servlet shell

Listing 11-5 shows the shell for this servlet. You will implement a `service()` method only, so the servlet will respond to all types of HTTP requests.

Listing 11-5: **ApplicationServlet shell**

```
package com.wiley.wlsbible.servlets.example;

import javax.servlet.*;
```

Continued

Listing 11-5 (continued)

```
import javax.servlet.http.*;
import java.io.*;
import java.util.*;

public class ApplicationServlet extends HttpServlet {

  public void service(HttpServletRequest request,
                      HttpServletResponse response)
  throws ServletException, IOException {
  }

}
```

`ApplicationServlet`'s job is to track the user's state through a series of five sequential Web pages. Therefore, it might be handy to define some class variables to track the first and last pages of this sequence. These variables are simply integer constants:

```
private static final int FIRST_PAGE = 1;
private static final int LAST_PAGE = 5;
```

The servlet will work with the session in order to track each user's state. It will also work with the servlet context in order to share that state with `AdminServlet`. Therefore, kick off the `service()` method by obtaining references to these structures:

```
ServletContext ctx = this.getServletContext();
HttpSession session = request.getSession();
```

Retrieving the username

Another piece of information you need is the name of the user because you plan to use that as part of the unique key that identifies each session in the servlet context. You also need the user's name to enforce the "one user, one session" rule spelled out in the requirements.

The problem is that the Web container handles form-based authentication automatically, so there's no obvious way for you to obtain the username from the login screen. One thing to notice is that the Web container automatically creates a session for users if they're authenticated. So maybe it copies the `j_username` attribute into the session, where you can retrieve it with the following call:

```
String userName = session.getAttribute("j_username");
```

Unfortunately, this is not the case. Even if it were, this code would not be portable because the `j_username` and `j_password` attributes are WebLogic-specific.

The good news is that the `ServletRequest` interface contains a call that gets the username for you: `getRemoteUser()`. And it just so happens that when a user logs in successfully, WebLogic stuffs its `j_username` attribute into the Web container, where it can be returned by `getRemoteUser()`:

```
String userName = request.getRemoteUser();
```

This is the perfect solution, because it is completely vendor-independent.

Tracking state in the session and in the servlet context

Now that you know who the user is, you can start tracking their state as they move through the application. At the session level, you do this with an attribute called `sessionInfo`, which you stuff with a `Hashtable` containing the user's name and current page. This attribute can have the same name for every session because every session is different.

At the servlet context level, things are slightly different. You stuff the same `Hashtable` into the context, but you must ensure that the attribute you map it to has a unique name because you're stuffing `Hashtables` for all users into the same context. You must also devise a way of naming your attributes that makes them distinguishable from attributes stuffed into the context by the Web container. Otherwise, you won't be able to reliably retrieve them later.

One other item: `ApplicationServlet` must be able to distinguish a new user from a returning user because its behavior is slightly different for the two groups. If users are new, `ApplicationServlet` must establish their initial state and save it to the session and servlet context. Then it sends them to the first page. If users are returning, `ApplicationServlet` must retrieve their state from the session, update their page number, and forward them to that page.

So how can `ApplicationServlet` tell a new user from a returning user? You can't do it by checking for a null versus non-null session because form-based authentication passes you a valid session for every authenticated user. A new session, however, does not contain any of the attributes you've defined. Therefore, you can detect whether the user is new by checking for a `sessionInfo` attribute in the session. If it doesn't exist, `session.getAttribute()` returns null, and you know that the user is new.

The first half of `ApplicationServlet` initializes a `sessionInfo` structure for a new user and then saves it to the session and servlet context. It uniquely names `sessionInfo` structures in the servlet context with the value `session_` plus the user's name, so you can reliably retrieve them later. And it checks to see whether a returning user is already logged in; in which case it invalidates the second user's session, redirects that user to the home page, and exits the servlet.

The second half of `ApplicationServlet` updates the state variables for your session based on the value of the query parameter passed to the servlet. It then forwards the request to `PageServlet`, which draws a Web page that reflects the state of the session.

The query parameter for `ApplicationServlet` is called `action`, and its legal values are `previous`, `next`, `logoff`, and `null` (if the session is new). The following URL, for example, invokes `ApplicationServlet` with an instruction to go to the next page:

```
http://localhost:7001/BibleServlets/appServlet?action=next
```

where `appServlet` is the URL that ApplicationServlet is mapped to in the deployment descriptor. Listing 11-6 contains the full implementation of `ApplicationServlet`.

Listing 11-6: **ApplicationServlet.java**

```
package com.wiley.wlsbible.servlets.example;

import javax.servlet.*;
import javax.servlet.http.*;
import java.io.*;
```

Continued

Listing 11-6 *(continued)*

```java
import java.util.*;

public class ApplicationServlet extends HttpServlet {

  private static final int FIRST_PAGE = 1;
  private static final int LAST_PAGE = 5;

  public void service(HttpServletRequest request,
                      HttpServletResponse response)
  throws ServletException, IOException {

    ServletContext ctx = this.getServletContext();
    HttpSession session = request.getSession();
    String userName = request.getRemoteUser();
    Hashtable sessionInfo = null;

    if (session.getAttribute("sessionInfo") == null) {
      // New user. Create a Hashtable to track their
      // session state.
      sessionInfo = new Hashtable();
      sessionInfo.put("userName", userName);
      sessionInfo.put("pageNumber", new Integer(FIRST_PAGE));
      session.setAttribute("sessionInfo", sessionInfo);
      // See if the new user is already logged in by checking
      // for their sessionInfo in the servlet context.
      if (ctx.getAttribute("session_" + userName) == null) {
        // Not already logged in. Save their sessionInfo to
        // the servletContext and continue.
        ctx.setAttribute("session_" + userName, sessionInfo);
      } else {
        // Already logged in elsewhere. Invalidate this session
        // and kick this user out.
        session.invalidate();
        response.sendRedirect(
          response.encodeURL("/BibleServlets/Home.html"));
        return;
      }
    } else {
      // Returning user. Retrieve their state from the session.
      sessionInfo = (Hashtable) session.getAttribute("sessionInfo");
      Integer pageNumber = (Integer)sessionInfo.get("pageNumber");
      int nextPage = pageNumber.intValue();
      pageNumber = null;
      // Read the query string to determine the user's desired
      // action. Update their state in the session accordingly.
      if (request.getParameter("action").equals("next")) {
        // Go to the next page. Wrap around to the
        // first page after passing the last page.
        nextPage++;
        if (nextPage > LAST_PAGE) {
          nextPage = FIRST_PAGE;
```

```
        }
        sessionInfo.put("pageNumber", new Integer(nextPage));
      } else if (request.getParameter("action").equals("previous")) {
        // Go to the previous page. Wrap around to the last page
        // after passing the first page.
        nextPage--;
        if (nextPage < FIRST_PAGE) {
          nextPage = LAST_PAGE;
        }
        sessionInfo.put("pageNumber", new Integer(nextPage));
      } else if (request.getParameter("action").equals("logoff")) {
        // User wants to log off. Invalidate their session,
        // remove their session info from the servlet context,
        // redirect them to the home page, and then quit.
        session.invalidate();
        ctx.removeAttribute("session_" + userName);
        response.sendRedirect(
          response.encodeURL("Home.html"));
        return;
      }
    }
    // Forward all non-logoff requests to the PageServlet.
    request.getRequestDispatcher("pageServlet").forward(request, response);
  }
}
```

Writing the page-rendering servlet

Listing 11-7 contains the full implementation of PageServlet, which simply renders HTML
for the browser that reflects the user's current position within the application.

Listing 11-7: **PageServlet.java**

```
package com.wiley.wlsbible.servlets.example;

import javax.servlet.*;
import javax.servlet.http.*;
import java.io.*;
import java.util.*;

public class PageServlet extends HttpServlet {

  public void service(HttpServletRequest request,
                       HttpServletResponse response)
  throws ServletException, IOException {
    HttpSession session = request.getSession();
    Hashtable sessionInfo =
      (Hashtable) session.getAttribute("sessionInfo");
    String userName = (String) sessionInfo.get("userName");
```

Continued

Listing 11-7 *(continued)*

```
    Integer pageNumber = (Integer) sessionInfo.get("pageNumber");

    response.setContentType("text/html");
    PrintWriter out = response.getWriter();
    out.println("<html>");
    out.println("<head><title>PageServlet</title></head>");
    out.println("<body>");
    out.println("<p>Welcome to the PageServlet.</p>");
    out.println("<p>Your name is " + userName + " and you are on page " +
      pageNumber.intValue() + ".</p>");
    out.println("<p></p>");
    out.println("<p><a href=\"" +
      response.encodeURL("appServlet?action=next") +
                        "\">Next Page</a></p>");
    out.println("<p></p>");
    out.println("<p><a href=\"" +
      response.encodeURL("appServlet?action=previous") +
                        "\">Previous Page</a></p>");
    out.println("<p></p>");
    out.println("<p><a href=\"" +
      response.encodeURL("appServlet?action=logoff") +
                        "\">Log Off</a></p>");
    out.println("</body></html>");
  }
}
```

Writing the administrative servlet

Listing 11-8 contains the full implementation of AdminServlet. This servlet loops through all the attributes stored in the servlet context. If it recognizes an attribute as one of our sessions, it writes a single line of HTML describing that session. After AdminServlet loops through all the sessions, the HTML is returned to the browser. The user may also elect to log off, in which case AdminServlet sends a redirect to Home.html.

Listing 11-8: **AdminServlet.java**

```
package com.wiley.wlsbible.servlets.example;

import javax.servlet.*;
import javax.servlet.http.*;
import java.io.*;
import java.util.*;

public class AdminServlet extends HttpServlet {

  public void service(HttpServletRequest request,
                  HttpServletResponse response)
```

```
    throws IOException {

  ServletContext ctx = this.getServletContext();
  HttpSession session = request.getSession();
  String servletName = this.getServletName();

  if (request.getParameter("action") == null) {
    // Generate an HTML page listing all active sessions.
    // This servlet does NOT store data into the session
    // or the servlet context.
    response.setContentType("text/html");
    PrintWriter out = response.getWriter();
    out.println("<html>");
    out.println("<head><title>" + servletName + "</title></head>");
    out.println("<body>");
    out.print("<p>Welcome to the " + servletName + ". ");
    out.print("Click your browser's Refresh button ");
    out.print("to update the display.</p>");
    // Get the names of all attributes in the servlet context.
    Enumeration sessions = ctx.getAttributeNames();
    int numSessions = 0;
    // Loop through the attributes, rendering the ones we recognize
    // as our sessions to the HTML output.
    while (sessions.hasMoreElements()) {
      String sessionName = (String) sessions.nextElement();
      if (sessionName.startsWith("session_")) {
        Hashtable sessionInfo =
          (Hashtable) ctx.getAttribute(sessionName);
        String userName = (String) sessionInfo.get("userName");
        Integer pageNumber = (Integer) sessionInfo.get("pageNumber");
        out.println("<p>" + userName + " is on page " +
                    pageNumber.intValue() + ".</p>");
        numSessions++;
      }
    }
    // If there are no sessions, indicate that as well.
    if (numSessions == 0) {
      out.println("<p>There are no active sessions.</p>");
    }
    out.println("<p></p>");
    out.println("<p><a href=\"" + response.encodeURL(
                "adminServlet?action=logoff") + "\">Log Off</a></p>");
    out.println("</body></html>");
  } else if (request.getParameter("action").equals("logoff")) {
      // User wants to log off. Invalidate their session and
      // redirect them to the home page.
    session.invalidate();
    response.sendRedirect(
      response.encodeURL("Home.html"));
  }
  }
}
```

Creating the deployment descriptors

You will now create the two deployment descriptors required for a Web application in WebLogic Server: `web.xml`, and `weblogic.xml`.

web.xml

Listing 11-9 shows `web.xml`, the J2EE deployment descriptor for your application. It begins with the `<welcome-file-list>` and `<login-config>` entries you created before.

The four `<servlet>` entries define your application's servlets. They give a logical name for the servlet and then give the fully qualified name of the servlet's class.

Next come four `<servlet-mapping>` entries that map the logical names of the servlets to URL patterns in the browser. To invoke a servlet, you enter a URL that follows this pattern:

```
http://<host-name>/<app-name><servlet-url-pattern>
```

In this example, `LoginServlet` is invoked as follows:

```
http://localhost:7001/BibleServlets/loginServlet
```

because the servlet class `com.wiley.wlsbible.servlets.example.LoginServlet` with the logical name `LoginServlet` is mapped to the URL `/loginServlet`.

The `<security-role>` entries define the security roles recognized by your application. In this case, you recognize two classes of users: normal users and administrators. The role names can be anything you want.

Finally, the `<security-constraint>` entries define which roles are allowed to access which servlets. The constraints you've defined specify that `ApplicationServlet` and `PageServlet` are available to normal and administrative users, whereas `AdminServlet` is available only to administrators. The restrictions apply for HTTP `GET` and `POST` requests alike, and you're not requiring a secure sockets connection to access any of these resources.

Notice that there is no `<security-constraint>` entry for `LoginServlet`. This is because `LoginServlet` is available to everyone; it sits outside the security perimeter of your application. The same applies for `Home.html` and `LoginError.html`.

Listing 11-9: **web.xml**

```
<!DOCTYPE web-app PUBLIC "-//Sun Microsystems, Inc.//DTD Web
Application 2.3//EN" "http://java.sun.com/dtd/web-app_2_3.dtd">

<web-app>

  <welcome-file-list>
    <welcome-file>Home.html</welcome-file>
  </welcome-file-list>

  <login-config>
    <auth-method>FORM</auth-method>
    <realm-name>default</realm-name>
    <form-login-config>
      <form-login-page>LoginServlet</form-login-page>
      <form-error-page>LoginError.html</form-error-page>
    </form-login-config>
```

```
    </login-config>

    <servlet>
      <servlet-name>LoginServlet</servlet-name>
      <servlet-class>
com.wiley.wlsbible.servlets.example.LoginServlet
      </servlet-class>
    </servlet>

    <servlet>
      <servlet-name>ApplicationServlet</servlet-name>
      <servlet-class>
com.wiley.wlsbible.servlets.example.ApplicationServlet
      </servlet-class>
    </servlet>

    <servlet>
      <servlet-name>PageServlet</servlet-name>
      <servlet-class>
com.wiley.wlsbible.servlets.example.PageServlet
      </servlet-class>
    </servlet>

    <servlet>
      <servlet-name>AdminServlet</servlet-name>
      <servlet-class>
com.wiley.wlsbible.servlets.example.AdminServlet
      </servlet-class>
    </servlet>

    <servlet-mapping>
      <servlet-name>LoginServlet</servlet-name>
      <url-pattern>/loginServlet</url-pattern>
    </servlet-mapping>

    <servlet-mapping>
      <servlet-name>ApplicationServlet</servlet-name>
      <url-pattern>/appServlet</url-pattern>
    </servlet-mapping>

    <servlet-mapping>
      <servlet-name>PageServlet</servlet-name>
      <url-pattern>/pageServlet</url-pattern>
    </servlet-mapping>

    <servlet-mapping>
      <servlet-name>AdminServlet</servlet-name>
      <url-pattern>/adminServlet</url-pattern>
    </servlet-mapping>

    <security-role>
      <role-name>admin_user</role-name>
```

Continued

Listing 11-9 *(continued)*

```
</security-role>

<security-role>
  <role-name>normal_user</role-name>
</security-role>

<security-constraint>
  <web-resource-collection>
    <web-resource-name>
      ApplicationServlet
    </web-resource-name>
    <description>
      Security constraint for ApplicationServlet.
    </description>
    <url-pattern>/appServlet</url-pattern>
    <http-method>POST</http-method>
    <http-method>GET</http-method>
  </web-resource-collection>
  <auth-constraint>
    <description>
      Constraint for all users
    </description>
    <role-name>admin_user</role-name>
    <role-name>normal_user</role-name>
  </auth-constraint>
  <user-data-constraint>
    <description>SSL not required</description>
    <transport-guarantee>NONE</transport-guarantee>
  </user-data-constraint>
</security-constraint>

<security-constraint>
  <web-resource-collection>
    <web-resource-name>
      PageServlet
    </web-resource-name>
    <description>
      Security constraint for PageServlet.
    </description>
    <url-pattern>/pageServlet</url-pattern>
    <http-method>POST</http-method>
    <http-method>GET</http-method>
  </web-resource-collection>
  <auth-constraint>
    <description>
      Constraint for all users
    </description>
    <role-name>admin_user</role-name>
    <role-name>normal_user</role-name>
  </auth-constraint>
  <user-data-constraint>
```

```
        <description>SSL not required</description>
        <transport-guarantee>NONE</transport-guarantee>
      </user-data-constraint>
    </security-constraint>

    <security-constraint>
      <web-resource-collection>
        <web-resource-name>
          AdminServlet
        </web-resource-name>
        <description>
          Security constraint for AdminServlet.
        </description>
        <url-pattern>/adminServlet</url-pattern>
        <http-method>POST</http-method>
        <http-method>GET</http-method>
      </web-resource-collection>
      <auth-constraint>
        <description>
          Constraint for admin users
        </description>
        <role-name>admin_user</role-name>
      </auth-constraint>
      <user-data-constraint>
        <description>SSL not required</description>
        <transport-guarantee>NONE</transport-guarantee>
      </user-data-constraint>
    </security-constraint>

</web-app>
```

If you study the `<url-pattern>` tags within the security constraints, you'll see that they map directly to the protected servlets. This is because your servlets all reside within the root of your application. Suppose that your application was much larger, and that you had several administrative servlets instead of just one. You could map all these servlets to an administrative area called /admin and then protect them all in one stroke, as shown by the bold lines in the following code sample:

```
<servlet>
  <servlet-name>AdminServlet</servlet-name>
  <servlet-class>
 com.wiley.wlsbible.servlets.example.AdminServlet
  </servlet-class>
</servlet>

<servlet-mapping>
  <servlet-name>AdminServlet</servlet-name>
  <url-pattern>/Admin/adminServlet</url-pattern>
</servlet-mapping>

//and so on for the other admin servlets

<security-constraint>
```

```
    <web-resource-collection>
      <web-resource-name>
        Administrative resources
      </web-resource-name>
      <description>
        Security constraint for administrative resources.
      </description>
      <url-pattern>/Admin/*</url-pattern>
      <http-method>POST</http-method>
      <http-method>GET</http-method>
    </web-resource-collection>
    <auth-constraint>
      <description>
        Constraint for admin users
      </description>
      <role-name>admin_user</role-name>
    </auth-constraint>
    <user-data-constraint>
      <description>SSL not required</description>
      <transport-guarantee>NONE</transport-guarantee>
    </user-data-constraint>
  </security-constraint>
```

weblogic.xml

Listing 11-10 shows `weblogic.xml`, your application's WebLogic-specific descriptor. This file serves as a bridge between `web.xml` and features specific to WebLogic, for which there is no support in the `web.xml` DTD. In the `BibleServlets` application, `weblogic.xml` uses security role assignments to map WebLogic users from the File realm to role names in `web.xml`, which enables you to specify which users belong to which roles. In this example, `Joe` is an administrator, whereas `Gary` and `Roya` are normal users.

Note   User and role names are case-sensitive. The users must match exactly those you defined in the WebLogic Console, and the role names must match exactly those you defined in `web.xml`.

Listing 11-10: **weblogic.xml**

```
<!DOCTYPE weblogic-web-app PUBLIC "-//BEA
Systems, Inc.//DTD Web Application 7.0//EN"
"http://www.bea.com/servers/wls700/dtd/
weblogic-web-jar.dtd">

<weblogic-web-app>

  <description>
    Demo of servlet features.
  </description>

  <security-role-assignment>
    <role-name>admin_user</role-name>
    <principal-name>Joe</principal-name>
```

```
    </security-role-assignment>

    <security-role-assignment>
      <role-name>normal_user</role-name>
      <principal-name>Joe</principal-name>
      <principal-name>Lou</principal-name>
      <principal-name>Karen</principal-name>
    </security-role-assignment>

  </weblogic-web-app>
```

The application is now complete. Let's try it out!

Running the application

Figure 11-8 shows the application home page you receive when you point your browser to `BibleServlets`. If you click User, you're taken to the login page, as shown in Figure 11-11.

Figure 11-11: The BibleServlets login page

First, log in as `Karen`. At this point, `ApplicationServlet` creates a session for `Karen` and dispatches her to the first page, as shown in Figure 11-12.

Figure 11-12: Karen on Page 1

Leave this browser window open and point a second browser window to BibleServlets. This time, enter the Administrator area, and log in as Joe. Figure 11-13 shows the resulting administrative screen.

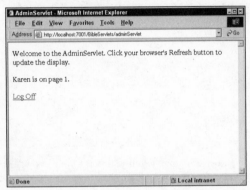

Figure 11-13: The BibleServlets administrative screen

Next, log into the User area as Lou and advance to Page 4, as shown in Figure 11-14.

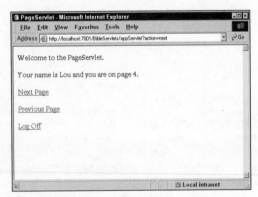

Figure 11-14: Lou on Page 4

Return to your administrative window and click the browser's Refresh button to update the display, as shown in Figure 11-15.

Figure 11-15: Admin screen showing two active sessions

This is a very simple example, but it gives you a good idea of the power behind servlets.

Deploying the application as a WAR file

When you finish the development and testing of an application, you'll want to convert it to a WAR file for easy deployment. WAR files are essential for two reasons:

✦ WebLogic Server, when running in Production mode, recognizes only WAR files. It will not recognize or deploy exploded directory structures.

✦ To deploy a Web application to a WebLogic cluster, you must copy the application to every machine in the cluster. This is easier and quicker to do with a WAR file.

To deploy the `BibleServlets` application as a WAR file, follow these steps:

Note

If you're building and deploying the WAR from the source code from the book's Web site, it uses Ant to perform the build, so follow the instructions provided there.

1. In the WebLogic Console, delete the `BibleServlets` application from the list of deployed Web applications. Exit from the Console and stop WebLogic Server.

2. Open a command window and change to the `BibleServlets` directory.

3. Use the WebLogic `setenv.cmd` utility to set your classpath; then enter the following command:

```
jar cvOf BibleServlets.war *
```

This instructs the JAR utility to create a WAR file called `BibleServlets.war` and to copy every file in the `BibleServlets` directory into it. The third parameter is a zero, and it instructs the JAR utility not to compress the file. WebLogic can load resources from uncompressed files more quickly, so this is a good option if you need maximum performance.

4. Move `BibleServlets.war` out of the `BibleServlets` directory and into the applications directory of your WebLogic domain.

5. Move the `BibleServlets` directory to another location outside of the applications directory or simply delete it.

6. Start WebLogic Server. `BibleServlets.war` will automatically deploy, and you can use the application exactly as before.

Summary

Servlets are one of the most important features of J2EE because they enable you to deliver the full power of J2EE, as well as your organization's critical data, to any user with a Web browser. Most companies buy WebLogic Server precisely because of this capability. If you master the concepts behind servlets and learn how to exploit their many capabilities, there is almost no limit to the power and functionality you can deliver to your browser-based users.

✦   ✦   ✦

Developing JavaServer Pages

The JavaServer Pages API defines a mechanism for server-side scripting within the J2EE environment. WebLogic Server provides an implementation of the API in the form of its JSP container.

Early in the chapter, we provide an overview of the JavaServer Pages architecture and the coding syntax. We then show how to configure WebLogic deployment descriptors and deploy JSPs within the WebLogic environment. Along the way, we provide several code examples that demonstrate the various features available, including using JSPs with JavaBeans.

Understanding JavaServer Pages

To gain a full appreciation of why JavaServer Pages exist and what advantages the JSP API brings to J2EE development, you should know something about how server-side scripting was done before JSPs.

Product of evolution

Server-side scripting is not a new concept to Web development. Back in the days when only static content was being delivered to Web browsers, developers were already looking for ways to deliver dynamic content and make the user experience more robust.

Along came server-side scripting in the form of Common Gateway Interface (CGI). CGIs are either interpreted scripts or compiled executables that can be accessed on the Web server, can access databases, and can generate dynamic responses. The downside of using CGIs is performance. Because every CGI runs as a separate process, every request to the server results in a CGI process being created and destroyed, which is very resource-expensive. Therefore CGIs do not scale well when going from tens of users to thousands of users.

Microsoft eventually introduced Active Server Pages (ASPs), which allowed for inline scripts that used either VBScript or JScript commingled with HTML for generating dynamic content. ASPs are interpreted on the Microsoft IIS server (plug-ins are available for other platforms) and allow access to Component Object Model (COM) objects for external functions such as database calls. Although ASPs offered great leaps in developer usability over CGI scripts because of their interpretive environment, the downside was again performance and scalability, not to mention the dependence on the Microsoft Windows environment.

In 1998, Sun Microsystems introduced the first draft of the Java Server Pages (JSP) API specification. JSP provided a means of inline scripting utilizing Java, and excelled in performance by leveraging its powerful and very successful servlet technology. From the developer's point of view, JSP provided the desired level of ease of use by providing the capability to embed HTML-like tags and Java scriptlets into your Web pages. JSP also enabled the developer to take full advantage of Java as an object-oriented language. Sun addressed scalability concerns by precompiling JSPs into servlets, thereby inheriting all the performance benefits of executing as "lightweight processes," or threads within the Java Virtual Machine.

Note JSP scripting is typically done in Java, but the JSP specification allows for alternative scripting languages. Later in the chapter, we'll show you how to specify the language you want to use, but we'll assume that it is Java.

WebLogic Server 7.0 supports the JSP 1.2 specification and the Servlet 2.3 specification. You can download copies of these specifications at the following URLs, respectively:

```
http://java.sun.com/products/jsp/download.html
http://java.sun.com/products/servlet/download.html
```

How JSPs work

In the simplest case, users invoke JSPs by requesting files ending in .jsp. For example:

```
http://www.bigbank.com/mystatement.jsp
```

The first time a JSP is requested, WebLogic forwards the JSP to the JSP compiler, which converts the JSP to a servlet and then compiles the servlet.

Note By default, the Java compiler is Sun Microsystems' javac compiler, but WebLogic lets you configure a different Java compiler. This topic is covered later in the chapter.

Assuming that the JSP compiles successfully, WebLogic Server executes the corresponding servlet and returns its response to the user. For all subsequent requests for the JSP, WebLogic automatically executes the servlet unless WebLogic detects that the JSP's code has changed since it was last compiled. In this case, WebLogic resubmits the JSP for compilation and then executes the new version of the servlet.

Note The code in your JSPs will not be visible to users; that is, users cannot see the JSP code with the "View Source" command in their browsers. Users can see only the HTML your JSP (actually, its servlet) generates.

JSPs are converted into servlets for performance reasons, but an important by-product of this design is that anything you can program in a servlet, you can also program in a JSP. This makes JSPs very powerful and flexible.

Figure 12-1 illustrates the full cycle of JSP requests, compilation, execution, and response.

Tip You can configure WebLogic Server to precompile your JSPs when starting WebLogic Server by setting the precompile parameter to true in the weblogic.xml deployment descriptor. You can also run the JSP compiler yourself from within your build scripts. Either approach saves your users from having to wait for JSPs to compile. The latter approach is better, however, because it won't increase the startup time of your WebLogic Server, and it also ensures that the JSPs are recompiled only when they change, instead of every time the server restarts. We'll cover both techniques later in the chapter.

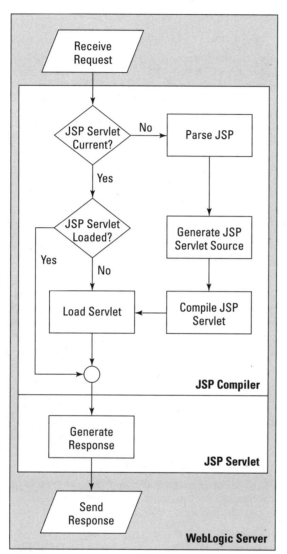

Figure 12-1: WebLogic's JSP request and compilation process

Model-View-Controller

JSPs are a great way of implementing the Model-View-Controller design pattern. Separating code by functionality, a concept known as *decoupling*, is especially useful in the View layer, which is by far the most changeable layer of an application. JSPs allow you to do just that — separate the presentation or View layer from the implementation or Controller layer.

Cross-Reference   See Chapter 3 for a complete discussion of Model-View-Controller.

JSPs provide the capability to decouple the View layer by providing you with all the capabilities of the Java language. You can embed Java scriptlets within HTML or other markup languages to generate dynamic content, access the Controller layer, or do anything else you want. As a result, JSPs enjoy all the benefits of Java: an object-oriented language with strong typing, encapsulation, and polymorphism; exception handling; automatic memory management; platform independence; and portability of code, to name a few.

Note   JSPs are for generating markup, not just HTML. You can, for example, generate XML with JSPs. In this chapter, however, we will generate HTML only.

JSPs also provide access to other Java-based objects such as JavaBeans. *JavaBeans* are objects written in Java that encapsulate data and behavior in a way that allows them to be reused. JSPs access JavaBeans via standard tags in an HTML-like syntax to request data or services, but without regard for how they are implemented. A typical bean might have a set of values or properties. The JSP will request these properties for the sake of displaying them as dynamic content. Because the properties were set by some other process with its own methodology, the JSP does not know nor need to know how the properties were derived.

JSPs also can use custom tag extensions in an HTML-like syntax. *Tag extensions* are a mechanism that enables developers to create libraries of custom tag classes written in Java that can be used in a JSP page. This is a great way of separating presentation from implementation by minimizing the Java code in the JSP. Tag extensions allow you to minimize the amount of programming logic commingled with your code by enabling you to call Java objects that encapsulate that logic.

With a robust collection of JavaBeans and tag library extensions, JSPs provide an even greater level of layer separation — syntax. JSPs provide the capability to minimize code and give user interface designers a language format with which they are familiar. A traditional UI developer proficient in HTML doesn't need to learn the Java syntax, but needs only to become familiar with a new set of tags. A traditional Java developer can create reusable routines for the UI developer to leverage or standard objects encapsulating display data. This perfectly matches division of labor sought by most development teams.

You may be wondering if anything can stop you from using Java code in your JSPs. Is there anything wrong with JavaBeans or tag library extensions generating HTML? Well, no, not really. It will work, but you don't achieve the level of separation as defined by the Model-View-Controller design pattern.

By using a significant amount of Java code in your JSPs, you force your UI developer to learn Java and potentially introduce controller level logic. You may end up with the need to make logic changes in your JSP every time you make logic changes in your controller layer.

You give up the reusability of your JavaBeans or tag library extension classes if they generate HTML. Maybe some other server-side Java classes would benefit from using them, but they have no need for HTML. Likewise, your UI developer now needs to ask your Java developer to make changes to modify the presentation layer.

You can be quite successful by implementing JSPs without regard for the MVC design pattern, but sticking with the pattern pays dividends in programmer productivity and code maintainability.

Configuring WebLogic Server for JSPs

Before using JSPs with WebLogic Server, you should configure the server to handle JSPs exactly the way you want. This section explains the various aspects of configuring WebLogic Server to handle JSPs, and shows you how to do so.

The JSP compiler

As discussed earlier, the JSP compiler is provided by WebLogic Server. It's responsible for converting JSP source into JSP servlet source. WebLogic Server automatically invokes the compiler when a requested JSP's source is new or has changed.

In some scenarios, such as debugging, it might be useful to access the JSP compiler directly. To start the JSP compiler, enter the following command:

```
java weblogic.jspc [-options] fileName
```

Replace fileName with the name of the JSP file to compile. You can specify any options before or after the target fileName. For information on the compile options, see the WebLogic Server documentation on compiling JSPs at the following URL:

```
http://edocs.bea.com/wls/docs70/jsp/reference.html#57794
```

The location of the generated JSP servlet source file (.java) and the compiled JSP servlet file (.class) depend upon the working directory and package prefix settings in the WebLogic Application Extension Deployment Descriptor (weblogic.xml). Whether to keep the source file depends upon the keepgenerated setting; this is discussed further in the next section.

Configuring the WebLogic Application Extension Deployment Descriptor

WebLogic Server allows you to configure the JSP container by setting the WebLogic Application Extension Deployment Descriptor (weblogic.xml). This descriptor is located in the WEB-INF directory of your Web application. It is defined by and verified against the BEA Web Application Document Type Definitions (DTD) file at

```
http://www.bea.com/servers/wls700/dtd/weblogic700-web-jar.dtd
```

After starting the default WebLogic Server and the default WebLogic Console, expand the Web Applications branch on the navigation tree. For this example, you'll define the deployment descriptor associated with the DefaultWebApp. After clicking the DefaultWebApp Web application node, the page shown in Figure 12-2 appears.

Next, click the Edit Web Application Deployment Descriptors link. A new window opens, displaying the page shown in Figure 12-3.

Notice that the left navigation pane has a navigation tree of the various categories of descriptors that can be defined. The right pane provides you with a couple of buttons to persist the changes made to the descriptors and to validate the descriptors. We use these buttons a few steps later.

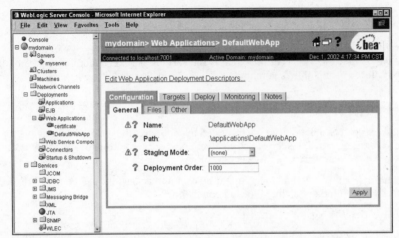

Figure 12-2: WebLogic Server console for the default server instance

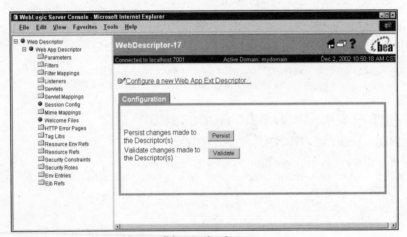

Figure 12-3: Web Descriptor editing navigation

Because you have not yet created a Web App Ext Descriptor, the `weblogic.xml` file, for this application, click the Configure a new Web App Ext Descriptor link to instruct the console to create one. The page shown in Figure 12-4 appears.

Figure 12-4: Confirmation that the Web App Ext Descriptor was created

This page confirms that the console was successful. Notice that there is a new branch of nodes in the left navigation pane. The Continue link will forward you back to the previous page, but you want to configure the JSP Descriptor. Click that node. The page shown in Figure 12-5 appears.

Figure 12-5: Configuring the JSP Descriptor

Here's the page you've been waiting for. A whole series of options is available to configure the WebLogic Server JSP container. We'll describe each option for you.

Compile Command

This option specifies the full pathname of the standard Java compiler used to compile the generated JSP servlets. The default value is `javac`, or the Java compiler defined for a server under the Configuration/Tuning tab of the WebLogic Server Administration Console.

Compiler Class

This option specifies the name of a Java compiler that is executed by WebLogic Server. It is used in place of an executable compiler such as `javac`. This class must reside within the WebLogic Server classpath. If not specified, there is no default value.

Compile Flags

This option specifies one or more command-line flags for the JSP compiler. If specifying multiple, enclose them in quotes and separate them by a space. If not specified, there is no default value.

Working Dir

This option specifies the name of a directory in which WebLogic Server saves the generated JSP servlet source file (`.java`) and the compiled JSP servlet file (`.class`). If specified, it is either located or created within the `WEB-INF` directory of the Web application. If not specified, WebLogic Server uses an internally generated directory. WebLogic Server, for example, will generate a directory in the server directory of the domain the application is deployed in. For example, for server `myserver` in domain `mydomain` for the default web application, WebLogic Server creates a directory `/mydomain/myserver/.wlnotdelete/Default WebApp_DefaultWebApp_2458792`. Within that directory, both servlet Java source and compiled class files will be placed in a subdirectory named `jsp_servlet` based upon the Package Prefix value. They will have the same name as your JSP file, but will be prefixed with a double underscore (_).

Verbose

This option instructs WebLogic Server to output debugging information to the browser, the command prompt, and the WebLogic Server log file. If not specified, the default value is `true`.

Keepgenerated

This option specifies that the JSP compiler keep the generated JSP servlet source file upon completion of the JSP compilation process. Otherwise, the intermediate Java files are deleted after they are compiled. If not specified, the default value is `false`.

Page Check Seconds

This option specifies the interval, in seconds, which WebLogic Server will check the JSP files to determine whether they have changed and need recompiling. Dependent JSPs are also checked and recompiled if changed. If not specified, the default value is 1. If set to 0, JSPs are checked on every request. If set to -1, page checking and recompiling is disabled.

Encoding

This option specifies the default character set used in the JSP page. Note that the `contentType` attribute of the page directive overrides this setting for that particular JSP page. If not specified, the default value is the encoding for your platform. See the following URL for more information:

```
http://java.sun.com/j2se/1.3/docs/guide/intl/encoding.doc.htm
```

Package Prefix

This option specifies the package into which all JSP pages are compiled. If not specified, there is no default value.

No Try Blocks

If a JSP file has numerous or deeply nested custom JSP tags and you receive a `java.lang. VerifyError` exception when compiling, use this flag to allow the JSPs to compile correctly. If not specified, the default value is `false`.

Precompile

This option specifies whether WebLogic Server should automatically compile all JSPs on startup. If not specified, the default value is `false`.

Compiler Supports Encoding

This option specifies the encoding used by the JSP compiler to create the intermediate JSP servlet source file. To use the encoding as defined in this descriptor (see "Encoding") or over-ridden by the JSP's page directive, specify `true`. To use the default encoding for the JVM, specify `false`. If not specified, the default value is `false`.

Suggested settings for development

When developing, we like to have as much information about what's happening as possible; we're not too worried about the performance of the JSP container. Therefore, we usually use the following settings:

```
Verbose = true
Keepgenerated = true
Page Check Seconds = 1
Precompile = false
```

Suggested settings for production

In production, however, performance is critical, so we want to turn off unwanted processing steps. We are not in development mode, so we have no need for verbose messages. Also, we are deploying an Enterprise Application Archive (`.ear`) file with all the JSP files already compiled, so there is no need to check for new versions of JSPs and to set compiling options. Therefore, we usually use the following settings:

```
Verbose = false
keepgenerated = false
Page Check Seconds = -1
Precompile = false
```

After setting the descriptors according to your needs, click the Apply button. A yellow triangle blinks next to Keepgenerated to let you know you need to restart the server for the changes to take effect. Then, at the top of the navigation tree, click Web Descriptor and you'll see the page shown in Figure 12-6.

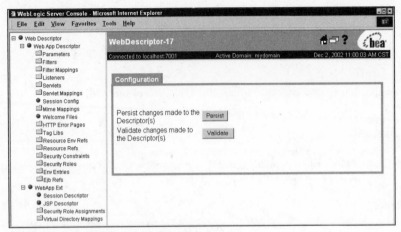

Figure 12-6: Validating the Web Descriptor

This is essentially the same page as Figure 12-3, but there's no longer a Configure link, and the left navigation tree shows the WebApp Ext branch that you created. Next, instruct the WebLogic Console to validate your descriptor against the DTD file (`http://www.bea.com/servers/wls700/dtd/weblogic700-web-jar.dtd`) by clicking the Validate button. The page shown in Figure 12-7 appears.

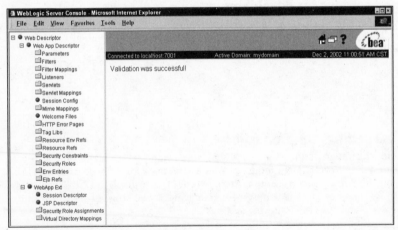

Figure 12-7: Web Descriptor Validation confirmation

After receiving validation that your Web Descriptor is correct, click the Web Descriptor node to redisplay the following page, as shown in Figure 12-8.

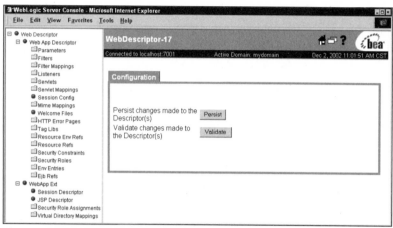

Figure 12-8: Persisting the Web Descriptor

Next click the Persist button to persist your changes to the weblogic.xml file. Additionally, WebLogic Server loads these changes immediately for the JSP container. The page shown in Figure 12-9 appears.

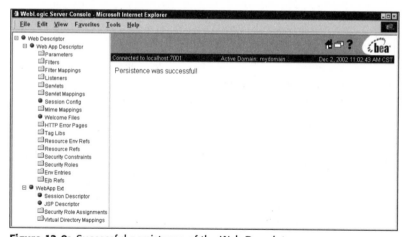

Figure 12-9: Successful persistence of the Web Descriptor

The changes have been persisted to the file system and loaded in WebLogic Server. Listing 12-1 is a listing of the weblogic.xml file that was created in our Web application's WEB-INF directory.

Listing 12-1: **weblogic.xml**

```
<!DOCTYPE weblogic-web-app PUBLIC "-//BEA Systems, Inc.//DTD Web Application
7.0//EN" "http://www.bea.com/servers/wls700/dtd/weblogic700-web-jar.dtd">

<weblogic-web-app>
  <jsp-descriptor>
    <jsp-param>
      <param-name>compileCommand</param-name>
      <param-value>javac</param-value>
    </jsp-param>
    <jsp-param>
      <param-name>verbose</param-name>
      <param-value>true</param-value>
    </jsp-param>
    <jsp-param>
      <param-name>keepgenerated</param-name>
      <param-value>true</param-value>
    </jsp-param>
    <jsp-param>
      <param-name>pageCheckSeconds</param-name>
      <param-value>1</param-value>
    </jsp-param>
    <jsp-param>
      <param-name>packagePrefix</param-name>
      <param-value>jsp_servlet</param-value>
    </jsp-param>
    <jsp-param>
      <param-name>noTryBlocks</param-name>
      <param-value>false</param-value>
    </jsp-param>
    <jsp-param>
      <param-name>precompile</param-name>
      <param-value>false</param-value>
    </jsp-param>
    <jsp-param>
      <param-name>compilerSupportsEncoding</param-name>
      <param-value>true</param-value>
    </jsp-param>
    <jsp-param>
      <param-name>superclass</param-name>
      <param-value>weblogic.servlet.jsp.JspBase</param-value>
    </jsp-param>
    <jsp-param>
      <param-name>exactMapping</param-name>
      <param-value>true</param-value>
    </jsp-param>
    <jsp-param>
      <param-name>debug</param-name>
      <param-value>false</param-value>
```

```
   </jsp-param>
  </jsp-descriptor>

</weblogic-web-app>
```

Deploying your first JSP in WebLogic Server

In this section, we show you how to deploy and run your first JSP. Because this will be the first time you call it, the JSP will be converted to a servlet and compiled. Then it will be loaded and executed, generating output to the browser. Finally, we show you how to find the generated JSP servlet source so you can look at it.

Start with a simple JSP, named First.jsp, as shown in Listing 12-2. If you take a close look, you'll see that it's a simple HTML page with a small scriptlet to get the current date from the server and output it.

Listing 12-2: **First.jsp**

```
<html>
<head>
  <title>First JSP</title>
</head>

<body>
Welcome! It is currently: <%= new Date() %>
</body>
</html>
```

Place the servlet in the root level of your Web application directory (named BibleApp), as you would an HTML document. Unlike servlets, there are no deployment descriptor entries necessary to register the JSP. WebLogic Server looks for the document based upon the URL in the client's request. However, WebLogic Server 7 requires a minimal web.xml file, so create one in the /BibleApp/WEB-INF directory, as follows:

```
<!DOCTYPE web-app PUBLIC "-//Sun Microsystems, Inc.//DTD Web Application
2.3//EN" "http://java.sun.com/dtd/web-app_2_3.dtd">
<web-app>
  <welcome-file-list>
    <welcome-file>index.html</welcome-file>
  </welcome-file-list>
</web-app>
```

Configure your Web application's JSP deployment descriptor for a development environment. As a result, WebLogic Server will compile your JSP and retain the generated JSP servlet source file.

Note   The generated servlet source files (.java files) are written to X/Y/.wlnotdelete/ Z_Z_nnn/jsp_servlet, where X is the name of the administrative server for your WebLogic domain, Y is the name of the WebLogic server to which the JSP is deployed, Z is the name of your application, and nnn is a random number.

Type http://localhost:7001/BibleApp/First.jsp to run the JSP. After a few seconds in which to create the JSP servlet and compile it, the page shown in Figure 12-10 appears.

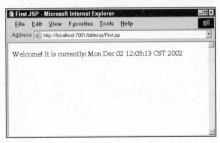

Figure 12-10: Executing First.jsp

Within the domain's server directory, in the .wlnotdelete directory, there is now a BibleApp_BibleApp_nnn directory, and within that a jsp_servlet directory. Again, these directory names are based upon the settings in your JSP deployment descriptor.

If you examine the contents of the jsp_servlet directory, there are now two files: __first. class and __first.java. The .java file is the generated JSP servlet source, and the .class filed is the compiled JSP servlet. If you open the __first.java file in an editor, the source shown in Listing 12-3 appears.

Listing 12-3: **__first.java**

```java
/* compiled from JSP: /First.jsp
*
* This code was automatically generated at 12:05:11 PM on Dec 2, 2002
* by weblogic.servlet.jsp.Jsp2Java -- do not edit.
*/

package jsp_servlet;

import java.io.*;
import java.util.*;
import javax.servlet.*;
import javax.servlet.http.*;
import javax.servlet.jsp.*;
import javax.servlet.jsp.tagext.*;

// User imports

// built-in init parameters:
// boolean          _verbose -- wants debugging
```

```
// Well-known variables:
// JspWriter out                -- to write to the browser
// HttpServletRequest  request  -- the request object.
// HttpServletResponse response  -- the response object.
// PageContext pageContext      -- the page context for this JSP
// HttpSession session          -- the session object for the client (if any)
// ServletContext application   -- The servlet (application) context
// ServletConfig config         -- The ServletConfig for this JSP
// Object page                  -- the instance of this page's implementation
class (i.e., 'this')

/**
 * This code was automatically generated at 12:05:11 PM on Dec 2, 2002
 * by weblogic.servlet.jsp.Jsp2Java -- do not edit.
 *
 * Copyright (c) 2002 by BEA Systems, Inc. All Rights Reserved.
 */
public final class __first
extends
weblogic.servlet.jsp.JspBase
implements weblogic.servlet.jsp.StaleIndicator
{

    // StaleIndicator interface
    public boolean _isStale() {
        weblogic.servlet.jsp.StaleChecker sci
=(weblogic.servlet.jsp.StaleChecker)(getServletConfig().getServletContext());
        java.io.File f = null;
        long lastModWhenBuilt = 0L;
        if (sci.isResourceStale("/First.jsp", 998778420000L, "7.0.1.0")) return
true;
        return false;
    }

    public static boolean _staticIsStale(weblogic.servlet.jsp.StaleChecker sci)
{
        java.io.File f = null;
        long lastModWhenBuilt = 0L;
        if (sci.isResourceStale("/First.jsp", 998778420000L, "7.0.1.0")) return
true;
        return false;
    }




    public void _jspService(javax.servlet.http.HttpServletRequest request,
javax.servlet.http.HttpServletResponse response) throws java.io.IOException,
javax.servlet.ServletException
    {

        // declare and set well-known variables:
```

Continued

Listing 12-3 *(continued)*

```
        javax.servlet.ServletConfig config = getServletConfig();
        javax.servlet.ServletContext application = config.getServletContext();
        javax.servlet.jsp.tagext.Tag _activeTag = null;
        // variables for Tag extension protocol

        Object page = this;
        javax.servlet.jsp.JspWriter out;
        javax.servlet.jsp.PageContext pageContext =
        javax.servlet.jsp.JspFactory.getDefaultFactory().getPageContext(this,
request, response, null, true, 8192, true);

        out = pageContext.getOut();
        JspWriter _originalOut = out;

        javax.servlet.http.HttpSession session = request.getSession(true);


        try { // error page try block

                out.print("<html>\r\n<head>\r\n\t<title>First
JSP</title>\r\n</head>\r\n\r\n<body>\r\nWelcome! It is currently: ");
                out.print(String.valueOf( new Date() ));  //[ /First.jsp; Line: 7]
                out.print("\r\n</body>\r\n</html>\r\n");
        } catch (Throwable __ee) {
                while (out != null && out != _originalOut) out =
pageContext.popBody();

((weblogic.servlet.jsp.PageContextImpl)pageContext).handlePageException((Throwab
le)__ee);
        }

        //before final close brace...
    }


}
```

Wow, a lot of code was generated from a relatively small JSP! If you read through the servlet code, you'll see there is a lot there to support the variety of functionality a JSP can contain.

Take some time to examine this source. Pay particular attention to the package name, import statements, parent class and interface, method names, declaration of implicit objects, and so on. Also notice that the lines of the servlet that directly correlate to the JSP are commented and that they reference line numbers in the JSP.

Support for JSP 1.2

As of this writing, the current release from Sun Microsystems is JavaServer Pages API specification Version 1.2. WebLogic Server 7.0 completely supports this spec, including the following features of JSP 1.2:

✦ **<jsp:include flush="false">**: Allows you to buffer the page output and then flush the buffer before including another resource.

✦ **TryCatchFinally**: Allows you to catch exceptions thrown from within a tag by implementing the `doCatch()` and `doFinally()` methods of the `javax.servlet.jsp.tagext.TryCatchFinally` interface.

✦ **Tag Library Validator**: Allows you to write a Java class that you can use to perform custom validation on a JSP page. The validator class takes the entire JSP page as an input stream, and you can validate the page based on criteria that you write into the validator class.

✦ **Iteration Tag Class**: Allows tag handler classes to implement a new `javax.servlet.jsp.tagext.IterationTag` interface to conditionally re-evaluate the tag body.

✦ **Scripting Variables**: Allows you to define scripting variables within a Tag Library Descriptor (TLD).

A JSP page can be written directly as an XML document, so you can use XML authoring tools. The XML document can be delivered to a JSP container for processing.

Programming Java Server Pages

Now that we've covered what JSPs are and how to deploy them in WebLogic Server, we will cover the rules and syntax to build them. In this section, we cover tag conventions, directives, scripting, comments, implicit objects, and actions. Then we provide you with a simple example that uses a little bit of everything and talk about error handling and debugging.

Tag conventions

JSP pages have two styles of syntax. Both always enclose their statements in angle brackets (< >). This is the obvious reason why JSP tags are said to be like HTML.

The first syntax style, which is used for scripting, always begins with <% and ends with %>. Those familiar with Microsoft's ASP will recognize this syntax style. An additional character may appear after the <% to further identify the type of tag. These characters are @ for directives, ! for declarations, and = for expressions. Following are some examples:

```
<%@ include file="header.jsp" %>
<%! int lineNumber = 0 %>
<% if (lineNumber % 2 > 0) { lineClass = "detailLineOdd";
} else { lineClass = "detailLineEven"; } %>
<%= lineClass %>"
```

The second syntax style is based upon the XML syntax. They are case-sensitive, all values must appear in single or double quotes, and belong to the `jsp` namespace. They also make the distinction between those that contain a body versus those that don't.

An XML-based tag with body content (enclosed statements) has both a starting tag `<jsp: ... >` and ending tag `</jsp: ... >`. For example:

```
<jsp:useBean id="testBean" class="bible.jsp.TestBean">
<jsp:setProperty name="testBean" property="*"/>
</jsp:useBean>
```

An XML-based tag without a body begins with a `<jsp:` and ends with `/>`. For example:

```
<jsp:include help="helpMain.htm" />
```

Directives

Directives are a set of tags with specific instructions to the JSP container about the JSP page. They do not affect request processing nor produce any output that is visible to the end user. Instead, they change the way the JSP container processes the page.

Directives support both styles of syntax, but it's a good idea to choose one and stick with it to make your code more readable. The scripting syntax uses an at sign (@) to uniquely identify directives. The XML syntax uses the directive action. These two tag styles are interchangeable. Following are some examples:

```
<%@ page import="java.util.*, bible.jsp.*" %>
<jsp:directive.page import="java.util.*, bible.jsp.*" />
```

page directive

The `page` directive defines attributes that apply to an entire JSP page. For convenience, you are allowed to specify multiple `page` directives on a single page. But no individual attribute of the `page` directive can be specified multiple times on a page. Any attempt to do so will result in a JSP-to-servlet translation-time error.

The basic syntax of the directive is the same in both script-based and XML-based syntax, namely

```
<%@ page attribute="value" attribute="value" ... %>
<jsp:directive.page attribute="value" attribute="value" ... />
```

The `page` directive supports a number of attributes, which are listed and described in the following sections.

info

The `info` attribute enables the developer to include textual information about the page. The `String` is then available to the JSP container and any other object that has access to the JSP servlet. If not specified, there is no default value.

```
<%@ page info="Application Main Page" %>
<jsp:directive.page info="Application Main Page" />
```

language

The `language` attribute identifies the scripting language to be used by the JSP. JSP containers are required to support Java, but they allow for other languages to be used based upon a set of rules defined in the JSP API specification. If not specified, the default value is `"java"`. This is typically not specified unless a unique situation warrants it.

```
<%@ page language="java" %>
<jsp:directive.page language="java" />
```

contentType

The `contentType` attribute identifies the MIME type of the generated response. If not specified, the default value is `"text/html"`. A common alternative would be `"text/xml"`.

```
<%@ page contentType="text/xml" %>
<jsp:directive.page contentType="text/xml" />
```

extends

The `extends` attribute identifies the class by which the generated JSP servlet will extend. If not specified, WebLogic Server will extend `weblogic.servlet.jsp.JspBase`. This attribute is typically not specified unless a unique situation warrants it.

```
<%@ page extends="bible.jsp.myParentJspClass" %>
<jsp:directive.page extends="bible.jsp.myParentJspClass" />
```

import

The `import` attribute identifies Java classes and packages to be imported for successful compilation of the generated JSP servlet. This works identically to the Java import statement. Multiple packages and classes can be specified, separated by a comma. As a convenience, WebLogic will automatically import the following packages: `java.lang`, `java.io`, `java.util`, `javax.servlet`, `javax.servlet.http`, `javax.servlet.jsp`, `javax.servlet.jsp.tagext`. If not specified, there is no default value.

```
<%@ page import='bible.jsp.*, bible.jsp.taglib.*" %>
<jsp:directive.page
   import="bible.jsp.*, bible.jsp.taglib.*" />
```

session

The `session` attribute indicates the page's participation in session management. In other words, the JSP servlet will either use URL rewriting or cookies to maintain state. Note that the implicit object `session` is available only if this attribute is set to `"true"`. If not specified, the default value is `true`.

```
<%@ page session="false" %>
<jsp:directive.page session="false" />
```

buffer

The `buffer` attribute indicates whether or not the generated response should be buffered, and if so, the buffer size. Because WebLogic Server actually uses a pool of buffers and may allocate more if needed, consider this more of a minimum size. The valid values are either `none` or the buffer size in kilobytes. If not specified, the default value is `"8kb"`.

```
<%@ page buffer="12kb" %>
<jsp:directive.page buffer="12kb" />
```

autoFlush

The `autoFlush` attribute is used for controller buffered output and indicates whether the output should automatically be flushed or sent when the buffer is full. If set to `"false"`, WebLogic Server will raise an exception. Note that after a buffer has been flushed, it is no longer possible to set HTTP headers or forward the request to another JSP for processing. If not specified, the default value is `"true"`.

```
<%@ page autoFlush="false" %>
<jsp:directive.page autoFlush="false" />
```

isThreadSafe

The isThreadSafe attribute indicates whether the generated JSP servlet is capable of running multiple threads successfully. If set to "false", WebLogic Server will queue requests for this servlet and process them sequentially. If not specified, the default value is "true".

```
<%@ page isThreadSafe="false" %>
<jsp:directive.page isThreadSafe="false" />
```

errorPage

The errorPage attribute identifies the URL of an alternate JSP to display if an uncaught exception occurs. After output has been flushed and an exception occurs, it is no longer possible to forward the request. If not specified, there is no default value.

```
<%@ page errorPage="/BibleApp/Error.jsp" %>
<jsp:directive.page errorPage="/BibleApp/Error.jsp" />
```

isErrorPage

The isErrorPage attribute indicates that the current JSP is behaving as an error page for another JSP. Note that the implicit object "exception" is available only if this attribute is set to "true". If not specified, the default value is "false".

```
<%@ page isErrorPage="true" %>
<jsp:directive.page isErrorPage="true" />
```

include directive

The include directive defines a file to be included by the JSP compiler. The file is identified by either a relative or explicit URL or path to the file. The end result is the tag replacing itself with the contents of the specified file.

No restrictions exist on the number of include directives nor on the number of nesting levels. The included file can contain any combination of static HTML and JSP tags. It is the final combined source that is parsed and compiled, and it therefore must follow all JSP rules to compile successfully. Additionally, because you are logically combining the source, it's perfectly legal to reference a variable in the child file from the parent file, and vice versa.

As described earlier in the chapter, WebLogic Server will automatically rebuild and recompile the JSP when it determines that the JSP source has changed. This is, of course, based upon the deployment descriptor settings detailed previously. WebLogic Server is able to determine when an included file has changed, and as a result will rebuild and recompile all parent JSPs.

```
<%@ include file="header.jsp" %>
<jsp:directive.include file="header.jsp" />
```

taglib directive

The taglib directive defines a tag library and prefix for the custom tags used in the JSP page. The uri attribute is the logical name to identify the location of the Tag Library Descriptor (TLD) as defined by the Web application deployment descriptor (web.xml). The prefix is the XML namespace identifier used by all custom tags referencing classes in the tag library.

```
<%@ taglib uri="BibleTagLib" prefix="bible" %>
<jsp:directive.taglib uri="BibleTagLib" prefix="bible" />
```

Scripting

Scripting tags are used to embed programming code within the body of a JSP to be executed during the process of each request. They are written in the designated processing language, which is typically Java. Note that the language can be changed in the `language` attribute of the `page` directive.

Declarations

Declarations are used to define instance level or class level variables and methods. Subsequently, they may be referenced by other scripting elements on the page.

Declarations support both styles of syntax. The scripting syntax uses an exclamation (!) to uniquely identify declarations. The XML syntax uses the `declaration` action. These two tag styles are interchangeable. Following are some examples:

```
<%! int x = 0; %>
<jsp:declaration> int x = 0; </jsp:declaration>
```

Variable declarations

Variable declarations have the net effect of defining instance level variables within the JSP servlet. Multiple variables can be declared within a single tag. Keep in mind that your JSP servlets are running multithreaded, so if one thread changes an instance level variable, any other thread that has a reference to that variable may be affected. This is not a consideration, however, if you have set the `isThreadSafe` attribute of the `page` directive to `"false"`. Another option is to use local variables, which are always thread safe and usually the better choice, anyway.

```
<%! int x = 0; int y = 1; %>
<jsp:declaration> int x = 0; int y = 1; </jsp:declaration>
```

Class level variables can also be defined by using the static keyword within the declaration. Because this is defined at the class level, any thread of any instance of this JSP servlet may be affected by changes to this value, regardless of the `isThreadSafe` attribute setting.

```
<%! static public boolean validate = true; %>
<jsp:declaration>
  static public boolean validate = true;
</jsp:declaration>
```

Method declarations

Method declarations define methods of the JSP servlet class. They can be called from any scripting element within the page. Multiple method declarations can be declared within a single tag.

```
<%@ page import="java.text.*" %>

<%!
// Get a formatted current date and time
public String getCurrentDateTime() {
  Date date = new Date();
  DateFormat dateFormat =
    DateFormat.getDateTimeInstance(DateFormat.FULL,
    DateFormat.SHORT);
  return dateFormat.format(date);
}
%>
```

A very specific usage for method declarations is to define logic associated with the initialization and destruction of a JSP servlet. By defining methods `jspInit()` and `jspDestroy()`, the corresponding `_jspInit()` and `_jspDestroy()` methods of the JSP servlet are defined.

Cross-Reference   See Chapter 11 for a complete discussion of servlet initialization and destruction.

```
<%!
public void jspInit() {
  // initialization logic ...
}
public void jspDestroy() {
  // destruction logic ...
}
%>
```

Expressions

Expressions are used to output the evaluated value of an individual variable, calculation, or method call. All expression results are converted to character strings before being added to the page's output. Java primitives are converted via the static `toString()` method on the corresponding Java object (for example, an integer uses the `Integer.toString()` method, and so on). Java objects use their own `toString()` method.

Note that no semicolon is required at the end of an expression because the JSP compiler is concerned with evaluating the code, not with its side effects.

Expressions support both styles of syntax. The scripting syntax uses an equal sign (=) to uniquely identify expressions. The XML syntax uses the `expression` action. These two tag styles are interchangeable. Following are some examples:

```
<%= 365 * 24 %>
<%= x %>
<%= getDate() %>
<jsp:expression> 365 * 24 </jsp:expression>
<jsp:expression> x </jsp:expression>
<jsp:expression> getDate() </jsp:expression>
```

Conditional output is usually handled by using scriptlets in combination with expressions, but expressions do support the tertiary condition operator.

```
<%= hours < 12 ? "am" : "pm" %>
<jsp:expression> hours < 12 ? "am" : "pm" </jsp:expression>
```

Scriptlets

Scriptlets are tags that contain code fragments of one or more lines. Although all the tags that we've covered are for specific purposes, scriptlets are general-purpose and allow you to embed Java code within your JSP. Each line of code within a scriptlet must be a complete line of code and therefore should end with a semicolon where appropriate.

Variables can be declared and set, methods can be called, return values can be evaluated, implicit objects can be referenced — virtually any Java code you want to embed within your JSP is valid. This is because scriptlets undergo no translation at all during the creation of the JSP servlet source, but are simply inserted as-is into the `_jspService()` method.

Scriptlets support both styles of syntax. The scripting syntax doesn't use any specific character to uniquely identify it; therefore, all scriptlet tags begin with the base `<%` designation. The XML syntax uses the `scriptlet` action. These two tag styles are interchangeable. Following are some examples:

```
<% String fullName = firstName + " " + lastName; %>
<jsp:scriptlet>
  String fullName = firstName + " " + lastName;
</jsp:scriptlet>
```

Conditional processing

One of the strengths of a scriptlet is JSP's support of code blocks left open across multiple statements. In other words, scoped blocks of code can be broken into multiple tags with HTML or any other valid code text intermingled. A good example of using this is conditional output based upon a dynamic variable. Look at the following example:

```
<% Random rand = new Random();
if (rand.nextBoolean()) { %>
<strong>Do something.</strong>
<% } else {  %>
<strong>Do nothing.</strong>
<% } %>
```

Notice the if/else statement with two blocks of code based upon a random Boolean value. Through use of the begin and end scope notations using curly braces {}, you can span the logic across three scriptlet tags. In addition, notice that intermingled with the scriptlet tags is basic HTML code. Execution of this code will randomly output "Do something." or "Do nothing."

Iterative processing

Another way to take advantage of this technique is with iterative processing. Java provides for loops, while loops, and do/while loops as iterative constructs. Again, by using the scope notations, blocks can be left open across multiple statements to create the desired results. The following code iteratively computes a table of squares and cubes for the integers between 1 and 10:

```
<table>
  <tr>
    <td>Number</td>
    <td>Squared</td>
    <td>Cubed</td>
  </tr>

<% for (int i = 1; i <= 10; i++ ) { %>
  <tr>
    <td><%= i %></td>
    <td><%= i * i %></td>
    <td><%= i * i * i %></td>
  </tr>
<% } %>

</table>
```

Comments

Comments are used to document various types of code that can be found in a JSP page. You can use three styles of comments in JSPs; these types are discussed in the following sections.

Content comments

Content comments are an HTML-style comment that is converted by the JSP compiler and is output as a `String` by the corresponding JSP servlet. Subsequently, the comment is sent to the client in the viewable page source. Any JSP statement in an HTML comment is still evaluated, thereby allowing the comment to contain dynamic content.

```
<!-- HTML comment -->
<!-- Table line number <%= lineNumber %> -->
```

JSP comments

A JSP-style comment is filtered out during the JSP conversion process and therefore cannot be found in the JSP servlet source. It is viewable only in the original JSP source. Any JSP statement between the beginning and end tags of a JSP comment is ignored by the JSP compiler.

```
<%-- JSP comment --%>
<%-- <jsp:getProperty name="bean" property="newAttribute" /> not yet
implemented -->
```

Scripting comments

Scripting comments are comments within the scriptlets themselves. They are in the style as defined by the scripting language. Java, for example, supports multiline comments beginning with `/*` and ending with `*/` as well as line level comments beginning with `//`. They are converted by the JSP compiler into the corresponding JSP servlet as a Java comment.

```
<% /* Scripting comment */ %>
<% int workHours = 178 /* number of workdays */ * 8 %>
<%  int hours = 365 * 24; // number of hours per year %>
```

Implicit objects

To expose all the capabilities of executing as servlets, WebLogic Server exposes a number of internal objects to the JSP developer. They are referred to as *implicit objects* because their availability is automatic and they're referenced by reserved names. Implicit objects are always either an instance of a class or interface adhering to the specific API and are always scoped at the same level. The following sections provide the details of each of the nine implicit objects.

page

The `page` object represents an instance of the JSP Servlet class corresponding to the JSP page. It can be used to call any of the methods defined by the servlet class. But because these methods will be accessible automatically, this object is typically not implicitly referenced in the body of the JSP.

Type: `java.lang.Object`

Scope: `page`

Some useful methods: Not typically referenced

Note Scope is discussed in the "Programming JSPs with JavaBeans" section of this chapter.

config

The `config` object represents the JSP servlet configuration data accessible in the form of initialization parameters.

Type: `javax.servlet.ServletConfig`

Scope: `page`

Some useful methods: `getInitParameter, getInitParameterNames`

request

The `request` object represents the request received by WebLogic Server to initiate processing. It provides information regarding the requested URL, HTTP headers, parameters, and cookies associated with the request.

Type: `javax.servlet.ServletRequest` or `javax.servlet.http.HttpServletRequest`

Scope: `request`

Some useful methods: `getAttribute, getParameter, setParameterNames, getParameterValues, setAttribute`

response

The `response` object represents the response that will be returned by WebLogic Server upon completion of processing.

Type: `javax.Servlet.ServletResponse` or `javax.servlet.http.HttpServletResponse`

Scope: `page`

Some useful methods: `setHeader, addHeader, encodeURL`

out

The `out` object represents the output stream for the page. The contents of the `out` object will be sent as the body of the response.

Type: `javax.servlet.jsp.JspWriter`

Scope: `page`

Some useful methods: `clear, clearBuffer, flush, getBufferSize, getRemaining`

session

The `session` object represents an individual user's current session. The session persists as long as that user continues to send requests to the server frequently enough that it does not time out. It is available only if the `session` attribute of the `page` directive indicates that this JSP is participating in session management.

Type: `javax.servlet.http.HttpSession`

Scope: `session`

Some useful methods: `getAttribute, getId, setAttribute`

application

The `application` object represents the application to which the JSP belongs and is an instance of the `ServletContext`. It can be used to share information with other JSPs and servlets running as part of other sessions within an application.

Type: `javax.servlet.ServletContext`

Scope: `application`

Some useful methods: `getAttribute, getMimeType, getRealPath, setAttribute`

pageContext

The `pageContext` object is an instance of the servlet `PageContext` and provides program-matic access to all the other implicit objects as well as methods for forwarding requests to or including responses from other URLs.

Type: `javax.servlet.jsp.PageContext`

Scope: `page`

Some useful methods: `findAttribute, getAttribute, getAttributesScope, getAttributeNamesInScope, setAttribute`

exception

The `exception` object represents the exception that is thrown as the result of execution of another JSP. It can be used to retrieve and display information about the exception. It is available only if the `isErrorPage` attribute of the `page` directive indicates that the JSP page is an error page.

Type: `java.lang.Throwable`

Scope: `page`

Some useful methods: `getMessage, getLocalizedMessage, printStackTrace, toString`

Actions

Actions are the final type of JSP tag. They are used to transfer control between pages, support applets in a browser-independent manner, and interact with JavaBeans. Unlike the other types of tags, actions support only the XML-based syntax. Following are some examples:

```
<jsp:forward page="<%= nextPage %>">
  <jsp:param name="cmd" value="load"/>
</jsp:forward>
<jsp:include page="Header.jsp" flush="true">
  <jsp:param name="helpTag" value="help_Main.htm"/>
</jsp:include>
<jsp:plugin type="applet" codebase="plugins"
  code="bible.jsp.myplugin.class"/>
<jsp:useBean id="account" class="bible.jsp.AccountBean"/>
<jsp:setProperty name="account" property="accountNumber"
  value="110-12345"/>
<jsp:getProperty name="account" property="accountNumber"/>
```

forward

The `forward` action permanently forwards a client request to another server location for processing. The recipient can be an HTML file, CGI, JSP file, or servlet.

A new `pageContext` object will be assigned to the forwarded page. The `request` and `session` objects remain the same. The `application` object will be shared only if both the from and to pages are part of the same Web application.

Because the same `request` object is available to the forwarded page, the URL remains the same and the request parameters are still available. Additional parameters can be specified via the `param` tag within the body of the tag to add name-value pairs to the request. The number of parameters that you can specify in this manner is unlimited. Larger amounts of data are typically stored in the `request` or the `session` objects. Note that to reference the `session` object, both pages need to participate in session management. See the `session` attribute of the `page` directive for more information.

After control is passed to the new page, processing of the originating page is immediately terminated. If the originating page buffered any data for output and that output has not yet been flushed, it can be cleared. But if output has already been flushed and an attempt to clear the buffer is made, an `IllegalStateException` will be thrown.

Following are some examples:

```
<jsp:forward page="Main.jsp"/>
<jsp:forward page="Confirm.jsp">
  <jsp:param name="cmd" value="load"/>
</jsp:forward>
```

For dynamic flow of control, embedding expressions within the body of the `forward` tag is supported. This allows the request to be forwarded to a location that is derived or passed as a parameter. Following is an example:

```
<% if (rows == 1) {
    nextPage = "Detail.jsp";
  } else {
    nextPage = "List.jsp";
  } %>

<jsp:forward page="<%= nextPage %>"/>
```

include

The `include` action allows the generated content of another file to be included into the output of the current JSP. Control is temporarily passed to the other location; upon completing, it returns to continue processing immediately after the action tag.

Unlike the `include` directive, the `include` action is resolved during the processing of the request. The included page's output is resolved and added to the output buffer, as opposed to processing the commingled source.

The `flush` attribute controls whether the output buffer is flushed prior to transferring to the included file's location. JSP 1.1 restricted usage of this attribute to allow only `false`. WebLogic supports some prerelease features of JSP 1.2, including support for this attribute's value as `true`. This allows the page output to be buffered and then `flush` the buffer before including another resource.

As with the `forward` action, a new `pageContext` object is assigned, the `request` and `session` objects remain the same, and the `application` object is shared only if both the from and to pages are part of the same Web application. Likewise, an unlimited number of additional parameters can be specified via the `param` tags. In addition, expressions may be embedded for dynamic includes.

Following are some examples:

```
<jsp:include page="<%= helpTag %>"/>
<jsp:include page="Header.jsp" flush="true">
  <jsp:param name="helpTag" value="help_Main.htm"/>
</jsp:include>
```

plugin

The `plugin` action downloads plug-in software to the browser to execute an applet or bean. Because this book focuses on the development of server-side applications using WebLogic Server, this is outside of the scope of this book. See the complete JavaServer Pages specification at the following URL for more information:

```
http://java.sun.com/products/jsp/download.html
```

Bean tags

Three additional tags exist for interacting with JavaBeans. They are `useBean`, `setProperty`, and `getProperty` (we cover them in the "Programming JSPs with JavaBeans" section later in this chapter). The following list is provided as a quick reference.

useBean

The `useBean` action locates or instantiates a bean with a specific name and scope. Example:

```
<jsp:useBean id="account" class="bible.jsp.AccountBean"
  scope="request" />
```

setProperty

The `setProperty` action sets a property value or values in a bean. Example:

```
<jsp:setProperty name="account" property="accountNumber"
  value="110-12345"/>
```

getProperty

The `getProperty` action gets the value of a bean property so that you can display it in a result page. Example:

```
<jsp:getProperty name="account" property="accountNumber"/>
```

JSP example

Now that we've covered all the different types of tags and their syntax, let's dive into a fairly meaty example and try to use a little bit of everything. We'll keep it simple by writing a JSP that prompts for the high value of a range of numbers, calculates the square and cube values of all the numbers in the range, and displays them in a table.

`Simple.jsp`, as shown in Listing 12-4, is the JSP to do exactly that. We'll walk you through this JSP and point out the various features.

First, we'll define our page directive and state that we're not participating in session management and to define our error page as `Error.jsp`.

Next, we'll make a variable declaration for the integer variable that we'll use to store the end of our range.

In this example, we want to use stylesheets and JavaScript to make sure that everyone is clear on how to commingle the various technologies necessary to build a robust application. Therefore, further down we define our stylesheet and include a function to open a new window to display help text. Note that we're using Microsoft's Internet Explorer version 5.5, and therefore using Microsoft stylesheet syntax and JavaScript 1.2.

Next of note is the `include` directive including our application's standard header, `Header.jsp`. In this case, it is a JSP file because it contains JSP tags to dynamically retrieve the server's current date and time for display.

An HTML anchor tag displays a Help link. This link calls `Help.jsp` passing the document name containing the help text for this page.

Next is a scriptlet that gets a parameter "end" from the request. Note that all parameters are of type `java.lang.String`, therefore it is parsed by using the static `Integer.parse()` method before being set as the "end" variable.

Immediately after that is an HTML form tag enclosing an input prompt for the end of the range. Note that the value of the input field uses an expression tag to substitute the value of the "end" variable. Also note that upon submittal, this form calls `Simple.jsp` again using the `get` method.

Now that we have all the information we need, we have a scriptlet with a conditional if statement checking for a valid value for the end of our range. If it's not 0 and not greater than 20 then we'll proceed with displaying the result table. Otherwise, we'll bypass that and display a validation error message. Notice that the end variable is referenced within the scriptlet. Also, notice that we use the scope notations to create the blocks of code necessary for this logic.

After we've passed our validation check, we have another scriptlet with an iterative for loop, looping from 1 through our end number. Again, notice the usage of the end variable and the code block created by the scope notations.

Now that we've either output our result table or issued a validation error, we want to end our output with our application's standard footer, `Footer.htm`. This time we include an HTML document because the footer is static.

Finally, we'll inline some JavaScript to set the focus on our input field and end our HTML.

Listing 12-4: **Simple.jsp**

```
<%-- Page Directives --%>
<%@ page session="false" errorPage="Error.jsp" %>

<%-- Declarations --%>
<%! int end; %>

<html>
<head>
```

Continued

Listing 12-4 *(continued)*

```
    <title>Simple JSP</title>
    <link href="jsp.css" type=text/css rel=stylesheet>
    <script language=JavaScript1.2>
    function openHelp(url) {
      var winname = "help"
      var winprops = "toolbar=0, location=0, status=1, menubar=0, scrollbars=1,
resizable=1, width=450, height=300"
      var win = window.open(url , winname, winprops);
      win.window.focus();
    }
    </script>
</head>

<body>
<%@ include file="Header.jsp" %>

<table width="100%">
  <tr>
    <td>
      <span class="sectionTitle">Simple JSP</span>
    </td>
    <td align=right><A href="Help.jsp?helpdoc=help_simple.htm"
onclick="javascript:openHelp(this.href);return false;">Help</A>
    </td>
  </tr>
 </table>

<%
// get the request parameter for the input field
String endParm = request.getParameter("end");
if (endParm != null) end = Integer.parseInt(endParm);
%>

<form action="Simple.jsp" method="get" name="prompt" id="prompt">
  <span class="prompt">Last number: </span>
  <input type="text" name="end" size="10" maxlength="2" value="<%= end %>">
  <span class="prompt">(1 - 20)</span>
</form>

<% // only output table if valid value
if (end > 0 && end <= 20) { %>
<table>
  <tr>
    <td>Number</td>
    <td>Squared</td>
    <td>Cubed</td>
  </tr>

  <% // Share square and cube of 1 through 10
  for (int i = 1; i <= end; i++ ) { %>
  <tr>
```

```
      <td align=center><%= i %></td>
      <td align=center><%= i * i %></td>
      <td align=center><%= i * i * i %></td>
    </tr>
  <% } %>
</table>

<% // otherwise display error message
} else if (endParm != null) { %>
<span class="errorText">Only values between 1 and 20 are allowed.</span>
<% } %>

<%@ include file="Footer.htm" %>

<script language=JavaScript1.2>
// set focus
document.prompt.end.focus();
</script>

</body>
</html>
```

Listing 12-5 is the `jsp.css` stylesheet source we're using for this example. Note that we are using Internet Explorer syntax.

Listing 12-5: **jsp.css**

```
TD {
  FONT-WEIGHT: normal;
  FONT-SIZE: 9pt;
  COLOR: #000000;
  FONT-FAMILY: 'Arial', 'Helvetica';
  TEXT-DECORATION: none
}
.pageTitle {
  FONT-WEIGHT: bold;
  FONT-SIZE: 11pt;
  COLOR: #000000;
  FONT-FAMILY: 'Arial', 'Helvetica';
  TEXT-DECORATION: none
}
.sectionTitle {
  FONT-WEIGHT: bold;
  FONT-SIZE: 10pt;
  COLOR: #000000;
  FONT-FAMILY: 'Arial', 'Helvetica';
  TEXT-DECORATION: none
}
.prompt {
```

Continued

Listing 12-5 *(continued)*

```
    FONT-WEIGHT: normal;
    FONT-SIZE: 10pt;
    COLOR: #000000;
    FONT-FAMILY: 'Arial', 'Helvetica';
    TEXT-DECORATION: none
}
.footer {
    FONT-WEIGHT: normal;
    FONT-SIZE: 8pt;
    COLOR: #666666;
    FONT-FAMILY: 'Arial', 'Helvetica';
    TEXT-DECORATION: none
}
.errorText {
    FONT-WEIGHT: bold;
    FONT-SIZE: 9pt;
    COLOR: Red;
    FONT-FAMILY: 'Arial', 'Helvetica';
    TEXT-DECORATION: none
}
```

Header.jsp, as shown in Listing 12-6, is the standard header for the application. It first uses the page directive to import the java.text package. Note that even though Simple.jsp already defined a page directive, this second page directive is valid. Next is the declaration of method getCurrentDateTime(), which gets the current date and time and formats it by using the java.text.DateFormat class. Finally, it outputs an HTML table by using an expression to call the getCurrentDateTime() method.

Listing 12-6: Header.jsp

```
<!-- Standard Header ------------------------------------------------------>
<%@ page import="java.text.*" %>

<%!
// Get a formatted current date and time
public String getCurrentDateTime() {
    Date date = new Date();
    DateFormat dateFormat =
        DateFormat.getDateTimeInstance(DateFormat.FULL,
        DateFormat.SHORT);
    return dateFormat.format(date);
}
%>

<table cellSpacing=0 cellPadding=0 border=0 width="100%">
    <tr>
        <td align=middle class="pageTitle">WebLogic Bible JSP Examples</td>
    </tr>
```

```
<tr>
  <td align=middle><%= getCurrentDateTime() %></td>
</tr>
</table>
<hr>
<!-- End Header ------------------------------------------------------>
```

Footer.htm, as shown in Listing 12-7, is a simple HTML document representing the application's standard footer. HTML comments surround the code and will be included in the source output to the browser.

Listing 12-7: **Footer.htm**

```
<!-- Standard Footer ----------------------------------------------->
<hr>
<table cellSpacing=0 cellPadding=0 border=0 align=center>
  <tr>
    <td class=footer>Copyright (c)2001 Your Company  All rights reserved.</td>
  </tr>
</table>
<!-- End Footer ---------------------------------------------------->
```

Help.jsp, shown in Listing 12-8, is the standard help page for the application. This design allows for a standard help page with dynamic help text through the usage of the JSP include action. Because it is resolved at request time, the help text document to be displayed can vary from page to page but continue to have the same look. Putting the finishing touches on this approach is the usage of the standard application header and footer JSPs.

Listing 12-8: **Help.jsp**

```
<%-- Page Directives --%>
<%@ page session="false" errorPage="Error.jsp" %>

<html>
<head>
  <title>Help Page</title>
  <link href="jsp.css" type=text/css rel=stylesheet>
</head>

<body>
<%@ include file="Header.jsp" %>

  <span class="sectionTitle">Help</span>
  <br><br>
<% String helpdoc = request.getParameter("helpdoc"); %>
```

Continued

Listing 12-8 *(continued)*

```
<jsp:include page="<%= helpdoc %>" />

  <br>
  <form>
    <input type="button" value="Close" onClick="window.close()">
  </form>

<%@ include file="Footer.htm" %>
</body>
</html>
```

The help text for the `Simple.jsp` is found in an HTML document, `help_simple.htm`, as shown in Listing 12-9. The nice thing about this approach is that not only does it allow for a standard help page, but it also enables nondevelopers using tools such as Microsoft Word to create the online help.

Listing 12-9: help_simple.htm

```
This is sample help text for the Simple.jsp example. This is a good way to
provide simple online help text while demonstrating the <em>jsp:include</em>
action. Any changes made to this page will take effect immediately without
recreating or recompiling the JSP.
```

Each of these files is placed in the root level of our Web application directory, `BibleApp`. We'll run the example by typing `http://localhost:7001/BibleApp/Simple.jsp` in the address field of our browser. The first time, it takes a few seconds while WebLogic Server combines `Simple.jsp`, `Header.jsp`, and `Footer.htm` into one source file, `_simple.java`, and compiles it into a servlet, `_simple.class`.

Because there is no parameter named "end" in the request, the page will not display a table the first time it appears. We'll type the number **6** in the entry field and press Enter. The page shown in Figure 12-11 appears.

If we enter a value of 0 or greater than 20, such as 25, the entry does not pass validation and an error message is shown, as shown in Figure 12-12.

If we click the Help link, a new window opens, displaying the help text for this page (see Figure 12-13). Again, this will take a few seconds the first time around so that `Help.jsp`, `Header.jsp`, and `Footer.htm` can be combined into one servlet and compiled. The help document, `help_simple.htm`, is included at request time.

Figure 12-11: A simple calculator of squared and cubed values

Figure 12-12: Displaying validation error text using conditional scriptlets

Figure 12-13: Displaying a dynamic help page

Error handling

As described earlier in the chapter, JavaServer Pages have built-in support for error handling. A JSP can be set to automatically forward to another page by setting the errorPage attribute of the page directive. Upon an uncaught error being thrown, processing is forwarded to the JSP defined in the errorPage attribute.

```
<%@ page errorPage="Error.jsp" %>
```

The page to receive the request as a result of an error also uses a page directive to set the isErrorPage to true. By defining this attribute, the implicit object exception is available to the page.

```
<%@ page isErrorPage="true" %>
```

Then anything can be done within that error page to elegantly handle the error, log it, and report it as required. Listing 12-10 of Error.jsp is our error page for this application.

We've defined an error page to display the exception message, the stack trace, and the URL to the browser. A lot more information is available that could also be displayed, such as request header information, request parameters, and cookie information. The information could also be logged or e-mailed. We suggest that you take time to develop an error page that will work for all your applications and that provides you with all the information you need.

Listing 12-10: **Error.jsp**

```
<%@ page isErrorPage="true" %>

<html>
<head>
  <title>Error Page</title>
</head>

<body>
  <strong>There was an error processing this request ...</strong><br><br>
  <strong>Error Message:</strong><br>
<%= exception %>
  <br><br><strong>Stack Trace:</strong><br>
<% exception.printStackTrace(response.getWriter()); %>
  <br><br><strong>Request URL:</strong><br>
<%
out.print(HttpUtils.getRequestURL(request));
String query = request.getQueryString();
if (query != null) out.print("?" + query);
%>
</body>
</html>
```

We intentionally left a bug in the code so that we could demonstrate JSP error handling. When running the Simple.jsp example in Listing 12-10, blank out the input field and press Enter. As a result, the "end" parameter exists, but with an empty String. The Integer. parseInt() method throws a NumberFormatException. The JSP error handling catches this and forwards the request to Error.jsp.

The error page, `Error.jsp`, receives the request and takes control of the processing. It uses the `exception` object to display the exception message, stack trace, and URL. The page shown in Figure 12-14 appears.

Figure 12-14: Displaying the error page

Another way that this could have been handled, assuming that the developer expected this type of exception to be thrown, is through the use of Java's try/catch statements. JSP scriptlets also support the definition of try/catch blocks, and therefore the `NumberFormat Exception` could have been caught and handled within `Simple.jsp`.

In fact, it is good practice to eliminate the error or use the try/catch methodology to avoid the error page in future requests.

Debugging

During the course of JSP development, every developer inevitably encounters syntax errors or logic errors. These errors could result in compile errors or undesirable execution results.

Compilation errors are reported to the browser and the WebLogic Server console. Both the JSP and the servlet compilers write error messages, referencing line numbers in your code or in the generated servlet code when appropriate. Each compiler identifies the error situation and tries to point out exactly where and why the error may have occurred.

Here's an example of a compile error. If we change line 11 of `Header.jsp` to misspell the `date` variable, this statement should no longer be able to compile properly:

```
return dateFormat.format(dat);
```

Figures 12-15 and 12-16 show the browser and WebLogic Console display of the compilation errors.

Figure 12-15: Compile errors displayed to the browser

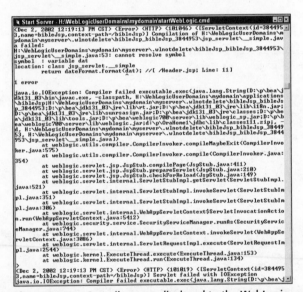

Figure 12-16: Compile errors displayed to the WebLogic
Server console

To determine the exact cause of the compilation error, sometimes it's necessary to examine the JSP servlet source that was created. As mentioned earlier, the `keepgenerated` tag of the JSP descriptor can be set to retain the generated JSP servlet source. The `package prefix` tag determines where the source will be located. We are using the default; therefore, the source can be found in our Web application's directory: `mydomain\myserver\.wlnot delete\BibleApp_BibleApp_nnn\jsp_servlet`.

Execution or logical errors are debugged as usual. Most developers use the standard `System.out.println()` or `out.println()` methods to display variables and informational text.

```
<%
boolean debug = true;

System.out.println("Debug mode = " + debug);
out.println("Debug mode = " + debug);
%>
```

The `weblogic.logging.NonCatalogLogger.info()` method can also be used to log information messages to the WebLogic Server log or a custom application log. See `http://edocs.bea.com/wls/docs70/logging/index.html` for more information on logging.

```
<%@ page import="weblogic.logging.NonCatalogLogger" %>

<%
NonCatalogLogger mylogger = new NonCatalogLogger("BibleApp");
boolean debug = true;

mylogger.info("Debug mode = " + debug);
%>
```

Programming JSPs with JavaBeans

The JavaBeans API specification version 1.01 describes the core specification for the JavaBeans component architecture. JavaBeans are Java objects whose implementation conforms to a set of conventions designed to promote modularity and reusability. They encapsulate data and behavior in a way that allows them to be reused without knowing how they are implemented. In fact, their implementation can be changed completely as long as their public methods provide the same interface. Separating presentation from implementation is the primary goal of JavaBeans.

The benefit is simple: developer productivity. Because JavaBeans are modular, they can be reused by multiple JSP pages or other server-side objects as necessary.

When a bean object is defined for use by a JSP, the JSP container searches for an existence of the bean instance in the defined scope. If not found, a new bean is instantiated with that scope. JavaBeans are scoped to the page, request, session, or application level, just like implicit objects.

When scoping beans to the session or application, it is then up to WebLogic Server to determine how to manage those beans and its own internal resources. It may choose to temporarily persist a dormant object such as the bean or the session to disk in order to free memory resources. For this reason, it's a good convention to make your beans serializable. This means that the bean should implement the `java.io.Serializable` interface. It also means that the bean properties should use either primitives or object types that likewise implement the `java.io.Serializable` interface.

For more information on JavaBeans, download the JavaBeans 1.01 specification at the following URL:

```
http://java.sun.com/products/javabeans/docs/spec.html
```

Deploying your first JavaBean

Listing 12-11 is a simple JavaBean that represents a brokerage account. It has three properties with their corresponding accessor methods — getter and setter. It implements the java.io.Serializable interface, and each of its properties is serializable.

Basing your JavaBeans on a custom interface and/or partially implemented abstract class is good development practice. This process enables you to code your Java code to the interface while enforcing that the beans have a common methodology. The AccountBean also implements a custom ValueBean interface (see Listing 12-12), and therefore defines another method for setting the bean with static test data.

Because the package name is com.wiley.wlsbible.jsp, we'll compile both files into the WEB-INF\classes\com\wiley\wlsbible\jsp of our BibleApp Web application.

Listing 12-11: **AccountBean.java**

```
package com.wiley.wlsbible.jsp;


public class AccountBean implements ValueBean, java.io.Serializable {

  // private properties
  private String accountNumber;
  private String accountName;
  private String status;

  /**
   * Account Number
   */
  public String getAccountNumber() {
    return accountNumber;
  }
  public void setAccountNumber(String accountNumber) {
    this.accountNumber = accountNumber;
  }

  /**
   * Name
   */
  public void setAccountName(String accountName) {
    this.accountName = accountName;
  }
  public String getAccountName() {
    return accountName;
  }

  /**
   * Status
   */
  public void setStatus(String status) {
    this.status = status;
  }
```

```
  public String getStatus() {
    return status;
  }

  /**
   * Sets the bean with static test data
   */
  public void setTestData() {
    setAccountNumber("110-12345");
    setAccountName("Martin Moneybags");
    setStatus("Active");
  }
}
```

Listing 12-12, `ValueBean.java`, is the ValueBean interface.

Listing 12-12: **ValueBean.java**

```
package com.wiley.wlsbible.jsp;


public interface ValueBean {

  /**
   * Sets the bean with static test data
   */
  public void setTestData();

}
```

JSP bean tags

As described earlier in the chapter, there are three action tags that exist for interacting with JavaBeans. They allow the JavaBean object to be instantiated and used within a JSP. We explain each of these tags in detail in the following sections so that you can understand how it all works.

useBean

The `useBean` action tag is used to locate an existing bean instance or instantiate a new bean. That bean is assigned a logical name as it is known and referenced throughout the JSP. The lifetime or scope of the object is also specified. Depending upon the scope, the object may also be referenced by other JSPs. Following are some examples:

```
<jsp:useBean id="account" class="com.wiley.wlsbible.jsp.AccountBean"
scope="request"/>
<jsp:useBean id="pageBean" class="AccountPageBean" type="PageBean" />
<jsp:useBean id="userBean" class="UserBean" scope=session />
```

The attributes of the `useBean` tag are described in the following sections:

id

The id attribute identifies the name assigned to the bean object instance. It is referenced by this name throughout the JSP. This attribute is required.

scope

The scope attribute identifies the lifespan of the object. It is implemented by actually binding the bean object to the implicit object representing that level of scope. Possible values are page, request, session, and application. If not specified, the default value is page.

The different scope values are explained as follows:

- ✦ **page:** The bean instance is associated with this page for the processing of this particular request. An object with page scope is bound to javax.servlet.jsp.PageContext.

- ✦ **request:** The bean instance is associated with the processing of this particular request. The bean will be available to any JSP upon which control has been transferred using the forward or include action. An object with page scope is bound to javax.servlet.ServletRequest.

- ✦ **session:** The bean instance is available during any requests made by the same client in the same session.

- ✦ **application:** The bean instance is available to any JSP with the same Web application. An object with page scope is bound to javax.servlet.jsp.ServletContext.

class

The class attribute identifies the fully qualified class name.

beanName

The beanName attribute specifies the name of the bean as it would be supplied to the Java.beans.Beans.instantiate() method.

This attribute supports request time evaluation through the use of an expression.

type

The type attribute specifies the object type to which an existing bean should be cast. It must be the bean's class, a superclass of the bean's class, or an interface implemented by the bean's class. If not, a ClassCastExeption will be thrown. This attribute is optional, and if not specified, will default to the value of the class attribute.

JavaBean instantiation

WebLogic Server uses the following logic to instantiate a new JavaBean instance or to locate an existing instance:

1. An attempt is made to locate an object that has the same id in the specified scope.

2. If the bean instance is found, and the type attribute has been specified, the object is cast to the specified type. If the cast fails, a ClassCastException is thrown.

3. If the bean instance is not found in the specified scope and no class or beanName attribute is specified, an InstantiationException is thrown.

4. If the bean instance is not found in the specified scope and the class attribute is specified, the bean specified in the class attribute is instantiated associating it with the id in the specified scope. Upon failure, an InstantiationException is thrown.

5. If the bean instance is not found in the specified `scope` and the `beanName` attribute is specified, the `java.beans.Beans.instantiate()` is invoked, associating it with the `id` in the specified `scope`. Upon failure, either a `ClassNotFoundException` or `IOException` is thrown.

6. If a bean is instantiated, the `useBean` tag is processed initializing the variable. It is now available for scriptlets, the `setProperty` action, and the `getProperty` action to reference.

getProperty

The `getProperty` action tag returns the value of a bean property so that it can be displayed in a result page. The bean property is accessed by using the corresponding getter method, converted to a `String`, and returned. Following are some examples:

```
<jsp:getProperty name="account" property="accountNumber"/>
<jsp:getProperty name="position" property="shares"/>
```

When properties are returned from a bean, the value is converted to a `String`. If the property is an object, that object's `toString()` method is used. If it is a primitive, the `valueOf()` method of the corresponding wrapper class is used. If the bean property is an integer primitive, for example, the `Integer.valueOf()` method is used.

The `getProperty` tag has the following attributes.

name

The `name` attribute identifies the name assigned to the bean object instance in the `useBean` tag. This attribute is required.

property

The `property` attribute identifies the name of the bean property to be returned. This attribute is required.

setProperty

The `setProperty` action tag sets a property value or values in a bean. It is used to map the data from the request to the bean. Bean properties, such as arrays, can be simple or indexed.

Bean properties are set at request time from request parameters, evaluated expressions, or hard coded `Strings`. Following are some examples:

```
<jsp:setProperty name="account" property="*"/>
<jsp:setProperty name="account" property="accountNumber"/>
<jsp:setProperty name="position" property="shares"
  param="quantity"/>
<jsp:setProperty name="account" property="status"
  value="Active"/>
```

One method for setting bean properties is to set them at request time from parameters in the `request` object. A single property can be set by simply specifying the bean name and the property to be set. Note that the `param` attribute needs to be specified only if the request parameter name doesn't match the bean property name.

```
<jsp:setProperty name="account" property="accountNumber"/>
```

The JSP can also set all the properties of a bean by specifying an asterisk (*). It will automatically map all the properties in the request to those in the bean. Note that this will work only when the request parameter name matches the bean property name.

```
<jsp:setProperty name="account" property="*"/>
```

Caution   It's important to note that no exception will be thrown if there are request parameters that do not have matching bean properties. Therefore, pay special attention that you achieve the desired results.

When properties are assigned from request parameters or `String` constants, the value is converted to the appropriate type if the bean property is not of type `String`. This is done by using the `valueOf()` method of the corresponding wrapper class. If the bean property is an integer primitive or `Integer`, for example, the `Integer.valueOf()` method is used. No conversion is performed if the property is being set from an evaluated expression. Indexed properties must be set with an array.

The `setProperty` tag has the following attributes.

name
The `name` attribute identifies the name assigned to the bean object instance in the `useBean` tag. This attribute is required.

property
The `property` attribute identifies the name of the bean property to be set. If this property has a value of *, all the parameters of the request are mapped to the bean attributes and the appropriate setter methods are called. If the request parameter is `""`, the bean property is left unaltered. This attribute is required.

param
The `param` attribute is used to specify the name of the request parameter to be mapped to the specified property. This attribute is unnecessary if the request parameter name is identical to the bean property name. If there is no request parameter with this name, the bean property is left unaltered. This attribute cannot be specified if the value of the `property` attribute is *.

value
The `value` attribute specifies the value to assign to the bean property. This can be a request time attribute or an expression. A tag cannot have both the `param` and `value` attributes.

Introspection
You may be wondering how the `setProperty` and `getProperty` action tags know what methods to call against the bean to set and return values. How do they determine the property type and therefore when to perform data type conversions?

These tags use a process called *introspection* to discover the bean's properties, whether they are simple or indexed, their type, and their accessor methods. Because the JSP container does not have any common interface or base class to rely upon for interaction with a bean, it must rely upon conventions to establish properties.

Introspection uses *reflection* to examine the bean class at request processing to determine its methods. Through detailed examination of each method, introspection can determine the corresponding private or protected variable and its type. Therefore, bean properties are defined by simply creating the appropriate accessor methods for them. Note that only one method needs to exist to define the existence of a bean's property.

Accessor methods are defined as the corresponding setter and getter methods for a property. They must be defined as public and named as the property with the word `get` or `set` prefixed. The setter should be declared void and accept one argument of the appropriate type. The getter should return the appropriate type and doesn't accept any arguments. The declaration of a property named `description` and its accessor methods are as follows:

```
private String description;

public void setDescription(String description) {
  this.description = description;
}
public String getDescription() {
  return description;
}
```

The corresponding `getProperty` and `setProperty` action tags are as follows:

```
<jsp:setProperty name="bean" property="description" />
<jsp:getProperty name="bean" property="description" />
```

Invoking bean methods

Note that it is valid to directly invoke the accessor methods or any other methods in a bean. To refer to the bean object, the same name as in the `id` attribute of the `useBean` tag is used. Other than that, it's the same as invoking a method in any other instantiated object. Note, however, that because the JSP compiler simply transfers the scriptlet code to the JSP servlet, there is no introspection or type conversion that takes place when using the accessor methods.

```
<% positions.next();
   position.getSymbol();
   position.getShares();
%>
```

JSP and JavaBean example

Now we'll walk you through an example of a JSP using a JavaBean. `AccountEdit.jsp` in Listing 12-13 represents a page that displays the details of a brokerage account for the purposes of editing the information.

This is not a complete example because we want to keep it simple and show you a JSP that demonstrates only the bean tags recently discussed. We will not provide the implementation of creating and setting the bean. Instead, we'll use the `setTestData()` method of the `AccountBean` and/or specify the name-value pairs in the URL request.

Looking at the source example, the first thing to notice is the `import` attribute of the `page` directive. The `bible.jsp` package is needed for the bean and any helper classes that may potentially be needed.

A `useBean` tag identifies a bean named `account` of class `bible.jsp.AccountBean` scoped to the `request`. Again, if the bean of this name and type is not found in the request, a new bean will be instantiated and bound to the request.

The `setProperty` tag immediately following will set the bean properties with the parameters in the request.

Next is a little scriptlet for use in development only. It looks for a parameter indicating that the JSP is being run in test mode, and if so, it instructs the bean to set itself with test data. This is nice to have for UI design and debugging the JSP tags.

Further down are JSP tags that get the account number and name from the bean for display in the input text boxes. Note how these tags are used with the `value` attribute of the HTML input tag. Also notice that we name the input fields the same as the bean properties so that when this page is submitted, the receiving JSP can successfully use `property="*"` in the `setProperty` tag.

To set the HTML select list with the proper status value is a bit trickier. First, we'll use a scriptlet to set a local status variable directly via the bean's `get` method. Next, we'll use an expression with a tertiary statement with each option tag to determine if it should be flagged as selected. Again, the select list is named the same as the bean property.

Normally, when the request is submitted, it's sent to a servlet of JSP that exists to process the request and forward to the next page to be displayed. But for the sake of easily demonstrating this example, this JSP submits the request to itself. This means that the new request gets created and forwarded to the JSP page. Because the `account` bean is scoped to the `request`, a new instance is created and set from the request parameters. The form submits the request by using the `get` method so that you can see the name-value pairs in the URL.

Listing 12-13: **AccountEdit.jsp**

```
<%-- Page Directives --%>
<%@ page session="false" errorPage="Error.jsp"
import="com.wiley.wlsbible.jsp.*"%>

<%-- Bean Tags  --%>
<jsp:useBean id="account" class="com.wiley.wlsbible.jsp.AccountBean"
scope="request"/>
<jsp:setProperty name="account" property="*" />

<%  // Test Mode
if ("true".equals(request.getParameter("testmode"))) {
  account.setTestData(); // Create test data
} %>

<html>
<head>
  <title>Edit Account Information</title>
  <link href="jsp.css" type=text/css rel=stylesheet>
</head>

<body>
<%@ include file="Header.jsp" %>
```

```
<form action="AccountEdit.jsp" method="get" name="prompt" id="prompt">
 <table cellSpacing=1 cellPadding=0 border=0 width="100%">
   <tr>
     <td colspan=2 class="sectionTitle">Edit Account Information</td>
   </tr>
   <tr>
     <td class="columnHead" align=right width="20%">Account Number: </td>
     <td><input type="hidden" name="accountNumber" size="9" maxlength="9"
       value="<jsp:getProperty name="account" property="accountNumber"/>">
       <jsp:getProperty name="account" property="accountNumber"/></td>
   </tr>
   <tr>
     <td class="columnHead" align=right width="20%">Name: </td>
     <td><input type="text" name="accountName" size="40" maxlength="40"
       value="<jsp:getProperty name="account" property="accountName"/>"></td>
   </tr>
   <tr>
     <td class="columnHead" align=right width="20%">Status: </td>
     <td><select name="status">
<% String status = account.getStatus(); %>
       <option value="A" <%= status.equals("A") ? "selected" : "" %>>Active
       </option>
       <option value="I" <%= status.equals("I") ? "selected" : "" %>>Inactive
       </option>
       </select>
       </td>
   </tr>
 </table>

 <br>
 <input type="Button" value="Submit" onclick="javascript:submit(); return
false;">
 </form>

<%@ include file="Footer.htm" %>

</body>
</html>
```

First, request the `AccountEdit.jsp` with the `testmode` parameter. The JSP will look at this parameter and instruct the bean to set itself with test data. This enables you to display the JSP with data.

```
http://localhost:7001/BibleApp/AccountEdit.jsp?testmode=true
```

The page shown in Figure 12-17 appears.

Now change the account name and status. When you submit this request, the request is actually submitted to the same JSP. The HTML form uses the `get` method; therefore, you can see the name-value pairs in the URL.

Another way to test this same JSP is by typing in the complete URL with a complete set of parameters. Either way, the parameters from the request are mapped to the AccountBean's properties, so the values are properly displayed on the page (see Figure 12-18).

Figure 12-17: Displaying the account edit page with test data

Figure 12-18: Displaying the account edit page with the request data

Using servlets to handle requests

A common methodology is to use servlets to receive and process requests and control navigation. Upon receiving a request for data, a servlet might get a connection from a JDBC connection pool, request data from the database, and forward the request to the next JSP.

In order to get the requested data to the JSP, the servlet could map all the data into the parameter portion of the URL before calling the bean. The bean would then map the parameters to the bean properties, as seen previously. Sounds a bit cumbersome, doesn't it?

A simpler and more elegant solution is for the servlet to actually use the bean to send the data to the JSP. It could instantiate the bean, map the data from the result set to the bean's properties, and manually bind the bean to the proper scope.

The bean must have the same name, be the same type, and have the same scope in order for the JSP to locate the bean via the useBean tag. If the JSP scoped the bean to the request, for example, the servlet would bind the bean to the request object. It would do this by creating the bean of the proper type and setting it in a parameter in the HttpServletRequest object. The parameter would have the same name as specified by the id attribute in the useBean tag.

To demonstrate this, we introduce the new AccountSearch.jsp in Listing 12-14. It prompts for the account and provides the option of editing it or viewing the details. The request is sent to the AccountServlet, as shown in Listing 12-15. The servlet loads the selected account information into an AccountBean instance, binds the bean to the request object, and forwards the request to AccountEdit.jsp. Listing 12-16 provides the web.xml application deployment descriptor to deploy the AccountServlet.

Listing 12-14: **AccountSearch.jsp**

```
<%-- Page Directives --%>
<%@ page session="false" errorPage="Error.jsp"
import="com.wiley.wlsbible.jsp.*"%>

<html>
<head>
  <title>Account Search</title>
  <link href="jsp.css" type=text/css rel=stylesheet>
</head>

<body>
<%@ include file="Header.jsp" %>

  <form action="loadaccount" method="get" name="prompt" id="prompt">
    <input type="hidden" name="cmd" value="">
    <table cellSpacing=1 cellPadding=0 border=0 width="100%">
      <tr>
        <td colspan=2 class="sectionTitle">Account Search</td>
      </tr>
      <tr>
        <td class="columnHead" align=right width="20%">Select Account: </td>
        <td><select name="accountNumber">
          <option value="">--Choose One--
          <option value="110-12345">Martin Moneybags
          <option value="110-98765">Lois Lottamoney
```

Continued

Listing 12-14 *(continued)*

```
        <option value="110-13579">Greg Goinbroke
        </option></select>
        </td>
    </tr>
  </table>

  <br>
  <input type="Submit" name="btnEdit" value="edit" >
  <input type="Submit" name="btnDetail" value="detail">
</form>

<%@ include file="Footer.htm" %>


</body>
</html>
```

Listing 12-15: **AccountServlet.java**

```java
package com.wiley.wlsbible.jsp;

import java.io.*;
import javax.servlet.*;
import javax.servlet.http.*;

public class AccountServlet extends HttpServlet {

  private AccountBean account;
  private String accountNumber;

  public void service(HttpServletRequest request, HttpServletResponse response)
    throws ServletException, IOException {

    // get the account number from the request
    accountNumber = request.getParameter("accountNumber");

    // create the band, set its properties, and scope it to the request
    account = new AccountBean();
    loadAccount();
    request.setAttribute("account", account);


    // determine next page based upon cmd
    String nextPage = "/AccountSearch.jsp";
    if ("edit".equals(request.getParameter("cmd"))) {
      nextPage = "/AccountEdit.jsp";
```

```
      } else if ("detail".equals(request.getParameter("cmd"))) {
        nextPage = "/AccountDetail.jsp";
      }

      // forward the request to the next page
      try {
        RequestDispatcher rd = getServletContext().getRequestDispatcher(nextPage);
        rd.forward(request, response);
      } catch (Exception e) {
        throw new ServletException(e);
      }
    }

  private void loadAccount() {
    // connect to the database here and load bean from account data; however
    // this example will set the static data based upon the request parameter

    if (accountNumber.equals("110-12345")) {
      account.setAccountNumber("110-12345");
      account.setAccountName("Martin Moneybags");
      account.setStatus("A");

    } else if (accountNumber.equals("110-98765")) {
      account.setAccountNumber("110-98765");
      account.setAccountName("Lois Lottamoney");
      account.setStatus("A");

    } else if (accountNumber.equals("110-13579")) {
      account.setAccountNumber("110-13579");
      account.setAccountName("Greg Goinbroke");
      account.setStatus("A");
    }
  }
}
```

Listing 12-16: **web.xml**

```
<!DOCTYPE web-app PUBLIC "-//Sun Microsystems, Inc.//DTD Web Application
2.3//EN" "http://java.sun.com/j2ee/dtds/web-app_2.3.dtd">
<web-app>
  <servlet>
    <servlet-name>AccountServlet</servlet-name>
    <servlet-class>com.wiley.wlsbible.jsp.AccountServlet</servlet-class>
    <load-on-startup>0</load-on-startup>
  </servlet>
  <servlet-mapping>
    <servlet-name>AccountServlet</servlet-name>
    <url-pattern>/loadaccount</url-pattern>
```

Continued

Listing 12-16 *(continued)*

```
    </servlet-mapping>
    <welcome-file-list>
      <welcome-file>index.html</welcome-file>
    </welcome-file-list>
</web-app>
```

To execute this example, type `http://localhost:7001/BibleApp/AccountSearch.jsp` to request the account search. The page shown in Figure 12-19 appears. Choose one of the accounts and click the Edit button. The account information appears for edit, as shown in Figure 12-20.

Figure 12-19: Selecting an account to edit

Figure 12-20: Displaying the selected account

Summary

JavaServer Pages represent the next generation of Web development architecture. Because they leverage the existing servlet technology, they offer excellent performance due to highly optimized use of processing and memory resources. WebLogic Server's implementation adds container management of JSP servlets and JavaBeans to optimize the handling of requests.

JSPs are also positioned perfectly for today's developers. They map better to the Model-View-Controller design pattern than to any other technology. They allow the User Interface and server-side developers to separate tasks cleanly and cooperate at the highest levels of efficiency. They allow for the development of reusable JavaBeans that take advantage of the OO strengths of Java. They allow the UI developer to utilize XML-like tags to interact with JavaBeans and tag extensions.

This chapter covered the basics of JSPs and used them with JavaBeans and servlets. Chapter 13 takes a look at tag extensions.

✦   ✦   ✦

Developing Tag Libraries

✦   ✦   ✦   ✦

In This Chapter

Understanding
tag libraries

Programming and using
a tag extension

Programming a
TagExtraInfo class

WebLogic tag libraries

WebLogic EJB-to-JSP
integration tool

✦   ✦   ✦   ✦

The JavaServer Pages API defines tag libraries that contain
reusable and modular functionality that can be invoked by custom tags within a JSP page. They reduce the necessity to embed large
amounts of Java code in JSP pages by moving the functionality into
tag implementation classes.

In the first part of this chapter, an overview of the interfaces, convenience classes, and support classes that are the core of the tag extension architecture is provided. You learn how to program tag handler
classes, create a descriptor for the tag library, and deploy the tag handler class and tag library within WebLogic Server. Then you learn how
to access your tag library with custom tag extensions in JSPs. Finally,
you learn about WebLogic's custom tags and the JSP Standard Tag
Library (JSTL), and how they can help make your JSP coding easier.

Understanding Tag Libraries

The JavaServer Pages API version 1.1 was the first version to define
tag extensions or custom tags that can be used in a JSP. Tag extensions reference custom tag handlers to extend the functionality of a
page. Tag handlers are custom Java classes that provide additional
functionality to the JSP page.

JavaServer Pages API version 1.2 offers additional interfaces and convenience classes that provide base implementations of commonly
coded functionality such as iteration and validation.

Note   At the time of this writing, Sun is finalizing the JSP 2.0 specification. This will be part of the J2EE 1.4 spec, which is also currently
being finalized. The big push here is for Web Services, and the JSP
2.0 spec will also make using tag libraries easier. The specifications will probably be finalized by the time you are reading this,
and will likely be supported in a future version of WebLogic Server.

Four components are required to define and utilize tag extensions in
a JSP:

✦ A Java class called a tag handler with the desired functionality
of a tag extension

✦ An XML document called a Tag Library Descriptor (TLD) that
contains information about a library and one or more tag handler classes

✦ An entry in the Web Application Deployment Descriptor (web.xml) defining the tag library to the Web application

✦ Taglib directive and tag extension statements referencing the tag handlers within the JSP

Tag handler lifecycle

The tag handler interfaces define methods that are invoked by the JSP engine at specific points during the processing of the JSP page. As shown in Figure 13-1, they signify points in the lifecycle of the tag. Therefore, understanding this lifecycle is important for proper implementation of your tag handlers.

1. When the JSP engine encounters a tag in a JSP page, a new tag handler is initialized. The setPageContext(), setParent(), and custom setter methods of the class are invoked to set up the environment context for the tag handler.

2. The doStartTag() method is invoked. At the end of the doStartTag() method, one of the following constants is returned:

   • SKIP_BODY directs the JSP engine to skip the processing of the tag's body content and continue to the doEndTag() method (as shown in Step 6).

   • EVAL_BODY_INCLUDE directs the JSP engine to evaluate and include the content of the tag body but skip the processing of the body content. Processing continues with the doEndTag() method (as shown in Step 6).

   • EVAL_BODY_BUFFERED directs the JSP engine to evaluate the tag body content and invoke the doInitBody() method. This is valid only if the tag handler implements the BodyTag interface or extends BodyTagSupport.

3. If the body is to be processed by the tag handler, the tag content is evaluated and appended to a BodyContent object's buffer. The setBodyContent() method is invoked to store a reference to the object in the tag handler.

   At this point in the cycle, if the tag is to output to the JSP page, the BodyContent.getEnclosingWriter().write() method should be used to gain access to the parent-scoped JspWriter.

4. The doInitBody() method is invoked to allow for processing before the tag body is evaluated for the first time.

5. The doAfterBody() method is invoked to perform some work based on the evaluated tag body. If the tag handler extends the BodyTagSupport convenience class, the getBodyContent() method can access the evaluated body. At the end of the doAfterBody() method, one of the following constants is returned:

   • SKIP_BODY directs the JSP engine to end any iteration of body evaluation and continue to the doEndTag() method (Step 6).

   • EVAL_BODY_AGAIN directs the JSP engine to append evaluated body to the BodyContent object and begin another iteration of the body by invoking doAfterBody() again.

   • The BodyContent is appended to the existing BodyContent upon each iteration through the body. Care must be taken to avoid repeating the content of each subsequent iteration in the output. A common approach is to hold the evaluated body content in a StringBuffer while iterating through the body content. The content of the StringBuffer should be written to the JspWriter only after it is determined that iteration is complete and SKIP_BODY will be returned.

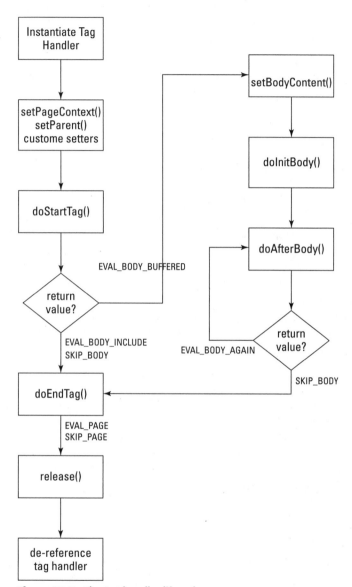

Figure 13-1: The tag handler lifecycle

At this point in the cycle, output needs to be written to the surrounding scope by using either the BodyTagSupport.getPreviousOut().write() method or the BodyContent.getEnclosingWriter().write() method. Either method obtains the same enclosing writer.

6. The doEndTag() method is invoked to perform processing at the end tag, such as writing output in a noniterative tag or cleaning up resources. At the end of the doEndTag() method, one of the following constants is returned:

- EVAL_PAGE directs the JSP engine to continue processing the rest of the JSP page.

- SKIP_PAGE directs the JSP engine to skip the rest of the JSP page. Caution should be taken when using this return value because it can be complicated to debug.

At this point in the cycle, output needs to be written to the surrounding scope by using the pageContext.getOut().write() method.

7. The release() method is invoked to release state. This occurs just before the tag handler instance is de-referenced by the JSP page and made available for garbage collection.

Tag handlers and the Tag Extension API

A *tag handler* is a request-time, container-managed Java object that evaluates tag extensions or custom tags during the execution of a JSP page. It must implement or extend a set of interfaces and convenience classes provided by Sun within the javax.servlet.jsp.tagext package. These interfaces ensure that the custom tag handler classes are capable of supporting a protocol to interact with the JSP container.

This protocol provides for passing of parameters, the evaluation and re-evaluation of the body content of a tag extension, and for getting access to objects and other tag handlers in the JSP page.

A tag extension can contain attributes that, in turn, set properties on a tag handler by the JSP container. Similar to JavaBeans, the JSP container uses introspection to discover the properties and setter methods of the tag handler. It then generates the appropriate code during JSP servlet generation to interact with the tag handler.

WebLogic manages tag handlers much like JavaBeans, in that it creates and manages a pool of tag handlers to handle requests. Unlike JavaBeans, tag handlers do not need to be thread-safe. WebLogic will only choose a tag handler that is not being used to process a request. If none is available, WebLogic will either add a new tag handler to the pool or queue up the request (Figure 13-2).

Main interfaces

A tag handler class must implement one of three main interfaces: Tag, InterationTag, or BodyTag. They define methodology that the JSP container expects to invoke upon encountering a tag extension.

Tag interface

The javax.servlet.jsp.tagext.Tag interface is used by tag handlers that don't contain body content or desire to process the body content.

Any tag handler class implementing the Tag interface must define the following methods: doStartTag(), doEndTag(), getParent(), setPageContext(), and release(). Complete descriptions of these methods are provided in the upcoming section that describes the TagSupport class.

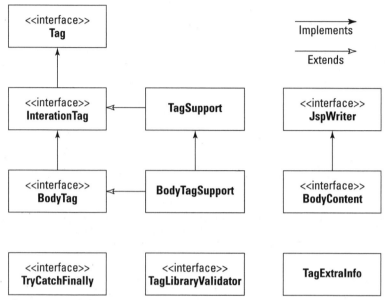

Figure 13-2: The Tag Extension API

IterationTag interface

Tag handlers that need to iteratively process the body content of the tag without manipulating its content use the `javax.servlet.jsp.tagext.IterationTag` interface. It extends the `Tag` interface and defines one additional method, `doAfterBody()`, to handle body-content iteration. This method will be covered in detail in the upcoming section that describes the `TagSupport` class.

BodyTag interface

Tag handlers that want access to the body content of the tag and the capability to manipulate it use the `javax.servlet.jsp.tagext.BodyTag` interface. It extends the `IterationTag` interface and defines two additional methods to process and set the body content.

Any tag handler class implementing the `BodyTag` interface must define the following methods: `doInitBody()` and `setBodyContent()`. Complete descriptions of these methods are provided in the upcoming section that describes the `BodyTagSupport` class.

Convenience classes

The API also provides two convenience classes: `TagSupport` and `BodyTagSupport`. They are provided as base classes for your tag handler classes. They are concrete classes that provide properties, convenience methods, and default implementations of the methods defined in the interfaces.

These classes are provided with the intent that they be extended to develop your own custom tag handler classes. Because they provide a set of default properties and methods, only the methods that need custom definition need to be coded.

TagSupport

The `TagSupport` convenience class implements both the `Tag` and `InterationTag` interfaces. Therefore, this class supports both simple tags and tags that desire tag body iteration. This is the base class that should be used for most tag handlers unless they need to access and manipulate the body content. In this case, see the `BodyTagSupport` convenience class described in a later section.

The `TagSupport` class provides a lot of base functionality that should be useful for most tag handlers. It provides convenience methods for getting, setting, and managing the tag handler's attributes. It also provides access to the `pageContext` object and methods for coordination among cooperating tags.

Tag extensions are typically used to write dynamic content to the page, replacing the start and end tags. To do this from a class that extends the `TagSupport` class, the `pageContext.getOut().write()` method should be used. This accesses and uses the `JspWriter.out` object.

The most commonly used `TagSupport` methods are described in the following sections. See the JSP API specification for a complete reference of its fields and methods.

doStartTag()

The `doStartTag()` method is called at request time when the start tag has been encountered and initialized. You should override this method if you want processing to occur before the body content and end tag are processed.

This method assumes that the properties `pageContext` and `parent` have been set. It also assumes that any properties exposed as attributes have been set as well. The `TagSupport` convenience class provides a default implementation that automatically takes care of these prerequisites.

This method can throw a `JspException` if an error condition occurs that the JSP should know about and perhaps handle through its error page. Otherwise, it's recommended that the JspException should be handled within the tag handler.

This method should return `Tag.EVAL_BODY_INCLUDE` or `Tag.SKIP_BODY` class constants. `EVAL_BODY_INCLUDE` indicates that upon return to the JSP, the body content should be evaluated and the end tag should be processed. `SKIP_BODY` indicates that the body content should be ignored and processing should continue and process the end tag only. If the action is an empty action, the `doStartTag()` method must return `SKIP_BODY`.

The default implementation of this method returns `SKIP_BODY`.

doEndTag()

The `doEndTag()` method is called by your JSP page servlet at request time when the end tag has been encountered and following execution of the `doStartTag()` method. The developer can override this method with whatever processing is desired by the tag extension after processing the start tag and body content.

This method can throw a `JspException` if an error condition occurs that the JSP should know about and perhaps handle through its error page. Otherwise, it's recommended that it should be handled within the tag handler.

This method should return either the `Tag.EVAL_PAGE` or `Tag.SKIP_PAGE` class constants.
`EVAL_PAGE` indicates that upon return to the JSP, processing should continue evaluation of
the page. `SKIP_PAGE` indicates that processing should terminate evaluation of the page. This
should be used only with very good reason. Because it's not immediately apparent to the
JSP developer why execution is being stopped, it can be confusing to determine what is
happening.

The default implementation of this method returns `EVAL_PAGE`.

getParent()

The `getParent()` method gets the parent or enclosing tag handler for this tag handler. This
method is used by the `findAncestorWithClass()` method in `TagSupport`.

The default implementation of this method is typically sufficient for most developers' needs.

setParent()

The `setParent()` method sets the parent or enclosing tag handler for this tag handler. This
method is automatically invoked by your JSP page servlet prior to `doStartTag()`. Note that
this value is not reset by the `doEndTag()` method and must be explicitly reset by a JSP if it
changes between calls to the `doStartTag()` method.

The default implementation of this method is typically sufficient for most developers' needs.

setPageContext()

The `setParent()` method sets the current page context and a default implementation is provided by the class. This method is automatically invoked by your JSP page servlet prior to
`doStartTag()`. Note that this value is not reset by the `doEndTag()` method and must be
explicitly reset by a JSP if it changes between calls to the `doStartTag()` method.

The default implementation of this method is typically sufficient for most developers' needs.

release()

The `release()` method is invoked by your JSP page servlet to release state. Therefore, the
developer would override this method if special processing related to the tag handler's state
is required. Note that the `doStartTag()` and `doEndTag()` methods may be invoked multiple
times in between initial invocation and release.

The default implementation of this method is typically sufficient for most developers' needs.

doAfterBody()

The `doAfterBody()` method allows you to conditionally re-evaluate the body of the tag. It is
invoked by your JSP page servlet after every evaluation of the body, so it's not invoked if
there is no body. The developer would override this method with whatever processing is
desired upon each iteration of the body content. This method is defined as a result of implementing the `IterationTag` interface.

This method can throw a `JspException` if an error condition occurs that the JSP should
know about and perhaps handle through its error page. Otherwise, it's recommended that it
should be handled within the tag handler.

This method should return either the `IterationTag.EVAL_BODY_AGAIN` or `Tag.SKIP_BODY`
class constants to control the iteration. `EVAL_BODY_AGAIN` indicates that a new evaluation of
the body should occur, followed by another invocation of `doAfterBody()`. `SKIP_BODY` indicates that no more body evaluations should occur and processing should continue and evaluate the end tag.

Note that the `BodyTag.EVAL_BODY_TAG` constant has been deprecated in JSP version 1.2 to encourage the use of the more descriptive term `EVAL_BODY_AGAIN`.

The JSP container will resynchronize any variable values that are indicated as such in `TagExtraInfo` after the invocation of `doAfterBody()`.

The default implementation of this method returns `SKIP_BODY`.

BodyTagSupport

The `BodyTagSupport` convenience class implements the `BodyTag` interface. `BodyTagSupport` supports tags that need to access and manipulate the body content.

In addition, it extends the `TagSupport` convenience class and has access to its fields and convenience methods. It provides two new methods to set the body content and define body initialization processing.

A `BodyContent` object is available to any tag handler class implementing the `BodyTag` interface or extending the `BodyTagSupport` class. The JSP page servlet will create a `BodyContent` object at request time that contains the evaluation of the body content. This is done only if the `doStartTag()` method returns a `EVAL_BODY_BUFFERED`. The `BodyContent` instance remains available until completion of the `doEndTag()` method. An upcoming section gives a complete description of the `BodyContent` class.

Tag extensions that extend `BodyTagSupport` are used to write dynamic content to the page, iterating through the body content, modifying the body content along the way. The `doAfterBody()` method, as described in the previous `TagSupport` section, is the appropriate place to do this. The main difference is that the `BodyContent` object is available to alter and output new body content.

The `BodyContent` is appended to the existing `BodyContent` upon each iteration through the body. Care must be taken to avoid repeating the content of each subsequent iteration in the output. A common approach is to hold the evaluated body content in a `StringBuffer` while iterating through the body content. The content of the `StringBuffer` should be written to the `JspWriter` only after it is determined that iteration is complete and `SKIP_BODY` will be returned.

The `BodyContent` object extends `JspWriter`. Therefore, to write output to the page while processing the body, the `bodyContent.getEnclosingWriter().write()` method should be used to access the enclosing `JspWriter.out` object. But after the body content processing has completed and processing continues with the `doEndTag()` method, output needs to be written to the surrounding scope by using the `pageContext.getOut().write()` method.

The most commonly used `BodyTagSupport` methods are described in the following sections. See the JSP API specification for more information about TagSupport's fields and methods.

doStartTag()

The `doStartTag()` method is as described earlier in the `TagSupport` convenience class. But this method can also return `BodyTag.EVAL_BODY_BUFFERED` as a constant value. `EVAL_BODY_BUFFERED` indicates that the body content should be evaluated and buffered in a `BodyContent` object and that the body processing should be initiated.

Note that the `BodyTag.EVAL_BODY_TAG` constant has been deprecated in JSP version 1.2 to encourage the use of the more descriptive term `EVAL_BODY_BUFFERED`.

The default implementation of this method returns `EVAL_BODY_BUFFERED`.

doEndTag()

The `doEndTag()` method is as described earlier in the `TagSupport` convenience class. Likewise, the default implementation of this method returns `EVAL_PAGE`.

setBodyContent()

The `setBodyContent()` method is the setter for the `bodyContent` field and supplies the class with the `BodyContent` object. This method is automatically invoked by your JSP page servlet prior to `doInitBody()`.

The default implementation of this method is typically sufficient for most developers' needs.

doInitBody()

The `doInitBody()` method is invoked immediately after `setBodyContent()` and just before the first body evaluation. It can be overridden to include processing to prepare for evaluation of the body. This method is only invoked if `doStartTag()` returns `EVAL_BODY_BUFFERED`.

This method can throw a `JspException` if an error condition occurs that the JSP should know about and perhaps handle through its error page. Otherwise, it's recommended that it should be handled within the tag handler.

Unlike the other methods that allow processing of tags or tag bodies, this method does not return any value to control processing.

doAfterBody()

The `doAfterBody()` method is as described earlier in the `TagSupport` convenience class. Likewise, the default implementation of this method returns `SKIP_BODY`.

This method should be overridden to define processing associated with body content iteration. The `BodyContent` object is available to manipulate its content.

Supporting interfaces and classes

The Tag Extension API also provides supporting interfaces and classes, some of which have been mentioned previously. They are described in detail in the following sections.

BodyContent class

The `BodyContent` class is an object that contains the body content of the tag extension to be accessible for a tag handler. It extends `JspWriter` and has additional methods to convert the tag body into a `String`, manage its contents, and ensure that buffer size will never be exceeded.

A `BodyContent` object is available to any tag handler class implementing the `BodyTag` interface or extending the `BodyTagSupport` class. The JSP page servlet will create a `BodyContent` object at request time that contains the evaluation of the body content. This is done only if the `doStartTag()` method returns a `EVAL_BODY_TAG`. The `BodyContent` instance remains available until completion of the `doEndTag()` method.

Note   Note that a `BodyContent` object contains the evaluation of the body content, rather than the body text itself. The significance of this is that it will not contain actions; it will contain their evaluated results.

A `BodyContent` object is enclosed within the JSP `JspWriter` object. It could also be enclosed in another `BodyContent` object if the JSP defines the body tag nested within another body tag. Instances of `BodyContent` are created by invoking the `pushBody()` and `popBody()` methods of the `PageContext` class.

clearBody()
The `clearBody()` method clears the body content.

flush()
The `flush()` method is redefined from `JspWriter` to be invalid. It is not valid to flush a `BodyContent` object because there is no backing stream behind it. It can throw an `IOException` if an error situation occurs.

getEnclosingWriter()
The `getEnclosingWriter()` method gets the enclosing `JspWriter`. It can either be a `JspWriter` object or another `BodyContent` object. This is set at the time the `BodyContent` object is constructed.

getReader()
The `getReader()` method returns the value of the `BodyContent` object as a `Reader` object.

getString()
The `getString()` method returns the value of the `BodyContent` object as a `String` object.

writeOut()
The `writeOut()` method writes the contents of the `BodyContent` object into a `Writer`. The `Writer` is passed as a parameter. It can throw an `IOException` if an error situation occurs.

TagExtraInfo class

The `TagExtraInfo` class is an optional class provided by the tag library author to describe additional translation-time information not described in the TLD file. It is used to define scripting variables used by the tag or to provide translation-time validation of the tag attributes. In other words, it does not create markup but instead provides information to the JSP compiler about the tag handler class.

The `TagExtraInfo` class is an abstract class that must be extended by your custom extra info class. It is associated with a tag extension by the `teiclass` attribute in the TLD file.

The most commonly used `TagExtraInfo` methods are described in the following sections. See the JSP API specification for a complete reference of its fields and methods.

setTagInfo()
The `setTagInfo()` method sets an object of type `TagInfo` that contains the tag information from the TLD. This information is available to the JSP translator at translation time and is invoked by the JSP translator to set its initial value. This invocation is prior to any invocation of `isValid()` or `getVariableInfo()`.

Note that if an explicit call is made to `setTagInfo()`,the object passed will be returned in subsequent calls to `getTagInfo()`.

The default implementation of this method is typically sufficient for most developers' needs.

getTagInfo()

The `getTagInfo()` method returns an object of type `TagInfo` that contains the tag information from the TLD.

The default implementation of this method is typically sufficient for most developers' needs.

getVariableInfo()

The `getVariableInfo()` method is used to introduce new or use existing variables to return data to the JSP. This allows the JSP to use expressions to access the returned variables as opposed to receiving generated markup.

The `getVariableInfo()` method receives a `TagData` object as input and returns an array of `VariableInfo` objects. Each `VariableInfo` object represents a variable to be returned to the JSP.

`VariableInfo` objects are created using its single constructor, which takes the variable name, class name, a Boolean indicating whether this is a new variable to be declared, and the variable's scope.

A variable's scope can be defined as one of three values. If `VariableInfo.NESTED` is specified, the variable is available to the calling JSP only within the body of the tag. If `VariableInfo.AT_BEGIN` is specified, the variable is available to the calling JSP from the start tag through the end of the page. If `VariableInfo.AT_END` is specified, the variable is available to the calling JSP from the end tag through the end of the page.

See the JSP API specification for more information. A working example of a `TagExtraInfo` class introducing a new scripting variable into a JSP is provided later in this chapter.

isValid()

The `isValid()` method provides translation-time validation of the attributes of a tag extension. It receives a `TagData` object as a parameter and returns a Boolean indicating if the tag instance is valid.

Validation occurs subsequent to the validation performed by a `validator` class implementing the `TagValidator` interface. Upon completion of the `validator` class processing, the `TagExtraInfo` classes for all tags will be consulted by invoking their `isValid()` method. The order of invocation is undefined. See the following section for an explanation of the `TagValidator` interface.

This method should be defined if validation on a custom tag extension is desired.

TryCatchFinally interface

A new interface defined in the JSP version 1.2 API is the `TryCatchFinally` interface. It allows for exceptions thrown from within a tag to be caught and handled by a custom tag handler implementing the `doCatch()` and `doFinally()` methods of the `javax.servlet.jsp.tagext.TryCatchFinally` interface.

doCatch()

The `doCatch()` method is invoked if a `Throwable` exception occurs while evaluating the body inside a tag or in any of the `doStartTag()`, `doEndTag()`, `doAfterBody()`, and `doInitBody()` methods. It is not invoked if an exception occurs during one of the setter methods.

This method is intended to handle the exception. But it can throw a `Throwable` exception if it is determined that there are exceptions that should still be thrown to the JSP.

doFinally()

The doFinally() method is invoked after doCatch() if a Throwable exception occurred or after doEndTag() if not. But as with doCatch(), it is not invoked if an exception occurs during one of the setter methods.

A JSP servlet that implements the TryCatchFinally interface looks something like this:

```
setPageContext(pc);
setParent(null);
...
try {
  doStartTag()...
  ...
  doEndTag()...
} catch (Throwable t) {
  doCatch(t);
} finally {
  doFinally();
}
...
release();
```

TagLibraryValidator interface

Another new interface defined in the JSP version 1.2 API is the TagLibraryValidator interface. Whereas the TagExtraInfo class allows for a specific action to be validated, a Java class that implements the javax.servlet.jsp.tagext.TagLibraryValidator interface can perform custom validation on the entire JSP page. A common use of a validator class is to use an XML parser to validate the page against a document type definition (DTD) file.

The validator class is invoked by the JSP compiler. It presents the entire JSP page via the PageData object, which abstracts the XML view of the JSP page and provides a read-only InputStream on the page. The validator class then utilizes its custom internal logic to validate the page. It returns a null String if the page is valid or a String with error information if it is determined to be invalid.

The validator class must be defined within the TLD. Initialization parameters for the class can also be defined.

Methods defined by the interface are setInitParameters(), getInitParameters(), validate(), and release(). The getter and setter methods are used in conjunction with the initialization parameters defined in the TLD. The validate() method is intended to be used for the validation logic of the JSP. The release() method is used to release any resources referenced during processing. See the JSP API specification for more information.

Programming and Using a Tag Extension

Now that we've covered the architecture, let's build and deploy a custom tag extension and utilize it within a JSP. For our example, we'll write a tag extension that will set the appropriate selected values in an HTML select list based upon a value or list of values.

Programming a tag handler class

The `SelectOption` tag handler, shown in Listing 13-1, is the tag handler class that will alter the contents of an HTML select list. The begin and end tags will enclose the option tags of the select list; therefore, the tag handler will process the body and modify it according to the selected values. The tag handler will extend the `BodyTagSupport` convenience class, which enables us to modify body content.

A private `String` array is declared to hold a list of values to be selected. A getter method is defined for this property along with two setters. Our tag will accept either a `String` with a single value or a `String` array with multiple values, so the setter has an overloaded method.

A `doStartTag()` method is not defined because the default method from the `BodyTagSupport` class is sufficient. It will return `BODY_TAG_BUFFERED`, which will trigger the creation of the `BodyContent` object and invoke the `setBodyContent()` method. Again, the `BodyTagSupport`'s default implementation of this method is sufficient.

The `doInitBody()` and `doAfterBody()` methods are not defined as well because we're not iterating through the body content. Instead, we're processing it once as a whole, modifying it as we go, and writing back to the JSP once completed. Therefore, we use the `doEndTag()` method because it still has access to the `BodyContent` object.

The `doEndTag()` method sets the body content into a `String`, uses a `StringTokenizer` to assist in finding each option tag's value, compares it to the value array, and sets `"SELECTED"` in the appropriate option tags. The significant thing to note is that the output is written to a `StringBuffer` while processing and then written to the enclosing JSP's out object upon completion.

No `release()` method is necessary because no resources were acquired that need to be de-referenced.

Listing 13-1: **SelectOption.java**

```
package com.wiley.wlsbible.jsp.tags;

import java.io.*;
import java.util.*;
import javax.servlet.jsp.*;
import javax.servlet.jsp.tagext.*;

public class SelectOption extends BodyTagSupport {

  /** Array of values to be selected */
  String[] values;

  /**
   * Returns an array of selected values.
   * @return     the array of selected values.
   */
  public String[] getValue() {
    return values;
```

Continued

Listing 13-1 *(continued)*

```java
}

/**
 * Sets the array of selected values to the array parameter.
 * @param      newArrayValues  the desired array of selected values.
 */
public void setValue(String[] newArrayValues) {
  values = newArrayValues;
}

/**
 * Creates an array of selected values from the single value parameter.
 * @param      newValue  the desired array of selected values.
 */
public void setValue(String newValue) {
  if (newValue != null) {
    values = new String[1];
    values[0] = newValue;
  }
}

/**
 * Creates an array of selected values from the single value parameter.
 * @return     the desired character.
 * @exception JspTagException
 *             if an error occurs while writing to the JSP writer.
 * @see        javax.servlet.jsp.JspWriter#write()
 */
public int doEndTag() throws JspTagException {

  // get body content
  String bodyString = bodyContent.getString();

  if(values != null && values.length > 0) {

    // make a string array of option tags
    StringTokenizer bodyTokens = new StringTokenizer(bodyString,"\n");
    ArrayList optionsList = new ArrayList();
    while (bodyTokens.hasMoreTokens()) {
      optionsList.add(bodyTokens.nextToken());
    }
    String[] optionsArray = new String[optionsList.size()];
    optionsArray = (String[])optionsList.toArray(optionsArray);

    // declare work fields
    String optionBeforeValue;
    String optionAfterValue;
    String optionValue;
    String opt;
    StringBuffer optionsOut = new StringBuffer();
    boolean found = false;
```

```
      // parse through the array looking for selected values
      for (int i = 0; i < optionsArray.length; i++) {
        opt = optionsArray[i];
        if (opt.trim().length() > 0) {

          // before option value
          optionBeforeValue = opt.substring(0,opt.indexOf("value="));

          //option value
          optionValue = opt.substring(opt.indexOf("value=")+6,opt.indexOf(">"));
          if (optionValue.startsWith("\""))
            optionValue = optionValue.substring(1,optionValue.length());
          if (optionValue.endsWith("\""))
            optionValue = optionValue.substring(0,optionValue.length()-1);

          // after option value
          optionAfterValue = opt.substring(opt.indexOf("value="),opt.length());

          // if a selected value is found, add to the buffer with "SELECTED"
          found = false;
          for (int j = 0; j < values.length ; j++) {
            if (optionValue.equals(values[j])) {
              found = true;
              optionsOut.append(optionBeforeValue + "SELECTED " +
optionAfterValue + "\n");
            }
          }

          // if not found, add to the buffer as is
          if (found == false) {
            optionsOut.append(opt + "\n");
          }
        }
      }

      // write the buffer
      try {
        pageContext.getOut().write(optionsOut.toString());
      } catch (IOException ex) {
        throw new JspTagException("Fatal IO error");
      }

    // no values, write the body content as is
    } else {
      try {
        pageContext.getOut().write(bodyString);
      } catch (IOException ex) {
        throw new JspTagException("Fatal IO error");
      }
    }
    return EVAL_PAGE;
  }
}
```

Defining a Tag Library Descriptor

The Tag Library Descriptor (TLD) is a file that defines the tag library and all the details of its tag extensions and corresponding tag handler classes. It's essentially an XML document with a .tld extension that is defined and validated against a DTD definition file provided by Sun. The latest version can be found at the following URL:

```
http://java.sun.com/dtd/web-jsptaglibrary_1_2.dtd
```

The main element of the TLD is taglib:

```
<!ELEMENT taglib (tlib-version, jsp-version, short-name,
                  uri?, display-name?, small-icon?,
                  large-icon?, description?, validator?,
                  listener*, tag+) >
```

The meanings of the taglib attributes are as follows:

tlib-version

The tlib-version attribute represents the version of the tag library implementation as defined by the developer. This attribute is optional.

jsp-version

The jsp-version attribute identifies the version of the JSP specification that the tag library depends on. This attribute is now mandatory.

short-name

The short-name attribute identifies a short name for the tag library. This should be specified as the prefix used by JSPs. This attribute is optional.

uri

The uri attribute uniquely identifies this tag library. If used, the value will be the URL of the definitive version of the tag library descriptor. This attribute is optional.

display-name

A short name for the tag library intended for use by development tools.

small-icon

An optional small icon (16x16 pixels) for use by development tools. Each icon must be a standalone file in either JPEG or GIF format, and with either a .jpg or .gif extension. The file name is given as a relative path within the tag library.

large-icon

An optional large icon (32x32 pixels) for use by development tools.

description

An arbitrary text string describing the tag library.

validator

An optional reference to a class that verifies correct usage of the tag library from within the calling JSP page.

listener

An optional event listener class that is instantiated and registered automatically.

tag

The `tag` attribute defines and describes a tag extension and its corresponding tag handler. This attribute is required and is defined as follows:

```
<!ELEMENT tag (name, tag-class, tei-class?, body-content?,
               display-name?, small-icon?, large-icon?,
               description?, variable*, attribute*,
               example?) >
```

The meanings of these attributes are as follows:

name

The `name` attribute identifies the tag. It is the same name used in the tag extension following the prefix. This attribute is required.

tag-class

The `tag-class` attribute identifies the fully qualified name of the tag handler class. It is expected that this class either implements the `javax.servlet.jsp.tagext.Tag` interface directly or extends one of its support classes. This attribute is required.

tei-class

The `tei-class` attribute identifies the `TagExtraInfo` class that will provide extra information about this tag at runtime to the JSP. It is expected that this class extends the `javax.servlet.jsp.tagest.TagExtraInfo` class. This attribute is optional.

body-content

The `body-content` attribute specifies the type of body content the tag contains. This attribute instructs the JSP engine on how it should process the body content upon completing execution of the tag handler class. This attribute can contain only one of three acceptable values. A value of `JSP` indicates that the tag content will be evaluated at runtime like any other JSP content. A value of `tagdependent` signifies that the JSP engine should pass the content to the tag handler unchanged and not attempt to evaluate it. A value of `empty` is useful when a tag should not have any body content. JSP translation will fail if this tag is used and the tag is not empty. If not specified, the default value is `JSP`.

display-name

An optional short name for the tag intended for use by development tools.

small-icon

An optional small icon for use by development tools.

large-icon

An optional large icon for use by development tools.

description

An arbitrary text string describing the tag.

variable

Scripting variable information, which is optional.

attribute

A list of all attributes accepted or required by the tag. Each attribute contains the following elements:

- ✦ **name:** The name of the attribute as it is referenced in the tag extension.

- ✦ **required:** A Boolean indicating whether or not the attribute is required. JSP translation will fail if `true` is specified and the attribute is not defined in the tag extension.

- ✦ **rtpexprvalue:** A Boolean specifying whether the attribute can be the result of an expression or whether it must be a fixed value. JSP translation will fail if `false` is specified and the tag extension attribute is an expression. If not specified, the default value is `false`.

- ✦ **type:** The Java type of the attribute value. Those determined at JSP translation time are assumed to be `java.lang.String`.

- ✦ **description:** A text description of the attribute for use by development tools.

Example of usage

This section describes an optional example demonstrating usage of the tag.

Listing 13-2 contains the TLD for our sample application. We'll explain the important components of a TLD by referencing this example.

First, we define the tag library by indicating that this is version 1.1 of our example and that we're using JSP version 1.2. We use the same `short-name` as our prefix to document to others that this is the suggested prefix for tag extensions using this tag library.

Next, we describe our tag extension and handler, specifying the name that matches the name in our JSP tag. The tag class is the fully qualified name of the tag handler class. This class evaluates standard HTML code and modifies it, so we specify that the body content is JSP. We use the `info` attribute to provide a short description of this tag.

This tag uses one attribute named `value`. It's required and allows a value evaluated from an expression.

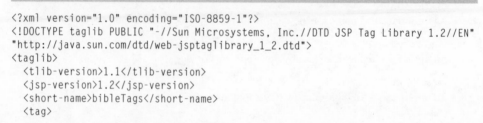

Listing 13-2: bible.tld

```
<?xml version="1.0" encoding="ISO-8859-1"?>
<!DOCTYPE taglib PUBLIC "-//Sun Microsystems, Inc.//DTD JSP Tag Library 1.2//EN"
"http://java.sun.com/dtd/web-jsptaglibrary_1_2.dtd">
<taglib>
  <tlib-version>1.1</tlib-version>
  <jsp-version>1.2</jsp-version>
  <short-name>bibleTags</short-name>
  <tag>
```

```
    <name>selectOption</name>
    <tag-class>com.wiley.wlsbible.jsp.tags.SelectOption</tag-class>
    <body-content>JSP</body-content>
    <description>Set selected option in select list</description>
    <attribute>
      <name>value</name>
      <required>true</required>
      <rtexprvalue>true</rtexprvalue>
    </attribute>
  </tag>
</taglib>
```

Configuring the WebLogic Web application deployment descriptor

The final step is to configure the Web application deployment descriptor in WebLogic Server by using the WebLogic Console. For this example, we'll define the deployment descriptor associated with the `BibleApp`. We click the `BibleApp` Web application node and then the Edit Web Application Deployment Descriptors link. (Refer to Figures 12-2 and 12-3 if you want a reminder on how to do this.) After clicking the Tag Libs node, the page shown in Figure 13-3 appears.

Figure 13-3: Configuring a new Tag Library Descriptor

Next, we click the Configure a new Tag Lib link. The page shown in Figure 13-4 appears.

Figure 13-4: Tag library configuration page

We type **/bibleTags** as the URI, which directly corresponds to the uri property of the taglib directive. The Location is entered as /WEB-INF/tlds/bible.tld, which is the path within the Web application directory to the Tag Library Descriptor file. Next, we click the Create button. The page shown in Figure 13-5 appears. Note that /bibleTags now shows up under Tag Libs on the navigation tree on the left.

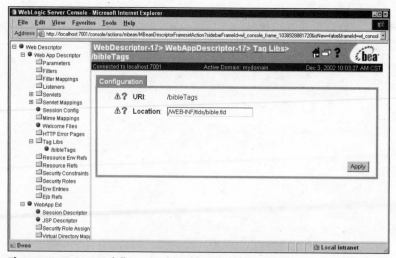

Figure 13-5: Successfully created tag library configuration

To complete this process, we validate and persist our Web descriptor. (Refer to Figures 12-6 through 12-9 for a reminder on how to do this.)

If you look at before and after versions of the Web application's web.xml deployment descriptor, you'll see that the following lines were added.

```
<taglib>
  <taglib-uri>/bibleTags</taglib-uri>
  <taglib-location>/WEB-INF/tlds/bible.tld</taglib-location>
</taglib>
```

Using a tag extension within a JSP

You must use two types of statements in a JSP to utilize a tag handler from within a JSP. First, a taglib directive statement must define the tag library and indicate the prefix by which it will be referred. Second, a custom tag extension references the tag library prefix and the logical name of the tag extension.

taglib directive

The taglib directive defines a tag library and prefix for the tag extensions used in the JSP page. It allows a JSP page to use tag handler classes by naming the tag library that contains the compiled Java code defining the tags to be used.

```
<%@ taglib uri="/bibleTags" prefix="bible" %>
<jsp:directive.taglib uri="/bibleTags" prefix="bible" />
```

The taglib directive supports two attributes, which are described in the next two sections.

uri

The uri attribute identifies the Uniform Resource Identifier (URI) for the Tag Library Descriptor (TLD) file. This value is matched against the taglib entries in the Web application deployment descriptor (web.xml) to physically locate the corresponding TLD file. This attribute is required.

prefix

The prefix attribute identifies the XML namespace identifier used by all tag extensions referencing classes in the tag library. It directly corresponds to the tag extensions in the JSP to associate those tags with this tag library definition. The prefixes jsp, jspx, java, javax, servlet, sun, and sunw are reserved. This attribute is required.

Tag extensions (or custom tags)

To actually reference a tag handler class within a JSP, tag extensions are used. The JSP compiler interprets the tag extension statements by replacing the tags with method calls to your tag handler class. The tag handler class is a Java class that actually performs the work. We'll cover tag handler classes shortly.

Tag extensions use an XML format similar to the standard JSP tags described earlier in this chapter. But instead of using the jsp prefix, the prefix identified in the taglib directive is used. This prefix identifies the XML namespace used by all tag extensions referencing classes in the tag library.

Immediately following the prefix is the logical name of the tag handler class. This name is matched against entries in the Tag Library Descriptor (TLD) file to identify the location of the class file.

Tag extensions can have any number of attributes that can be specified. Attributes are the means by which information is passed to the tag handler class. They are defined in the TLD as part of tag definition.

These attributes are what allow tag extensions to be dynamic. They are essentially input parameters for the tag handler class that allows it to respond with different results. The most powerful way of leveraging this is in combination with expressions. Attributes are allowed to contain an evaluation of an expression statement, thereby allowing request-specific data to be used.

Because tag extensions follow XML conventions, an end tag is required, which can be specified by either ending the begin tag with `/>` or with a separate end tag specifying prefix and tag name. Following are some examples:

```
<bible:debugData/>
<bible:selectOption value="<%= color %>">
</bible:selectOption>
```

JSP example

Now let's bring it all together with a JSP that uses the tag handler class just created and configured. The `TestTags.jsp` in Listing 13-3 represents a simple JSP that exists merely to test the tag in two different scenarios: an option list with only one selected value and an option list with multiple selection values.

The first thing to notice is the `taglib` directive. It defines the `uri` and `prefix`, as described earlier.

Next there is an options list with a selection of five colors. The options tags are surrounded by begin and end tag extensions for the tag handler. The correct prefix and tag are referenced to call the extension class. The value passed is a `String`; therefore, the extension class's overloaded `getValue()` method that expects to receive a `String` will be called. This `String` is initialized with a valid value for testing purposes.

Finally, there is another options list with five colors. But the tag extension passes a `String` array as its value, thereby calling the other `getValue()` method. This `String` array is initialized with two values for testing purposes.

Listing 13-3: TestSelectOptionTag.jsp

```
<%-- Page Directives --%>
<%@ page session="false" errorPage="Error.jsp" %>

<%-- Taglib Directives --%>
<%@ taglib uri="/bibleTags" prefix="bible" %>

<html>
<head>
  <title>Test Select Option Tag</title>
</head>

<body>
<%@ include file="Header.jsp" %>
```

```
    <h3>SelectOption with single value</h3>
<%-- Set color for testing purpose only --%>
<% String color = "2"; %>
  Color: 
  <select name="color">
    <bible:selectOption value="<%= color %>">
      <option value="0">--Select One--</option>
      <option value="1">Red</option>
      <option value="2">Green</option>
      <option value="3">Blue</option>
      <option value="4">Yellow</option>
      <option value="5">Orange</option>
    </bible:selectOption>
  </select>
   (value selected = <%= color %>)


  <h3>SelectOption with multiple values</h3>
<%-- Set colors for testing purpose only --%>
<%
String[] colors = new String[2];
colors[0] = "1";
colors[1] = "4";
%>
  Colors: 
  <select name="colors" size="6" multiple>
    <bible:selectOption value="<%= colors %>">
      <option value="0">--Select Multiple--</option>
      <option value="1">Red</option>
      <option value="2">Green</option>
      <option value="3">Blue</option>
      <option value="4">Yellow</option>
      <option value="5">Orange</option>
    </bible:selectOption>
  </select>
   (values selected =
<%
boolean needComma = false;
for (int i = 0; i < colors.length; i++) {
  if (needComma) out.print(", ");
  out.print(colors[i]);
  needComma = true;
} %>
)

<br><br>

<%@ include file="Footer.htm" %>

</body>
</html>
```

Our WebLogic Server is running on our local machine, so we type **http://localhost:7001/
BibleApp/TestSelectOptionTag.jsp** to run the JSP. After a few seconds to create the JSP
servlet and compile it, the page shown in Figure 13-6 appears.

Figure 13-6: Testing the tag extension

Notice that both tags worked as expected, selecting the appropriate values for display.
Viewing the source from the browser shows the select list tags generated as a result of
processing the tag extension. Listing 13-4 shows a subset of this source.

Notice that the tag extensions are not present in the output. Also notice that the appropriate
values are selected.

Listing 13-4: **Generated source from selectOption tag**

```
<h3>SelectOption with single value</h3>

Color: 
<select name="color">
<option value="0">--Select One--</option>
<option value="1">Red</option>
<option SELECTED value="2">Green</option>
<option value="3">Blue</option>
<option value="4">Yellow</option>
<option value="5">Orange</option>
</select>
 (value selected = 2)


<h3>SelectOption with multiple values</h3>

Colors: 
```

```
<select name="colors" size="6" multiple>
<option value="0">--Select Multiple--</option>
<option SELECTED value="1">Red</option>
<option value="2">Green</option>
<option value="3">Blue</option>
<option SELECTED value="4">Yellow</option>
<option value="5">Orange</option>

</select>
 (values selected =
1, 4
)
```

Resolving a tag extension

Let's review how a tag extension is resolved by the JSP engine to find the tag handler class.

1. A JSP encounters a tag extension and looks at the prefix to determine the tag library and the logical tag name (following the colon).

2. The `taglib` directive of the JSP defines the tag library by a logical name that is defined by the Web application deployment descriptor (`web.xml`).

3. The Web application deployment descriptor (`web.xml`) defines the tag library by a logical name and identifies the location of the tag library descriptor (TLD).

4. The tag library descriptor defines the tag by identifying its logical name as referred by the JSP. It also defines the location of the tag handler class file. The tag handler's attributes, `TagExtraInfo` class, and `TagValidator` class can also be defined.

5. The JSP engine instantiates the tag handler class and begins invoking methods against it.

Programming a TagExtraInfo Class

One useful way to use this class is to introduce new scripting variables into the page. This allows the JSP to have variable content while externalizing the processing to define the new scripting variables. To do this, there are three major steps.

First, add the following lines to the TLD file to describe a new tag named `lineClass`. Notice that the `tei-class` attribute must define the `TagExtraInfo` class, as described earlier in this chapter.

```
<tag>
  <name>lineClass</name>
  <tag-class>com.wiley.wlsbible.jsp.tags.LineClass</tag-class>
  <tei-class>com.wiley.wlsbible.jsp.tags.LineClassTEI</tei-class>
  <body-content>JSP</body-content>
  <info>Determine stylesheet class based upon line#</info>
  <attribute>
    <name>lineNumber</name>
```

```
      <required>true</required>
      <rtexprvalue>true</rtexprvalue>
    </attribute>
    <attribute>
      <name>oddClass</name>
      <required>true</required>
      <rtexprvalue>true</rtexprvalue>
    </attribute>
    <attribute>
      <name>evenClass</name>
      <required>true</required>
      <rtexprvalue>true</rtexprvalue>
    </attribute>
  </tag>
```

Next you need to write a custom class that extends `TagExtraInfo`. The only method that needs to be overridden is the `getVariableInfo()` method. This method returns an array of `VariableInfo` objects. Therefore, your class should create and add to the array a new `VariableInfo` object for each new variable being introduced.

An example is shown in Listing 13-5. This class defines a new scripting variable named `className` of type `java.lang.String`. It is being declared by this class and has a scope available from the end tag onward.

Listing 13-5: **LineClassTEI.java**

```java
package com.wiley.wlsbible.jsp.tags;

import javax.servlet.jsp.tagext.*;

public class LineClassTEI extends TagExtraInfo {

  /**
   * Returns an array of VariableInfo objects defining new scripting
   * variables.
   * @return    the array of scripting variables.
   * @see       javax.servlet.jsp.tagext.TagExtraInfo#getVariableInfo()
   */
  public VariableInfo[] getVariableInfo(TagData tagData) {

    // return VariableInfo array with the new scripting variable
    return new VariableInfo[] {
      new VariableInfo("className", "java.lang.String", true,
VariableInfo.AT_END)
    };

  }
}
```

Finally, the tag handler class must add the new variables to the PageContext by using the pageContext.setAttribute() method. They cannot be available to the JSP unless this occurs. A good place to do this is in the doStartTag() method of the tag handler.

Listing 13-6 is an example of a tag handler class that uses the Extra info class defined in Listing 13-5. It extends the TagSupport class because that listing requires processing only of the tag, not the body content. It is invoked by the JSP and passed a line number and two class names. Based upon the line number, the stylesheet class is determined, based, and set in the PageContext. The JSP uses an expression to output the returned class name to the browser, as shown in Listing 13-7.

Listing 13-6: **LineClass.java**

```java
package com.wiley.wlsbible.jsp.tags;

import javax.servlet.jsp.*;
import javax.servlet.jsp.tagext.*;

public class LineClass extends TagSupport {

  /** tag properties */
  private int lineNumber;
  private String oddClass;
  private String evenClass;

  /** getters and setters */
  public int getLineNumber() {
    return lineNumber;
  }
  public void setLineNumber(int lineNumber) {
    this.lineNumber = lineNumber;
  }
  public String getOddClass() {
    return oddClass;
  }
  public void setOddClass(String oddClass) {
    this.oddClass = oddClass;
  }
  public String getEvenClass() {
    return evenClass;
  }
  public void setEvenClass(String evenClass) {
    this.evenClass = evenClass;
  }

  /**
   * Returns the stylesheet class based upon the HTML table line
   * number.
   * @return    the desired stylesheet class.
   * @exception JspException
```

Continued

Listing 13-6 *(continued)*

```
 * @see        javax.servlet.jsp.tagext.TagSupport#doStartTag()
 */
public int doStartTag() throws JspException {
   String className = (lineNumber % 2 == 0 ? evenClass : oddClass);
   pageContext.setAttribute("className", className);
   return EVAL_BODY_INCLUDE;
 }
}
```

Now that everything is in place, the JSP can use the tag and is able to refer to the new scripting variable in an expression without ever declaring it within the JSP itself. An example is shown in Listing 13-7. Notice that the variable className isn't declared anywhere within the JSP.

Listing 13-7: **TestLineClassTag.jsp**

```
<%-- Page Directives --%>
<%@ page session="false" errorPage="Error.jsp" %>

<%-- Taglib Directives --%>
<%@ taglib uri="/bibleTags" prefix="bible" %>

<html>
<head>
  <title>Test Line Class Tag</title>
</head>

<body>
<%@ include file="Header.jsp" %>

  <h3>LineClass with odd value</h3>
  <% int lineNumber = 5; // for testing purposes only %>
  <bible:lineClass lineNumber="<%= lineNumber %>" oddClass="oddLine"
   evenClass="evenLine"/>
  Line Number = <%= lineNumber %>  Stylesheet Class = <%= className %>

  <h3>LineClass with even value</h3>
  <% lineNumber = 8; // for testing purposes only %>
  <bible:lineClass lineNumber="<%= lineNumber %>" oddClass="oddLine"
   evenClass="evenLine"/>
  Line Number = <%= lineNumber %>  Stylesheet Class = <%= className %>

  <br><br>

<%@ include file="Footer.htm" %>

</body>
</html>
```

Now we type **http://localhost:7001/BibleApp/TestLineClassTag.jsp** to run the JSP. After a few seconds to create the JSP servlet and compile it, the page shown in Figure 13-7 appears.

Figure 13-7: Declaring a new scripting variable using the TagExtraInfo class

WebLogic Tag Libraries

WebLogic Server provides a library of custom tag extensions that you can access and use in your JSP pages. In this section, we provide a quick overview of these tags along with a link to WebLogic's documentation Web site with more detailed descriptions and JavaDocs of the tag handler classes.

Note   Be aware that using WebLogic specific tag libraries means this part of your application will not be portable to other J2EE-compliant servers. That's not to say that you shouldn't use them, but rather that you should carefully balance the pros and cons of useful tags versus portability. You might also consider the recently released JSP Standard Tag Libraries (JSTL) which are discussed later in this chapter.

WebLogic JSP form validation tags

WebLogic JSP form validation tags are used with HTML forms to validate user entry. They can validate required fields, validate text fields against regular expressions, compare fields on a form, and allow custom validation logic.

You can find this tag library in a `.jar` file named `weblogic-vtags.jar`, which is in the `ext` directory of your WebLogic implementation. To use these tags, copy this JAR file to your Web application and define it in the Web application deployment descriptor (`web.xml`).

Validator classes

Three `validator` tag handler classes are provided in the `weblogicx.jsp.tags.validators` package. They are fully implemented and invoked directly by the validation tags in the JSP. A custom tag handler class that implements a WebLogic provided interface or abstract class must handle custom validation.

Required field validator

The `weblogicx.jsp.tags.validators.RequiredFieldValidator` class is used to validate that a required field has been entered. It is invoked directly from the JSP via the `<wl:validator>` tag.

Regular expression validator

The `weblogicx.jsp.tags.validators.RegExpValidator` class is used to validate text in a form field against a regular expression. It is invoked directly from the JSP via the `<wl:validator>` tag.

Compare validator

The `weblogicx.jsp.tags.validators.CompareValidator` class is used to validate a form field against another form field. They must be `Strings`. It is invoked directly from the JSP via the `<wl:validator>` tag.

Custom validator

Custom `validator` classes can be written to implement any logic that needs to be performed to complete form field validation. To write a custom `validator`, the tag handler must implement the `weblogicx.jsp.tags.validators.Customizable` interface or extend the `weblogicx.jsp.tags.validators.CustomizableAdapter` abstract class. The `validate()` method must be defined to implement the custom validation logic and return a Boolean indicating whether it passed.

Validator tags

Three `validator` tags are provided for use within a JSP page. They are nested within each other to reference attributes defined by the parent tag. Each tag has a set of attributes required for proper use.

Summary tag

The `summary` tag, `<wl:summary>`, wraps the HTML code and subsequent `validator` tags. It is used to define attributes to be used across all page validation. This could include a vector of error messages to be used, header text to be displayed only when there is an error, or a page that a request is directed to when there are no errors.

Form tag

The `form` tag, `<wl:form>`, is similar to the HTML form tag. It is used to define attributes associated with a form. This could include the `GET` or `POST` methods, the action or URL if there are no errors, and the form name (significant if there are multiple errors).

Validator tag

The `validator` tag, `<wl:validator>`, is used to define a validation rule for a form field. Multiple `validator` tags may exist for any form field. A blank text field, for example, will always be evaluated as valid by the regular expression `validator`. Therefore, the required field `validator` may need to be used in conjunction if entry is required. Attributes associated with this tag define the error message text, the regular expression if using the regular expression `validator`, the field to validate, and the `validator` class to use for validation.

When a validation tag determines that data in a field has not been input correctly, the page is redisplayed and the fields that need to be re-entered are flagged with text or an image to alert the end user. After the form is correctly filled out, the end user's browser displays a new page specified by the validation tag.

The preceding information is intended to provide you with just an overview of the tag library. For more information, see `http://edocs.bea.com/wls/docs70/jsp/validation_tags.html`.

WebLogic custom JSP tags

WebLogic provides a library of three custom tags that you can use to code your JSPs. They include a cache, process, and repeat tag.

You can find this tag library in a `.jar` file named `weblogic-tags.jar` in the `ext` directory of your WebLogic implementation. To use these tags, you copy this JAR file to your Web application and define it in the Web application deployment descriptor (`web.xml`).

Custom tags

Three custom tags are provided for use within a JSP page. They are completely independent of each other and can be used as necessary within the same JSP. Each tag has a set of attributes required for proper use.

Cache tag

The `cache` tag, `<wl:cache>`, provides the capability to cache data during processing of the tag body. It supports caching of the evaluated body prior to processing and the transformed body upon completion. This can be useful if the page needs to display either the evaluated or transformed body content based upon some other criteria.

Process tag

The `process` tag, `<wl:process>`, provides the capability to conditionally execute the statements between start and end tags based upon attribute values. It can also declaratively process the results of form submissions.

Repeat tag

The `repeat` tag, `<wl:repeat>`, provides the capability to iterate over many different types of sets, including Enumerations, Iterators, Collections, Arrays of Objects, Vectors, ResultSets, ResultSetMetaData, and the keys of a Hash table. It can also loop base upon a counter.

The preceding information is intended to provide you with only an overview of the tag library. For more information, see the following URL:

```
http://edocs.bea.com/wls/docs70/jsp/customtags.html
```

JSTL: JSP Standard Tag Library

The power of developing custom tag libraries was such that a lot of people were creating very similar libraries over and over again. The Java community realized this and thus was born JSTL 1.0, the JavaServer Pages Standard Tag Library.

Version 1.0 of the specification was released in the summer of 2002. It provides support for things that any JSP developer could want:

✦ Iteration and conditional processing

✦ XML

✦ SQL

✦ Internationalization

You can read more about the specification at Sun's JSTL Web site at the following URL:

```
http://java.sun.com/products/jsp/jstl/
```

WebLogic Server 7.0 does not come with an implementation of this specification, but you can easily add it. The reference implementation was created by the Apache Jakarta group and can be found at the following site:

```
http://jakarta.apache.org/taglibs/doc/standard-doc/intro.html
```

Just download a binary distribution and add it to your Web Application, just as you do with any other tag library described in this chapter.

WebLogic EJB-to-JSP Integration Tool

WebLogic provides an EJB-to-JSP integration tool that can generate a JSP tag extension library based upon an EJB JAR file. By referencing the EJB's remote interface, tags are created for invoking methods of an EJB. The generated tag libraries support stateless and stateful session beans, and entity beans.

Traditionally, a JSP would contain Java code within a scriptlet to invoke the EJB directly. Through the use of this tool, JSPs can use custom XML tags to access EJBs through the associated tag handler objects. The tag handler encapsulates the code to invoke the EJB and its methods.

See the following URL for more information:

```
http://edocs.bea.com/wls/docs70/jsp/ejb2jsp.html
```

Summary

Tag libraries can help dramatically reduce or even eliminate Java scriptlets from within your JSPs. At the same time, they provide a powerful mechanism to produce reusable components for your JSPs. A rich set of tag libraries can increase a JSP developer's productivity and efficiency.

In this chapter, we discussed the basics of JSP tag libraries and deployed a couple of examples to transform HTML and introduce new scripting variables as well as definitions of the appropriate XML descriptors and deployment in WebLogic. We also gave you an overview of two tag libraries and a generation tool provided by WebLogic.

You've probably thought of many ideas while reading this chapter on how tag libraries can improve your Web applications. So go to it!

✦ ✦ ✦

Developing EJB Components

◆ ◆ ◆ ◆

Understanding Enterprise JavaBeans

*E*nterprise JavaBeans (*EJBs*) are software components written in Java that encapsulate a system's business logic and data access and make it available to Java clients running anywhere on the network. When you consider the architecture of EJBs plus the runtime services they provide — high availability, transactions, session management, persistence, and security — no other technology comes as close to delivering on the promise of reusable software components for the distributed enterprise. EJBs are at the heart of what J2EE is all about; in fact, whenever developers think of J2EE, they usually think of EJBs.

The next four chapters of this book guide you through the complex world of EJB development and deployment with WebLogic Server. This chapter begins with an overview of EJB technology and discusses issues that pertain to all four types of EJBs (see the following section for a description of these types). The other three chapters cover the different types of EJBs in detail — with Chapter 15 devoted to stateless and stateful session EJBs, Chapter 16 to entity EJBs, and Chapter 17 to message-driven EJBs.

EJB Basics

This section gets you up-to-speed on the basics of EJBs, from the architecture of EJBs to the different types of EJBs to how clients access the EJBs, to the components that make up the EJBs, to some of the changes in the most recent specification.

EJB architecture

Enterprise JavaBeans are simply Java classes written to the EJB specification and deployed within a J2EE-compliant EJB container. The J2EE standard mandates that the EJB container must provide well-defined deployment support, as well as certain runtime services and behavior. The EJB container, in turn, runs within a J2EE-compliant Application Server. This allows it to provide the required access to the J2EE APIs, while making the EJBs available to Java clients over the network via JNDI and RMI. Figure 14-1 shows the interactions among the EJB container, the Web container, the J2EE APIs, the Application Server, and EJB clients.

Figure 14-1: EJB architecture

Application software vendors, such as BEA, implement EJB containers, while end-user developers implement EJBs and their clients. The container, the EJBs, and the clients each have certain roles and responsibilities within the overall system, which the J2EE specification spells out in the form of contracts. If an EJB container is written to fulfill *its* responsibilities with the contract and if we write our EJBs to fulfill *their* responsibilities, our EJBs will work within the container.

One of the most powerful aspects of EJB architecture is that the services provided by the container — transactions, persistence, security, and so on — are completely transparent to EJBs deployed within the container. In other words, it's possible to write an EJB that is fully transactional, secure, and persistent without writing a single line of Java code in support of these services. This is a tremendous boon for developers because writing code to support these services is notoriously difficult. Nevertheless, the EJB standard and the J2EE APIs still make it possible for developers to code these services themselves, but it's generally better to avoid doing so if you can.

EJB types

The J2EE specification defines four different types of EJBs, each designed to meet a specific category of software development challenges. The following list briefly describes each type so that you can get an overview of the four types; the following sections go into more detail on each type.

EJBs come in four different varieties:

✦ *Stateless session EJBs* execute business logic on behalf of any client; they usually perform relatively quick and simple tasks, such as returning a current stock price given a ticker symbol.

✦ *Stateful session EJBs* execute business logic on behalf of a specific client with whom they are maintaining a conversational state; the classic example of a stateful session EJB is an online shopping cart that tracks a user's purchases until checkout.

✦ *Entity EJBs* manage low-level database storage and retrieval and also provide some degree of related business logic. They are typically used in conjunction with session EJBs. A good example is an entity EJB that manages a customer's stock portfolio.

✦ *Message-driven EJBs*, which are new with the EJB 2.0 specification, work hand-in-hand with JMS (see Chapter 9) to provide asynchronous processing capabilities to any client that sends them a message. A good use for a message-driven EJB is to handle the confirmation and settlement of a securities trade.

The J2EE specification mandates that EJBs run within an *EJB container* that not only provides a runtime environment for them, but also provides the enterprise-class services that we mentioned before: high availability, transactions, session management, persistence, and security. The container must also provide support for *declarative services*, which allow the users of EJBs (referred to in J2EE parlance as *application assemblers*) to configure many aspects of EJB runtime behavior through the use of XML deployment descriptors. WebLogic Server's EJB container provides all these services and more, as you will see in the rest of this chapter.

Enterprise JavaBeans are different from "plain" JavaBeans, which are written to a completely different specification (originally intended for implementing client-side GUI components) and which do not participate in the EJB container architecture.

Cross-Reference

You can learn more about JavaBeans in Chapter 12.

Session beans

Session beans are generally used to implement control, process, and workflow in an application. In the Model-View-Controller world, session beans almost always live in the Controller realm.

Session beans come in two flavors: *stateless* and *stateful*. These beans are so named because they are commonly invoked directly by clients in the context of a client session. But their usage and treatment by the EJB container are completely different, as discussed in the following sessions.

Stateless session beans

As their name implies, stateless session beans do not maintain client state across method calls — when a method call completes, the bean's state is exactly the same as it was before the call. Multiple instances of the same session bean are, therefore, identical to each other and can be shared or pooled among multiple clients.

Stateless session beans are used to perform simple, self-contained tasks that don't require the preservation of state, such as verifying a user's identity, returning the current time from an atomic clock, performing a database search, and so on.

Stateful session beans

Stateful session beans, in contrast with stateless session beans, *do* preserve state across method calls and execute on behalf of a single client. As the client performs tasks supported by the bean, the bean's state changes as needed to reflect the current status of the interaction. The bean maintains its state by using Java instance variables.

Stateful session beans are used to support prolonged interactions between individual clients and the system. The most common example is an online shopping cart. A client might use a stateless session bean to find products in an online catalog, but when he adds an item to his cart, a stateful session bean is created for his exclusive use that tracks the items he has added to his cart. The same bean might also track the overall state of his visit (shopping, checkout pending, checkout completed, and so on).

Entity beans

Entity beans are Java representations of items stored in a database. Most often, the database is relational, and the entity bean represents a row in a relational table. Entity beans make programming easier because they allow developers to work with Java objects and methods, rather than using JDBC or some other protocol to interact with the underlying data store.

Entity beans possess the quality of *persistence* — they work in conjunction with the EJB container and the database to keep the bean's state in memory synchronized with the data in the store. In most cases, this persistence is accomplished by making JDBC calls to select, insert, update, or delete the row represented by the bean in a relational database. These calls can be hand-coded by the developer directly in the bean (an approach called *bean-managed persistence,* or *BMP*), or they can be automatically generated by the EJB container (an approach called *container-managed persistence,* or *CMP*). You can find more info about BMP and CMP in the "WebLogic's EJB Container Services" section later in this chapter.

Cross-Reference

JDBC, Java Database Connectivity, is covered in Chapter 5.

Message-driven beans

Message-driven beans are deployed as listeners for JMS queues and topics, and execute their business logic in response to incoming JMS messages. This enables developers to write beans that can be invoked asynchronously.

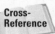

Cross-Reference

JMS, the Java Messaging Service, is covered in Chapter 9.

Unlike session and entity beans, client code cannot obtain references to message-driven beans, nor can it invoke the methods of message-driven beans directly. Instead, the client invokes the beans' methods indirectly by posting JMS messages to the queues or topics to which the beans are listening.

Message-driven beans are well-suited for deferred processing or the completion of time-consuming tasks that don't require the client's attention. You can use message-driven beans, for example, to queue up overnight processing tasks, implement logging functions, or process orders for online purchases. In the last case, the message-driven bean can transmit a pick list and shipping instructions to the warehouse, a credit card transaction to the bank, and a confirmation e-mail to the customer, all without requiring the customer to wait for any of these tasks to complete.

EJB client-access models

EJBs can be called from Java code running with the same JVM as the EJB or from a different JVM elsewhere on the network. The first form of access is called *local* access, and the second is called *remote* access. With either form of access, the initial reference to an EJB is obtained in client code by performing a JNDI lookup on one of the EJB's home interfaces, which we discuss in the next section.

In the EJB 1.1 specification, there is no difference in the way an EJB is programmed to accommodate local versus remote access. EJBs are implemented as RMI objects, so access to their methods always takes place through the bean's remote interface and traverses RMI's server and client stacks. Note, however, that WebLogic Server short-circuits the access path, if the client code and EJB code both reside within WebLogic's JVM, by transparently replacing remote calls with local calls. This increases performance by eliminating the overhead of building serialized remote method calls.

 Cross-Reference See Chapter 7 for a complete description of this process. Specifically, see Figure 7-3 for a diagram comparing the two access methods.

Unlike the EJB 1.1 specification, the EJB 2.0 specification defines separate programmatic interfaces for local and remote access to EJBs. This allows developers to formally design and implement EJBs whose calling semantics explicitly support the two types of access. When developing EJBs under the 2.0 specification, developers can implement the remote interface only, the local interface only, or both.

EJB components

With the exception of message-driven beans, EJBs are deployed as RMI objects, and therefore possess many of the same structural elements as RMI servers. As a result, programming EJBs is much like programming RMI servers with some important differences.

In this section, we explain the components common to all EJBs, which are as follows:

✦ Home interface

✦ Remote interface

✦ Implementation class

✦ Deployment descriptor

To make the explanations concrete, we present the code and deployment descriptors for a simple session EJB that implements business logic surrounding a company's revenues. Such an EJB might be part of an accounting package or an executive reporting system.

Home interface

An EJB's *home interface* controls the bean's lifecycle within the EJB container, including creating, removing, and locating the bean. As the bean developer, you don't need to implement the interface; its implementation is provided by the EJB container. The home interface merely identifies to the container the type of bean it is dealing with; it has nothing to do with actual bean instances. Think of the home interface as a factory for the type of bean you seek to create.

When deploying a bean to WebLogic Server, you register the home interface with JNDI. Then, when client code wants to work with the bean, it obtains a reference to the bean's home interface via a JNDI lookup and uses it to work with the bean.

Tip

JNDI lookup is too slow for repeated lookups of EJBs. If you want your applications to be fast and scalable, you should avoid doing a JNDI lookup for the home interface in every page or every client of your application.

A better solution is to implement a *service locator class* that keeps a cache (implemented as a static Hash table or something similar) of all EJB home interfaces. When a client requests a home, the service locator checks the cache to see whether it has already been looked up. If so, it simply returns the cached copy. If not, it performs a JNDI lookup and adds the home interface to its cache before returning it to the client.

You can learn more about the service locator design pattern at http://developer.java. sun.com/developer/restricted/patterns/ServiceLocator.html.

For remote clients, the EJB's home interface extends from the javax.ejb.EJBHome interface. For local clients, the home interface extends from javax.ejb.EJBLocalHome. The latter interface is new with EJB 2.0.

The following is the "remote" home interface for our Revenue EJB, intended for use by remote clients:

```
package com.wiley.wlsbible.ejb;

import java.rmi.*;
import javax.ejb.*;

public interface RevenueHome extends EJBHome {
   public Revenue create()
   throws RemoteException, CreateException;
}
```

Here is the "local" home interface, intended for use by local clients:

```
package com.wiley.wlsbible.ejb;

import java.rmi.*;
import javax.ejb.*;

public interface RevenueLocalHome extends EJBLocalHome {
   public RevenueLocal create()
   throws CreateException;
}
```

Note that the only differences between these two interfaces are their base classes, the type of objects their create() methods return, and the types of exceptions they throw. With regard to exceptions, the "remote" home interface throws a RemoteException, whereas the "local" home interface does not. Otherwise, the interfaces are identical—they simply provide a create() method that clients can use to obtain a runtime reference to the appropriate underlying bean.

Remote interface

The EJB's *remote interface* is where you define the signatures of business methods that are visible to clients using the EJB. The create() method of the home interface returns a reference to this remote interface, which clients use to invoke methods on the bean.

As with the home interface, you can write separate remote interfaces for remote and local clients. For remote clients, the remote interface extends the `javax.ejb.EJBObject` interface; and for local clients, it extends the `javax.ejb.EJBLocalObject` interface. Again, the latter interface is new with EJB 2.0.

The following is the "remote" remote interface for our Revenue EJB:

```
package com.wiley.wlsbible.ejb;

import java.rmi.*;
import javax.ejb.*;
import java.util.Date;

public interface Revenue extends EJBObject {
   double getYTD() throws RemoteException;
   double getForPeriod(Date startDate, Date endDate)
   throws RemoteException;
}
```

In this interface, we exposed two business methods to clients: `Revenue.getYTD()` and `Revenue.getForPeriod()`. Note that these methods must throw `javax.rmi.RemoteExceptions` because `EJBObject` extends the `java.rmi.Remote` interface.

You can define any number of business methods to your remote interface, just as you would in a normal Java class.

The "local" remote interface for our Revenue EJB is as follows:

```
package com.wiley.wlsbible.ejb;

import javax.ejb.*;
import java.util.Date;

public interface RevenueLocal extends EJBLocalObject {
   double getYTD();
   double getForPeriod(Date startDate, Date endDate);
}
```

In most cases, the business methods in your "remote" and "local" remote interfaces will be identical. The only difference is that the "local" methods will not throw `RemoteExceptions`. Another difference, not reflected in the code itself, is that arguments are passed to "remote" methods by value and to "local" methods by reference.

Implementation class

The EJB's *implementation class* is where you provide the code behind the methods defined in the remote interfaces. The interface you implement depends on the type of bean you are writing:

✦ Session beans (stateful and stateless) implement `javax.ejb.SessionBean`

✦ Entity beans implement `javax.ejb.EntityBean`

✦ Message-driven beans (new with EJB 2.0) implement `javax.ejb.MessageDrivenBean`

For session beans, you must implement the `ejbCreate()` method. Implementing the other lifecycle methods — `ejbRemove()`, `ejbActivate()`, and `ejbPassivate()` — is optional.

For session beans, you must also define a private instance variable of type `javax.ejb.SessionContext` and a setter method called `setSessionContext()` that the container can call to set the value of the `SessionContext`. Entity beans and message-driven beans have similar methods — for entity beans the method is called `setEntityContext()`, and for message-driven beans it is called `setMessageDrivenContext()`. All three methods perform the same function: to provide the bean instance with information about its container that can be used by the bean or its clients at runtime. Each method accepts an extension of the `javax.ejb.EJBContext` interface as a parameter — for session beans it is `javax.ejb.SessionContext`, for entity beans it is `javax.ejb.EntityContext`, and for message-driven beans it is `javax.ejb.MessageDrivenContext`.

In our example, we will not provide implementations for the lifecycle methods, but rather will rely on the default implementations provided by WebLogic's EJB container.

Listing 14-1 shows the implementation class for our Revenue bean, including the lifecycle methods and business methods. But instead of providing code for the business methods, we merely wrote comments explaining what they might do so that you can focus on the structure of the class rather than the details of its implementation.

If you want your implementation class to support both local and remote clients, as ours does, you may have to duplicate some of your business methods — one for each case. The only difference is that the implementations for local clients must not throw `RemoteExceptions`. As you can see from the code, our local implementations simply call the remote implementations and catch the `RemoteExceptions`. This saves us from writing the same code twice.

Listing 14-1: **RevenueEJB.java**

```
package com.wiley.wlsbible.ejb;

import java.rmi.*;
import javax.ejb.*;
import java.util.*;
import javax.naming.*;
import java.sql.*;

public class RevenueEJB implements SessionBean {

  // Mandatory instance variable.
  private SessionContext sessionContext;

  // Mandatory setter for the SessionContext.
  public void setSessionContext(SessionContext sessionContext) {
    this.sessionContext = sessionContext;
  }

  // Mandatory bean lifecycle methods.
  public void ejbCreate() throws CreateException {
  }

  public void ejbRemove(){
  }

  public void ejbActivate(){
```

```
    }

    public void ejbPassivate(){
    }

    // Business method to return YTD revenues.
    public double getYTD(){
      double revenue = 0.0;
      // Insert code here to read revenues from
      // a data source, such as a relational database.
      return revenue;
    }

    // Local version of getYTD(). Calls getYTD() but does not
    // throw the RemoteException.
    public double getYTDLocal() {
      double revenue = 0.0;
      try {
        revenue = getYTD();
      }
      catch (RemoteException re) {
      }
      finally {
        return revenue;
      }
    }

    // Business method to return revenues realized between
    // the given date range.
      public double getForPeriod(java.sql.Date startDate,
        java.sql.Date endDate) throws RemoteException {
      double revenue = 0.0;
      // Insert code here to read revenues from
      // a data source, such as a relational database.
      return revenue;
    }

    // Local version of getForPeriod(). Calls getForPeriod()
    // but does not throw the RemoteException.
    public double getForPeriodLocal(java.sql.Date startDate,
      java.sql.Date endDate) {
      double revenue = 0.0;
      try {
        revenue = getForPeriod(startDate, endDate);
      }
      catch (RemoteException re) {
      }
      finally {
        return revenue;
      }
    }
  }
}
```

Deployment descriptors

The EJB's deployment descriptors define how the EJB should be deployed within WebLogic Server. Every EJB deployed to WebLogic requires two deployment descriptors:

✦ `ejb-jar.xml`: the deployment descriptor required by J2EE. This descriptor defines the bean's deployment structure and maps its internal dependencies and application assembly information.

✦ `weblogic-ejb-jar.xml`: the WebLogic-specific deployment descriptor, which specifies the bean's caching, clustering, and performance behavior. This descriptor also defines the bean's JNDI identity, security roles, and dependencies on other WebLogic Server resources such as JMS connection factories, JDBC connection pools, and other deployed EJBs.

Notice that EJB deployment descriptors are analogous to Web application descriptors, consisting of a J2EE-specific descriptor plus a WebLogic-specific descriptor. Unlike Web applications, however, you cannot omit the WebLogic-specific descriptor — *all* EJBs require *both* deployment descriptors.

Listing 14-2 shows `ejb-jar.xml` for our sample session bean. Note that it is based on the XML DTD for EJB 2.0. The DTD for EJB 1.1 is

```
<!DOCTYPE ejb-jar PUBLIC '-//Sun Microsystems, Inc.//DTD Enterprise JavaBeans
1.1//EN' 'http://java.sun.com/j2ee/dtds/ejb-jar_1_1.dtd'>
```

Listing 14-2: **ejb-jar.xml for the Revenue bean**

```xml
<?xml version="1.0"?>

<!DOCTYPE ejb-jar PUBLIC '-//Sun Microsystems, Inc.//DTD Enterprise
JavaBeans 2.0//EN' 'http://java.sun.com/dtd/ejb-jar_2_0.dtd'>

<ejb-jar>
  <enterprise-beans>
    <session>
      <ejb-name>Revenue</ejb-name>
      <home>bible.ejb.RevenueHome</home>
      <remote>bible.ejb.Revenue</remote>
      <local-home>bible.ejb.RevenueLocalHome</local-home>
      <local>bible.ejb.RevenueLocal</local>
      <ejb-class>bible.ejb.RevenueEJB</ejb-class>
      <session-type>Stateless</session-type>
      <transaction-type>Container</transaction-type>
    </session>
  </enterprise-beans>
  <assembly-descriptor>
    <container-transaction>
      <method>
        <ejb-name>Revenue</ejb-name>
        <method-name>*</method-name>
      </method>
      <trans-attribute>Required</trans-attribute>
```

```
      </container-transaction>
    </assembly-descriptor>
  </ejb-jar>
```

From top to bottom, the elements of this deployment descriptor are as follows:

✦ `<ejb-jar>`: The top-level document type.

✦ `<enterprise-beans>`: A listing of all the enterprise Java beans contained in this deployment. It can include any number of `<session>`, `<entity>`, or `<message-driven>` descriptors.

✦ `<session>`: The descriptor for the session bean included in this deployment.

✦ `<ejb-name>`: A descriptive name for the bean.

✦ `<home>`: The fully qualified class name of the home interface used for remote clients.

✦ `<remote>`: The fully qualified class name of the remote interface.

✦ `<local-home>`: The fully qualified class name of the home interface used for local clients.

✦ `<local>`: The fully qualified class name of the local interface.

✦ `<ejb-class>`: The fully qualified name of the class implementing the bean, including its lifecycle methods and the business methods defined in the local and remote interfaces.

✦ `<session-type>`: This tag, which applies to session beans only, indicates whether the bean is stateless (as ours is) or stateful.

✦ `<transaction-type>`: Indicates how transactions are demarcated. In this example, transaction demarcation is handled by the EJB container. We discuss transactions and EJBs later in this chapter in the section called "WebLogic's EJB Container Services."

✦ `<assembly-descriptor>`: This tag defines transaction control on a method-by-method basis for the bean.

✦ `<container-transaction>`: Indicates that attributes for container-managed transactions are now being defined.

✦ `<method>`: The list of EJBs and methods to which a container-managed transaction attribute applies.

✦ `<ejb-name>`: The name of the EJB owning the method(s).

✦ `<method-name>`: The method(s) to be controlled by the transaction attribute. An asterisk (*) indicates the attribute applies to all methods of the EJB.

✦ `<trans-attribute>`: The transaction attribute to apply to the methods just listed. In this example, our methods all require a transaction context to be established by the EJB container before they are called.

Cross-Reference

See Chapter 6 for a complete description of transaction attributes and their meanings.

Listing 14-3 shows `weblogic-ejb-jar.xml` for our sample session bean.

Listing 14-3: weblogic-ejb-jar.xml for the Revenue bean

```
<?xml version="1.0"?>

<!DOCTYPE weblogic-ejb-jar PUBLIC '-//BEA Systems, Inc.//DTD WebLogic
7.0.0 EJB//EN' 'http://www.bea.com/servers/wls700/dtd/weblogic-ejb-
jar.dtd'>

<weblogic-ejb-jar>
    <weblogic-enterprise-bean>
        <ejb-name>Revenue</ejb-name>
        <jndi-name>Revenue</jndi-name>
        <local-jndi-name>RevenueLocal</local-jndi-name>
    </weblogic-enterprise-bean>
</weblogic-ejb-jar>
```

This deployment descriptor simply maps EJB names (as defined in `ejb-jar.xml`) to JNDI names corresponding to the local and remote implementations of the beans. Clients invoke the EJBs by performing lookups against these JNDI names.

For each bean, you should only define JNDI names for the type(s) of beans you're deploying; don't define a local JNDI name for a bean unless it actually contains a local home interface, and so on.

Our sample bean contains no descriptors for caching, clustering, or other WebLogic services. You'll see examples of those in upcoming chapters.

EJB 1.1 versus 2.0

Two versions of the EJB specification are now in use:

✦ EJB 1.1, which was released in December, 1999

✦ EJB 2.0, which was released in September, 2001

Note   At the time this chapter was being written, the EJB 2.1 specification was in draft form and was not currently supported by WebLogic Server.

A detailed discussion of the features of the two versions is beyond the scope of this book, but this section alerts you to some of the most important additions and enhancements Sun introduced with the EJB 2.0 specification. To fill in the blanks, you should download copies of both specifications at `http://java.sun.com/products/ejb/docs.html` and study them carefully. You should also carefully review *Programming WebLogic Enterprise JavaBeans,* which is part of WebLogic's documentation set.

According to the EJB specification, EJB 2.0-compliant containers must support beans written to the EJB 1.1 specification, and WebLogic's does. But you must write each of your beans to one version of the specification or the other; you cannot mix and match features from both versions in the same bean.

EJB 2.0 expands and improves upon the EJB architecture in response to suggestions from developers, vendors, and customers. What follows are some of the most important changes.

New: Message-driven beans

Message-driven beans, discussed in a previous section, are completely new with EJB 2.0 and have no counterpart in EJB 1.1. Message-driven beans attach themselves to JMS queues and topics and provide a component-based solution for managing messaging.

 Cross-Reference   Chapter 17 covers message-driven beans.

Improved: CMP for entity beans

As mentioned earlier, container-managed persistence is dramatically improved in EJB 2.0. These improvements are embodied in the following new features:

✦ Abstract accessor methods

✦ Container-managed relationships

✦ Local interfaces and local home interfaces

✦ Enterprise JavaBeans Query Language (EJB QL)

Abstract accessor methods

Abstract accessor methods are abstract getters and setters that manipulate an object's persistent state. All access to the persistent state passes through these accessors, so the container can interpose code of its own that efficiently manages exchanges between the bean and its underlying data store.

Container-managed relationships

With EJB 2.0, you can now represent various types of data relationships with collections of entity beans that work together at runtime. These relationships map to the same ones that have been modeled in relational databases for years:

✦ One-to-one, unidirectional

✦ One-to-one, bidirectional

✦ One-to-many

✦ Many-to-many

Such relationships were difficult, if not impossible, to model in EJB 1.1, both for technical and performance reasons.

Local interfaces and local home interfaces for session and entity beans

The concept of local interfaces (and corresponding local home interfaces), which we demonstrated earlier in this chapter, is new with EJB 2.0. In EJB 1.1, all access to EJBs was through their remote interfaces, whether the client code resided in the same JVM as the EJB or not. Now developers can write separate interfaces to explicitly support clients that are local *or* remote relative to the bean, thereby maximizing performance.

Enterprise JavaBeans Query Language (EJB QL)

The *Enterprise JavaBeans Query Language,* or *EJB QL,* is used to define queries for entity beans with container-managed persistence (for *all* entity beans in EJB 2.0). Because it's based on the SQL 92 standard, EBJ QL makes it possible to shift the parsing and execution of queries from the runtime representations of data in beans to the underlying data stores. This results in greater portability and performance, as well as enhanced functionality, for clients who want to query schemas of entity beans based on arbitrary criteria.

WebLogic Server Utilities

Before you go off and start hand-coding dozens of EJBs, keep in mind that WebLogic Server provides a variety of tools to cut down dramatically on the amount of manual work you need to do. The following list briefly describes some of the most useful tools:

✦ **Ant Tasks.** Ant is a very powerful Java-based build tool from the Apache Jakarta group. It uses XML build files to configure what actions to take, so its files are very human-readable. Out of the box, it can do everything from compiling Java source to building JARs, EARs, and WARs; to automating source code check-ins; to performing FTP transfers. Ant is without question the build tool of choice for Java developers. WebLogic Server comes with some specialized Ant tasks (Ant is extendable) to precompile JSPs, automate the creation of deployment descriptors, and perform several other tasks.

✦ **BEA XML Editor.** This freely downloadable tool ensures that you generate valid XML.

✦ **WebLogic Builder.** Builder is a tool for packaging J2EE applications, creating and modifying their deployment descriptors, and deploying them to WebLogic Server.

✦ **EJBGen.** You don't have to create your Home, Local, and Remote interfaces by hand. Use this handy tool to generate them automatically from Javadoc comments you put in your EJB 2.0 classes.

✦ **weblogic.Deployer.** This command-line tool enables you to automate the deployment process. It replaces the `weblogic.deploy` tool that came with previous versions of WebLogic Server.

Cross-
Reference

More information on these tools is included in Appendix B.

For more information about the tools that WebLogic Server provides to make your life easier, visit the following site:

```
http://edocs.bea.com/wls/docs70/toolstable/index.html
```

WebLogic's EJB Container Services

Maximizing the performance and scalability of your EJBs requires a clear understanding of how WebLogic's EJB container works. This section gives you an overview of the services that WebLogic's EJB container provides. These services are highly configurable and tunable; consult the WebLogic Server documentation for more information on the multitude of options available.

Lifecycle management

WebLogic Server's EJB container, like all J2EE-compliant EJB containers, provides full lifecycle management for the beans you deploy, which means the container assumes responsibility for the following tasks:

✦ Creating new bean instances, either in response to demand from clients or to populate predefined bean pools at startup time.

✦ Passivating bean instances that are still in use, but are idle. This process involves serializing the contents of the bean and saving it to disk.

✦ Activating bean instances that have been passivated. In this case, the passivated beans are deserialized from disk and restored to active memory, where they are once again available for use.

✦ Destroying bean instances that are no longer in use, usually to make memory available for other functions or to prepare for a shutdown of WebLogic Server.

✦ Handling the create, load, store, and delete operations for entity EJBs.

✦ Binding message-driven EJBs to the appropriate JMS queues and topics.

✦ Managing failover operations in clustered environments.

Transaction support

EJBs, by definition, operate in a transactional environment. When you deploy EJBs, you specify the level of transaction support you expect from the EJB container in your `ejb-jar.xml` deployment descriptor.

Recall from Chapter 6 that *transaction demarcation* is the process of specifying when a transaction is started, suspended, resumed, committed, and rolled back. With J2EE, transactions can be manually demarcated in code by using calls to the JTA, or they can be automatically demarcated by using declarative rules stored in XML deployment descriptors.

Because writing transaction code is such a difficult and error-prone process, it is almost always better to take advantage of automatic transaction demarcation. Nevertheless, you can manually demarcate transactions in session and message-driven EJBs; these transactions are called *bean-managed transactions*. The EJB 2.0 specification, however, prohibits the use of bean-managed transactions in entity EJBs; entity EJBs must always use container-managed transactions (which, of course, are available to the other bean types as well).

Container-managed transactions

The EJB specification defines several attributes for container-managed transactions that control the way EJB methods participate in transactions. You specify the attributes you want in `ejb-jar.xml` by using the `<trans-attribute>` element of the `<assembly-descriptor>` tag.

The following sections summarize how EJB 2.0 specification defines the container's behavior for each attribute, but you should consult the EJB 2.0 specification for more details (`http://java.sun.com/products/ejb/`).

NotSupported

This attribute applies to EJB methods that do not support transactions. The container invokes the EJB method with an unspecified transaction context. If the caller has a transaction in progress when such a method is invoked, the container suspends the transaction before invoking the method and then resumes it when the method completes.

Required

The container must establish a valid transaction context before invoking an EJB method with this attribute. If a transaction is already under way, the container will associate the method with that transaction. If not, the container will start a new transaction, invoke the method, and then commit the transaction when the method completes.

Note, however, that message-driven EJB methods *never* execute within the context of an existing transaction, so the container *always* creates a new transaction context for them prior to executing the onMessage() method. After onMessage() completes, the container commits the transaction. If the container rolls back the transaction, the message is marked for redelivery in accordance with the JMS specification.

Supports

This attribute is a cross between NotSupported and Required. If the EJB method is invoked with a transaction in progress, the container proceeds as in the Required case. If not, the container proceeds as in the NotSupported case.

RequiresNew

This attribute always forces the new container to start a new transaction for the EJB method and to commit that transaction when the method completes. If the caller has a transaction under way, that transaction is suspended until the method completes; it is then resumed again.

Mandatory

The caller is required to have a transaction under way before calling EJB methods with this attribute set, and the container executes the methods within the context of the caller's transaction. If no transaction is under way, the container throws an exception.

Never

This attribute is the opposite of Mandatory. The caller must invoke the EJB method with no transaction under way. If a transaction is under way, the container throws an exception; otherwise, it proceeds as in the NotSupported case.

Bean-managed transactions

To use bean-managed transactions, you omit the <trans-attribute> tag for the affected bean methods and write your own transaction demarcation code, as explained in Chapter 6.

Persistence

The EJB container provides persistence services for stateful session beans and entity beans. For stateful session beans, the container automatically serializes the bean's state to disk when the bean is passivated, assuming that the bean is still in use (and the client session with the bean has not expired or otherwise ended). When the same bean is activated later, the container reloads its state from disk into main memory.

Persistence services for entity beans, which almost always represent data in relational or object-relational databases, are far more advanced. Here, the programmer has two persistence models to choose from:

✦ Container-managed persistence (CMP): The container automatically synchronizes the bean instance in memory with the underlying data it represents

✦ Bean-managed persistence (BMP): The developer writes code to maintain this synchronization

In theory, it is always better for developers to use CMP because developers can focus on implementing business logic while leaving the details of entity persistence to the container. It also enables developers to write code that is independent of the underlying data source used because the container correctly manages persistence for any data source with a compliant JDBC driver.

In practice, it's not always that easy. With EJB 1.1, CMP has a lot of usability and performance problems that force developers to use BMP almost exclusively. EJB 2.0, however, promises to be a different story. Sun has completely rewritten CMP in EJB 2.0 to address developer concerns with the previous version. It's too early to tell whether they did a good job, but you should probably give CMP a try in EJB 2.0 to see if it works for your project before taking on the formidable task of implementing BMP.

Clustering support

WebLogic Server provides full clustering support for EJBs, which enables you to deploy your EJBs in an environment that requires high scalability and availability. WebLogic uses cluster-aware stubs for bean home interfaces, along with cluster-aware EJBObjects, to implement clustering for EJBs. These cluster-aware entities are aware of the locations of all other instances of the bean in the cluster. Drawing from this information, the stub manages load balancing and failover for bean invocations, whereas the EJBObjects manage failover to bean instances on healthy servers if the servers on which the beans are executing go down.

Security

You can control user access to the methods of your EJBs by using the same mechanisms available for controlling access to Web applications. In your deployment descriptors, you can declare users, roles, and security role assignments; at runtime, the EJB container automatically restricts access to EJB method calls based on your security role assignments.

Summary

In this chapter, we discussed the basics of EJBs, including what they are, how they are constructed, the extensive runtime services that are available to them, and the way some of those services are implemented in WebLogic Server. You also learned about the two versions of the EJB specification now in use, 1.1 and 2.0, and how to properly structure your EJBs to support either version.

The next three chapters explore the three types of EJBs in detail: session EJBs, entity EJBs, and message-driven EJBs — J2EE's newest bean type.

✦　　✦　　✦

Developing Session Beans

In Chapter 14, you learned that session EJBs are used to represent control, process, and workflow in an application. This chapter provides concrete examples of this theory in action and shows how to build and deploy session EJBs in WebLogic Server.

Introducing Session Beans

Session EJBs come in two flavors: *stateful* and *stateless*. Stateful session beans maintain ongoing conversations with clients, whereas stateless beans do not. The classic example of a stateful session bean is an online shopping cart that keeps track of the items a customer intends to purchase until the customer checks out or otherwise concludes the shopping session. Stateless beans, on the other hand, are used to perform simple, one-off tasks, such as updating the customer's mailing address or adding an item to her wish list. These are atomic functions that do not require an ongoing dialogue between the client and the server.

Stateful session beans maintain their state in memory, not in a database. Therefore, if the WebLogic EJB container crashes or destroys a session bean instance for some reason, the state of the bean is lost. But stateful beans can be clustered, which provides a failover capability for applications that need it.

WebLogic's EJB container manages the lifecycle of session EJBs, including their creation, caching, and destruction. For the most part, WebLogic's bean lifecycle management occurs automatically in response to client demand for beans. In this chapter, we show how this occurs and discuss steps that you can take to override the container's behavior in certain situations.

Before you can invoke a session EJB's methods, you must obtain a reference to either its local or remote interface. The first step is to perform a JNDI lookup to obtain a reference to the bean's home interface. This reference, in turn, is used to retrieve a reference to the bean's local or remote interface. The local or remote interface is then used to invoke the bean's methods.

Which interface you'll use (local or remote) depends partially on where the client code lives in relationship to the bean and partially on how portable you want your application's components to be. If the client code is a Java class, servlet, or another EJB, it can use the local interface as long as it is deployed in the same EAR file as the EJB or as part of a standalone JAR that is loaded into the same JVM as the EJB. The local interface is more efficient than the remote interface because method calls are made directly within the same JVM, with parameters being passed by reference instead of by value. Local calls, however, are location-specific — if you decide to move the calling code or the EJB to a different server, you will have to rewrite your code to use the EJB's remote interface.

> **Tip**   Chapter 7 discusses WebLogic's implementation of RMI as an alternative to the Sun implementation. Although it's possible to have your EJBs use the `weblogic.rmi` package instead of the standard `java.rmi` implementation, it is not recommended. By using Sun's RMI, your beans will be easily portable to non-WebLogic application servers, which is one of the most profound benefits of using EJBs. When writing remote EJBs, your developers will never need to worry about method invocations passing parameters by reference — when using `java.rmi` they can count on parameters being passed by value. If a developer wants to increase the efficiency of his EJBs and knows his EJBs will be accessed from clients within the server, he can now write a local EJB.

Common session bean uses

Any business logic that will be used by clients in your WebLogic applications can be encapsulated in session EJBs. Session EJBs can update and fetch shared data as long as they do not directly represent that data. In other words, you could write `FooDataFactory` as a session EJB to obtain references to a non-EJB `Foo` class. They can be used to do business calculations, obtain references and call other EJBs, or even help facilitate the model role in the MVC design architecture. Session beans can be used instead of entity beans to persist objects representing data in your business model, but this approach is not recommended. This scenario is often seen when an application has an existing object database or developers have been using an object-relational mapping tool.

Using session EJBs to model workflow

Many good reasons exist for choosing to model workflow and business processes in session EJBs instead of normal Java classes.

Client-server architecture

When you encapsulate business logic in a session EJB, you maximize the benefits of client-server computing. Logic implemented in session EJBs is executed inside the WebLogic EJB Container on the server. Client code not running on the server can remain lightweight and avoid the expense and details of local method invocations.

EJB Container functionality

By choosing session EJBs to model workflow, a good deal of complex functionality is provided by the EJB Container. Security issues, transactional capabilities, and other complicated issues will be easier to implement than if you had to start from scratch. Because the WebLogic EJB Container has been built with lots of these issues in mind, you only need to implement your EJBs correctly, leaving these complex details to the WebLogic Server. This also ensures that your security and transactional issues will be standardized across your application, making your application easier to support over time.

No synchronization issues

The WebLogic EJB Container, as part of implementing the EJB specification, ensures that no EJB instance will be accessed by multiple clients across method invocations. Thus, application developers don't need to deal with somewhat complicated threading details.

Inherently reusable

The logic session EJBs contain can be reusable across many applications in the WebLogic application environment or even in non-WebLogic J2EE applications. Session beans can be deployed with different security settings and environment settings across many applications or even servers with no change to the underlying Java classes. This is accomplished by using the bean's deployment descriptors to encapsulate environment-specific information.

Scalability

The WebLogic EJB Container provides a runtime environment that scales exceptionally well. WebLogic Server provides the capability to have a pool of session EJBs that dynamically grow and shrink with the real-time needs of your application. This concept is a powerful one, especially when you look closely at how WebLogic Server handles pools of stateless session EJBs.

Comparing Stateless and Stateful Beans

Stateless and stateful session beans are completely different, both in terms of the way they are used and the way they are managed by WebLogic Server.

Stateless session beans are used to perform simple, one-off tasks that are not client-specific and often involve only a single method call. Stateful session beans, by contrast, are used to maintain conversational state with clients, and the conversation may span several method calls against the bean.

When a client uses a stateless session bean, it's not pinned to a specific instance of that bean because the bean doesn't care who the client is. The beans are all alike, and any bean is capable of servicing any client. Because of this, the client-to-bean ratio for stateless session beans is potentially many-to-many.

When a client uses a stateful session bean, it's pinned to a specific instance of the bean for the duration of its conversation with that bean. No two beans are alike because each bean represents the unique state of its client. Because of this, the client-to-bean ratio for stateful session beans is always one-to-one.

Figure 15-1 illustrates these client-to-bean relationships for the two types of session beans.

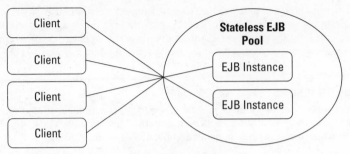

Stateless EJB Clients
Remote reference actually a proxy to pool of EJB instances

Stateful EJB Clients
One to One Relationship with EJB instances

Figure 15-1: Client-to-bean relationships for session beans

WebLogic Server takes these session bean usage patterns into account and manages the two types of session beans within the EJB container in completely different ways.

Stateless session beans are managed like independent truckers — if you make a shipment to Des Moines every Tuesday, you might get Eddie one week, Vern the next week, and Eddie again the week after — but WebLogic has the singular advantage that it can create new truckers out of thin air! WebLogic creates a pool of bean instances, and when a client requests a bean, WebLogic hands it an unused (or *unbound*) bean from the pool. If no unbound beans are available, WebLogic creates one or more new bean instances, depending on how the pool is configured. When a client is finished with a bean, it is returned to the pool. This is illustrated in Figure 15-2.

When a client requests a new stateful session bean, WebLogic Server creates a new instance of the bean for that client. Every subsequent method call the client makes to the bean is funneled to the same bean. The bean remains in WebLogic's stateful session bean cache either until the client removes it (by calling its `remove()` method) or until WebLogic *passivates* it to free up memory for other needs. Passivating a bean involves serializing its contents and writing them to disk. If a client calls a method on a passivated bean, WebLogic *activates* it by reading it from disk back into the cache. Passivation and activation are completely transparent to clients. Figure 15-3 illustrates the lifecycle of stateful session beans.

Figure 15-2: WebLogic Server stateless session bean lifecycle

Figure 15-3: WebLogic Server stateful session bean lifecycle

When programming stateful session beans, you must ensure that their internal member variables are serializable, and you must respond intelligently when WebLogic passivates and activates your beans. WebLogic Server calls your bean's ejbPassivate() method when passivation occurs; this is your opportunity to perform cleanup tasks, such as closing open network sockets or database connections, before the bean instance is written to disk. Likewise, you should code the ejbActivate() method to reverse these operations when the bean is read back into the cache.

Cross-Reference   Refer to Chapter 7 for more details on object serialization.

Programming Session Beans

Now we'll discuss the EJB components that you will have to create in your session EJB development process. The mandatory components that you must provide the WebLogic Server during a session EJB deployment are a home interface, a local or remote interface to interact with a client of the bean, an implementation class, and two deployment descriptors.

We'll examine each piece of the session EJB development process in detail and give an example in the form of two stateless session EJBs. The first session EJB you will develop will be called RequestResearch and will be used by a remote client to request research on a particular security. The second example session EJB, RequestDataManager, is a local EJB that will act as a helper bean to the remotely accessible RequestResearch.

Home interfaces

Home interfaces are the conduits that allow clients to communicate with the WebLogic EJB Container to obtain references to session EJBs. All stateless session beans must supply a create() method with no parameters as they have no state to initialize.

When developing a home interface, the first decision that you must make is whether the home is remote or local. Because the home interface is what clients use to obtain EJBs, your client's location is the major factor in determining which to use. If you don't know where your clients will be located or if you don't want to mandate that the clients will be living locally on the WebLogic Server, simply choose to use a remote home interface.

The decoupling of a bean's functionality and access location is a powerful design concept that you inherit by implementing a remote session EJB. It enables you to reuse a session EJB in many applications without worrying about where the client is located.

Example remote home: RequestResearchHome

As shown in Listing 15-1, this remote home interface has a create() method that returns a remote reference, RequestResearchRemote, to the RequestResearch session EJB. Because the bean home is being accessed remotely, the create method throws a java.rmi.Remote Exception and will also throw CreateException if a problem occurs during creation.

Listing 15-1: **RequestResearchHome.java**

```
package com.wiley.wlsbible.ejb.session.stateless;

import java.rmi.*;
import javax.ejb.*;

public interface RequestResearchHome extends EJBHome {
  public RequestResearchRemote create() throws RemoteException,
CreateException;
}
```

Example local home: RequestDataManagerLocalHome

As shown in Listing 15-2, this local home interface has a single `create()` method that returns a local reference, `RequestDataManagerLocal`. Notice that there's no need to import the `java.rmi` package because the bean is accessing a local interface that isn't passed via RMI.

Listing 15-2: **RequestDataManagerLocalHome.java**

```
package com.wiley.wlsbible.ejb.session.stateless;

import javax.ejb.*;

public interface RequestDataManagerLocalHome extends EJBLocalHome {
  public RequestDataManagerLocal create() throws CreateException;
}
```

Session EJB interfaces

The second component to develop is the bean's client interfaces. Remote and local interfaces to session beans are essentially the client's view of the bean, and they contain the methods that define those session beans. These methods represent the business logic supplied by the session EJBs. If you've chosen a remote home, you must use a remote interface here, and vice-versa.

Remote session EJB interfaces

Remote interfaces are what clients will actually obtain and use from remote home interfaces. Remote interfaces extend from `javax.ejb.EJBObject`. Because this is a remote reference to an object living on the WebLogic Server, you must adhere to proper RMI standards. Methods must throw `java.rmi.RemoteExceptions`, and all method parameters, return-types, and application exceptions must be serializable.

Cross-Reference   See Chapter 7 for further details on object serialization.

Listing 15-3 shows `RequestResearchRemote.java`, a sample remote interface. Note that `RequestResearchRemote` extends `EJBObject` because it's a remote interface. Also, note that the return types and parameters are of type `String`, which are serializable and therefore RMI-compliant.

Listing 15-3: **RequestResearchRemote.java**

```
package com.wiley.wlsbible.ejb.session.stateless;

import java.rmi.*;
import javax.ejb.*;

public interface RequestResearchRemote extends EJBObject {

  /**
   * Fetches and returns research for a security.
   */
  public String requestResearch(String symbol)
      throws RemoteException;
}
```

Local session EJB interfaces

Local interfaces are obtained by clients from the local home EJB interface. Local interfaces extend `javax.ejb.EJBLocalObject`. Because local objects live within the same JVM, they are passed by reference, not by value.

Listing 15-4 shows `RequestDataManagerLocal.java`, a sample local interface. To demonstrate that parameters are passed by reference with local EJBs, note that we pass a `String Buffer` as a parameter to the local EJB and have that EJB alter it. Note also that the methods in this interface need not throw `java.rmi.RemoteException` because they cannot be invoked remotely.

Listing 15-4: **RequestDataManagerLocal.java**

```
package com.wiley.wlsbible.ejb.session.stateless;

import javax.ejb.*;

public interface RequestDataManagerLocal
   extends EJBLocalObject {
```

```
/**
 * Returns research data about a particular security.
 */
public String getResearchData(String symbol);

/**
 * Appends research data about a particular security
 * to this buffer.
 */
public void appendResearchData(StringBuffer buffer,
                               String symbol);
}
```

Implementation class

The next component to define after the home and client interfaces is the implementation class. These classes must implement the `javax.ejb.SessionBean` so that the container can notify them of the bean's lifecycle events. They will also implement `create()` methods matching the signatures of the `create()` methods in the their home interfaces. Finally, they will implement all the methods defined in their local or remote interfaces.

The SessionBean lifecycle methods in `javax.ejb.SessionBean` are as follows:

✦ `ejbActivate()`: Called when the instance is activated from its passive state. Stateless session beans will have nothing to activate because they have no state, whereas stateful beans will contain logic to refresh their states and obtain necessary external resources.

✦ `ejbPassivate()`: Called before the instance enters the passive state. Stateless session beans should have nothing to passivate and should implement an empty `ejbPassivate` method. Stateful beans should deallocate any external resources here.

✦ `ejbRemove()`: Called before the WebLogic EJB Container ends the life of the session object.

✦ `setSessionContext()`: WebLogic Server will call this to set the associated session context.

Note

During activation and passivation, the WebLogic Server may serialize and deserialize your instance, so it will be necessary that any internal variables are serializable. It is also legal to mark members *transient*, although those members will be lost upon serialization.

Cross-Reference

See Chapter 14 for discussion of the EJBContext.

RequestResearch implementation

The implementation class for the remote stateless session bean must provide methods for all the previously discussed components. First, it will implement the ejbCreate() method from RequestRequestHome. Then it will implement all the necessary lifecycle methods, as defined by the SessionBean interface. Because this is a stateless session bean that doesn't use any external resources, note that the ejbActivate() and ejbPassivate() methods are empty. Don't forget that you must provide these methods, even if they are empty. Finally, the implementation class provides the functionality for RequestResearchRemote that the remote clients will use.

Note   The implementation class does not directly implement the home or the remote interfaces. The WebLogic Server will use our deployment descriptors to make the logical connection.

Note that the implementation class clients will call the requestResearch() method that returns a String containing research for a particular security. When this method is invoked, it will first call a private method useRequestDataManager() to determine how it will process the request. If useRequestDataManager() returns false, the bean itself will generate test research with the private method createRandomResearch(). Otherwise, it will call the RequestDataManager EJB to obtain the research for the client.

The useRequestDataManager() method actually will do an environment entry lookup in order to determine whether to use the RequestDataManager. We'll discuss how this works in more detail a little later when we cover the bean's deployment descriptor.

Note that because the RequestResearch EJB lives inside the WebLogic Server, it can use the default empty constructor for InitialContext. This is different from client code, in which you must use the Environment configuration class to obtain the InitialContext.

Listing 15-5 contains RequestResearch.java, the code for the implementation class.

Note   Pay special attention to the getResearchFromDataManager() method, in which the RequestDataManagerLocalHome reference is obtained through a normal casting operation on the object it obtains via the JNDI lookup. When obtaining a reference to a remote interface, it's necessary to invoke javax.rmi.PortableRemoteObject.narrow on the object obtained through JNDI, which is less efficient than simply casting.

Listing 15-5: **RequestResearch.java**

```
package com.wiley.wlsbible.ejb.session.stateless;

import java.rmi.*;
import javax.ejb.*;
import java.util.*;
import javax.naming.*;

public class RequestResearch implements SessionBean {
   //Implemented create method required by RequestResearchHome.
   public void ejbCreate() {
   }
```

```
//Implemented methods required by SessionBean.
private SessionContext sessionContext;
public void ejbRemove() throws RemoteException {
}
public void ejbActivate() throws RemoteException {
}
public void ejbPassivate() throws RemoteException {
}
public void setSessionContext(
  SessionContext sessionContext) throws RemoteException {
  this.sessionContext = sessionContext;
}

//Methods for processing requests for research as required
//for the RequestResearchRemote interface.
/**
 * Fetches and returns research for a security.
 */
public String requestResearch(String symbol)
throws RemoteException {
  //CheckEnvironment flag here to see whether to route
  // the call to the internal system.
  String research = null;

  if (this.useRequestDataManager()) {
    System.out.println("Locally calling RequestDataManager for
research.");
    research = getResearchFromDataManager(symbol);
  }
  else {
    System.out.println("Randomly generating research for this
symbol.");
    research = createRandomResearch(symbol);
  }
  return research;
}

/**
 * Randomly creates 'research' for this security.
 */
private String createRandomResearch(String symbol) {
  Random rand = new Random();
  int x = rand.nextInt();
  x = x % 3;
  String research = null;
  switch(x) {
    case 0:
      research = "Zeetrade recommends you buy "+ symbol;
      break;
```

Continued

Listing 15-5 *(continued)*

```
      case 1:
        research = "Zeetrade recommends you hold "+ symbol;
        break;
      default:
        research = "Zeetrade recommends you sell "+ symbol;
        break;
    }
    return research;
  }

  /**
   * Does an environment entry lookup to determine where or not to use
   * the DataManager or randomly generate data here. This field can be
edited in
   * the ejb-jar.xml before EJB deployment.
   */
  private boolean useRequestDataManager() {
    System.out.println("Checking the env-entry for
useRequestDataManager");
    InitialContext ctx = null;
    boolean useManager = false;

    try {
      //Because Request Research is a bean living in the EJB container,
      //no need to specify server parameters to obtain the correct
context.
      ctx = new InitialContext();
      Boolean useManagerBool =
(Boolean)ctx.lookup("java:comp/env/useRequestDataManager");
      useManager = useManagerBool.booleanValue();
    } catch (Exception e) {
      e.printStackTrace();
    } finally {
      try {
        ctx.close();
      } catch (Exception e) {}
    }
    return useManager;
  }

  /**
   * Calls local EJB RequestDataManager to get research.
   */
  private String getResearchFromDataManager(String symbol) {
```

```
InitialContext ctx = null;
StringBuffer sb = new StringBuffer();

try {
//Because Request Research is a bean living in the EJB container,
//no need to specify server parameters to obtain the correct
context.
ctx = new InitialContext();
Object objref = ctx.lookup("RequestDataManager");

//No need to do narrow, simply cast as this is a local object to
this JVM.
RequestDataManagerLocalHome home =
(RequestDataManagerLocalHome)objref;

RequestDataManagerLocal dataBean = home.create();

sb.append("**Data Retrieved from the local datasource**");
//Call the dataBean, this is not pass by value as in RMI (Remote
//beans included) Instead the stringbuffer is passed by reference,
// and therefore when the local session EJB RequestDataManager
//appends to it, the appends are altering this buffer (sb).
dataBean.appendResearchData(sb, symbol);

} catch (Exception e) {
  e.printStackTrace();
} finally {
  try {
    ctx.close();
  } catch (Exception e) {}
}

return sb.toString();
  }
}
```

RequestDataManager implementation

Listing 15-6 is the implementation of the local helper bean. It's similar to the previous implementation in that it defines methods in its home interface and also implements nearly empty methods to fulfill its SessionBean interface requirements. It defines two business methods: getResearchData() and appendResearchData(). Both simply call the private method checkResearchDatasource(), which checks a hard-coded list of securities. This example could be extended to do a symbol lookup on an external datasource such as a database. Note that in appendResearchData() the results are returned through the client by appending to a StringBuffer the client provides as a parameter, thus showing that parameters are passed by reference when invoking methods on local EJBs.

Listing 15-6: RequestDataManager.java

```java
package com.wiley.wlsbible.ejb.session.stateless;

import javax.ejb.*;
import java.util.*;

public class RequestDataManager implements SessionBean {
  private SessionContext sessionContext;
  public void ejbCreate() {
  }
  public void ejbRemove() {
  }
  public void ejbActivate() {
  }
  public void ejbPassivate() {
  }
  public void setSessionContext(SessionContext sessionContext) {
    this.sessionContext = sessionContext;
  }

  /**
   * Returns research data about a particular security.
   */
  public String getResearchData(String symbol) {
    return checkResearchDatasource(symbol);
  }

  /**
   * Appends research data about a particular security to this buffer.
   */
  public void appendResearchData(StringBuffer buffer, String symbol) {
    buffer.append(checkResearchDatasource(symbol));
  }

  /**
   * Checks a hard-coded list of securities for a match and returns
recommendations.
   * This has been kept simple for the sake of the example, but
potentially
   * could be doing a database lookup here.
   */
  private String checkResearchDatasource(String symbol) {
    if(symbol.equals("BEAS"))
      return "(Zeeware Internal System Lookup) BEAS is rated at a
Strong Buy";
    else if(symbol.equals("YHOO"))
      return "(Zeeware Internal System Lookup) YHOO is rated at a Buy";
```

```
    return "(Zeeware Internal System Lookup Failed) No research
available for security: "+ symbol;
  }
}
```

Session EJB deployment descriptors

Because the deployment descriptors for session beans are the same deployment descriptors used by entity beans, you should refer to Chapter 14 for an overview of `weblogic-ejb-jar.xml` and `ejb-jar.xml`. Here, we'll discuss a few of the deployment descriptors important to deploying session beans in WebLogic and look at the two deployment descriptors for the two session beans.

ejb-jar.xml

Both beans declare a `<session-type>` with value stateless because they are stateless session EJBs. Note that you're declaring a Boolean environment entry `useRequestDataManager` in the `RequestResearch` deployment descriptor. This flag tells `RequestResearch` whether or not to use the data manager bean. Also of note is that `RequestResearch` declares `<home>` and `<remote>` tags, whereas the local EJB `RequestDataManager` has `<local-home>` and `<local>` tags.

Notice that an environment entry has been declared in the `RequestResearch` descriptor marked by the `<env-entry>` flag. The entry type is defined by the `<env-entry-type>` tag, and must be a fully qualified object relating to the eight Java primitives. In the sample application (see Listing 15-7), the `RequestResearch` EJB uses the entry `useRequestData Manager` to decide whether or not to route a method call to the local helper EJB, `Request DataManager`.

Listing 15-7: **ejb-jar.xml**

```
<!DOCTYPE ejb-jar PUBLIC '-//Sun Microsystems, Inc.//DTD Enterprise
JavaBeans 2.0//EN' 'http://java.sun.com/dtd/ejb-jar_2_0.dtd'>

<ejb-jar>
  <enterprise-beans>
    <session>
      <ejb-name>RequestResearch</ejb-name>

<home>com.wiley.wlsbible.ejb.session.stateless.RequestResearchHome
</home>

<remote>com.wiley.wlsbible.ejb.session.stateless.RequestResearchRemote
</remote>
      <ejb-
class>com.wiley.wlsbible.ejb.session.stateless.RequestResearch</ejb-
class>
```

Continued

Listing 15-7 *(continued)*

```
      <session-type>Stateless</session-type>
      <transaction-type>Container</transaction-type>
      <env-entry>
        <env-entry-name>
          useRequestDataManager
        </env-entry-name>
        <env-entry-type>java.lang.Boolean</env-entry-type>
        <env-entry-value>true</env-entry-value>
      </env-entry>
    </session>
    <session>
      <ejb-name>RequestDataManager</ejb-name>
      <local-home>

com.wiley.wlsbible.ejb.session.stateless.RequestDataManagerLocalHome
      </local-home>

<local>com.wiley.wlsbible.ejb.session.stateless.RequestDataManagerLocal
</local>
      <ejb-
class>com.wiley.wlsbible.ejb.session.stateless.RequestDataManager</ejb-
class>
      <session-type>Stateless</session-type>
      <transaction-type>Container</transaction-type>
    </session>
  </enterprise-beans>

  <assembly-descriptor>
    <container-transaction>
      <method>
        <ejb-name>RequestResearch</ejb-name>
        <method-name>*</method-name>
      </method>
      <method>
        <ejb-name>RequestDataManager</ejb-name>
        <method-name>*</method-name>
      </method>
      <trans-attribute>Required</trans-attribute>
    </container-transaction>
  </assembly-descriptor>
</ejb-jar>
```

weblogic-ejb-jar.xml
This is the WebLogic-specific deployment descriptor. Table 15-1 shows some of the more important properties relating to session EJBs. For a complete list, see the WebLogic documentation.

Table 15-1: Session EJB Properties

Property	Description	Default Value
allow-concurrent-calls	If this is set to `true`, the WebLogic Server will not throw `RemoteExceptions` when a client tries to make concurrent calls to the EJB; instead, it blocks the second call until the first has completed.	FALSE
idle-timeout-seconds	The maximum amount of time a stateful EJB should stay in the cache.	600s
initial-beans-in-free-pool	Amount of stateless beans in the free pool on initialization.	0
max-beans-in-cache	The maximum number of stateful bean instances allowed in memory.	100
max-beans-in-free-pool	Maximum number of stateless session beans allowed in the pool.	max Int

Cross-Reference   See Chapter 14 for a more detailed look at this deployment descriptor.

Note that the `RequestResearch` EJB declares a `<jndi-name>` tag while `RequestDataManager` uses a `<local-jndi-name>` tag (see Listing 15-8).

Listing 15-8: **weblogic-ejb-jar.xml**

```
<!DOCTYPE weblogic-ejb-jar PUBLIC '-//BEA Systems, Inc.//DTD WebLogic
7.0.0 EJB//EN' 'http://www.bea.com/servers/wls700/dtd/weblogic-ejb-
jar.dtd'>

<weblogic-ejb-jar>
  <weblogic-enterprise-bean>
    <ejb-name>RequestResearch</ejb-name>
    <stateless-session-descriptor>
      <pool>
        <max-beans-in-free-pool>1000</max-beans-in-free-pool>
        <initial-beans-in-free-pool>
          0
        </initial-beans-in-free-pool>
      </pool>

      <stateless-clustering>
        <stateless-bean-is-clusterable>
          True
```

Continued

Listing 15-8 *(continued)*

```xml
          </stateless-bean-is-clusterable>
          <stateless-bean-methods-are-idempotent>
            False
          </stateless-bean-methods-are-idempotent>
        </stateless-clustering>

      </stateless-session-descriptor>

      <transaction-descriptor>
        <trans-timeout-seconds>0</trans-timeout-seconds>
      </transaction-descriptor>

      <enable-call-by-reference>True</enable-call-by-reference>
      <jndi-name>RequestResearch</jndi-name>
    </weblogic-enterprise-bean>

    <weblogic-enterprise-bean>
      <ejb-name>RequestDataManager</ejb-name>
      <stateless-session-descriptor>
        <pool>
          <max-beans-in-free-pool>1000</max-beans-in-free-pool>
          <initial-beans-in-free-pool>
            0
          </initial-beans-in-free-pool>
        </pool>

        <stateless-clustering>
          <stateless-bean-is-clusterable>
            True
          </stateless-bean-is-clusterable>
          <stateless-bean-methods-are-idempotent>
            False
          </stateless-bean-methods-are-idempotent>
        </stateless-clustering>

      </stateless-session-descriptor>

      <transaction-descriptor>
        <trans-timeout-seconds>0</trans-timeout-seconds>
      </transaction-descriptor>

      <enable-call-by-reference>True</enable-call-by-reference>
      <local-jndi-name>RequestDataManager</local-jndi-name>
    </weblogic-enterprise-bean>
</weblogic-ejb-jar>
```

Client example – Using RequestResearch EJB

The client will periodically obtain a reference to a `RequestResearch` session EJB, ask it about a couple of securities, and dump those results to standard out. Because the simple client will be running in its own Java Virtual Machine (JVM), it will need to do a little more work to access the proper `InitialContext`. The `Environment` class is used to accomplish `Initial Context` lookup. The `Environment` class makes assumptions about your WebLogic configuration, including listening ports and URL. You may need to edit this file to match your exact configuration.

The client extends `TimerTask` and implements the `Runnable` interface so that it will continue to poll the WebLogic Server over time.

Because the client code shown in Listing 15-9 is running outside the server, the client code must obtain a reference to the `RequestResearchHome` by using `javax.rmi.PortableRemote Object.narrow()` instead of simply casting.

Listing 15-9: **ResearchClient.java**

```
package com.wiley.wlsbible.ejb.session.stateless;

import java.rmi.*;
import java.util.*;
import javax.naming.*;

/**
 * ResearchClient periodically asks server for research.
 */
public class ResearchClient extends TimerTask implements Runnable {

  private Random rand = new Random();
  private String[] securities = null;

  /**
   * Initializes an InitialContext, gets a reference to a remote EJB on
the server,
   * and asks that EJB for research.
   */
  public void run() {
    System.out.println("ResearchClient calling remote EJB.");
    System.out.println(" Time: "+ new
Date(System.currentTimeMillis()));

    try {
      InitialContext ctx = Environment.getInitialContext();
```

Continued

Listing 15-9 *(continued)*

```
      Object objref = ctx.lookup("RequestResearch");
      RequestResearchHome home = (RequestResearchHome)
javax.rmi.PortableRemoteObject.narrow(objref,
RequestResearchHome.class);

      RequestResearchRemote requestResearchBean = home.create();

      StringBuffer sb = new StringBuffer();
      sb.append(requestResearchBean.requestResearch("YHOO")+"\n");
      sb.append(requestResearchBean.requestResearch("BEAS")+"\n");
      sb.append(requestResearchBean.requestResearch("WAG")+"\n");

      System.out.println(sb.toString());
    }
    catch(Exception e) {
      e.printStackTrace();
    }
  }

  /**
   * Declare a new client and schedule it on a timer.
   */
  public static void main(String [] args) {
    Timer t = new Timer();
    ResearchClient client = new ResearchClient();
    //Starting in 5 secs, run every 5 seconds.
    t.schedule(client, 5000, 5000);
  }
}
```

Because the simple client will be running in its own Java Virtual Machine (JVM), it will need to do a little more work to access the `InitialContext`. This `Environment` class has a static method `getInitialContext`, which returns an `InitialContext`. The `Environment` class makes assumptions about your WebLogic configuration, including listening ports and URL. You may need to edit this file, shown in Listing 15-10, to match your exact WebLogic Server configuration.

Listing 15-10: **Environment.java**

```
package com.wiley.wlsbible.ejb.session.stateless;

import javax.naming.*;
import java.util.*;

public class Environment {
```

```
  public final static String
JNDI_FACTORY="weblogic.jndi.WLInitialContextFactory";
  public final static String WEBLOGIC_URL = "t3://localhost:7001";

  public static InitialContext getInitialContext()
   throws NamingException {

    Hashtable env = new Hashtable();
    env.put(Context.INITIAL_CONTEXT_FACTORY, JNDI_FACTORY);
    env.put(Context.PROVIDER_URL, WEBLOGIC_URL);
    return new InitialContext(env);
  }
}
```

Figure 15-4 shows how the components of the application work together. The research client, running in its own JVM, accesses a `RequestResearch` EJB via the `RequestResearchRemote` remote interface. Client method invocations on `RequestResearchRemote` are proxied to a pool of `RequestResearch` EJB instances by the Weblogic Server. The `RequestResearch` EJB then acts as a client and accesses a `RequestDataManager` EJB through `RequestDataManager`'s local interface. Method invocations on the local interface are again proxied to a pool of `RequestDataManager` instances. Non-remote invocations are possible because all EJB instances in this example live within the same JVM.

Figure 15-4: RequestResearch design diagram

Building and Deploying EJBsTo test the EJBs we've just created, let's build and deploy the EJBs to the WebLogic Server and run the client.

Building EJBs consists of compiling the .java files into .class files and packaging them along with the deployment descriptors in a .jar file. This tedious process is made much easier by using Ant, an open source Java build tool from the folks at the Apache Jakarta project. Ant version 1.4 is included along with WebLogic Server 7.0. For more information on Ant, visit http://jakarta.apache.org/ant/.

Cross-Reference   Ant and other helpful tools are described in Appendix B.

All the source code examples from this book are built by using Ant. Ant uses XML-based configuration files — typically named build.xml — as input, so they're easy to read and modify.

Note   You can download the source files and Ant configuration scripts from http://www.wiley.com/compbooks/zuffoletto by following the links on the main page.

Build the EJB JAR file

First, you must build the JAR file to deploy to the server (see Figure 15-5). This JAR file will contain all the EJB components (the classes, interfaces, and deployment descriptors) for the two beans. Running the Ant configuration file named build.xml in the WLSBible\ejb\session\ directory results in the following output.

```
Command Prompt                                              _ □ x
To build the Stateful Session Bean
        ant stateful.build
To run the Stateful Session Client
        ant stateful.client.run

BUILD SUCCESSFUL

Total time: 1 second

H:\WebLogicUserDomains\myCode\src\WLSBible\ejb\session>ant stateless.build
Buildfile: build.xml

stateless.build:

ejb.build:
    [javac] Compiling 8 source files to H:\WebLogicUserDomains\myCode\src\WLSBib
le\ejb\session\stateless
    [ejbjar] building RequestEJB.jar with 10 files

BUILD SUCCESSFUL

Total time: 4 seconds

H:\WebLogicUserDomains\myCode\src\WLSBible\ejb\session>
```

Figure 15-5: Building the EJB JAR file

Deploy the beans to WebLogic Server

Deploying an EJB is simplified in WebLogic Server 7.0. You start out in the WebLogic Server Console by right-clicking on the EJB element and selecting Configure a New EJB, as shown in Figure 15-6.

The next step is telling WebLogic where the jar is that you want to deploy. You can either click the upload it through your browser link in Step 1 (see Figure 15-7), or you can traverse your file system in Step 2 (see Figure 15-7) and then click the select link next to your EJB. That's what we did for RequestEJB.jar.

Figure 15-6: The first step in EJB deployment

Figure 15-7: Locating the EJB that you want to deploy

After selecting your EJB, the console displays a list of available servers in the current domain (Figure 15-8). So far, all you've done is told WebLogic about your EJB—you haven't yet assigned it to a server. Just select a server in the list on the left and then click the right arrow to move it into the list on the right (you can select more than one server if you want to deploy to multiple servers at once). You can leave the default name alone. Then click the Configure and Deploy button, and WebLogic Server will deploy it to the server(s) you've chosen.

Figure 15-8: Assigning an EJB to one or more servers in the domain

Deployment is a multistage process in WebLogic Server 7.0. After you click the Configure and Deploy button, the console will show a temporary screen for a few seconds, informing you that it is currently attempting to deploy your EJB to the server (you'll see a rotating arrow near the top right of the console window). Then the page will automatically refresh, and if all goes well, you'll see that your deployment has succeeded, as shown in Figure 15-9.

Now that the EJB has been deployed, it's time to run the client to show that it works.

Figure 15-9: A successfully deployed EJB

Run the client

Run the client using the Ant script, as shown in Figure 15-10. Ensure that you have run the `\mydomain\setEnv.cmd` (or `setEnv.sh` for Unix) script so that Ant is your `PATH` and `weblogic.jar` in your classpath because this is required to get access to the JNDI tree.

```
Command Prompt - ant stateless.client.run
Total time: 4 seconds

H:\WebLogicUserDomains\myCode\src\WLSBible\ejb\session>ant stateless.client.run
Buildfile: build.xml

stateless.client.run:
    [java] ResearchClient calling remote EJB.
    [java]  Time: Tue Nov 26 18:36:45 CST 2002
    [java] Zeetrade recommends you sell YHOO
    [java] Zeetrade recommends you sell BEAS
    [java] Zeetrade recommends you sell WAG
    [java]
    [java] ResearchClient calling remote EJB.
    [java]  Time: Tue Nov 26 18:36:50 CST 2002
    [java] Zeetrade recommends you buy YHOO
    [java] Zeetrade recommends you buy BEAS
    [java] Zeetrade recommends you hold WAG
    [java]
    [java] ResearchClient calling remote EJB.
    [java]  Time: Tue Nov 26 18:36:55 CST 2002
    [java] Zeetrade recommends you buy YHOO
    [java] Zeetrade recommends you buy BEAS
    [java] Zeetrade recommends you buy WAG
    [java]
```

Figure 15-10: Client running with environment entry set to false, not routing calls to the RequestDataManager EJB

Modify the Deployment Descriptor and Redeploy

Change the environment entry that tells the bean to use the local helper bean `RequestData Manager`. Rebuild your JAR file and redeploy the bean, as shown in Figure 15-11.

Note If you deployed your EJB from the directory you built it in, you may have trouble rebuilding it because WebLogic Server may have a file lock on the jar file. Make sure that you un-deploy and delete the EJB from the console. To delete the EJB, click the EJB node in the console's tree and then click the trashcan icon to the right of the EJB you want to delete.

```
Command Prompt - ant stateless.client.run
Total time: 4 seconds

H:\WebLogicUserDomains\myCode\src\WLSBible\ejb\session>ant stateless.client.run
Buildfile: build.xml

stateless.client.run:
    [java] ResearchClient calling remote EJB.
    [java]  Time: Tue Nov 26 17:45:48 CST 2002
    [java] **Data Retrieved from the local datasource**<Zeeware Internal System
Lookup> YHOO is rated at a Buy
    [java] **Data Retrieved from the local datasource**<Zeeware Internal System
Lookup> BEAS is rated at a Strong Buy
    [java] **Data Retrieved from the local datasource**<Zeeware Internal System
Lookup Failed> No research available for security: WAG
    [java]
    [java] ResearchClient calling remote EJB.
    [java]  Time: Tue Nov 26 17:45:53 CST 2002
    [java] **Data Retrieved from the local datasource**<Zeeware Internal System
Lookup> YHOO is rated at a Buy
    [java] **Data Retrieved from the local datasource**<Zeeware Internal System
Lookup> BEAS is rated at a Strong Buy
    [java] **Data Retrieved from the local datasource**<Zeeware Internal System
Lookup Failed> No research available for security: WAG
    [java]
```

Figure 15-11: Client running with environment entry set to true, routing calls to the RequestDataManager EJB

Stateful EJB example — AnalyzePortfolio

Now that you're familiar with all the components of session beans, let's create a stateful session bean. The AnalyzePortfolio bean, whose remote and home interfaces are given in Listings 15-11 and 15-12, is a stateful session bean to which you can pass holdings and debts. As you add to the bean by invoking addHolding() and addDebt(), the bean will keep track of all client holdings in internal state variables. At any time, a client may ask for a summary of his account, including whether or not he has enough assets to qualify for a gold plan. The minimum assets required to qualify are set in the ejb-jar.xml deployment descriptor of the bean.

Listing 15-11: **AnalyzePortfolioRemote.java**

```java
package com.wiley.wlsbible.ejb.session.stateful;

import java.rmi.*;
import javax.ejb.*;

public interface AnalyzePortfolioRemote extends EJBObject {

  /**
   * Adds a holding.
   */
  public void addHolding(String name, Integer amount) throws
RemoteException;

  /**
   * Adds a debt.
   */
  public void addDebt(String name, Integer amount) throws
RemoteException;

  /**
   * Returns a detailed analysis of the current state.
   */
  public String getAnalysis() throws RemoteException;

  /**
   * Returns true if they have the financial strength to qualify for
   * a gold account.
   */
  public boolean qualifiesForGoldAccount() throws RemoteException;
}
```

Listing 15-12: AnalyzePortfolioHome.java

```
package com.wiley.wlsbible.ejb.session.stateful;

import java.rmi.*;
import javax.ejb.*;

public interface AnalyzePortfolioHome extends EJBHome {
  public AnalyzePortfolioRemote create() throws RemoteException,
CreateException;
}
```

AnalyzePortfolio

Note that you now declare some internal variables to maintain state in the stateful bean. Note that java.util.Hashmap, Integer, and String all implement java.io.serializable, so you're okay for passivation and activation (see Listing 15-13).

Listing 15-13: AnalyzePortfolio.java

```
package com.wiley.wlsbible.ejb.session.stateful;

import java.rmi.*;
import javax.ejb.*;
import java.util.*;

public class AnalyzePortfolio implements SessionBean {
  private SessionContext sessionContext;
  public void ejbCreate() {
  }
  public void ejbRemove() throws RemoteException {
  }
  public void ejbActivate() throws RemoteException {
  }
  public void ejbPassivate() throws RemoteException {
  }
  public void setSessionContext(SessionContext sessionContext) throws
RemoteException {
    this.sessionContext = sessionContext;
  }

  //Internal state variables
  private HashMap holdings = new HashMap();
  private HashMap debts = new HashMap();
```

Continued

Listing 15-13 *(continued)*

```java
/**
 * Adds a holding.
 */
public void addHolding(String name, Integer amount) throws
RemoteException {
    holdings.put(name, amount);
}

/**
 * Adds a debt.
 */
public void addDebt(String name, Integer amount) throws
RemoteException {
    debts.put(name, amount);
}

/**
 * Returns a detailed analysis of the current state.
 */
public String getAnalysis() throws RemoteException {
    StringBuffer sb = new StringBuffer();
    sb.append("**Current Portfolio Analysis**\n");

    sb.append(analyzeMap("Your Holdings", holdings));
    sb.append(analyzeMap("Your Debts", debts));

    sb.append("  Total Cash Value: " + this.getTotalCash());
    sb.append("Currently qualifies for Zeetrade Gold plan: "
      + this.qualifiesForGoldAccount());

    return sb.toString();
}

/**
 * Returns true if they have the financial strength to qualify for
 * a gold account.
 */
public boolean qualifiesForGoldAccount() throws RemoteException {
    if(this.getGoldAccountMinimum() > this.getTotalCash())
        return false;
    else
        return true;
}

/**
 * Checks the deployment descriptor for the minimum amount of
 * total cash is needed to qualify.
 */
```

```java
private int getGoldAccountMinimum() {
  InitialContext ctx = null;
  Integer minimum = new Integer(10000); //10000 for default.

  try {
    ctx = new InitialContext();
    minimum =
(Integer)ctx.lookup("java:comp/env/goldAccountMinimum");
  } catch (Exception e) {
    e.printStackTrace();
  } finally {
    try {
      ctx.close();
    } catch (Exception e) {}
  }
  return minimum.intValue();
}

private int getTotalCash() {
  return getTotalHoldings() - getTotalDebt();
}

private int getTotalHoldings() {
  return calculateTotal(holdings);
}

private int getTotalDebt() {
  return calculateTotal(debts);
}

private int calculateTotal(HashMap map) {
  Iterator iter = map.values().iterator();
  int total = 0;
  Integer tmp = null;
  while(iter.hasNext()) {
    tmp = (Integer)iter.next();
    total += tmp.intValue();
  }
  return total;
}

private String analyzeMap(String name, HashMap map) {
  StringBuffer sb = new StringBuffer();
  sb.append("  **" + name + "**\n");
  Iterator iter = map.keySet().iterator();
  String key = null;
  Integer tmpInt = null;
  int total = 0;
```

Continued

Listing 15-13 *(continued)*

```
    while(iter.hasNext()) {
      key = (String)iter.next();
      tmpInt = (Integer)map.get(key);
      sb.append("     " +key + ": "+ tmpInt.intValue() + "\n");
      total += tmpInt.intValue();
    }
    sb.append("  Total: " + total+ "\n\n");
    return sb.toString();
  }
}
```

ejb-jar.xml

Listing 15-14 shows ejb-jar.xml for AnalyzePortfolio. Note that the session-type property is now *stateful*. Also take notice of the environment entry, in which you're setting the minimum portfolio value to qualify for a gold account.

Listing 15-14: ejb-jar.xml

```
<!DOCTYPE ejb-jar PUBLIC '-//Sun Microsystems, Inc.//DTD Enterprise
JavaBeans 2.0//EN' 'http://java.sun.com/dtd/ejb-jar_2_0.dtd'>

<ejb-jar>
  <enterprise-beans>
    <session>
      <ejb-name>AnalyzePortfolio</ejb-name>
      <home>portfolioanalyzer.AnalyzePortfolioHome</home>
      <remote>portfolioanalyzer.AnalyzePortfolioRemote</remote>
      <ejb-class>portfolioanalyzer.AnalyzePortfolio</ejb-class>
      <session-type>Stateful</session-type>
      <transaction-type>Container</transaction-type>
      <env-entry>
        <env-entry-name>goldAccountMinimum</env-entry-name>
        <env-entry-type>java.lang.Integer</env-entry-type>
        <env-entry-value>15000</env-entry-value>
      </env-entry>
    </session>
  </enterprise-beans>

  <assembly-descriptor>
    <container-transaction>
      <method>
```

```
      <ejb-name>AnalyzePortfolio</ejb-name>
      <method-name>*</method-name>
    </method>
    <trans-attribute>Required</trans-attribute>
  </container-transaction>
</assembly-descriptor>

</ejb-jar>
```

Listing 15-15 shows `weblogic-ejb-jar.xml` for `AnalyzePortfolio`.

Listing 15-15: **weblogic-ejb-jar.xml**

```
<!DOCTYPE weblogic-ejb-jar PUBLIC '-//BEA Systems, Inc.//DTD WebLogic
7.0.0 EJB//EN' 'http://www.bea.com/servers/wls700/dtd/weblogic-ejb-
jar.dtd'>

<weblogic-ejb-jar>
  <weblogic-enterprise-bean>
    <ejb-name>AnalyzePortfolio</ejb-name>
    <stateful-session-descriptor>
      <stateful-session-cache>
        <max-beans-in-cache>1000</max-beans-in-cache>
        <idle-timeout-seconds>600</idle-timeout-seconds>
        <cache-type>NRU</cache-type>
      </stateful-session-cache>

      <lifecycle>
        <passivation-strategy>Default</passivation-strategy>
      </lifecycle>

      <stateful-session-clustering>
      </stateful-session-clustering>

      <allow-concurrent-calls>False</allow-concurrent-calls>
    </stateful-session-descriptor>

    <transaction-descriptor>
      <trans-timeout-seconds>0</trans-timeout-seconds>
    </transaction-descriptor>

    <enable-call-by-reference>True</enable-call-by-reference>
    <jndi-name>AnalyzePortfolio</jndi-name>
  </weblogic-enterprise-bean>
</weblogic-ejb-jar>
```

PortfolioClient

Notice that the bean maintains state by remembering the holdings and debts passed to it. Additionally, because the stateful EJB is tied to this client and not to a free-pool, it's imperative that you call the `remove()` method on your EJB to free it when you're done with it (see Listing 15-16).

Listing 15-16: **PortfolioClient.java**

```
package com.wiley.wlsbible.ejb.session.stateful;

import java.rmi.*;
import java.util.*;
import javax.naming.*;

/**
 * ResearchClient periodically asks server for research.
 */
public class PortfolioClient extends TimerTask implements Runnable {

  public void run() {
    System.out.println("PortfolioClient running:" + new Date());

    try {
      InitialContext ctx = Environment.getInitialContext();

      Object objref = ctx.lookup("AnalyzePortfolio");
      AnalyzePortfolioHome home = (AnalyzePortfolioHome)
javax.rmi.PortableRemoteObject.narrow(objref,
AnalyzePortfolioHome.class);

      AnalyzePortfolioRemote analyzer = home.create();

      //Add some debts and some holdings.
      analyzer.addHolding("BEAS", new Integer(20000));
      analyzer.addHolding("WAG", new Integer(10000));
      analyzer.addHolding("MSFT", new Integer(150));
      analyzer.addDebt("Car Loan", new Integer(20000));
      analyzer.addDebt("Mortgage", new Integer(30000));

      //Ask for first analysis.
      System.out.println(analyzer.getAnalysis());

      //Add a big holding and ask for second analysis.
      analyzer.addHolding("PETS", new Integer(200000));
      System.out.println(analyzer.getAnalysis());

      analyzer.remove();
    }
```

```
    catch(Exception e) {
      e.printStackTrace();
      return ;
     }
  }

  /**
   * Declare a new client and schedule it on a timer.
   */
  public static void main(String [] args) {
    Timer t = new Timer();
    PortfolioClient client = new PortfolioClient();
    //Starting in 5 secs, run every 5 seconds.
    t.schedule(client, 5000, 5000);
  }
}
```

Because the simple client will be running in its own Java Virtual Machine (JVM), it will need to do a little more work to access the InitialContext. This Environment class has a static method getInitialContext() that returns a InitialContext. The Environment class makes assumptions about your WebLogic configuration, including listening ports and URL. You may need to edit the file shown in Listing 15-17 to match your exact WebLogic Server configuration.

Listing 15-17: **Environment.java**

```
package com.wiley.wlsbible.ejb.session.stateful;

import javax.naming.*;
import java.util.*;

public class Environment {

  public final static String
JNDI_FACTORY="weblogic.jndi.WLInitialContextFactory";
  public final static String WEBLOGIC_URL = "t3://localhost:7001";

  public static InitialContext getInitialContext()
   throws NamingException {

    Hashtable env = new Hashtable();
    env.put(Context.INITIAL_CONTEXT_FACTORY, JNDI_FACTORY);
    env.put(Context.PROVIDER_URL, WEBLOGIC_URL);
    return new InitialContext(env);
  }
}
```

Figure 15-12 shows the results of running PortfolioClient. The client makes multiple calls to the stateful session bean AnalyzePortfolio and outputs them via standard out. Notice that the EJB remembers the client's portfolio details from previous method invocations.

```
Command Prompt - ant stateful.client.run
H:\WebLogicUserDomains\myCode\src\WLSBible\ejb\session>ant stateful.client.run
Buildfile: build.xml

stateful.client.run:
     [java] PortfolioClient running:Tue Nov 26 18:42:26 CST 2002
     [java]
     [java]
     [java] **Current Portfolio Analysis**
     [java]  **Your Holdings**
     [java]      BEAS: 20000
     [java]      VRG: 10000
     [java]      MSFT: 150
     [java]  Total: 30150
     [java]
     [java]  **Your Debts**
     [java]      Mortgage: 30000
     [java]      Car Loan: 20000
     [java]  Total: 50000
     [java]
     [java]  Total Cash Value: -19850
     [java] Currently qualifies for Zeetrade Gold plan: false
     [java]
     [java]
     [java] **Current Portfolio Analysis**
     [java]  **Your Holdings**
     [java]      BEAS: 20000
     [java]      VRG: 10000
     [java]      PETS: 200000
     [java]      MSFT: 150
     [java]  Total: 230150
     [java]
     [java]  **Your Debts**
     [java]      Mortgage: 30000
     [java]      Car Loan: 20000
     [java]  Total: 50000
     [java]
     [java]  Total Cash Value: 180150
     [java] Currently qualifies for Zeetrade Gold plan: true
```

Figure 15-12: Running the PortfolioClient

Clustering Session Beans

The WebLogic Server provides failover services for all stateless session bean method calls, but only if the failure occurs between those method calls. That is, if there is a failure during a method call, that method call will not failover to a replica stateless session bean on another server. This default behavior will prevent potential errors in most systems by ensuring that a failure does not cause a unit of work to be accidentally done more than once. WebLogic does allow you to configure this setting in the stateless-bean-methods-are-idempotent property of the weblogic-ejb-jar.xml file. If this property is set to true, the methods are assumed to be repeat-safe and the WebLogic Server will provide failover when a failure occurs during a method call.

With stateful session EJBs, the WebLogic Server provides failover only for stateful EJB lookups. Unlike stateless session EJBs, there is no failover service for method calls to stateful session EJBs unless those stateful session EJBs have been in-memory replicated to another server.

Cross-Reference   For more information on in-memory replication for stateful session EJBs, see Chapter 24.

Programming Transactions in Session BeansIf one or more of your beans is used as part of a larger transaction, and you want those beans to be notified of events about that transaction, you can have your session EJBs implement the javax.ejb.SessionSynronization interface. Using this interface, you can provide necessary functionality or efficiently allocate/deallocate resources in the context of that external transaction. To implement the interface, you must program the following methods:

✦ `public void afterBegin()`: This method will be called on the bean to notify it that a new transaction has started and that it can expect further method invocations in the context of that transaction. You could use this method to obtain necessary resources during the transaction.

✦ `public void beforeCompletion()`: This method will be called on the bean to notify it that the transaction is about to be committed. You could put logic in this method to push any cached data to a database.

✦ `public void afterCompletion(Boolean committed)`: This method will be called on the bean to notify it that the transaction has completed and will pass `true` if the transaction has successfully completed.

✦ Session beans can also manage transaction demarcation themselves using the `javax.transaction.UserTransaction` interface. For information regarding this interface and transactions, see Chapter 6.

Summary

Session EJBs encapsulate business logic and workflow in your WebLogic applications. They do not represent data such as entity beans, but they can manipulate data and interact with entity beans. They are not persisted to disk, and will be lost when the EJB container crashes or the server shuts down. From the bean's client perspective, the bean was obtained by creation through the bean's home interface. The client gets a reference to the bean's home interface through a JNDI lookup.

Stateless session beans do not maintain state between a client's method invocations. They are shared in a pool and never assigned to a particular client. They are the most efficient type of EJB.

Stateful session beans maintain a conversational state with a client, but not a transactional state. They cannot be pooled, but the WebLogic Server does maintain a cache to increase efficiency. The server may choose to passivate these beans, which is the process of serializing a bean to disk to free up memory. Upon the next client invocation, the bean can be deserialized from disk and put back into memory during the process of activation.

✦   ✦   ✦

Developing Entity Beans

Session beans represent business processes. Although they can be used to persist data, they do not represent persistent data. This is the role of entity beans, which may be used to represent things such as orders, products, and employees — things that you want to keep track of across sessions and server crashes.

Entity beans are much more complex than session beans, and a full discussion would have to go into the intricacies of object-relational mapping and transactions, among other things. In this chapter, we provide an overview of basic entity bean development and discuss some WebLogic-specific features relating to them.

Note   Unless otherwise noted, this discussion will deal with the WebLogic 7.0 EJB 2.0 implementation.

Understanding Entity Beans

We'll begin by discussing basic entity bean concepts, including persistence, entity bean types, and the entity bean lifecycle within the EJB container.

Entity beans and persistence

Representing and accessing persistent data in an object-oriented system is always a major effort. Some of the approaches include using something like SQL (in the case of relational databases) or a mapping tool, such as an object-relational mapping tool (again in the case of relational databases). Another approach is to use an object-oriented database (OODBMS), which reduces the impedance of trying to map one paradigm to another. Although this approach has much to offer, most object-oriented systems still use relational databases.

Entity beans offer a uniform way to represent persistent objects in Java. The type of storage in which the persistent entities reside does not matter. In the case of container-managed entities (more on this later), this should make it easier to port from one type of storage to another.

Types of entity beans

Two types of entity beans exist: those with bean-managed persistence (BMP) and those with container-managed persistence (CMP). With BMP entities, the developer codes data access functionality in the bean by using SQL, an O/R mapping tool, or whatever other programmatic tools are available in Java to access the persistent store. With CMP, beans and their attributes are mapped to objects in the persistent store by using deployment descriptors, not code.

The advantage of using BMP is that you have complete control over the persistence. This means that you can use whatever tricks you need to eke out as much performance as you can. Of course, this also means that you have to write and maintain all that code.

The advantage of using CMP is that the container does all the work. All you need to do is populate deployment descriptors with mapping information that tells the container which tables and fields should map to specific entity bean classes and attributes. This mapping was severely limited in EJB 1.1 and earlier, but as you'll see in this chapter many new features were added in EJB 2.0, which is supported by WebLogic Server 7.0.

So which should you choose? There's no simple answer, of course. Considering how little time it takes to set up CMP beans, however, it makes a lot of sense to try CMP first. If you run into limitations or performance problems, nothing says you can't move to BMP.

As you read through this chapter and run the examples, keep in mind how much code the BMP example uses and contrast that with the simplicity of CMP entity beans.

Note   Don't confuse bean- and container-managed persistence with bean- and container-managed transactions. Entity beans, whether BMP or CMP, use container-managed transactions.

Entity bean lifecycle

The lifecycle of an entity bean, like all enterprise beans, is controlled by its container. This allows the container to optimize performance and memory-usage through techniques such as reusing pooled objects and passivating objects. Most servers allow a certain amount of configuration of the object pool. WebLogic, for example, allows you to set bean cache sizes and the number of beans to create on startup.

An entity bean instance is first created through a call to newInstance(), followed by a call to setEntityContext(). It is said to be in the pooled state and is not yet associated with an entity in the persistent store. Thus, you may have an entity bean of type Employee, but this bean will not be associated with any specific employee.

Before the bean instance can be useful, it must be associated with a persistent entity, after which it is said to be in the ready state. This can happen in two ways. The first is when a client calls a create method on the home interface. This results in the container picking an entity instance and calling its ejbCreate() and ejbPostCreate() methods. This results in the creation of a new entity in the persistence store, with which the bean instance is associated.

The second way for a bean instance to enter the ready state is if a business method is called on an entity for which no suitable bean instance currently exists. In this case, the container takes an entity instance and calls its ejbActivate() method followed by its ejbLoad() method. Then it calls the business method.

As an example, suppose that you have configured your Application Server to put three `Employee` bean instances (call them A, B, and C) in the bean pool on startup. They are not associated with actual employees in your database. At this point, the personnel department inputs information on John Smith, who has just joined the company. When the `create()` call comes to the container, it plucks bean instance A from anonymity in the pool and calls its `ejbCreate()` and `ejbPostCreate()` methods. It is now associated with John Smith (or at least his data).

Next, personnel must update data on Sally Johnson, who has just gotten a raise. They do a search that results in a call to a finder method. The finder method itself does not result in the bean being put in the ready state, but when personnel updates the salary, the container chooses bean instance B, calls `ejbActivate()`, and then `ejbLoad()`, followed by the call to the business method, say `setSalary()`. Now A and B are associated with entities in the persistent store, with C in reserve for when another employee needs to be created or have its data updated.

A bean instance in the ready state can transition back to the pooled state if any of three actions take place. First, the container may call `ejbPassivate()`, which disassociates the bean instance from the persistent entity (while maintaining the persistent entity in storage). Second, the container may call `ejbRemove()` as a result of a client `remove()` call, which will remove the entity from persistent storage. Finally, the bean instance may return to the pooled state if the `ejbCreate()`, `ejbPostCreate()`, or `ejbRemove()` method is called from within a transaction that rolls back.

When the instance is back in the pool, the container can assign it to a new persistent entity as before. If it decides it no longer needs the instance, it can remove it from the pool by calling the instance's `unsetEntityContext()` method.

EJB 2.0

This section provides a brief overview of the major features in EJB 2.0 in relation to entity beans.

CMP relationships

The EJB 2.0 spec fills a major void in CMP development with support for relationships. Previously, this could be done only with a nonstandard O/R mapping tool such as TopLink or Cocobase. Now, relationships are specified explicitly in the EJB deployment descriptor (`ejb-jar.xml`). Relationships can be one-to-one, one-to-many, or many-to-many. In addition, relationships can be unidirectional or bidirectional, depending on whether only one or both beans have references to one another.

CMP entities in a relationship must be local to each other and access each other through local interfaces (discussed in the next section). WebLogic 7.0 actually supports both local and remote CMP relationships but, according to the documentation, "relationships in CMP that use remote interfaces should probably not be used in new code."

Local interfaces

EJB 2.0 adds local interfaces, originally intended only for session beans, to entity beans. A local interface exposes methods that can only be called from a client residing in the same

Java virtual machine (including another bean). Local methods calls are, needless to say, quicker and less resource-intensive than remote methods, which involve network calls.

Local interfaces were extended to entity beans to provide support for relationships, especially between beans and fine-grained objects. Previously, it was not efficient to code fine-grained objects as entity beans. If modeling order and line items, for example, it was recommended that you implement the line item as an ordinary Java class, not an entity bean. Otherwise, remote calls between remote order and line item beans would generate too much network traffic. The problem then became how to model the line item. One solution was serialization, but then the line item became a monolithic blob in the database, which was not ideal.

Local interfaces solve the problem by lowering the overhead for fine-grained objects. Now, instead of modeling a line item as a regular object, it's recommended that you model it as an entity bean with all the advantages that go with this. Also, because beans with relationships will generally be accessing each other frequently, all entities with relationships must be local to one another and must access each other through each other's local interfaces.

CMP abstract persistence schema

In EJB 1.1, a CMP entity bean class was a concrete class that specified its fields as instance variables. This has changed in 2.0. Now the entity bean class is an abstract class that specifies abstract getter and setter methods for the persistent fields and relationships declared in its EJB deployment descriptor. The container is responsible for generating the concrete class that implements the abstract entity bean class.

EJB QL

EJB 2.0 also features the introduction of EJB Query Language (EJB QL), an SQL-like language for querying entities and related objects. This serves two functions:

✦ To specify the expressions the container uses to fulfill finder methods. This takes the place of proprietary finder query languages such as WebLogic Query Language (WLQL), which vendors supplied for lack of a standard facility.

✦ To enable developers to express query methods, which are used for queries the bean may use internally. They are not exposed to the client.

EJB QL methods take the following form:

```
select_clause from_clause [where_clause]
```

You will see some EJB QL in the example CMP beans. For more information on EJB QL, visit Sun's J2EE tutorial at the following location:

```
http://java.sun.com/j2ee/tutorial/1_3-fcs/doc/EJBQL.html
```

Entity Bean Component Files

As with session beans, entity beans are composed of both Java classes and deployment descriptors. Chapter 14 explains the various remote, local, and home interfaces that apply to all EJBs. Entity beans have an additional requirement for a *primary key class* and *finder methods* that live in the home interface and return one or more bean instances matching search criteria given by clients.

Every entity bean must have a primary key class. This may be specific to that entity bean type, but doesn't have to be. Any class that is a legal `Value` type in RMI-IIOP will do, and different entity bean types may have the same primary key. The primary key must implement `java.io.Serializable`. A custom primary key class is needed for a compound primary key (consisting of more than one data field), whereas an ordinary Java type such as `String` or `Integer` may be used when the key has only one data field.

A finder method called `findByPrimaryKey()`, which takes a primary key class instance as an input parameter, is also required. This method allows clients to retrieve specific existing data elements. You can optionally write additional finder methods that return individual bean instances, similar to the `findByPrimaryKey()` method or collections of instances. You can write any number of finder methods to match the needs of your application.

CMP entity beans also require an additional deployment descriptor: `weblogic-cmp-rdbms-jar.xml`. The name and content of this descriptor depend on the persistence-mapping framework being used, and this can be configured in the WebLogic deployment descriptor.

Programming BMP

In this section, we describe the steps needed to implement a BMP entity bean. As an example, we use a `Student` entity, perhaps part of an online learning system.

Define the home interface

As with session beans, the home interface of an entity bean contains factory methods for obtaining beans. Two types of methods exist: creation methods and finder methods, as discussed in the following sections.

Creation methods

Creation methods take the following form where `<args>` are arguments:

```
public void create(<args>)
   throws CreateException, Remote Exception;
```

As with session beans, the create method corresponds to an `ejbCreate()` method in the bean class (along with an `ejbPostCreate()` method to be discussed later). In the example, you have one create method that takes a value object as a parameter.

```
public Student create(StudentVO student)
   throws CreateException, RemoteException;
```

Finder methods

Finder methods are used to retrieve existing objects from persistent storage. They are analogous to database queries. There must always be a finder method called `findByPrimaryKey(<arg>)`, which takes the entity's primary key class as an argument. The example has two custom finders:

```
public Student findBySSNum(String ssNum)
   throws FinderException, RemoteException;

public Collection findByLastName(String lastName)
   throws FinderException, RemoteException;
```

The first returns an instance of the remote interface—in this case, an instance of Student. The second finder can potentially return more than one object. In this case, the return type must be specified as a Collection (this has changed since 1.1, when an Enumeration was also allowed).

The complete remote home interface is as follows:

```
package com.wiley.wlsbible.ejb.entity.bmp;

import javax.ejb.*;
import java.rmi.RemoteException;
import java.util.Collection;

public interface StudentHome extends EJBHome
{
  public Student create(StudentVO student)
    throws CreateException, RemoteException;

  public Student findByPrimaryKey(StudentPK key)
    throws FinderException, RemoteException;

  public Student findBySSNum(String ssNum)
    throws FinderException, RemoteException;

  public Collection findByLastName(String lastName)
    throws FinderException, RemoteException;
}
```

Define the local home interface

You'll see examples of local home interface in the CMP example, but the Student entity does not have one.

Define the remote interface

The entity's remote interface is used to define business methods accessible by remote callers. These can be a variety of things, but because entity beans deal with state, you will usually have methods for accessing state.

One way to expose the state of an entity bean via a remote interface is to have getter and setter methods for each attribute. The disadvantage of getters and setters for each attribute is that it can result in many fine-grained calls from a client. Although this is okay for a regular Java object, one must remember that entity beans are remote objects, and remote method calls are expensive. For this reason, value objects are often used to aggregate state and effectively batch remote calls, as explained in Chapter 3. The example bean has both fine-grained methods and value object methods.

The complete remote interface is as follows:

```
package com.wiley.wlsbible.ejb.entity.bmp;

import javax.ejb.EJBObject;
import java.rmi.RemoteException;
```

```
public interface Student extends EJBObject
{
  public String getFirstName() throws RemoteException;

  public void setFirstName(String firstName)
    throws RemoteException;

  public String getLastName() throws RemoteException;

  public void setLastName(String lastName)
    throws RemoteException;

  public String getEMailAddr() throws RemoteException;

  public void setEMailAddr(String eMailAddr)
    throws RemoteException;

  public String getPhone() throws RemoteException;

  public void setPhone(String phone) throws RemoteException;

  public String getSSNum() throws RemoteException;

  public void setSSNum(String ssNum) throws RemoteException;

  public void setStudentData(StudentVO student)
    throws RemoteException;

  public StudentVO getStudentData() throws RemoteException;
}
```

Define the local interface

The example bean will not define a local interface. Instead, we will demonstrate the use of a local interface in the CMP example.

Create the bean

The bean file contains the code to persist entity state. The developer must code both call-back methods and any bean business methods.

The ejbCreate() methods

The bean class must contain an `ejbCreate()` method for each `create()` method on the remote interface (the argument list must be the same).

In the `ejbCreate()` method, you typically set bean attributes and then manually persist the bean. If using SQL, this will involve an `INSERT` statement. As with any `INSERT` statement, all constraints, such as field uniqueness and nullability, must be respected, or else an exception will be thrown.

The `ejbCreate()` method returns an instance of the entity's primary key class. Note that this differs from the home interface `create()` method, which returns an instance of the remote interface.

The ejbPostCreate() methods

Each `ejbCreate()` method has a corresponding `ejbPostCreate()` method, which is called after `ejbCreate()`. The `ejbPostCreate()` method differs from `ejbCreate()` in that the entity's object identity is available. This allows a reference to a remote interface instance to be passed during the creation process, as shown in the following code:

```
EntityContext context;
...
public void ejbPostCreate(StudentVO) {
    Student thisStudent = (Student) context.getEJBObject();
    SchoolEJB schoolEJB = getSchoolEJB();
    schoolEJB.addStudent(thisStudent);
}
```

The ejbLoad() method

The `ejbLoad()` method is called to synchronize the bean's state with the persistent store. Generally, it's called whenever a new transaction involving the entity begins, but may be configurable depending on the application server.

When using SQL and JDBC, `ejbLoad()` generally involves executing a SELECT statement and setting entity attributes based on the values returned in the ResultSet.

The ejbStore() method

This method is called to update the persistent store with the entity's current state. It's generally called at transaction commit, but may be configurable based on the application server. When using SQL, this involves an UPDATE statement.

The ejbRemove() method

The `ejbRemove()` method gets called by a client to remove an entity from persistent storage. With SQL, this involves a DELETE statement.

Finder methods

Finder methods are used by the container to service calls to the finder methods on the entity's home interface. Each `findBy<someCriteria>(<args>)` in the home interface will have a corresponding `ejbFindBy<someCriteria>(<args>)` with matching parameters. Note that finders returning a single object do not return an instance of the remote interface, but an instance of the primary key. This is used by the container to get the instance of the remote interface that is returned to the client. Finders returning collections are similar—the finder returns a collection of primary key instances that the container uses to return a collection of remote interface instances.

The ejbActivate() and ejbPassivate() methods

These methods serve the same purpose as in stateful session beans. The `ejbActivate()` method should be used to initialize any resources (such as socket connections) needed by the bean before being activated, whereas `ejbPassivate()` should be used to release these resources on passivation.

Business methods

Business methods correspond to methods in the entity's remote interface. In your case, these are getter and setters for the entity's attributes and for StudentVO, its value object.

Note that the setStudentData() method does not set the primary key field (ID). According to the EJB 2.0 spec, the primary key field should not be reset. This suggests that any field that may change, even if unique, should not be used as a primary key. You might, for example, have a UserProfile bean with a userName field. You might require this to be unique, but allow users to change it. If so, you should not use this field as a primary key. One commonly used technique is to have a separate field whose sole purpose is to serve as a primary key and generate unique primary keys. This is the purpose of the ID field in the Student entity.

The complete bean class is given in Listing 16-1.

Listing 16-1: StudentEJB.java

```java
package com.wiley.wlsbible.ejb.entity.bmp;

import javax.ejb.*;
import java.sql.*;
import javax.sql.DataSource;
import javax.naming.InitialContext;
import java.util.Collection;
import java.util.Vector;

public class StudentEJB implements EntityBean
{
  private EntityContext context;
  private static final String DATASOURCE
    = "java:comp/env/jdbc/connectionPool";

  public String id;
  public String firstName;
  public String lastName;
  public String eMailAddr;
  public String phone;
  public String ssNum;


  public void setEntityContext(EntityContext ec) {
    context = ec;
  }

  public void unsetEntityContext() {
    this.context = null;
  }

  public StudentPK ejbCreate(StudentVO student)
      throws CreateException
  {
    this.id = student.getId();
    setStudentData(student);

    Connection con = null;
```

Continued

Listing 16-1 *(continued)*

```java
    PreparedStatement ps = null;
    StudentPK key = null;
    try {
      con = getConnection();
      ps = con.prepareStatement("insert into STUDENT (ID,
                FIRST_NAME, LAST_NAME, EMAIL_ADDR, PHONE,
                SSNUM) values (?, ?, ?, ?, ?, ?)");
      ps.setString(1, id);
      ps.setString(2, firstName);
      ps.setString(3, lastName);
      ps.setString(4, eMailAddr);
      ps.setString(5, phone);
      ps.setString(6, ssNum);
      int ret = ps.executeUpdate();
      if (ret != 1) {
        throw new CreateException("Create failed");
      }
      key = new StudentPK();
      key.id = id;
      return key;
    }
    catch (Exception e) {
      throw new CreateException(e.getMessage());
    }
    finally {
      cleanup(con, ps);
    }
  }

  public void ejbPostCreate(StudentVO student) {
  }

  public void ejbLoad()
  {
    StudentPK key = (StudentPK)context.getPrimaryKey();

    try {
      readData(key);
    }
    catch(Exception e) {
      throw new EJBException(e.getMessage());
    }
  }

  public void ejbStore()
  {
    Connection con = null;
    PreparedStatement ps = null;
```

```
      try {
        con = getConnection();
        StudentPK key =
          (StudentPK)context.getPrimaryKey();

        ps = con.prepareStatement("update STUDENT set
                FIRST_NAME = ?,LAST_NAME = ?,EMAIL_ADDR = ?,
                PHONE = ?,SSNUM = ? where ID = ?");
        ps.setString(1, firstName);
        ps.setString(2, lastName);
        ps.setString(3, eMailAddr);
        ps.setString(4, phone);
        ps.setString(5, ssNum);
        ps.setString(6, key.id);
        int ret = ps.executeUpdate();
        if (ret == 0) {
          throw new EJBException("ejbStore failed");
        }
      }
      catch (Exception e) {
        throw new EJBException(e.getMessage());
      }
      finally {
        cleanup(con, ps);
      }
    }

    public void ejbRemove() throws RemoveException
    {
      Connection con = null;
      PreparedStatement ps = null;
      try {
        con = getConnection();
        StudentPK key =
            (StudentPK) context.getPrimaryKey();

        ps = con.prepareStatement("delete from STUDENT where
                ID=?");
        ps.setString(1, key.id);
        int result = ps.executeUpdate();
        if (result == 0) {
          throw new RemoveException("Remove failed");
        }
      }
      catch (Exception e) {
        throw new RemoveException(e.getMessage());
      }
      finally {
        cleanup(con, ps);
      }
    }
```

Continued

Listing 16-1 *(continued)*

```java
public void ejbActivate() {
}

public void ejbPassivate() {
}

public StudentPK ejbFindByPrimaryKey(StudentPK key)
    throws FinderException
{
  try {
    readData(key);
    return key;
  }
  catch (Exception e) {
    throw new FinderException(e.getMessage());
  }
}

public StudentPK ejbFindBySSNum(String ssNum)
  throws FinderException
{
  Connection con = null;
  PreparedStatement ps = null;
  try {
    con = getConnection();
    ps = con.prepareStatement("select ID, FIRST_NAME,
            LAST_NAME,EMAIL_ADDR,PHONE,SSNUM from STUDENT
            where SSNUM = ?");
    ps.setString(1, ssNum);
    ResultSet rs = ps.executeQuery();
    if (!rs.next()) {
      throw new FinderException("Record not found");
    }
    else {
      loadAttributes(rs);
    }
    rs.close();
    StudentPK key = new StudentPK();
    key.id = id;
    return key;
  }
  catch (Exception e) {
    throw new EJBException(e.getMessage());
  }
  finally {
    cleanup(con, ps);
  }
}
```

```
public Collection ejbFindByLastName(String lastName)
  throws FinderException
{
  Connection con = null;
  PreparedStatement ps = null;
  try {
    con = getConnection();
    ps = con.prepareStatement("select ID from STUDENT where
            LAST_NAME = ?");
    ps.setString(1, lastName);
    ResultSet rs = ps.executeQuery();
    Vector students = new Vector();
    StudentPK key = null;
    while (rs.next()) {
      key = new StudentPK();
      key.id = rs.getString(1);
      students.addElement(key);
    }
    rs.close();
    return students;
  }
  catch (Exception e) {
    throw new FinderException(e.getMessage());
  }
  finally {
    cleanup(con, ps);
  }
}

private void loadAttributes(ResultSet rs)
    throws SQLException
{
  id = rs.getString(1);
  firstName = rs.getString(2);
  lastName = rs.getString(3);
  eMailAddr = rs.getString(4);
  phone = rs.getString(5);
  ssNum = rs.getString(6);
}

private void cleanup(Connection con, PreparedStatement ps)
{
  try {
    if (ps != null) {
      ps.close();
    }
    if (con != null) {
      con.close();
    }
  }
```

Continued

Listing 16-1 *(continued)*

```
    catch (Exception e) {
      throw new EJBException (e);
    }
  }

  public StudentVO getStudentData()
  {
    StudentVO student = new StudentVO();
    student.setFirstName(firstName);
    student.setLastName(lastName);
    student.setPhone(phone);
    student.setEMailAddr(eMailAddr);
    student.setSSNum(ssNum);
    return student;
  }

  public void setStudentData(StudentVO student)
  {
    firstName = student.getFirstName();
    lastName = student.getLastName();
    eMailAddr = student.getEMailAddr();
    phone = student.getPhone();
    ssNum = student.getSSNum();
  }

  public String getFirstName() {
    return(firstName);
  }

  public void setFirstName(String firstName) {
    this.firstName = firstName;
  }

  public String getLastName() {
    return lastName;
  }

  public void setLastName(String lastName) {
    this.lastName = lastName;
  }

  public String getEMailAddr() {
    return eMailAddr;
  }

  public void setEMailAddr(String eMailAddr) {
    this.eMailAddr = eMailAddr;
  }
```

```java
public String getPhone() {
  return phone;
}

public void setPhone(String phone) {
  this.phone = phone;
}

public String getSSNum() {
  return ssNum;
}

public void setSSNum(String ssNum) {
  this.ssNum = ssNum;
}

private Connection getConnection() throws EJBException
{
  try {
    InitialContext ic = new InitialContext();
    DataSource ds = (DataSource)ic.lookup(DATASOURCE);
    return ds.getConnection();
  }
  catch (Exception e) {
    throw new EJBException(e.getMessage());
  }
}

private void readData(StudentPK key) throws
      FinderException, EJBException
{
  Connection con = null;
  PreparedStatement ps = null;
  try {
    con = getConnection();
    ps = con.prepareStatement("select ID, FIRST_NAME,
            LAST_NAME,EMAIL_ADDR,PHONE,SSNUM from STUDENT
            where ID = ?");
    ps.setString(1, key.id);
    ResultSet rs = ps.executeQuery();
    if (!rs.next()) {
      throw new FinderException("Record not found");
    }
    else {
      loadAttributes(rs);
    }
    rs.close();
  }
  catch (Exception e){
    throw new EJBException(e.getMessage());
  }
```

Continued

Listing 16-1 *(continued)*

```
      finally {
        cleanup(con, ps);
      }
   }
}
```

Create the primary key class (optional)

Entities must have a primary key class, which is used to find a unique entity. The primary key class may be a special-purpose class (required if the key has multiple fields) or an ordinary Java class such as `String` or `Integer`.

If constructing a specific primary key class, the class must have a public no-argument constructor. The fields in the primary key class must be public and must be some subset of the attributes of the bean (every primary key class field must have the same name as that of a field of the bean).

Though not strictly necessary, the example bean uses a custom primary key class, which is given in Listing 16-2.

Listing 16-2: Student primary key class

```
package com.wiley.wlsbible.ejb.entity.bmp;

import java.io.Serializable;

public class StudentPK implements Serializable
{
  public String id;

  public int hashCode() {
    return id.hashCode();
  }

  public boolean equals(Object that)
  {
    if (that == null || !(that instanceof StudentPK))
      return false;

    String otherId = ((StudentPK) that).id;
    return id.equals(otherId);
  }
}
```

Create value object class (optional)

As mentioned, the Student class uses a value object to minimize network calls. The value object contains attributes corresponding to the fields of the entity. As the value object is passed over the wire, it must implement java.io.Serializable. Listing 16-3 shows a value object implementation for the Student class.

Listing 16-3: Value object for the Student class

```
package com.wiley.wlsbible.ejb.entity.bmp;

public class StudentVO implements java.io.Serializable
{
  private String id;
  private String firstName;
  private String lastName;
  private String eMailAddr;
  private String phone;
  private String ssNum;

  public StudentVO() {
  }

  public String getId() {
    return id;
  }

  public void setId(String id) {
    this.id = id;
  }

  public String getFirstName() {
    return firstName;
  }

  public void setFirstName(String firstName) {
    this.firstName = firstName;
  }

  public String getLastName() {
    return lastName;
  }

  public void setLastName(String lastName) {
    this.lastName = lastName;
  }

  public String getEMailAddr() {
    return eMailAddr;
```

Continued

Listing 16-3 *(continued)*

```
    }

    public void setEMailAddr(String eMailAddr) {
      this.eMailAddr = eMailAddr;
    }

    public String getPhone() {
      return phone;
    }

    public void setPhone(String phone) {
      this.phone = phone;
    }

    public String getSSNum() {
      return ssNum;
    }

    public void setSSNum(String ssNum) {
      this.ssNum = ssNum;
    }
  }
```

Create the deployment descriptors

As with all EJBs, BMP entities have an EJB deployment descriptor. BMP beans developed with WebLogic will also have a WebLogic deployment descriptor. We'll discuss the properties in each relevant to BMP entities.

The EJB deployment descriptor (ejb-jar.xml)

The following sections discuss the properties specific to entity beans.

<persistence-type>

For BMP, this is set to Bean.

<prim-key-class>

This is the bean's primary key class. In your case, it's the fully qualified class name of the custom class you developed.

<reentrant>

This indicates whether the bean is reentrant or not. *Reentrant* means that a thread can enter the bean more than once within a method call. In a loopback call, for example, bean A may call bean B, which then calls bean A again.

Whenever possible, loopback calls should be avoided and <reentrant> should be set to false. This is because it's difficult for containers to distinguish loopback calls from calls from other threads, which are illegal and, as the specification warns, it may lead to unpredictable results.

<resource-ref>

The <resource-ref> element is not specific to entity beans, but this element is where you specify the DataSource for use within the bean. This, in turn, is mapped to a connection factory supplied by the container using container-specific mappings.

The complete EJB deployment descriptor for the Student bean is as follows:

```
<?xml version="1.0"?>

<!DOCTYPE ejb-jar PUBLIC '-//Sun Microsystems, Inc.//DTD Enterprise
JavaBeans 2.0//EN' 'http://java.sun.com/dtd/ejb-jar_2_0.dtd'>

<ejb-jar>
  <enterprise-beans>
    <entity>
      <ejb-name>Student</ejb-name>
      <home> com.wiley.wlsbible.ejb.entity.bmp.StudentHome</home>
      <remote> com.wiley.wlsbible.ejb.entity.bmp.Student</remote>
      <ejb-class> com.wiley.wlsbible.ejb.entity.bmp.StudentEJB</ejb-
class>
      <persistence-type>Bean</persistence-type>
      <prim-key-class>
com.wiley.wlsbible.ejb.entity.bmp.StudentPK
      </prim-key-class>
      <reentrant>False</reentrant>
      <resource-ref>
        <res-ref-name>jdbc/connectionPool</res-ref-name>
        <res-type>javax.sql.DataSource</res-type>
        <res-auth>Container</res-auth>
      </resource-ref>
    </entity>
</enterprise-beans>

<assembly-descriptor>
  <container-transaction>
    <method>
      <ejb-name>Student</ejb-name>
      <method-intf>Remote</method-intf>
      <method-name>*</method-name>
    </method>
    <trans-attribute>Required</trans-attribute>
  </container-transaction>
</assembly-descriptor>
</ejb-jar>
```

The WebLogic deployment descriptor (weblogic-jar.xml)

The weblogic-ejb-jar.xml file contains WebLogic-specific deployment settings.

The <reference-descriptor> element is what WebLogic uses to map a connection pool to the DataSource required by your bean in the EJB deployment descriptor. The <resource-descriptor> corresponds to a <res-ref-name> in the EJB deployment descriptor, whereas the <jndi-name> is used to look up a connection pool set up in a WebLogic Server instance by an administrator.

The complete WebLogic deployment descriptor is as follows:

```
<?xml version="1.0"?>

<!DOCTYPE weblogic-ejb-jar PUBLIC '-//BEA Systems, Inc.//DTD WebLogic
7.0.0 EJB//EN' 'http://www.bea.com/servers/wls700/dtd/weblogic-ejb-
jar.dtd'>
<weblogic-ejb-jar>
  <weblogic-enterprise-bean>
    <ejb-name>Student</ejb-name>
    <reference-descriptor>
      <resource-description>
        <res-ref-name>
          jdbc/connectionPool
        </res-ref-name>
        <jndi-name>
          OraclePool
        </jndi-name>
      </resource-description>
    </reference-descriptor>

    <jndi-name> com.wiley.wlsbible.ejb.entity.bmp.Student</jndi-name>
  </weblogic-enterprise-bean>
</weblogic-ejb-jar>
```

Database table

To run this example, you need to create a table on your database. You can use the following:

```
CREATE TABLE STUDENT
  (
      ID VARCHAR(50) NOT NULL,
      LAST_NAME VARCHAR(50) NOT NULL,
      FIRST_NAME VARCHAR(50) ,
      EMAIL_ADDR VARCHAR(50) ,
      PHONE VARCHAR(20) ,
      SSNUM VARCHAR(50)
  )
```

In practice, it is a good idea to define indexes on columns used by the finder methods in your EJBs. In this case, you (or your DBA) would create indexes on ID, LAST_NAME, and SSNUM to improve the performance of the EJB's finder methods.

Notes

In the example, you used straight SQL to persist your entity to a relational database. If using another type of persistent store, you would use whatever persistent layer that store had available in Java.

Also, an RBDMS does not limit you to SQL. Within your BMP entity, you can also use any technique available to a regular Java program, such as SQLJ or an O/R mapping tool.

Programming CMP

In this section, we show you how to program CMP beans. As you will see, there is a lot less coding, but a lot more configuration than BMP beans.

In order to demonstrate relationships (and local interfaces), you will develop two beans: Department and Course. Department will encapsulate information about departments at your online educational institution, whereas Course will represent the courses offered. Department will be in a one-to-many relationship with Course. Course will not expose a remote interface, but will instead use Department as a façade for remote access.

We'll discuss the bean classes of Department and Course separately and then look at the deployment descriptors.

Create the Department bean

For the Department bean, we will implement remote home and remote interfaces, local home and local interfaces, and an abstract bean class. We will also write a value object (optional) for the bean.

Define the remote home interface

Your remote home interface will have a create method that takes a value object. In addition, it will have two custom finder methods: findAll(), which returns a collection, and findByName(), which returns the bean's remote interface.

The remote interface is as follows:

```
package com.wiley.wlsbible.ejb.entity.cmp;

import java.util.Collection;
import java.rmi.RemoteException;
import javax.ejb.CreateException;
import javax.ejb.EJBHome;
import javax.ejb.FinderException;

public interface DepartmentRemoteHome extends EJBHome
{

  public DepartmentRemote create(DepartmentVO Department)
    throws CreateException, RemoteException;

  public DepartmentRemote findByPrimaryKey(Integer
      primaryKey) throws FinderException, RemoteException;

  public Collection findAll()
    throws FinderException, RemoteException;

  public DepartmentRemote findByName(java.lang.String name)
    throws FinderException, RemoteException;
}
```

Define the remote interface

You have dispensed with individual field access methods in this interface and instead will rely on value objects to retrieve and update Department fields. This is a design decision that will depend on your application's needs. You will also allow callers to add courses and retrieve course data from a Department through value objects.

The remote interface is as follows:

```
package com.wiley.wlsbible.ejb.entity.cmp;

import java.rmi.RemoteException;
import javax.ejb.*;
import javax.naming.*;

public interface DepartmentRemote extends EJBObject
{
  public DepartmentVO getDepartmentData()
    throws RemoteException;

  public void setDepartmentData(DepartmentVO dept)
    throws RemoteException;

  public void addCourse(CourseVO courseData)
    throws NamingException, CreateException, RemoteException;

  public CourseVO[] getAllCourses() throws RemoteException;
}
```

Define the local home interface

According to the EJB 2.0 spec, beans must refer to each other through their local interfaces. Because the Course beans will reference Department beans, the Department bean must have a local and local home interface. The latter must have a findByPrimaryKey() method, which is the only method you will need.

The local home interface is as follows:

```
package com.wiley.wlsbible.ejb.entity.cmp;

import javax.ejb.*;

public interface DepartmentLocalHome extends EJBLocalHome
{
  public DepartmentLocal findByPrimaryKey(Integer primaryKey)
    throws FinderException;
}
```

Define the local interface

As noted, this interface exists so that the Course bean can reference the Department bean. It doesn't have any methods.

The local interface is as follows:

```
package com.wiley.wlsbible.ejb.entity.cmp;

import javax.ejb.*;

public interface DepartmentLocal extends EJBLocalObject
{
}
```

Create the abstract bean class

Unlike BMP, the bean developer does not write the actual bean class used by the container. Instead, the developer writes an abstract bean class, for which the container generates a concrete class based on the bean's abstract persistence schema.

Specify abstract methods for persistent fields and relationships

Persistent fields and relationships are not declared or implemented in the bean class. Instead, abstract getter and setter methods are *declared* in the bean class, but these methods are *implemented* in the concrete class generated by the container at deployment. The abstract getter and setter methods must be named to correspond to fields specified in the deployment descriptor. In the deployment descriptor, the field name must be lowercase. In the bean class, the method names will be get and set followed by the field name with the first letter capitalized. The pattern should be familiar — if the field were name, for example, the methods would be declared as getName() and setName().

The ejbCreate() methods

In your sole ejbCreate() method, you call the setDepartmentData() method, which uses the abstract set methods (actually only one in our case) to set persistent fields. Note also that you're not setting the ID field — you'll see why shortly.

The ejbPostCreate() methods

Nothing is needed here.

Business methods

In addition to a getter and setter, you have two methods relating to Course: addCourse() and getAllCourses(). addCourse() finds Course's local home interface through its local JNDI name, which is defined in the WebLogic deployment descriptor.

```
public void addCourse(CourseVO courseData)
    throws NamingException, CreateException
{
  Context ctx = new InitialContext();
  CourseLocalHome courseHome = (CourseLocalHome)
  ctx.lookup("cmp.Course");
  CourseLocal course = courseHome.create(courseData);
      getCourses().add(course);
}
```

The getAllCourses() method obtains a Collection of Courses by using the getCourses() method, which is abstract in the bean class and implemented in the concrete class generated by the container. It iterates over the returned collection and creates an array of value objects.

```
public CourseVO[] getAllCourses()
{
  Collection courses = getCourses();
  CourseVO[] courseArray = new CourseVO[courses.size()];
  Iterator courseIterator = courses.iterator();
  for (int i=0; courseIterator.hasNext(); i++) {
    CourseLocal course = (CourseLocal) courseIterator.next();
    courseArray[i] = course.getCourseData();
  }

  return courseArray;
}
```

That's it for code. The other methods, `ejbLoad`, `ejbStore`, and `ejbRemove` are left blank and handled by the container. Finder methods will be configured in the EJB deployment descriptor using EJB QL.

The complete bean class is given in Listing 16-4.

Listing 16-4: **DepartmentEJB.java**

```
Package com.wiley.wlsbible.ejb.entity.cmp;

import java.util.*;
import javax.ejb.*;
import javax.naming.*;

abstract public class DepartmentEJB implements EntityBean
{
  private EntityContext ctx;

  public void setEntityContext(EntityContext ctx) {
    this.ctx = ctx;
  }

  public void unsetEntityContext() {
    this.ctx = null;
  }

  abstract public Integer getId();
  abstract public void setId(Integer id);

  abstract public String getName();
  abstract public void setName(String val);

  abstract public Collection getCourses();
  abstract public void setCourses(Collection courses);


  public void ejbActivate() {
```

```
}

public void ejbPassivate() {
}

public void ejbLoad() {
}

public void ejbStore() {
}

public void ejbRemove() throws RemoveException
{
}

public Integer ejbCreate(DepartmentVO dept)
  throws CreateException
{
  setDepartmentData(dept);
  return null;
}

public void ejbPostCreate(DepartmentVO dept)
  throws CreateException
{
}

public void addCourse(CourseVO courseData)
    throws NamingException, CreateException
{
  Context ctx = new InitialContext();
  CourseLocalHome courseHome = (CourseLocalHome)
  ctx.lookup("cmp.Course");
  CourseLocal course = courseHome.create(courseData);
      getCourses().add(course);
}

public CourseVO[] getAllCourses()
{
  Collection courses = getCourses();
  CourseVO[] courseArray = new CourseVO[courses.size()];
  Iterator courseIterator = courses.iterator();
  for (int i=0; courseIterator.hasNext(); i++) {
    CourseLocal course = (CourseLocal)
        courseIterator.next();
    courseArray[i] = course.getCourseData();
  }

  return courseArray;
}
```

Continued

Listing 16-4 *(continued)*

```
public DepartmentVO getDepartmentData()
{
  DepartmentVO dept = new DepartmentVO(this.getId());
  dept.setName(this.getName());
  return dept;
}

public void setDepartmentData(DepartmentVO dept) {
  setName(dept.getName());
}
}
```

Create the value object (optional)

The Department value object has two constructors: a default constructor and one that takes an Integer and sets the ID field. The latter is so that the bean can set the ID when returning DepartmentVO objects for existing beans. You don't have a setId() method to emphasize the fact that clients will not set the ID field. Client programmers should be made aware of this fact through documentation or other means.

The Department class value object is given in Listing 16-5.

Listing 16-5: Value object for the Department class

```
public class DepartmentVO implements java.io.Serializable
{
  private Integer id;
  private String name;

  public DepartmentVO() {
  }

  public DepartmentVO(Integer id) {
    this.id = id;
  }

  public Integer getId() {
    return id;
  }

  public void setName(String name) {
    this.name = name;
  }

  public String getName() {
```

```
      return name;
   }
}
```

Define the Course bean

For the Course bean, we will implement local home and local interfaces and an abstract bean class. We will also write a value object (optional) for the bean.

Define the local home interface

Because your Course bean is in a relationship, it must be accessible through a local home interface. You will have one create method, which takes a value object in addition to the required findByPrimaryKey. Both methods return a reference to Course's local interface.

```
package com.wiley.wlsbible.ejb.entity.cmp;

import javax.ejb.*;

public interface CourseLocalHome extends EJBLocalHome
{
   public CourseLocal create(CourseVO course)
     throws CreateException;

   public CourseLocal findByPrimaryKey(Integer primaryKey)
     throws FinderException;
}
```

Define the local interfaces

Your local interface will include methods for accessing Course data and establishing the relationship with a Department bean.

The local interface is as follows:

```
package com.wiley.wlsbible.ejb.entity.cmp;

import javax.ejb.*;

public interface CourseLocal extends EJBLocalObject
{
   public CourseVO getCourseData();
   public void setCourseData(CourseVO course);

   public void setDepartment(DepartmentLocal dept);
   public DepartmentLocal getDepartment();
}
```

Create the abstract bean class

Creating the abstract bean class requires a few simple steps, as discussed in the following sections.

Specify abstract methods for persistent fields and relationships

You specify the abstract getters and setters for persistent fields and your reference to Department.

ejbCreate method

As with Department, you pass in a value object and let WebLogic set the ID field.

ejbPostCreate methods

You don't need to do anything special here.

Business methods

There's nothing new here. You have a getter and setter by using value objects.

The complete Course bean is given in Listing 16-6.

Listing 16-6: CourseEJB.java

```
package com.wiley.wlsbible.ejb.entity.cmp;

import java.io.Serializable;
import java.util.*;

import javax.ejb.*;
import javax.naming.InitialContext;
import javax.naming.NamingException;
import javax.sql.DataSource;

abstract public class CourseEJB implements EntityBean
{
  private EntityContext ctx;

  public void setEntityContext(EntityContext ctx) {
    this.ctx = ctx;
  }

  public void unsetEntityContext() {
    this.ctx = null;
  }

  abstract public Integer getId();
  abstract public void setId(Integer id);

  abstract public String getName();
  abstract public void setName(String name);

  abstract public double getCredits();
  abstract public void setCredits(double credits);

  abstract public void setDepartment(DepartmentLocal dept);
  abstract public DepartmentLocal getDepartment();
```

```
    public void ejbActivate() {
    }

    public void ejbPassivate() {
    }

    public void ejbLoad() {
    }

    public void ejbStore() {
    }

    public void ejbRemove()
      throws RemoveException {
    }

    public Integer ejbCreate(CourseVO course)
      throws CreateException
    {
      setCourseData(course);
      return null;
    }

    public void ejbPostCreate(CourseVO course) {
    }

    public CourseVO getCourseData()
    {
      CourseVO course = new CourseVO(this.getId());
      course.setName(this.getName());
      course.setCredits(this.getCredits());
      return course;
    }

    public void setCourseData(CourseVO course)
    {
      setName(course.getName());
      setCredits(course.getCredits());
    }

  }
```

Create the value object (optional)

The CourseVO value object, which is similar to the DepartmentVO value object, is given in
Listing 16-7.

Listing 16-7: Value object for the Course class

```
package com.wiley.wlsbible.ejb.entity.cmp;

public class CourseVO implements java.io.Serializable
{
  private Integer id;
  private String name;
  private double credits;

  public CourseVO() {
  }

  public CourseVO(Integer id) {
    this.id = id;
  }

  public Integer getId() {
    return id;
  }

  public void setName(String name) {
    this.name = name;
  }

  public String getName() {
    return name;
  }

  public void setCredits(double credits)   {
    this.credits = credits;
  }

  public double getCredits() {
    return credits;
  }
}
```

Create the deployment descriptors

Our CMP entity beans require three deployment descriptors: `ejb-jar.xml`, `weblogic-ejb-jar.xml`, and `weblogic-cmp-rdbms-jar-.xml`.

ejb-jar.xml

The `ejb-jar.xml` file, or EJB deployment descriptor, has two sections with properties relating specifically to CMP entity beans. The `<enterprise-beans>` section contains an `<entity>` element for each entity bean and describes, among other things, persistent fields and queries. The `<relationships>` section, new in EJB 2.0, describes logical relationships between CMP entities. The `<assembly-descriptor>` section doesn't contain any entity-specific properties. Following is a discussion of elements that pertain to CMP beans.

<entity>

Each entity bean must be declared in an `<entity>` element, which contains a number of other elements, such as those relating to the classes of the bean and interfaces, persistent fields, and queries.

<local-home>

This element is where you specify the bean's local home interface. It isn't specific to entity beans, but we mention it because you will need to use it if using CMP entities with relationships.

<local>

This element is where you specify the bean's local interface. We mention it again because you will need to use it if using CMP entities with relationships.

<persistence-type>

For CMP, this is set to `Container`.

<prim-key-class>

As with BMP, this is where the type of the primary key class is specified.

<cmp-version>

This specifies which EJB CMP version this bean uses. Possible values are 1.*x* and 2.*x*, with the latter being the default.

<abstract-schema-name>

This element specifies a name for the bean that can be used in EJB QL queries. In the example, the `Department` bean has an abstract schema name of `DepartmentSchema`; the choice of schema name is entirely up to you. The following query demonstrates how the abstract schema name is used.

```
<entity>
...
  <abstract-schema-name>
    DepartmentSchema
  </abstract-schema-name>
...
  <query>
   ...
    <ejb-ql>
      <![CDATA[SELECT OBJECT(d) FROM DepartmentSchema AS d
        WHERE d.name = ?1]]>
    </ejb-ql>
  </query>
...
</entity>
```

<cmp-field>

The complete syntax for the `<cmp-field>` element is

```
<cmp-field><field-name>name</field-name></cmp-field>
```

This element is where persistent entity fields are declared. Field names must begin with a lowercase letter and have corresponding get and set methods within the bean class. For example, the following

```
<cmp-field>
  <field-name>name</field-name>
</cmp-field>
```

will correspond to the following methods within the bean:

```
abstract public String getName();
abstract public void setName(String name);
```

`<cmp-field>` elements may be serializable dependent classes as well as simple attributes.

<primkey-field>

This element specifies which field is the bean's primary key field. It must be a field declared in a `<cmp-field>` element. It is not used if the primary key consists of multiple CMP fields.

<query>

Query elements map EJB QL statements to queries on the bean's home interface and bean select methods. The `<query>` element has two subelements: `<query-method>` and `<ejb-ql>`.

<query-method>

This element has two subelements, `<method-name>` and `<method-params>`, which map the query to a method on the bean's home interface.

<ejb-ql>

This element is where the query's EJB QL statement is specified.

To illustrate a `<query>` element, the following home interface method

```
findByName(java.lang.String name)
```

is mapped to an EJB QL statement as follows:

```
<query>
  <query-method>
    <method-name>findByName</method-name>
    <method-params>
      <method-param>java.lang.String</method-param>
    </method-params>
  </query-method>
  <ejb-ql>
    <![CDATA[SELECT OBJECT(d) FROM DepartmentSchema AS d
        WHERE d.name = ?1]]>
  </ejb-ql>
</query>
```

The EJB QL statement in this case returns all `Department`s where the name field equals the value of the `String` passed in to the method.

<relationships>

The `<relationships>` element is the other major section pertaining to entities and describes the logical relationship between them. The `<relationships>` section consists of `<ejb-relation>` elements.

\<ejb-relation\>

This element describes the relationship between two entity beans. In turn, it consists of an optional `<ejb-relation-name>` element and two `<ejb-relationship-role>` elements, one to describe each side of the relation.

\<ejb-relation-name\>

This is the name given to the relation. Although it's optional from the J2EE spec point of view, it is used by WebLogic, which refers to it in its persistence descriptor.

\<ejb-relationship-role\>

As mentioned, each `<ejb-relation>` has two `<ejb-relationship-role>` elements, each describing the relationship from one entity's point of view. This is specified with the `<multiplicity>` and `<relationship-role-source>` elements. This element also has optional `<ejb-relationship-role-name>`, `<cascade-delete>`, and `<cmr-field>` elements.

\<ejb-relationship-role-name\>

As with `<ejb-relation-name>`, this element is optional from the J2EE spec point of view, but is used by WebLogic to map the relationship in the database.

\<multiplicity\>

This element specifies the multiplicity of the entity in this `<ejb-relationship-role>` and can have values of one or many. In the example, `Department` and `Course` are in a one-to-many relationship, so the `<ejb-relationship-role>` describing `Department` will have a `<multiplicity>` of one, whereas `Course` will have a `<multiplicity>` of many.

\<cascade-delete\>

This element can be used to specify that any deletes of entities should be cascaded to related entities. It can be used only for beans where the related bean has a multiplicity of one. In the example, `Course` has `<cascade-delete>` set, which is allowable because `Department` has a multiplicity of one.

\<relationship-role-source\>

This element specifies which entity this `<ejb-relationship-role>` describes. It has an `<ejb-name>` subelement whose value must correspond to an `<ejb-name>` element of an `<entity>` element declared in the `<enterprise-beans>` section.

\<cmr-field\>

This element specifies what field will store the reference to the other bean in the relationship. Each element listed here will have corresponding abstract getter and setter methods using the same naming pattern as with `<cmp-field>` elements.

The complete EJB deployment descriptor is given in Listing 16-8.

Listing 16-8: **ejb-jar.xml**

```
<?xml version="1.0"?>
<!DOCTYPE ejb-jar PUBLIC '-//Sun Microsystems, Inc.//DTD Enterprise
JavaBeans 2.0//EN' 'http://java.sun.com/j2ee/dtd/ejb-jar_2_0.dtd'>
```

Continued

Listing 16-8 *(continued)*

```xml
<ejb-jar>
  <enterprise-beans>
    <entity>
      <ejb-name>DepartmentEJB</ejb-name>
      <home>
com.wiley.wlsbible.ejb.entity.cmp.DepartmentRemoteHome</home>
      <remote>
com.wiley.wlsbible.ejb.entity.cmp.DepartmentRemote</remote>
      <local-home>
 com.wiley.wlsbible.ejb.entity.cmp.DepartmentLocalHome
      </local-home>
      <local> com.wiley.wlsbible.ejb.entity.cmp.DepartmentLocal</local>
      <ejb-class>
 com.wiley.wlsbible.ejb.entity.cmp.DepartmentEJB
      </ejb-class>
      <persistence-type>Container</persistence-type>
      <prim-key-class>java.lang.Integer</prim-key-class>
      <reentrant>False</reentrant>
      <cmp-version>2.x</cmp-version>
      <abstract-schema-name>
        DepartmentSchema
      </abstract-schema-name>
      <cmp-field>
        <field-name>id</field-name>
      </cmp-field>
      <cmp-field>
        <field-name>name</field-name>
      </cmp-field>
      <primkey-field>id</primkey-field>
      <query>
        <query-method>
          <method-name>findByName</method-name>
          <method-params>
            <method-param>java.lang.String</method-param>
          </method-params>
        </query-method>
        <ejb-ql>
          <![CDATA[SELECT OBJECT(d) FROM DepartmentSchema AS d
            WHERE d.name = ?1]]>
        </ejb-ql>
      </query>
    <query>
      <query-method>
        <method-name>findAll</method-name>
        <method-params>
        </method-params>
      </query-method>
      <ejb-ql>
        <![CDATA[SELECT OBJECT(d) FROM DepartmentSchema AS
          d]]>
```

```
        </ejb-ql>
      </query>
  </entity>

  <entity>
    <ejb-name>CourseEJB</ejb-name>
    <local-home>
com.wiley.wlsbible.ejb.entity.cmp.CourseLocalHome
    </local-home>
    <local> com.wiley.wlsbible.ejb.entity.cmp.CourseLocal</local>
    <ejb-class> com.wiley.wlsbible.ejb.entity.cmp.CourseEJB</ejb-class>
    <persistence-type>Container</persistence-type>
    <prim-key-class>java.lang.Integer</prim-key-class>
    <reentrant>False</reentrant>
    <cmp-version>2.x</cmp-version>
    <abstract-schema-name>CourseSchema</abstract-schema-name>
    <cmp-field>
      <field-name>id</field-name>
    </cmp-field>
    <cmp-field>
      <field-name>name</field-name>
    </cmp-field>
    <cmp-field>
      <field-name>credits</field-name>
    </cmp-field>
    <primkey-field>id</primkey-field>
    </entity>
</enterprise-beans>

<relationships>
  <ejb-relation>
    <ejb-relation-name>
      Department-Course</ejb-relation-name>
    <ejb-relationship-role>
      <ejb-relationship-role-name>
        Department-Has-Courses
      </ejb-relationship-role-name>
      <multiplicity>one</multiplicity>
      <relationship-role-source>
        <ejb-name>DepartmentEJB</ejb-name>
      </relationship-role-source>
      <cmr-field>
        <cmr-field-name>courses</cmr-field-name>
        <cmr-field-type>
          java.util.Collection
        </cmr-field-type>
      </cmr-field>
    </ejb-relationship-role>
    <ejb-relationship-role>
      <ejb-relationship-role-name>
        Course-Has-Department
```

Continued

Listing 16-8 *(continued)*

```
            </ejb-relationship-role-name>
            <multiplicity>many</multiplicity>
            <cascade-delete/>
            <relationship-role-source>
              <ejb-name>CourseEJB</ejb-name>
            </relationship-role-source>
            <cmr-field>
              <cmr-field-name>department</cmr-field-name>
            </cmr-field>
            </ejb-relationship-role>
      </ejb-relation>
   </relationships>

   <assembly-descriptor>
     <container-transaction>
     <method>
       <ejb-name>DepartmentEJB</ejb-name>
       <method-name>*</method-name>
     </method>
     <trans-attribute>Required</trans-attribute>
     </container-transaction>
     <container-transaction>
     <method>
       <ejb-name>CourseEJB</ejb-name>
       <method-name>*</method-name>
     </method>
     <trans-attribute>Required</trans-attribute>
     </container-transaction>
   </assembly-descriptor>
</ejb-jar>
```

weblogic-ejb-jar.xml

The WebLogic deployment descriptor allows you to specify the JNDI name for your beans as well as use value-added WebLogic features. Many of them will be discussed in the "Advanced WebLogic Features for Entity Beans" section.

<entity-descriptor>

This section is used to specify options for the entity bean named by the `<ejb-name>` parent element.

<persistence-use>

This element specifies a persistent service that the container can use to persist an entity. I specify WebLogic's (`WebLogic_CMP_RDBMS`), but you can specify others such as Oracle9iAS TopLink as well.

The `<type-identifier>` and `<type-version>` specify the persistent service, whereas the `<type-storage>` element specifies the location of a persistence descriptor used by this persistence service.

<local-jndi-name>

Although not specific to entities, we mention this element because entities may need it to obtain a reference to one another's home interface.

The WebLogic deployment descriptor is given in Listing 16-9.

Listing 16-9: weblogic-ejb-jar.xml

```
<?xml version="1.0"?>

<!DOCTYPE weblogic-ejb-jar PUBLIC
'-//BEA Systems, Inc.//DTD WebLogic 7.0.0 EJB//EN'
'http://www.bea.com/servers/wls700/dtd/weblogic-ejb-jar.dtd'>

<weblogic-ejb-jar>

  <weblogic-enterprise-bean>
    <ejb-name>DepartmentEJB</ejb-name>
    <entity-descriptor>
      <persistence>
<persistence-use>
        <type-identifier>
          WebLogic_CMP_RDBMS
        </type-identifier>
        <type-version>7.0</type-version>
        <type-storage>
          META-INF/weblogic-cmp-rdbms-jar.xml
        </type-storage>
      </persistence-use>
    </persistence>
    </entity-descriptor>
    <jndi-name>cmp.Department</jndi-name>
    <local-jndi-name>cmp.Department-Local</local-jndi-name>
  </weblogic-enterprise-bean>

  <weblogic-enterprise-bean>
    <ejb-name>CourseEJB</ejb-name>
    <entity-descriptor>
      <persistence>
<persistence-use>
        <type-identifier>
          WebLogic_CMP_RDBMS
        </type-identifier>
        <type-version>7.0</type-version>
        <type-storage>
          META-INF/weblogic-cmp-rdbms-jar.xml
        </type-storage>
      </persistence-use>
    </persistence>
```

Continued

Listing 16-9 *(continued)*

```
      </entity-descriptor>
      <local-jndi-name>cmp.Course</local-jndi-name>
    </weblogic-enterprise-bean>
</weblogic-ejb-jar>
```

weblogic-cmp-rdbms-jar-.xml

The EJB deployment descriptor specifies entities' abstract persistence schemas. But it does not specify how entities map to an underlying persistent store. This must be done by the persistence service specified in the WebLogic deployment descriptor. We discuss the descriptor used by WebLogic's default implementation in the following sections.

Like the EJB deployment descriptor, the WebLogic persistence descriptor contains a section that deals with beans and their fields (`<weblogic-rdbms-bean>`) and another that deals with relationships (`<weblogic-rdbms-relation>`).

<weblogic-rdbms-bean>

There is one `<weblogic-rdbms-bean>` element for each CMP bean declared in the EJB deployment descriptor. This element maps the entity to a table and its persistent fields to table columns and additionally specifies the database connection pool to use.

<ejb-name>

This element maps the entity to this `<weblogic-rdbms-bean>` description. It must correspond to the `<ejb-name>` of an `<entity>` element in the EJB deployment descriptor.

<data-source-name>

This element specifies which database connection pool to use to persist the bean. It must be a connection pool set up on the WebLogic Server instance used.

<table-map>

Consists of `<table-name>` and `<field-map>` entries.

<table-name>

This is the name of the database table to which to persist the bean.

<field-map>

This element maps an entity field to a column in the table specified in `<table-name>` through its `<cmp-field>` and `<dbms-column>` subelements. There is one of these elements for each of the entity's persistent fields.

```
<field-map>
  <cmp-field>id</cmp-field>
  <dbms-column>id</dbms-column>
</field-map>
```

<automatic-key-generation>

WebLogic 7.0 includes a useful feature for generating primary keys for CMP entities. You can use this feature by including an `<automatic-key-generation>` element in the `<weblogic-rdbms-bean>` section. There are two types of generation. One involves using native facilities of supported databases, which are Oracle using Oracle sequences or Microsoft SQL Server using its `IDENTITY` column. For more information on using these facilities, consult the WebLogic documentation.

The other method, which can be used with any database, involves setting up a sequence table with a single column and single record that serves as a counter. All entities using this facility will get keys from this field. This is the method your example beans use.

The SQL to create the sequence table is the following where *table_name* is specified by the user:

```
CREATE table_name (SEQUENCE int)
INSERT into table_name VALUES (0)
```

The `<automatic-key-generation>` setting you use in your example is as follows:

```
<automatic-key-generation>
  <generator-type>NAMED_SEQUENCE_TABLE</generator-type>
  <generator-name>SEQUENCE</generator-name>
  <key-cache-size>10</key-cache-size>
</automatic-key-generation>
```

The `<generator-type>` element can have values of `NAMED_SEQUENCE_TABLE` when using a user-specified table, or `ORACLE` or `SQL-SERVER` if using the native facilities of those databases.

The `<generator-name>` element specifies the name of the sequence table (or the Oracle sequence object if using Oracle).

The `<key-cache-size>` enables WebLogic to cache primary key values so that it doesn't have to call the database every time a new primary key in needed. In your example, `<key-cache-size>` is set to 10, so a database call will be needed only after every tenth primary key is requested.

Here are a couple of notes about using automatic primary key generation. Your primary key must be a single field and it must be of type `Integer`. This means that you have about four billion unique primary keys shared among all the entities that use this facility. This may not be sufficient for all applications. Also, to get all four billion IDs, you should start your counter (in the sequence table) at -2147483648 (the value of `Integer.MIN`), because going from 0 to `Integer.MAX` gives you only half of your potential values.

It should be stressed that this facility is specific to WebLogic. If you switch to another application server, you will have to find another way to generate your primary keys.

<weblogic-rdbms-relation>

The `<weblogic-rdbms-relation>` section handles persisting bean relationships to the database. In databases, relationships are expressed using foreign keys, so this section specifies what columns in what tables that foreign keys are stored.

<relation-name>

This element maps this WebLogic relation to an `<ejb-relation>` in the EJB deployment descriptor. Its value must be the same as the `<ejb-relation-name>` element of the mapped `<ejb-relation>`.

<weblogic-relationship-role>

This element is used to map any keys needed by the relationships expressed in the EJB deployment descriptor. For each relationship needing a key mapping, there is an element of this type. Specifically, this element's `<relationship-role-name>` value will be the value of an `<ejb-relationship-role>` element's `<ejb-relationship-role-name>` value in the EJB deployment descriptor. For each `<relationship-role-name>` there is a `<relationship-role-map>`.

In your example, you have a one-to-many relationship between `Department` and `Course`. In relational tables, a one-to-many relationship is implemented by the many table having a column to store a foreign key to the one table. In your example, `dept_id` in `Course` (the many table) will be a foreign key corresponding to an ID in `Department` (the one table). This mapping is expressed in the `<column-map>` element through the `<foreign-key-column>` and `<key-column>` subelements.

```
<column-map>
  <foreign-key-column>dept_id</foreign-key-column>
  <key-column>id</key-column>
</column-map>
```

Tables 16-1 and 16-2 give an example of how this might look in the database.

Table 16-1: The Department Table within the Database

Id	Name
1	English
2	Computer Science

Table 16-2: The Course Table within the Database

Id	dept_id	Name
1	1	Composition
2	1	Creative Writing
3	2	Data Structures

The complete `weblogic-cmp-rdbms-jar.xml` file is given in Listing 16-10.

Listing 16-10: **weblogic-cmp-rdbms-jar.xml**

```
<!DOCTYPE weblogic-rdbms-jar PUBLIC
'-//BEA Systems, Inc.//DTD WebLogic 7.0.0 EJB RDBMS Persistence//EN'
'http://www.bea.com/servers/wls700/dtd/weblogic-rdbms20-persistence-700.dtd'>
<weblogic-rdbms-jar>

  <weblogic-rdbms-bean>
    <ejb-name>DepartmentEJB</ejb-name>
    <data-source-name>
```

```
      OraclePool
   </data-source-name>
   <table-map>
     <table-name>department</table-name>
     <field-map>
       <cmp-field>id</cmp-field>
       <dbms-column>id</dbms-column>
     </field-map>
     <field-map>
       <cmp-field>name</cmp-field>
       <dbms-column>name</dbms-column>
     </field-map>
   </table-map>

   <automatic-key-generation>
     <generator-type>NAMED_SEQUENCE_TABLE</generator-type>
     <generator-name>SEQUENCE</generator-name>
     <key-cache-size>10</key-cache-size>
   </automatic-key-generation>

</weblogic-rdbms-bean>

<weblogic-rdbms-bean>
   <ejb-name>CourseEJB</ejb-name>
   <data-source-name>
      OraclePool
   </data-source-name>
   <table-map>
     <table-name>Course</table-name>
     <field-map>
       <cmp-field>name</cmp-field>
       <dbms-column>name</dbms-column>
     </field-map>
     <field-map>
       <cmp-field>id</cmp-field>
       <dbms-column>id</dbms-column>
     </field-map>
     <field-map>
       <cmp-field>credits</cmp-field>
       <dbms-column>credits</dbms-column>
     </field-map>
   </table-map>

   <automatic-key-generation>
     <generator-type>NAMED_SEQUENCE_TABLE</generator-type>
     <generator-name>SEQUENCE</generator-name>
     <key-cache-size>10</key-cache-size>
   </automatic-key-generation>
</weblogic-rdbms-bean>

<weblogic-rdbms-relation>
   <relation-name>Department-Course</relation-name>
```

Continued

Listing 16-10 *(continued)*

```
        <weblogic-relationship-role>
          <relationship-role-name>
            Course-Has-Department
          </relationship-role-name>
          <relationship-role-map>
            <column-map>
              <foreign-key-column>dept_id</foreign-key-column>
              <key-column>id</key-column>
            </column-map>
          </relationship-role-map>
        </weblogic-relationship-role>
      </weblogic-rdbms-relation>
    </weblogic-rdbms-jar>
```

Building and Deploying to WebLogic

The section on "Building and Deploying to WebLogic" in Chapter 15 contains details on how to build and deploy EJBs. It also contains instructions about where to download the sample source code from this chapter and how to build and deploy these examples.

With entity EJBs, you must also make sure that you have properly set up your connection pool and any tables that you might need.

Before running (deploying) the bean, the database tables to which the bean maps must be created.

DDL for your tables are as follows:

```
CREATE TABLE DEPARTMENT
  (
    NAME CHAR(50) NOT NULL,
    ID INT NOT NULL
  )

CREATE TABLE COURSE
  (
    CREDITS DECIMAL(2) NOT NULL,
    NAME CHAR(50) NOT NULL,
    DEPT_ID INT ,
    ID INT NOT NULL
  )
```

Advanced WebLogic Features for Entity Beans

This section discusses some advanced features that WebLogic offers for entity beans. Most are performance enhancements. For a complete list, see the WebLogic documentation.

Concurrency and locking

By default, WebLogic calls `ejbLoad` on an entity when a transaction is initiated on that entity, and `ejbStore` when the transaction commits. This behavior can be modified by using the features discussed in this section.

<concurrency-strategy>

WebLogic offers several ways to optimize concurrency by using the `<concurrency-strategy>` element. This element has three options: `Exclusive`, `Database`, and `ReadOnly`, which can be set for each entity bean type in the WebLogic deployment descriptor as follows:

```
<weblogic-enterprise-bean>
  <ejb-name>AccountBean</ejb-name>
  <entity-descriptor>
    <entity-cache>
      <concurrency-strategy>ReadOnly</concurrency-strategy>
    </entity-cache>
  </entity-descriptor>
</weblogic-enterprise-bean>
```

`Exclusive` locking places an exclusive lock on an entity instance until transaction commit, which means that other requests, including read requests, block until transaction completion. This was the default up through WebLogic Server 5.1.

`Database` locking defers locking requests to the underlying datastore. It's the current default and can increase throughput over exclusive locking.

The `ReadOnly` option can be used in cases in which bean clients are only reading, perhaps because updates are performed by an external system. Your system, for example, may have stock quotes streamed from an external system. Bean clients will use this data but will never change it. In this case, it's unnecessary to ever call `ejbStore()`. You can turn this off by setting your bean's `<concurrency-strategy>` to `ReadOnly`. Note that this also requires a `transaction-attribute` setting of `NotSupported`.

<read-timeout-seconds>

Setting a bean's concurrency strategy to `ReadOnly` not only affects calls to `ejbStore()`, but also to `ejbLoad()`. The `ejbLoad()` method gets called only at bean startup and then at an interval defined in the `<read-timeout-seconds>` element. In the stock quotes example, you might update quotes every second or every few seconds (depending on requirements). For a quote being requested multiple times a second, this could offer a large performance savings.

WebLogic has also introduced a feature called *read-only multicast invalidation*, which can be a more efficient way to update cached data when updates to read-only beans occur infrequently. This involves programmatically calling an `invalidate()` method on the `CachingHome` interface, which gets implemented by the concrete class WebLogic generates to implement the home interface of read-only entities.

Calling `invalidate()` invalidates the read-only entity bean on the local server and, if the bean is clustered, causes a multicast message to be sent out that invalidates copies of the bean on the other servers in the cluster. A call to an invalidated read-only entity causes `ejbLoad()` to be called on that bean.

The `invalidate()` method can take an entity's primary key object or `Collection` of primary keys as parameters. There is also an `invalidateAll()` method. An example of calling `invalidate()` is

```
((CachingHome) home).invalidate(someBeansPrimaryKey)
```

\<invalidate-target\>

This subelement of the `<entity-descriptor>` enables you to automatically invalidate a read-only entity when the CMP entity bean in whose descriptor this element appears gets modified.

```
<invalidate-target>
  <ejb-name>SomeReadOnlyEntity</ejb-name>
</invalidation-target
```

\<db-is-shared\>

This is another way to optimize calls to `ejbLoad()`. By default, WebLogic Server calls `ejbLoad()` at the beginning of each transaction. This is to avoid missing any updates to the database from other database clients (including other WebLogic instances). But if a single (nonclustered) WebLogic instance is the only client updating the database, the data cached in the entity will always be synched with the database, and the calls to `ejbLoad()` will be unnecessary. You can configure this behavior by setting `<db-is-shared>` to `false` (the default is `true`).

\<delay-updates-until-end-of-tx\>

This property enables you to control the timing of when updates can be read by other transactions. By default, WebLogic writes data (calls `ejbStore()`) only when a transaction commits. But there may be cases where you want to allow other database users to see uncommitted data. If so, you can set this property to `false`, which will cause `ejbStore()` to be called whenever there is an update. The data will not actually be committed after each `ejbStore()` call, only when the transaction commits.

Automatic table creation

WebLogic enables you to specify that tables be automatically created for beans and relationship join tables if they don't already exist. This feature is meant to be used only in development because production tables will probably need more precise table schemas than WebLogic can generate. To turn this feature on, add the following line to the WebLogic persistence deployment descriptor:

```
<create-default-dbms-table>True</create-default-dbms-table>
```

CMP, BMP, and Other Options

In this section, we'll briefly discuss trade-offs between BMP and CMP and describe some other alternatives.

Trade-offs between BMP and CMP

When should you use BMP or CMP? It depends on what you are doing. Following are some guidelines to help when choosing:

✦ BMP may be more efficient if well coded.

✦ BMP allows you greater scope for customization, although EJB 2.0 greatly extends what you can do with CMP.

✦ CMP is easier to program and maintain.

✦ CMP is more easily ported because persistence-related functionality is configured, not hard-coded.

Session beans

Entity beans are slower than session beans, and in database-intensive applications, entity beans may not be suitable. One alternative is to put persistence code in session beans. The trade-off here is that, like BMP, you have a lot of code to manage. Using an O/R tool or other persistence-mapping framework can mitigate this.

Java Data Objects

Java Data Objects (JDO) is a new specification from Sun that seeks to offer developers a standard view of persistent entities in Java, regardless of what type of persistent store those objects reside in. JDO is similar to O/R mapping frameworks, but allows mapping schemes to different persistent storage types to be plugged in without changing code.

Before local interfaces, a major difference between JDO objects and entity beans was that JDO objects are not remote objects. Many seized on this and were advocating a pattern where session beans provide a façade to allow remote access to JDO objects. With local interfaces, the gap is much less, but JDO proponents argue it is simpler to use.

Third-Party Tools

Tools should be an integral part of EJB development to help ease the burden of the countless configuration details and patterns to which developers must adhere. The spec explicitly acknowledges the role of tools. In the following sections, we discuss some of the major EJB tools. The tools' arena is constantly changing, so it's a good idea to check sites such as theServerside.com and vendor Web sites for new developments.

Oracle 9iAS TopLink

TopLink, originally from The Object People, was sold to WebGain, who then sold it to Oracle shortly before going belly up. Oracle recently refreshed the product — it now supports EJB 2.0 — and has reiterated that it will continue to support BEA WebLogic. It's a complex product that has a devoted following.

JBuilder

JBuilder is Borland's general purpose Java IDE with features to create, configure, and deploy EJB. It also includes an O/R mapping tool for EJB 1.1 entity beans. JBuilder 8 has a new EJB 2.0 visual designer for EJB 2.0 session, entity, and message beans. In addition, BEA and

Borland recently announced a joint technology and marketing agreement to integrate JBuilder WebLogic Edition more tightly with WebLogic Server and WebLogic Workshop.

Cocobase Enterprise O/R

Enterprise O/R is a mapping tool from Thought, Inc. that enables you to do complex entity bean mappings. Other features include auto-generation of entity beans from database tables and integration with IDEs such as JBuilder. As of this writing, they had just announced support for EJB 2.0 CMP in WebLogic 7.0.

TogetherSoft Control Center

Control Center is a modeling and code generation tool that allows you to model EJB and their configurations in UML diagrams. The recently released Control Center 6.0 now supports EJB 2.0 CMP. At the time of this writing, Borland just announced its purchase of TogetherSoft.

Summary

Entity beans are used to offer an object representation of persistent objects. Two types of entity beans exist: bean-managed (BMP) and container-managed (CMP). BMP entities require the developer to handle bean persistence in code, whereas CMP beans use deployment descriptors that get interpreted by the EJB container. A key benefit of entity beans is that they are transaction-aware. WebLogic offers bean developers a variety of configuration settings to optimize performance. Tools can greatly simplify bean development, over and above the advances in EJB 2.0.

✦　　✦　　✦

Developing Message-Driven Beans

In Chapters 15 and 16, we examined the features of session beans
and entity beans. As we mentioned in Chapter 14, the EJB 2.0 specification introduces *message-driven beans,* which are essentially Java
Message Service (JMS) clients that live within the EJB container and
benefit from its component-based architecture and transactional
services.

This chapter introduces you to message-driven beans, showing you
the advantages of this new technology, the ins and outs of message-
driven bean development and deployment, and the essentials you
need to program message-driven beans. The chapter also explores a
real-world application of message-driven beans: a B2B application
that makes use of XML and a message-driven bean. When you're finished with this chapter, you will have a complete understanding of
how to implement message-driven beans, enabling you to build transactional components that are tied into asynchronous messaging.

 **Cross-
Reference** Message-driven beans rely on the Java Message Service (JMS) to
function. Therefore, you should read Chapter 9 on WebLogic JMS
before beginning this chapter. The remainder of this chapter
assumes that you are familiar with the material in Chapter 9.

Understanding Message-Driven Beans

Message-driven beans, a significant addition to the EJB 2.0 specification, provide a simple component-based way to process asynchronous messages. Recall that an asynchronous message is a
message that does not require an immediate response. But most Web
applications respond to requests synchronously. For example, a
request is sent to a servlet, and the servlet immediately returns a
response. To send a message to a server that requires no response,
you can use JMS. A message-driven bean is an EJB that can consume
asynchronous JMS messages, either by listening to a queue or by subscribing to a topic.

Versions and packages

EJB 2.0, released in mid-September 2001, is not just an updated version of the EJB specification, but a new release altogether. It's nearly twice as long as the EJB 1.1 specification. The largest changes in the specification are the introduction of message-driven beans, as well as several changes to container-managed beans (see Chapter 14 for a comparison of EJB 1.1 and 2.0).

How message-driven beans differ from other EJBs

Unlike session beans and entity beans, clients cannot directly invoke a message-driven bean's methods. The only way to invoke a message-driven bean is to send it a JMS message. For this reason, there are no home or remote interfaces for message-driven beans, and message-driven beans are always invoked asynchronously. Figure 17-1 shows how client code accesses the different types of EJBs.

Figure 17-1: Client access to the three types of EJBs

Deciding whether to write a message-driven bean or a JMS client

Developers familiar with WebLogic JMS may wonder: When should I write conventional JMS applications, and when should I write message-driven beans?

The answer depends partly on how much control over the environment your application requires and partly on how much coding you want to do. Conventional WebLogic JMS, for example, provides features such as load balancing and stability, but taking advantage of these features is left up to the application developer. This is fine if you need fine-grained control over the JMS infrastructure, transactions, and data access. But if you're simply writing queue listeners and topic subscribers that perform relatively simple processing, you should seriously consider implementing them as message-driven beans. This way, you'll benefit from the EJB container's transparent support for managing the JMS infrastructure, controlling transactions, enforcing security, and managing database access. You'll also be able to make certain changes to your code's runtime behavior, such as changing the target queue or topic, simply by modifying the beans' deployment descriptors.

Table 17-1 lists key differences between message-driven beans and JMS clients. Consider these differences before writing your code so you can be sure to choose the right approach for your project.

Table 17-1: Message Beans versus JMS Clients

Feature	Message Bean	JMS Client
Transaction support	Built-in transaction support the EJB container)	Transaction support must be (via coded by the developer
Binding	Can bind to only one JMS topic or queue	Can bind to any number of JMS topics or queues
JMS infrastructure management	JMS infrastructure (references to connection factories, sessions, queues, and topics) managed by the EJB container	JMS infrastructure managed by the developer
Runtime JMS behavior	Runtime JMS behavior controlled by deployment descriptors	Runtime JMS behavior controlled by code and WebLogic Console settings

Programming Message-Driven Beans

Now that you have learned some basics about message-driven beans, let's look at them in more detail. Just like entity beans and session beans, there are a few programming constructs you must follow when developing message-driven beans.

The MessageDrivenBean interface — javax.ejb.MessageDrivenBean

Just like entity beans and session beans, message-driven beans require you to implement standard interfaces. The methods defined in the `javax.ejb.MessageDrivenBean` interface are shown in Table 17-2.

Table 17-2: The javax.ejb.MessageDrivenBean Interface

Method Name	Purpose
`onMessage (javax.jms.Message messageName )`	This method is called when a message is received by a bean from a topic or queue. Most of the business logic for your bean should be implemented in this method.
`ejbCreate()`	This method is called when the MDB is created by the EJB container.
`ejbRemove()`	This method is called when the MDB is removed from the EJB container.
`setMessageDrivenBeanContext(MessageDrivenContext context`	This method, which is called before `ejbCreate()`,is invoked by the EJB container. The `MessageDrivenContext` object describes the environment-specific information for the MDB. If you want to obtain any type of environment- or transaction-specific information in your bean, you should do it in this method by invoking the methods in the context object (this will be explained further in the next section).

The message-driven bean context

When an instance of a message-driven bean is created, the EJB container passes it an instance of the `MessageDrivenContext`. Table 17-3 shows methods for obtaining useful information from this context.

Table 17-3: MessageDrivenContext Methods

Method Name	Purpose
`setRollbackOnly()`	If transaction demarcation is container-managed, `setRollbackOnly()` marks a transaction so that it cannot commit.
`getRollbackOnly()`	If the transaction demarcation is container-managed, `getRollbackOnly()` returns a Boolean indicating whether the transaction can be committed.
`getUserTransaction()`	If the transaction demarcation is bean-managed, `getUserTransaction()` returns the User Transaction interface, which can allow the bean to explicitly manage transaction boundaries.

Implementing business logic

Recall that message-driven beans cannot be accessed directly by client code; the only way to trigger the business logic in message-driven beans is to send them JMS messages. Such logic resides in the bean's onMessage() method, a simple example of which is given in Listing 17-1.

Listing 17-1: **A Simple onMessage() Method**

```
public void onMessage(Message incomingMsg) {
  TextMessage msg = null;
  String msgType = null;
  String msgPayload = null;

  try {
    if (incomingMsg instanceof TextMessage) {
      msg = (TextMessage) inMessage;
      msgType = msg.getStringProperty("messageType");
      msgPayload = msg.getText();

      if (msgType.equals("PriceAlert"))
        processAlert(msgPayload);
      else if (msgType.equals("FullQuote"))
        processFullQuote(msgPayload);
    } else {
      log.append("Only accepting text messages");
    }
  } catch (JMSException e) {
    log.append("Exception: " + e.printStackTrace());
  } catch (Throwable te) {
    log.append("Throwable: " + te.printStackTrace());
  }
}
```

Notice the similarity between this code and the code for asynchronous message listeners discussed in Chapter 9. In fact, the code is functionally identical. A message-driven bean is nothing more than an asynchronous message listener implemented within the EJB container.

It's important to note that if any bean method throws an exception, WLS immediately removes the bean instance from the EJB container without calling ejbRemove(), and creates a new one. This behavior may be undesirable for your application, especially if the bean instance must re-establish database connections or perform other time-consuming setup tasks. A more serious problem is that beans removed in this manner don't get a chance to clean up after themselves, which can lead to memory leaks and wasted resources. To prevent these problems, program the bean to catch its own exceptions so they don't propagate to WebLogic. The code in Listing 17-1 accomplishes this by embedding its logic in a try-catch block.

Deploying Message-Driven Beans in WebLogic Server

Before deploying a message-driven bean, you must create its deployment descriptors and then bundle the bean's classes and deployment descriptors into a `jar` file.

Deployment descriptors

Just like entity beans and session beans, message-driven beans use XML-based deployment descriptors. WebLogic requires two deployment descriptors: a JavaSoft-compliant message-driven bean descriptor and a WebLogic-specific descriptor.

ejb-jar.xml

The JavaSoft deployment descriptor, `ejb-jar.xml`, gives basic information about the message-driven bean's deployment, such as its class name, type of transaction support, and so on. The DTD for the generic message-driven bean descriptor is shown in Listing 17-2.

Listing 17-2: DTD for the Message-Driven Bean's Deployment Descriptor

```
<!ELEMENT message-driven (description?,
  display-name?, small-icon?,
  large-icon?, ejb-name?, ejb-class,
  transaction-type, transaction-scope?,
  jms-message-selector?, jms-acknowledge-
  mode?, message-driven-destination?,
  env-entry*, ejb-ref*, security-
  identity?, resource-ref*, resource-
  env-ref*)>
```

As you can see, the deployment descriptor for a message-driven bean is similar to the entity and session bean deployment descriptors discussed in Chapters 15 and 16. One new field is the `message-driven-destination` field, which specifies the type of messaging destination (queue or topic) to which the message-driven bean will be bound. The value of this field should be the fully qualified class name of the destination type; for example, `javax.jms.Queue` or `javax.jms.Topic`.

Note   If a JMS `topic` is specified, a `subscription-durability` tag must also be added. The two values for this field are either `durable` or `nondurable`. See Chapter 9 for more information on durable and nondurable topic subscribers.

Listing 17-3 is an example of a completed deployment descriptor.

Listing 17-3: ejb-jar.xml

```
<!DOCTYPE ejb-jar PUBLIC "-//Sun Microsystems, Inc.//DTD Enterprise
JavaBeans 2.0//EN" "http://java.sun.com/dtd/ejb-jar_2_0.dtd">
<ejb-jar>
  <enterprise-beans>
    <message-driven>
      <ejb-name>prescriptionConsumer</ejb-name>
      <ejb-class>bible.chapter17.PrescriptionBean</ejb-class>
      <transaction-type>Container</transaction-type>
      <message-driven-destination>
        <destination-type>
          javax.jms.Queue
        </destination-type>
      </message-driven-destination>
    </message-driven>
  </enterprise-beans>
</ejb-jar>
```

weblogic-ejb-jar.xml

The WebLogic-specific deployment descriptor `weblogic-ejb-jar.xml` is used to specify WebLogic-specific bean behavior, such as cache pool behavior, the name of the WebLogic JMS queue or topic to which the bean will listen, and so on. To map a message-driven bean to a topic or queue, simply specify the JNDI name of the topic or queue in the bean's WebLogic deployment descriptor. Listing 17-4 shows an example of a WebLogic-specific message bean deployment descriptor. The JMS mapping information is in bold type.

Listing 17-4: weblogic-ejb-jar.xml

```
<?xml version="1.0"?>
<!DOCTYPE weblogic-ejb-jar PUBLIC "-//BEA Systems, Inc.//DTD WebLogic 7.0.0
EJB//EN" "http://www.bea.com/servers/wls700/dtd/weblogic-ejb-jar.dtd">
<weblogic-ejb-jar>
  <weblogic-enterprise-bean>
    <ejb-name>prescriptionConsumer</ejb-name>
    <message-driven-descriptor>
      <pool>
        <max-beans-in-free-pool>50</max-beans-in-free-pool>
        <initial-beans-in-free-pool>10</initial-beans-in-free-pool>
      </pool>
      <destination-jndi-name>PrescriptionQueue</destination-jndi-name>
    </message-driven-descriptor>
    <jndi-name>prescriptionConsumer</jndi-name>
  </weblogic-enterprise-bean>
</weblogic-ejb-jar>
```

Transaction attributes

Like entity and session beans, message-driven beans can have either container-managed transactions or bean-managed transactions. For container-managed transactions, two trans-action attributes are supported: `Required` and `NotSupported`. By indicating `Required` as the transaction type, WebLogic Server makes the JMS message receipt "required" as part of the bean's transaction. This transactional attribute is useful if the `onMessage` method invokes other enterprise beans. Because the container passes the transaction context with the invo-cation, the transaction started at the `onMessage` method execution may involve several oper-ations such as accessing a database (via entity bean or JDBC calls) or sending messages (by using a connection factory resource). By indicating `NotSupported`, the message receipt is "NotSupported" as part of the transaction. This should be used when enterprise beans are not accessed from your `onMessage()` method.

The following assembly descriptor specifies that all methods of the `prescriptionConsumer` bean must be executed within the scope of a transaction. The assembly descriptor appears in `ejb-jar.xml`:

```
<assembly-descriptor>
  <container-transaction>
    <method>
      <ejb-name>prescriptionConsumer</ejb-name>
      <method-name>*</method-name>
    </method>
    <trans-attribute>Required</trans-attribute>
  </container-transaction>
</assembly-descriptor>
```

When using bean-managed transactions, WebLogic server allows message-driven beans to use one of two acknowledge modes: `AUTO_ACKNOWLEDGE` or `DUPS_OK_ACKNOWLEDGE`. See Table 9-1 for a complete listing of JMS non-transacted acknowledge modes. If your message bean was designed to handle duplicate JMS message requests, use the `DUPS_OK_ACKNOWLEDGE` mode. An example of specifying bean-managed transactions in the deployment descriptor is the following:

```
<transaction-type>Bean</transaction-type>
<acknowledge-mode>Auto-acknowledge</acknowledge-mode>
```

Deploying message-driven beans using WebLogic Console

After you successfully compile your message beans, you must deploy them to WebLogic Server. The deployment process has two steps:

1. Create a standard JAR file.

2. Deploy the EJB JAR file to WebLogic Server.

 Cross-Reference   An automated method of building EJB JAR files using the Ant tool is given in Chapter 15. This method is used for the demo projects for this book. Note also that the source code for this book is available at the book's Web site at the following URL:

```
http://www.wiley.com/compbooks/zuffoletto
```

Create a standard JAR file

The first step in this process is to create a META-INF directory in the same directory in which your compiled message-bean classes are stored. After you create this directory, move the ejb-jar.xml and weblogic-ejb-jar.xml deployment descriptors into the directory. The following command creates the file, message-bean.jar, which you will deploy to WebLogic Server:

```
d:\MYBEANS> jar cvf message-bean.jar *.*
```

Deploy the EJB JAR file to WebLogic Server

The final step in the deployment process is to deploy the EJB JAR file to WebLogic Server. First, open the WebLogic Console and click Deployments ➪ EJB ➪ Configure a new EJB. Your browser will appear as shown in Figure 17-2. In Chapter 15, we explained how you could deploy your EJB JAR from the directory you built it in. Here, we'll show you how to copy your EJB to your domain and deploy the copy. This allows you to rebuild your EJB without having to un-deploy it (because WebLogic will no longer have a file lock on the original JAR), but you need to re-deploy it every time you rebuild it.

Figure 17-2: The first step in deploying a message bean by using the WebLogic Console

The WebLogic Server Console page shown in Figure 17-2 shows from where you perform these steps:

1. Click the upload through your browser link to upload a JAR to a directory, which takes you to the page shown in Figure 17-3.

2. Click the Browse... button, navigate to and select the EJB JAR you just created; then click Upload. WebLogic uploads (copies) your EJB to your domain directory.

3. The Upload and Install an Application window reappears with a [deploy] link to the left of the filename of the file you just copied. Click this link. Your message bean is now deployed to WebLogic Server.

Figure 17-3: Browsing to the location of your message-driven EJB JAR file

Building an Application Using Message-Driven Beans and XML

Recall that message-driven beans are used exclusively for asynchronous message processing. One application domain that relies heavily on asynchronous messaging is that of wireless services. Therefore, to demonstrate the use of message-driven beans in the real world, we show you how to include them as part of a wireless application solution in this section.

Because current wireless transfer rates are still too unreliable to host mission-critical applications, asynchronous messaging plays an important role in application development for wireless devices. By using JMS and message-driven beans, you can design an application with quick response times that can still connect to enterprise resources and business partners.

Cross-Reference   This example makes use of a number of different J2EE technologies, including servlets, XML, and JMS. If you are unfamiliar with these topics, you may want to review Chapters 9 and 11 through 13 before continuing.

The business problem: Sending medical prescriptions over a wireless network

A physician examining patients is always on the move, whether traveling from one examining room to the next or (for family practitioners in rural areas) making house calls. Having immediate access to medical history or drug information while writing the prescription is a clear benefit, as is the ability to transmit the prescription immediately to a pharmacy. Finally, writing a prescription requires quick response time because a physician's time is of the essence. The challenge we present in this section is to write a wireless application that caters to the mobile physician's need to quickly and reliably transmit prescriptions to a remote pharmacy.

Application design issues

Processing a prescription on the server side is a rather time-consuming task: It must be logged to a database, and information about the prescription must be sent to various pharmaceutical companies. Because it's possible that these transactions might take 20 to 30 seconds to complete, you must devise a way to handle this processing asynchronously so that you don't keep busy physicians waiting.

Figure 17-4 illustrates the architecture of a possible solution. The following list discusses each action individually.

1. The physician uses a tablet PC to write and submit a prescription request, which is transmitted via a radio or cellular network to the Internet.

2. A URL embedded in the prescription request routes it to a servlet running on a designated Web server.

3. The servlet parses the data in the HttpRequest object and constructs an XML document from the information.

4. The XML document is then embedded in a TextMessage and published to a predefined JMS queue.

5. The servlet forwards the HttpRequest to a JSP, which renders an acknowledgment message that is returned immediately to the physician.

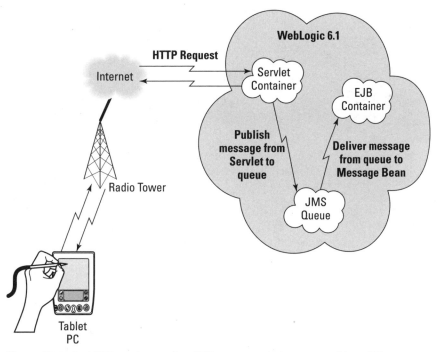

Figure 17-4: An HTTP servlet sending JMS messages to a message-driven EJB

Although the physician has received acknowledgment of a successful transmission, processing continues asynchronously on the server. A message-driven bean retrieves the `TextMessage` from the queue and processes the XML embedded within it according to the pharmacy's business rules, which may include checking the patient's medical background, routing the prescription to a fulfillment center, and sending a bill to the patient's insurance carrier. The system is designed so that the physician does not have to wait for any of this back-end processing to finish; all he or she is concerned with is that the prescription request was successfully sent and received.

Source code

Listing 17-5 displays the code for `SendPrescriptionServlet`. Notice the initialization of the JMS queue in the `init()` method of the servlet.

Listing 17-5: **SendPrescriptionServlet.java**

```
package com.wiley.wlsbible.ejb.message.prescription;

import java.io.*;
import javax.servlet.*;
import javax.servlet.http.*;
import java.rmi.RemoteException;
import java.util.*;
import javax.naming.*;
import javax.jms.*;


public class SendPrescriptionServlet extends HttpServlet {
  SessionContext sc = null;
  ServletContext context = null;
  QueueConnection qConnection = null;
  Queue q = null;

  public void init(ServletConfig config)
  throws ServletException {
    super();

    Context context = null;
    QueueConnectionFactory qConnectionFactory = null;
    context = getServletContext();

    try {
      q = (Queue) context.lookup("PrescriptionQueue");

      // Create a TopicConnection
      qConnectionFactory = (QueueConnectionFactory)
        context.lookup("PrescriptionConnectionFactory");
```

```
      qConnection =
        qConnectionFactory.createQueueConnection();

    } catch (Throwable t) {
      log.append(t.toString());
    }
  }

  public void service(HttpServletRequest req,
                      HttpServletResponse res)
  throws ServletException, IOException
  {

    QueueSession qSession = null;
    QueueSender qSender = null;
    TextMessage message = null;

    try {
      // retrieve parameters from request
      String physicianId =
        (String)req.getParameter("physicianId");
      String patientId =
        (String)req.getParameter("patientId");
      String drug = (String)req.getParameter("drug");
      String note = (String)req.getParameter("note");

      // create a jms session
      qSession = qConnection.createQueueSession(true, 0);
      qSender = qSession.createSender(queue);

      // create a message
      message = qSession.createTextMessage();
      message.setStringProperty("necessity", "immediate");
      message.setText(
        generatePrescriptionXML(physicianId,
                                patientId,
                                date,
                                drug,
                                note));

      // send the message to the queue
      qSender.send(message);
    } catch (Exception e) {
      pageToReturn = "error.jsp";
      e.printStackTrace();
      context.getRequestDispatcher(pageToReturn).forward(req,
        res);
    }
  }
```

Continued

Listing 17-5 *(continued)*

```
// generate XML for a prescription
private String generatePrescriptionXML(String physicianId,
  String patientId, String drug, String note )
{
  StringBuffer sb = new StringBuffer();

  sb.append("<?xml version=\"1.0\" ?>");
  sb.append("<PRESCRIPTION>");
  sb.append("<PHYSICIAN_ID>" + physicianId +
    "</PHYSICIAN_ID>");
  sb.append("<PATIENT_ID>" + patientId + "</PATIENT_ID>");
  sb.append("<DRUG>" + drug + "</DRUG>");
  sb.append("<NOTE>" + note + "</NOTE>");
  sb.append("</PRESCRIPTION>");

  return sb.toString();
}

// close the queue connection here
public void destroy()
{
  if (qConnection != null) {
    try {
      qConnection.close();
    } catch (Exception e) {
      e.printStackTrace();
    }
  }
}
}
```

Now that the prescription message was sent successfully, it's time to process the information sent. Listing 17-6 shows the code for PrescriptionBean, which listens for prescription requests on PrescriptionQueue. As mentioned earlier, the onMessage() method is the central location for developing your business logic. In this case, you will process only JMS messages that were sent with the tag immediate, which is accomplished by reading the message's necessity property. After a message is processed, the processPrescription() method is called with the message payload as a parameter. Using the SAX parser shown in Listing 17-7, a Java Prescription object, defined in Listing 17-8, is generated from the data in the XML document.

Listing 17-6: **PrescriptionBean.java**

```java
package com.wiley.wlsbible.ejb.message.prescription;


import java.rmi.RemoteException;
import javax.ejb.EJBException;
import javax.ejb.MessageDrivenBean;
import javax.ejb.MessageDrivenContext;
import javax.ejb.CreateException;
import javax.jms.*;


public class PrescriptionBean
implements MessageDrivenBean ,javax.jms.MessageListener {

  public MessageBean() {
  }

  public void setMessageDrivenContext(
    MessageDrivenContext mdc)
  {
  }

  public void ejbCreate() {
  }

  public void onMessage(Message incomingMsg) {
    TextMessage msg = null;
    String msgType = null;
    String msgPayload = null;

    try {
      if (incomingMsg instanceof TextMessage) {
        msg = (TextMessage) inMessage;
        msgType = msg.getStringProperty("necessity");
        msgPayload = msg.getText();

        if (msgType.equals("immediate"))
          processPrescription(msgPayload);
      } else {
        System.out.println("Only accepting text messages");
      }
    } catch (JMSException e) {
      e.printStackTrace();
    } catch (Throwable te) {
```

Continued

Listing 17-6 *(continued)*

```
      te.printStackTrace();
   }
}
public void ejbRemove() {
}

public void processPrescription(String prescriptionXmlDoc)
{
   PrescriptionXmlParser parser =
      new PrescriptionXmlParser(
         handlerContext.getConnection());

   // Create SAX 2 parser...
   XMLReader xr =
      XMLReaderFactory.createXMLReader(
         "org.apache.xerces.parsers.SAXParser");

   // Set the ContentHandler...
   xr.setContentHandler(parser);
   xr.parse(prescriptionXmlDoc);

   Prescription currentPrescription =
      parser.getPrescription();

   // Now that you have the prescription object
   // you can make calls to various backend order
   // management systems
   }
}
```

Listing 17-7: PrescriptionXmlParser.java

```
Package com.wiley.wlsbible.ejb.message.prescription;

import org.xml.sax.*;
import org.xml.sax.helpers.*;

import java.io.*;
import java.util.*;
import java.text.ParseException;
```

```java
public class PrescriptionXmlParser extends DefaultHandler {

  private Prescription prescription = new Prescription();

  public void startElement(String namespaceURI,
    String localName,
    String qName,
    Attributes attr ) throws SAXException {

    contents.reset();
  }

  public void endElement(String namespaceURI,
    String localName,
    String qName ) throws SAXException{

    try {
      if (localName.equals("physician_id")) {
        prescription.setPhysicianId(
          Integer.parseInt(contents.toString()));
      }

      if (localName.equals("patient_id")) {
        prescription.setPatientId(
          Integer.parseInt(contents.toString()));
      }

      if (localName.equals("note")) {
        prescription.setNote(contents.toString());
      }

      if (localName.equals("drug")) {
          prescription.setDrug(contents.toString());
      }
    } catch (ParseException p) {
      System.out.println("Here" + p.toString());
    }
  }

  public void characters(char[] ch, int start, int length)
  throws SAXException {
    contents.write( ch, start, length );
  }

  public Prescription getPrescription() {
    return prescription;
  }
}
```

Listing 17-8: **Prescription.java**

```java
package com.wiley.wlsbible.ejb.message.prescription;


public class Prescription {
  private int physicianId;
  private int patientId;
  private String note;
  private String drug;

  public void setPhysicianId(int physicianId) {
    // SBgen: Assign variable
    this.physicianId = physicianId;
  }

  public int getPhysicianId() {
    // SBgen: Get variable
    return(physicianId);
  }

  public void setPatientId(int patientId) {
    // SBgen: Assign variable
    this.patientId = patientId;
  }

  public int getPatientId() {
    // SBgen: Get variable
    return(patientId);
  }

  public void setDrug(String drug) {
    // SBgen: Assign variable
    this.drug = drug;
  }

  public String getDrug() {
    // SBgen: Get variable
    return(drug);
  }
}
```

Deploying the message-driven bean

Now that the message-driven bean is written, it's time to deploy it.

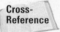
Cross-Reference   For instructions on how to deploy the servlet and set up the JMS queue, refer to the chapters on servlets (Chapter 11) and JMS (Chapter 9).

The first step is to create a deployment descriptor for your bean. As with entity and session bean deployment descriptors, the file must be called `ejb-jar.xml` and it must be in the directory `META-INF`, which resides in the directory in which your compiled classes are stored. Listing 17-9 shows `ejb-jar.xml` for `PrescriptionBean.java`.

Listing 17-9: **ejb-jar.xml**

```
<!DOCTYPE ejb-jar PUBLIC "-//Sun Microsystems, Inc.//DTD Enterprise
JavaBeans 2.0//EN" "http://java.sun.com/dtd/ejb-jar_2_0.dtd">

<ejb-jar>
 <enterprise-beans>
    <message-driven>
       <ejb-name>prescriptionConsumer</ejb-name>
       <ejb-class>
com.wiley.wlsbible.ejb.message.prescription.PrescriptionBean</ejb-
class>
       <transaction-type>Container</transaction-type>
       <message-driven-destination>
         <jms-destination-type>
           javax.jms.Queue
         </jms-destination-type>
       </message-driven-destination>
    </message-driven>
 </enterprise-beans>
</ejb-jar>
```

Looking at the file, you can see that the JNDI name for `PrescriptionBean` is `prescriptionConsumer`, the transaction type is `container-managed`, and the destination type is a JMS queue. To specify the exact queue to which the bean will listen, you must modify the WebLogic-specific deployment descriptor (`weblogic-ejb-jar`), which is shown in Listing 17-10. This file also belongs in the `META-INF` directory mentioned earlier.

Listing 17-10: **weblogic-ejb-jar.xml**

```
<?xml version="1.0"?>
<!DOCTYPE weblogic-ejb-jar PUBLIC "-//BEA Systems, Inc.//DTD WebLogic
7.0.0 EJB//EN" "http://www.bea.com/servers/wls700/dtd/weblogic-ejb-
jar.dtd">
<weblogic-ejb-jar>
  <weblogic-enterprise-bean>
    <ejb-name>prescriptionConsumer</ejb-name>
    <message-driven-descriptor>
    <pool>
      <max-beans-in-free-pool>
        50
```

Continued

Listing 17-10 *(continued)*

```
        </max-beans-in-free-pool>
        <initial-beans-in-free-pool>
          10
        </initial-beans-in-free-pool>
      </pool>
      <destination-jndi-name>
        PrescriptionQueue
      </destination-jndi-name>
      </message-driven-descriptor>
      <jndi-name>prescriptionConsumer</jndi-name>
    </weblogic-enterprise-bean>
</weblogic-ejb-jar>
```

Now that the deployment descriptors are ready, the next step is to create a standard JAR file that contains the class and interface files of each message-driven bean. Follow the instructions earlier in this chapter (in the section "Deploy the EJB JAR file to WebLogic Server") for building and deploying the EJB in WebLogic Server.

Summary

In this chapter, we explained the fundamental concepts behind message-driven EJBs, which are a new type of EJB introduced in the EJB 2.0 specification.

Message-driven beans enable you to easily write asynchronous message-handling code that lives within the EJB container and benefits from the services the container provides, such as automatic caching, transaction control, and management of the JMS infrastructure.

Message-driven beans are for asynchronous message-handling only. They can listen to any JMS queue or subscribe to any JMS topic defined in your WebLogic Server.

Unlike other types of EJBs, the business logic in message-driven beans can be invoked only by sending the bean a JMS message. You cannot directly invoke any of the bean's methods from code living outside the bean.

Writing a message-driven bean is as simple as writing an `onMessage()` method, creating deployment descriptors, and deploying the bean's JAR file to WebLogic Server. Of course, you must also create the JMS queue or topic to which the message-driven bean will be attached.

✦   ✦   ✦

Deploying and Testing Enterprise Applications

Assembling and Deploying WebLogic Applications

Packaging J2EE Applications

The J2EE specification offers a number of packaging formats for wrapping up everything from Java client applications to JSPs and servlets to Enterprise JavaBeans in standardized formats that are generic and portable to all platforms. Proper packaging enables you to configure your applications via deployment descriptors, which are text documents written in XML. Proper use of packaging and deployment descriptors allows you to change

✦ The URL a browser uses to point to a servlet in a Web application

✦ Database connection pools for a container-managed entity EJB

✦ Security constraints on any part of an application

without rewriting a single line of code. Simply change the deployment descriptors and redeploy the application from WebLogic Console. In most cases, you don't even have to restart the server if it is running in Development mode because every application in WebLogic gets its own area of memory to work in; that is, each is loaded by a separate ClassLoader — more on this later in the section "Classloading in Enterprise Applications and WebLogic Server." An application can be destroyed and re-created without affecting anything else on the server.

In addition to the J2EE standard package and descriptors, each application server usually adds deployment descriptors of its own to a package. Sometimes these descriptors are optional; in other cases, they're required by the server for proper deployment of the package. In some cases, WebLogic requires additional files used by the container to be included. Usually a WebLogic-specific compiler like the EJB or the RMI compiler generates these files; you just have to feed them your package.

Deployment descriptors

Table 18-1 shows the different application types supported by WebLogic and the names and locations of J2EE and WebLogic-specific deployment descriptors that go with them.

Table 18-1: Deployment Descriptor Files and Locations

Application	J2EE	WebLogic
Web applications	`WEB-INF/web.xml`	`WEB-INF/weblogic.xml`
Enterprise JavaBeans	`META-INF/ejb-jar.xml`	`META-INF/weblogic-ejb-jar.xml`
		`META-INF/weblogic-cmp-rdbms-jar.xml`
Enterprise applications	`META-INF/application.xml`	`META-INF/weblogic-application.xml`
Client applications	`application-client.xml`	`client-application.runtime.xml`
Resource adaptors	`META-INF/ra.xml`	`META-INF/weblogic-ra.xml`

Writing deployment descriptors can be confusing at first. The order of elements in the XML files is important, and translating examples from a book into a working descriptor for your application involves a lot of cutting and pasting, which is a time-consuming process dependent on trial and error. Luckily, WebLogic7.0 simplifies this process by including deployment descriptor editors for each of the application types listed in the table. You still must create the basic descriptor, but tweaking settings and configuration from the WebLogic Console makes these descriptors much more manageable.

If you choose to create all your descriptors by hand, there are many good XML editors available, including ones that will let you check your files against the document type definition (DTD — a set of rules for what constitutes a valid form of that type of XML document) for validity. Many Java IDEs also include auto-generation of deployment descriptors for your application, complete and ready to go.

 Note   The BEA XML Editor, a free downloadable XML editor, is described in Chapter 27.

WebLogic also provides a number of Java-based utilities for generating deployment descriptors by scanning your application directory. This is a best-effort attempt at creating your deployment descriptors. The files generated may be syntactically correct, but you should review the files to make sure that the content is correct. In any case, it saves a lot of typing.

The two utilities are the following:

✦ `weblogic.ant.taskdefs.ejb20.DDInit`: Generates Enterprise JavaBeans 2.0 deployment descriptors

✦ `weblogic.ant.taskdefs.war.DDInit`: Generates Web application deployment descriptors

An example of using this on a Web application located at c:\testwebapp is the following:

```
$ java weblogic.marathon.ddinit.WebInit c:\testwebapp
```

This command generates the web.xml and weblogic.xml files and places them in the c:\testwebapp\WEB-INF directory.

JAR — Java archive format

The Java .jar utility allows you to bundle files together into a single .jar (*Java AR*chive) file. This format maintains the directory structure of your application, and by default uses ZIP compression to reduce the amount of space the application takes up. WebLogic does not require that you deploy applications in the .jar format because the classloader can read both "exploded" directory structures and JAR files with equal ease.

Developing your applications in the exploded directory makes life easier because WebLogic can detect when single files have been changed and load them individually without reloading the application. But when it comes time to deploy your application into production, bundling it into a JAR file saves space and ensures a neat package.

Note
To get WebLogic 7.0 to automatically deploy "exploded" or JAR'd applications, you must be running your server in development mode. For more about development and production modes on your WebLogic Server, see Chapter 4.

The .jar format is not always optional, either. If you are deploying your application from an administration server that manages a domain with many WebLogic Servers (clustered or not), you have to deploy your file in the .jar format.

The jar utility is included in the bin directory of any Java Development Kit. And because the JDK 1.3 is included with the WebLogic distribution, you probably have it available to you. We'll go into details of how to use the jar utility when we talk about how to build each package format later in this chapter.

Web Applications Structure and Packaging

Web applications provide a J2EE-standard application structure (defined in the servlet 2.2 + 2.3 specification) for deploying resources for availability via HTTP, WAP, and other network protocols. The application structure

- ✦ Can contain an application's resources such as servlets, JavaServer Pages (JSPs), JSP tag libraries, and static resources such as HTML pages and image files.

- ✦ Can contain links to resources outside of the application, such as Enterprise JavaBeans (EJB).

- ✦ Are described by a J2EE web.xml file and a WebLogic weblogic.xml file.

- ✦ Can be standalone or part of an Enterprise Application (more on this later).

- ✦ Has a standard directory structure, known as the exploded directory form (handy during development). You can also run the jar utility, as described previously, on the directory to create a .war file (recommended for production).

Steps to creating a Web application

Web applications are fairly simple structures, requiring only a single subdirectory (WEB-INF) and a single file (web.xml) to become a valid application. Now a Web application without any content would be pretty boring, so this is where a little help getting set up is useful. Following is a rough sketch of where to put things and what you need to do to get a typical J2EE Web application up and running. The following sections discuss each step in more detail.

1. Arrange files in the proper directory structure. JSPs and tag libraries, servlet classes, helper classes and libraries, static files, and deployment descriptors all have their proper place in a Web app, some dictated by the J2EE Servlet specification; some only by convention.

2. Create the web.xml deployment descriptor. It is in this file that you register servlets and map them to URLs, define servlet initialization parameters, register JSP tag libraries, define security constraints, and so on.

3. Create the weblogic.xml deployment descriptor (optional). This file allows you to configure WebLogic-specific Web application features such as JSP properties and HTTP session parameters. It also maps web.xml configurations into WebLogic-specific configurations, which includes EJB and JNDI resources and security role mappings.

4. jar the directory structure into a .war file (optional). Using the Java jar utility, you can package your Web application into a single file (giving it a .war extension instead of a .jar extension). As mentioned, this is not always necessary for WebLogic Server to deploy the application.

5. Deploy the Web application to your WebLogic Server. During development, this is as easy as dropping the folder structure or .war file in the applications directory under your domain root (for example, on Windows c:\WebLogicUserDomains\mydomain\applications\webapp.war). For clustered or managed WebLogic Server the location is different, but we'll get to that in good time.

Web application directory structure

In a Web application, all your documents are arranged as part of directory hierarchy. Files must be in their proper places for WebLogic to be able to deploy the application properly.

The root of this hierarchy is called the document root. In "exploded" directory format, the name of the document root folder is also the name of your Web application when it is deployed, so choose carefully. In the case in which you jar the Web application, the deployed name is the name of the .war file (sans extension). Directory or filenames should not contain spaces.

With the exception of two special directories, WEB-INF and META-INF directly under the document root (these directories are private), anything under the document root can be served to a client browser. So, in a manner similar to static content Web servers, you can create an orderly directory structure to help in the management of files.

The META-INF directory is not used in the Web application specification, but it is created to hold the manifest file when you jar a Web application. This folder can also be handy for storing files that you want to package with a Web application, but do not want to be available to the client. Good examples of this are documentation about the application and source files. Files not directly accessed by the server for deployment and running of the Web application are not loaded into memory, so you don't have to worry about using up valuable RAM by putting some potentially handy documentation here.

The `WEB-INF` directory contains many files necessary to the working of the Web application. These files are not served directly to the client, but many are mapped via the `web.xml` file to resources available to the client.

Here's the basic directory structure of a Web application.

```
WebAppName/
          |   All static files and JSP pages are placed
          |   here or in subdirectories of your choosing.
          WEB-INF/web.xml (required)
          WEB-INF/weblogic.xml (optional)
          WEB-INF/classes
          |   Contains server-side classes such as HTTP servlets
          |   and utility classes. All class files under this
          |   directory are loaded automatically by the web
          |   application classloader.
          WEB-INF/lib
          |   By convention, this is the area you should put any
          |   jar files referenced by the Web Application (jars
          |   must be referenced in the web.xml file to be
          |   loaded by the web application class loader)
          WEB-INF/tlds
              Again by convention this is where JSP tag library
              definition files often go. The actual java classes
              go in either the lib or classes directory as
              appropriate.
```

Here's a sample Web application directory structure with "real" files. You'll build and deploy this application in the following pages.

```
accountManager/
    login.jsp
    /errors
        login_error.jsp
    /accounts
        myAccount.jsp
    /images
        logo.gif
        navbar.gif
    /WEB-INF
        web.xml
        weblogic.xml
        /lib
            jspTagLibrary.jar
        /classes
            /bible
                /deployment
                    AcctReport.class
        /tlds
            jspTags.tld
```

Configuring your Web application

In WebLogic, a Web application is configured via two XML deployment descriptor files: One is the `web.xml` file specified by the J2EE servlet specification; the second is specific to

WebLogic and is named `weblogic.xml`. This optional file is used to configure WebLogic-specific features.

Note that the document type definitions (DTDs) of the XML deployment descriptors specify a certain order to the XML file's contents. You'll walk through some parts of the descriptors in order, but this is not the venue for an exhaustive description of all the portions of the `web.xml` file. You can view Sun's DTD for `web.xml` at the following URL:

```
http://java.sun.com/dtd/web-app_2_3.dtd
```

Table 18-2 gives a simple listing of the elements in a `web.xml` file and their use. The order in which the tags appear in the list is the order that should be in your `web.xml` file.

Table 18-2: web.xml elements

Element	Description
`<icon>`	An optional icon for the Web application. Not used by WebLogic.
`<display-name>`	An optional display name for the application. Not used by WebLogic.
`<description>`	An optional short description of the application. Not used by WebLogic.
`<distributable>`	Indicates that the Web application can be deployed into a distributed servlet container. Not used by WebLogic.
`<context-param>`	Servlet context initialization parameters.
`<filter>`	Filters can intercept servlet requests and response objects and examine or modify the object before passing it on (part of the Servlet 2.3 spec).
`<filter-mapping>`	Maps a filter to a URL pattern.
`<listener>`	Application listeners fire events when the servlet context changes state (part of the Servlet 2.3 spec).
`<servlet>`	Defines servlets available to the Web application.
`<servlet-mapping>`	Maps a servlet or JSP to a URL pattern.
`<session-config>`	Used only to set the session time out.
`<mime-mapping>`	Allows association between a mime extension and return mime type associating .txt with text/plain).
`<welcome-file-list>`	Defines default filenames when a URL request is a directory.
`<error-page>`	Allows mapping between HTTP error codes and error handling pages.
`<taglib>`	Defines JSP tag libraries available to the Web application.
`<resource-env-ref>`	Declares a Web application's reference to another administered entity on the server, such as a JMS queue or topic.
`<resource-ref>`	Used with the `<resource-description>` element in the `weblogic.xml` file, it maps resources used in your Web application to objects listed in the JNDI tree.
`<security-constraint>`	Used with the `<security-role-assignment>` element in the `weblogic.xml` file, it defines the access privileges for a `<security-role>` element to a group of resources via their URL pattern.

Element	Description
`<login-config>`	Defines how a user is authenticated in a Web application.
`<security-role>`	Used with the `<security-role-assignment>` element in the `weblogic.xml` file, it maps role names to principal in the WebLogic security domain.
`<env-entry>`	Declares an environment entry for the Web application.
`<ejb-local-ref>`	Declares a reference to an EJB's local home interface.
`<ejb-ref>`	sed with the `<ejb-reference-description >` element in the `weblogic.xml` file, it creates references to EJB resources used within the Web application.

Although the `weblogic.xml` file is optional, many features defined in the `web.xml` will not work without corresponding entries in a `weblogic.xml`. These entries include security constraints and roles and EJB and resource references. Table 18-3 shows the elements of a `weblogic.xml` deployment descriptor. We'll discuss a couple of the features that are available, but you should refer to the WebLogic documentation for a complete explanation.

Table 18-3: weblogic.xml elements

Element	Description
`<description>`	Description of the Web application.
`<weblogic-version>`	WebLogic version for which the application is designed. This element is no longer used.
`<security-role-assignment>`	Used with the `<security-contraint>` element in the `web.xml` file, it maps between a role defined in the `web.xml` file to principals in the WebLogic security realm.
`<reference-descriptor>`	Used with the `<resource-ref>` element in the `web.xml` file to map resources used in the Web application to objects listed in the JNDI tree.
`<session-descriptor>`	Contains parameters for the way WebLogic configures the session.
`<jsp-descriptor>`	Contains parameters for the way WebLogic handles JSPs.
`<auth-filter>`	Fully qualified name of a servlet that extends the AuthFilter abstract servlet; methods on this servlet are called just before and after authentication and authorization.
`<container-descriptor>`	Contains the `<check-auth-on-forward/>`, `<redirect-content>`, and `<redirect-content-type>` flags to force reauthentication on forwarded requests.
`<charset-params>`	Used to define character set mappings from incoming POSTs and GETs to the Java character set.

Creating the web.xml deployment descriptor

First, you need to create the basic framework of the deployment descriptor and then you can begin to add elements in the proper order. As mentioned earlier, you can do this by hand using a text editor, you can use an editor specifically made for XML, or you can have WebLogic generate a descriptor for you using its Ant deployment descriptor utilities.

After you create the basic descriptor, you can deploy your application and use the WebLogic Console's deployment descriptor editors to add references and configurations to all parts of your application.

The basic outline of a web.xml file begins with a header declaring the type of XML file and showing where to find the definition.

```
<!DOCTYPE web-app PUBLIC
"-//Sun Microsystems, Inc.//DTD Web Application 2.3//EN"
"http://java.sun.com/dtd/web-app_2_3.dtd">
```

Note   If your WebLogic Server resides behind a firewall, make sure that your server has access to the public DTD, or make a copy of the DTD onto a stable Web server (not the WebLogic Server in which the application is being deployed) and point your header to that location.

Cross-Reference   See the *Configuring an external entity* subsection of the *XML* section in Chapter 23 for information on hosting and caching DTDs locally.

All the following entries should be contained between a pair of opening and closing <web-app> tags.

```
<web-app>
   <!-- All other elements between these two elements -->
</web-app>
```

For the example Web application, you'll begin with the web.xml file because this is required for any Web application to work. After that, you'll walk through the options available to you by creating a weblogic.xml file.

Deploying your basic Web application

Because you're developing a new application, you should be running your WebLogic Server in development mode (see Chapter 4 for an explanation of how to do this). By doing so, applications you place in the applications folder under your domain root will be automatically deployed.

You'll deploy the Account Manager Web application by placing the accountManager folder in your applications folder.

On Windows 2000, the path might look something like this:

C:\WebLogicUserDomains\mydomain\applications\accountManager

As discussed earlier, the bare minimum required for WebLogic to recognize a Web application is a directory root and a subfolder called WEB-INF containing a well-formed web.xml file.

You'll start out with a deployment descriptor that looks like the following:

```
<!DOCTYPE web-app PUBLIC
"-//Sun Microsystems, Inc.//DTD Web Application 2.3//EN"
"http://java.sun.com/dtd/web-app_2_3.dtd">
<web-app>
</web-app>
```

Now go to the WebLogic Console and edit your deployment descriptor from there. Figure 18-1 shows the console screen for doing so.

Figure 18-1: Editing a Web application's deployment descriptor

Click the Edit Web Application Descriptor link, and a new window pops up with all the possible settings for your Web application.

Servlet configuration

Because your Web application contains an HTTP servlet, you need to put in several references to the Java class in order for clients to be able to access it. You'll put in only the required subelements, but be aware that there are many optional elements for most deployment descriptor tags (see the references at the end of this chapter for links to the full servlet specification for information on all tags).

Click the Servlets folder in the left frame, followed by the Configure a New Servlet link. Figure 18-2 shows the resulting screen as we've filled it in for our example.

From here, you'll fill in information about your servlet. Servlet Name is the name by which the servlet will be referred to throughout the deployment descriptor. Servlet Class is the fully qualified name of the Java servlet class. Usually the class is in WEB-INF/classes, but this location is not required. The class should be in the classpath at deployment.

Click Create to save the web.xml file.

Now you need to map your servlet reference to a URL pattern so that the browser can connect to it. Again, Servlet Name is the name defined in the servlet declaration, and the URL pattern is the portion of the URL that comes after http://server:port/WebApplication Name (more on URL patterns in a bit).

Figure 18-2: Configuring a new servlet

Click the Servlet Mappings folder in the left frame, followed by the Configure a New Servlet Mapping link. Figure 18-3 shows the resulting console screen as we've filled it in for our example. Click the Create button when finished.

Figure 18-3: Configuring the servlet mapping

What this accomplishes is that when a client connects to the following URL, he is directed to the `AcctReport` servlet class:

```
http://www.zeetrade.com/accountManager/acct_report
```

You can also have as many `<servlet-mapping>` elements per `<servlet>` element as you want. It is worthwhile to play around with the `<url-pattern>` subelement of `<servlet-mapping>` because you can be quite flexible with what client requests get mapped to your servlet.

Table 18-4, for example, lists changes to the `<url-pattern>` element associated with the `Login` servlet and the HTTP requests that could connect to them.

Table 18-4: URL Patterns

URL pattern	HTTP request
/acct_report/*	http://www.zeetrade.com/accountManager/acct_report/index.html
/myaccount/report	http://www.zeetrade.com/accountManager/myaccount/report
/*.report	http://www.zeetrade.com/accountManager/anypage.report
/	http://www.zeetrade.com/accountManager/

JSP tag libraries

The example includes a JSP tag library, so you have to put a reference for that in your deployment descriptor for your JSPs to be able to use those custom tags.

Click the Tag Libs folder in the left frame, followed by the Configure a New Tag Lib link. Figure 18-4 shows the resulting console screen after we've filled it in. Click the Create button to create the library reference.

Figure 18-4: Creating a new TagLib

The URI that you enter is the URI that you will refer to in the `<%@ taglib %>` declaration in your JSP pages. The Location is the location of the tag library definition file (`.tld` file) relative to the `WEB-INF` directory.

Cross-Reference

For more on how to write `.tld` files, see Chapter 12.

In this case, your JSP pages might reference the tab library this way:

```
<%@ taglib uri="/jspTags" prefix="bible" %>
```

Application security

Now let's tighten up the security on your Web application. First, create some roles for your applications. Think of roles as groups of users who have similar privileges in your application. They may be administrators, general users, managers — whatever titles and descriptions make sense for your environment. You'll create the roles in your Web application and then you'll map them to WebLogic-specific principals in the WebLogic extension descriptor (`weblogic.xml`).

To create a security role, click the Security Roles folder in the left frame, followed by the Configure a New Security Role link.

You'll create a single group (Users) that represents the users who are allowed access to the application. Figure 18-5 shows the Create a New SecurityRole page after we've filled it in. Click Create to create the role.

Figure 18-5: Creating a new security role

Now you need to map this security role to actual principals (either users or groups) with a WebLogic security realm.

Cross-Reference   For more information on configuring a WebLogic security realm, see Chapter 22.

If you haven't already created the WebLogic Web application extension descriptor (`weblogic.xml`), you can create it now.

Click the Web Descriptor link at the top of the left frame and then click the Configure a New Web App Ext Descriptor link. Then click the Continue link.

You now have a new link in the left frame called WebApp Ext (see Figure 18-6). Inside the WebApp Ext folder, click the Security Role Assignments folder and then click the Configure a New Security Role Assignment link.

On this screen, choose the Users role you just created. In the Principal Names text area, type the names of the users and groups that are part of the WebLogic security realm that you are using. (Asking a user for validation of a particular security realm by using the `login-config` element is discussed in a following section.) Click the Create button.

Because WebLogic 7.0 Web applications are running on the same server and share user authentication information, you don't necessarily need to have a login page associated with this Web application. The user may have been authenticated in a different application altogether. Just in case, you'll make one of your own.

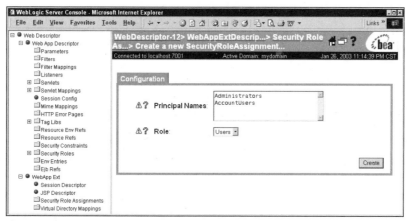

Figure 18-6: Creating a security role assignment

To create a new login configuration element to your deployment descriptor, click the Web App Descriptor link in the left frame and then click the Configure a New Login Config link. The screen in Figure 18-7 appears.

Figure 18-7: Creating a LoginConfig

Fill it in as shown and click the Create button. You have now specified that you want to use your own login form page, that you want to authenticate against the WebLogic file realm, and that your login page will be `login.jsp`. Upon errors in the login process, you will send browsers to the `login_error.jsp` file.

Validation using an HTML form and WebLogic requires that the field names of the form's input boxes be as follows:

```
<form method="POST" action="j_security_check">
    Name: <input type="text" name="j_username"><br>
    Password: <input type="password" name="j_password"><br>
            <input type="submit" name="login">
</form>
```

Now you must create a security constraint to define which resources of your Web application you want to protect. To do so, click the Security Constraints link in the left frame and then click the Configure a New Security Constraint link. Figure 18-8 shows the resulting page. Fill it in as shown and click Create.

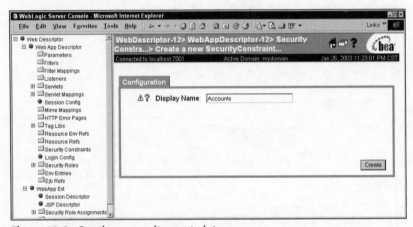

Figure 18-8: Creating a security constraint

After creating the constraint, you need to add some URL patterns to determine which resource on the site gets restricted.

Click the Web Resource Collections folder under the newly created Accounts Security Constraint and then click the Configure a New Web Resource Collection link.

On this screen, pick the URL pattern you want to protect (see the earlier section on URL patterns for more help choosing an appropriate pattern). In this case, you will protect everything under the accounts folder in your Web application. You may also choose the HTTP protocols that will be allowed, which includes the standard GET and POST, but can also include other HTTP methods such as PUT and DELETE, which are useful for managing upload folders (see Figure 18-9). Click Create.

Now you need to assign the security roles that will be allowed access to this particular Web resource.

Click the Account Security Constraint in the left frame and then click the Configure a New Auth Constraint link. Type in the auth constraint Description, click Create, choose the role you want to include, and then click Apply. Figure 18-10 shows the resulting screen.

Note   You *must* click Create after entering a Description before any Roles show up in the list.

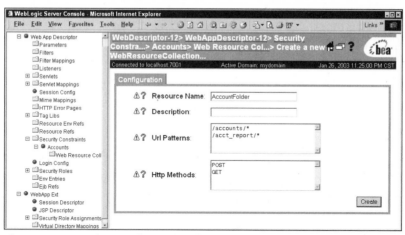

Figure 18-9: Creating a Web resource definition

Figure 18-10: Creating an authentication user constraint

Well, that should secure our application a bit. To validate your changes, click the Web Descriptor node on the left and then click Validate. To save your changes, click the Web Descriptor node on the left and then click Persist.

Suppose that you will test this out by pointing your browser to

```
http://localhost:7001/accountManager/accounts/myAccount.jsp
```

You would get redirected to your simple login page at

```
http://localhost:7001/accountManager/login.jsp
```

This page is shown in Figure 18-11.

Figure 18-11: The Login page

After your login is successful, you are forwarded to your original request page. If the login is invalid, you are redirected to the defined error page: `errors/login_error.jsp`.

Packaging Enterprise JavaBeans

Enterprise JavaBeans (EJBs) are server-side Java components created according to the EJB specification. WebLogic 7.0 supports the EJB 2.0 specification, which includes three types of Enterprise beans: session beans, entity beans, and message-driven beans.

Like Web applications, the deployment of EJBs is handled via XML deployment descriptors, and they are bundled up in JAR format for deployment.

Cross-Reference   Chapters 14–17 explain how to package and deploy the various types of EJBs.

Upon deployment, WebLogic's EJB compiler, `weblogic.ejbc`, is run to generate the RMI stub and skeleton classes that allow remote access to the EJBs. You may run the EJBC compiler separately if you wish, but when you deploy the EJB, WebLogic will run the compiler if you have not done so already.

Tip   It's a good habit to run `ejbc` yourself when you build EJBs, so you can catch errors in your code or deployment descriptors *before* deploying the EJBs to WebLogic Server.

Packaging Enterprise Applications

The Enterprise Application format can contain Web- and EJB-application components, as well as other supporting Java classes and files.

The files are bundled into an Enterprise Archive (.ear) file. This file has a META-INF directory that contains the application.xml deployment descriptor. application.xml contains an entry for each EJB and Web application. You may also describe security roles and other application resources here.

You can configure your Enterprise Application via the console. WebLogic provides a convenient XML deployment descriptor editor. Or if you choose to create one by hand, the DTD is

```
<!DOCTYPE application PUBLIC "-//Sun Microsystems,
Inc.//DTD J2EE Application 1.3//EN"
"http://java.sun.com/dtd/application_1_3.dtd">
```

The XML file has five sections that are contained within the <application></application> tags. They are as follows:

Web Modules:

```
<module>
  <web>
    <web-uri>webapp.war</web-uri>
    <context-root>mywebapp</context-root>
  </web>
</module>
```

EJB modules:

```
<module>
  <ejb>myEJB.jar</ejb>
</module>
```

Java Client Modules:

```
<module>
  <java>clientApp.jar</java>
</module>
```

Enterprise Connector Modules:

```
<module>
  <connector>myConnector.rar</connector>
</module>
```

Security Roles:

```
<security-role>
  <description>All Users</description>
  <role-name>Users</role-name>
</security-role>
```

Classloading in Enterprise Applications and WebLogic Server

Classloading can be a frustrating topic for J2EE programmers. Your Enterprise Application may contain many EJBs, servlets, JSPs, utility classes, third-party packages, and more. How do you make sure that your Java classes have appropriate access to each other without putting everything everywhere?

A *classloader* is a Java class that locates a requested file and loads it into the memory space of the Java Virtual Machine (JVM) for use by the requestor. A classloader finds these files by looking though the JARs and directories listed in its classpath.

WebLogic, in complying with the Enterprise Application specification, creates a number of classloaders to deploy an Enterprise Application:

✦ An Enterprise classloader (effectively the EJB classloader) that contains all the EJBs in an Enterprise Application.

✦ Any number of "children" Web application classloaders, loaded beneath the EJB classloader. There is one such class loader for each Web application in the Enterprise Application.

WebLogic creates the separate children classloaders so that the server may dynamically deploy and undeploy any one particular application without affecting any other on the server (thus avoiding having to reboot the entire server to change one application).

These classloaders are created in a specific hierarchy in which resources at any one level may see the resources only at their own level and above, as shown in Figure 18-12. What this means in practical terms is that Web applications can see files in their own classloader and those in its parent EJB classloader, but not those files in other sibling Web applications within the Enterprise Application. EJBs in the EJB classloader can only see files listed in the EJB classloader. And, of course, all levels can see files listed in the WebLogic classloader created at server startup. It is important to note that when a resource is requested, the topmost classloader will be queried first (for an identically named resource, the copy in the root class-loader will be returned in preference to a copy in the EJB classloader).

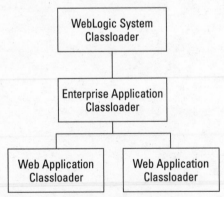

Figure 18-12: Classloader hierarchy

Third-Party and Utility Classes

Dealing with third-party classes is another area that can be quite frustrating. You have your favorite third-party package, `randomWords.jar`, which you use all over your Enterprise

Application, in EJBs, and Web applications alike. Where should you put it? Here are some choices with their pros and cons.

Root classloader

One place that would guarantee its universal availability is in the root system level classpath that is used when WebLogic starts up (`java -cp`).

Pros: Files placed here would be available to everything in the entire server.

Cons: One downside is that to change files here you have to reboot the entire server. Also, you potentially face the problem of versioning. Suppose that three different Enterprise Applications on the server use three different versions of the Xerces XML parser. Placing `xerces.jar` in the root classloader will not work for you then.

Keep in mind, too, that classes in the root classloader are by nature not distributed as part of your application. Maintaining boot scripts for all your applications on multiple clustered servers could be a hassle.

Put it everywhere

This means placing the JAR in every Web application's `WEB-INF/lib` directory and placing dependent files in every EJB JAR file.

Pros: You know that any particular application will have access to the files it needs, no matter how you slice and dice your application. This makes for very portable components.

Cons: Without meticulous care and/or good build scripts, versioning can become a nightmare.

Suppose that you've always used one version of `xerces.jar` in your Web application. But any EJB new to your Enterprise Application has a more recent version of the `xerces.jar` bundled in its JAR file. Due to the hierarchical nature of classloading, the EJB version will be loaded by your Web app before the version actually contained in the Web application.

The JAR manifest file classpath header

This is a handy way to reference dependency classes without having to leave copies of them everywhere. The manifest file (`manifest.mf`) contained in the `META-INF` directory of every JAR-packaged application can contain numerous bits of meta information about the package, useful for security, versions, and many other things. For your purposes though, you are interested in the classpath entry in the manifest file. This entry is a space-delimited list of JARs and folders (either absolute or relative to the location of the JAR file) that the deploying application container should make available to the files in the JAR.

WebLogic makes good use of the classpath entry (the implementation of which is left to the application vendor). Within an Enterprise Application, if any `.jar` file (including `.war` files) refers to a file in its manifest classpath entry, that file will be loaded at the Enterprise Application classloader level. This means that if a Web application refers to a file in its classpath entry, not only will EJBs be able to reference it, but other Web applications will be able to load it as well.

Here's an example of how you could structure your Enterprise Application to efficiently use this.

Place all third-party and utility classes in a `lib` directory under the root of your Enterprise Application directory. An example application might look like the following:

```
EntApp/
       accountEJB.jar
       accountManager.war
       /lib/
            xerces.jar
            xalan.jar
            myFormat.jar
       /META-INF/
                 application.xml
```

Now you'll create a manifest update file that contains the classpath listings for the utility files located in your `lib` directory and call it manifest.update. Note that classpath listings should be space-delimited and all on the same line as the classpath header (though you may have as many classpath header lines as you like).

```
Manifest-Version: 1.0
Class-Path: lib\xerces.jar lib\xalan.jar lib\myFormat.jar
```

As part of whatever build method you are using for your application, ensure that the following command is run on every `.jar` or `.war` file:

```
jar -umf manifest.update myJarlib.jar
```

Summary

The capability to configure the runtime behavior of applications and components at deployment time is one of J2EE's greatest strengths. In this chapter, you learned how to configure J2EE Web applications, EJBs, and Enterprise Applications using XML deployment descriptors, and how to package these entities into WAR files, JAR files, and EAR files for easy deployment to one or more WebLogic Server instances.

✦   ✦   ✦

Testing and Tuning WebLogic Applications

CHAPTER

19

Building your J2EE application and testing its functionality in a development environment is only half the battle. Having constructed a logical and sound business application for your clients, the next step is to ensure that your application yields acceptable performance in a production environment. WebLogic Server enables you to tailor its internal settings to your application's needs.

In this chapter, we provide an overview of monitoring your application's performance by using the WebLogic Console. We define load testing and profiling tools that may help you simulate users and analyze performance, and explain many possible environment settings for your WebLogic Server and Java Virtual Machine. We also mention various tips on tuning your application, touching on JDBC, EJB, and other WebLogic J2EE features and then provide an overview of profiling, load testing, and clustering. Finally, we wrap things up with an example WebLogic Server and application tuning process.

Understanding Performance Tuning

The first step of performance tuning is to define what you are trying to achieve. A developer's time is expensive to any business. A clear understanding of performance goals is necessary to ensure that developers don't waste time unnecessarily tuning applications that already perform well enough. After performance goals are defined, the next step is to determine whether your application is meeting those goals through testing. By monitoring your application and server when under simulated load, you can analyze your server's performance. If you determine that your application is falling short of its performance goals, it's time to tune the application and potentially tweak the server itself, tweak the JVM, or even change the amount or configuration of your hardware environment. Tuning is the process of changing various aspects of your application and its environment to achieve those goals.

Determining performance goals

Before spending a lot of time tuning and tweaking your application, you should first identify your client's needs and performance expectations. The foundation for performance tuning is to examine performance expectations and expected user population and behavior.

Identifying critical user actions

Rather than setting broad goals of having fast search queries or quick file downloads, look at specific user actions. Find the most time-critical and the most frequently used user actions in your application. Write these actions down and prioritize performance in these core pieces of your application. Come up with a list of performance goals in a scientific manner. Perhaps one of your goals is to ensure that a customer running a search query on your product database never has to wait more than five seconds for a response. This goal could take priority over another piece of your application, such as a user downloading documentation.

In the "Monitoring active queues, connections, and sockets" section later in this chapter, we discuss how you can focus the WebLogic Server to prioritize specific mission-critical facets of your application by assigning a group of server threads, called an *execute queue,* to specific servlets or JSPs.

Determining user population

After you come up with a prioritized list of client expectations, you must then study your expected user population. What is the maximum and average amount of users who will be using your application simultaneously?

Studying user behavior

After determining the maximum number of simultaneous users, you must then focus on the users' behavior. Maybe the most users you will ever expect to see are 1,000, but that doesn't necessarily mean that those users are all doing performance-intensive activities. Perhaps most of your users spend time browsing static content, whereas only a few run expensive queries.

Also, keep in mind how active your users are during their application sessions. Some applications may see users that have a request from the server every 30 seconds of their session, whereas other applications may see fairly inactive users that hit the server only once every couple of minutes.

Finalizing performance goals

Now that you have at least roughly identified your user population and behaviors, you should finalize your application performance goals. These goals consist of various user actions and usage scenarios. For example, you can now define a goal of product queries taking a maximum of five seconds each, while 1,000 users simultaneously run these queries at one-minute intervals.

Knowing performance goals will help you determine your performance-testing needs. If you determine that you require the use of commercial load-testing software or service, this information will help you pick one to best suit your needs. Having well-defined goals can also help you determine in which area of performance-tuning to start your tuning efforts.

Load testing

Load testing is the process of simulating your user base for the purposes of testing your application performance and finding bottlenecks.

A performance bottleneck occurs when a facet of your application environment is found to be responsible for performance degradation. Generally, you will be able to see only the very worst bottlenecks during a load test because they will tend to mask smaller issues. For instance, an improper network configuration between the database server and your WebLogic Server could be a huge bottleneck. Only after you fix the largest problem, the network latency, will you be able to determine whether your database queries are well designed.

Load testing is therefore a fairly iterative process of pounding the server with users, finding a performance bottleneck, fixing that bottleneck, and again pounding the server. Depending on the amount of users who will be using your application, it can become a critical piece of your development process. You will sleep better at night knowing that you have tested your applications under a load similar or even more extreme than you will see in production. This process is over when your application has met its performance goals.

Simulating hundreds or thousands of simultaneous users, and recording performance results from these simulated users, is not an easy task. There are many commercial and some noncommercial tools available for this purpose. Knowing your load-testing needs before entering into a commercial agreement for load-testing tools is truly important because you can identify specific things to look for in your tool. Here are a few questions you need to answer:

 ✦ How important is it to you to simulate real user behavior?

 ✦ How many users do you need to simulate to feel comfortable moving into a production environment?

 ✦ Will the service allow you to iteratively run tests and tune your servers?

 ✦ Will it require purchasing extra hardware to simulate the load?

 ✦ Will it require one of your developers or QA engineers to install and run the software?

To further your understanding of these tools and what they do, we have provided a simplistic class that illustrates load-testing behavior. Listing 19-1 shows `CheapLoadTester.java`, a class that uses internal WebLogic classes to test a system's response to heavy bursts of HTTP requests. `CheapLoadTester` simulates users by making multiple HTTP connections to URLs defined in the `main()` method. When run, the class creates a number of "users" equal to `NUM_CLIENTS` and waits `SLEEP_INTERVAL` milliseconds between initiating user requests.

Note that this class provides only a first-order approximation to actual Web browser behavior. For example, it does not spawn multiple threads for downloading images and framesets as real browsers do; nor does it handle cookies or sessions. Nevertheless, it might be useful for testing certain parts of your application, and it might help you determine whether you really need more realistic (and expensive) load-testing tools. Many commercially available load-testing suites simulate real browsers and also install performance-monitoring hooks into your systems while the tests are running. Some vendors will sell you software and some will perform the tests over the Internet from their own data centers.

One important point is to run `CheapLoadTester` on separate hardware from the system you are testing, so it doesn't affect the results of the tests.

Listing 19-1: **CheapLoadtester.java**

```java
package com.wiley.wlsbible.performance;

import java.io.*;
import java.net.*;
import java.util.*;
import weblogic.net.http.HttpURLConnection;

/**
 * This class uses the WebLogic HttpURLConnection
 * class to do a HTTP request and time the contents. It does not
 * do a good job of simulating a real browser's behavior; real
 * browsers are far more complex. Many testing suites do a much
 * better job of simulating browsers by doing multi-threaded
 * image downloading, paying attention to cookies, etc.
 * Remember to run load testing software on separate hardware from
 * your WebLogic server so you don't taint testing results.
 */
public class CheapLoadtester
    extends TimerTask implements Runnable {

  /**
   * Milliseconds of sleeps between requests, used for initializing
   * the timertask and as sleeps between URL hits during the run
   * method.
   */
  private static final int SLEEP_INTERVAL = 1000*10;

  /**
   * Number of users to simulate.
   */
  private static final int NUM_CLIENTS = 10;
  private ArrayList urlsToHit = null;
  private String testerName;

  /**
   * Instanciates a new CheapLoadtester.
   * @param name Name this tester for display purposes.
   */
  public CheapLoadtester(String name) {
    urlsToHit = new ArrayList();
    this.testerName = name;
  }

  /**
   * Adds a URL to iteratively test.
   */
  public void addURL(URL url) {
    urlsToHit.add(url);
  }

  public String getName() {
```

```
    return testerName;
  }

  /**
   * Hits all this tester's URLs and pushes timing info to standard
   * out.
   */
  public void run() {
    URL[] urls = new URL[urlsToHit.size()];
    urls = (URL[]) urlsToHit.toArray(urls);

    long start = 0;
    String contents = null;
    float runtime, total = 0;
    for(int i = 0; i < urls.length; i++) {
      start = System.currentTimeMillis();
      try {
        contents = getPage(urls[i]);
        System.out.println(
          testerName + " contents returned: " + contents);
      } catch (Exception e) {
        System.out.println(testerName +
          testerName + ": Exceptions occurred attempting to hit URL.");
        e.printStackTrace();
      }

      runtime = (float)(System.currentTimeMillis() - start)/1000;
      total += runtime;
      System.out.println(testerName + " took " + runtime +
        " seconds to process: " +  urls[i].toString());

      try { //Sleep between requests.
        Thread.sleep(CheapLoadtester.SLEEP_INTERVAL);
      } catch(Exception e) {
        e.printStackTrace();
      }
    }
    System.out.println("*****************************************");
    System.out.println("** " + testerName +
      ": Total time (not including sleeps) to process " +
      urls.length + " URLs: " + total + " seconds **");
    System.out.println("*****************************************");
  }

  /**
   * Opens a HttpURLConnection to the URL and returns the contents.
   */
  private String getPage(URL url) throws Exception {
    StringBuffer sb = new StringBuffer();

    HttpURLConnection conn = new HttpURLConnection(url);
    conn.connect();
```

Continued

Listing 19-1 *(continued)*

```
    DataInputStream dis = new DataInputStream(conn.getInputStream());
    String nextline;

    while((nextline = dis.readLine()) != null) {
     sb.append(nextline);
    }
    dis.close();
    return sb.toString();
}

/**
 * Declares multiple new 'clients' and schedules them on a timer.
 */
public static void main(String[] args) {
  ArrayList clients = new ArrayList(); //holds clients.
  try {
    for(int i = 0; i < NUM_CLIENTS; i++) {
      CheapLoadtester client = new CheapLoadtester("User"+i);
      //Add URLs for client to hit.
      URL tmpURL = new URL("http://servername:7001/APP/index.html");
      client.addURL(tmpURL);
      tmpURL = new URL(
       "http://servername:7001/APP/ProductDetail.jsp?productID=12345");
      client.addURL(tmpURL);
      tmpURL = new URL(
       "http://servername:7001/APP/ProductSearch.jsp?searchName=Potter");
      client.addURL(tmpURL);
      clients.add(client);
    }
  } catch(Exception e) {
    System.out.println("Exceptions occurred building clients, exiting.");
    e.printStackTrace();
    System.exit(1);
  }

  CheapLoadtester[] testerArray = new CheapLoadtester[clients.size()];
  testerArray = (CheapLoadtester[]) clients.toArray(testerArray);
  for(int i = 0; i < testerArray.length; i++ ) {
    Timer t = new Timer();
    t.schedule(testerArray[i], 500, CheapLoadtester.SLEEP_INTERVAL);
    //Start clients a second off from each other.
    try {
      Thread.sleep(1000);
    } catch(Exception e) {}
  }
 }
}
```

If you want to investigate more sophisticated load-testing tools, the Jakarta Foundation has a Jmeter project for performance testing. Information can be found at the following URL:

```
http://jakarta.apache.org/jmeter/index.html
```

Mercury Interactive also has performance-testing solutions, which you can find at the following site:

```
http://www-svca.mercuryinteractive.com
```

Note   During load testing, you may find that many client connections are being dropped. This could be because the server is bogged down and you have the accept backlog attribute set too low (see the section "Accept Backlog attribute" later in this chapter).

Areas of performance tuning

Many different factors can degrade application performance. This section focuses on some different options for configuring and tuning your WebLogic Server environment. We will touch on the tuning hardware and operating systems, but extensive coverage of these topics is beyond the scope of this book.

If there are configuration problems with your hardware, operating system, or JVM, it may be that no amount of WebLogic Server or application tuning will increase application performance. For instance, if you have allotted only 64 megabytes of RAM to your JVM when much more is available, WebLogic Server may be forced to use massive amounts of CPU swapping from memory to disk in its internal operations. Rather than start your tuning efforts at the lowest application level, it is wise to familiarize yourself with the bigger picture.

WebLogic Server tuning

You can configure the WebLogic Server to suit your application's needs. We examine many of these settings later in the chapter. One example of tuning WebLogic Server's environment is that you can modify the total amount of threads the server is allowed to spawn. Another example of WebLogic Server tuning is tweaking a JDBC connection pool to have a different initial size or maximum size.

Java Virtual Machine tuning

All instances of WebLogic Server run inside a Java Virtual Machine, or JVM. WebLogic Server 7.0 is distributed with and runs on the Java HotSpot JVM. One example of tuning the JVM is the ability to change the algorithm the JVM uses for garbage collection. For more information, see the section "Garbage collection" later in this chapter.

WebLogic application tuning

In your application code are many potential performance improvements. One example of improving your WebLogic application's performance is by using value objects to create an entity EJB, instead of calling individual setters, to decrease network and database traffic.

Cross-Reference   See Chapter 3 for information about using value objects with EJBs.

Hardware and operating system tuning

Some of the most important performance tuning of your production environment will be in ensuring a proper amount of CPU power, memory, throughput, and other hardware tuning. Also, your choice of operating system and its settings will drastically affect the performance of your applications. Be sure to read your platform's performance-tuning documentation and work with your IT-Operations team to ensure that your environment is properly tuned for your needs.

As already mentioned, WebLogic Server runs on the HotSpot JVM, and your applications run on the WebLogic Server. In a clustered environment, you will have multiple servers running on multiple JVMs. Figure 19-1 is a reminder that performance tuning for WebLogic applications must occur on several fronts.

Figure 19-1: Performance tuning occurs on several fronts for WebLogic applications.

WebLogic Server Performance Monitoring

The key to making your WebLogic Server environment faster and more efficient is being able to quickly identify bottlenecks in WebLogic Server's performance. There are also different command-line arguments to your JVM that can provide some performance-monitoring information. Finally, we'll mention some popular commercial tools that interface with the WebLogic Server to assist in performance monitoring.

Monitoring WebLogic Servers with the console

Understanding the WebLogic Console will be critical to helping you identify exactly why you may or may not be meeting your performance needs. The console will also be critical in providing evidence that a performance bottleneck has been solved.

Monitoring performance graphs from the console

The WebLogic Console provides a great tool for monitoring application performance. From the Console, go to your domain and select a server. Click the Monitoring tab and then the Performance tab, as shown in Figure 19-2.

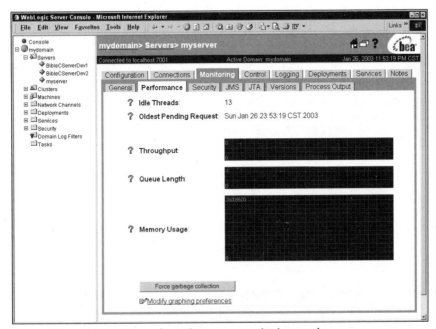

Figure 19-2: WebLogic Console performance monitoring graphs

These graphs provide visual real-time performance monitoring of some aspects of your server's performance. Table 19-1 describes the attributes shown on the screen.

Table 19-1: WebLogic Console Performance Monitoring Attributes

Attribute	Description
Idle Threads	The amount of the server's threads that are currently sitting idle.
Oldest Pending Request	The amount of time the oldest server request has been waiting to be serviced.
Throughput	The rate at which this server processes requests.
Queue Length	The total number of requests waiting to be serviced.
Memory Usage	The amount of memory currently being used by this server.

These graphs are ideal for easily understanding how your WebLogic Server is performing. If the number of idle threads approaches zero, it reflects a potential server-performance bottleneck. New client requests coming to the server in this state will be queued because the server will not have available threads to immediately service the requests. Alternatively, if the number of idle threads is very high when your server is at its peak usage, it could also hurt performance. Each server thread costs a certain amount of server resources to keep around and alive. Therefore, having more server threads than you require may hurt performance.

The queue length and pending oldest request times provide a great insight into your server's performance. A growing queue implies that your server is receiving more requests than it can handle. As this queue gets larger, the amount of lag-time before new requests can be serviced will increase. You'll notice that when your queue is growing, the oldest pending request time will also tend to increase.

If your memory usage is approaching 60 to 70 percent of the total available, it may start to degrade performance. As the server starts running out of memory, it will start pushing in-memory pieces of your applications to disk to free up memory and also run the garbage collector more frequently than it would normally.

Note   In the "Heap sizes" section later in the chapter, we explain how to allocate more memory to the JVM as well as how to tweak the number of threads available to the server.

Monitoring active queues, connections, and sockets

Still having your server selected on the console, choose Monitoring ➪ General (see Figure 19-3).

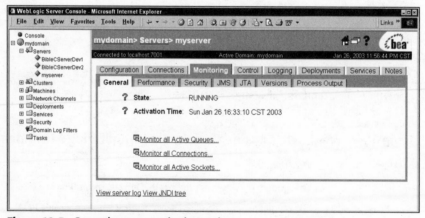

Figure 19-3: General server monitoring options

From the page shown in Figure 19-3, you can get a more detailed look at the server queues, connections, and sockets by clicking those links. If you noticed that your request queues were getting large from the graph, you could come here to determine which execute queues were having poor performance.

Execute queues in the WebLogic Server are essentially a group of execute threads that the server has at its disposal to assign work. New execute queues can be created and assigned to particular servlets of your application. Each queue has a configurable amount of threads assigned to it and also a configurable thread priority. The normal WebLogic configuration is to have one execute queue named "default" that all JSPs and servlets share. We will discuss the implications of creating and modifying execute queues in the "Modifying execute thread counts" section later in this chapter.

As seen in Figure 19-3, clicking the Monitor all Active Queues link takes you to the Active Execute Queues page. In Figure 19-4, you can see the total number of server threads allocated, idle threads, request queue length, and throughput of each execute queue. Clicking a particular queue will allow you to see the threads and the latest actions they have performed.

Figure 19-4: Examining active execute queues

The first thing to check when monitoring execute queue performance is the idle thread count. This is the number of execute threads that aren't currently doing anything and are waiting to process requests.

If the number of idle threads in the queue is zero, all the execute threads in this queue are busy and the next request to this queue will be blocked until one becomes available. This isn't necessarily a bad thing as long as requests aren't being timed out and are being processed within an acceptable time frame. On this page, you can see how many requests are currently waiting for an execute thread to become available. You can also see the time the oldest request was made to give you an idea of how long a client is waiting for a response from the server. If an HTTP request from a servlet is waiting for an execute thread for too long, as defined by your Web-server and HTTP configuration, the client's request will time out.

Having too many idle threads in an execute queue, especially when your server is under maximum load, can also potentially lead to performance problems. With each execute thread comes a performance cost because each thread owns its own stack and some system resources are required for its creation and maintenance. If your server is under maximum load and execute threads are still available, you may have assigned too many to this queue and you may see a performance increase when reducing the number of threads available to it.

The WebLogic Console enables you to see performance bottlenecks at a high level and then gives you the power to drill down into low-level details of your server performance.

Monitoring CPU utilization

Another important metric for monitoring your server's performance is CPU utilization. Familiarize yourself with your operating system and research the performance-monitoring tools you have at your disposal. For example, knowing that your server has a good amount of idle CPU under maximum load might be a sign that you can add a few more execute threads to the server. Alternatively, if you see that the server does not have any idle CPU and is consistently above 90 percent utilization, that's a good sign that you will not be able to improve performance by adding additional threads and could even hinder performance by doing so. Under these circumstances, it might be time to add another CPU to your server computer or possibly add another computer.

JVM options for performance monitoring

The Java HotSpot JVM provides some command-line flags that you may find useful. Although a complete analysis of their output data is outside the scope of this book, we will briefly mention them and point you in the right direction if you choose to investigate further.

Garbage collection monitoring

Garbage collection can sometimes cause noticeable pauses in Java applications. The Hotspot JVM allows you to tune garbage performance behavior and get garbage collection information. To get a detailed analysis of your JVM's garbage-collecting behavior, use the option for verbose garbage collection, -verbosegc. See your JVM documentation for detailed analysis and explanation of the output.

 Caution   Be sure to turn off verbose garbage collection when you move to a production environment because there is a performance hit associated with using it.

-Xprof JVM profiling

Edit your scripts to start WebLogic by adding an -Xprof to the server startup call. This flag tells the JVM that you want to get some JVM profiling information, as shown in Figure 19-5.

```
Command Prompt                                                        _ □ ×
Flat profile of 354.84 secs (34371 total ticks): ExecuteThread: '14' for queue:
'default'

  Interpreted + native   Method
  99.8%     0  +  20817   weblogic.socket.NTSocketMuxer.getNextSocket
   0.1%     0  +     14   weblogic.kernel.ExecuteThread.notifyRequest
   0.0%     0  +      6   java.net.PlainSocketImpl.socketGetOption
   0.0%     0  +      3   weblogic.transaction.internal.ServerCoordinatorDescript
or$1.execute
   0.0%     0  +      2   weblogic.socket.NTSocketMuxer.processSockets
   0.0%     0  +      2   java.io.FileOutputStream.openAppend
   0.0%     0  +      1   java.net.PlainSocketImpl.socketSetOption
   0.0%     1  +      0   weblogic.servlet.internal.ServletRequestImpl.<init>
   0.0%     0  +      1   weblogic.servlet.internal.WebAppServletContext.findInde
xFile
   0.0%     1  +      0   weblogic.servlet.internal.MuxableSocketHTTP.getBuffer
   0.0%     0  +      1   weblogic.servlet.internal.RequestParser.parse
   0.0%     0  +      1   weblogic.servlet.internal.RequestParser.getFirstLine
 100.0%     3  +  20848   Total interpreted

   Compiled + native     Method
   0.0%     1  +      0   weblogic.servlet.internal.RequestParser.getFirstLine
   0.0%     1  +      0   Total compiled
```

Figure 19-5: Sample standard output from running your JVM with -Xprof

Running your JVM with `-Xprof` will push some profiling information to standard out. You can find more information on `-Xprof` output at the following URL:

    http://java.sun.com/products/hotspot/2.0/README.html

-Xrunhprof JVM profiling

Another way to get more profiling information about your JVM is to put the `-Xrunhprof` flag in your WebLogic Server startup scripts, as shown in Figure 19-6.

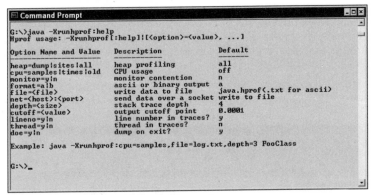

Figure 19-6: -Xrunhprof JVM profiling options

Running your WebLogic Server with the `-Xrunhprof` flag can give you a lot more detailed JVM information, including heap profiling and CPU usage. You can have this information pushed to an ASCII text file for later review. You can find more information on `-Xrunhprof` profiling at the following URL:

    http://developer.java.sun.com/developer/onlineTraining/Programming/JDCBook/
    perf3.html

Caution   When moving your WebLogic applications into production, be sure to remove these profiling flags from your server startup scripts.

Commercial tools for performance monitoring

If you need more detailed or easier-to-understand performance analyses, there are a number of commercially available Java profilers. Many of them even integrate easily with the WebLogic Server. Borland's (formerly Intuitive Systems') profiler Optimizeit and Quest's (formerly Sitraka's) Jprobe are just a few you may want to research for your WebLogic Server profiling needs.

Tuning WebLogic Server

Now you have put some thought into performance expectations of your WebLogic application and also learned some methods to monitor WebLogic Server's performance. You can use these skills to find critical bottlenecks. This section discusses some methods to solve these bottlenecks.

Basic server configuration

A number of basic configuration options are available from the WebLogic Console tuning page. Enabling native I/O using performance packs, creating and adjusting WebLogic's internal execute queues, and configuring connection buffer sizes are just a few.

WebLogic Server performance packs

WebLogic provides performance packs for certain platforms. These performance packs tie I/O operations more closely to the platform and thereby increase application performance because platform-independent I/O is not as efficient. Depending on which platform you are running WebLogic Server, you may be able to enable these platform-native I/O operations, which will yield a significant performance boost. See the WebLogic documentation to see whether your platform has a performance pack available. If one is available for your platform, you should use it.

To activate the native I/O performance pack, go to the WebLogic Console, select your server, click Configuration, and then click the Tuning tab, which is shown in Figure 19-7.

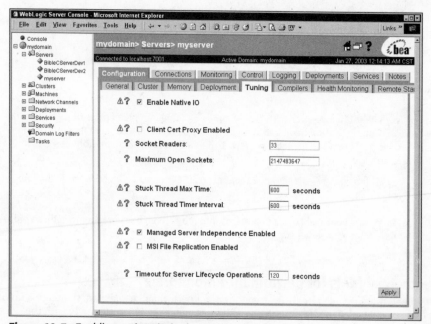

Figure 19-7: Enabling native I/O in the WebLogic Console

Select the Enable Native IO checkbox and click Apply. When you restart your server, you will now be using native I/O.

If no performance pack is available for your platform, WebLogic Server will allocate a certain percentage of its execute threads to be available as socket readers. This percentage is also available for adjustment on the console, also seen in Figure 19-7. If your application heavily uses I/O, you may get a performance boost by raising this percentage.

Modifying execute thread counts

The number of execute threads that WebLogic Server has allotted to it affects its internal operations and your applications drastically. The more threads allotted, the more simultaneous actions can take place within the server. During the course of your testing, look for the situation in which the waiting request queues are building up and your CPU utilization isn't 100 percent. This implies that although there is CPU time available to the server, all the threads are potentially blocked and not available to service a new request. This is a situation in which raising the execute thread count could improve your server's performance.

You can adjust the number of threads from the WebLogic Console. From the Examining Active Execute Queues page (see Figure 19-4), click the link to Configure Execute Queue. This will bring up a list of all the execute queues. Click one to configure it, as shown in Figure 19-8.

Figure 19-8: Modifying thread count on execute queues

Adjusting the thread count will take effect after restarting your WebLogic Server. The queue length is the maximum length of the execute queue. Raising thread priority will result in this queue taking CPU priority over threads with lower priority.

Caution   Raising the server thread count can sometimes increase application performance, but there are many factors to consider before raising the count. Setting the count too high will degrade server performance.

The number of simultaneous actions that can happen on your server is dependent on the number of CPUs on your server hardware. The more processors available, the more threads you can give the server and expect a performance boost.

Another factor to consider when deciding to modify the thread counts is the operating system you are running because some operating systems can handle higher numbers of threads than others. Also, keep in mind that the more threads you allocate to the server, the more *context-switching* will occur. Context-switching occurs when one thread stops and another takes over on the CPU—and you pay a performance price when that happens. Also, by increasing the number of server threads, you're increasing the amount of memory the server uses, which can degrade performance.

Accept Backlog attribute

The WebLogic Server will allow a certain number of connections, 50 by default, to be placed in the connection backlog when all execute threads in the queue are busy. The amount is configurable by changing the accept backlog attribute on the Server Tuning page of the console, as seen in Chapter 23, Figure 23-30. If you notice that many of your clients are having their connections refused by your WebLogic Server, you could increase this number accordingly to allow the buffer to grow larger.

Creating new execute queues

The WebLogic Server allows you to create new execute queues as well. This is generally only a good idea if you have pieces of your application that you can define as far more or far less critical than the rest of your application. Even in that case, use extreme caution when configuring new queues because taking this step unnecessarily could easily create new performance issues.

For example, imagine that there is a certain set of JSPs that your company provides free of charge that see lots of traffic. You may need to take steps to ensure that these users don't interfere with a set of pages your customers use during payment. This is because there is a good chance that customers will not proceed with a purchase if the pages are taking too long. In this case, you could create a new execute thread with a small number of execute threads at a low priority and assign the freely available JSPs to use that execute thread. This way, the JSPs or servlets will get only so much attention from the WebLogic Server and will not directly interfere with the execute queues of the mission-critical JSPs. Alternatively, you could create a new execute queue with threads at a higher priority and assign your mission-critical pages to that thread.

To bind servlets or JSPs to a specific execute queue, you must alter the web.xml file entry to set the wl-dispatch-policy initialization parameter to the proper execute queues name. An example of this is seen in Listing 19-2.

Listing 19-2: **Binding Servlets or JSPs to Execute Queues**

```
<servlet>
  <servlet-name>ServletName</servlet-name>
  <jsp-file>/applicationname/dopayment.jsp</jsp-file>
  <init-param>
    <param-name>wl-dispatch-policy</param-name>
    <param-value>NewExecuteQueueName</param-value>
  </init-param>
</servlet>
```

JDBC tuning considerations

Correctly configuring your JDBC connection pools and using the correct drivers can increase the performance of your WebLogic Server applications. Using precompiled prepared statements is another method of increasing performance. Also, sometimes the best way to improve database performance is to avoid the database as much as possible through the use of object caches.

Connection pool settings

Making your database connection pool too small can drastically degrade application performance. In most applications, the ideal number of maximum connections in a pool is equal to the amount of simultaneous users using the application, assuming those users could cause database hits. If your pool has reached its maximum number of connections, and all connections are in use by other users, a new database connection request will block until one becomes available.

Alternatively, if the number of database connections is set too high, this could also cause performance issues. Each database connection you create has a performance cost in terms of memory and also in ongoing maintenance as the WebLogic Server pool will monitor its connections.

Also, some databases will kill idle connections, causing the WebLogic Server to re-create the connections at a high performance cost. You must work with your DBAs to determine your connection pool settings in production and development.

Driver-type considerations

Not all JDBC drivers perform alike. Much like how using a performance pack can use native I/O, some drivers are more optimized and closely tied to the platform. If your application is database-intensive, be sure and research what driver you are using and what other drivers are available to you.

Cross-Reference　　See Chapter 5 for more detailed information on driver types, pool settings, and general JDBC concerns.

EJB tuning considerations

You can find many potential performance improvements by correctly tuning the EJB pools for your applications. This section discusses a few of them, but be sure to look at Part IV for information on database-locking issues, detailed analyses of deployment descriptors, and other performance-related information.

EJB pool settings

As with JDBC connection pools, the WebLogic Server saves the cost of allocating some types of EJBs by using pooling. If you set the maximum size of the pools too low, you will degrade application performance. The maximum size of these pools is found in the `weblogic-ejb-jar.xml` descriptor under the attribute `max-beans-in-free-pool`. If all of a pool's EJBs are in use by a client and a new client requests an EJB from the pool, the client must wait until one becomes available. You have the option of setting the initial size of these pools high as well: At server startup, a certain number will be created, increasing memory usage but potentially improving performance.

Stateful and entity EJB caching

Another potential area to focus your tuning efforts is in the caching of the stateful session EJBs. Stateful session EJBs are never persisted to a database, so the server must keep them in a memory cache or push them to disk for temporary storage. The process of pushing these beans to disk and retrieving them when needed — called *activation* and *passivation* — is expensive. The most stateful session EJBs that the server will keep in the cache are set in the `weblogic-ejb-jar.xml` file under the attribute `max-beans-in-cache`. If this attribute is set too low, your server may do an excessive amount of passivation of these EJBs, which will degrade performance. Raising the maximum cache size excessively could cost your server in memory availability.

Defer locking to database with entity EJBs

By default, the WebLogic Server will defer entity locking to the database, which is more efficient than having the EJB container do it.

Tuning the WebLogic Server's JVM

The Hotspot Java Virtual Machine (JVM) is highly tunable for boosting your server performance. We'll discuss a few common options for tuning your JVM when launching your WebLogic Servers. Be sure to research in more detail in the documentation for the Hotspot JVM. Pay particular attention to options available to the platform on which you are running WebLogic because they vary. You will tune the JVM by editing the server startup scripts.

 Note   BEA also has the new WebLogic JRockit server side optimized JVM available. More information is available at BEA's Web site at `http://www.bea.com/framework.jsp?CNT=index.htm&FP=/content/products/jrockit`

Heap sizes

One of the most important steps of starting the WebLogic Server in your production environment is setting the maximum and minimum sizes of the memory heap, as shown in Figure 19-9. It's a good general practice to set the minimum and maximum equal to each other because it ensures that the JVM will not waste resources resizing the heap. Tuning the size of this heap will greatly affect server performance. You want to set it as high as your hardware will allow, but at a point prior to reaching that maximum you may encounter performance degradation. Having too much memory allocated can sometimes cause garbage collection to be overly slow. To change these sizes, adjust the JVM options `-Xms` and `-Xmx` by modifying the allotted memory in your scripts that start the WebLogic Server JVM. In Figure 19-9, you can see that the startup script has set the minimum and maximum memory to be 64MB.

Garbage collection

The Hotspot JVM uses a generational garbage-collection algorithm. Rather than scan the entire heap for all dereferenced objects, it keeps track of the age of the objects and uses the information to increase its efficiency. You may see a performance boost by playing with more options for setting the heap. The options `-XX:NewSize` and `-XX:MaxNewSize` set the size of the portion of the heap that will house relatively new objects. These objects are the most frequently garbage-collected, and this area will be garbage-collected more than some other areas of the heap. WebLogic recommends setting these sizes to approximately one-fourth the total size of the heap. If your application tends to allocate large quantities of objects only to have them dereferenced shortly thereafter, you may want to tune this number higher. For a more complete discussion of the Hotspot Garbage Collector and settings, go to `http://java.sun.com/docs/hotspot/PerformanceFAQ.html`.

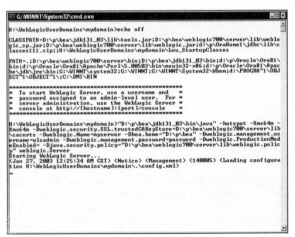

Figure 19-9: Starting the WebLogic Server JVM with heap sizes of 64MB

Client/Server JVM options

Multiple JVMs come with Hotspot. By running with a `-hotspot` flag or a `-client` flag, you are running the client version. The client version is optimized for a small scope. Alternatively, running your server with a `-server` flag will run the Hotspot JVM that has been optimized for a server environment.

Caution   Be sure to retest your applications if you choose to try and switch JVMs in this manner. Changing the JVM is a fundamentally radical change in environment and should be taken seriously.

Tuning WebLogic Server Applications

Now that you know about tuning your WebLogic Server and also its JVM, let's look at some performance considerations for your applications.

Tuning JDBC modules within your application

Not only must you properly set up your WebLogic Server connection pools and datasources, but you must also make sure that your applications use those resources intelligently. Here are a few simple JDBC tuning considerations when examining your application code.

ResultSet concurrency and direction

Make sure that when you are doing normal forward-only and read-only processing that you are using the most efficient ResultSet concurrency and direction modes. When the statements are initialized to return forward-moving and read-only results, they are generally far more efficient. See the `java.sql.Statement` and static constants on the `java.sql.ResultSet` interface documentation and your database driver documentation for further details.

Prepared statements

Use JDBC optimizations like prepared statements whenever possible, including in your session EJBs that perform database operations. To learn more about what prepared statements are, research the `java.sql.PreparedStatement` interface as defined by Sun.

Java object caches

Caching information in memory on the server can prevent unnecessary database hits. Often, these caches are loaded on application startup and are serializable objects registered with JNDI. For example, an application may be able to keep its entire product catalog in memory, in a collection keyed by a unique product identifier. This would be an alternative to doing a database query to load product information on demand.

Depending on the type and configuration of the database you are using, it's possible that it is doing some complex caching on its end to improve query performance. However, no matter how fast the JDBC queries come back from the database, you still will have to parse the ResultSet into a Java object at some point in order to use it. Also, it's possible that your database lives on a separate piece of hardware and must communicate over a network. This network communication will use bandwidth and also increase the latency of the queries. For those reasons, there is always a performance gain from keeping some commonly used objects in a cache.

EJB considerations

When developing EJBs that you know will not be accessed remotely via Remote Method Invocation (RMI), define local interfaces for those EJBs. This is a new option in the EJB 2.0 specification.

The WebLogic Server is extremely efficient at supplying stateless session EJBs to clients; it is far more efficient than when you use stateful beans. Clients do not actually hold onto a reference to a stateless session EJB, but a proxy to the pool of EJBs.

Tip   Use value objects to populate entity EJBs rather than individual setters. Each set method call is potentially a remote method call, as well as a database hit! By passing a serializable object that represents all the values to set, you can accomplish this all at once.

Cross-Reference   See Part IV for a more detailed discussion of these types of EJB considerations.

Asynchronous components

By keeping your application components asynchronous, you often increase performance (or at least response times) to the client. Research some of the different J2EE technologies that can help achieve this, including JMS messaging and message-driven EJBs.

For instance, let's say one result of a user's action is that an e-mail should be sent to an administrator. Instead of doing that processing synchronously, in which the user doesn't receive confirmation until the e-mail has been sent, you could post the user's message to some JMS destination and then immediately respond to the user. A message-driven EJB could be listening on the JMS destination and sending the e-mail asynchronously. So if the WebLogic Server was very busy and it takes lots of time to build and send that e-mail, the user would not notice that performance issue. This is only one example of improving performance via asynchronous behavior.

Singletons

A *singleton* is a design pattern in which only one of a certain facet of your application exists. This pattern can be useful when making performance-tuning decisions. Let's say there is a certain process, for example performing a massive data conversion, that takes an enormous amount of CPU and memory to run. You want to make a design decision to enforce that this process can be running by only one thread at any given moment in time to limit the amount of server resources it can take up. You would therefore implement this class as a singleton.

Transaction considerations

In general, make sure that you keep your transaction scopes as small as possible. Don't have unnecessary systems or modules inside a transaction because large scope and duration can be extremely expensive. Also, make it a rule to never have a transaction spanning a user's input.

 Cross-Reference   See Chapter 6 for more information about transaction scopes.

Logging considerations

Anyone who has coded in Java is familiar with the tendency to put lots of `System.out.println` lines in code for debugging purposes. It's important to try and limit these logging messages when you move to production because there is a performance cost to this extra messaging to the standard output stream.

Even if you use WebLogic Server's logging subsystem or some configurable logging system such as log4j, there may be a cost in every method call to those subsystems, regardless of priority of the log message. It is possible that in your strings you are calling lots of `toString()` methods during those log statements. Even if there is no I/O cost relating to the logging call because you have logging turned off, you still will be using the CPU with the unnecessary method calls and string building.

Compiler settings

You can configure your EJBC and JSP compiler settings to use more-efficient compilers if you have them. These optimizing compilers may create more-efficient Java classes. Also, you can configure your JSPs to precompile on server startup to avoid situations in which a JSP compiler causes brief but noticeable spikes in your CPU utilization when compiling JSPs.

Nonsynchronized collections

You can achieve some significant performance boosts by using nonsynchronized collections, such as `java.util.HashMap`, instead of synchronized collections such as `java.util.HashTable`. Of course, this assumes that you don't have concurrent access of these collections.

Placing objects in sessions

Placing Java objects in a client session can drastically improve performance. For example, it's a much better idea to place a user's personal data in her session than to load it from a database on every one of her page clicks. However, there is a server-side cost relating to placing objects in the session.

Every object you keep in the session has a performance cost related to the object's in-memory size. Every data member of the object increases the amount of memory it will take to store it in the session. Suppose that when monitoring your server's performance, you notice that the server is using near its maximum allotted memory, and you detect a direct correlation between the number of users logged in and the amount of memory used, regardless of user behavior. This would indicate a large memory cost per client session, and could point to a case with large data objects or large numbers of objects in session.

Before putting a large object into the session, take the time to think of potential design alternatives. For example, let's look at an e-commerce site's decision to place a UserBean object into all user sessions. The UserBean contains other data members relating to the user's preferences, request history, general account information, and a product wish list. Perhaps all those data members are loaded when a user logs in and are then placed into that user's session. Instead of keeping a user's wish list in memory as a UserBean data member, perhaps you want that information to be loaded from the database on every HTTP request or to get loaded into memory only when they visit a specific subset of application pages relating to the wish-list functionality. With these alternatives, when the user is not building or viewing a wish list, the data members relating to the wish list aren't eating up precious memory resources.

You also want to analyze all the objects you put in the session to see whether they are holding redundant information. Perhaps you are actually storing product names and descriptions in the user's wish list when you only need to keep around the product's unique integer identifier.

Make sure that your application is intelligent enough to remove objects from the session when it is no longer necessary to keep them around. Instead of keeping the user's entire product history in the session, you should keep data around that relates only to the last four products he viewed. This would cut down the amount of memory the product history takes up in the session and free valuable server resources.

WebLogic Server clustering overview

At some point in your load-testing and tuning process, you may realize that you've made lots of improvements, but you are still unable to meet your performance goals. You've worked with IT to ensure that the hardware is properly configured and has a good amount of memory and fast CPUs. However, all your execute queues are busy, requests are still being dropped, there is no idle CPU and available memory is running low, so creating extra execute threads or object caches don't seem like good solutions.

No matter how finely tuned, there is only so much that one WebLogic Server can do. If your application has a large audience whose performance demands have your single server peaked, clustering is the answer. Instead of running one server, you run your applications on many servers, and WebLogic is intelligent enough to distribute the load across the different servers. Clustering also has the added bonus of providing failover. When one of your servers goes down, there are more to fill in the gaps, and your clients may not even notice. Assuming that you wrote your application components in a somewhat standard J2EE fashion by using EJBs, JSPs, servlets, and so on, there is a good chance your application performance will improve linearly as you add hardware and servers.

Take special care when tuning WebLogic Servers in a cluster. A WebLogic Server in a cluster will tend to use more execute threads as socket readers than a non-clustered server will. This is due to the overhead of the clustered servers interacting via socket communication. As seen in Figure 19-7, you can adjust the number of execute threads and also increase the percentage of those threads available as socket readers. If you are encountering performance problems with your cluster under load, pay special attention to the number of idle execute threads. If there are a good number of idle execute threads available to the server, you can increase performance by increasing the percentage available. If there are no execute threads idle, you may need to increase the overall number of execute threads on the server, taking into consideration your hardware and platform constraints.

It is generally best to performance tune and test your applications in a single-server environment before adding the complexity of a server cluster into the mix.

 Cross-Reference See Chapter 24 for more information about clustering WebLogic Server.

Tuning Process Example

In this section, we'll examine the steps of a fictitious development and its iterative tuning, load-testing, and analysis process. This case study will not contain code, specific details about load-testing suites, profilers, or hardware. It is of a walkthrough of simple tuning steps and high-level tuning thoughts. The purpose is to illustrate a simple process that may be similar to those used in many development shops.

Define performance goals

After the project team had completed the project's functional specifications, it was time for the software engineers to focus on the design specifications and high-level architecture. Before starting this design, they laid out detailed thoughts on user behavior, expected user populations, and application performance goals in specific application modules.

For this example, we will focus on three of the project team's goals:

✦ To be able to support 1,000 concurrent users, which is twice as many as they have ever seen in production. By overshooting the amount of users they expect to see, they should be able to develop their application and tune their environment to handle a potential unexpected growth in users.

✦ To return "critical" Web pages; that is, pages central to the user's purpose for using the application, in two seconds or less. On an online brokerage site, for example, such pages might include forms to buy and sell securities, or pages that display individual account statements.

✦ To return "non-critical" Web pages to users in five seconds or less. Considering again an online brokerage site, such pages might include the brokerage firm's quarterly financial statements, delivery of lengthy research reports, explanations of trading regulations, and so on.

Now that the project team has laid down goals, it must define what it means by 1,000 users. When analyzing user behavior of similar sites and of its own current user population, the team has found the following:

✦ The average user is estimated to issue one request every 45 seconds.

✦ Forty percent of the requests are for portfolio analysis or to view breaking news about companies.

✦ Forty percent of the requests are for research on specific stocks and mutual funds, including getting real-time quotes of stocks.

✦ Twenty percent of the requests are directly related to the trading of stocks, such as a request to enter an order to buy a security.

The application-tuning process

Having a great iterative tuning process is no substitute for good initial architecture and engineering practices. Many of the performance problems seen in the testing phase of applications reflect a poor initial architecture or an architecture that was created without detailed performance goals and scalability in mind. For this example, let's assume that the application's architects did a mediocre job, so during their tuning process, we'll see some architecture decisions rethought, as well as tweaking of the server, JVM, database, and EJB settings.

The process employed by the project team is to load test the application with an accurate portrayal of the user population. During the test, developers will monitor the server's performance from the WebLogic Console and by monitoring the hardware's CPU metrics. After analyzing the test data to see whether they met their performance objectives, the team will decide when it's time to end the tuning process and proceed to staging the application in production.

Load testing

The development team leverages its knowledge of expected user behavior and performance goals to create its load-testing suite. The team configures its load-testing suite to create a user population that is similar to the one it will see in production. The team also has configured the testing suite to gradually increase users over time, until it reaches the 1,000-user limit. Starting small and increasing the amount of users over time enables the team to monitor the performance at a wide range of stresses and help it pinpoint an approximate number of maximum users with the current application and server configuration.

The team will then correlate data returned from its simulated users with data gained from monitoring the server. When the simulated users start to see large response times, server timeouts, or refusing connections, that is the time to closely inspect the WebLogic Console and the CPU Utilization for evidence of where the bottlenecks are occurring. After they have theorized where the bottleneck lies, they will attempt to fix the issue and then move forward with the next load-testing phase to see if the server performance has improved, stayed the same, or become worse.

Now let's examine the specific iterations of load testing and taking a WebLogic Server and application configuration to production.

Iteration 1

Test results: At the first run of the load testing, the test got up to 40 users before the users started to experience response times slower than five seconds. At 60 users, many user connections were getting dropped and an inspection of the WebLogic Server logs indicated out-of-memory exceptions. Meanwhile, the WebLogic Console performance graph showed that the server had indeed consumed its entire memory allocation of 64MB.

Solution: After checking the staging server's hardware and speaking with IT-Operations, the team decided to give the server's JVM maximum and minimum heap size to 512MB of memory.

Iteration 2

Test results: This time, the team started encountering "connection refused" errors when the test got to 100 total users. All the users previous to that moment had been getting server responses within acceptable time frames.

Solution: Because all the users who got any responses got acceptable ones, and the rest of the user connections were refused, the engineering team thinks that the server could accept more connections and increases the Accept Backlog attribute on the WebLogic Console tuning page from 50 to 100. This forces the server to allow the backlog to grow so it can continue to service those requests.

Iteration 3

Test results: This time, the test got up to 250 users, at which point server response times on a specific page fell below acceptable limits, taking over five seconds. This page is related to looking up a detailed view of a stock's metrics.

Solution: The engineers looked at the code for looking up the stock metrics, and noticed that it was a JDBC query against the stock database. They worked with the DBAs to create indexes on the columns of data that the users could search on, and changed their result sets to be forward moving and read-only.

Iteration 4

Test results: This time the test got up to 300 users, at which point server response times on all JDBC-related pages fell below acceptable limits, taking over five seconds. The engineers inspected the JDBC connection pools and noticed that all the connections were busy, and therefore all new database requests started to queue up waiting for connections from the pool.

Solution: The engineers worked with the DBAs and decided to triple the amount of maximum database connections. They also decided to build an in-memory cache of objects encapsulating data about the top 1,000 stocks.

Iteration 5

Test results: The test got up to 400 users before users started to get unacceptable response times on all pages. Using the WebLogic Console to examine the execute queues, the engineers noticed that there were no available execute threads and requests had started piling up. Inspection of the CPU Utilization at the same moment shows that there is still 50 percent CPU idle time.

Solution: The engineers researched WebLogic documentation about their operating system and hardware configurations, and decided to increase the number of threads on the default execute queue from 15 to 40.

Iteration 6

Test results: The test approached 700 users before server response times fell well below acceptable limits. The idle CPU time was less than one percent, free memory available to the server was also less than one percent, no free database connections were seen, and the backlog had overflowed. The engineers had cached everything possible, inspected the user sessions for unnecessary objects, and worked with DBAs to build all the necessary database tuning.

Solution: The engineers now feel it is time to cluster and add hardware. Not only will this provide another server to disperse the load to, but it has the added bonus of giving the Web site some measure of failover. They decide to purchase two additional servers. The current server seems to be able to service 700 users before peaking out. By purchasing two additional servers, they estimate they will be able to service almost 2,000 simultaneous users. And if one server happens to go down, they will still be able to service the performance goals with the other two. A three-server cluster is implemented.

Iteration 7

Test results: The test approached 900 users before the performance on the mission-critical pages fell below acceptable range, and trades started approaching three-second response times. All other page requests were well within acceptable range. There was plenty of memory available across the cluster, and CPU Utilization was relatively low. When examining the execute queues, the engineers realized all execute threads were busy.

Solution: The mission-critical pages are using the same execute queues as the rest of the pages. The engineers decide to create separate execute queues for the mission-critical pages. These new queues are assigned 15 threads each, while moving the default queues down to 25 execute threads. The priority of the mission-critical execute queues is set higher than the default queues.

Iteration 8

Test results: The test approached 1,800 users before performance was unacceptable. Engineers then dropped one server from the cluster and ran the test again to simulate a server crash at a critical time. The test was still within acceptable parameters, allowing 1,300 users.

Summary

WebLogic Server supplies you with lots of help in measuring and monitoring its performance. The real-time graphing and thread-queue monitoring from the console are especially helpful. You must also familiarize yourself with tools to monitor performance in your operating system in order to help you tune applications.

Load testing is the process of simulating a user base in order to measure your application and server performance during development. Profiling is the process of using tools to inspect the application and server environments and help you troubleshoot bottlenecks. Many commercial tools are available to help you load test and profile your server's performance. Define your application-testing needs before investigating these potentially commercial solutions. Look for tools that easily interface with the WebLogic Server.

Because your WebLogic Server has many components, they can cause performance bottlenecks when improperly tuned. Use the console to investigate and tailor these components for your platform and application.

WebLogic Server runs on the Java Hotspot JVM. Hotspot gives you many options for tuning it to your particular operating system and hardware.

Assuming that your application was written with scalability in mind, WebLogic Server clustering scales almost linearly by adding new server instances to the cluster.

✦　　✦　　✦

Implementing Security

◆ ◆ ◆ ◆

◆ ◆ ◆ ◆

Understanding Security Fundamentals

In This Chapter

Understanding security principles and layers

Working with security perimeters

Dealing with security attacks

Understanding ciphers, keys, and secure sockets

Almost all enterprise applications today, especially those being deployed to the Internet, require some level of security and protection. Sometimes the requirement is to protect consumers from fraud (such as credit card theft); other times, the requirement is to protect internal corporate data (such as payroll information) from access by unauthorized persons; and other times, the requirement is something completely different. This chapter helps you understand the need for enterprise application security, the fundamental concepts of enterprise application security, and the properties of effective security solutions. In Chapters 21 and 22, you'll learn how to apply these concepts in the context of WebLogic Server to build secure WebLogic applications.

Understanding Enterprise Security

Enterprise security concepts closely parallel the security concepts you encounter in daily life. Security is the capability to enforce some level of trust among people, organizations, and systems, including the capability to protect assets belonging to those entities. Just as people have different levels of trust, so do organizations. You encounter different levels of trust in your daily lives. When getting change from a cashier, for example, do you count it? Do you trust your daughter with the car keys? Do you lock up your jewelry and cash when a maid cleans your hotel room? Do you believe your co-worker about the lay-off rumors without asking anyone else? All these questions imply some form of security layering. The more valuable you believe an object is, the more security you apply to it. You may, for example, forget about change on the nightstand in a hotel room, but you will likely pick up 50 dollars before you leave the room.

Just as you apply different levels of security to items of different perceived value, so do organizations. An online trading firm's home page, for example, is visible to everyone; whereas only customers can view their accounts. The firm's internal mail system is protected from everyone except employees. The question then becomes: How valuable is the enterprise data?

Customers and their data are at the mercy of how an organization manages that data. When a credit card number is stored into the Web site for an order, that number is now stored by the system that the customer placed the order in. If that same customer places many orders at different systems, his credit card number is managed by each of them, and the security of that important data depends on the security of those systems. The question is, how secure must enterprise data be, and how do you go about securing it?

Security Layers

Security principles are the answers to the questions of how secure and how valuable the enterprise data needs to be. *Security layers* refer to the way those answers are modeled in the system. Before you give access to your objects (*authorization*), you first have to know the person (*authentication*). If you have any doubts about the state of something you own, you check up on it (*integrity*). If the person seems untrustworthy, you keep mental notes on what to trust to him, what to double-check, and what not to share (*auditing*). A typical security-layering system may look like Figure 20-1.

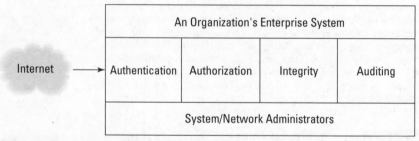

Figure 20-1: Security layers

You apply security levels throughout your everyday life. The following list describes each of these levels.

Authentication

The first level is authentication. You use authentication whenever you answer a phone and give a name, or whenever you try to recognize someone's face. Authentication knows with whom you are communicating to determine how much access you will give that person. If a telemarketer calls me in a cold call, for example, I'm unlikely to give him my credit card number. Yet, sometimes I find myself ordering from a site without truly knowing the company at the other end. Even if I know the company, such as ABCD.com, how do I know that it is the one at the other end? How do I know that ABCD.com, instead of someone pretending to be, is getting my credit card number? If I ask ABCD.com to verify itself by answering some questions about the company that only it would know, it's called *one-way authentication*. If it finishes answering my questions and starts asking me questions, such as my mother's maiden name, to also verify me, the authentication becomes *mutual authentication*.

Authorization

After a customer talks to ABCD.com and believes it is who it says it is, and if he needs to purchase something, he might give it access to his credit card, one of his objects. Now ABCD.com has entered the authorization layer. It's like a person who has entered my house after I let him through my front door. Now I have given that person permission to touch something that I own. Depending on how much I trust that person, I might allow him to pick it up and look at it (read permission), I might allow him to modify it (write permission), or I might allow him to use it (execute permission).

Another example is when I give my car keys to my daughter. After she has access to the car, she can lend the keys to a friend. But if I want to limit her access to the car, I might give her the keys only when she asks for them. Not giving users access to resources unless they ask for them is a common idea in a lot of organizations — this is known as the *least privileged method.*

Integrity

To continue with the car scenario, let's look at the next layer of security: integrity. After my daughter drives my car for the first time, I might go outside and look at it to ensure that the car is in the same condition. That is called integrity. If you upload a file to an FTP site and later download it, how do you know the file has not changed? You trust that no one has gone into your Web site; but that might not be true. You might check the byte size and date/time of the file, and if it is the same, you might assume that the file has not been modified. But changing the file and setting the original file information is a trivial exercise. The same could hold true with my daughter. She may have banged up the car over the weekend but then repaired it. Because I know my car well, I can tell the difference — or so I hope.

Auditing

If my car seems different and I'm unsure what is different about it, I have to figure it out. I might not even know the extent of the damage unless I examine the car in detail. I might have to take it to a mechanic and get an estimate of the damage. That is the next layer: auditing. In this layer, not knowing the extent of the damage is the worst thing that can happen. Perhaps the brakes on the car are good only for another 40 miles. I cannot blame my daughter for not knowing the extent of the damage of the car; she isn't a mechanic. The same applies to hackers: Many hackers use tools that someone else invented, and they're not even sure about the extent of damage that they might do to a system. If a hacker is caught and questioned about what is now wrong with the system, it's possible that he won't know the answer.

Therefore, there should always be monitoring techniques to detect changes in the system and the system's data. If a hacker intercepted your credit card, for example, you could cancel the credit card. If the hacker found a hole in the firewall, you could plug it up next time, setting a redirector to fake him out, while monitoring and tracking his moves to find out where he's originated. For every enhancement to security, there have been enhancements to hacking skills to break these securities. If it weren't for auditing records, nobody would know how hackers break in.

Some organizations see security in a negative light — as something that must be accomplished to protect their data. But I have seen many instances in day-to-day development where security could have helped the development process. Not long ago, there were some issues at an organization where it could have easily applied some of these concepts. The organization was using properties files inside Java Archive (JAR) files, and developers were changing these files at will, without regard to the way they would affect other programs. Because of this incident, the organization decided to avoid properties files. The organization could have saved a lot of time and trouble by just changing the permissions on the file to be read-only. Auditing records could have been applied to find out who was changing the file. In the end, applying security could have saved more time than changing the architecture based on security issues.

The following sections explore each of the four security layers — authentication, authorization, integrity, and auditing — in greater detail.

Authentication layer

As mentioned earlier, authentication is simply asserting the originator of a message. When a client needs to assert that the server is who it claims to be, it is a one-way authentication. Sometimes, especially in business-to-business (B2B), it's necessary for both parties to ensure that they have verified each other's identification as the originator. Mutual authentication occurs when both parties need to know that the other is the originator.

An important issue with Internet authentication is that you cannot see exactly whom you are authenticating. An attacker could intercede and try to pass for the other party. In the B2B world, for example, if a party such as ABCD.com were placing a batch of orders into XYZ.com, and competitor company DEF.com interceded and deterred the batch process, it would be bad business for XYZ.com.

Basic terms

Before discussing how you can establish a counterdefense, you need to understand some terms (you can find some of these terms in the *Java Authentication and Authorization Service* [*JAAS*]).

✦ The term *subject* refers to any user of computing services; it's a user or another computing service.

✦ A *principal* is a name associated with a subject. Because of issues with using straight subjects across systems, principals are further defined in JAAS. A set of principals might exist for one subject across an enterprise in case the same name does not exist for the same subject. Principals are associated to a subject only after it has a successful authentication into a system, but principals solve the issue of resolving name issues across systems.

✦ Some services may want to associate more security-related information. These generic security attributes are credentials. *Credentials* may include passwords, Kerberos tickets, and other types of data used for verifying the principal throughout the system.

Certificates and Certificate Authorities

JAAS uses principals and credentials to authenticate throughout an enterprise system. Another form of principal authentication is incorporated into the Java Servlet v2.2 and EJB v1.1 specifications to pass principal information through Java Naming and Directory Interface (JNDI) context. This authenticates the original user through the Java Enterprise systems.

These techniques help authentication throughout the enterprise; however, there are still issues of getting into the system. When a user tries to authenticate to a proprietary system, he still runs the risk of an attacker intercepting his call, especially in getting the exchange of public keys for encryption. This attack is called the man-in-the-middle attack. For this reason, digital certificates were invented to thwart potential attackers. *Digital certificates* are remote documents that are maintained through a trusted third party to uniquely identify the user, or principal, over the Internet to another party.

The trusted third party is a *Certificate Authority (CA)*. The primary standard for certificates is X.509, which has been around since 1988. The X.509 scheme has a public key associated with each CA. The recipient of the certificate uses this public key from the CA to decrypt a digital signature. If he can decrypt it, it follows that it was encrypted with the CA's private key in the key pair algorithm. In the certificate is the public key of the owner of the certificate that the recipient wishes to communicate with by using ciphers. This ensures that a valid key pair matches the certificate from the CA and that the public key of the owner is valid. A chain of responsibility can grow here because a certificate can contain another certificate, and so on. Then the signature can be matched with another signature of another authority and so on. When the certificate is a top-level certificate, implying a self-signed signature, it's called the *root certificate;* thus, no public key is needed to certify it. Root certificates are used to check with other third parties for trust of the CA itself.

The application server receives only a copy of the certificate; the original remains with and can be modified by the CA. The CA ensures that no changes can be made in the user's certificate, and the CA is responsible for ensuring that you receive the correct public key for that user. The certificate will contain several elements, including the owner of the certificate, the key associated with this owner, and a digital signature to verify the integrity of the certificate. If there is any doubt from the CA that tampering may appear or integrity is lost, the CA can revoke the certificate and inform the owner of the certificate revocation. The CA can identify the owner of the certificate through the owner's key pair and IP address. For specific information about a CA, two companies come to mind: VeriSign and Entrust. For more information in the Java API for X.509, refer to the `java.security.cert` package from the JAAS distribution or JDK 1.4 distribution.

To get a certificate, you have to contact a CA. In most cases, after paying money and sending the machine name and IP address of the authentication server to the CA, you will receive information about your certificate, including a directory on the CA where it will be located and the key to access it. You can then configure your Web and application servers to communicate with the CA via HTTPS.

Secure protocols

The Web Server protocol that uses these certificates for authentication is called HTTPS, or *HTTP Secure*. HTTPS is also referred to as HTTP over SSL and HTTP over TLS (Transport Layer Security). TLS is the successor of SSL v3 after the IETF (Internet Engineering Task Force) created it as an Internet standard when they took it over from Netscape Communications.

An example of when to use HTTPS is when you log on to a secure Web site to download a chapter of a book using a URL such as `www.cliffsnotes.com`. After accessing the URL, a login prompts you for secure authentication. In this scenario, only one certificate is used at the Web site to pass you the encryption keys through the HTTPS protocol on port 443. This messaging is encrypted by using the public keys that the CA distributes to the SSL handshaking.

Netscape to the rescue with SSL

The key and cipher techniques are applied by using many algorithms; however, those techniques do not solve the problems of building programs that support network protocols. In the early 1990s, the Socket Application Program Interface (API) was used to develop network protocols in the C language on Unix by using BSD Sockets, and later on the NT Operating System by using WinSock. Cipher libraries for programming were available at the time from different vendors. But they were not standardized at the time, and handshaking with the client and servers to exchange keys was not established as a standard in the protocols. There was no way of ensuring that the other client vendors were using the same package.

Netscape took the challenge in 1994 and created a wrapper on top of the Socket API that became known as Secure Socket Layer (SSL V1.0). This evolved into what is today the Secure Socket Layer (SSL V3.0) protocol. SSL is a security protocol that provides communications privacy over the Internet. The protocol allows client/server applications to communicate in a way that is designed to prevent eavesdropping, tampering, or message forgery. This figure illustrates the Secure Sockets Layering.

Secure Socket Layer (SSL)		Encryption Algorithms and Keying
Socket Layer (BSD Sockets or WinSocks)		
Transmission Control Protocol (TCP)	User Datagram Protocol (UDP)	
Internet Protocol (IP)		

SSL layering

SSL was designed as a programming interface for network protocols that provided functionality for connecting and transporting data across TCP and UDP. TCP is a connection across the Internet that guarantees delivery; UDP does not guarantee delivery. UDP is used mostly in sending a one-way message or message broadcasting, such as for a stock ticker. The SSL's primary goal is to provide privacy and reliability between two communicating applications. The SSL has two layers: the SSL Record and the SSL Handshake Protocol. The SSL Record is at the lowest level that handles the transport of the data; the SSL Handshake Protocol allows the server and client to authenticate each other and to negotiate the keys before the data is transmitted and received. The advantage of SSL is that it is protocol-independent.

The SSL protocol has many more properties. SSL can handshake by using the key-pair algorithm and encrypt by using a secret key. Its transport includes message integrity, and it can support digital signatures such as MD5 and SHA, which are discussed later. This makes SSL a very powerful instrument in the arsenal against attackers.

For this application, you need to provide confidentiality for the data passing between client and server, and the user needs to be sure that his client is connected to the correct server and is using the correct key pair. Behind the scenes, a digital certificate is being received through the X.509 protocol, the handshaking and socket encryption is being handled by SSL, and the overall protocol for the Web interfacing is being handled through HTTPS.

Authorization layer

Authentication verifies that the correct user is logged into the system, but after the user is logged in, there's still a need to ensure that the user is only allowed certain resources.

Authorization entails applying security policies to regulate which resources the specific users, or groups of users, can access in the system. In order to access any given resource, the user needs privileges for that resource. The *privilege* is the level of access granted to that user for a particular resource. Each user will have a collection of privileges for the system, which is the user's *role*. The basic system usually consists of four roles: user, group, other, and super-user. As the system grows, more and more roles will be added, such as network and database administrator.

The Unix operating system has always accessed resources in this way. The owner of the resource determines who has access to the resource. The Unix system has three privilege levels that are of interest to most users: read access, write access, and execute access. Each of these levels must be set from the owner for it to be allowed for a particular user or group. A *group* is a logical set of users; groups are used because they are more efficient to manage than individual users. It's simply easier to set the accesses to groups and to have all the users that need that access to belong to that group. This security follows the *Discretionary Access Control* (DAC) model, in which the owner of each file can determine who else can access it by setting the file's permission bits.

Note   One of the issues with this model is that anyone who has read access to a file can copy the file and give it to another user. DAC is called *discretionary* because it is up to the owner's discretion to give others permission to that file or resource. DAC is also sometimes referred to as the owner-based model.

Another authorization model is the *Mandatory Access Control* (MAC) model. In the MAC security model, each user and resource is assigned a security level, such as classified, secret, and top secret. These security levels are usually ordered, thereby creating a *lattice*. Top secret, for example, is higher than secret, which is higher than classified. Each user has a security clearance, such as secret. If the user has a secret clearance, he has access only to resources that are classified and secret, not top secret resources. This security model follows the way sensitive data is used in the military and other Department of Defense organizations. Many systems, however, do not currently support this type of security model.

Access Control Lists

The DAC model has been enhanced over the years. From the structure of Unix files and directories, it has moved into the Java world of enterprise development for EJB and JSP resources. For enterprise systems, DAC policies are implemented in the form of *access control lists* (ACLs), in which each resource has an ACL administered by its owner. The purpose of the ACL and its entries is to ensure that a user can perform an action on a resource, based on the action and user having the correct permission on the resource. Because this model is very generic, it can easily suit access control requirements for any system.

The biggest issue with ACLs is that as the number of users grows, so does the administration of the DAC model. An ACL is a data structure that guards access to resources. Each ACL has a list of `AclEntry` objects. An `AclEntry` associates a principal, such as the user `rhelton`, with a permission object, such as `read`. An `AclEntry` has a positive number if it grants permission and a negative number to deny the permission. This paradigm can also be displayed in the form of tables, not just objects. A table can have the ACL IDs and normalize to an `AclEntry` that can then normalize to a table of principals and permissions. Figure 20-2 illustrates this relationship.

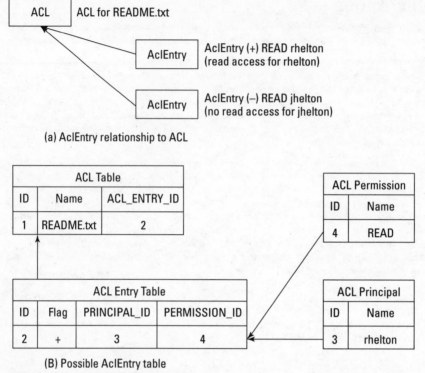

(a) AclEntry relationship to ACL

(B) Possible AclEntry table

Figure 20-2: ACL and AclEntry objects

If the user or the group to which the user belongs has the correct rights, the user can perform the desired operation. This security architecture is incorporated into the Java Development Kit 1.3 as a separate distributed package. The advantage of this architecture is that it decouples the authorization process from the authentication process. Decoupling the authentication protects the certificates from corruption if the authorization gets corrupted. This also provides a central location to store all access across the enterprise system. The central location for storing information across an enterprise system is typically referred to as a *security realm*.

Figure 20-3 shows how a Web container can decouple the actions of authentication and authorization by using the access control list. Note that the ACL table is just an example to show the separation, and is not normalized. The table stores relationships between principals and permissions. Even though the AclEntry is calculated by using positive and negative algorithms, the permissions are normally in the form of read, write, execute, and delete. As you can see from Figures 20-2 and 20-3, you load the principals, permissions, and resource names from the tables to check the user's access level.

Figure 20-3: Access versus authentication tables

LDAP

Not long ago, most organizations had their own interfaces and schema for implementing access lists such as the one shown in Figure 20-3. The problem was that there was no common interface to this data. Most organizations created these tables from scratch, which was a lot of work, and they could not reuse this work across organizations. That changed, however, with the implementation of *Lightweight Directory Access Protocol (LDAP)*.

An LDAP service provides a generic directory service, which stores information of all sorts. LDAP was created to do much more than just store user and group information; it can store a server's configuration, certificates, EJB and JSP objects, file system information, and customer information. LDAP excels at authorization because it can centralize all the user information for an entire enterprise. Using LDAP can be another centralized choke point for attackers; it can force the authorization into one point. That is, just as the firewall forces the attacker to enter at a predetermined point on the network, the LDAP server forces the attacker to use a predetermined store of user and group access. This can aid the system and network administrators to audit specific points and carefully monitor those points that the attacker is forced to go through to gain any control of the system.

Another feature in administrating the LDAP service is that owners can modify groups. Groups are a subset of any users, which can modify many users at the same time. The LDAP server itself has authorization for a user to modify these records, like an owner. The owner can add, modify, and delete any record by using the LDAP SDK or console. The console will change depending on the manufacturer, such as the Netscape's Directory Server or Active Directory from Microsoft. This gives the administrator a GUI-like tool for administering user rights instead of traversing multiple Unix stations and proprietary databases to accomplish the same goals.

Since LDAP was invented in 1995, the technology opened the doors to many possibilities for centralizing enterprise directories. The motivation was to first store a distributed directory structure. But because a directory structure has attributes, files, and subdirectories in them, it formed a basis for storing information about machines, objects, and services. Tree-like directory structures and file systems are traversed like any other file system, as shown in Figure 20-4.

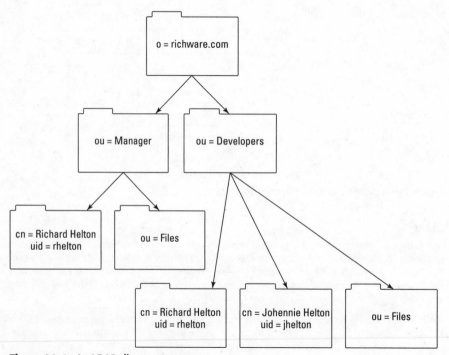

Figure 20-4: An LDAP directory structure

The first things that you might notice in Figure 20-4 are some of the symbols used to define the structures. The symbol to define the overall organization that owns the enterprise system is o=richware.com. Because there is normally one LDAP server at a given organization, it uses the organization as the root and initial name. In this diagram, the organization is defined as richware.com. This folder can contain any number of attributes about the organization, such as the location of the headquarters, the CEO, and more. This is for referencing organizational data.

The next folder in the directory structure is ou=Manager, which belongs to the organization richware.com because it is part of the same tree. The ou in ou=Manager stands for organizational unit and acts as a directory that can contain files, attributes, or users. This ou contains one user, who is Richard Helton and has the user identity of rhelton. This is the user's ID that is used so that the user may get a connection to the LDAP service. In the figure, the user

`Richard Helton` can get a connection from the `Manager` folder or the `Developers` folder. When logging in, this user can specify which `ou` that he is logging in under. Depending on which one he uses, he may set his permissions differently. Another `ou` is the `Files` subdirectory under the `Manager` `ou`. This `ou` contains all the manager's files (text- or binary-based). If the user `Richard Helton` logged in under the `Manager` `ou` and had his permissions set, he can access these `Manager` files in the `ou=Files` subdirectory. These permissions are set through the LDAP service from an administrator. After `Richard Helton` logs in through the LDAP SDK, he can start accessing files if the permissions are set in the LDAP ACL table.

The permissions that are allowed in LDAP are read, write, search, compare, selfwrite, delete, add, and proxy. These permissions can be applied to the `ou` folder or any resource that may belong to that `ou` folder. These resources can be in the form of files or even objects. In this scenario, an LDAP administrator had the role of an owner that set the permissions of the files for the `Richard Helton` user.

One of the biggest security features that should be mentioned about LDAP servers is that they have their own internal ACL for handling users and groups of the elements inside the LDAP directory tree. LDAP servers have authentication protocols that they follow to get a *bind*, which is an association of a name with an object. An EJB client, for example, binds to an EJB's home name to access the home object. A single bind or multiple binds can be stored in a context object. To get a bind, there must be access to a *namespace*, which contains all the names within a naming system that can be used for the association. A namespace can be in the form of all the names in an LDAP directory tree. To get a specific name, normally you would have to traverse a namespace. In finding the file `etc/hosts` in Unix, for example, the traverse would need to start at the root directory, form the root, traverse to the subdirectory `etc` and then traverse the file `hosts`. This is how directory trees are normally traversed.

As mentioned earlier, LDAP provides its own authentication mechanisms. These mechanisms can be anonymous, simple, none, and SASL. SASL is the most secure, and it stands for *Simple Authentication and Security Layer*. RFC 2222 defines SASL. LDAP uses this protocol to identify and authenticate a user in the server. The command built into LDAP requires that it specify the name and mechanism to use for authentication. When the client makes an authentication request of the server, the server can challenge the authentication. The client sends responses to the server, which can challenge as many times as it deems necessary. If the authentication succeeds, it will get a SUCCESS message; otherwise, the client will receive an `INVALID_CREDENTIALS` error. SASL is part of the JAAS product, and further information can be found in the `javax.security.sasl` package.

This was a brief introduction to the LDAP server, but there are many other mechanisms that a Java Servlet, or EJB, may use to get permissions to resources. The most common are locally stored deployment descriptors, which eliminate the need to make network calls to an LDAP server (you may, however, decide to put some of these resources in the LDAP server later because the maintenance of these files becomes complex). Because of such complexities, Sun has provided an architecture in which both LDAP and file systems can be used interchangeably. This specification is called *Java Naming and Directory Interface* (JNDI).

JNDI

The purpose of the JNDI interface is to provide a single API to access different directory structures using different protocols. It hides the implementation details for accessing protocols such as LDAP. JNDI makes it possible to link different types of directories, such as a file directory on Unix and an LDAP service.

JNDI has a client API (shown in Figure 20-5) for getting the object from the contexts. It also has a service provider interface that wraps around the various directory and naming services. Both the file system and LDAP server can act as a service provider.

Figure 20-5: The JNDI API Layer

A code example of JNDI looks like the following:

```
// Start the environment settings
Hashtable env = new HashTable();
env. put(Context.INITIAL_CONTEXT_FACTORY,
"com.sun.jndi.ldap.LdapCtxFactory");
env.put(Context.PROVIDER_URL,"ldap://localhost:389/o=JNDIServer");
// Authenticate user "Rich" with password "password".
// Start with Authentication Type
env.put(Context.SECURITY_AUTHENTICATION,"simple");
env.put(Context.SECURITY_PRINCIPAL","cn=Rich,ou=Author,o=richware.com")
;
env.put(Context.SECURITY_CREDENTIALS,"password");
// Create the Initial Context
DirContext ctx = new InitialDirContext(env);
//  Work with the newly created Context
```

In the preceding code, there is a communication directly to the LDAP server. To change the code to access the File System Provider, a file system in Unix, simply change two of the functions and reuse the rest of the code to produce the following code:

```
// Start the environment settings
Hashtable env = new HashTable();
env. put(Context.INITIAL_CONTEXT_FACTORY,
"com.sun.jndi.fscontext.LdapCtxFactory");
env.put(Context.PROVIDER_URL,"file:/tmp");
// Authenticate user "Rich" with password "password".
// Start with Authentication Type
env.put(Context.SECURITY_AUTHENTICATION,"simple");
env.put(Context.SECURITY_PRINCIPAL","cn=Rich,ou=Author,o=richware.com")
;
env.put(Context.SECURITY_CREDENTIALS,"password");
// Create the Initial Context
DirContext ctx = new InitialDirContext(env);
//  Work with the newly created Conext
```

Cross-Reference   See Chapter 8 for additional LDAP programming examples.

JAAS

Introducing LDAP may be overkill for some applications or for smaller organizations. The Java Authentication and Authorization Service (JAAS) provides a simpler alternative for these situations. Because it is built into J2EE, JAAS can be used in a WebLogic environment without adding an additional server.

Just as the JDK 1.2 provides a `SecurityManager` class implementation that can enforce access control on source code and classes, there is a JAAS SecurityManager that augments the JDK 1.3 version that can enforce access control to sensitive resources. Augmenting the security in the newer versions of the JDK is just an example of the way the Java 2 SecurityManager from Sun continues to evolve.

To use the JAAS SecurityManager, a policy file must be maintained. This policy file is simply a variation of the JDK 1.2 `SecurityManager` policy file. This form of access control is referred to as *principal-based access control* because it is based on the policy file's principals. Only authorized principals can access the resources. You can grant access to non-principals, however, as shown in the following code:

```
// Java 2 codesource-based policy
grant Codebase "http://richware.com", Signedby "rich" {
  permission java.io.FilePermission "/cdrom/-", "read";
}
```

In this example, because the policy file has `grant Codebase` instead of `grant Principal`, all Java code trying to access the CD-ROM through `http://richware.com` will have access to it. The files will have the signature of `rich`, regardless of who executes it. To demonstrate a principal using JAAS, see the following policy file:

```
// Java 2 codesource-based policy
grant Principal com.sun.security.auth.SolarisPrincipal "rich" {
  permission java.io.FilePermission "/cdrom/-", "read";
}
```

In this example, only the subjects associated with the `SolarisPrincipal` principal type that has the name `rich` associated with it can have access to the CD-ROM. The `com.sun.security.auth.SolarisPrincipal` is a Sun principal for a Solaris user.

When accessing a resource, such as the CD-ROM in the preceding example, the JAAS API will need many properties in the policy file for the policy file to be sufficient. The properties that are needed are the subject, the set of name properties associated with the subject (called principals) and the security-related attributes (called credentials). To execute the subject, one of the easiest ways is to use the static function "doAs" that associates a function with a subject:

```
class ExampleAction implements java.security.PrivilegedAction {
      public Object run() {
          java.io.File f = new java.io.File("/cdrom/-");

          // the following call invokes a security check
          if (f.exists()) {
              System.out.println("cdrom exists");
          }
          return null;
```

```
        }
    }

    public class Example1 {
        public static void main(String[] args) {

            // Authenticate the subject, "rich".
            // This process is described in the
            // LoginContext section.

            Subject rich;
            ...

            // perform "ExampleAction" as "rich"
            Subject.doAs(rich, new ExampleAction());
        }
    }
```

The preceding code will check to see if it can read the CD-ROM as the user rich. If the user rich is logged into a Solaris machine, it will work.

Enterprise principals

As mentioned before, principals are used in other enterprise system architectures besides JAAS; they are also used in EJBs and Java Servlets. In EJB 1.1/2.0, you may get a principal by calling the function getCallerPrincipal(). After the principal is received, the name of the principal can be retrieved by calling the getName() function. You can see an example of this in the following code:

```
//Obtain the default initial JNDI context
Context initCtx = new InitialContext();
// get the home interface
Object result = initCtx.lookup("java:comp/env/ejb/UserRecord");
// narrow to the proper type
UserRecordHome userRecordHome = (UserRecordHome)
javax.rmi.PortableRemoteObject.narrow(result, UserRecordHome.class);
// get the caller principal
userPrincipal = ejbContext.getCallerPrincipal();
// get the user's name
String username = userPrincipal.getName();
// Lookup or execute something on the user's name
```

This code creates an EJB and retrieves the current user's name in the getName() function. After the user's name is returned, a lookup in the ACL, database server, or LDAP server can be performed to get the permissions of this user. Another function, isCallerInRole(), is used to see if the current user is in the group that is authorized to perform actions on the resources in that thread of execution. Using it as ejbContext.isCallerInRole("admin") will return true if the user belongs to the admin group.

Java Servlets provide the same functionality as EJBs, but the method names are different. The method names servlets used to check the user's role and principal are isUserInRole() and getUserPrincipal().

The focus of this section has been on authorization; but it has been very difficult to separate some of the other layers, such as authentication, because the security layers overlap each other and are needed to work with each other every step of the way.

Authorization can be implemented in various different methods, but they all implement the DAC model in various forms. Securing the organization's data is very important if that organization wants to stay in the market. We cannot think of a single company that can freely distribute its information and data and still survive the market. All companies have some form of data that it does not wish to distribute, such as financial records or the CEO's home phone number. Guarding that information should be of the utmost importance with several people allocated to it.

Integrity layer

Integrity is the assurance that data has not been modified without knowledge of its modification in an enterprise system. Adding a signature to a document or having a digest to compare against provides data integrity, which is especially important for organizations that are disseminating files to the public. These organizations would not want to inadvertently transmit viruses in their files because it could damage their credibility with the public.

Some of the concepts of digital signatures were already mentioned in the authentication layer section because these security principles constantly rely on each other for support.

Digital signatures

Digital signatures are based on the same concept as a person signing a document. If a person receives a document in the mail from a bank, signs it, and returns it to the bank, how does the bank know that it is a valid signature? Even if the person were authenticated (if, for example, a package sent by registered mail is signed for in the presence for the postal carrier), the signature might still be forged. If the bank has the person's signature on file for comparison purposes and the two signatures appear the same, this would furnish validation. Another validation method is to use a certified, trusted third party. When the person seeking validation presents an ID to the trusted third party, he can put a seal on the document. The issue is that sometimes more than authentication is needed, as when there is no trust between the sender and the receiver or when it is possible to forge the message.

Two types of digital signatures exist: *direct signatures* and *arbitrated signatures.* The direct digital signature is just between the sender and receiver; the arbitrated digital signature is between the sender, a trusted third party, and the receiver. The direct digital signature is the use of either a secret key or public key to decrypt a message. If the message uses a secret key, and if there are only two people in the group that share the key, trusting that it came from the other person who has the secret key can be somewhat valid. If more than two people are involved, copies could start to appear and managing the keys becomes an issue.

One method of ensuring who encrypted a message is by applying the key pair algorithm. If a person receives a message from Jane, for example, as long as the message decrypts with Jane's public key using the key pair algorithm, you can somewhat trust that Jane had to use her private key to encrypt the message and therefore the message is considered valid. But what if the secret key or the private key were stolen? Messages could be sent and received, and the integrity of the message is compromised between parties.

The arbitrated digital signature has a trusted third party to ensure authenticity, such as a Certificate Authority in the authentication principle. The idea is that every signed message between the sender and receiver goes through an arbitrator. All parties must trust the arbitrator. The arbitrator will receive the message from the sender, validate that it came from the sender, sign it saying that it was verified, and forward it to the receiver. One method of verification is that the sender and the arbitrator share a secret key, and the arbitrator and the receiver share a different secret key. The arbitrator receives the message from the sender, decrypts it, and then encrypts it with the other secret key to send it to the sender, thus playing a middleman to ensure trust between the sender and the receiver. The man-in-the-middle becomes very difficult to implement with an arbitrator because all sets of keys would have to be impersonated, both from the receiver and the sender. Also, because there are trusted third-party servers used from the arbitrator to transport the certificate to both the receiver and the sender, impersonations are more complex because of information used to set up the HTTPS to the arbitrator to both the sender and receiver. The arbitrator establishes the connection between the sender and receiver. This makes destroying the integrity of the message a little more difficult.

Message digests

A message digest, illustrated in Figure 20-6, is normally referred to as a digital fingerprint. Its purpose is to take a stream of data as the input to a hash algorithm and produce an output called a *digest*. The digest is a representation of the input data and does not change unless the input data changes. This allows you to compare the digests that are computed at different times to determine whether the data has been altered. An example is the Java utility `jar-signer`. `Jarsigner` signs a Java Archive (JAR) file, which packages related files together. An example is the JSSE (Java Secure Socket Extension) distribution from Sun in the `jsse.jar`. The `jarsigner` utility is advisable when extending the functionality of WLS and adding JAR files to WebLogic applications. When giving these files to a client as a deliverable, the creator of these files doesn't know if they have tampered with unless they were signed.

Figure 20-6: Using the message digest

Message digests are also called *one-way hash algorithms*, which work in only one direction, taking plaintext data and computing it into a unique hash. If one byte has changed in the plaintext, it will create a hash different from the previous hash. The same input will always produce the same hash. If the data is different, the hash output will be different. The hash will always be the same size, regardless of the size of the data. The hash is also referred to as a *digest* because it is a digest of the data or, put simply, a description of the byte pattern that obscures the original data. The word *hash* is taken from the hashing algorithms that are involved in producing the result. Most algorithms will iterate through the data, XORing each byte and then rehashing that result into the next byte. The hash is the result of the hashing algorithm. The digest, or hash, was originally used mostly in messaging protocols such as SSL, which coined its name: the *message digest*. The one-way hash is never reversed; that is, the digest cannot be used to reconstruct the original data. This ensures that the original data is never compromised.

Types of message digest algorithms

Several message digest algorithms exist, including MD2, MD4, and MD5. (MD stands for *message digest*.) These algorithms produce 128-bit hash values. MD2 is used for Privacy Enhanced Mail (PEM). It's byte-oriented in its checksums calculations and requires input that is multiple of 16 bytes. Padding has to be done to ensure that it is a multiple. This algorithm has been cracked. The MD5 was created to enhance MD4 because it was rumored that it would be broken. MD5 is slower and more robust because it has more hashing loops than MD4. MD4 wasn't broken as promised, and it is still used today. MD5 and MD4 both use 512-bit blocks. These fit the block cipher paradigm as far as hashing a 64-bit block at a time. It has to be padded if not divisible by 64 bits. Both algorithms produce a 128-bit message digest.

Secure Hash Algorithm

Besides the MD series of message digests, there is another very common message digest called the *Secure Hash Algorithm* (SHA). A revised copy, called SHA-1, was developed in 1995. SHA is based on the MD4 algorithm, and its design closely models MD4. SHA takes an input message with a maximum length of less than $\frac{3}{4}$ bits and produces a 160-bit message digest as output. The input is processed in 512-bit blocks. This produces a full 32 bits wider than the other hash algorithms, so it is stronger than the other hash algorithms.

Java Cryptography Architecture

Because the message digest is so widely used, it was included in the *Java Cryptography Architecture* (JCA) that will work with JDK 1.3. It is part of the JDK 1.4 distribution. WLS has support for this functionality in the `weblogic.security.MessageDigest` class. This class supports the SHA and MD5 algorithms. To use this class, first you get an instance of the class using the `MessageDigest.getInstance("MD5")` function. The input of this function is a case-insensitive string that states that it is either MD5 or SHA. A provider may also be included in this function if other algorithms are desired from a provider. Next you need to use an `update` function and pass in the input stream as a byte or byte array. After data has been inputted to the class, the digest is returned using the `digest` function. Here is a code example:

```
MessageDigest sha = MessageDigest.getInstance("SHA");
byte [] i1;
// Initialize i1with some data here
sha.update(i1);
byte[] hash = sha.digest();
```

The digital signature standard

The *digital signature standard* (DSS) exists to handle digital signatures. DSS uses the SHA algorithm as well as a key pair algorithm. The first thing that DSS does to a message is to get a digest of the message through the SHA algorithm. Then it encrypts the digest by using a private key to form a signature. Both message and signature are sent to the receiver. On the receiver's end, the receiver first produces a digest by using the SHA algorithm. Then the receiver decrypts the signature by using the public key of the sender. If both digests match, the one from the receiver and the one from the sender, the message is considered valid. An example of DSS in Java code is as follows:

```
/* Get Signature object */
Signature sig = Signature.getInstance("DSS");
/* Initialize for signing */
sig.initSign(myPrivateKey);
/* Process the document */
sig.update(document);
/* Sign it */
byte[] signature = sig.sign();
```

Verifying the authenticity of a signed document in Java code looks like the following:

```
/* Get Signature object */
Signature sig = Signature.getInstance("DSS");
/* Initialize for verifying */
sig.initSign(myPublicKey);
/* Process the document */
sig.update(document);
/* Verify authenticity */
Boolean authentic = sig.verify(signature);
```

Ciphers and Keys

Before much more is said about security, you need to be a familiar with ciphers and keys.

Several components are involved in encryption, as shown in Figure 20-7. There is the *plaintext,* which is the input, or unencrypted data, to the encryption engine. The output, which is the encrypted data, is called *ciphertext.* The encryption/decryption algorithm is called a *cipher. Keys* are a block of bytes that will produce a ciphertext when used with the plaintext. When a different key is used with the same plaintext, it will produce a different ciphertext. Simply put, it's used to keep attackers guessing about when they have access to the cipher. Because a key and cipher are used to create ciphertext, it's part of the measurement of most algorithms.

Most ciphers' strength is measured against the *brute-force* attack. The brute-force attack is walking through all the possible keys in order until the ciphertext produces readable plaintext in the decryption cipher. Another measurement is the level of complexity involved with possible systems to break the algorithm; it sets the differentiation between strong and weak algorithms.

Figure 20-7: Brute force attack

Keys, not just ciphers, also can take on many forms, as shown in Figure 20-8. The *secret key* is a key that a group agrees to use and not to change. A secret key is a key, such as 90909090, that Alice and John agree upon to decrypt and encrypt messages when communicating with each other.

Figure 20-8: Secret key algorithm

The *key-pair*, sometimes called the public key algorithm or asymmetric ciphering, starts with two keys generated from a key utility, such as RIPEMD or the `KeyPairGenerator` class in the Java Cryptography Extension (JCE). Figure 20-9 illustrates the key-pair algorithm. The generated pair is made up of a public key and a private key. The public key is given out to people in your group to encrypt, and the private key is used to decrypt the message. This algorithm makes it infeasible to determine the private key, thus hiding half of the keying technology from anyone.

Figure 20-9: The key-pair algorithm

Auditing layer

Auditing is simply a practice of keeping records for the purpose of capturing security-related events. One purpose is to hold users or systems accountable, but most important, to know whether any damage is done to your systems if security has been breached. A lot of this functionality relies on the services and servers that you use in the organization's enterprise system. All firewalls, application servers, Web servers, and LDAP servers come with logging and monitoring features. But when developing your enterprise systems, a good place to start is to log any security exceptions that have taken place. When logging exceptions, capture the principal and user information when the exception happens. Ensure that these files are protected and trusted with integrity and review them constantly. Files like these will report issues across the enterprise system.

Another approach is to try to break in the system while the auditing techniques are in place to ensure that they work. Many cracking packages are available on the Web. Try some out against an isolated section of your site—by isolated, we mean one that is in test and not production—and see what the log files generate. Try spoofing the firewall to see if the firewall catches it.

Security Perimeters

Before getting into a discussion about types of security attacks, we must discuss the perimeters within which these attacks can take place.

Points of entry

Every organization has perimeters around its systems, with specific points in the network where users can enter, such as the following:

✦ The point where a customer enters the system through the Web farm

✦ The point where other organizations enter the system

✦ The point where administrators enter to monitor system status

It is to these entry points that most of the concentration of security techniques is usually applied. The premise is that if a hacker cannot enter the system, the system is safe. There are two tiers of concern: the outside world (the entry from the Internet) and the inside world (the entry from the internal servers). The internal servers must also have a form of security for securing the objects between each other.

Figure 20-10 shows a few entry points to the system; these entry points *must* be protected against attackers.

Figure 20-10: An organization's enterprise

Firewalls

The most common technique to protect a network is to install a *firewall*. A firewall provides a protective perimeter that prevents hackers from entering through the organization's front door. Firewalls use one or more of the following types of filtering to protect the network's front door:

✦ *Port filtering:* Port filtering allows certain network ports to be seen from the outside world, while rendering others invisible. Access is almost always provided for port 80, which is the default for Hypertext Transfer Protocol (HTTP). The firewall is supposed to block other ports to ensure that the attacker can enter only specific ports that are monitored.

✦ *Protocol filtering:* Protocol filtering ensures that the only protocol entering the port is the protocol permitted by the firewall. In most cases, it is the HTTP protocol that is passed from the Web server to the application server via an application server port that is unknown to the outside world. Usually, this port is an uncommon one; so it's hard to find.

✦ *Trusted machines:* One of the filters that most firewalls take into consideration is the knowledge of which originating machines allow connections to the application server. The knowledge is based on recognizing the DNS name of the client machine or its IP address; that is the basis for IP/DNS name filtering. The firewall will check to see if the client originated on that machine inside the DMZ to ensure that the connection to the application server doesn't originate outside of the DMZ. These machines that are in the perimeter of the firewall are considered *trusted machines*.

The demilitarized zone

A secure perimeter around a network is commonly known as a *demilitarized zone (DMZ)*, a term borrowed from battlefield tactics. A DMZ blocks the enemy (hackers) while permitting access to allies (customers and other authorized users). A DMZ is formed by the combination of two firewalls. One firewall is between the Web server and the outside world. The other firewall is between the Web and application servers; it prevents outside connections, other than that of the known Web server, from accessing the application server as a client. The *client* is the process that initiates the connection into the system. These firewalls can be implemented in hardware or software; they provide filters by port, protocol, or IP/DNS name. Figure 20-11 shows the location of the two firewalls that make up the DMZ and shows a typical attack at this level.

Figure 20-11: A DMZ with firewalls

The technique of a DMZ is fundamental to force attackers to enter through a single choking point in which they must apply their attack techniques. The entry points are the gates they must pass through to get into an organization's enterprise world. There are other tactics that must be applied against hackers and their attacks; these will be discussed in the "Security Attacks" section. But it's quite obvious that the firewall must support auditing. If the attacker tries to gain any access, records need to be created to monitor the techniques. This not only gives a performance report of the existing firewall structure, but also gives information to network administrators on the directions that attackers are taking. It also provides information about the attackers that allows administrators to prepare for future attacks. It could even point out a specific tool that the attacker is using — it's useful to get details on such a tool and prevent its use. Integrity is used to ensure that no one is trying to change the startup information to the firewalls and, at various points, to ensure that attackers are not introducing their own files for an attack.

Security Attacks

Some people spend hours studying the specifications for a particular firewall and try to break it. Attackers are not limited to individuals sitting in their parents' basement with limited resources. Some may have bigger labs than the companies designing the firewalls! Some may be in the organization that they plan to attack. Some may be disgruntled employees who get laid off and then develop a program to execute vengeance on the system. Some attackers even do it for fun, or just to see if they have the technical abilities to accomplish their tasks. In this section, I'll explore common techniques employed by attackers to gain unauthorized access to computers and data.

Not all the attacks are intended to reach valuable data on the other side; they might originate with a competitor trying to bring down an organization's site to get its business. The motivation of attackers is as diverse as the attacks themselves.

IP spoofing

Referring to Figure 20-11, you can see that the firewall on the right is filtering all addresses and ports except port 9001 from host 166.99.99.99. An attack that circumvents this barrier is one in which the attacking machine pretends to have the IP address 166.99.99.99, transmitting on port 9001. Such an attack is called *IP spoofing*.

The IP spoofing attack begins by knowing the address of the Web server. This can be easily found by doing a ping to the Web host if it is a direct connection. A ping establishes a short connection to a host to determine whether it exists. A ping will work only if the Web server is the physical host to a WWW site and the ping port is active. In many systems, the Web server may not be connected directly to the Internet through the firewall. When you are accessing a Web host, it could be through a load balancing router or proxy server. But after an IP address is found, the idea is to build an IP packet with the Web server's IP address as the return address to pretend that the packet originated on the Web server. After the address is inserted and no other filtering is applied, the firewall believes that the packet is from the company's Web server. Usually, the Web server is considered a *trusted machine* because it belongs to the company. IP spoofing breaks this trust between machines by pretending to be one of the trusted machines.

DNS spoofing

Firewalls may be configured to filter by host name instead of IP address. In this case, if the intruder assumes the name of a trusted host, the intruder is performing *Domain Name*

Service (DNS) spoofing, which has the same net effect as IP spoofing—unauthorized access to the protected machine.

A common way to affect DNS spoofing is to change the DNS entry to reflect that of the attacker's machine and fake the firewall into believing that this machine is valid. The DNS uses a table lookup usually found in the `etc/host` file on the network administration server. Changing the entry to this table to point to other machines triggers the spoof.

IP and DNS spoofing defeat firewall security only if the firewalls employ IP filtering exclusively. But most firewalls employ multiple layers of filtering, making spoofing difficult. Most firewalls, for example, employ an HTTP protocol filter, which permits HTTP connections only. The downside of such filters is that they restrict other potentially friendly protocols, such as RMI. The workaround for this is called *HTTP tunneling,* shown in Figure 20-12, in which the packets of a nonpermitted protocol (such as RMI) are wrapped within the packets of a permitted protocol (such as HTTP), causing the firewall to let them through. Of course, the recipient of these tunneled packets must be able to recognize them, unwrap them, and act on them accordingly.

Figure 20-12: HTTP tunneling

Trapdoors

A *trapdoor,* also known as a *back door,* is a secret entry point into a system that allows someone access without going through the normal security routines. Developers have been adding trapdoors to systems for decades to help in the testing and debugging of programs. It may take time, for example, to go through the security setup; and because of time constraints, the developer will take shortcuts in testing. These developers may also be responsible for fixing bugs in the programs even after the testing phase, so they leave doors in the program to update classes to fix the bugs discovered at a later date. Some developers don't even consider them as trapdoors because the developers might be trying to build something that is experimental for dynamically configuring their system and its security to enhance system functionality.

An example of a trapdoor may be a database table that dynamically changes the organization's enterprise system, and that database system has privileges set to bypass the system's security. A trapdoor is any door that can access the system without going through the normal security access procedure. The threat is that these doors allow accesses to the system without going through security, and the threat is extended if any of the developers with trapdoors ever leave the organization or let others know of them. The ex-employees that have access to the ex-employer's software are no longer held responsible for the consequences, and they no longer have the threat of being fired from the organization. A disgruntled employee could be very dangerous with a trapdoor.

Logic bombs

The *logic bomb* is a program requiring that some condition be met in the program before the bomb explodes into the system to do some damage. One example is a program that deletes system files unless it is disabled before a particular date. The motivation here may be for an insecure contractor to ensure that he gets paid; a logic bomb might go off if he doesn't turn it off. Again, it's important to have auditing in place to help monitor any of these possibilities. A very strong monitoring system would reveal improper logins and could catch changes in files that might indicate logic bombs if done at regular intervals.

Worms

A *worm* is a virus that crawls through the Internet to make its way to other systems. Worms are commonly spread via e-mail; the "Nimda" virus is a recent example. E-mail has become a popular delivery method for worms because it is easy to fool unwitting users into executing damaging programs disguised as harmless e-mail attachments. A common trick is for the worm to send itself to every address in the victim's e-mail address book. This not only causes the worm to propagate at an exponential rate, but it fools recipients into believing that the worm is harmless because it was apparently sent by someone they know.

Trojan horses

A *Trojan horse* does something harmful when invoked, but disguises itself as a valid program. It can be in the form of a useful utility program that, when executed, captures the keystrokes of the user and monitors for any sites that the user may be logging into at that time. These keystrokes could be saved to a file or be sent to a waiting server on the Internet to collect keystrokes from various users and organizations that use this utility. A database could be built from the number of users accessing this utility program. The utility program from myfavoriteutility.com might not even be from myfavoriteutility.com, but a modified version uploaded to a shareware site with a Trojan horse hidden in it. Anyone who uses it would invoke the Trojan horse. Integrity could help out in this area because of the capability to ensure that the version from the shareware site matches a valid version from myfavorite utility.com.

Books could easily be written about the many different server attack types. The attacks that were mentioned can also contain various combinations. A worm attack, for example, could easily contain a logic bomb that was transported to the machine by using the worm but set to explode based on a specific date.

Summary

This chapter gave you a short introduction into some security fundamentals. Many organizations employ full-time security experts because attackers are becoming more sophisticated and aggressive every day, and more data is at risk as organizations become more networked. To keep the site up and the data safe should be a daily goal in every organization. Some malicious hackers have nothing better to do than to get your data and bring your machines down. Disgruntled employees who start working for your competitors can probably do the most damage. The best advice is to have your security systems protected by people that you trust and who understand the hacker mentality and toolsets.

You may be asking yourself, how much security is enough? We recommend that all organizations have a security department whose job is to stay one step ahead of hackers. Just because you're not aware of any attacks doesn't mean that they didn't happen. It may be that the auditing is not adequate enough to discover attacks. The leadership in the organization needs to constantly ask the question about the value of the data in the organization being made public. Organizations need to have a set of procedures to follow when their sites have been hacked. It's better to be overprepared than to suffer the consequences. For a secure system, all layers and resources need to be marked off in a checklist as being secured.

✦   ✦   ✦

Understanding WebLogic's Security Architecture

✦ ✦ ✦ ✦

In This Chapter

Using the New 7.0
Security Architecture

Creating custom security
providers

Accessing the
embedded LDAP server

Upgrading from
WebLogic Server 6.x

✦ ✦ ✦ ✦

Security awareness has been raised to a much higher level over the past few years in step alongside the growth of the Internet. Prominent news stories of security debacles abound in the news these days; with Internet viruses and worms hitting our networks from every side, hackers exposing credit card numbers and other sensitive and/or personal information, and the threat of e-terrorism, it's impossible not to become ever more mindful of security.

Remember that security is more than keeping out hackers; you have to be equally concerned with employees (current and former) and contractors who may have a grudge against the company or just think they have something to gain.

Designing and executing a security plan is a complex process, although having the right hardware and software can make things easier. With version 7.0, BEA has introduced a vastly more sophisticated security system in WebLogic Server. This introduces significant new complexity in the short term, but it makes security configuration much more granular, robust, and able to meet the specific business needs of your company in the long run.

This chapter explains the big picture behind WebLogic's new security architecture. We highly recommend that you read this chapter before trying to configure security for your domain and applications. After you understand the architecture, it's much easier to configure WebLogic security.

 Cross-Reference For information on setting up security policies that restrict access to server side applications and using JAAS with Java clients, see Chapter 22. See Chapter 25 for information on domain-level security, such as setting up users, groups, and roles; integrating external LDAP servers; and links to other security configuration procedures.

The New 7.0 Security Architecture

WebLogic Server 7.0 introduces a completely new and comprehensive security architecture. Sounds scary, doesn't it? Take comfort in the fact that it still has users, groups, and the concept of a security realm, but these have been extended and modularized. It also now comes with an embedded LDAP server that makes it easier to administer.

Roles and policies

Users and groups have been extended with the concept of roles and policies. A *role* is similar to a group in that it can be composed of users and other groups, but it extends that functionality with the concept of dynamic business rules. Currently, *dynamic business rules* are composed of time-of-day limitations, but the architecture is there for other types of business rules. A *policy* is the application of a role to a specific WebLogic resource, such as a Web application.

For an example of time limitations, you can create a role called DayShift. This role might be composed of all employees on the production line who work on shift 1. "Big deal!" you might say, "I can do that with groups!" Ah, but now you can limit their membership in the DayShift role to the hours from 8 a.m. to 5 p.m.; if they log in before 8 or after 5, they're not considered to be in the DayShift role. You can then apply this DayShift role to, say, a product-tracking Web application. Applying this DayShift role to the Web application is called creating a policy. This has the effect of limiting their access to your product tracking Web application to 8 a.m. through 5 p.m.. If they try to access it after 5 p.m., authorization will fail. Try that with a simple group!

Another special feature of roles is that you can create either global roles or scoped roles. A *global role* applies to the entire WebLogic domain. Global roles are created when you create a role at the level of the realm, as described in Chapter 25. A *scoped role*, on the other hand, applies to a specific WebLogic resource, such as an enterprise application, a Web URL, a JNDI branch, or an EJB method. Scoped roles are created when you create a role on a WebLogic resource, as described in Chapter 22. Scoped roles can also be inherited. For example, you can create a scoped role at the level of an EJB and another at the level of a single EJB method. All the EJB methods will inherit the EJB scoped role, and the role defined at the one EJB method will supplement or override its inherited scoped role.

Users and groups can only be global; you cannot define a user or group scoped to a WebLogic resource.

Realms and the WebLogic Security Service Provider Interface (SSPI)

At a view from 30,000 feet, security can seem quite simple. As shown in Figure 21-1, a browser makes a call to a protected Web (URL) resource. The WebLogic Web container intercepts the call and calls a security "black box" to make sure that the user can access that resource. The black box then calls an externally available LDAP server that has been configured for use. The user is found in the appropriate group and, assuming that the user has supplied the correct password, the black box gives the okay back to the Web container. The Web container then allows the client access to the URL it was calling because the authentication and authorization succeeded.

Figure 21-1: Security is simple at a high level: It's just a black box.

Looking closer at security, it turns out that the black box is a WebLogic Server security realm that uses the WebLogic Security Service Provider Interface (or SSPI). This may sound intimidating, but this too is very simple in theory. Refer to Figure 21-1, but this time think of it in terms of JDBC. Replace "web container" with "JDBC code," replace "black box/SSPI" with "JDBC API/Driver," and replace "LDAP Security Store" with "Oracle Database." See, it's simple. The SSPI is just a standardized interface to third party (or custom or WebLogic default) security service providers. Thus, the name *security service provider interface*. This concept is illustrated in more detail in Figure 21-2, in which we magnify the view of the black box to see what's really inside it.

SSPI provides the same benefits to security that JDBC provides to database code. Your code is completely independent of the security system (or database) that you're using. In fact, you can change the security system (or database) without affecting your code.

Figure 21-2: The black box in detail: the Security Service Provider Interface

The analogy between SSPI and JDBC can be extended to the libraries that implement the interfaces: you usually don't write SSPI or JDBC drivers yourself. Theoretically, you could write them yourself, but pragmatically you just use or buy drivers from third parties, such as Sun's JDBC-ODBC bridge or Oracle's thin driver. Likewise, you generally don't write security providers yourself, but you can if you need to. BEA has a Web page that describes the third parties that are certified to work with the WebLogic security framework at the following URL:

```
http://www.bea.com/products/security
```

Figure 21-2 shows some of the requirements that make up the SSPI, as well as a sample config-ured component in the form of an LDAP server (iPlanet). Remember, the SSPI is just an inter-face; you need to configure and instantiate components to do the work (much as you configure a specific JDBC driver, such as the Oracle thin driver, when you work with JDBC).

Configuring these components is what you do when you create a WebLogic security realm. When you create a new realm, it's initially completely empty. This is illustrated in Figure 21-3 and shown in practice in Figure 21-4. You can't use this empty realm because it's like using an unconfigured JDBC connection pool. If you don't configure a specific JDBC driver, how will the connection pool know what to connect to? Likewise, if you don't specify an authentica-tion provider, authorization provider, and so on, the SSPI won't know what to do with security requests.

Whether you're reconfiguring the default realm (myrealm) or creating a new one from scratch, there are a number of components that need to be defined. Table 21-1 lists these components and their requirements, based on three groups of related concepts: Authentication, Authorization, and Auditing.

Figure 21-3: A newly configured security realm has no providers configured.

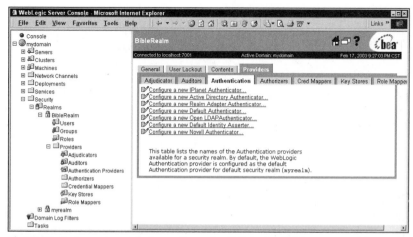

Figure 21-4: A newly created security realm (`BibleRealm`) has no providers configured.

Table 21-1: Security Realm Requirements

Authentication-Related Requirements

Provider Type	Number of Instances Allowed	Comments
Authentication Provider and/or Identity Assertion Provider	1+ (one or more required)	• Provides a JAAS LoginModule. • Identity Assertion Provider is a subtype of the Authentication Provider; either can be used (need at least one of either or both). • Identity Assertion Providers may support multiple token types, but can have only one type active per instance.

Continued

Table 21-1 *(continued)*

Authentication-Related Requirements

Provider Type	Number of Instances Allowed	Comments
Principal Validation Provider	1 per Authentication Provider	Not configurable in the WebLogic Console.
Credential Mapping Provider	1+	Maps a credential (for example, username/password or username/certificate) configured in the WebLogic Security realm to an external (for example, legacy or database or CRM) system, thus allowing WebLogic Server to "log in" to the external system as a WebLogic user.
Keystore Provider	0+	Obtains secured private keys from a keystore which stores private keys and public key certificates and trusted CAs (certificate authorities).

Authorization-Related Requirements

Provider Type	Number of Instances Allowed	Comments
Authorization Provider	1+	Can segment: 1 for JNDI tree, one for EJBs, and so on.
		Restricts user access to resources based on role.
Adjudication Provider	0 or 1	Required only if multiple authorization providers.
		Resolves multiple authorization conflicts.
Role Mapping Provider	1+	• Supplies authorization providers with *dynamic* role information by using security roles from deployment descriptors and configured role information in the Console.
		• Can have, for example, one provider per LDAP server or one provider per resource type (one for the JNDI tree and one for EJBs, for example).
		• If there are multiple results (more than one role is returned) the results are merged.

Auditing-Related Requirements

Provider Type	Number of Instances Allowed	Comments
Auditing Provider	0+	• Can save the audit trail anywhere that it knows how to (database, LDAP server, log file, port, and so on). • Can specify criteria such as an auditing threshold.

The following sections give you more information about some of the WebLogic (Default) providers.

 Note The WebLogic documentation refers to these as the WebLogic providers, whereas the Console refers to these as the Default providers. In this book, we refer to them as WebLogic (Default) providers to cover all our bases!

Authentication

This provider implements a JAAS LoginModule to perform the authentication. Because WebLogic Server 7.0 requires JDK 1.3, it also uses the JAAS 1.0 specification. (JDK 1.4 has JAAS built in.)

The WebLogic (Default) provider uses an embedded LDAP server that comes with WebLogic. The embedded LDAP server cannot have custom fields added to it. If you need custom fields, you need to use a third-party authentication provider, such as iPlanet (Sun ONE), Novell Netware, or Microsoft Active Directory.

The embedded LDAP server is case-insensitive; all users and groups must be unique within the realm, regardless of their case. For example, after you add a user named Lou, you cannot also have a user named lou or LOU.

Authorization

WebLogic does not use JAAS for authorization; it uses it only for authentication. So you will not see JAAS policy files. Instead, you use the WebLogic Console to edit the realm, as we describe in Chapter 25.

Adjudication

Because the purpose of an adjudicator is to make a final decision based on feedback from each of multiple authorization providers, this setting is crucial to understand. When a request is made for a particular resource, each authorization provider returns PERMIT, DENY, or ABSTAIN.

Keystore providers

Keystore providers are deprecated in this release of WebLogic Server. Writing your own is not supported.

Realm Adapter providers

These providers are for using the WebLogic 6.x realms, and are not discussed further in this book. See the WebLogic Server security documentation for more information on configuring and using them, along with significant caveats. They are introduced and deprecated in WebLogic Server 7.0, so if you do choose to use them, you should have a road map to using the 7.0 providers as soon as possible.

Note   "What?! They're introduced and deprecated in the same release?!" Yes, and it makes sense if you understand BEA's intent. The Realm Adapter providers are introduced in WebLogic Server 7.0 so that your migration from 6.x is as easy as possible. However, they are deprecated because BEA probably doesn't want to spend the resources to maintain this backwards compatibility. Think of it as a crutch, and a temporary one at that. If you do decide to use the Realm Adapter providers, make sure you have a plan for moving to the new WebLogic 7.0 providers. These Realm Adapter providers won't be hanging around for long.

Creating Custom Security Providers

In Chapter 25, we describe how to use the built-in and provided third-party security providers. If none of these providers meets your needs, you can write your own custom security providers.

See the example code and PDF documentation on BEA's dev2dev Web site at the following URL:

```
http://dev2dev.bea.com/codelibrary/code/security_prov.jsp
```

Accessing the Embedded LDAP Server

You can access the embedded LDAP server with any generic LDAP browser or editor. To show you how, we'll configure a new connection in a commonly available LDAP browser, which is available at the following URL:

```
http://www.openchannelfoundation.org/projects/LDAP_Browser_Editor
```

First, you must explicitly configure the WebLogic Server domain's security credential. In the WebLogic Console, this is set at mydomain ⇨ Security ⇨ EmbeddedLDAP ⇨ Credential. See Chapter 23 (Figure 23-13) for complete details. After you set the credential, restart the Server for the change to take effect.

After you restart the WebLogic Server, open your LDAP browser/editor and configure it as follows (the result of the Session tab is shown in Figure 21-5):

1. Set the Host field to **localhost**.

2. Set the Port field to **7001** (7002 if SSL is being used).

3. Set the Base DN field to **dc=mydomain**.

4. Uncheck the Anonymous Bind option.

5. Set the User DN field to **cn=Admin**.

6. Set the `Password` field to the password you specified in [change Credential in console for embedded LDAP].

Figure 21-5: Configure the first tab of the LDAP browser.

Click the `Options` tab and ensure the options are set as shown in Figure 21-6.

Figure 21-6: Configure the second tab of the LDAP browser.

When you are finished entering the options, click Save. You will be prompted for a name for your new configuration. Enter an appropriate name, such as **WLS7 Embedded LDAP** and click OK. You are then brought back to the Connect dialog, shown in Figure 21-7. Next time you start the LDAP browser, you can connect directly from this dialog, without going through the steps above.

Figure 21-7: A list of configurations including your new configuration

Select your new configuration from the Session List and click the Connect button to connect to the embedded WebLogic LDAP server. If you get an error, make sure you've changed the domain-level security credential and rebooted the server, as described earlier. After you successfully connect, your LDAP browser should look something like Figure 21-8.

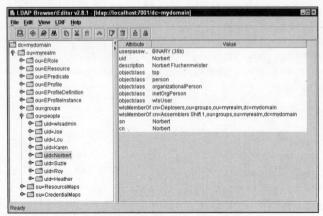

Figure 21-8: An LDAP browser with information on a user configured in the `myrealm` realm

Now you can browse and edit the embedded LDAP server's contents.

Upgrading from WebLogic Server 6.x

There are no equivalents to the WebLogic Server 6.x Windows NT, Unix, or RDBMS security realms in WebLogic Server 7.0. Therefore, BEA recommends using the Realm Adapter Authentication provider to access the users and groups stored in these security realms.

When using Compatibility Security, a Realm Adapter Authentication provider is by default configured for the CompatibilityRealm. However, you can configure a Realm Adapter Authentication provider in any security realm.

Note   The Realm Adapter Authentication provider is the only Realm Adapter provider that can be configured in a realm other than the CompatibilityRealm.

By default, the CompatibilityRealm is configured with a Realm Adapter Adjudication provider, a Realm Adapter Authentication provider, a WebLogic Authorization provider, a Realm Adapter Authorization provider, a WebLogic Credential Mapping provider, and a WebLogic Role Mapping provider.

See the WebLogic Server security documentation on Compatibility Security and the Realm Adapter Authentication Provider for information on migrating from WebLogic Server 6.x to 7.0.

Summary

WebLogic Server 7.0 introduced a dramatically improved security system. In this chapter, you learned about the architecture of the system and its advanced features.

As do most security systems, WebLogic Server 7.0 includes the concepts of users and groups. But it extends these concepts with roles and policies. Roles allow you to apply business rules — such as time-of-day limits — to groups of users. Policies are the application of users, groups, and roles to WebLogic resources, such as Web applications and EJBs.

You can create separate security infrastructure instances called realms. Although you can configure multiple realms, only one realm can be active at a time. WebLogic ships with a default realm that is preconfigured using an embedded LDAP server. Each realm can be configured with different providers for authentication, authorization, and adjudication. These providers together comprise the WebLogic Security Service Provider Interface, or SSPI. SSPI providers constitute a plug and play architecture much like JDBC providers or JNDI providers do. In addition to using out-of-the-box providers, SSPI enables you to create your own custom security providers, or use third-party providers.

The embedded LDAP server is convenient, but BEA provides no way to browse or edit its contents other than through the simple Console security realm interface. We showed you how to configure your own general LDAP browser to view the contents of the embedded LDAP server.

The security system in WebLogic Server 7.0 is sufficiently different from that of the 6.*x* series that we provided a section on migrating from one to the other.

After reading this chapter you should have a basic understanding of the overall architecture of the new security system. With this under your belt, you can read Chapter 22 to learn how to protect WebLogic resources or read Chapter 25 to learn how to configure the default security realm.

✦   ✦   ✦

Securing WebLogic Resources and Programming JAAS

♦   ♦   ♦   ♦

In This Chapter

Securing WebLogic
resources

Introduction to JAAS
programming

♦   ♦   ♦   ♦

Now that you understand security fundamentals and the way WebLogic implements them, it's time to see how to configure and program security for WebLogic applications. This chapter provides you with the configuration steps and source code required to effectively secure a WebLogic system.

Securing a WebLogic Resource

As we described in Chapter 21, security policies are created when you secure a WebLogic Server resource. These security policies use roles, called scoped roles, to define access to the resource.

Cross-Reference In Chapter 25, we discuss creating global roles at the realm level, instead of scoped roles at the resource level, which is what we discuss in this chapter.

In version 6.1 of WebLogic Server, you could apply security only at the EJB or Web Application level. In version 7.0, you can specify security policies at the resource level. Resources include Web applications, servlets, JARs, EJBs, EJB methods, and JNDI branches. A full list of resource types is in the WebLogic documentation at the following URL:

```
http://edocs.bea.com/wls/docs70/secwlres/wlres.html#
1190651
```

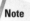
Note Web services can be secured at various levels using the WebLogic Console. You can secure the entire Web service or any individual component of that service, such as at the level of a component EJB. If the Web service is implemented by a simple Java class, however, the Web service can be secured only by securing the entire Web service's URL.

Cross-Reference   See also Chapter 11 for information on setting up security information in deployment descriptors for servlets.

Let's configure the security for a few resources to see how it's done.

First, let's configure a policy for an EJB. As shown in Figure 22-1, in the WebLogic Console, you right-click an EJB in the domain tree on the left and then choose Define Policy from the context menu.

The panel on the right then changes to that shown in Figure 22-1. A policy is a (scoped) role applied to a resource. So this pane is where you define the role. Here, we specified that the caller is granted the role of Tester. Notice also that there is an Inherited Policy Statement. This defaults to Caller, which is a member of the group everyone. This policy is inherited because all resources have this by default. But it gets more interesting. Because policies can be applied at many levels—an enterprise application, an EJB, and an EJB method, for example—policies at the lowest level (an EJB method, for example) inherit the policies from higher levels (at the EJB and enterprise application levels). For example, when you right-click the EJB in the domain tree on the left, the context menu also shows a Define Policies and Roles for Individual Beans option. If we choose that option, we get Figure 22-2, which shows a list of beans and how they can be configured. After you've made your changes, click the Apply button at the bottom to save your changes.

Figure 22-1: Fill out the policy information for an EJB

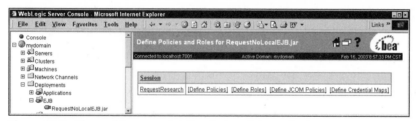

Figure 22-2: Show all beans and define their policies and roles

Now let's look at configuring a Web application. Right-click a Web application in the Console and choose Define a Policy from the context menu. You'll see the pane shown in Figure 22-3. Specify a URL pattern (we've chosen `*.jsp`) and then click Define Policy.

Figure 22-3: Specify a URL pattern to secure

Figure 22-4 appears. This looks identical to the policy configuration for an EJB (refer to Figure 22-2), except for the Methods drop-down list at the top. Here you can specify which HTTP method you want to protect: `GET`, `POST`, `DELETE`, or `ALL`. After you've defined it, don't forget to click the Apply button way at the bottom. Otherwise, your changes won't be saved.

You can also define a role at this level. Go back to the Web application's node in the Console, right-click, and select Define Role (refer to Figure 22-4). The pane will change to one very similar to that shown in Figure 22-3. Enter a URL, such as `*.html`, and click the Define Role button. If this URL has not yet been configured, you'll see an empty panel with a single link that says Configure a New Role.... Click the link and the pane shown in Figure 22-5 will appear. Enter a name and click Apply. You'll now see the typical role-definition pane, shown in Figure 22-6. As you can see, we added some users to the role and clicked Apply to save our changes.

Figure 22-4: Fill out the policy information for a Web application

Figure 22-5: Enter a role name to configure

Figure 22-6: Fill out the role information, such as a few users

If you now go back to the same Web application, right-click it, select Define Roles, and enter the same *.html URL. Click Define Role and you'll see the pane that shows up in Figure 22-7. As you can see, we have just defined a scoped role for this URL, so now it appears in the list.

Figure 22-7: Our previously defined role shows up

If you want to see all the scoped roles (as well as the global roles) that you have defined, you can view them in the security realm section of the Console. On the left side of the Console, open the Security node and then open the Realms node inside that. Click the name of the realm (in our case, myrealm) and then select the Contents tab, which is shown in Figure 22-8.

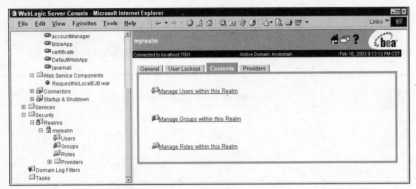

Figure 22-8: Accessing global and scoped roles

Note   Don't click the Roles node on the left under the realm name's node. Doing this will show you only the global roles, not the global *and* scoped roles.

In Figure 22-8, click the Manage Roles within this Realm link, which will bring you to a list of all global and scoped roles, as shown in Figure 22-9.

Figure 22-9: List of all global and scoped roles in the realm

As described earlier, there are many types of Resources in WebLogic Server. Try setting policies at different levels and see how the inheritance works. This is a powerful yet simple-to-use technique for locking down your applications at a very fine resolution.

Introduction to JAAS Programming

JAAS 1.0 is a separate software package provided by Sun to extend the Java Software Development Kit version 1.3 as an alternative to the JNDI authentication process. (It now comes standard with the Java SDK 1.4.) This implies that, at a minimum, version 1.3 of the Java Software Development Kit must be installed and used for development. The JAAS mechanism is used for authentication from the Java client through WebLogic Server to authenticate a subject. The authorization components are not provided in JAAS for the WebLogic Server because of the use of the security realms. To understand how to program to the WebLogic Server's implementation of JAAS, you must first understand how to program to Sun's implementation of JAAS.

 Note   More information on WebLogic-specific JAAS considerations is available at `http://edocs.bea.com/wls/docs70/security/fat_client.html`.

Start the architecture by defining the various classes that make up JAAS in the following classes that comprise the JAAS v1.0 architecture:

✦ `javax.security.auth.Subject`: Represents the source of the request that can be an individual or group with a set of public and private credentials. A `Subject` object is created at the completion of a successful user authentication or login.

✦ `javax.security.auth.login.LoginContext`: Provides the base API for initiating login and logout, and acquires the authenticated `Subject` for the purpose of authorization.

✦ `javax.security.auth.login.Configuration`: The configuration object that specifies which `LoginModule` to use from the `LoginConext`.

✦ `javax.security.auth.spi.LoginModule`: The object that provides a module for a specific implementation of an authentication technology from the providers that support JAAS. This object is also the actual object that performs the authentication.

✦ `javax.security.auth.callback.Callback`: The object that interfaces with the `CallbackHandler`. This allows the security services to interact with the calling application to retrieve specific data such as usernames and passwords. The type of `Callbacks` used is based on the type of `LoginModule`.

✦ `javax.security.auth.callback.Callback.CallbackHandler`: The object that is passed as a mechanism between the `LoginContext` and the `LoginModule` to communicate with a subject to obtain the authentication mechanism. This mechanism is used to both provide information and to get information to the `LoginModule`. The information is passed through the `Callback` object.

Writing and configuring the LoginContext

To create the Java Client for authentication, the first step is to associate the login mechanism to the `LoginContext`. The login mechanism is in an implementation of `LoginModule`. When the `LoginContext` is constructed, the `LoginModule` and `CallbackHandler` instances are associated with it at that time. The `LoginModule` is not hard-coded to the `LoginContext`, but is distributed through a `Configuration` object. All that will be called in the `LoginContext` is a reference that is stored in the configuration file to specify which login mechanism to install. This is so that login mechanisms can be plugged in without changing code, just the configuration. Listing 22-1 starts the `LoginContext`:

Listing 22-1: Using a LoginContext in Sample.java

```java
/**
 * Sample client for JAAS user authentication
 */
public class Sample {

  /**
   * Attempt to authenticate the user.
   */
  public static void main(String[] args) {

    LoginContext loginContext = null;

    /**
     * Set JAAS server url system property and create a LoginContext
     */
    try {
      // Create LoginContext
      loginContext = new LoginContext("Sample",
        new MyCallbackHandler());
    } catch (SecurityException se) {
      se.printStackTrace();
    } catch (LoginException le) {
      le.printStackTrace();
    }

    /**
     * Attempt authentication
     */
    try {
      // If we return without an exception, authentication succeeded
      loginContext.login();
    } catch (FailedLoginException fle) {
      System.out.println("Authentication Failed, " +
        fle.getMessage());
    } catch (AccountExpiredException aee) {
        System.out.println("Authentication Failed: Account Expired");
    } catch (CredentialExpiredException cee) {
        System.out.println("Authentication Failed: CredentialsExpired");
    } catch (Exception e) {
        System.out.println("Authentication Failed: Unexpected Exception, "
          + e.getMessage());
      e.printStackTrace();
    }

    /**
     * Retrieve authenticated subject, perform SampleAction as Subject
     */
    Subject      subject      = loginContext.getSubject();
```

```
    SampleAction sampleAction = new SampleAction();
    Subject.doAs(subject, sampleAction);
    System.exit(0);
  }
}
```

Figure 22-10 shows a lot of work being done "under the hood" in the process of the LoginContext creation. The instance of the CallbackHandler is passed to the underlying LoginModule in order for the Subject and the LoginModule to communicate. The configuration of the LoginModule must succeed in order for the authentication to succeed. One thing that becomes clear regarding communication between the LoginModule and LoginContext is that they never interact directly, but rather through mediators such as the Configuration object and CallbackHandler.

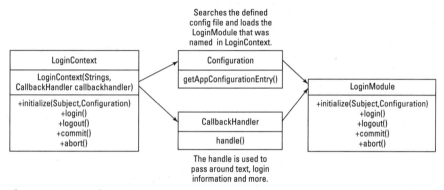

Figure 22-10: LoginContext

After the Java client creates the LoginContext object, it must then invoke the login() function. This login() function will, in turn, invoke the login() function from each of the LoginModule objects defined in the creation of the LoginContext. Regardless of whether the login() function fails or succeeds, this method will complete a two-phase authentication process by calling either the commit or abort functions of the LoginModules. The commit() function gets called for every successful authentication of the login() function to associate the Principals and Credentials to the Subject. The abort() function gets called for every unsuccessful attempt of the login() function to clean up any resources used for the verification. A successful login() of the Subject is when the login() function completes and no exception was thrown; otherwise, the authentication was unsuccessful. After a successful authentication, a getSubject() function can be called on the LoginContext to get the current Subject that was authenticated in the Java client. To get the Principals on the Subject, a getPrincipals() function can be called on the Subject object. To get the current Credentials, a getCredentials() function can be called on the current Subject object.

The configuration determines the LoginModule that will be applied to the LoginContext. The configuration for the example is defined by the environment properties — Djava. security.auth.login.config==sample_jaas.config:

```
/** Login Configuration for the JAAS Sample Application **/

Sample {
  SampleLoginModule required debug=true;
};
```

The file is set for the `Sample` name, but more names can be named in this file for multiple configurations. The `java.auth.login.config` setting to define the configuration file can also be changed by overwriting the `Configuration` object's `getAppConfigurationEntry()` function. The `debug=true` is a name and value pair that are parameters that can be passed into the `LoginModule` initialization. The `SampleLoginModule` is the class that will be loaded up and become the running instance of the `LoginModule`. It is normally referred to as the `ModuleName`. The Authentication Flag is required and is not case-sensitive; its legal values are as follows:

✦ **Required:** The associated `LoginModule` must succeed for the authentication to be considered successful. The next modules will still continue to load, even if a failure condition is encountered.

✦ **Requisite:** The `LoginModule` must succeed for the authentication process to be considered successful, but the subsequent modules will not be attempted if a failure occurs.

✦ **Sufficient:** The `LoginModule` is not required to succeed. If it does succeed, it will not proceed to the next `LoginModule`. But if it doesn't succeed, it will proceed to the next `LoginModule` that is specified.

✦ **Optional:** The `LoginModule` is not required to succeed. Whether it succeeds or not, it will proceed to the next `LoginModule` down the chain.

This solves the issue of configuring the `LoginModule`. You can also give access to the `SampleAction` and the rest of the sample code by configuring policy files. You can use the `policytool` that comes with the JDK 1.3 to configure policy files. These policy files can grant permissions to JAR files, directories, or even URLs. The `SampleAction` was put into a JAR to assign the permissions and a principal to it:

```
/** Subject-Based Access Control Policy for the JAAS Sample Application **/

grant codebase "file:D:/Working/jaas/jaas/SampleAction.jar",
  Principal sample.SamplePrincipal "rich" {
  permission java.util.PropertyPermission "java.home", "read";
  permission java.util.PropertyPermission "user.home", "read";
  permission java.io.FilePermission "sample_jaas.config", "read";
};
```

Because the `SampleAction.class` is saved in the `SampleAction.jar` and the `Principal` is set to `rich`, the user `rich` will have read permissions to the `user.home` and `java.home` properties and read permissions for the file sample `jaas.config`. The type of permissions that are allowed depends on the permission class name. The permission class name in the example given is `java.io.FilePermission` that can have a read, write, delete, and execute permission on a particular file. The same type of permission structure is applied to the rest of the JARs and sample code. We recommended that you keep the `LoginModules` in separate JARs to decouple them from the rest of the sample code. Separating the `LoginModules` models maintains the pluggable behaviors of these authentication mechanisms. The other file that is part of the sample code is shown in Listing 22-2.

Listing 22-2: **sample_java2.policy**

```
/** Java 2 Access Control Policy for the JAAS Sample Application **/

/* grant the JAAS core library AllPermission */
grant codebase "file:D:/Working/jaas/jaas/jaas.jar" {
  permission java.security.AllPermission;
};

/* grant the sample LoginModule AllPermission */
grant codebase "file:D:/Working/jaas/jaas/LoginModule.jar" {
  permission java.security.AllPermission;
};

/*grant permissions for the Sample Class */
grant {
  permission javax.security.auth.AuthPermission "modifyPrincipals";
  permission javax.security.auth.AuthPermission "createLoginContext";
  permission javax.security.auth.AuthPermission "doAs";
  permission java.util.PropertyPermission "java.home", "read";
  permission java.util.PropertyPermission "user.home", "read";
  permission java.io.FilePermission "sample_jaas.config", "read";
};
```

Note   To enable the use of loading property files, the `java.security.manager` must be enabled in the environment.

Writing a LoginModule

The first function in the `LoginModule` is the `initialize()` function. This function receives the `Subject`, `CallbackHandler`, and any shared states and options that were started from the `Configuration` object loading the configuration file. The `initialize()` function is associated with the `Configuration` object settings and the `CallbackHandler` functionality when it is started by the JVM. The `initialize()` function needs to set these parameters to the `LoginModule`'s global variables for future reference. The `LoginModule` will use the `Callback Handler` to establish any interaction with the `LoginContext`, such as getting a password.

The next function is the `login()` function, which is called when the `login()` function of the `LoginContext` starts. In this code, a simple authentication was written to compare the username to `rich` and the password `richpass`. In the WebLogic implementation, WebLogic Server provides a helper class `weblogic.security.auth.Authenticate` that will be used with these principals to authenticate through WebLogic Server. The `Authenticate` class uses a JNDI `Environment` object and returns the authenticated subject. This implies that if the `Credential` and `Principals` are defined in the JNDI environment, it will associate those `Credentials` and `Principals` to that `Subject` after there is a successful login into WebLogic Server. This authentication method will interface to WebLogic's security realm to access the permissions and the authentication of the users. If the user is not defined in WebLogic Server security realm, or if the password is not valid, the user cannot be authenticated.

Using standard JAAS conventions would make the developer copy the PasswordCallback and NameCallback directly into the Subject object and start an authentication process. These are the callbacks that will retrieve the values from the CallbackHandler that interfaces between the Java client and the LoginModule. The login() function associates Principals and Credentials with the Subject. A commit() function is called if the login is successful; otherwise, it is an abort() function. These functions simply finish the work of either continuing to notify the LoginModule to change to a confirmation state of a login or, in an abort, cleaning up the Subject to ensure that it returns that there were errors. Listing 22-3 shows an example of the login() function:

Listing 22-3: **Login example**

```
/**
 * Authenticate the user by username and password passed in
 *
 * @return true in all cases
 *
 *
 * @exception LoginException if this LoginModule
 *             is unable to perform the authentication.
 */
public boolean login() throws LoginException {

  // Verify that the client supplied a callback handler
  if (callbackHandler == null) {
    throw new LoginException("No CallbackHandler Specified");
  }

  // Populate callback list
  Callback[] callbacks = new Callback[2];
  callbacks[0] = new NameCallback("username: ");
  callbacks[1] = new PasswordCallback("password: ", false);

  try {
    // Prompt for username and password
    callbackHandler.handle(callbacks);

    // Retrieve username
    username = ((NameCallback) callbacks[0]).getName();

    // Retrieve password, converting from char[] to String
    char[] charPassword = ((PasswordCallback) callbacks[1]).getPassword();

    if (charPassword == null) {
      // Treat a NULL password as an empty password, not NULL
      charPassword = new char[0];
    }

    password = new String(charPassword);
  } catch (IOException ioe) {
    throw new LoginException(ioe.toString());
  } catch (UnsupportedCallbackException uce) {
```

```
      throw new LoginException("Error: Callback "
        + uce.getCallback().toString() + " Not Available");
    }

    // Populate weblogic environment and authenticate
    /* WebLogic Only */
    //     Environment env = new Environment();
    //     env.setProviderUrl(url);
    //     env.setSecurityPrincipal(username);
    //     env.setSecurityCredentials(password);
    try {
      // Authenticate user credentials, populating Subject
      /* WebLogic Specific */
      //       Authenticate.authenticate(env, subject);

      /* Non-WebLogic Function for Login */
      authenticate(username, password);
    } catch (LoginException le) {
      System.err.println("Error: Login Exception on authenticate, "
        + le.getMessage());
      throw new LoginException(le.toString());
    }

    // Successfully authenticated subject with supplied info
    succeeded = true;
    return succeeded;
}
```

The last function that the `LoginModule` needs to define is the `logout()` function. This function is called in the `LoginModule` when the `LoginContext` executes its `logout()` function. The purpose of this function is simply to release its resources by setting its global variables to null, as Listing 22-4 shows.

Listing 22-4: **Logout function example**

```
/**
 * Logout the user.
 *
 * @exception LoginException if the logout fails.
 *
 * @return true in all cases since this LoginModule
 *         should not be ignored.
 */
public boolean logout() throws LoginException {
  succeeded = false;
  commitSucceeded = false;
  username = null;
  password = null;
  return true;
}
```

Writing the CallbackHandler

The `CallbackHandler` is the object that populates the callbacks from the Java client for the `LoginModule` to use for authentication. These include the `ChoiceCallback`, `ConfirmationCallback`, `LocaleCallback`, `NameCallback`, `PasswordCallback`, `TextInputCallback`, and `TextOutPutCallback`. These are all the callbacks for handling the various authentication mechanisms and their protocols for passing information from and to the Java client. The ones that are emphasized in most `LoginModules` are the `NameCallback` for the username and the `PasswordCallback` for retrieving the user's password. `TextInputCallback` retrieves arbitrary text from the user, and `TextOutputCallback` sends messages such as warnings back to the user. The `ConfirmationCalllback` asks for confirmation from the user to ensure that he is who he claims to be. If it's a choice selection and the `LoginModule` needs to examine the choice, it would use a `ChoiceCallback`. The `LocaleCallback` provides the `LoginModule` with locale information such as the current country being executed in for language constraints. Listing 22-5 shows an example of populating the callbacks.

Listing 22-5: **Populating callbacks**

```
/**
 * Implementation of the CallbackHandler Interface
 */
class MyCallbackHandler implements CallbackHandler {

    /**
     * Method handle
     *
     * @param callbacks
     *
     * @throws IOException
     * @throws UnsupportedCallbackException
     */
    public void handle(Callback[] callbacks)
            throws IOException, UnsupportedCallbackException {

        for (int i = 0; i < callbacks.length; i++) {
            if (callbacks[i] instanceof TextOutputCallback) {

                // Display the message according to the specified type
                TextOutputCallback toc = (TextOutputCallback) callbacks[i];

                switch (toc.getMessageType()) {

                case TextOutputCallback.INFORMATION :
                    System.out.println(toc.getMessage());
                    break;
```

```
                    case TextOutputCallback.ERROR :
                        System.out.println("ERROR: " + toc.getMessage());
                        break;

                    case TextOutputCallback.WARNING :
                        System.out.println("WARNING: " + toc.getMessage());
                        break;

                    default :
                        throw new IOException("Unsupported message type: "
                                            + toc.getMessageType());
                }
            } else if (callbacks[i] instanceof NameCallback) {

                // Prompt the user for the username
                NameCallback nc = (NameCallback) callbacks[i];

                System.err.print(nc.getPrompt());
                System.err.flush();
                nc.setName((new BufferedReader(new InputStreamReader(System
                    .in))).readLine());
            } else if (callbacks[i] instanceof PasswordCallback) {

                // Prompt the user for the password
                PasswordCallback pc = (PasswordCallback) callbacks[i];

                System.err.print(pc.getPrompt());
                System.err.flush();

// Note: JAAS specifies that the password is a char[] rather than a String
                String tmpPassword =
                    (new BufferedReader(new InputStreamReader(System.in)))
                        .readLine();
                int     passLen     = tmpPassword.length();
                char[] password     = new char[passLen];

                for (int passIdx = 0; passIdx < passLen; passIdx++) {
                    password[passIdx] = tmpPassword.charAt(passIdx);
                }

                pc.setPassword(password);
            } else {
                throw new UnsupportedCallbackException(
                    callbacks[i], "Unrecognized Callback");
            }
        }
    }
}
```

Summary

In this chapter, we showed you how to set security policies at the WebLogic resource level. Resources on which you can set security policies include EJBs and EJB methods, URLs, and Web services. Security policies are inherited, in that a policy applied to an EJB applies to all the EJB's methods and yet you can override the policy on one or more individual methods of the EJB. It's also possible to apply different security policies to different URLs on a single Web application or Web service.

To further refine your security, you can create new roles that apply only to a single WebLogic resource. They are called scoped roles, as opposed to the global roles that we'll be creating in Chapter 25.

We also showed how to use JAAS to connect a fat client to a WebLogic Server resource. JAAS is a Java implementation of Sun's PAM (Pluggable Authentication Module), allowing authentication to be performed in a technology-independent manner. Programming JAAS on WebLogic Server means you avoid having to use a configuration file, since WebLogic will use the default realm for authentication.

✦   ✦   ✦

WebLogic Server
Administration

◆　◆　◆　◆

In This Part

◆　◆　◆　◆

Working with WebLogic's Administration Tools

♦ ♦ ♦ ♦

In This Chapter

Understanding the
WebLogic Server
Console

Administering domain
information, servers,
clusters, and machines
from the Console

Administering
deployments, services,
security, and domain
log filters from the
Console

Administering
WebLogic Server using
command-line tools

♦ ♦ ♦ ♦

WebLogic Server provides two separate methods for accessing the WebLogic Server administration tools and configuration settings. The primary administration tool available to WebLogic developers and administrators is the WebLogic Console. The Console, which is a Web application implemented by using JSPs, was introduced with WebLogic 6.0 and has been improved with the release of WebLogic 7.0. The Console provides an easy-to-use interface that replaces the old, error-prone method of directly editing XML or properties files.

The majority of this chapter explores the Console and the different WebLogic services that can be administered and monitored with it. The Console section is broken down into the different major headings of the Console and the subsections of those headings. These subheadings are then explained and their use is demonstrated.

The second method of accessing the WebLogic Server administration tools is from the command line. WebLogic offers extensive command-line support for most major functionality. But because the Server Console is the main tool for administering a WebLogic environment, it's covered in greater detail.

Note Many aspects of WebLogic Server administration and the WebLogic Console have already been covered in other chapters (for example, JDBC in Chapter 5 and JMS in Chapter 9). Therefore, if the Console settings for a particular section are covered in a previous chapter, we will give a short description and a reference to that chapter, rather than duplicating the material here.

Administering WebLogic Server Using the WebLogic Console

When you open the WebLogic Console, a screen similar to the one shown in Figure 23-1 appears.

The left side of the screen is a view of the current WebLogic Server domain, organized in a tree structure. This is called, appropriately enough, the *domain tree*. To select a node in the domain tree, click it with the left mouse button. To bring up a shortcut menu for a node, right-click it.

The right side of the screen is where configuration information appears for the item you have selected in the domain tree. Initially, no item is selected on the left, so the right side contains links to all the items in the domain tree, organized by topic. If for some reason the domain tree (a Java applet) doesn't work, you can access almost all of the functionality using the simple Web links on the right pane.

Notice the three icons adjacent to the BEA logo. From left to right, they are as follows:

✦ **Home.** Click the home icon (it looks like a house) to get to this page from anywhere in the Console.

✦ **Window.** Click the window icon (it looks like two overlapping windows) to open the current right side pane in its own window.

✦ **Help.** Click the help icon (a question mark) to bring up context-sensitive help for the current pane.

Figure 23-1: WebLogic Console opening screen

The following sections discuss the items in the domain tree in the order in which they appear.

Note For ease of reading, each section is named after its menu, each subsection is named after its submenu, and so on. Because this results in some sections being named identically, when referring to a section we will use the same convention that we use for menu paths; placing a command arrow (⇨) between each menu and/or submenu. So, for example, when we say "See the 'Services ⇨ Configuration' section later in this chapter," simply find the "Services" section and see the "Configuration" subsection under it.

Console

The Console node is for configuring the appearance of the Console itself, as well as for viewing version information about the Console and WebLogic Server. Figure 23-2 shows the Preferences tab of the Console Preferences page.

Figure 23-2: The Preferences page of Console Preferences

The entries on this page are as follows:

✦ **Language:** The language in which you want the Console and its help system displayed. The choices are English and Japanese, with the default being English.

✦ **Auto-refresh every:** The Console screens automatically refresh themselves at the interval, in seconds, given by this number. The default is 10 seconds.

✦ **Poll for graph data every:** The Console includes graphical monitoring screens, discussed later in this chapter, that give real-time displays of server traffic and memory usage. This setting determines the interval, in milliseconds, at which the graphs poll the server for data. The default is 500 milliseconds (½ second).

✦ **Remember Last Tab:** Many Console pages, including this one, contain multiple configuration tabs. If this option is checked, the Console remembers which tab you last visited for each node in the domain tree and returns you to that tab the next time you go to that node. If unchecked, you will always be sent to the first (leftmost) tab. The default is checked.

✦ **Use Navigation Tree:** If checked, the Console displays the navigation (domain) tree on the left side. If unchecked, the navigation tree disappears, and you must navigate using the menu on the opening screen (see Figure 23-1). We find it much easier to navigate by using the tree, which is the default. However, if for some reason the domain tree Java applet isn't working, you can unselect this option to display the right pane in the full width of the Console.

Figure 23-3 shows the Versions tab of the Console Preferences page, which shows version information for the Console and the underlying WebLogic Server.

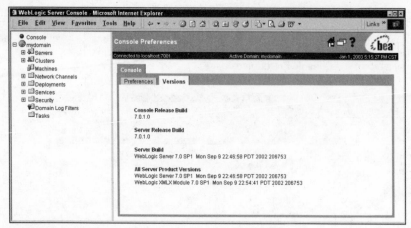

Figure 23-3: The Versions page of Console Preferences

Domain information

The node below Console is the node for the WebLogic domain you are administering. My domain is called dev. This node contains subnodes for administering all aspects of the domain.

Cross-Reference   See Chapters 4 and 24 for information on how to set up and configure WebLogic domains.

Clicking the name of the domain itself brings up several pages for adjusting domain-wide preferences. These pages are organized under four tabs: Configuration, Security, Monitoring, and Notes (discussed in the following sections).

Configuration

The Configuration tab contains general domain settings, as well as settings for JTA, SNMP, Logging, and Applications.

General

Figure 23-4 shows the General page. You should never have to change the settings on this page. Notice, however, the two kinds of icons that appear next to the entry fields: A yellow triangle with an exclamation point and an orange question mark. The yellow icons indicate that changes to those attributes require a restart of the affected WebLogic Server. The orange icons can be clicked on to get context-sensitive help for the specific entry field.

The entries on this page are as follows:

✦ **Name:** The name of the domain. This attribute cannot be changed. Nevertheless, a caution icon appears next to it, presumably in case you figure out how to hack it.

✦ **Console Enabled:** If checked, the domain can be managed with the WebLogic Console. Otherwise, you must manage the domain by using command-line tools. This is primarily a security feature.

✦ **Console Context Path:** This entry enables you to change the servlet context for the Console application itself. The default is `console`, which means that when you invoke the Console in a Web browser, you enter **http://127.0.0.1:7001/console**. If you change this value, say, to `hiddenconsole`, the required URL becomes `http://127.0.0.1:7001/hiddenconsole`. The value you enter is case-sensitive.

✦ **Enable Domain Wide Administration Port (Please configure SSL):** Changes the routing of administration commands from the server's configured HTTP port (7001 by default, where it competes with client traffic) to an administration-command-only HTTPS port specified as follows. It also enables you to start up servers in STANDBY mode. For more information, including setting up administration ports on a server-by-server basis, view the WebLogic documentation at the following site:

`http://e-docs.bea.com/wls/docs70/admin_domain/network.html#administration_port_and_administration_channel`

✦ **Domain Wide Administration Port:** Specify the SSL port for domain administration if the checkbox above is selected.

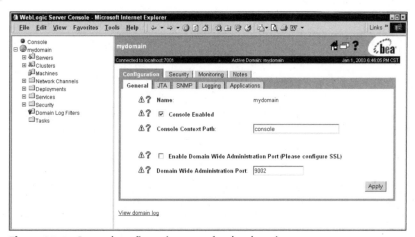

Figure 23-4: General configuration page for the domain

Note   The `View domain log` appears at the bottom of every page in this set. Click it to view the domain-wide log for all servers.

JTA

This tab, shown in Figure 23-5, contains configuration settings for the Java Transaction API (JTA), which is the J2EE component that manages user transactions.

Cross-Reference   For more information about JTA, see Chapter 6.

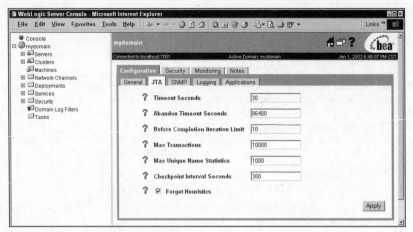

Figure 23-5: JTA configuration page

The entries on this page are as follows:

✦ **Timeout Seconds:** The number of seconds that must elapse before a transaction is rolled back automatically by WebLogic. The default is 30 seconds. When testing your applications, you need to adjust this value to be greater than your longest-running transaction, or else that transaction will never commit.

✦ **Abandon Timeout Seconds:** The maximum amount of time a transaction coordinator will attempt to complete a transaction before abandoning it. The default is 86,400 seconds, or 24 hours. Whereas `Timeout Seconds` controls how long WebLogic waits *each time* it tries to commit a transaction, `Abandon Timeout Seconds` controls how long WebLogic will keep trying, even in the face of timeouts, before it completely gives up.

✦ **Before Completion Iteration Limit:** The number of `beforeCompletion()` callbacks (implemented by EJB developers using the `javax.ejb.SessionSynchronization` interface) that WebLogic will process before forcing the rollback of a transaction. This setting prevents the server from getting bogged-down with too many `beforeCompletion()` calls.

✦ **Max Transactions:** The maximum number of transactions that may be active on a server at one time. The default is 10,000. The setting you choose will depend on a number of factors, including the traffic on your site, the availability of licenses for databases and drivers, and performance.

✦ **Max Unique Name Statistics:** Programmers have the option of giving their transactions unique names. This setting determines how many such names the server will track when collecting performance statistics.

✦ **Checkpoint Interval Seconds:** The transaction manager will always check for old transaction log files that are ready to be deleted and will create new ones as necessary. This specifies the number of seconds between such checks. The default is 300 (five minutes).

✦ **Forget Heuristics:** This tells the transaction manager not to track heuristic completions of transactions for monitoring purposes. *Heuristic completions* are those that occur outside the control of the transaction manager.

SNMP

Figure 23-6 shows the SNMP page, which contains configuration settings for WebLogic's Simple Network Management Protocol (SNMP) agent. The agent runs on the administration server for the domain and reports information for every server and/or cluster in the domain to a third-party SNMP management tool, which you must purchase separately. Step-by-step instructions for configuring SNMP appear later in this chapter in the section titled "Services ⇨ SNMP."

Cross-Reference   See Chapter 4 for more information on WebLogic administration servers.

Figure 23-6: SNMP agent configuration page

The entries on this page are as follows:

✦ **Enabled:** If checked, the SNMP agent is enabled and will transmit data to the BEA management information base (MIB), which is the database that contains information about the WebLogic Server's state.

✦ **SNMP Port:** The network port on which the WebLogic SNMP agent listens for requests from SNMP managers. The default is 161.

✦ **MIB Data Refresh Interval:** The amount of time that elapses, in seconds, between updates to the MIB. The data in the MIB is what gets transferred to the SNMP agent when it makes a request. The default is 120.

✦ **Server Status Check Interval Factor:** The SNMP agent multiplies this number by the Mib Data Refresh Interval to determine how often to check whether managed servers in the domain are up or down. If this value is set to 2, for example, and the Mib Data Refresh Interval is 120, the SNMP agent polls the managed servers every 240 seconds. The default is 1.

✦ **Community Prefix:** This is a string that's used to determine what level of information is sent back to the SNMP manager. The default value is `public`, which means that the agent retrieves data only for the WebLogic administration server running in the `public` community. You can change this to any community name, and the effect will be the same. If this value is of the form `community_prefix@server_name`, WebLogic returns data for that managed server only; if it is of the form `community_prefix@domain_name`, WebLogic returns data for the entire domain.

✦ **Debug Level:** An integer between 0 and 3 that determines how verbose the SNMP debugging messages will be. A value of 0 means no debugging messages are written, whereas a value of 3 means the messages will be most verbose. The default is 0.

✦ **Targeted Trap Destinations:** Select the previously defined trap destinations that you want to target to this domain. To create an SNMP trap destination, see the instructions in the "Services ⇨ SNMP" section later in this chapter.

Logging

Figure 23-7 shows the configuration page for the domain log file. To change the severity of errors posted to the domain log file, see the section "Domain log filters" later in this chapter for information on creating a Domain Log Filter.

Figure 23-7: Logging configuration page

The entries on this page are as follows:

✦ **File Name:** The full pathname of the file to which WebLogic Server writes domain log messages. The default is `.\wl-domain.log`.

✦ **Rotation Type:** Determines how additional log files are created over time. The default is `none`, which means all messages are written to the same login perpetuity. The other options are `by Size`, which means that a new log file is created after the current log file reaches a given size, and `by Time`, which means that a new log file is created every time a certain number of hours passes.

✦ **File Min Size:** If Rotation Type is set to `by Size`, this is the file size (in kilobytes) that must be exceeded by the current log file in order for the next log file to be created. The default is 500k.

✦ **Rotation Time:** If Rotation Type is set to `by Time`, this specifies the base for the rotation time calculation. In other words, a new log file is created every time File Time Span hours increment past the Rotation Time. It can be an absolute date/time or a recurring time and is specified using the layout specified in the `java.text.SimpleDateFormat` class (`MM-dd-yyyy-k:mm:ss` format; note that it uses `k` [1-24] for the hour, not `H` [0-23]). An example of a relative entry would be "`01:15:00`", which means start a new base sequence at 15 minutes past midnight every day. Absolute times, for example, would include a Rotation Time value of "`01-02-2003-2:00:00`" (Thursday, January 2nd 2003 at 1 a.m.) along with a File Time Span value of `168` hours (1 week) will result in a new log file being created every Thursday at 1 a.m. Alternatively, a Rotation Time value of "`01-02-2003-4:30:00`" combined with a File Time Span value of `12` will result in a new log file being created on January 2nd 2003 at 3:30 a.m. and every 12 hours thereafter. If an absolute date has already passed, it is internally converted to a day of week and time of day to use as the base. For example, if you want to start a new rotation sequence every Sunday morning at 3 a.m., enter the date of *any* Sunday (in the past) and a time of 3 a.m. like this: `01-29-2002-3:00:00` along with a File Time Span of `168` hours.

✦ **File Time Span:** If Rotation Type is set to `by Time`, this is the number of hours that will elapse between the creation of each additional log file. The default is 24 hours.

✦ **Number of Files Limited:** If this is checked, the total number of log files created is limited to the number given by File Count; otherwise, there is no limit. After the limit is reached, logging to files stops. Default is unchecked.

✦ **File Count:** If Number of Files Limited is checked, this gives the total number of files that will be created before the logging to files stops. The default is 7.

Applications

Figure 23-8 shows the Applications configuration page.

Figure 23-8: Applications configuration page

The entries on this page are as follows:

✦ **Auto Deployed Enabled:** When this is checked (the default), applications can be auto-matically deployed, without restarting WebLogic.

✦ **Auto Update Interval:** WebLogic Server checks for newly deployed applications at this interval, expressed in milliseconds. The default is 3,000 (3 seconds).

Security

The security pages are where you manage auditing, file realms, passwords, and other related parameters for WebLogic Server.

General

Figure 23-9 shows the General configuration page for WebLogic security.

Figure 23-9: Configuring general security parameters

The entries on this page are as follows:

✦ **Default Realm:** Specify which of the realms in this domain you want to use as the default realm.

✦ **Audit Provider Class:** The fully qualified name of the Java class you have written to provide auditing services for the domain, such as writing login attempts to a log file, and so on.

Cross-Reference

You can find more information about this feature in Chapter 22.

✦ **Guest Disabled:** Checking this box disables the domain's built-in guest account, for increased security.

Filerealm

Figure 23-10 shows the Filerealm configuration page.

The entries on this page are as follows:

✦ **Caching Realm:** The fully qualified name of the Java class that is providing auditing ser-vices for the domain, such as writing all login attempts to a log file, and so on.

✦ **Max Users:** The maximum number of users supported by the realm, which must be an integer between 1 and 10,000. The default is 1000. Exceeding the maximum has no effect except to generate a warning.

✦ **Max Groups:** The maximum number of groups supported by the realm, which must be an integer between 1 and 10,000. The default is 1000. Exceeding the maximum has no effect except to generate a warning.

✦ **Max ACLs:** The maximum number of access control lists supported by the realm, which must be an integer between 1 and 10,000. The default is 1000. Exceeding the maximum has no effect except to generate a warning.

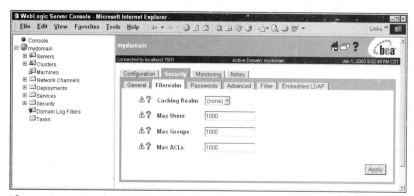

Figure 23-10: Configuring the Filerealm tab

Passwords

Figure 23-11 shows the Passwords configuration page.

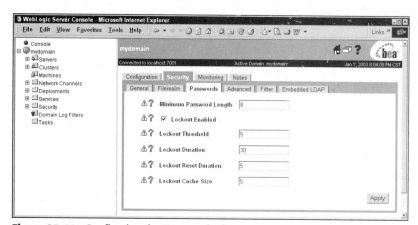

Figure 23-11: Configuring the Password tab

The entries on this page are as follows:

✦ **Minimum Password Length:** The minimum number of characters that user passwords must contain. It must be an integer greater than or equal to 8, and the default is 8.

✦ **Lockout Enabled:** When checked, user accounts will be automatically disabled (the user will be locked out) after a certain number of failed login attempts. This is checked by default.

✦ **Lockout Threshold:** The number of failed login attempts that causes a user to be locked out. The default is 5.

✦ **Lockout Duration:** The length of time, in minutes, a user will be locked out after exceeding the lockout threshold. The default is 30. During this time, all login attempts (even with a correct username and password) will generate security exceptions, unless the system administrator explicitly unlocks the account.

✦ **Lockout Reset Duration:** The length of time, in minutes, within which failed login attempts count against the lockout threshold. The default is 5. Therefore, if five failed login attempts occur within five minutes, the account is locked.

✦ **Lockout Cache Size:** The total number of failed login attempts WebLogic Server will track across all user accounts. The default is 5.

Advanced

Figure 23-12 shows the Advanced security configuration page.

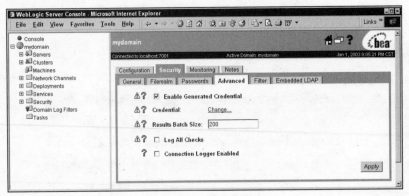

Figure 23-12: Configuring advanced security settings

The entries on this page are as follows:

✦ **Enable Generated Credential:** The credential specified in this pane refers to a domain password. In order for two domains to interact with each other (say, for example, for an EJB in one domain to call an EJB in another domain), they must share the same credential. By default, it is checked, which means that WebLogic generates a credential automatically. Therefore, if you leave this checked for both domains, WebLogic will automatically generate (different) credentials, and the domains will not be able to interact successfully. If you have two domains that you want to interact, you must uncheck this option in both domains and manually set the credential to the same value in both domains (see the next bullet).

✦ **Credential:** Here, you can manually set the credential for this domain (see the previous bullet). If you click here, the pane changes to show a password entry and confirmation field. Fill them out with the same password and click Apply. At that point, the credential you just specified will be applied to the domain and the Enable Generated Credential will automatically be unchecked (these are mutually exclusive options — either you specify the credential or WebLogic generates it — you can't have it both ways). You must reboot for it to take effect. Note that in WebLogic 6.*x*, the credential is the same as the system user's password and cannot be changed. Therefore, for WebLogic 6.*x* and 7.0 domains to interact, set the Credential on the WebLogic 7.0 domains to the system user's password on the WebLogic 6.*x* domain.

✦ **Results Batch Size:** The number of users, groups, and ACLs returned per batch. The default is 200. This allows you to fine-tune the size of the security information returned per RPC.

✦ **Log All Checks:** Determines whether all security checks are logged to the domain log. The default is false.

✦ **Connection Logger Enabled:** This is a dynamic feature (it doesn't require a server restart) that allows you to check incoming secure connections to see if an additional level of security might be needed. For example, if you turn this feature on and find out that secure requests are coming from outside your corporate network, you can create a connection filter (see the next section).

Filter

The filter tab allows configuration of a connection filter as well as rules for filtering.

Cross-Reference See Chapter 25 for more information on filters.

Embedded LDAP

Figure 23-13 shows the Embedded LDAP security configuration page. These settings are used to configure the LDAP server that is embedded in WebLogic Server.

Figure 23-13: Configuring Embedded LDAP security settings

The entries on this page are as follows:

✦ **Credential:** The credential used to authenticate to the embedded LDAP server. This is usually a password.

✦ **Backup Hour:** The hour, from 0 to 23, at which to back up the LDAP server. The default is 23. Also see the next bullet.

✦ **Backup Minute:** The minute, from 0 to 59, at which to back up the LDAP server; used in conjunction with Backup Hour. The default is 5. Combined with the default hour (23), the default minute results in a backup time of 11:05 pm.

✦ **Backup Copies:** The number of copies of the LDAP server to save. Because each backup is done daily, this represents the total number of days of backups to keep. So the default value of 7 means that a total of seven days' backup is kept.

✦ **Cache Enabled:** Determines whether the embedded LDAP server uses a cache. It is enabled by default.

✦ **Cache Size:** The size, in kilobytes, of the cache used (if enabled).

✦ **Cache TTL:** The TTL (time-to-live) of the embedded cache (if enabled).

✦ **Refresh Replica At Startup:** Determines whether replicas of the embedded LDAP server (that is, those copies running on managed servers) are refreshed at startup. This can be useful if a managed server is not booted until all data is updated on the admin server; the managed server will then get all updates at one time, upon startup.

✦ **Master First:** Forces all lookups to the LDAP server to go to the master server on the administration server. Lookups will not go to the local replicated (managed) servers.

Monitoring

This tab allows you to monitor the status of the domain, including clusters and servers. It shows a single link, `Monitor clusters and servers in this domain`. Clicking it will bring up a display such as that shown in Figure 23-14. This gives you immediate feedback on the status of the entire domain.

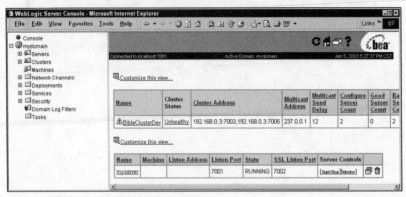

Figure 23-14: Monitoring the domain

Notes

The Notes page allows you to enter administrative notes about the domain configuration. The field accepts free-form text, up to 32,000 characters.

 Note Every Notes page in the Console works the same way, so we won't describe any of the others in the rest of this chapter.

Servers

Clicking the Servers node brings up a page that allows you to add new WebLogic Servers to your domain or to edit the settings of existing servers. You can also monitor the state of existing servers via the simple display that shows whether they are running or not. Figure 23-15 shows the Servers page.

Figure 23-15: Servers page

Our domain contains three servers from the development-style cluster described in Chapter 24. All the servers are listed below the Servers node on the left and also in the list of servers on the right. Clicking the name BibleCServerDev1 in either location brings up the server configuration page shown in Figure 23-16. This page contains several tabs and subtabs for configuring all aspects of the server, which we'll now explain. We specifically chose a cluster node so that we could see all the available options.

 Note BEA rearranged quite a number of options and tabs in the change from WebLogic Server 6.1 to 7.0. If you're migrating from 6.1 to 7.0, keep an eye on the Configuration tab (and the new Connections tab especially, for this is where many of the changes occurred). For example, the settings for HTTP, SSL, Protocols, and half of Tuning have moved from the Configuration tab to the Connections tab.

Configuration

The Configuration tab is where you manage the runtime aspects of your WebLogic Server, including its network identity, clustering behavior, compilers, and so on.

General

Figure 23-16 shows the General configuration page for a server.

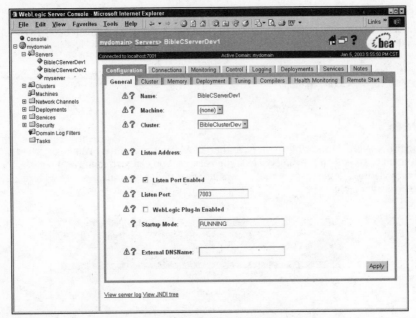

Figure 23-16: General configuration page for a server

The entries on this page are as follows:

✦ **Name:** The name of the server, which must be unique within the WebLogic domain and cannot contain spaces or commas. This name is set when you create a new server and cannot be changed after the server is defined.

✦ **Machine:** The name of the machine on which the server runs. This attribute is not required to have a value, and the default is none. Machine names and the requirements for their usage are covered later in this chapter.

✦ **Cluster:** The name of the cluster, if any, to which this server belongs. The default is none.

✦ **Listen Address:** The IP address on which the server is listening for requests. You are not required to enter a value for this attribute, but if the computer running your WebLogic Servers contains multiple network interface cards (each with a separate IP), you may want to map different servers to different cards. Addresses are entered in standard IP format (such as 192.168.0.10). The default is blank (no address).

✦ **Listen Port Enabled:** Determines whether the HTTP (non-secure) port is enabled. If false, the SSL (secure) port must be enabled and configured. To enable SSL and the secure port, go to the Connections tab and configure the items in the SSL and the SSL Port tabs.

✦ **Listen Port:** The network port on which the server runs, which must be unique for each listen address; no two WebLogic Servers running on the same listen address can listen on the same port. The default is 7001, but you can change it to any valid port that is not in use by other software on the machine.

✦ **WebLogic Plug-In Enabled:** To increase security, WebLogic 7.0 introduces a proprietary HTML header named WL-Proxy-Client-IP that is used when the WebLogic Plug-In is used on other HTTP servers. This setting ensures that the proprietary header's value is returned in any method calls to `HttpRequest.getRemoteAddr()`.

✦ **Startup Mode:** The mode that the server starts up in. The default is `RUNNING`. The only other valid value is `STANDBY`. (It's unclear why this is not a drop-down list, unless there are unpublished debugging modes that the server can be placed in.) This feature, which is new in WebLogic Server 7.0, allows you to start the server and keep it in a standby state. A thorough description of modes can be viewed at the following URL:

`http://e-docs.bea.com/wls/docs70/adminguide/startstop.html#1109112`

✦ **External DNSName:** If the WebLogic Server sits behind a firewall that performs network address translation, enter the DNS name defined for the server on the public side of the firewall.

Cluster

Figure 23-17 shows the Cluster configuration page for a server.

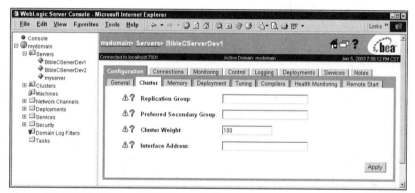

Figure 23-17: Cluster configuration page for a server

The entries on this page are as follows:

✦ **Replication Group:** The replication group within the cluster to which this server belongs. Replication groups are explained in detail in the WebLogic documentation at the following site:

`http://e-docs.bea.com/wls/docs70/cluster/failover.html#1019188`

✦ **Preferred Secondary Group:** The preferred replication group to be used as a backup if the primary replication group fails.

✦ **Cluster Weight:** The percentage of work to be performed by this server within the cluster. The default is 100. If all servers have equal cluster weights, the workload is split evenly among them.

✦ **Interface Address:** This server's physical IP address where cluster multicast traffic is directed.

Memory

Figure 23-18 shows the Memory configuration page for a server. These settings configure how WebLogic detects low memory conditions and how it goes about fixing the situation.

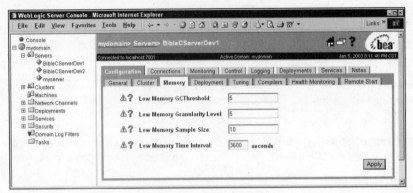

Figure 23-18: Memory configuration page for a server

The entries on this page are as follows:

✦ **Low Memory GCThreshold:** The threshold, as a percentage from 0 to 99, at which garbage collection is attempted after the granularity level is reached. The default is 5.

✦ **Low Memory Granularity Level:** The granularity level used in reporting low memory information. The default is 5.

✦ **Low Memory Sample Size:** The number of memory samples taken at each interval (see the next bullet). The default is 10, so 10 sequential samples are taken every hour for the default time interval.

✦ **Low Memory Time Interval:** The interval, in seconds, that memory samples are taken. The default is 3600, or one hour.

Deployment

The Deployment tab has settings for how applications are deployed from administration servers to managed servers. Figure 23-19 shows the configuration for an administration server, whereas Figure 23-20 shows the configuration for a managed server. We'll go over the options separately.

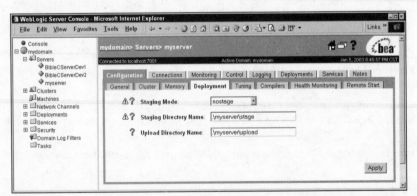

Figure 23-19: The Deployment configuration page for an administration server

The entries on this page for an administration server are as follows:

✦ **Staging Mode:** When WebLogic prepares an application for deployment to a managed server, the application can be copied from the administration server's Upload Directory Name (as follows) to the managed server's Staging Directory Name (also as follows). And this is in fact what happens if this entry is set to `stage`. If it is set to `nostage`, the files are not copied (for example, if the current server is a single server deployment, as for a developer's setup). If it is set to `external_stage`, the files are assumed to be in a shared staging area, so there is no need to copy (overwrite) them. The default is `nostage` for an administration server or single server domain.

✦ **Staging Directory Name:** The directory on the managed server in which WebLogic places all staged applications. An administration server that is in a single-server domain (in a typical developer situation, for example) can also use this setting.

✦ **Upload Directory Name:** The directory on the administration server in which WebLogic places all applications that are to be deployed to managed servers. An absolute path can be specified or a path relative to the server's name in the domain. The default is `.\myserver\upload`, which is relative to the domain's directory path.

Figure 23-20: Deployment configuration page for a managed server

The entries on this page for a managed server are as follows:

✦ **Staging Mode:** When WebLogic prepares an application for deployment to a managed server, the application can be copied from the administration server's Upload Directory Name (see the last bullet in the previous list) to the managed server's Staging Directory Name (see the next bullet). And this is in fact what happens if this entry is set to `stage`. If this is set to `nostage`, the files are not copied (for example, if the current server is a single server deployment, as for a developer's setup). If this is set to `external_stage`, the files are assumed to be in a shared staging area, so there is no need to copy (overwrite) them. The default is `stage` for a managed server.

✦ **Staging Directory Name:** The directory on the managed server in which WebLogic places all staged applications. The default is `.\myserver\stage`.

Tuning

Figure 23-21 shows the Tuning configuration page for a server.

Figure 23-21: Tuning configuration page for a server

The entries on this page are as follows:

✦ **Enable Native IO:** When checked, instructs WebLogic Server to use the native operating system's I/O routines instead of Java's. If the server can't find the native libraries while starting up, you'll see an exception. Make sure that the native libraries are in the correct location. Native I/O is always faster, so the default is checked.

✦ **Client Cert Proxy Enabled:** Enables proxying the client certificate in an HTTP header. The default is false. Setting it to true can be a security risk; see the following URL for more information:

```
http://e-docs.bea.com/wls/docs70/ConsoleHelp/domain_server_config_
tuning.html#1107447
```

✦ **Socket Readers:** The percentage of WebLogic threads to be allocated as socket readers. The default is 33.

✦ **Maximum Open Sockets:** The total number of sockets allowed for this server. After this threshold is reached, no more sockets will be opened and no requests will be accepted until the number of open sockets goes below this value. The default is 2147483647.

✦ **Stuck Thread Max Time:** The number of seconds a thread must be busy before it is considered stuck. The default is 600.

✦ **Stuck Thread Timer Interval:** How often WebLogic checks to see if any thread is stuck; the default is 600 seconds.

✦ **Managed Server Independence Enabled:** Enabling this option will cause WebLogic to store startup information for a managed server locally; this will enable it to start up in the absence of an administration server. The default is false.

✦ **MSI File Replication Enabled:** This enables file replication for the Managed Server Independence (MSI) option (see the previous bullet). MSI must be enabled for this to be enabled. Enabling it results in copies of the administrator's configuration files being replicated to the managed servers. There are some specific caveats that you can read by clicking the help icon.

✦ **Timeout for Server Lifecycle Operations:** The timeout period, in seconds, after which a shutdown will be performed unconditionally. Refers to the server lifecycle that is new in WebLogic Server 7.0 and discussed earlier in this chapter in the General section of the Configuration tab for servers. Currently, this is effective only for the shutdown and force shutdown commands. The default is 120 seconds, and a value of 0 means to wait indefinitely.

Compilers

Figure 23-22 shows the Compilers configuration page for a server. WebLogic uses these settings when generating RMI stubs for EJBs and RMI servers. This page has not changed from WebLogic 6.1.

Figure 23-22: Compilers configuration page for a server

The entries on this page are as follows:

✦ **Java Compiler:** The name of the Java compiler to use. This compiler must reside within your classpath. The default is `javac`.

✦ **Prepend to classpath:** Type directories into this space, separated by semicolons, that you want inserted before WebLogic's classpath when invoking the compiler. The default is blank.

✦ **Append to classpath:** Type directories into this space, separated by semicolons, that you want inserted after WebLogic's classpath when invoking the compiler. The default is blank.

✦ **Extra rmic Options:** Type extra command-line options you want WebLogic to pass to the RMI compiler (rmic) when compiling EJBs and RMI servers.

Health Monitoring

The Health Monitoring configuration is shown in Figure 23-23. This is new in WebLogic Server 7.0 and allows configuration of settings to detect failed managed servers and automatically restart them.

Figure 23-23: Health Monitoring configuration page for a server

The entries on this page are as follows:

✦ **Auto Restart:** Checking this will ensure that the Node Manager will automatically restart the managed server if it crashes. See the next section for information on the Node Manager. It is also discussed in the "Machines" section in this chapter.

✦ **Auto Kill If Failed:** If checked, the Node Manager will kill a server process that it has determined has failed based on the other properties set here.

✦ **Restart Interval:** The interval over which a server can be restarted, measured in seconds. The default is 3600.

✦ **Max Restarts within Interval:** The maximum number of times a server can be restarted within the Restart Interval (see the previous bullet).

✦ **Health Check Interval:** The number of seconds between each check of the server's health by its self-monitoring code and the Node Manager's monitoring.

✦ **Health Check Timeout:** The number of seconds the Node Manager waits to see if its health check fails.

✦ **Restart Delay Seconds:** The number of seconds the Node Manager waits before restarting a server it has determined has failed.

Remote Start

Figure 23-24 shows the Remote Start configuration page for a server. This page is used to configure a managed server so Node Manager can remotely start it.

Figure 23-24: Remote Start configuration page for a server

The entries on this page are as follows:

✦ **Java Home:** The full pathname (on the managed server's machine) to the Java home directory. The Java runtime executable located in the `bin` subdirectory will be used to start the managed server.

✦ **BEA Home:** The full pathname (on the managed server's machine) to the BEA Home directory. For example:

```
D:\bea\weblogic700\server
```

✦ **Root Directory:** The full pathname to the managed server's domain directory. For example:

```
D:\WebLogicUserDomains\mydomain
```

✦ **Class Path:** A valid classpath for use by this server instance. If none is provided, the machine's classpath will be used.

✦ **Arguments:** Command-line arguments you want Node Manager to pass to the `weblogic.Server` executable.

✦ **Security Policy File:** The full pathname to the security policy file you want Node Manager to pass to the `weblogic.Server` executable.

✦ **Username:** The username used to start the managed server. Because WebLogic 7.0 now allows the creation of administrator usernames other than `system`, this is required.

✦ **Password:** The password associated with the administration username above. Clicking this link will bring you to a pane in which you enter the password and re-enter it for confirmation.

Connections

The Connections tab is new in WebLogic Server 7.0, and brings together options that used to be widely dispersed.

SSL

Figure 23-25 shows the SSL configuration page for a server.

Figure 23-25: SSL configuration page for a server

The entries on this page are as follows:

✦ **Configure Key Store Providers:** Clicking this link is the same as going to the Security ➪ Realms ➪ <realm name> ➪ Providers ➪ Keystores node in the domain tree.

 See Chapter 25 on Security for more information.

✦ **Server Private Key Alias:** The string used to retrieve the server's private key in the keystore.

✦ **Server Private Key Passphrase:** Click here to set the password associated with the private key.

✦ **Server Certificate File Name:** The pathname to the file containing the server's private key file. The default is `<user domains>/<domain-name>/server-cert.der`.

✦ **Client Certificate Enforced:** When checked, WebLogic Server enforces mutual authentication with clients. The default is unchecked.

✦ **Client Certificate Requested But Not Enforced:** If this is checked, two-way SSL is enabled. It is off by default.

✦ **Export Key Lifespan:** Sets the number of times WebLogic Server uses an exportable (40-bit) key when communicating with a client using export-strength encryption before generating a new key. The smaller the number, the more secure the communication. The premise is that 40-bit keys can be hacked within relatively short timeframes. The default is 500.

✦ **Hostname Verification Ignored:** The installed implementation of the `weblogic.security.SSL.HostnameVerifier` class is disabled when WebLogic Server acts as a client to another application server.

✦ **Hostname Verifier:** The name of the class that implements the `weblogic.security.SSL.HostnameVerifier` class. This class verifies that the host name in the URL received from an SSL client matches the common name in the server certificate's distinguished name. This class prevents man-in-the-middle attacks. The `weblogic.security.SSL.HostnameVerifier` has a `verify()` method that WebLogic Server calls on the client during the SSL handshake.

✦ **Server Key File Name:** The pathname of the file containing the server's security key. The default is `server-key.der`.

✦ **Trusted CA File Name:** The pathname to the file containing the digital certificate provided by a certificate authority that is trusted by WebLogic Server. The default is `trusted-ca.pem`.

✦ **Cert Authenticator:** The name of the Java class that implements the `CertAuthenticator` interface. The default is `null`.

✦ **Server Certificate Chain File Name:** The pathname to the file containing the server's digital certificate. The default is `server-certchain.pem`.

✦ **Use Encrypted Keys:** When true, indicates that WebLogic Server's private key is encrypted with a password.

✦ **Use Java:** When true, enables the use of WebLogic's Java libraries for SSL operations. Uncheck this if you prefer to use faster native SSL libraries on the Solaris, Windows NT, and IBM AIX platforms.

✦ **Certificate Cache Size:** The number of digital certificates that are tokenized and stored by WebLogic Server. The default is 3.

SSL Ports

Figure 23-26 shows the SSL Ports configuration page for a server. This is used in combination with the SSL configuration page to define the Secure Sockets Layer for HTTP and administration.

Figure 23-26: SSL Ports configuration page for a server

The entries on this page are as follows:

✦ **Enable SSL Listen Port (Please configure SSL):** If checked, SSL is enabled (and must be configured) for this server. The default is unchecked.

✦ **Listen Port:** The network port on which to handle SSL requests. This port must be different from the server's HTTP port, as well as all other ports in use on the server's network interface. The default is 7002.

✦ **Enable Domain Wide Administration Port:** If true, the domain-wide admin port has been configured. See the "Domain ⇨ Configuration ⇨ General" section later in this chapter for more information.

✦ **Domain Wide Administration Port:** The TCP/IP port used for domain-wide administration (see the preceding bullet).

✦ **Local Administration Port Override (0: no override):** The domain-wide administration port can be overridden on a server-by-server basis. If you enable the domain-wide administration port, but desire a different port on this particular machine, set this option to the port's value (other than 0). The default is 0 (no override).

✦ **Channel Overrides:** Click this link to override any network channels that have been defined for this server (or the cluster this server is a part of). See Chapter 24 for more information on network channels and overrides.

HTTP

Figure 23-27 shows the HTTP configuration page for a server. In WebLogic Server 6.1, this page was under the Configuration tab.

Figure 23-27: HTTP configuration page for a server

The entries on this page are as follows:

✦ **Default Web Application:** The name of the Web application that serves as the default application for the server. It must conform to the Servlet 2.3 specification. This application must already be deployed to the server. Its home page will be displayed when the user accesses the server with the default URL (`http://localhost:<weblogic-port>`). `DefaultWebApp`, an application provided by BEA, displays the Web Server Index Page shown in Figure 23-28.

✦ **Frontend Host:** The name entered in this field, if any, will be returned as the host name in the HTTP response header.

✦ **Frontend HTTP Port:** The frontendHTTPPort.

✦ **Frontend HTTPS Port:** The frontendHTTPSPort.

✦ **Send Server Header Enabled:** When checked, WebLogic Server returns server information in the HTTP response header. The default is checked.

✦ **Post Timeout Secs:** Sets the amount of time, in seconds, that WebLogic waits between receiving HTTP POST requests. BEA added this feature to help administrators prevent denial-of-service (DOS) attacks that are caused by flooding the server with POST requests. The default value is zero, which makes the server vulnerable to attack. Increasing positive values makes the server less vulnerable, but slower under heavy loads.

Figure 23-28: Home page for DefaultWebApp

✦ **Max Post Time:** Sets the amount of time, in seconds, that WebLogic waits for individual HTTP POST requests to complete. The default value is zero, which means that WebLogic will wait indefinitely.

✦ **Max Post Size:** This is the maximum size, in bytes, of an HTTP POST request that will be accepted by WebLogic Server. POSTs larger than this size are truncated. A value of –1 (the default) indicates that the server accepts POSTs of any size.

✦ **Enable Keepalives:** Check this option if you want the HTTP responses generated by WebLogic to contain HTTP 1.0-compliant Keep-Alive headers. This option is not required for HTTP 1.1 (which *always* uses Keep-Alives), but you may want to keep it checked for backward compatibility.

✦ **Duration:** The number of seconds WebLogic's HTTP listener waits before closing an inactive HTTP connection.

✦ **HTTPS Duration:** The number of seconds WebLogic's HTTPS listener waits before closing an inactive HTTPS connection.

✦ **Accept Context Path In Get Real Path:** This is a temporary fix for the transition from WebLogic Server 6.1 to 7.0 and will be deprecated in the future. It's needed because version 7.0 doesn't allow the inclusion of the context path in the virtual path (having a subdirectory of the same name will cause confusion). It's here for backward-compatibility for those applications that may have been developed with the old behavior in mind. If you need to use this, make sure you change your code to get rid of this dependency as soon as is practical.

jCOM

Figure 23-29 shows the jCOM configuration page for a server. jCOM is new in WebLogic Server 7.0, but it is beyond the scope of this book. It allows COM clients to talk to WebLogic Server EJBs as if they were COM objects, and vice versa.

Figure 23-29: jCOM configuration page for a server

The entries on this page are as follows:

✦ **Enable COM:** If this is checked, COM is enabled on the plaintext (non-SSL) port configured for this server.

✦ **COM Max Message Size:** The maximum message size, in bytes, for an incoming COM message. This prevents the server from trying to allocate too much memory for DOS attacks. The max message size is reconfigurable on non-default ports on the channel overrides link (see the last bullet in this list).

✦ **COM Message Timeout:** The maximum number of seconds to wait for receiving an entire COM message. This, too, is reconfigurable for non-default ports on the channel overrides link (see the last bullet in this list).

✦ **NTAuth Host:** The address of the Windows PDC (primary domain controller) for authenticating COM clients. No authentication is performed if this value is null.

✦ **Native Mode Enabled:** If checked, WebLogic Server will use Windows native DLLs to interact with COM objects. This works only on WebLogic Servers running on the Windows platform.

✦ **Memory Logging Enabled:** All memory usage will be logged if this is checked.

✦ **Prefetch Enums:** When checked, jCOM will prefetch the next COM VariantEnumeration in between calls to `getNextElement( )`.

✦ **Apartment Threaded:** Controls the flag that is used to initialize COM in native mode. By default, jCOM initializes COM using the COINIT_MULTITHREADED_FLAG. If the server logs a Class Not Registered Message when using native mode, try setting this property (COINIT_APARTMENTTHREADED).

✦ **Channel Overrides:** Click this link to override any network channels that have been defined for this server (or cluster this server is a part of). See Chapter 24 for more information on network channels and overrides.

Tuning

Figure 23-30 shows the Tuning configuration page for a server.

Figure 23-30: Tuning configuration page for a server

The entries on this page are as follows:

✦ **Accept Backlog:** The number of connections WebLogic Server allows to "stack up" when the server is too busy to accept them. The default is 50. Backlogged connections become active when existing active connections drop.

✦ **Login Timeout:** The number of milliseconds WebLogic waits before timing out a login attempt on the plaintext port. The default is 5000 (five seconds).

✦ **SSL Login Timeout:** The number of milliseconds WebLogic waits before timing out a login attempt on an SSL port. The default is 25000 (25 seconds).

✦ **Reverse DNS Allowed:** When checked, indicates that reverse DNS lookups are allowed on this server. The default is unchecked.

✦ **Maximum Open Sockets:** The maximum number of sockets the server will open. No new sockets will be opened while this threshold is reached.

✦ **Channel Overrides:** Click this link to override any network channels that have been defined for this server (or cluster this server is a part of).

Cross-Reference   See Chapter 24 for more information on network channels and overrides.

Protocols

Figure 23-31 shows the Protocols configuration page for a server.

Figure 23-31: Protocols configuration page for a server

The entries on this page are as follows:

✦ **Default Protocol:** Select the protocol you want WebLogic Server to use for its internal communications. The choices are t3, t3s, HTTP, HTTPS, and IIOP. The default is t3, a BEA-proprietary protocol optimized for WebLogic Server.

✦ **Default Secure Protocol:** Select the secure protocol you want WebLogic Server to use for its internal secure communications. The choices are t3s and HTTPS. The default is t3s, a BEA-proprietary protocol optimized for WebLogic Server.

✦ **T3 Max Message Size:** If the t3 protocol is used, this is the maximum message size WebLogic will use for communicating. The default is 10,000,000 bytes.

✦ **T3 Message Timeout:** The number of seconds WebLogic waits before giving up on an unacknowledged t3 message. The default is 60.

✦ **HTTP Max Message Size:** Same as T3 Max Message Size, but for HTTP.

✦ **HTTP Message Timeout:** Same as T3 Message Timeout, but for HTTP.

✦ **Enable Tunneling:** When checked, all client interactions with WebLogic Server will be tunneled through the HTTP and HTTPS ports on which WebLogic is listening. This feature is useful if you are trying to support RMI clients through a firewall. The default is unchecked.

✦ **Tunneling Client Ping:** When a client is tunneling to WebLogic, the server pings the client every few seconds to make sure they are still connected. This is where you set the number of seconds between pings. The default is 45.

✦ **Tunneling Client Timeout:** The number of seconds WebLogic waits for a client ping to return before disconnecting the client. The default is 40.

✦ **Enable IIOP:** What does this mean? When checked, IIOP is enabled for this WebLogic Server instance. The default is checked.

✦ **IIOP Max Message Size:** Same as T3 Max Message Size, but for IIOP.

✦ **IIOP Message Timeout:** Same as the T3 Message Timeout, but for IIOP.

✦ **Default IIOP Password:** Sets the IIOP password for this server, if any. The default is `null`.

✦ **Default IIOP User:** Sets the default IIOP user for this server, if any. The default is `guest`.

✦ **Enable COM:** If checked, COM is enabled on the plaintext (non-SSL) port.

✦ **COM Max Message Size:** Same as T3 Max Message Size, but for IIOP.

✦ **COM Message Timeout:** Same as T3 Message Timeout, but for IIOP.

Summary

Figure 23-32 shows the Summary configuration page for a server.

This page shows a summary of all the configuration options entered for this server. This is a good way to get a bird's-eye-view of the way it's configured and to compare it to other servers.

Monitoring

The Monitoring tab gives you access to several subtabs that allow you to look into the current activities of your servers.

General

Figure 23-33 shows the General monitoring page for a server.

The entries on this page are as follows:

✦ **State:** The server's current state: either STANDBY, RUNNING, or null (shut down).

✦ **Activation Time:** The date and time the server was started.

Figure 23-32: Summary configuration page for a server

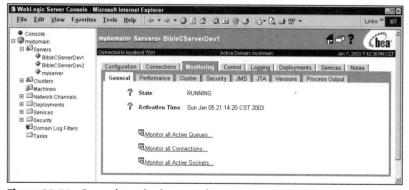

Figure 23-33: General monitoring page for a server

There are additional links to monitor the server's active execution queues, monitor connections to the server, and monitor active network sockets. For more information on these options, see the WebLogic documentation.

Performance

Figure 23-34 shows the Performance monitoring page for a server.

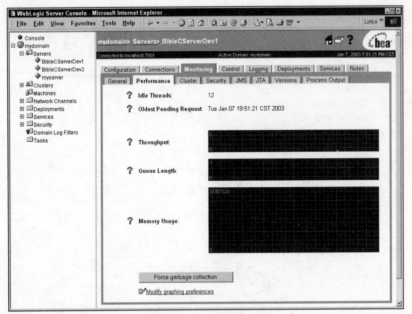

Figure 23-34: Performance monitoring page for a server

The entries on this page are as follows:

- ✦ **Idle Threads:** The number of execution threads that are idle and available for immediate use.

- ✦ **Oldest Pending Request:** The start time of the oldest pending request that has not been processed by the server.

- ✦ **Throughput:** The amount of data passing through the server, expressed in kilobytes per second.

- ✦ **Queue Length:** The number of pending requests waiting for execution threads to become available. For optimal performance, you want this number to be as close to zero as possible.

- ✦ **Memory Usage:** The number of megabytes of RAM currently being used by WebLogic Server.

In addition, there is a button to instantly force garbage collection within the server's JVM, and a link to modify the graphing preferences. You can find more information on these features in the WebLogic documentation.

Cluster

Figure 23-35 shows the Cluster monitoring page for a server. This tab shows up only for servers within a cluster because it describes the state of the cluster that the server is in. The administration server does not have this tab.

Figure 23-35: Cluster monitoring page for a server

The entries on this page are as follows:

✦ **Servers:** The number of *active* servers in this cluster. Note that it's not the total number of *configured* servers in the cluster.

✦ **Resend Requests:** The number of state-delta messages that had to be resent because a receiving server in the cluster missed a message.

✦ **Fragments Sent:** The number of multicast fragments sent from this server into the cluster.

✦ **Fragments Received:** The number of multicast fragments received on this server from the cluster.

✦ **Lost Multicast Messages:** The number of incoming multicast messages that were lost according to this server.

✦ **Known Servers:** The name of each *active* server in this cluster.

✦ **Primaries:** The number of objects that the local server hosts as primaries.

✦ **Secondary Distributions:** The names of the remote servers of which the local server is hosting secondary objects. A number is appended to each name, indicating the number of secondaries hosted on behalf of that server.

Security

Figure 23-36 shows the Security monitoring page for a server.

The entries on this page are as follows:

✦ **Total Users Locked Out:** The number of users locked out at this because of too many failed login attempts.

✦ **Invalid Logins Total:** The total number of failed logins logged by the server.

✦ **Total Login Attempts while Locked:** The number of times users who were locked out attempted to log in while still locked out.

✦ **Total Users Unlocked:** The number of users who have been unlocked by the administrator or who became unlocked because their lockout interval expired.

✦ **Invalid Logins High:** The highest number of users with failed logins at any one time.

✦ **Locked Users:** The number of users locked out at this moment because of too many failed login attempts.

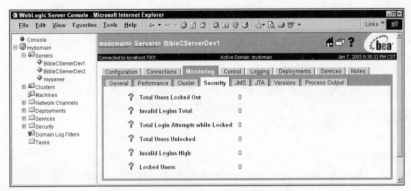

Figure 23-36: Security monitoring page for a server

JMS

Figure 23-37 shows the JMS monitoring page for a server.

Figure 23-37: JMS monitoring page for a server

The entries on this page are as follows:

✦ **Connections:** The number of JMS connections currently in use.

✦ **Connections High:** The peak number of JMS connections since the last server restart.

✦ **Connections Total:** The total number of JMS connections that have been made to the server since the last server restart.

✦ **Servers:** The number of JMS servers that are currently active.

✦ **Servers High:** The peak number of active JMS servers since the last server restart.

✦ **Servers Total:** The total number of JMS servers that have been created since the last server restart.

Additionally, the page contains links to monitor all active JMS connections and servers. See the WebLogic documentation for more information about these links.

Cross-Reference   For more information about JMS, see Chapter 9.

JTA

Figure 23-38 shows the JTS monitoring page for a server.

Figure 23-38: JTA monitoring page for a server

The entries on this page are as follows:

✦ **Total Transactions:** The total number of transactions that have been initiated since the last server restart. This includes container-managed transactions as well as transactions initiated in code.

✦ **Total Committed:** The total number of transactions that have been committed since the last server restart.

✦ **Total Rolled Back:** The total number of transactions that have been rolled back since the last server restart.

✦ **Timeout Rollbacks:** The total number of transactions that have been rolled back due to timeouts since the last server restart.

✦ **Resource Rollbacks:** The total number of transactions that have been rolled back by participating resources since the last server restart.

✦ **Application Rollbacks:** The total number of transactions that have been rolled back by application code since the last server restart.

✦ **System Rollbacks:** The total number of transactions that have been rolled back by WebLogic's transaction manager since the last server restart.

✦ **Total Heuristics:** The total number of heuristic completions that have been reported by the transaction manager in response to transactions that were manually completed outside the transaction manager. This usually occurs when there is a problem with a transaction, and a system administrator intervenes to end the transaction.

✦ **Transaction Abandoned Total Count:** The total number of transactions that were abandoned before being committed since the last server restart.

✦ **Average Commit Time:** The average time, in milliseconds, that a transaction took to commit.

Additionally, the page contains links to monitor transactions based on various criteria. See the WebLogic documentation for more information about these links.

Cross-Reference   For more information about JTA, see Chapter 6.

Versions

Figure 23-39 shows the Versions monitoring page for a server. It simply displays version information for WebLogic Server, the JDK that WebLogic Server is using, and the host operating system.

Process Output

Figure 23-40 shows the Process Output monitoring page. Click any of the links to see the associated output.

Control

This tab, which is new in WebLogic Server 7.0, incorporates subtabs that control server startup and shutdown, as well as migrating pinned services. *Pinned services* are those that are not distributed across a cluster, but instead run on only one server at a time. For more information on migrating pinned services, see the WebLogic Server documentation at the following URL:

```
http://e-docs.bea.com/wls/docs70/cluster/failover.html#1027954
```

Start/Stop

Figure 23-41 shows the Start/Stop control page for a server. The links become active when a particular action can be taken. The first three options are only for servers that are controlled by the node manager. Shutdown sends an administrative command to the server to shut down, whereas Force Shutdown will kill the OS process running the server.

Figure 23-39: Versions monitoring page for a server

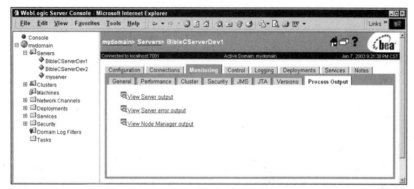

Figure 23-40: Process Output monitoring page for a server

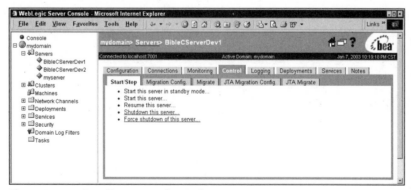

Figure 23-41: Start/Stop control page for a server.

Migration Config.

Figure 23-42 shows the Migration Config. control page for a server in a cluster. Non-clustered servers are not configurable here.

This page allows you to define which servers in a cluster can have a JMS server migrated to them in the case of server failure or for routine maintenance purposes.

Figure 23-42: Migration Config. Control page for a clustered server node

The Available list has a list of all servers in this cluster. If you want to restrict the servers that can host a migrated JMS server service, click its name and then click the right arrow to move it to the Chosen list and click the Apply button.

Migrate

Figure 23-43 shows the Migrate control page for a server in a cluster. Non-clustered servers are not configurable here.

This page allows you to go ahead with a migration to an available configured server.

Figure 23-43: Migration control page for a clustered server node.

JTA Migration Config.

This is the same as Migration Config., except that it is for JTA transaction-recovery service instead of JMS.

JTA Migrate

This is the same as Migrate, except that it is for the JTA transaction-recovery service instead of JMS.

Logging

WebLogic Server provides separate logging for many of its services, including the Application Server itself, the server's domain, HTTP, JDBC, and JTA. In addition, the server can log debugging messages for remote exceptions and stack traces.

General

Figure 23-44 shows the General logging page for a server, which is where logging options for the Application Server are set.

Figure 23-44: General logging page for a server

The entries on this page are as follows:

✦ **File Name:** The pathname to the log file for the Application Server. The default is `<server_name>/<server_name>.log`.

✦ **Log to Stdout:** If checked (the default), log messages are written to standard output — the WebLogic Server command window.

✦ **Debug to Stdout:** If checked, debug messages are written to standard output. The default is unchecked.

✦ **Stdout severity threshold:** Determines the severity of messages that are logged to standard output. Messages of the chosen severity and higher are written logged to standard output. The severity levels, from highest to lowest, are `Emergency`, `Alert`, `Critical`, `Notice`, `Error`, `Warning`, and `Info`. The default setting is `Error`.

Rotation

Figure 23-45 shows the Rotation logging page for a server. This page allows you to configure the rotation scheme for the Application Server's log file.

Figure 23-45: The Rotation logging page for a server

The entries on this page are as follows:

✦ **Rotation Type:** Determines the way log files are created over time. The default is none, which means all messages are written to the same log in perpetuity. The other options are by Size, which means that a new log file is created after the current log file reaches a given size, and by Time, which means that a new log file is created every time a certain number of hours passes.

✦ **File Min Size:** If Rotation Type is set to by Size, this is the file size (in kilobytes) that must be exceeded by the current log file in order for the next log file to be created. The default is 500k.

✦ **Rotation Time:** If Rotation Type is set to by Time, then this sets the rotation start time. See the description of this field in the "Domain ➪ Configuration ➪ Logging" section earlier in this chapter.

✦ **File Time Span:** If Rotation Type is set to by Time, this is the number of hours that will elapse between the creation of each additional log file. The default is 24 hours.

✦ **Number of Files Limited:** If this is checked, the total number of log files created is limited to the number given by File Count; otherwise, there is no limit. After the limit is reached, logging to files stops. Default is unchecked.

✦ **File Count:** If Number of Files Limited is checked, this gives the total number of files that will be created before logging to files stops. The default is 7.

Domain

Figure 23-46 shows the Rotation logging page for a server. This page allows you to configure the rotation scheme for the Application Server's log file.

Figure 23-46: Domain logging page for a server

The entries on this page are as follows:

✦ **Log to Domain Logfile:** If checked, log messages for the domain are written to a log file.

✦ **Domain Log Filter:** Domain log filters that you have previously defined, if any, appear in this list. Select one to use for the domain. The default is none. The configuration of Domain Log Filters is covered later in this chapter.

HTTP

Figure 23-47 shows the HTTP logging page for a server. This page allows you to configure the logging and rotation scheme for WebLogic's HTTP server log.

Figure 23-47: HTTP logging page for a server

The entries on this page are as follows:

✦ **Enable Logging:** If checked (the default), logging is enabled for the HTTP server.

✦ **Logfile Name:** The pathname of the file to which HTTP log messages are written. The default is `<server_name>/access.log`.

✦ **Format:** The HTTP log format. The choices are `common` (the default) and `extended`, which provides additional information.

✦ **Log Buffer Size:** This is the size, in kilobytes, of the in-memory buffer used for HTTP logging. When the buffer reaches this size, its contents are flushed to the log file on disk. This option is provided for increased performance. Generally speaking, the larger the buffer, the better the performance because expensive writes to disk will be minimized. But you stand to lose more information with large buffer sizes if the server crashes before the buffer is flushed to disk. The default size is 8k.

✦ **Max Log File SizeK Bytes:** This is the maximum size, in kilobytes, to which the log file can grow. After this size is reached, the contents of the log are overwritten.

✦ **Rotation Type, Period, and Time:** This is WebLogic's standard log file rotation scheme, as described in the "Domain ⇨ Configuration ⇨ Logging" section earlier in this chapter.

✦ **Flush Every:** At this interval, given as a number of seconds, the log file will be flushed to disk regardless of how full the log buffer is. The default is 60.

JDBC

Figure 23-48 shows the JDBC logging page for a server.

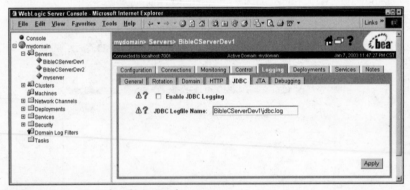

Figure 23-48: JDBC logging page for a server

The entries on this page are as follows:

✦ **Enable JDBC Logging:** If checked, logging is enabled for JDBC. The default is unchecked.

✦ **JDBC Logfile Name:** The pathname of the file to which JDBC log messages are written. The default is `<server_name>/jdbc.log`.

JTA

Figure 23-49 shows the JTA logging page for a server.

Figure 23-49: JTA logging page for a server

This page contains two entries:

+ **Transaction Log File Prefix:** The pathname to the folder that contains the JTA logs. It should *not* include the filename. The default is `./`.

+ **Transaction Log File Write Policy:** Defines the policy for writing the transaction log file, as described in Chapter 6 earlier in the book. Read the warnings carefully before changing this option. The options are `Cache-Flush` and `Direct-Write`.

Debugging

Figure 23-50 shows the Debugging logging page for a server.

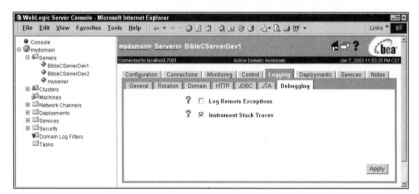

Figure 23-50: Debugging logging page for a server

The entries on this page are as follows:

+ **Log Remote Exceptions:** If checked, remote exceptions are logged to the debugging log. The default is unchecked.

+ **Instrument Stack Traces:** If checked, stack traces are logged to the debugging log. The default is unchecked.

Deployments

The Deployments section contains pages for EJB, Web Applications, Java Connector Architecture (JCA), and Startup and Shutdown classes. These configuration options are covered in Chapters 15, 16, and 17 (EJBs), 11 (Web Applications), 26 (Web Services), 28 (JCA), and 8 (Startup and Shutdown classes).

Services

The Services tab for a server allows you to configure attributes related to JDBC, JMS, XML, WebLogic Enterprise Connectivity (WLEC), WebLogic Jolt, WebLogic File T3, virtual hosts, and mail.

JDBC

The JDBC page allows you to activate and deactivate JDBC connection pools. This functionality is fully described in Chapter 5.

JMS

Figure 23-51 shows the JMS services page for a server.

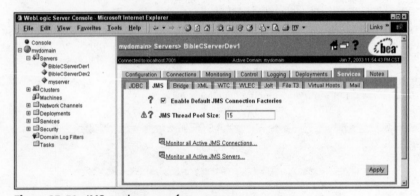

Figure 23-51: JMS services page for a server

The entries on this page are as follows:

✦ **Enable Default JMS Connection Factories:** If checked (the default), WebLogic Server creates a default JMS connection factory at startup for use by applications. This factory is accessible through the `weblogic.jms.connectionfactory` interface. Otherwise, you must create your own connection factories with the Console.

✦ **JMS Thread Pool Size:** The number of free threads WebLogic Server allocates for JMS requests at startup. The default is 15.

Cross-Reference

For more information about JMS, see Chapter 9.

Bridge

The Bridge page allows you to configure a single property for the messaging bridge — the number of threads in the message pool. The default is 5, as shown in Figure 23-52.

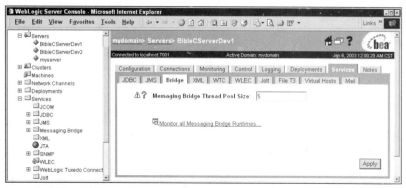

Figure 23-52: Bridge services page for a server

Bridges are set up in the Services node of the node tree on the left. Bridges, which control the way WebLogic and third-party tools communicate messages, are beyond the scope of this book.

XML

The XML page allows you to configure the XML registry and cache for your server. This functionality is covered later in this chapter in the Services ⇨ XML section.

WTC

The WTC page allows you to activate and deactivate WebLogic Tuxedo Connectors.

WLEC

The WLEC page allows you to activate and deactivate WebLogic Enterprise Connectivity (WLEC) connection pools. These pools are used to connect to CORBA objects running within BEA Tuxedo. WLEC configuration is discussed in the Services ⇨ WLEC section later in this chapter.

Jolt

The Jolt page allows you to activate and deactivate Jolt connection pools. These pools are used to connect to BEA Tuxedo, which is a dedicated transaction server. Jolt configuration is discussed in the Services ⇨ Jolt section later in this chapter.

File T3

The File T3 page allows you to activate and deactivate File T3 connections. This functionality is described in the Services ⇨ File T3 section later in this chapter.

Virtual Hosts

The Virtual Hosts page allows you to activate and deactivate virtual hosts. This functionality is described in the Services ⇨ Virtual Hosts section later in this chapter.

Mail

The Mail page allows you to activate and deactivate JavaMail sessions.

Cross-Reference This functionality is fully described in Chapter 10.

Clusters

This node allows you to create and configure clusters of WebLogic Servers.

Cross-Reference   See Chapter 24 for information on how to create and configure WebLogic clusters.

Machines

This panel is used to create entries for the physical machines that will participate in a cluster. WebLogic Servers, configured by using the Server node, are assigned to these machines. WebLogic uses this information to determine whether or not server instances reside on the same machine. If you don't map servers to machines, WebLogic assumes that each server runs on separate physical hardware. This may negatively impact the way WebLogic selects servers to host secondary HTTP session replicas, so you should always define machines for your clusters and map your WebLogic Server instances to the appropriate machines.

Note   The machines you define should map precisely to the physical machines in your installation. If two WebLogic Server instances are running on the same physical machine, map them to the same machine in the Console as well.

Creating a machine

Figure 23-53 shows the Console page for creating a machine.

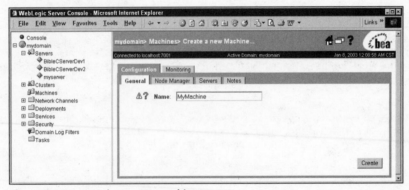

Figure 23-53: Creating a new machine

When you create a machine in the Console, you give it a logical name. You can give any name you want; the name doesn't have to match the machine's physical or DNS name. But the name must be unique among the machines present in your domain.

Configuring Node Manager for a machine

After creating the machine, you can move to the Node Manager tab to configure Node Manager settings. Node Manager is a Java program, introduced in WebLogic 6.1, which allows you to start and kill WebLogic-managed servers remotely from the Console. You use Node Manager when a server has hung or has become unresponsive. Figure 23-54 shows the Node Manager configuration page.

Figure 23-54: Node Manager configuration page for a machine

The only entry on this page is as follows:

✦ **Listen Address and Port:** The IP address and port on which Node Manager listens for commands to start or kill a server.

Assigning servers to a machine

After creating a machine and configuring Node Manager for it, use the Servers tab to assign existing WebLogic Server instances to the machine.

Deployments

The configuration steps for all types of deployments are covered elsewhere in this book. See the relevant chapters for more information.

Cross-Reference Deployments are covered in the following chapters: 15, 16, and 17 (EJBs), 11 (Web Applications), 26 (Web Services), 28 (JCA), and 8 (Startup and Shutdown classes)

Services

The configuration steps for JDBC, JMS, JTA, and Mail have been covered elsewhere in this chapter or in this book, and will not be covered here. This section focuses on the remaining services — JCOM, Messaging Bridge, XML, SNMP, WLEC, WebLogic Tuxedo Connector, Jolt, Virtual Hosts, and File T3 — that have not yet been discussed in this book. Administration nodes for these services can be found by expanding the Services node in WebLogic Console's domain tree.

XML

The XML section is where you configure XML registries, parsers, transformers, and so on for servers in your WebLogic domain.

Creating a new XML registry

By default, WebLogic uses Apache's implementations of DocumentBuilderFactory, SAXParserFactory, and TransformerFactory to parse and transform XML documents. But you can create your own XML registries that substitute alternative implementations of

DocumentBuilderFactory, SAXParserFactory and TransformerFactory. You can create any number of registries, but only one can be active per WebLogic Server. Figure 23-55 shows the configuration page for defining a new XML registry.

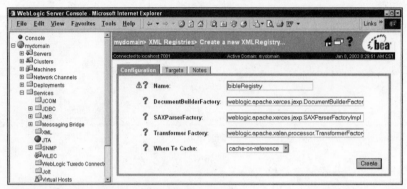

Figure 23-55: Configuring a new XML registry

To create a new XML registry, follow these steps:

1. Start WebLogic Server and WebLogic Console.

2. Expand the Services node in the domain tree and click the XML node.

3. Click the Configure a New XML Registry link on the right side of the Console. The screen shown in Figure 23-55 appears.

4. Give the new registry a unique name.

5. Enter a value for DocumentBuilderFactory if this XML registry will be used to produce `org.w3c.Document` objects, or leave the default in place (which is `weblogic.apache.xerces.jaxp.DocumentBuilderFactoryImpl`). You can also leave the field blank, which instructs WebLogic to use the default.

6. Enter a value for SAXParserFactory if this XML registry will be used to parse XML documents on an event-driven basis. The default is `weblogic.apache.xerces.jaxp.SAXParserFactoryImpl`, or you can leave the field blank to use the default.

7. Enter a value for TransformerFactory if this XML registry will be used to apply XSL stylesheets to XML documents. The default is `weblogic.apache.xalan.processor.TransformerFactoryImpl`, or you can leave the field blank to use the default.

8. Choose whether to have your XML components cache-on-reference (the first time WebLogic parses an XML document defined by these rules) or cache-on-initialization (WebLogic Server caches this on startup).

9. Click Create.

10. Click the Targets tab and move the desired server into the Chosen column. Don't forget to click Apply.

11. Expand the Servers node in the domain tree and click the server that will host the new XML registry.

12. Click the Services tab and then click the XML subtab. Figure 23-56 shows the resulting configuration page.

13. Use the drop-down list to select the XML registry to be associated with this server and then enter values for Cache Memory Size, Cache Disk Size, and Cache Timeout Interval. These values are defined in kilobytes, megabytes, and seconds, respectively.

14. Click Apply.

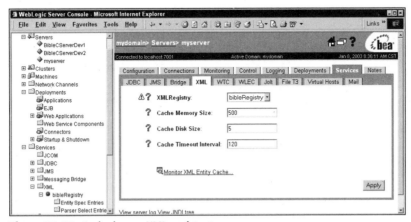

Figure 23-56: Assigning an XML registry to a server

Configuring an alternative parser for use with specific document types

Sometimes, it's desirable to have certain XML documents processed by a particular parser. To have WebLogic use an alternative parser automatically with certain XML documents, do the following:

1. Follow the preceding steps to create a new XML registry and associate it with a WebLogic Server.

2. Under the XML node in the domain tree, expand the node of the XML registry with which this parser is to be associated. Click the XML Parser Select Entries node and then click the Configure a New XML Parser Select Registry Entry link on the right side of the Console. Figure 23-57 shows the configuration page that appears.

3. Use either Public Id or System Id to specify the document type that will use the parser. Alternatively, a Root Element Tag can be specified for the parser. Only one of the three fields needs to have data.

4. Enter the class name for the parser that is to be used with the specified document type. Enter data either for DocumentBuilderFactory or SAXParserFactory, but not both. Parser Class Name is for backward-compatibility with older versions of WebLogic. In this example, only when a document uses the Bible DTD will the WebLogic fast parser be used.

5. Click the Create button.

Figure 23-57: Configuring a different SAX parser to use with the Bible DTD

Configuring an external entity

External entities are XML entities that live outside of the XML document that references them. DTDs are an example, as are namespaces or other XML documents. Usually, these documents are accessed remotely via the Internet. But WebLogic Server enables the user to specify different locations for these entities. For example, you can install the most frequently used ones locally and reference them via this mechanism. Users can also configure and monitor the caching of these entities.

To configure a new external entity resolution, follow these steps:

1. Follow the steps in the section Services ➪ XML ➪ Creating a new XML registry to create an XML registry and associate it with a WebLogic Server.

2. Expand the new XML registry in the domain tree and then click Entity Spec Entries. Click the Configure a New XML Entity Spec Registry Entry link on the right side of the Console. Figure 23-58 shows the resulting configuration page.

3. Enter the Public Id or System Id that will cause the external entity to be referenced. In the example, this is a reference to `bible.dtd` on my `mirandacorp.com` web site.

4. Enter the EntityURI. This is the path to the file containing the external entity. If the entity resides on the administration WebLogic Server, the entry should be relative to the registries entity directory. This directory is `<domain-name>/xml/registries/<XML Registry name>`. In this example, we specify `dtds/bible.dtd`, which means the file must be physically located at `H:\WebLogicUserDomains\mydomain\xml\registries\bibleRegistry\dtds\bible.dtd` for our mydomain domain.

5. If the entity is accessed over the Internet, a fully qualified URL is required. The entity can also be accessed from databases by using a JDBC connection. The entity can only be accessed by URIs that start with these qualifiers: `http://`, `ftp://`, `file://`, and `jdbc:`.

6. Select one of the caching settings. We chose `defer-to-registry-setting`, which uses the setting we just configured for `bibleRegistry`. The other cache settings were described in the setup for `bibleRegistry`.

7. Click Create.

Figure 23-58: Creating a new external entity resolution

SNMP

Before creating a SNMP trap, you need to enable the SNMP service in WebLogic Server. To do so, follow these steps:

1. Load the WebLogic MIB (filename: `BEA-WEBLOGIC-MIB.asn1`) into the SNMP management system. Consult your SNMP vendor documentation for directions on how to do this.

2. In the domain tree, expand the SNMP node and click the Trap Destination node.

3. The right side of the Console shows all SNMP Trap Destinations that exist for this WebLogic Server. Click the Configure a New SNMP Trap Destination link. Figure 23-59 shows the resulting configuration page and its default values.

Figure 23-59: Configuring a new SNMP trap destination

4. Define the destination where trap notification will be sent.

   - *Name*, which is a unique identifier for this SNMP trap, should describe what the trap is doing.

   - *Community* is the name of the group of managed machines to which this trap should be mapped by the SNMP management software.

- *Host* is either the host name or IP address of the SNMP management station.

- *Port* is the port number on which the SNMP management station listens. The default is 162.

5. Click Create.

6. In the domain tree, click the SNMP node. This takes you to the SNMP configuration tab for the domain, shown in Figure 23-60 (this screen was also shown in Figure 23-6, along with complete definitions of its entry fields).

Figure 23-60: Configuring an SNMP trap for the domain

7. Enter values for the following fields:

- Check the Enabled box. The SNMP agent will not be activated until this box is checked.

- Set SNMP Port to the port number the SNMP agent listens on.

- The Mib Data Refresh Interval is the interval that the SNMP Service updates its cache of WebLogic Server attribute values. The default value is 120 seconds, and the minimum value is 30 seconds. The closer the value is to 30 seconds, the worse the performance will be because the Console does a GET for each WebLogic attribute in the MIB.

- The Status Check Interval Factor is the interval that the SNMP Service checks to see if any managed servers are up or down. The Mib Data Refresh Interval is multiplied by this number, and status checks occur at that interval. The minimum value is 1; you will probably want to use a value between 1 and 3.

- Community Prefix is the SNMP community that the manager will be using for requests sent to the WebLogic SNMP agent.

- Set the Debug Level to the desired level, as described in the section Domain Information ⇨ Configuration ⇨ SNMP earlier in this chapter.

- Move the appropriate targeted trap destination to the Chosen list.

8. Click Apply.

WLEC

WebLogic Enterprise Connectivity is a component of WebLogic Server that allows you to create a pool of WLEC connections to WebLogic Tuxedo CORBA objects. WLEC connection pools operate under the same theory as JDBC connection pools; creating connections is expensive, so do it once at server startup; then share the connections among clients who need them.

To create a new WLEC connection pool, follow these steps:

1. In the domain tree, click the WLEC node. The right side of the Console displays all existing WLEC connection pools.

2. Click the Configure a New WLEC Connection Pool link. Figure 23-61 shows the General tab of the WLEC connection pool configuration page, which appears when you click the link.

Figure 23-61: Configuring a WLEC connection pool

3. Enter values for the following:

- *Name:* A name for the connection pool that is unique within the WebLogic domain.

- *Primary Addresses:* A comma-separated list of addresses for IIOP listeners/handlers that are used to create the connection pool between WebLogic Server and the Tuxedo domain. The format for each address is //hostname:port; for example, //tuxedo.zeeware.com:1024.

- *Failover Addresses:* A comma-separated list of addresses for IIOP listeners/handlers that are to be used if connections cannot be established with any of the addresses in the primary field. The entry format is the same. Entering data for this field is optional.

- *Domain:* The name of the WebLogic Tuxedo domain to which this connection pool connects. There can be only one connection pool per domain.

- *Minimum Pool Size:* The minimum number of IIOP connections that are to be created at startup. The default is 1.

- *Maximum Pool Size:* The maximum number of IIOP connections that are allowed. The default is 1.

4. Click Create.

5. Click the Security tab to propagate the security context for a WebLogic user to the BEA Tuxedo domain. This is needed only if the security level in Tuxedo is USER_AUTH, ACL, and MANDATORY_ACL. Figure 23-62 shows the configuration page.

Figure 23-62: Configuring security for a WLEC connection pool

6. Enter values for the following:

- *User Name:* A BEA Tuxedo username.

- *User Password:* The password for the username given.

- *User Role:* The BEA Tuxedo user role, chosen from among the roles defined in your Tuxedo installation.

- *Application Password:* The password for the BEA Tuxedo CORBA application.

- *Minimum Encryption Level:* The minimum SSL encryption level that WebLogic Server is allowed to communicate with Tuxedo. If this level is not met, the connection process will fail. Possible values are 0, 40, 56, and 128.

- *Maximum Encryption Level:* The maximum SSL encryption level that WebLogic Server is allowed to communicate with BEA Tuxedo.

- *Enable Certificate Authentication:* Check this box if certificates are to be used.

- *Enable Security Context:* Check this box if the user security information provided is to be passed to BEA Tuxedo.

7. Click Apply.

8. Run the `tpuseradd` command to define the WebLogic user as an authorized user in the BEA Tuxedo domain.

9. Set the `-E` option of the ISL command to propagate the User information for the WebLogic Server to the Tuxedo domain. The `-E` option requires that a principal username be provided. This is the same as the preceding username entry.

Jolt

BEA Jolt provides generic access to BEA Tuxedo. Jolt creates a pool of connections at startup, providing the same benefits as a JDBC connection pool.

To create a new Jolt connection pool, follow these steps:

1. In the domain tree, click the Jolt node to display all existing Jolt connection pools in the right side of the Console.

2. Click the Configure a New Jolt Connection Pool link. The configuration page shown in Figure 23-63 appears.

Figure 23-63: Configuring a Jolt connection pool

3. Enter values for the following parameters:

- *Name:* A unique identifier for this connection pool within the domain.

- *Minimum Pool Size:* The initial number of Tuxedo connections to create at startup. The default is 0.

- *Maximum Pool Size:* The maximum number of connections allowed. The default is 1.

- *Recv Timeout:* The amount of time to wait for a response from Tuxedo before timing out. The default is 0.

- *Security Context Enabled:* Check this box to enable WebLogic's security context for this connection pool.

4. Click Create.

5. Click the Addresses tab. Figure 23-64 shows the resulting configuration page.

Figure 23-64: Configuring addresses for the Jolt connection pool

6. Enter primary and failover connection addresses for the Tuxedo domain. Failover addresses are optional. The format for each address is //hostname:port; for example, //tuxedo.zeeware.com:1024.

7. Click Apply.

8. Click the User tab. These fields must be set if you enabled the WebLogic security context on the General page. The user must be a known BEA Tuxedo domain user; provide valid entries for User Name, User Role, User Password, and Application Password, as described in Figure 23-62.

9. Click Apply.

10. Click the Targets tab, and move the WebLogic Servers and/or clusters for which you want to activate the Jolt connection pool into the Chosen list. Click Apply.

Virtual hosts

Virtual hosts are host names that WebLogic Servers or clusters respond to. They allow you to have different Web applications respond to different host names, even if those applications are deployed on the same physical hardware. A retail banking application, for example, might respond to www.onlinebanking.com, whereas a stock trading application might respond to www.onlinetrading.com. The virtual host configuration screens enable you to define host names and map them to WebLogic Web applications.

Follow these steps to configure a new virtual host:

1. In the domain tree, click the Virtual Hosts node.

2. The right side of the Console displays all existing virtual hosts for this server. Click the Configure a New Virtual Host link at the top. Figure 23-65 shows the resulting configuration page with its default values.

Figure 23-65: Configuring a new virtual host

3. The entries on this page are as follows:

   • *Name:* The administrative name of the virtual host. This name must be unique within the WebLogic domain.

   • *Virtual Host Names:* Enter one or more virtual host names for the application, one per line. Example: www.onlinebanking.com.

   • *Default Web App:* Choose a deployed Web application from this list that will be invoked when the virtual host name is entered.

4. Click Create.

5. Enter the data for the Logging and HTTP tabs as you would for a normal WebLogic Server deployment. These configuration steps were described earlier in this chapter.

6. Click the Targets tab, and move the WebLogic Servers and/or clusters for which you want to activate the virtual host into the Chosen list. Click Apply.

Mail

This node is used to configure JavaMail sessions.

Cross-Reference   For more information on configuring mail, see Chapter 10.

File T3

File T3 allows WebLogic Server to create high-speed client access to native operating system files. The API extends the lowest-common-denominator Java classes (java.io.InputStream, java.io.OutputStream), thus allowing for seamless integration with a pre-existing code base. In several ways, WebLogic file services provide superior network performance compared with the standard Java implementation:

✦ Data is transmitted in buffers whose size is independent of the request that was sent. Thus, clients can send several small requests and not affect performance.

✦ Read-ahead buffering allows the WebLogic Server to load a buffer of data before it is actively processed by the application.

✦ Write-behind buffering allows the WebLogic application to write to a buffer beyond what has been flushed to disk. While the application writes to a buffer, other buffers are being written to disk. A flush operation blocks on the client until an acknowledgment is sent that all buffers have been written to disk.

Follow these steps to create and assign a File T3:

1. Click the File T3 node in the domain tree. The right side of the Console shows all File T3 definitions that exist on WebLogic Server.

2. Click the Configure a New File T3 link. Figure 23-66 shows the resulting configuration page.

Figure 23-66: Configuring a File T3 entry

3. Enter a unique administrative name for the File T3 and a valid path to the file.

4. Click Create.

5. Click the Targets tab and moved the desired server and or cluster name into the Chosen list.

6. Click Apply.

The new File T3 is now created and deployed.

Security

The configuration steps for security are covered elsewhere in this book. See Chapter 25 for more information.

Domain log filters

Domain log filters allow you to customize the information written to WebLogic Server's domain log. This is a useful feature for troubleshooting problems you may be having with a domain. You are allowed to have one active domain log filter per domain. You can, however, create multiple filters for different purposes and then swap them in and out depending on the troubleshooting you are trying to perform.

To create a domain log filter, click the Domain Log Filters node at the bottom of the domain tree. In the pane on the right, click the Configure a New Domain Log Filter link. Figure 23-67 shows the resulting configuration screen filled out with some sample data. Let's say we're having problems with an EJB, and we want to see all log messages having to do with EJBs.

Figure 23-67: Configuring a domain log filter

The entries on this screen are as follows:

✦ *Name:* The administrative name for the filter. It must be unique within the domain.

✦ *Severity Level*: Select a level from the drop-down list. Messages of this severity or higher are written to the log.

✦ *User Ids:* Enter one or more WebLogic user IDs, one per line. This causes logging to happen only for sessions that can be tracked to those IDs.

✦ *Subsystems:* A list of WebLogic Server's subsystems is given. You can move any number of these subsystems into the Chosen list. Logging occurs only for the subsystems you choose. If no subsystems are chosen, all are logged.

Click Create after configuring the filter. Then click the Targets tab, and select the WebLogic Servers or clusters in the domain to which you want to apply the filter.

Administering WebLogic Using Command-Line Tools

WebLogic Server also provides a command-line interface to its administration tools, along with many configuration and runtime management bean (Mbean) properties, for the following reasons:

✦ Command scripts for management and administration efficiency.

✦ Users who cannot access the administration Console via a browser.

✦ Users who prefer a command-line interface to a graphical user interface.

To execute a WebLogic command from the command line, perform these steps:

1. Start WebLogic Server. This is most easily done by running the `startWeblogic.cmd` script.

2. Open a new command window in your domain directory, such as `H:\WebLogicUserDomains\mydomain`.

3. Run the `setEnv.cmd` script that resides in the `mydomain` directory or add the necessary data to the classpath system environment variable. At the very least, classpath needs `<WL_HOME>\lib\weblogic.jar` and `<WL_HOME>\lib\weblogic_sp.jar`, where `<WL_HOME>` is the location of the WebLogic installation (usually the `\bea\weblogic700\server` directory). Any other classes that might be accessed from the command line also need to be added to the classpath variable.

4. Run the WebLogic Server command. These are always in the form `java weblogic.Admin [-url URL] [-username username] [-password password] COMMAND parameters`, where:

   • `url` is the URL that is used to access the WebLogic Server. By default, this is `localhost:7001`.

   • `username` is a valid user on the WebLogic Server. This parameter is optional and defaults to `guest` if not provided.

   • `password` is the password for the username provided. This is also optional.

These commands can be combined into command scripts. The following one-line command script, for example, shuts down the server specified in the `URL` parameter:

```
@rem shutdown the localhost server running on port 7001
java weblogic.Admin -url localhost:7001 -username wlsadmin -password
password SHUTDOWN 200 "Server localhost is shutting down."
```

The following debug script pings the WebLogic Server to see if it is still up, and then prints several pieces of information to the command screen:

```
@rem Ping the WebLogic Server to see if it is still running
java weblogic.Admin -url localhost:7001 -username wlsadmin -password
password PING 10

@rem print out the WebLogic Server JNDI binding list for the
```

```
@rem weblogic context
java weblogic.Admin -url localhost:7001 -username wlsadmin -password
password LIST weblogic

@rem print out the server logs contents for 8 AM till 10 AM
@rem on January 8 2003.
java weblogic.Admin -url localhost:7001 -username wlsadmin -password
password SERVERLOG "2003/01/08 08:00" "2003/01/08 10:00"
```

Most common administration and configuration duties can be performed from the command line. But coverage of all the commands and their parameters is beyond the scope of this chapter. For more information on available command-line commands, see the WebLogic Documentation at http://e-docs.bea.com/wls/docs70/adminguide/cli.html.

Summary

Administering and configuring WebLogic Server is made considerably easier with the WebLogic Server Console. The Console provides a user-friendly GUI that eliminates the need for direct editing of XML configuration documents. This prevents validation errors that can occur when users are forced to edit XML documents. For those who prefer command-line tools to GUI tools, WebLogic Server has extensive command-line support. Most major configuration and administration operations can be performed from the command line. Common administration tasks can thus be automated by using scripts that contain these commands. Because of these two powerful features, administering a WebLogic Server is a relatively simple task.

✦   ✦   ✦

Working with WebLogic Clusters

Have you ever found yourself with so much work to do that you wish you could clone yourself and delegate some of the work to the clone? Or maybe you've fallen ill with an important deadline looming, and you wish you had a clone that could finish the job while you recover. This kind of "cloning" is what WebLogic clusters are all about, except that clusters contain clones of WebLogic Servers, not people. A WebLogic cluster is a group of WebLogic servers working together to help your applications withstand heavier workloads and to continue functioning in the event of server failures.

Servers in a cluster cooperate in two ways. First, they share the workload of responding to incoming requests, allowing greater numbers of requests to be handled. This feature is called *load balancing*. Second, they cover for each other, so if one server "falls ill," the other servers in the cluster can instantly and transparently assume its workload, resulting in no service disruption to users. This is called *failover*.

Load balancing and failover imply *scalability* and *availability*. Scalability is an application's capability to handle any number of users with no appreciable degradation in performance, and clusters provide this by distributing the workload across multiple servers. If traffic increases, simply add more servers to the cluster. Availability is an application's capability to "be there" for the user, even in the face of hardware or network failures. Clusters provide this through their failover capability.

Nothing will solidify your understanding of clusters more than actually building a couple of clusters and watching them work. Therefore, in this chapter we walk you through the process of building two simple, multiple-server clusters that are accessed through a WebLogic Server instance acting as a proxy. We also show you how to deploy a Web application to this cluster and demonstrate how HTTP session replication works, even in the face of server failures. Toward the end of the chapter, we give you a brief overview of how J2EE services such as JDBC and JMS behave in clusters, and finally we explain the clustering implications behind RMI objects and EJBs.

Introduction to Clustering

Clustering is a simple concept, but it can be quite complicated in practice. One issue is that clusters can be designed lots of different ways, with some approaches working better than others for various types of applications. Another issue is that you must deal with a few gotchas when building even the simplest clusters, due to practical realities and limitations inherent in the J2EE architecture and computer networks.

BEA's documentation on clusters, which you can find online at the following URL, is essential reading and is especially strong at explaining cluster design strategies and their networking implications:

```
http://edocs.bea.com/wls/docs70/cluster/index.html
```

The coverage is good enough, so we won't repeat that information here. However, a number of new features have been added in WebLogic Server 7.0 that directly or indirectly affect clustering, and in this chapter we'll tie it all together so it's easier to digest.

In this chapter, we'll be building a development-style cluster and a production-style cluster. The idea behind a development-style cluster is that you want to be able to set up a cluster on a single machine to minimize hardware requirements during development. On the other hand, a production-style cluster typically would be hosted on multiple physical machines and should configured for maximum flexibility.

The development-style cluster will take advantage of new WebLogic Server 7.0 features that allow you to host two clustered servers on a single machine with a single IP address. This is a configuration that a developer can use while writing and testing an application. We'll also create a production-style cluster that will be hosted on different machines, with two types of hardware running three different operating systems. This production-style cluster will not only show you the power of WebLogic (and Java) running on different systems, but it will also take advantage of the latest WebLogic 7.0 features, including a template-like feature that allows simple configuration of multiple cluster nodes and the capability to override that template on a node-by-node basis.

By the time you finish reading this chapter, you will have the hands-on ability to deploy a session-based Web application to a WebLogic cluster. This will give you a strong foundation of knowledge and experience for building clusters of arbitrary complexity and designing applications to leverage their power.

Designing the Cluster Topology

For both the development-style cluster and the production-style cluster, we'll be setting up two-node WebLogic clusters. A two-node WebLogic cluster actually requires three WebLogic instances: one for each participant (node) in the cluster and one to be the administration point for the cluster. The latter server is configured as a WebLogic administration server, and the cluster participants (also called *nodes*) are configured as managed servers that "belong" to the administration server. This arrangement is illustrated in Figure 24-1.

Note   Figure 24-1 is a logical diagram, not a physical one. Each server or node in the diagram represents a WebLogic server instance, not (necessarily) a physical machine. You can run multiple WebLogic servers on a single physical machine. This will become clearer as you build the development- and production-style clusters in this chapter.

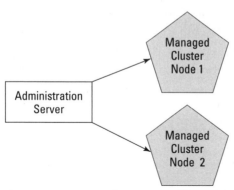

Figure 24-1: Managed servers (nodes) and
Administration server in a WebLogic cluster

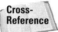

Cross-
Reference

Administration and managed servers are discussed in Chapter 4.

In the development-style cluster, the administration server and the two cluster nodes will all
be deployed and running on a single physical PC. In the production-style cluster, the administration server and the two cluster nodes will each be deployed and running on separate physical hardware (two PCs and a Unix machine).

The administration server should not participate in the cluster. There is no reason to put an
administration server in the cluster because the administration application is not clusterable.
And if the administration server goes down, the cluster can still operate without it. In that
case, just start a new instance of the administration server, and it will automatically discover
its managed servers as part of its bootup process.

The administration server, however, can still perform a useful role when it's not being used to
manage the cluster: It can be used as an HTTP proxy to the servers in the cluster, at least for
development purposes. We discuss this further in the "Accessing a Cluster through an HTTP
Proxy" section later in this chapter.

The machines themselves must be configured on the network according to a few simple rules:

✦ Each machine must have a static IP address. Machines participating in clusters must
not have their IP addresses assigned dynamically with DHCP or any other method.
Otherwise, the participants in the cluster will suddenly be unable to communicate with
each other if the addresses change.

✦ All machines participating in a cluster must be on the same local area network and
must be reachable by IP multicast. Although not a requirement, it is best if the
machines are on the same subnet as well. This greatly simplifies troubleshooting and
eliminates the possibility that you will have to reconfigure bridges or routers to support IP multicast.

✦ All machines participating in the cluster must be running the same version of WebLogic
Server.

Note The machines can be running different operating systems, as long as those operating systems are supported by WebLogic.

In the next two sections, we'll map the cluster shown in Figure 24-1 to a simple development-style cluster running on a single piece of hardware and a more complex production-style cluster running on multiple hardware/operating system combinations.

Building a Development-Style Cluster

Probably the best way to learn about clusters is to build one. In this section, we demonstrate how to build a two-node, development-style WebLogic cluster, deployed on one physical machine. This is the simplest possible WebLogic cluster, and understanding how to build such a simple cluster makes it easier to work with more complex clustering arrangements.

Figure 24-2 shows the cluster from Figure 24-1 assigned to a single machine on our network. For this development-style cluster, we're running the administration server and both managed servers (nodes) on a single physical server (a PC workstation).

For this development-style cluster, we are keeping things as simple as possible. We will reuse our existing domain and server — mydomain and myserver, respectively — that are created by default, as described in Chapter 4. The `myserver` server will become our administration server for the cluster, and we'll use the administration console to create two new server nodes for our cluster and set up the cluster itself.

Figure 24-2: A cluster mapped to a single machine on the network

In Chapter 4, we discuss how to disable the discovery of managed servers in order to speed up the server boot process. However, you don't want to do this for an administration server in a cluster. Set `weblogic.management.discover=true` to allow the administration server to find its managed nodes at startup. This process lets you administer a cluster even if the administration server goes down for some reason.

In this development-style cluster, we will be taking advantage of a new feature of WebLogic 7.0: the ability to have cluster nodes with different TCP port numbers. This is very useful for development, demonstration, and test purposes because it allows you to have multiple nodes running on a single machine, without resorting to multihoming. (It is less useful for production-style clusters because it prevents you from administering cluster nodes via a single DNS name and port number.)

To create a cluster like this, follow these steps:

1. Configure the first managed server (cluster node).

   Open the administration console, right-click the Servers node, and select Configure a New Server from the pop-up menu. (Or, click the Servers node and click Configure a New Server on the resulting Web page.) Fill out the page as shown in Figure 24-3. The important things to change from the defaults are Name and Port. For this example, the name should be `BibleCServerDev1`, where "BibleC" is short for BibleCluster and "Dev" is short for Development—this is descriptive without being overly long. The port is `7003`, which ensures that the port this node is using (7003) does not conflict with the port (7001) the administration server (myserver) is using. Click Create to create the node.

2. Configure the second managed server. Repeat Step 1, but this time using a name of `BibleCServerDev2` and a port of 7005.

3. Configure the cluster. To do so, right-click the Clusters node in the administration console and select Configure a New Cluster from the pop-up menu. Fill out the page as shown in Figure 24-4. The important fields here are Name, Cluster Address, and Default Load Algorithm. Use a Name of `BibleClusterDev`. For the Cluster Address, enter the IP addresses and port numbers of each cluster node that you configured in Steps 1 and 2. (For a production-style cluster, you would use a single DNS name that is mapped to multiple servers.) Note that the combination of IP address and port number *must be unique* for each entry (in the format of `<IP Address>:<Port>`), and each entry is separated by a comma. The Default Load Algorithm is used for any replicable service for which no specific algorithm has been chosen in its configuration. The default value is `round-robin`, which means that requests made to the cluster are distributed among the cluster members in alternating fashion. Other options are `weight-based`, in which requests are distributed according to numeric weights you assign to each server, and `random`, which is self-explanatory. We chose `round-robin` for our cluster because all participating nodes are on the same machine and are therefore equal in terms of power and performance. Click the Create button to create the cluster configuration.

4. Assign the nodes to the cluster by clicking the newly created `BibleClusterDev` cluster in the console's node tree and then click the Servers tab. Hold down the Ctrl key and click both `BibleCServerDev1` and `BibleCServerDev2` in the Available list; then click the right-facing arrow to move them to the Chosen list. Click Apply to save the changes, and the Servers tab should appear as shown in Figure 24-5. Note the server nodes shown under the cluster name in the tree on the left. Remember, don't add the administration server (myserver) to the cluster.

Figure 24-3: Creating a server for a development-style cluster

At this point, you have created the configuration for the cluster, but the only WebLogic Server that's running is the administration server myserver. (You can verify this by clicking the BibleClusterDev node and then clicking the Monitoring tab — you'll see that there are two servers configured, but none are running.) There are just a few small steps you need to do to get the two cluster nodes up and running:

Figure 24-4: Configuring the development-style cluster

Figure 24-5: Assigning the servers to the cluster

1. Create a command file to start the first node. If you look in the `mydomain` directory located in your user domains directory, you'll find the `startWebLogic.cmd` file that you use to start the administration server. In addition, there's a `startManagedWebLogic.cmd` file that's used to start a server instance as a managed server rather than an administration server. We'll create a copy specifically for our cluster node. Copy `startManagedWebLogic.cmd` to `startBibleCServerDev1.cmd`. Modify it as follows to match our cluster settings:

   ```
   set SERVER_NAME=BibleCServerDev1
   
   set ADMIN_URL=http://192.168.0.3:7001
   
   set WLS_USER=wlsadmin
   
   set WLS_PW=password
   ```

   The `SERVER_NAME` is the name of the node you created in the cluster. The `ADMIN_URL` is the IP address and port number of the administration server that controls the cluster. The `WLS_USER` and `WLS_PW` are the administration username and password for the domain. These last two items are optional, but make it easier to start the server on a development machine; you don't want to embed the password in a command file in clear text on a production machine, however.

2. Create a command file to start the second node. Repeat Step 1, but name the copied file `startBibleCServerDev2.cmd` and set `SERVER_NAME` to `BibleCServerDev2`.

3. Open two new command windows and run the commands you just created. This process will start the two new cluster nodes. As they start, they will join the cluster to get configuration information from the administration server.

At this point you have created a development-style cluster in WebLogic. If you're a developer who's just trying to get up and running — and you don't need a production-style cluster — you can skip ahead to the "Deploying a Web Application to the Cluster" section later in this chapter. If you can deploy a Web application to the cluster successfully, then you'll know your cluster is up and working correctly.

Building a Production-Style Cluster

In this section, we demonstrate how to build a two-node, production-style WebLogic cluster, deployed on three physical machines (one machine for each cluster node, plus an administration server on the third machine). This is a more complex configuration that more realistically represents a cluster in production. It also allows us to go over some exciting new features in WebLogic Server 7.0 that make managing multiple servers or nodes easier.

Figure 24-6 shows the cluster from Figure 24-1 assigned to three machines on a network. For this production-style cluster, we're running each server on its own physical machine. We're not running DNS on our network, so we use IP addresses instead of machine names in the configuration.

Managed Cluster Server 1
Name: *BibleCServerProd1*
IP: *192.168.0.2*
Port: 7001
Processor: *Intel Pentium 4, 1.6 GHz*
OS: *Windows XP*

Administration Server
Name: *BibleCServerAdmin*
IP: *192.168.0.3*
Port: 7001
Processor: *Intel Pentium III, 733 MHz*
OS: *Windows 2000*

Managed Cluster Server 2
Name: *BibleCServerProd2*
IP: *192.168.0.5*
Port: 7001
Processor: *Motorola G3, 800 MHz*
OS: *Mac OS X (Unix)*

Figure 24-6: A cluster mapped to a three machines on the network

Tip   In a production system, it makes configuration and changes easier if you use DNS names. It's also easier if the nodes all use the same port number, as we'll see in the discussion in the section titled "Configuring network channels and channel overrides."

For this production-style cluster, we cover a number of features new to WebLogic Server 7.0 that make creating and managing clusters easier. These include the Domain Configuration Wizard, network channels, and channel overrides.

Here's an overview of the process we'll be discussing in the following sections, just to help you get your head around it:

1. We'll first create an entirely new domain to hold our configuration information.

2. Next, we'll use the new Domain Configuration Wizard to create our administration server for the cluster and then start up the administration server.

3. Then, we'll use that same wizard running on different hardware (and operating systems) to create two new server nodes for our cluster.

4. We'll then start up those nodes and show how to monitor the cluster.

5. Next, we'll create and apply a network channel, which is like a template for managed servers.

6. Finally, we'll create a channel override, which lets you change a specific node's configuration and override its network channel.

Create the domain and administration server

The first thing we need to do is create a completely new domain and set up an administration server for it. In addition to the administration server, this domain will contain the configuration for the cluster nodes. Even though the cluster nodes will be running remotely on other physical machines, we need to set them up in the domain configuration so the cluster nodes can retrieve this information when they boot up and connect to the cluster domain.

1. If you haven't already done so, install WebLogic Server on the machine that will be the administration server. To keep things simple, we shut down any running instances of WebLogic Server on the same machine that we've been using for all our examples (the domain `mydomain` and server `myserver`).

Cross-Reference See Chapter 4 for information on installing WebLogic.

2. Start the Domain Configuration Wizard on this administration server PC. If you did a fresh install, the installation program will ask if you want to run the Domain Configuration Wizard. If the software is already installed, the wizard will appear as an entry on your Start menu in Windows. On Unix, you'll find the shell script that starts the wizard in `WL_HOME/common/bin/dmwiz.sh`.

3. The first page of the wizard will look like Figure 24-7. In the Template section, choose `WLS Domain` because you want to create an empty new domain. For the name, enter **BibleClusterDomain**. Click Next to continue.

4. Next, you get to choose your server type. In Chapter 4, we chose Single Server (Standalone Server), and we used it for all the other examples in this book. For this cluster, we'll choose Admin Server with Clustered Managed Server(s). Click Next to continue.

Note In the next section, we'll cover the Managed Server with Owning Admin Server Configuration. The remaining option, Admin Server with Managed Server(s), is for creating individual managed—but unclustered—servers that are controlled by an administration server.

Figure 24-7: The first page of the Domain Configuration Wizard for creating a new domain for the cluster

5. Choose the directory in which the new domain will be created. Our user projects directory is `H:\WebLogicUserDomains\`, so a directory with the domain's name will be created inside that directory. Click Next to continue.

6. An empty table appears. Click Add to create a new server node for the cluster. For the server name, enter `BibleCServerProd1`. For the listen address, enter the IP address (or DNS name) of the server; in our case, it's `192.168.0.2`. Use the default listen port of `7001` and SSL port of `7002`. Click Add.

7. The table now has the entry we just added, as shown in Figure 24-8. Click Add again to add the second cluster node.

8. Add another by entering the same settings into the fields as you did in Step 6, except change the server name to `BibleCServerProd2` and the IP address to `192.168.0.5`. For this production-style cluster, each server node is on a separate physical machine, so the port numbers are all the same. Click Add.

9. Now the table shows both newly configured nodes. Click Next to continue.

10. In the next window, you configure the cluster itself. This is similar to configuring the cluster through the administration console as we did for the development-style cluster. Enter `BibleClusterProd` as the name, and leave the cluster multicast address and port at their default values unless there is a conflict. For cluster address, enter a comma-separated list of IP (or DNS) addresses and port numbers. Click Next.

11. On this screen we configure the administration server for the cluster. Enter `BibleCServerAdmin` for the name, but leave the listen address blank. Leaving the listen address blank lets us use `http://localhost:7001/` to reach the server locally (say, through a local script), and it allows us to use `http://192.168.0.3:7001/` to reach the host from another machine. If you enter `localhost` instead of leaving it

blank, it will only be accessible locally; if you enter 192.168.0.3, it will only be accessible remotely. Leave the listen and SSL ports at their default values. Click Next.

12. Create the administrative user. Because we're in the process of creating a new domain, we can have a different administrative user than we had for mydomain, which we set up in Chapter 4. But to keep things simple, we'll use the same username (wlsadmin) and password (password) that we used previously. Click Next to continue.

13. The summary page displays everything we've entered. Confirm that Figure 24-9 matches your screen and then click Create to create the cluster domain. We're done with configuration now, so quit the Domain Configuration Wizard by clicking Exit.

14. Start the administration server by going into the domain directory that was just created (in our case, H:\WebLogicUserDomains\BibleClusterDomain), run startWebLogic.cmd in a command window, and enter the username and password that you just configured. (Recall from Chapter 4 that you can enter the administration username and password into this command file so you don't have to type it every time. You don't want to do this for a production server, however.)

15. Open a browser and go to the administration console by entering http://localhost:7001/console/, and you should see the node layout shown on the left of Figure 24-10. Click alternately on each server and you'll see the configuration information that you entered in the Domain Configuration Wizard.

Leave the administration server running while you continue to the next sections. Remember, the administration server must be running when you start the cluster nodes because that's where they get their configuration information from. Think of the nodes as blank slates, waiting to get configuration, services, and deployment information for their "master:" the administration server.

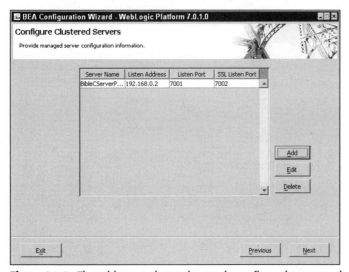

Figure 24-8: The table now shows the newly configured server node

Figure 24-9: This summary window shows all the configuration information you entered

Figure 24-10: The administration console displaying the cluster configuration

Creating the cluster nodes

Okay, so far the administration server is up and running, the cluster has been configured, and the nodes have been configured from an administrative standpoint, but the nodes have not actually been installed or run on the separate physical machines.

In this section, we'll get WebLogic Server installed on the node machines, minimally configure the nodes through the Domain Configuration Wizard, and then run the nodes so they can contact the administration server for configuration information.

Following are a few things to keep in mind before you begin:

✦ If you downloaded the installation files, as described in Chapter 4, you don't need to download them again to install WebLogic on the cluster nodes. Just make sure that the directory in which you saved the installation files is accessible over your network, and run the installation files from the node where you want to install WebLogic Server. Although the installation files can be run over the network, WebLogic itself should be installed locally on each node.

✦ It's important to remember that although you can run WebLogic Server cluster nodes on different operating systems, all the nodes must be running at the same version and service pack level of WebLogic Server. Only the administration server can be at a different service pack level, and it must be at the same or a higher service pack level than the nodes in the cluster.

✦ Because many of these steps are similar to previous steps, we won't be showing you screen shots of every single step. Instead, we'll refer to previous figures as reference. However, remember to enter the data we specify here, rather than the exact data in the referenced figure.

Caution　　We are installing WebLogic Server on a Windows XP machine with an Intel Pentium 4 processor and a Mac OS X (which OS essentially has a BSD Unix core) notebook with a Motorola G3 processor. This is useful because it serves to demonstrate that different nodes in a WebLogic Server cluster can run on different hardware and operating systems in a totally seamless manner. However, neither Windows XP nor Mac OS X is currently certified by BEA, so you should not install WebLogic Server on these operating systems in a test or production environment.

With those things in mind, follow these steps to create your cluster nodes:

1. Install WebLogic Server on each node's computer. Recall from Chapter 4 that the Domain Configuration Wizard runs at the end of installation; the first screen of the wizard is similar to Figure 24-7. Select WLS Domain to create a new blank domain, and enter BibleClusterDomain as the domain name. You don't actually need to use the same domain name as the one you configured for the administration server — the node will get all its configuration information from the administration server — but it just makes sense to give it the same domain name. Click Next.

2. Select Managed Server (with owning Admin Server configuration) from the next screen. When you select this, the wizard will ask you for details related to a managed server (node) configuration instead of an administration server configuration. Click Next.

3. On the next screen of the wizard, use a directory path that's relevant to the operating system the node is on. For example, on our Unix (Mac OS X) notebook, we chose `/Users/Lou/bea/user_projects`. Click Next.

4. Now we come to the Configure Administrative Server Connection page. Enter the administration server's IP address (`192.168.0.3`), and leave the port numbers at their defaults of 7001 and 7002. For the managed server name, enter `BibleCServerProd1` (or 2, for the second node) and click Next.

5. Now we're at the Configure Standalone/Administrative Server page. The name of this page is misleading: This page is for configuring a Managed Server (node) of the cluster. Therefore, use a server name of `BibleCServerProd1` (or 2, for the second node), leave the listen address blank, and leave the ports at their default values of 7001 and 7002. Click Next.

6. Next comes the Create Administrative User page. The username and password here *must* match the username and password you entered when you created the Administrative Server for this domain. So enter `wlsadmin` for the username and `password` as the password. Click Next.

7. If you're running Windows, you'll be asked if you want to install the server as a Windows service. This will start the server whenever Windows starts up, and runs independently of any user — so whether anyone is actually logged in to the machine is irrelevant. Generally, a better way of handling this is through WebLogic's Node Manager, but that's beyond the scope of this book. Click Next.

8. If you're running on Windows, you'll be asked if you want to install a link to the script that starts this server on the Windows Start menu. You'll probably want to select No for a production server. Click Next.

9. Finally, we're at the Summary page. Figures 24-11 and 24-12 show how the summary should look for our two nodes. Click Create to create the domain configuration for the node.

Figure 24-11: The Windows XP configuration summary for the first node

Figure 24-12: The Unix (Mac OS X) configuration summary for the second node

Starting the nodes

Now that we've configured the nodes, it's time to start them.

WebLogic has no magic command for starting a cluster. Instead, you must start each participating server separately, and it will join the cluster on its own. The usual sequence is to start the administration server first and then start the managed servers. You can do this using startup scripts or Node Manager; in this chapter, we use the startup script that is created automatically by the Domain Configuration Wizard.

> **Note** See the WebLogic Administration Guide for more information about using Node Manager.

Open a command-line window on the node machines and change to the domain directory we created on each machine. Start the startManagedWebLogic.cmd (or startManagedWebLogic.sh, for Unix) command file. You should see a flurry of resulting output similar to that shown in Figure 24-13, which shows a node starting up on Windows XP. Note especially the last 10 or so log events (those containing <Notice>) that show this managed server contacting the Administration Server for configuration and deployment information.

There are several things to notice about the results you see — it's not your typical WebLogic startup sequence:

✦ First, right after the startup begins, you see this line:

```
Connecting to http://192.168.0.3:7001...
```

Here, you see the managed server attempting to contact its administration server in order to receive the latest configuration information and deployments. If contact cannot be made, the managed server won't start; without an administration server, the managed server cannot function.

✦ Next, you see an entry indicating that the server is starting as a managed server called BibleCServerProd1 in the domain BibleClusterDomain.

✦ After that, the cluster service attempts to start. If the server's IP address and multicast address match those expected by the administration server, the cluster service will start successfully.

✦ Finally, you see messages indicating that the cluster service is listening for messages from the BibleClusterProd cluster on the appointed IP addresses and ports and that the WebLogic managed server is up and running under its given name and domain. Success!

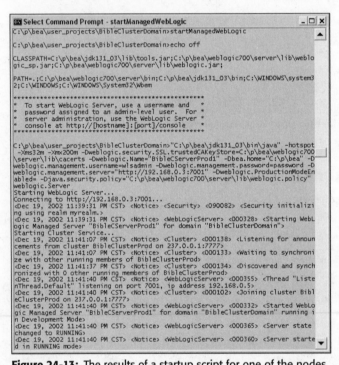

Figure 24-13: The results of a startup script for one of the nodes

Monitoring the status of the cluster

When you started up the individual nodes at the command-line window, you could see exactly what was happening during startup. The status was right there in front of you. But how do you see the status of the cluster after startup is finished?

We can remotely view the status of the cluster via the WebLogic Server administration console. If we go back to the administration server and open the console, we can click the plus sign next to the Clusters node in the tree on the left and then click on the BibleClusterProd node. On the window on the right, click the Monitoring tab. A window similar to Figure 24-14 should show up. This window shows the number of server nodes that have been configured and the number that are running.

Figure 24-14: Remotely monitor the status of the cluster

Click the link named Monitor server participation in this cluster. The result should be something like Figure 24-15, which shows the state of each node in the cluster.

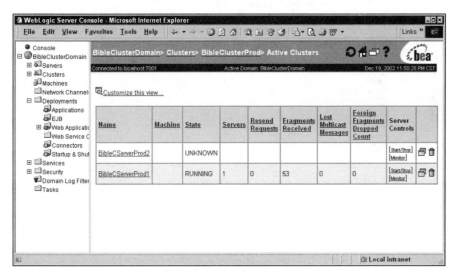

Figure 24-15: The status of each node in the cluster

Configuring network channels and channel overrides

New in WebLogic Server 7.0 are the concepts of *network channels* and *channel overrides*. Think of network channels as templates that can be applied to servers, and consider channel overrides as server-specific modifications to the template. Just as templates can make all your word processing documents have the same characteristics, network channels can give all the server nodes in your cluster the same configuration—whether HTTP is enabled and which port it's enabled on, or which port to use for SSL, for example.

Note   Network channels are cumulative. You can assign more than one to a server or cluster. This granularity gives you tremendous flexibility for setting up your cluster nodes or other servers.

Adding a network channel

To give a quick demonstration of a network channel and a channel override, we'll add a channel that listens for HTTP requests on port 8001. We'll assign this to the cluster rather than to an individual server. Because the servers are already configured to listen on port 7001, they are now reachable at both ports.

1. Open the administration console and click Network Channels in the tree on the left. In the pane on the right, click Configure a new network channel.

2. The panel should look like Figure 24-16. Enter a name of `BibleCProdChannel` and a description of `Cluster for Production`. Note that you can configure ports and protocols. Make sure that Listen Port Enabled is checked, that it's assigned to port 8001, and that HTTP Enabled is checked. Click Create to create this channel.

Figure 24-16: Configuring a new network channel that defines a Listen Port of 8001

Note   Because network channels are cumulative, if you don't check off an option, it doesn't necessarily mean that it's disabled; it just means that it hasn't been configured in this specific network channel.

3. After it's created, a channel has to be assigned to a server or cluster to take effect. Click the Targets tab and then click the Clusters tab. Move BibleClusterProd to the Chosen list and then click Apply. The window should look like Figure 24-17.

Figure 24-17: Assign the network channel to our production-style cluster

Stand back for a moment and think about what you just accomplished. Just by configuring a single network channel and assigning it to a cluster, we have now added specific protocol support and port configuration cluster-wide. No need to change each server node individually. Try adding additional network channels to test out more options. We'll leave that as an exercise for the reader.

Adding a channel override

Okay, so the capability to create network channels is a great new feature, but inevitably there are exceptions. Channel overrides allow you to continue to benefit from the ease of using standard network channels and still have the ability to tweak individual servers based on a need to override those standards.

The following list lets us create a channel override on one server. This will cause this one server to behave differently from all the other servers. (Remember Sesame Street: "One of These Things is Not Like the Others...")

1. In the administration console, click the server you want to modify. In our example, we click BibleCServerProd1. On the pane on the right, click the Connections tab and then click the Tuning tab (the console should now look something like Figure 24-18. Click the Channel Overrides link at the bottom.

2. The network channel we just created, BibleCProdChannel should appear (see Figure 24-19). Click this link to view it.

Figure 24-18: Viewing a server's configuration in preparation for overriding them

3. All the default values will be listed, whether as blanks or -1s. (You can click the help icons to see what the default value for each entry is.) We want to set the listen port to 8005 instead of the network channel's 8001, so enter **8005** for the Listen Port. Now the pane should look similar to Figure 24-20. Click Apply to apply your changes.

Figure 24-19: Listing of network channels assigned to this server

Figure 24-20: Overriding the network channel

Again, now is a good time to consider the implications of what you've just done. On a server-by-server basis, you now have the ability to override the template-like functionality of the network channel that you previously configured at will. This means your options are virtually unlimited for configuring clusters and servers in WebLogic Server.

Accessing a Cluster through an HTTP Proxy

At this point, if you start the administration server and the managed servers, you will techni-cally have a cluster in place, but it won't be easy to reach for your clients. Think about it: If you were to deploy a Web application to the cluster, what URL would you give clients to point them to the application? Which IP address should it resolve to?

You have many ways to solve this problem, but one approach is to insert an *HTTP proxy* between clients and the cluster. This server receives requests from clients and dispatches them to servers in the cluster according to the load-balancing algorithm specified in Step 3 of the "Building a Development-Style Cluster" section earlier in this chapter. The proxy can either be a WebLogic 7.0 server with the HttpClusterServlet installed or a third-party HTTP server with the WebLogic Proxy plug-in installed. Figure 24-21 illustrates these options.

For this example, we will install the HttpClusterServlet into my admin server and use it as an HTTP proxy for our cluster.

Note   Configuring your administration server to perform double duty as an HTTP proxy is fine for development, but in production you will probably want your HTTP proxy server(s) to be sep-arate from your administration server.

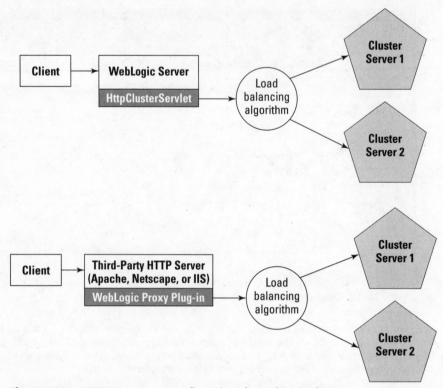

Figure 24-21: HTTP proxy server configurations for WebLogic clusters

To install the `HttpClusterServlet` on the administration server, follow these steps:

1. Open the WebLogic Console for the administration server.

2. The `HttpClusterServlet` must be attached to a default Web application for the server. Therefore, attach it to `DefaultWebApp`, which is the default Web application for all freshly installed WebLogic Servers. To do so, choose *<Domain>* ⇨ Deployments ⇨ Web Applications ⇨ DefaultWebApp and then click the Edit Web Application Descriptor link on the right side of the screen.

3. Choose Servlets ⇨ Configure a New Servlet. Set Servlet Name to `HttpClusterServlet` and Servlet Class to `weblogic.servlet.internal.HttpClusterServlet`, as shown in Figure 24-22. Click Create.

4. Expand the `HttpClusterServlet` node you just created. Click Parameters and then click Configure a New Parameter. Set Param Name to `defaultServers` and set Param Value to the IP addresses and ports of the clustered servers, separated by the pipe (|) character. The format for each entry is *<IP address>:<HTTP port>:<HTTPS port>*. For this example, the entry is `192.168.0.1:7001:7002|192.168.0.2:7001:7002`. Click Create.

Figure 24-22: Configuring `HttpClusterServlet`

5. Configure an additional parameter: Its name is `DebugConfigInfo`, and its value is `ON`. This parameter allows you to request debugging information from `HttpClusterServlet` by appending the request parameter `?_WebLogicBridgeConfig` to any request. Be sure to turn this parameter `OFF` for production environments.

6. Click Servlet Mappings and then click Configure a New Servlet Mapping. Set Servlet to `HttpClusterServlet` (choose it from the drop-down menu), and set URL pattern to `/` (forward slash). Click Create. This tells WebLogic to invoke `HttpClusterServlet` for all servlet requests, which is necessary for it to function correctly.

7. Add three more servlet mappings for `HttpClusterServlet`: `*.htm`, `*.html`, and `*.jsp`. These additional mappings ensure that `HttpClusterServlet` is invoked for all requests for HTML files and JSPs.

8. **Important!** Click the Web Descriptor node at the top-left corner of the screen and then click the Validate button on the right. You should get the message `Validation was successful`. Click the Web Descriptor node again and then click the Persist button. *You must do this, or all the changes you made in this window will be lost!*

Tip

If validation was not successful for some reason, persist the changes, and shut down the administration server and your cluster. Use a text editor to manually repair the domain's `config.xml` file on the administration server. If you're not an XML expert, you'll need to find someone who is because the only other way to repair the file is to throw it away and let WebLogic create a new empty one.

Figure 24-23 shows the deployment descriptor editor after making the changes we just described. Note the entries under HttpClusterServlet and ServletMappings in the domain tree on the left side of the figure.

Figure 24-23: The completed configuration of HttpClusterServlet, along with its parameters and servlet mappings

Deploying a Web Application to the Cluster

Now that the pieces of the cluster are in place, it's time to deploy a Web application to the cluster to see how everything works. We will deploy BibleServlets, the servlet example we created in Chapter 11 (you may want to refer to Chapter 11 as you read this to understand the functioning of the application) to our development-style cluster. Recall that Bible Servlets makes extensive use of HTTP sessions and the servlet context; deploying such an application gives you a chance to see how sessions and context are handled by the cluster.

BibleServlets is already deployed to our administration server, so all we need to do is remove it from that server and deploy it to the cluster. Here's how to do it:

1. Make sure the administration server is running and open the WebLogic Console against it.

2. Start the development-style cluster nodes, if they aren't already running. Each node's command-line window should look something like Figure 24-24.

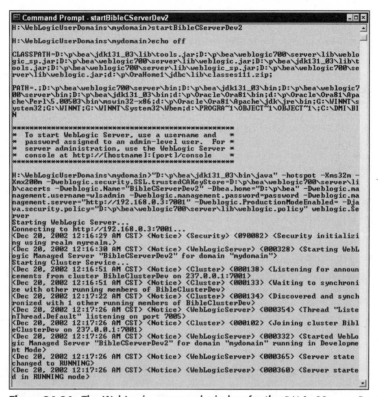

Figure 24-24: The WebLogic command window for the `BibleCServerDev2` clustered node

There are several things to notice about this window — it's not your typical WebLogic startup sequence:

First, right after the startup begins, you see this line:

```
Connecting to http://192.168.0.3:7001...
```

- Here, you see the managed server attempting to contact its administration server in order to receive the latest configuration information and deployments. If contact cannot be made, the managed server won't start; without an administration server, the managed server cannot function.

- Next, you see an entry indicating that the server is starting as a managed server called `BibleCServerDev2` in the domain `mydomain`.

- After that, the cluster service attempts to start. If the server's IP address and multicast address match those expected by the administration server, the cluster service will start successfully.

- Finally, you see messages indicating that the cluster service is listening on the appointed IP addresses and ports and that the WebLogic managed server is up and running under its given name and domain. Success!

3. Return to the WebLogic Console on the administration server. Here, you can deploy a Web application to the cluster just as you would to a single WebLogic Server instance. But first, it might be wise to verify that the administration server is aware of the cluster nodes. To do so, choose *<Domain>* ➪ Clusters and click the cluster name. On the right side of the display, click the Monitoring tab. It should look something like Figure 24-14. Click the Monitor server participation in this cluster link. Figure 24-15 shows the display for the nodes in our cluster. An indication that the server has a status of RUNNING means that it is both up and running, and the administration server is indeed aware of its existence on the network.

4. To deploy a Web application to the cluster, you can either install and deploy a new application (following the steps given in Chapter 11) or you can redeploy an existing application. Because BibleServlets is already deployed on our administration server, we'll perform the latter operation by choosing *<Domain>* ➪ Deployments ➪ Web Applications ➪ BibleServlets and then clicking the Targets tab. BibleServlets is already deployed to the administration server.

> We remove admin from the Chosen list and then click Apply. At this point, this Web application is not deployed to any server nor to any cluster. It's just configured, sitting around waiting to be deployed.

> Next, click the Clusters tab and move BibleClusterDev from the Available list to the Chosen list, similar to that shown in Figure 24-25. Click Apply.

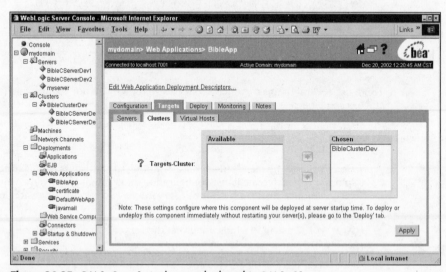

Figure 24-25: BibleServlets is now deployed to BibleCluster

When you click Apply, WebLogic Server copies the Web application (either its exploded directory format or its `.war` file, depending on what you installed) to every server in the cluster. It also sets up the runtime infrastructure to support clustered execution of the application. Your servers will chug along for a few moments while this happens.

5. The final step is to configure session replication for the application. Because `BibleServlets`'s execution relies heavily on session management, it's a good idea to configure the cluster to replicate session state, so that if one server fails, another server can pick up the user's session data. To better understand what we mean, imagine a shopping cart application that stores the user's purchases in the session. If the clustered server maintaining the session fails, the user is automatically routed to another server in the cluster; but without session replication, the contents of their shopping cart are lost. Session replication prevents this malady.

   Session state is maintained by a *primary cluster node,* which is the node to which the user initially connected. It is replicated to a *secondary node,* which is either the next node in round-robin sequence or the highest-ranked node as determined by the replication groups in effect for the cluster. (For more information about configuring replication groups, see the WebLogic documentation.)

   In order to replicate session state, you must somehow persist the state so it is available to the secondary node in case the primary node fails. WebLogic Server provides five types of persistence for session state: *none, memory-based, file-based, JDBC-based,* and *cookie-based.* In this example, we will configure memory-based persistence.

Note
We will discuss the pros and cons of the various persistence types in the "Session State Persistence Strategies" section later in this chapter.

   You specify the type of persistence you want in the `weblogic.xml` deployment descriptor for the application. You can use the WebLogic Console to make this change. To configure in-memory replication for `BibleServlets`, choose *<Domain>* ⇨ Deployments ⇨ Web Applications ⇨ BibleServlets and then click Edit Web Application Descriptor on the right side of the screen. In the secondary browser that appears, choose Web Descriptor ⇨ WebApp Ext ⇨ Session Descriptor. On the right side of the screen, use the drop-down menu to set Persistent Store Type to `replicated` and then click Apply. Figure 24-26 shows the resulting display.

Caution
Don't be fooled into selecting `memory` if you want in-memory replication — the correct choice is `replicated`. Selecting `memory` is equivalent to selecting `none` — the user's session is maintained on the node they are interacting with, but it is not persisted in any way, so it cannot be picked up by other nodes if the user's node fails.

6. Stop and restart the administration server and the cluster nodes (this is good practice any time you change a deployment descriptor for a Web application or an EJB component).

Figure 24-26: Configuring in-memory session state persistence for `BibleServlets`

Testing a Clustered Web Application

With the cluster up and running again, it's time to test the application by bringing it up in a Web browser. On our system, which has no DNS, we must navigate to the IP address and port of our proxy server. The full URL to `BibleServlets` on our system is

```
http://192.168.0.3:7001/BibleServlets
```

This URL brings up the home page for `BibleServlets`, as shown in Figure 24-27. We have great confidence that our proxy server and cluster are working. Why? `BibleServlets` is not physically deployed to our proxy server, so the request must have been forwarded to one of the servers in our cluster. Pretty cool, huh?

Figure 24-27: Navigating to the clustered version of `BibleServlets`

We tested this application by connecting two users and one administrator and then we observed the application's behavior when we brought down and restarted nodes in the cluster. The results are enlightening, especially if you've never worked with clusters before.

First, we found a bug in the `BibleServlets` code that prevented it from working properly in a clustered environment. The problem was that user sessions were being created and maintained by `ApplicationServlet`, but changes in session state weren't being picked up by `AdminServlet`. In the application, this problem was reflected by individual users' pages properly showing which page they were on, but the administrator's page always showing that the user was on page 1. Why on earth would this happen?

Recall that `ApplicationServlet` tracks session state in a `Hashtable`, which it stores in the `HttpSession`. In our code, we were updating the `Hashtable` with the new page number every time the user switched pages, but we weren't updating the session with a call to `setAttribute()` after making these changes. This works fine in a single-server application, but it fails in a cluster because WebLogic's session replication engine has no way of knowing that we changed the `Hashtable`, and therefore the changes don't get replicated. To fix this, simply be sure to call `setAttribute()` after every change to the session; it will trigger replication of the session data to the other nodes.

The bold text in Listing 24-1 shows additions we made to the body of `ApplicationServlet` to fix this bug. For good measure, we added calls to `setAttribute()` for the servlet context as well.

Listing 24-1: **Fixing** `ApplicationServlet` **so it works in the cluster**

```
// Returning user. Retrieve their state from the session.
sessionInfo = (Hashtable)
  session.getAttribute("sessionInfo");
Integer pageNumber = (Integer)sessionInfo.get("pageNumber");
int nextPage = pageNumber.intValue();
pageNumber = null;
// Read the query string to determine the user's desired
// action. Update their state in the session accordingly.
if (request.getParameter("action").equals("next")) {
  // Go to the next page. Wrap around to the
  // first page after passing the last page.
  nextPage++;
  if (nextPage > LAST_PAGE) {
    nextPage = FIRST_PAGE;
  }
  sessionInfo.put("pageNumber", new Integer(nextPage));
  session.setAttribute("sessionInfo", sessionInfo);
  ctx.setAttribute("session_" + userName, sessionInfo);
} else if (request.getParameter("action").equals("previous")) {
  // Go to the previous page. Wrap around to the last page
  // after passing the first page.
  nextPage--;
  if (nextPage < FIRST_PAGE) {
    nextPage = LAST_PAGE;
  }
```

Continued

Listing 24-1 *(continued)*

```
  sessionInfo.put("pageNumber", new Integer(nextPage));
  session.setAttribute("sessionInfo", sessionInfo);
  ctx.setAttribute("session_" + userName, sessionInfo);
} else if (request.getParameter("action").equals("logoff")) {
  ...
}
```

With these changes in place, we tested the cluster by executing various sequences of steps. These steps involved invoking servlets from multiple clients while stopping and restarting the two nodes in the cluster. Note that the `HttpClusterServlet` and the WebLogic proxy plug-ins always load-balance HTTP sessions by using the round-robin algorithm, with cluster nodes being served in the order in which they join the cluster. `BibleCServerDev1` joined our cluster first (because we started it first). With that in mind, here is what happens and why:

1. User A logs into `BibleServlets` and is proxied to `BibleCServerDev1`.

2. User B logs into `BibleServlets` and is proxied to `BibleCServerDev2`.

3. Administrator A logs into `BibleServlets` and is proxied to `BibleCServerDev1`. The only active session showing in the administrator's window is that of user A. But what about user B? Recall that `AdminServlet` uses the servlet context to display this information. Each node in the cluster has its own servlet context, separate from the others, which is why administrator A cannot "see" user B.

4. `BibleCServerDev2` goes down when we shut down its WebLogic instance. User B, however, continues to use the application normally because the cluster service transparently fails them over to `BibleCServerDev1`.

5. Administrator A refreshes the screen, and now both users appear! This is because when `BibleCServerDev2` fails, the cluster service merges its servlet context with that of `BibleCServerDev1`. It is able to do this because the servlet contexts are replicated along with the sessions—they're just not combined unless a server fails.

We continued to experiment by restarting `BibleCServerDev2` and stopping `BibleCServerDev1`, and then restarting `BibleCServerDev1` and stopping `BibleCServerDev2`. As expected, our three users were able to continue their sessions without interruption, and their session states were accurately preserved. This is the power of clustering.

Session State Persistence Strategies

As mentioned earlier, HTTP session state (and also session state for stateful session EJBs) can be persisted in five ways:

✦ **None:** No persistence

✦ **Memory-based:** Session state is maintained in active memory and replicated to in-memory caches on secondary replication nodes

✦ **File-based:** Session state is maintained in disk files that are stored in shared directories accessible to all nodes in the cluster

✦ **JDBC-based:** Session state is maintained in a JDBC-compliant database that is accessed via an associated connection pool created on each node of the cluster

✦ **Cookie-based:** Session state is maintained in client-side cookies

Each persistence type comes with its own trade-offs in terms of reliability and performance. With no persistence, reliability is zero but performance is spectacular because the overhead of persisting data is completely eliminated. Memory-based replication has excellent performance and good reliability, although session state can't survive server restarts or power outages. File-based and JDBC-based replication have mediocre performance but exceptional reliability because changes to session state are immediately written to disk. Cookie-based replication works okay if users have cookies enabled, but it's useless if they don't.

 Tip   We suggest that you plug your cluster nodes into UPSs and go with memory-based replication. If you're really paranoid, or if your session data is really important enough to warrant the significant performance hit, go with JDBC-based replication. We wouldn't bother with any of the other choices for production systems.

Clusters and J2EE Services

WebLogic clusters affect the way certain J2EE services behave, and you must take this into account if your clustered applications use these services. In this section, we give you an overview of clustering's impact on JNDI, JDBC, and JMS.

Cluster-wide JNDI tree

Recall that the JNDI tree enables you to look up objects and services that reside on a WebLogic server instance. A cluster-wide JNDI tree provides this capability as well, but it lists objects and services that reside on all nodes of a WebLogic cluster.

As you might imagine, WebLogic manages cluster-wide JNDI trees somewhat differently from single-server trees. Each node in a cluster builds and maintains its own local copy of the cluster-wide tree. When the node boots or if a service is added to the node while it is running, it first binds its services to its local copy of the tree. Then it uses IP multicast to broadcast availability of its clustered services to the other nodes in the cluster, and they add its services to their local copies of the tree. Meanwhile, the newly booted node receives notifications of services residing on the other nodes' trees, and it adds them to its local copy of the tree. The net effect is that all servers in the cluster maintain synchronized copies of the cluster-wide JNDI tree.

Of course, there are exceptions and caveats regarding the behavior of the cluster-wide JNDI tree, and you should study the WebLogic documentation to gain a better understanding of what they are.

Load balancing JDBC connections

WebLogic clusters do not provide failover support for JDBC connections, but you can configure a cluster to provide limited load balancing support for JDBC connection pools. To configure a cluster this way, simply create identically named JDBC datasources on each node, but
have the datasources point to different connection pools. Figure 24-28 shows such an
arrangement.

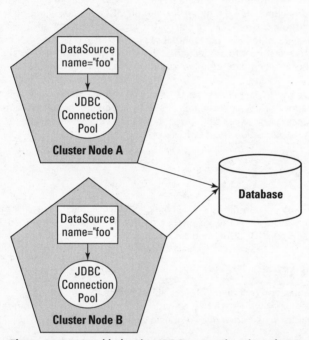

Figure 24-28: Load balancing JDBC connections in a cluster

As with unclustered JDBC, however, WebLogic has no way of knowing whether a pool has
available connections or not, so your code will get an exception if it's unlucky enough to execute on a node whose connection pool has run out of connections.

Load balancing JMS connection factories

Clustering support for JMS is similar to that for JDBC. Failover support is not provided for
queues and topics because they are pinned to specific WebLogic instances. But connection
factories pointing to the same queues and topics can be deployed on multiple cluster nodes,
allowing you to load balance access to the queues and topics. Figure 24-29 illustrates one way
to do this.

The problem with this approach is that cluster node C becomes a single point of failure; if it
goes down, no messages can be delivered. A better option is to create a JMS server on each
cluster node, create identical copies of the queues and topics on each node, and then have
the connection factory target the cluster. Figure 24-30 shows this arrangement.

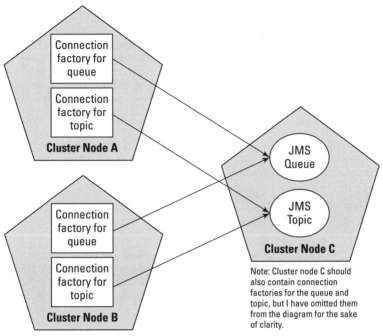

Figure 24-29: Load balancing JMS connection factories

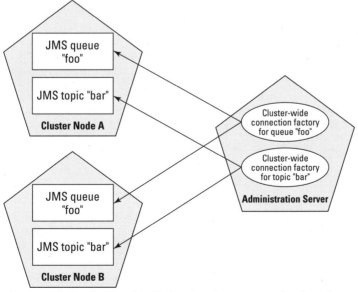

Figure 24-30: Redundant load balancing of JMS connection factories

Clustering of RMI Objects and EJBs

RMI objects and EJBs can be deployed to clusters, and WebLogic Server supports their run-time invocation through the use of *replica-aware stubs*. To calling clients, replica-aware stubs look the same as normal stubs, but they have embedded within them logic for finding all the instances of the objects they represent within the cluster and also for implementing the load balancing strategy that is being used by the cluster. Replica-aware stubs also provide failover capability by automatically rerouting calls to different object instances when runtime failures occur.

Generating replica-aware stubs for RMI objects is accomplished by invoking the RMI compiler (rmic) with the appropriate command-line options. For EJBs, the EJB compiler (ejbc) does this for you automatically if you send it a bean whose deployment descriptor specifies that it is cluster-aware.

When you invoke RMI objects, replica-aware stubs are returned for the local and remote interfaces, which allow load balancing and failover to occur for object lookups *and* method invocations.

For EJBs, replica-aware stubs are returned for all EJBHome interfaces. This provides load balancing and failover for EJB lookups. Whether you receive replica-aware stubs for EJBObject interfaces depends on the type of the bean. Replica-aware stubs are always returned for the EJBObject interfaces of stateless session beans, providing load balancing and failover for bean method invocations. The same applies for stateful session beans, but only if you specify that stateful session replication should be used for the bean. If not, the stub you receive is pinned to whatever bean instance was returned by the EJBHome.

Note   The load-balancing algorithm used for stateful EJB session replication is the same one used for HTTP session replication; primary session state is maintained on the node the client connected to, and secondary state on some other node, as determined by the round-robin algorithm or the replication groups in effect. This means that the load-balancing logic embedded in replica-aware stubs for stateful session EJBs is different from that in the stubs for stateless session EJBs, which implements the load-balancing algorithm assigned to the cluster.

For entity EJBs, the type of EJBObject stub you receive depends on whether the bean is read-only or read/write. If the bean is read-only, you will always receive a replica-aware stub. This stub provides load balancing for method calls, but it does not provide failover capability. Why not? Because entity EJBs are pinned to JDBC connections, for which there is no failover support. For the same reason, EJBObject stubs returned for read/write beans are always pinned to a specific bean instance.

Summary

WebLogic clusters are an essential tool for building scalable, fault-tolerant J2EE applications. Although the concepts behind clusters are simple, the mechanics of setting up even a simple cluster are fairly complex, especially when you include the effort required to properly deploy applications in a clustered environment.

In this chapter we set up both development-style clusters (all nodes running on a single piece of hardware) and production-style clusters (nodes running on independent hardware, with network channels and overrides), giving us a broad background on cluster configuration and new WebLogic 7.0 features.

Clustering requires application designers and developers to rethink everything, from HTTP session management to EJB deployment, and all the J2EE services in between. But the sturdiness of clustered applications, along with the peace of mind they offer to overworked developers, makes the effort more than worthwhile.

We hope you made the effort to set up your own clusters while you were reading this chapter. If you did so (and if you succeeded!), you'll have a major advantage when it comes time to build bigger, more complex clusters in your production environment.

✦   ✦   ✦

Security Administration in WebLogic

◆ ◆ ◆ ◆

In This Chapter

Configuring the default
realm

Configuring other
providers

Managing security
realms

Other security
configuration

◆ ◆ ◆ ◆

Administration is a comprehensive topic in WebLogic, but we put
security administration into its own chapter because of its complexity. WebLogic Server 7.0 introduces a comprehensive new security model, and we take you step by step through administering it in
this chapter.

In the following sections, we cover configuring the default WebLogic
security providers as well as third-party LDAP providers. We also discuss adding and removing realms, enabling trust between domains,
setting up SSL (Secure Sockets Layer), and setting up connection
filters.

Cross-Reference Before reading this chapter, you should have read Chapter 21.
That will give you the big picture of the theory behind why
WebLogic's security is set up the way it is. In this chapter, we have
room only for the *how*, not the *why*.

Cross-Reference For information on setting up security for a particular application,
see Chapter 22. For information on creating your own security
providers, see Chapter 21.

Configuring the Default Realm

WebLogic comes with a complete security implementation out of the
box. Creating a new domain with the Domain Configuration Wizard
(see Chapter 4) results in the creation of a default security realm,
which is called `myrealm`. In this default realm, one security provider
is automatically created for each provider type except auditing.

Note Many security configuration changes require a reboot of the
WebLogic Server instance. If you made a change and it's not working as expected, try rebooting the server to see if it works.
Remember that the configuration options that require a reboot
should have a yellow triangle to the left of their property name in
the Console as a reminder to reboot.

Note

If you find that you have somehow misconfigured the security system so that it won't allow you to boot WebLogic, use the following command-line argument to revert to the last security configuration:

```
-Dweblogic.safeCommoBoot=true
```

As WebLogic boots, you may get a notice from the server that the command-line parameter is not understood, but it will work nonetheless.

To work with the myrealm default realm, we need to go into the WebLogic Server Console and make all our configuration changes there. To view the default realm, follow these steps:

1. Open the WebLogic Server Console.

2. Click the plus symbol next to the Security tree element on the left; then open the Realms and myrealm nodes and all their children.

3. Click on Realms and the panel that is displayed should appear similar to that shown in Figure 25-1.

As you can see, one default provider has been created for each provider type with the exception of an auditing provider.

Figure 25-1: The default myrealm security realm in the Console

General configuration

If you click myrealm, you'll see a panel with four tabs. The first tab, General, is shown in Figure 25-2. It has the following attributes:

✦ **Name:** The name of this realm, which cannot be changed, is specified when creating a new realm, as we discuss later in this chapter.

✦ **Ignore Security Data in Deployment Descriptors:** If this option is selected, any user and group security information that's specified in WAR, JAR, EAR, or RAR deployment descriptors is ignored. Use this setting if you plan to perform all security configuration and administration from the Console, and if you want to ignore and override any configuration options specified in your applications. Don't change this option willy-nilly because it can delete configuration information. See the following site for more details:

http://e-docs.bea.com/wls/docs70//secwlres/wlres.html#1190721

✦ **Use Deprecated WebResource:** Starting with service pack 1, securing an application by using a WebResource is deprecated. You should secure against a URLResource instead. However, if you have already written or obtained a security service provider that implements this functionality, you'll need to enable this option.

Figure 25-2: The General tab in realm configuration

User lockout configuration

Clicking on the User Lockout tab brings up the panel shown in Figure 25-3. The top half of this window has a list of options, whereas the bottom half is a status display. The options are as follows:

✦ **Lockout Enabled:** Select this option to lock users out if any of the other configuration options have been met.

✦ **Lockout Threshold:** The number of times within a specified period that a user can attempt to log in incorrectly before being locked out. If set to the default value of 5, the user will be locked out on the sixth try (within the time frame defined in Lockout Reset Duration, following) with an invalid login.

✦ **Lockout Duration:** The number of minutes that a user will be locked out of his or her account after hitting the threshold and being locked out. Setting this value to 0 means that the user will not actually be locked out, but the status will still be tracked and shown in the status region at the bottom of this panel.

✦ **Lockout Reset Duration:** The number of minutes within which a user must enter consecutive incorrect login credentials before being locked out. This is used in conjunction with Lockout Threshold to define when users get locked out.

✦ **Lockout Cache Size:** The number of incorrect login attempts for a single user that the server puts in a cache.

✦ **Lockout GCThreshold:** The total number (for all users) of incorrect login attempts that the server keeps in its cache. When this number is reached, garbage collection is performed on any users who have actually been locked out. Basically, each failed login is added to the cache, and when the user is locked out, those failed logins are kept in the cache until this number of cache elements is reached.

The statuses listed at the bottom of the panel shown in Figure 25-3 show statistics on the number of lockouts. These are fairly obvious, so we'll skip to the next topic.

Figure 25-3: The User Lockout tab with options and status regions

Configuring realm contents

Clicking the Contents tab brings up the panel shown in Figure 25-4. This allows you to configure users, groups, and roles for this realm, as described in the following sections.

> **Note**   Configuring users and groups here is applicable only if you're using the default (WebLogic) authenticator that uses the embedded LDAP server. If you configure your own external LDAP server, as described later in this chapter, use that security provider's configuration tools to create and update users and groups.

Users

Click the Manage Users within this Realm link on the right (see Figure 25-4) or click the Users node under the realm name on the left. This will bring you to a panel that should look like Figure 25-5. This figure shows the system administrator you defined when you created this domain (in our case, wlsadmin) as well as the users we created (Joe, Lou, Karen) in Chapter 11.

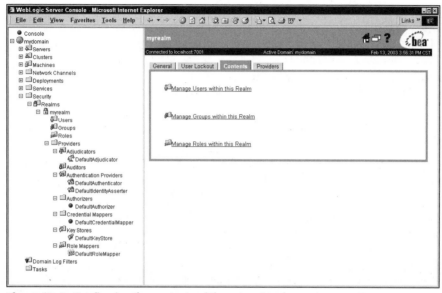

Figure 25-4: Configuring the contents of the current realm

Figure 25-5: Configuring users for the embedded LDAP server

To view or edit a user, click his or her name. To delete a user, click the trashcan icon at the right. If a user has been locked out because of too many invalid login attempts, a link will appear in the locked column. To unlock the user, click the link and then click Unlock.

As you add more and more users, you may want to filter the list of users displayed. Just enter a pattern with one or more asterisk wildcards and then click the Filter button. The filter works on the User field, not the Description field. In addition, one or more asterisks can be placed in the filter field; an asterisk matches zero or more characters. For example, to list only the users with a username that begins with "L," enter L* and click Filter. To show users that have an "a" anywhere in their name, enter *a*. To show users that end in "n," enter *n.

To show all users, clear out the text entry field so it is blank and then click Filter. Filtering is case-insensitive, so filtering by K* and k* yields the same results.

To create a new user, click the Configure a New User link. We filled out the pane as shown in Figure 25-6 and clicked Apply. The values you can modify are as follows:

✦ **Name:** Enter the username. Choose carefully because this name can never be changed. Users can be added and deleted, but their names cannot be modified.

✦ **Description:** Enter a description, such as the user's full name or the purpose for the user if it isn't a person. Descriptions can be changed at any time.

✦ **Password:** Enter the password for the user. The password length is enforced via the rules set up at the panel shown in <domain name> ⇨ Security ⇨ Passwords, as described in Chapter 23.

✦ **Confirm Password:** Re-enter the password to confirm it.

The pane shown in Figure 25-7 appears. This is the same pane that would appear if you clicked a user to edit it. You can edit the description, or click Change next to the Password field to change the password. You cannot edit a username.

Click the Groups tab to add or remove groups that the user will be in, as shown in Figure 25-8. Select one or more groups in the Possible Groups list, click the right arrow to move them to the Current Groups list, and click Apply. You can remove groups by selecting one or more groups in the Current Groups, clicking the left arrow button, and clicking Apply.

Caution   For the default (WebLogic) authenticator, usernames are case-insensitive. If you try to create a user named `karen` and a user named `Karen`, you will get an exception. Usernames must be unique, regardless of case/capitalization.

Groups

Click the Manage Groups within this Realm link on the right of Figure 25-4, or click the Groups node under the realm name on the left. This will display a panel that should look like Figure 25-9. This figure shows the groups that were populated when you created this domain with the Domain Configuration Wizard.

Figure 25-6: Create a new user

Figure 25-7: Edit a user

Figure 25-8: Change a user's groups

Figure 25-9: Configuring groups for the embedded LDAP server

To view or edit a group, click its name. To delete a group, click the trashcan icon at the right.

As you add more and more groups, you may want to filter the list of groups displayed. Use the same filter rules as explained in the previous section on filtering users.

To create a new group, click the Configure a New Group link. We filled out the pane as shown in Figure 25-10 and clicked Apply. The values you can modify are the following:

✦ **Name:** Enter the Group name. Choose carefully because this can never be changed. Groups can be added and deleted, but their names cannot be modified.

✦ **Description:** Enter a description, such as the purpose for the group. Descriptions can be changed at any time.

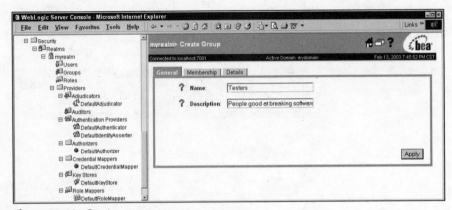

Figure 25-10: Create a new group

Caution   We had no trouble creating group names with spaces in them, but did have difficulty adding them to roles. We recommend you use group names without spaces.

Next the pane shown in Figure 25-11 appears. This is the same pane that would appear if you clicked on a group to edit it. You can edit the description; you cannot edit a group name.

Click the Membership tab to add or remove groups that the group will be in; groups can be nested within other groups, as is shown in Figure 25-12. Select one or more groups in the Possible Groups list, click the right arrow to move them to the Current Groups list, and click Apply. You can remove groups by selecting one or more groups in the Current Groups, clicking the left arrow button, and clicking Apply.

Notice that there is no good way to add a bunch of users to a group. You have to go to each user and add it to each group. You can't choose a group and then add multiple users at once. To do something like that, you can use an external tool to directly access WebLogic's internal LDAP server. We explain how to do that later in this chapter.

Note   If you're using the default (WebLogic) security service providers, BEA recommends that you use roles instead of groups because roles are more efficient.

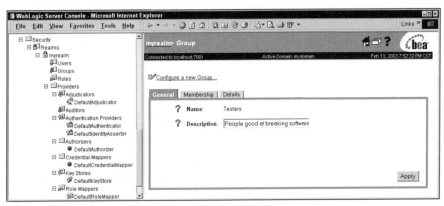

Figure 25-11: Edit a group

Figure 25-12: Change a group's groups

Roles

Click the Manage Roles within this Realm link on the right of Figure 25-4 or click the Roles node under the realm name on the left. This will display a panel, showing the roles that were populated when you created this domain with the Domain Configuration Wizard (see Figure 25-13).

> **Note**
>
> If you click the Manage Roles within this Realm link (shown in Figure 25-4), you'll get a list with three extra `admin` roles. These extra roles do not show up if you click the Roles node under the realm name in the tree on the left. Why the different results? What's happening is that two different kinds of roles can be configured. Clicking the Roles node shows only global roles, whereas clicking the Manage Roles within this Realm link shows both global and scoped roles.

This panel is where you create *global* roles; that is, roles that apply to an entire resource (Web application, EJB, and so on). To create a *scoped* role—one that applies to a sub-resource such as an EJB method or a URL pattern—see Chapter 22.

Figure 25-13: Configuring roles

Default global roles

The default global rules that are already there are preconfigured, they are not just samples. Table 25-1 shows a list of the roles and what their permissions are.

Table 25-1: Default Global Rules

Role	View Server Config	View Server Encrypted Attributes	Modify Server Config	Start, Resume, and Stop Servers	Deploy Apps and Components; Edit Deployment Descriptors
everyone					
Monitor	X				
Operator	X			X	
Deployer	X				X
Admin	X	X	X	X	X

Editing Roles

To view or edit a role, click its name. To delete a role, click the trashcan icon at the right.

There is no way to filter the list of roles displayed.

To create a new role, click the Configure a New Role link. We filled out the pane as shown in Figure 25-14 and clicked Apply. The only value you can modify is Name, in which you can enter the role name. Choose carefully because this name can never be changed. Roles can be added and deleted, but their names cannot be modified.

Figure 25-14: Create a new role

We'll call this role Day Shift. Click Apply and the pane shown in Figure 25-15 appears. This is the same pane that would appear if you clicked on a role to edit it. You cannot edit the role name.

Figure 25-15: Edit a role

Adding Conditions

Click the Conditions tab to add or remove conditions that define which users will end up in the role at any given instant of time. This panel is shown in Figure 25-16. You can add users and groups to a role, as well as define a time period in which the role is active. You can add multiple entries and combine them with and or or logic.

Note   You cannot define a role simply with a time constraint. You must also define one or more users or groups if you have a time constraint. Conversely, if you just want to define users and/or groups, you do not need a time constraint.

Figure 25-16: Change a role's conditions

We'll define the conditions for our sample role named Day Shift for our fictitious manufacturing company's assembly-line workers. For our role, let's add some users and groups and define a time period in which they can be active. In plain English, let's say that we want to have members of the Assembly group have access during business hours, but not during lunch. (We could also create a role called Night Shift that would contain the same group, but different allowable times, for example.)

We went ahead and created a new group named AssemblersShift1 and added some users to it (because we already explained how to create users and groups, we won't show you the screen-by-screen detail of the way we did that). Then we click the Roles node in the domain tree, click on the Day Shift role to edit it, and click the Conditions tab (now we're back to Figure 25-16). Next, it's time to define which groups go into this role and during what time period it will be valid.

On the pane shown in the Conditions tab, click Caller is a Member of the Group under Role Condition and then click Add. This brings up a new window that allows you to specify the group(s) that will comprise this role. We entered the name of our group, AssemblersShift1, in the field marked Enter Group Name and then clicked Add. The result is shown in Figure 25-17.

Caution   Be careful when typing the names of the groups that you are adding here. You don't get a list of groups to add; instead, you have to type the name from memory. Unfortunately, WebLogic does no checking and you will receive no warning if the group does not exist. We suggest that you copy the name from the Groups panel and paste it here so there's no problem with misspellings or typos.

Next, we added another group, TestersShift1, and clicked Add again. The result is shown in Figure 25-18.

Figure 25-17: Group-based roles are added in this window

Figure 25-18: Multiple group-based roles in a single window

Note that when you click various items in the Groups list, different buttons become enabled and disabled:

✦ When multiple groups are listed, you can click a group name and then click Move Up or Move Down to change its position in the list.

✦ Clicking a group enables the Remove button. Clicking this button will remove this condition from the list.

✦ Clicking a logical operator — the words or or and in the list — enables the Change button. Clicking this button will change it to the alternate logical operator.

Caution   If you click Caller is a Member of the Group and then click the Change button, the text will be changed to the word null. WebLogic will allow you to save this, and it will be propagated to the Conditions tab. We're not sure if this is a good thing or not, though, so we recommend that you not click the Change button for the first item in the Groups list.

Click the OK button to save your changes, which brings you back to the role's Conditions tab, as shown in Figure 25-19. So far, this is nothing that you can't already do with groups alone. But the power of roles is that they can be limited by business rules. In this version of WebLogic, BEA provides time-based rules. Because the WebLogic security provider APIs are open and published, you could create your own business rules with other kinds of logic. This is not a trivial undertaking, via the role-mapping provider, so you might want to wait for third-party providers to integrate into the new security model.

Figure 25-19: Our role's Conditions tab with our new group conditions

For now, we'll add time-based rules that limit our assembler users to a regular time frame. This will be 7:30 a.m. to 5:30 p.m., not including lunch. We do this by clicking the item Hours of Access Are Between in the Role Condition list and clicking the Add button. We changed the hours, as shown in Figure 25-20. Notice that time-based rules allow only one rule per dialog box (unlike group-based rules, in which we could add multiple groups within a single window). So we need to click OK to add it to our Conditions tab.

Figure 25-20: Time-based rules are added in this window

We need to click our Add button again and add a time limitation for 1:30 – 5:30 p.m. Then we click OK again and we are back at the Conditions tab with all our rules in place, as shown in Figure 25-21.

Figure 25-21: The role's Condition tab with multiple rules

If you look carefully at the rules, however, they don't make sense. Access to a resource based on this rule would always fail because the two time-based requirements are and-ed together. Well, it can never be 10:30 a.m. and 2:25 p.m. at the same time and in the same location — not in our universe, anyway. What we really want the rule to say is that access is allowed if it's in the morning *or* if it's in the afternoon. Just as we can change the elements in the list in the group conditions dialog box (refer to Figure 25-18), we can do that here as well. The elements that can be changed are the following:

✦ Click a group definition: You can click Move Up or Move Down or you can click Edit to edit the definition. If one or more groups are already defined, going up to the Role Condition list and clicking the Add button has the same effect as clicking Edit on a Role Statement. That is, the groups window will come up and it will be prepopulated with the existing group definition.

✦ Click a logical operand and then click the Change button to reverse its value.

✦ Click a time-based rule and click the Move Up or Move Down buttons to change its position. You can also click Edit to bring up the Time Constraint definition window.

Caution If you try to edit a time-based rule, the editor window that comes up defaults to a start time of 8 a.m. and an end time of 7 p.m., regardless of the values you originally entered. Don't go in there and change only the start or end time and think that it will remember your original values because it won't remember them.

Click the list item and Hours of Access Are Between and then click the Change button. The and will change to or, which changes the logic to what we wanted it to be. Click Apply to save your changes.

We now have a complex role based on group- and time-based information. This is a powerful technique that you should try to take advantage of if it fits your company's business.

Configuring the WebLogic default security providers

In addition to content—users, groups, and roles—WebLogic security has to deal with providers—which applications take care of authentication, authorization, and other security components. When you create a new domain, the Domain Creation Wizard automatically populates your new domain with a default realm that has default providers. Those providers all come with WebLogic, and most use the built-in LDAP server. We'll spend some time configuring the default providers to show you what flexibility you have, even just with the default providers.

Cross-Reference   For more information on how WebLogic security providers function, and how you can extend them, see Chapter 21.

Note   Most changes to security providers require a reboot of the WebLogic Server for the changes to take effect.

DefaultAdjudicator

To bring up the pane that allows you to edit the configuration for the DefaultAdjudicator, open the Security node in the WebLogic Console; then choose Realms ⇨ myrealm ⇨ Providers ⇨ Adjudication and click on the DefaultAdjudicator node (see Figure 25-22).

Figure 25-22: Configuring the DefaultAdjudicator

The only option is Require Unanimous Permit. If this is checked, all configured authorizers must return PERMIT if the authorization is to succeed; if even one of them returns ABSTAIN, the authorization fails. If this is unchecked, one or more ABSTAINs can be returned and they will not prevent a successful authorization. Whether this option is checked or not, if even one authorization returns DENY, the entire authorization fails.

Cross-Reference   For more information on the role of adjudication providers; authorization providers; and the PERMIT, DENY, and ABSTAIN results, see Chapter 21.

Auditors

By default, no auditors are configured (probably for performance reasons). That's not to say that you shouldn't use auditors; instead, you should consider carefully when you need them and how much detail you need to have in your audit trail. This is specific to your business, or even to a department in your business. A bank, health insurer, or medical device manufacturer might need very different auditing from a widget manufacturer. Even though an auditor is not configured by default, let's go ahead and configure one so you can see what options are available for the default auditing provider.

In the domain tree on the left of the Console, click the Auditors node and then click the Configure a New Auditor link. The resulting pane is shown in Figure 25-23. Enter a name, but choose carefully; you cannot modify this name later. You'll need to delete and re-create an auditor if you want one with a different name. The only real option you have is Severity. You can set it to any of the values shown in Figure 25-23. Any event with the chosen severity or a higher severity will be logged to `<WL_HOME>\<domain name>\DefaultAuditRecorder.log`. Click Apply to save your changes.

Figure 25-23: Configuring a new default auditor

Authentication providers

In the Security node in the Console (under Authentication Providers), WebLogic installs two default providers: the DefaultAuthenticator and the DefaultIdentityAsserter.

DefaultAuthenticator

The DefaultAuthenticator uses the embedded LDAP server in WebLogic to store users, groups, and roles. (We defined these users, groups, and roles earlier in this chapter.) Keep in mind that alternative providers may not (and probably don't) use the embedded LDAP server, and thus do not use the users, groups, and roles that are set up under the `myrealm` node in the WebLogic Console.

Cross-Reference
You can access the embedded LDAP server by using any general LDAP directory tool. The parameters needed to configure your LDAP browser/editor are detailed in Chapter 21.

If you click the DefaultAuthenticator node in the Console, you'll see the configuration panel shown in Figure 25-24. There are two options that you can modify:

✦ **Minimum Password Length:** The minimum number of characters needed for creating a new password.

✦ **Control Flag:** A value of OPTIONAL, SUFFICIENT, REQUISITE, or REQUIRED. These values relate how this authenticator's results are used in conjunction with additional authenticators' results.

- OPTIONAL means that this authenticator may or may not succeed, but control will pass on to the next authenticator in any case; in other words, this authenticator by itself will not make or break authentication if other authenticators are configured and in the chain.

- SUFFICIENT means that no other authenticators are checked; if this authentication check succeeds, control immediately returns and login is allowed.

- REQUISITE means that this authenticator must succeed for this login attempt. If it succeeds, control passes to the next authenticator; if it fails, however, control passes back to the application and login does not proceed.

- REQUIRED means that this authenticator must succeed for this login attempt; other authenticators are checked whether this one passes or not. This means that if authentication fails for this provider and then moves on to additional authentication providers, authentication will ultimately fail, regardless of what the other authenticators return.

Figure 25-24: Configuring the DefaultAuthenticator

DefaultIdentityAsserter

The DefaultIdentityAsserter supports identity assertion using X509 certificates and Common Secure Interoperability version 2 (CSIv2). Multiple Identity Assertion providers can be configured in a security realm, but none is required. Click the DefaultIdentityAsserter node in the WebLogic Console, and the configuration panel shown in Figure 25-25 appears.

Figure 25-25: Configuring the DefaultIdentityAsserter

There are three options you can configure:

✦ **User Name Mapper Class Name:** The name of the Java class that maps X509 digital certificates and X501 distinguished names to WebLogic usernames. This option is required
only if X509 is configured and active (see following).

✦ **Trusted Client Principals:** The list of trusted client principals to use in CSIv2 identity
assertion. An asterisk (*) can be used as a wildcard to specify that all principals are
trusted. If a client is not listed as a trusted client principal, the CSIv2 identity assertion
fails and the invoke is rejected.

✦ **Active Types:** Identity Assertion providers can support more than one token type, but
only one token type can be active at a given time for each Identity Assertion provider.
So this should probably be called Active Type, rather than Active Types. The supported types that you can choose from are listed directly above this field.

DefaultAuthorizer

Authorizers are responsible for authorizing access to a resource to a particular user. Clicking
its name in the Console's domain tree node results in the configuration panel shown in
Figure 25-26. You have only one option: Policy Deployment Enabled. If this is checked, policies can be applied to EJBs and Web applications.

**Cross-
Reference**   See Chapter 22 for information on policies.

Figure 25-26: Configuring the DefaultAuthorizer

DefaultCredentialMapper

Credential Mappers are used to map users to authentication and authorization credentials stored in a legacy resource. Click DefaultCredentialMapper in the Console's security realm to display the configuration panel shown in Figure 25-27. There is only one option to configure: Credential Mapping Deployment Enabled. This setting interacts with the Ignore Security Data in Deployment Descriptors setting on the realm (look at the configuration panel for myrealm, shown earlier in this chapter). If Credential Mapping Deployment Enabled is checked, security information from the weblogic-ra.xml deployment descriptor will overwrite any changes made in the Console whenever the application is redeployed unless Ignore Security Data in Deployment Descriptors is checked.

Figure 25-27: Configuring the DefaultCredentialMapper

DefaultKeyStore

This provider was introduced in WebLogic Server 7.0 and then deprecated in service pack 1, so we won't discuss it here. Suffice it to say that its purpose is to store keys from Certificate Authorities (CAs). For information on what these fields mean, if you insist on using them, click the question mark help icon in the WebLogic Console on the DefaultKeyStore's configuration panel (Figure 25-28).

Figure 25-28: Configuring the DefaultKeyStore

DefaultRoleMapper

Role Mapping Providers are optional; and zero, one, or more may be configured. If more than one is configured, the intersection of all role mappings is returned. Click on DefaultRoleMapper in the security realm in the WebLogic Console to display the panel shown in Figure 25-29. You have only one option: Role Deployment Enabled. This setting interacts with the Ignore Security Data in Deployment Descriptors setting on the realm (look at the configuration panel for myrealm, shown earlier in this chapter). If Role Deployment Enabled is checked, security information from the weblogic.xml and weblogic-ejb-jar.xml deployment descriptors will overwrite any changes made in the Console whenever the application is redeployed unless Ignore Security Data in Deployment Descriptors is checked.

Figure 25-29: Configuring the DefaultCredentialMapper

Configuring Other Providers

WebLogic allows you to configure multiple security providers and also allows you to use third-party or custom providers. (Custom providers are explained in Chapter 21.) In this section, we'll concentrate on non-WebLogic provider interfaces that come with WebLogic.

As of service pack 1 of WebLogic Server 7.0, only the authentication providers come with third-party interfaces. That's what we'll discuss in this section.

Cross-Reference   If you're interested in writing your own providers and generating MBeans, see Chapter 21.

Note   If you already configured the Administrators group in your LDAP server for some other reason, you can easily use any other group in your LDAP server for your WebLogic Server administrators. For example, create a group in your LDAP server named `WebLogicAdmins` and make sure you add your WebLogic administrators' usernames to this group. Then go into the WebLogic Console and edit the Admin role to include your `WebLogicAdmins` group.

To see which provider interfaces are available, click Authentication Providers under your security realm name in the domain tree in the WebLogic Console. The panel on the right should appear, as shown in Figure 25-30. Authentication provider interfaces are supplied for iPlanet (now Sun ONE), Active Directory, OpenLDAP, and Novell LDAP servers. BEA does not certify any particular LDAP servers, but any LDAP server that's compliant with v2 of the specification should work with WebLogic Server 7.0.

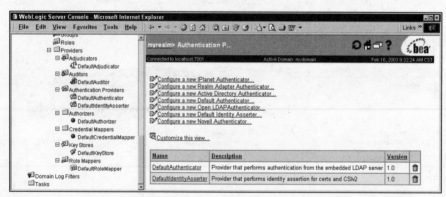

Figure 25-30: WebLogic and third-party authenticators supported out of the box

Note that the providers all currently have the same options, but the default values for those options differ based on the requirements of the LDAP server. For this reason, we'll cover the configuration options of just one LDAP source: iPlanet/Sun ONE.

Click the Configure a new iPlanet Authenticator, and you'll see what's shown in Figure 25-31. Your two configurable options are the following:

✦ **Name:** As we've seen with other parts of the security realm, make your decision carefully because you cannot change the name later.

✦ **Control Flag:** If there are multiple authenticators configured, this JAAS control flag determines how the authentication proceeds after the results of this authenticator's login attempts are returned. Its values are OPTIONAL, SUFFICIENT, REQUISITE, and REQUIRED (described previously in Default Authenticator). We set it to OPTIONAL because we haven't configured a user in iPlanet who is mapped to the Admin role. If we set it to REQUIRED and still didn't have a user defined for that role, we wouldn't be able to boot up WebLogic Server.

Figure 25-31: General options for the iPlanet LDAP server

Click the Create button to create the new authenticator. Click the iPlanet LDAP tab to configure how to connect to the LDAP server. The window shown in Figure 25-32 appears. You have the following options:

✦ **Host:** Enter the DNS host name or the numeric IP address of your LDAP server.

✦ **Port:** Enter the port number of the LDAP server, typically 389. (Do not enter the LDAP server's administration port, typically 16279.)

✦ **SSLEnabled:** Check this option if you have configured iPlanet to use secure communications.

✦ **Principal:** Enter the Distinguished Name (DN) of the LDAP user that WebLogic Server uses to connect to the LDAP server.

✦ **Credential:** Click the Change link to open up a window that allows you to change the password for the principal that you entered previously.

✦ **Cache Enabled:** Check this if you want WebLogic to cache requests to the LDAP server. If cache is enabled, the next two options are used.

✦ **Cache Size:** The size of the cache, in kilobytes, that WebLogic uses to communicate with the LDAP server.

✦ **Cache TTL:** The Time-to-Live (TTL) of the cache, in seconds.

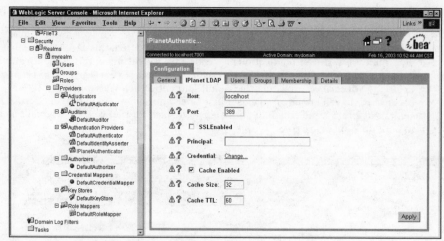

Figure 25-32: Configure your external LDAP server

Click Apply to save your changes. Then click the Users tab to configure how WebLogic gets user information from your LDAP server.

Note   You do not create or edit users and groups on the Users or Groups tabs here in the LDAP authenticator configuration. These tabs are used to configure how to get user and group information from the LDAP server. You also do not create or edit users or groups for an external LDAP server in your WebLogic realm's Users or Groups nodes in the domain tree. Instead, those nodes are used to configure users and groups for the embedded LDAP server within WebLogic itself. To configure users and groups in an external LDAP server such as iPlanet, you use the configuration tools that came with the LDAP server itself.

You'll see the window shown in Figure 25-33. The options are as follows:

✦ **User Object Class:** The name of the object class iPlanet uses to store users. WebLogic will create users using this object class.

✦ **User Name Attribute:** The name of the attribute on the LDAP user object class, specified previously, that contains the username. WebLogic will store and retrieve usernames from this attribute.

✦ **User Dynamic Group DNAttribute:** The name of the attribute on the user object class, specified previously, that specifies the distinguished names (DNs) of dynamic groups that a user belongs to. If nothing is specified, WebLogic can determine whether a user is a member of a dynamic group by looking at their URLs.

✦ **User Base DN:** The base distinguished name (DN) of the tree in the LDAP directory that contains users.

✦ **User Search Scope:** Specifies whether to search for users only at the current level or through the subtree.

✦ **User From Name Filter:** The LDAP search that's used to find a user, given a username. If you don't enter anything, a filter is generated by default.

✦ **All Users Filter:** The LDAP search that's used to find all users under the user base DN. If you don't enter anything, a filter is generated by default.

Click Apply to save your changes.

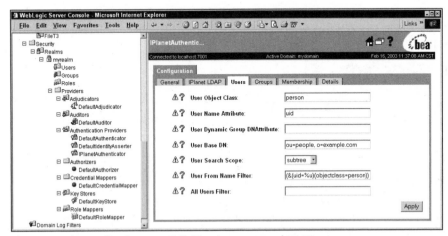

Figure 25-33: Configuring user definition in an external LDAP server

Click on the Groups tab to configure how WebLogic accesses group information on iPlanet (see Figure 25-34). Your options are the following:

✦ **Group Base DN:** Similar to the User Base DN on the previous screen, except that it's for group information.

✦ **Group Search Scope:** Similar to the User Search Scope on the previous screen, except that it's for group information.

✦ **Group From Name Filter:** Similar to the User From Name Filter on the previous screen, except that it's for group information.

✦ **All Groups Filter:** Similar to the All Users Filter on the previous screen, except that it's for group information.

✦ **Static Group Object Class:** The name of your LDAP server's object class that stores static group information.

✦ **Static Group Name Attribute:** The name of the attribute on the static group object class, specified previously, that stores the group's name.

Click Apply to save your changes.

Figure 25-34: Specifying group configuration information for an external LDAP server

Click the Membership tab to define how WebLogic uses membership information in iPlanet (users are members of groups, for example), as shown in Figure 25-35. The options available are the following:

✦ **Static Member DNAttribute:** The name of the attribute on the static group object, specified on the previous panel, that specifies the DNs of the members of a static group.

✦ **Static Group DNsfrom Member DNFilter:** An LDAP search filter that takes a group member DN and returns all the static groups that the specified member is a member of. If you don't specify a search filter, one will be generated automatically.

✦ **Dynamic Group Object Class:** The LDAP server's object class name that stores dynamic groups.

✦ **Dynamic Group Name Attribute:** The name of the attribute on the dynamic group object class, specified previously, that stores the group name.

✦ **Dynamic Member URLAttribute:** The name of the attribute on the dynamic group object class, specified previously, that stores the URLs referencing the members of the group.

Click Apply to save your changes.

Click the Details tab to view iPlanet-specific configuration details. Currently, all external LDAP providers have the same Details tab, but this could change in the future. The options are shown in Figure 25-36 and are detailed as follows:

✦ **Follow Referrals:** Specifies whether referrals are followed or whether the query is stopped at the referral.

✦ **Bind Anonymously On Referrals:** If this is checked, the binding is done anonymously when following referrals.

Click Apply to save your changes.

Figure 25-35: Specifying membership configuration information for an external LDAP server

Figure 25-36: Specifying iPlanet-specific LDAP configuration options

You have now configured a new authentication provider, but you must reboot WebLogic Server for it to be able to communicate with your external LDAP server.

Managing Security Realms

We just described how to configure the default realm, `myrealm`, which is provided by WebLogic Server when you create a new domain. But what if you want a different configuration for security? You don't need to delete `myrealm` or even reuse it. You can have multiple security realms within a WebLogic Server domain, so you can just create a new realm with the providers and configuration that you need. However, only one realm can be active at a time. This active realm is called the default realm. So you could have two realms: one that connects to a development LDAP server and the other that connects to a test LDAP server. And you could even have a third realm that uses the built-in LDAP server in WebLogic, but you could use only one at a time. In this section, we describe how to create realms, delete realms, and make a particular realm into the default (active) realm.

Creating a new realm

To create a new realm, click the Realms node under the Security node in the WebLogic Console. In the panel on the right (shown at the beginning of this chapter in Figure 25-1), click Configure a New Realm. The resulting panel is shown in Figure 25-37. You can specify a name, and the other options are as described earlier in this chapter (refer to Figure 25-2).

Figure 25-37: Configuring a new security realm

Click Create to create the new realm. The other options on the tabbed panels were described at the beginning of this chapter, so we won't go into them here.

By default, nothing is created or configured for the new realm. There are no users, no groups, no roles, and no security providers.

As you might expect, you can't boot with this configuration. (If you somehow managed to mess up the security configuration, see one of the notes near the beginning of this chapter for a command-line parameter that will allow you to revert to the previous security configuration on bootup.) You can't set this new realm as the default realm until you configure an Authentication provider, an Authorization provider, an Adjudication provider, a Credential Mapping provider, and a Role Mapping provider.

After configuring all these providers and creating an Admin role with at least one user (you'll use this as the username/password to boot WebLogic), you must reboot WebLogic after creating a new realm for WebLogic to be able to use it.

Changing the default realm

As described in the last section, you must configure a number of providers and at least one user in an Admin role in order to use a new realm as the default realm. And after creating a new realm, you must reboot the server instance in order for WebLogic to make it available as a default realm option.

Note   For our example, we just went ahead and created new default (WebLogic) providers for all the security providers that are required. We accepted the default names and values to make it go as quickly as possible. Therefore, we will not show you all the screens. Note, however, that if you do this, you'll suddenly find that some default users, groups, and roles are automatically populated. These are generated automatically by WebLogic. If you use an external LDAP browser, you'll see that a new organizational unit ("ou") is created for each realm in the embedded LDAP server if you use the WebLogic default security providers.

After you've met the conditions of setting up providers, changing the default realm is very easy. In the Console domain tree on the left, select the `mydomain` node and then click the Security and General tabs. The first option is the default realm, and it shows all properly configured security realms, as shown in Figure 25-38. Click Apply to save your changes and then reboot for the new security realm to be used as the default.

Note   The WebLogic documentation makes it sound like you have to reboot the server in order for a new realm to show up in the list of available default realms, but actually the realm will show up as soon as you've configured all the required providers. Rebooting doesn't seem to be necessary.

Note   If you don't see your new realm in the list of available realms for the default realm, it means you haven't configured it properly. Reread the previous section for the providers and user you have to configure in order to have a valid realm that can be configured as a default realm.

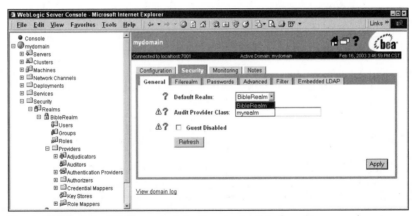

Figure 25-38: Selecting the new default realm for this domain

Deleting a realm

Deleting an existing realm is easy: In the WebLogic Console, click the Realms node under the Security node. (The browser will look something like Figure 25-39.) Just click the trashcan icon at the end of the row of the realm you want to delete. You'll get a confirmation dialog box; just click Yes to confirm the deletion or No if you change your mind.

Caution   Deleting a realm will delete all the configuration information you have painstakingly entered. Think twice about doing this on a development machine. If you ever think you'll need the realm again, just change the default realm to a different realm rather than deleting it. Of course, in a production environment, you probably don't want rogue realms hanging around; that's a security risk.

Figure 25-39: Selecting a realm to delete

Other Security Configuration

Security is such a pervasive feature that many elements of it are configured elsewhere in WebLogic Server 7.0 and in this book.

Security settings found elsewhere in this book

In addition to the entire chapters dedicated to security (Chapters 20, 21, 22, and this chapter), there are a variety of places in this book where security configuration is discussed.

Cross-Reference
This section contains cross-references to security configuration items that could have been described in this chapter, but are described elsewhere. This will make it easier for you to find related security items.

✦ **Embedded LDAP Configuration:** Some configuration items for the embedded LDAP server are specified at the domain node (for example, `mydomain`) in the Security tab's Embedded LDAP and General tabs (see Chapter 23 for more information).

✦ **Compatibility Realm Configuration:** Many items relating to the Compatibility realm (including ACLs and the deprecated FileRealm) are on the domain node's Security tab (see Chapter 23 for details).

✦ **Enabling Trust between Domains:** When you want two WebLogic domains running independently of each other to interact in a secure manner (such as having a servlet in one domain securely call an EJB in another domain), you can set up interdomain security, or a trust relationship. You specify this in the domain's node in the WebLogic Console, under the Security—Advanced tab (see Chapter 23 for a description).

✦ **Configuring SSL and a Domain-Wide Administration Port:** Configuring the Secure Sockets Layer protocol for a server is described in Chapter 23. It is found on a server's node in the WebLogic Console (for example, `myserver`) on the Configuration—General tab, and in the Connections—SSL and Connections—SSL Ports tabs. New in WebLogic Server 7.0 is the ability to have a secure, domain-wide administration port. This is also described in Chapter 23 in the domain node of the WebLogic Console under the General tab.

Configuring a connection filter

When you want to protect your systems that are exposed to the Internet, you'll always have a firewall between your servers and the Internet. This is to protect your systems from attack by outside intruders. A firewall allows you to define rules for which systems and clients can connect to your servers. WebLogic Server has a similar functionality built in to provide an additional layer of security. You can define a connection filter that accepts or rejects connections based on the client's address, the protocol, the server listen address, and the port number.

This functionality is set up on in the WebLogic Server Console. Click the domain name at the top of the domain tree on the left and then choose Security ➪ Filter tabs. You have two options:

✦ **Connection Filter:** Enter the name of the Java class that implements the connection filtering logic. WebLogic provides a built-in class that can read its configuration from the Connection Filter Rules option, following this list, and apply them to incoming requests. This class is named `weblogic.security.net.ConnectionFilterImpl` and is part of the `weblogic.jar` file (so it's already in the classpath). You can use this class or create your own; if you write your own class, the class must be part of the classpath that WebLogic Server sees as it boots.

✦ **Connection Filter Rules:** Here is where you enter the rules that the connection filter will implement. This configuration information is read only if you use the default implementation (`weblogic.security.net.ConnectionFilterImpl`) or if you create your own implementation that implements the `ConnectionFilterRulesListener` interface.

In our example, we specified the built-in class and a simple rule, as shown in Figure 25-40. Then we clicked Apply and rebooted the server so that WebLogic picked up and used the connection filter class as it boots. Note that once you've rebooted the server so that the connection filter class is used, you can then make any changes to the rules and the new rules will be applied as soon as you click the Apply button; there's no need to reboot the server after the first time.

Connection filter rules are in the form of

```
target localAddress localPort action protocols
```

where

✦ `target` specifies one or more systems to filter, either an IP address or a domain name. An asterisk (*) can be used at the beginning of a domain to specify multiple matches, such as `*.evilempirez.com`, but this is referred to as a slow rule because it requires a DNS lookup for each call.

✦ `localAddress` defines the host address of the server. (An asterisk matches all local IP addresses.)

✦ `localPort` defines the port on which the server is listening. (If you specify an asterisk, the match returns all available ports on the server.)

✦ `action` specifies either `allow` or `deny` for the connection.

✦ `protocols` is the list of protocol names to match. You can specify one or more of the following protocols: HTTP, HTTPS, T3, T3S, GIOP, GIOPS, DCOM, and FTP. If none is defined, all protocols will match a rule.

The hash (#) can be used as a comment character.

Figure 25-40: Configuring a connection filter and rules

For more information on connection filter rules and writing your own connection filters, see the WebLogic documentation at the following URL:

`http://e-docs.bea.com/wls/docs70/security/con_filtr.html#1029527`

Summary

WebLogic Server 7.0 has an enormous amount of flexibility when it comes to defining and configuring its security. Security configuration is encapsulated in the concept of a realm, and the default configuration uses an embedded LDAP server, new to WebLogic Server 7.0.

We showed you how to create users, groups, and roles in the embedded LDAP server and how to configure each of the default (WebLogic) security providers.

You can have more than one realm within a domain, but only one realm can be the default for that domain. Only the default realm is active. We showed you how to create and delete realms, and how to set a new realm to be the default realm for the domain.

Because security is such an overwhelming part of any production deployment nowadays, we also provided links to other security configuration items that you may need to set up.

Lastly, we discussed how to set up a connection filter to help keep unwanted users out of your system. Connection filters can allow or deny connections from specific hosts using specific protocols, giving you a powerful tool in your security toolbox.

✦   ✦   ✦

Enterprise Application Integration

P A R T

VIII

✦   ✦   ✦   ✦

In This Part

Chapter 26
Web Services with
WebLogic Server

Chapter 27
Web Services with
WebLogic Workshop

Chapter 28
Working with WebLogic
and the J2EE Connector
Architecture

✦   ✦   ✦   ✦

Web Services with WebLogic Server

From a view of 20,000 feet, Web Services seem simple. The whole concept comprises just two different software processes — potentially on different hardware, operating systems, and computer languages — talking to each other, typically via XML over HTTP.

You can think of Web Services as Web pages for machines. Instead of a human sending and receiving HTML Web pages via HTTP at an online store, a software process sends and receives XML documents via HTTP to another automated business process. Instead of a user going to Google or Yahoo to do an online search, a Web service uses a UDDI registry to search for compatible services. Easy, right?

Unfortunately, at a view of two feet, the concepts behind Web Services get much more complicated quickly.

In this chapter, we'll cover creating a Web Service using WebLogic Server's automated tools to help get you up and running right away. We'll show you exactly what WebLogic's tools generate and the Web Services standards they represent. Then, we'll discuss some manual processes for creating Web Services and finish up with a discussion of the custom Ant tasks that WebLogic provides.

Introducing Web Services

Web Services, as WebLogic Server implements them, are built on the SOAP 1.1 specification. Here's a quick rundown of some of the most common acronyms you'll see in Web Services:

✦ **Simple Object Access Protocol (SOAP):** SOAP is not really object-oriented, but it does typically use HTTP to send XML documents to and from Web Services. The format of those documents, including the SOAP header and body, are defined in the specification. The SOAP header contains information about how to direct the request to the correct service, whereas the body contains XML markup for the actual operations and parameters to be used.

✦ **Web Services Description Language (WSDL; pronounced wiz-dull):** Each Web service has its own WSDL document, which describes the protocols used, the operations available, as well as their parameters and return types. Think of a WSDL document serving a similar function as a Java interface: It tells other services what operations are supported and how to call them (number and type of parameters, and so on).

✦ **Universal Description, Discovery, and Integration protocol (UDDI):** UDDI is the yellow pages and the white pages of Web Services. A person or a program can search one or more UDDI registries to find services that use the protocols and understand the XML documents that they understand.

The key words to remember about Web Services are *integration* and *interoperability*. That is, you use Web Services to integrate disparate systems. Those systems could be in the same company or communicating over the Internet, but they need to share data or functionality. To do that, those services need to be interoperable. Web Services you create in WebLogic Server can interoperate with other Web Services, whether hosted on other WebLogic Servers, on other J2EE servers, or even hosted on Microsoft .Net servers.

Generating a Web Service Automatically

There are two ways to develop Web Services: the hard way and the easy way. The hard way entails writing new Web Services from scratch, and hand coding the parsing and generation of the SOAP XML documents. Basically what the easy way is saying is this: "OK, let's just put a Web Services facade on top of our existing J2EE applications."

Cross-Reference Actually, BEA provides a third way — the *really* easy way — in the form of WebLogic Workshop. See Chapter 27 for coverage of WebLogic Workshop.

In this section, we'll jump right into creating a Web service the easy way. We could have provided a nice theoretical framework upon which we could then build a Web service manually. Although that would have been very instructive, we fear that by the time we would cover all the standards and technologies, you'd have long since become confused — or bored — and not kept up with us. We figure it's far more instructive to just get down-and-dirty with Web Services and learn the technologies as we go along, so that's how this chapter is structured.

Another reason we're doing things this way is to show you that you *can* do it the easy way. There's no reason to do it the hard way if you have relatively simple requirements and your purpose is to quickly integrate multiple processes. After all, that's the purpose of Web Services: to integrate things, not to force you to study for a Ph.D.

To show the easy way to Web Services, in this chapter, we will take a slightly modified EJB that we created earlier in the book (a stateless session EJB from Chapter 15) and make it into a full-fledged Web service in a remarkably short period of time.

Note In addition to converting EJBs, you can also convert simple Java classes or JMS destinations to Web Services in this manner. See the WebLogic Server documentation at the following URL:

```
http://e-docs.bea.com/wls/docs70/webserv/anttasks.html
```

Converting an EJB to a Web service

In Chapter 15, we developed the RequestResearch stateless session EJB. As you'll recall, that EJB provided a method to get a buy, sell, or hold recommendation for a passed-in stock symbol. In our example, we'll take that EJB and make a Web service out of it, thereby providing a public interface that can be called by any other Web service.

Cross-Reference

The book's Web site has the complete code for the EJB. Note that we had to modify the code slightly from Chapter 15. Because WebLogic's automated Web Services tools do not currently (as of Service Pack 1 of WLS 7.0) support EJB local interfaces, we had to remove the bean's interaction with another EJB through a local interface.

Caution

Before continuing, remember to un-deploy the RequestResearch EJB from Chapter 15 from your WebLogic Server instance. The modified EJB will be deployed in our Web service with the same JNDI name, and you won't be able to deploy the Web service EJB because of a JNDI naming conflict if you don't first un-deploy the existing EJB.

This simple process of converting an EJB to a Web service consists of just four steps:

1. Build the EJB into a JAR file. Nothing special here, it's just a good old EJB.

2. Run the `servicegen` WebLogic custom Ant task to generate an Enterprise application (EAR file).

3. Deploy the EAR in the WebLogic Server Console.

4. Test your new Web service by pointing your browser to `http://<hostname>:<port>/<contextURI>/<serviceURI>` (for example, `http://localhost:7001/web_services/RequestService`), enter any parameters, and click Submit. The Web-based client will parse your entry, send the appropriate SOAP envelope to your new Web service, and display the returned results.

Now, we'll explain these four steps in greater detail.

Build the EJB

There's nothing much to say here, except that you'll want to download the source from the book's Web site. Make sure that you use the EJB in the `webservices` directory; if you use the EJB from the `EJB/session/stateless` directory, you'll get an error because WebLogic Server's `servicegen` task can't use introspection on EJBs that have local interfaces. (We used the name `RequestNoLocalEJB.jar` to distinguish this from the jar in the EJB chapter, which was called `RequestEJB.jar`. The "NoLocal" in the name refers to the fact that this EJB does not use an EJB with a local interface.) Build the EJB using the provided Ant `build.xml` file, just as you do all the other examples.

Run the Ant task to Convert the EJB

Next, we use Ant to convert the EJB into a full-blown Web service. This involves using WebLogic's custom Ant task named `servicegen`. An Ant `build.xml` build file that uses `servicegen` is shown in Listing 26-1.

Listing 26-1: The Ant build.xml file for Converting an EJB into a Web Service

```xml
<project name="webServicesExample" default="build">

  <taskdef name="servicegen"
classname="weblogic.ant.taskdefs.webservices.servicegen.ServiceGenTask"/>

  <taskdef name="clientgen"
classname="weblogic.ant.taskdefs.webservices.clientgen.ClientGenTask"/>

  <target name="build">
    <delete dir="build_dir"/>
    <mkdir dir="build_dir"/>
    <copy todir="build_dir" file="RequestNoLocalEJB.jar"/>
    <servicegen
        destEar="build_dir/RequestNoLocalEJB.ear"
        warName="RequestNoLocalEJB.war"
        contextURI="web_services">
      <service
          ejbJar="build_dir/RequestNoLocalEJB.jar"
          targetNamespace="http://www.wiley.com/wlsbible"
          serviceName="RequestService"
          serviceURI="/RequestService"
          generateTypes="True"
          expandMethods="True">
        <client
            packageName="com.wiley.wlsbible.ejb.session.stateless"
            clientJarName="requestNoLocalEJB_client.jar"/>
      </service>
    </servicegen>
  </target>

  <target name="build.client" >
    <property name="wsdlUrl"
        value="http://localhost:7001/web_services/RequestService?WSDL" />
    <clientgen wsdl="${wsdlUrl}"
packageName="com.wiley.wlsbible.requestservice.client"
        clientJar="requestClient.jar" />
  </target>

</project>
```

Define the WebLogic servicegen Ant Task

Note in Listing 26-1 that near the top of the build.xml file is this declaration:

```xml
<taskdef name="servicegen"
classname="weblogic.ant.taskdefs.webservices.servicegen.ServiceGenTask"/>
```

This defines a new Ant task, `servicegen`, so that Ant knows where to find the Java executable to run this task. This is necessary because `servicegen` is not a built-in Ant task; it's provided by BEA with WebLogic Server 7.0.

Cross-Reference   Using Ant and defining new Ant tasks is covered more generally in Appendix B.

Add a target

Now that we've defined the `servicegen` task, we can use it in an Ant target. We create a target named `build` (see Listing 26-1) that clears out any existing temporary build files, re-creates the build directory, and copies our EJB there. Then, we add our `servicegen` task. This task can take more parameters than shown here in our example; full documentation is available at `http://e-docs.bea.com/wls/docs70/webserv/anttasks.html`. Our `servicegen` task takes the following parameters:

✦ **destEar:** The destination of the EAR file that is generated by this task. This EAR file contains all the components needed for the Web service. We gave it the same name as our EJB jar file, except with an `ear` extension. If you leave off the `ear` extension, it will generate an exploded directory structure.

✦ **warName:** The generated EAR file contains both the original EJB and a Web application. The warName specified here is the name given to the generated WAR file. This Web application displays the input parameters for the Web service, processes the user input, converts it to a SOAP message, and passes it off to the Web service. It also processes and displays the resulting SOAP reply message. We gave it the same name as our EJB jar file, except with a `war` extension. If you leave off the `war` extension, it will generate an exploded directory structure.

✦ **contextURI:** This entry becomes the base URI for our Web service, as described earlier in the four steps of creating a Web service automatically.

✦ **service:** This describes the Web service that is to be built. You can have multiple Web Services in a single EAR. The `ejbJar` attribute gives the name of the original EJB jar that we are converting to a Web service. The `targetNamespace` is the XML namespace that is used in the WSDL file to define our service (we talk about the WSDL file and XML namespaces a little later on). The `serviceName` is the name assigned to our Web service in the WSDL file (again, more on WSDL later). If you have multiple services, giving them all the same name will cause `servicegen` to package all the methods together under a single service name. The `serviceURI` is the final part of the URL that is used to access our Web service, as described earlier in the four steps of creating a Web service automatically. `generateTypes` defines whether custom data types (classes) will be interpreted automatically; we could leave this as False because our EJB's method uses only Java standard types (String), but you would generally leave this as True. `expandMethods` determines whether each method is created individually in the Webservices.xml file or whether they're treated together via the * notation.

✦ **client:** This optional tag lets you define the package name and jar name for the generated client that's packaged in the EAR file. If you don't generate the client jar here, you can use the `clientgen` task, as shown in Listing 26-1, to generate the client after the fact.

Run build.xml in Ant

After creating the `build.xml` file, we need to provide it to Ant so that it can generate our EAR file. Open a command-line window and change to the directory you created with the `build.xml` and `RequestNoLocalEJB.jar` files. You first want to set your WebLogic environment and then run the Ant command (which uses `build.xml` by default). The two commands on the command line are simply the following:

```
H:\WebLogicUserDomains\mydomain\setenv.cmd
ant
```

In this example, `H:\WebLogicUserDomains\mydomain` is the location of the WebLogic Server domain that you will be running your Web service in. When finished, Ant should display its `BUILD SUCCESSFUL` message. There should now be a `RequestNoLocalEJB.ear` file in the `build` subdirectory.

Deploy the Web Service EAR

Now that we've created our EAR with the Web service, we need to deploy it. The simplest way is to use the WebLogic Console. Point your browser to `http://localhost:7001/console/` to open the console; then log in with the username and password you defined when you created the domain in the Domain Configuration Wizard.

There are two ways to deploy a Web Services application in the console, and they both end up doing the exact same thing. The first way is to click on the Deployments ⇨ Applications node; the other way is to click on the Deployments ⇨ Web Services node. Then select the Configure a New Application link. This brings you to the same application deployment pane that you saw in the chapters on Web applications and EJBs (see Figure 26-1). First, upload it through your browser link to navigate to the `RequestNoLocalEJB.ear` file you just created and then click OK to copy it to the domain directory. Next click the [Select] link next to the EAR file you just copied.

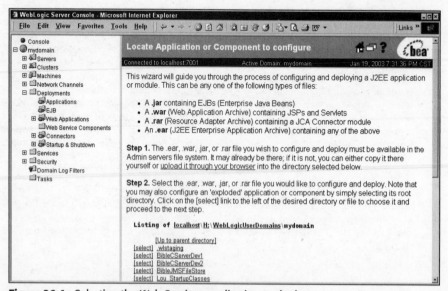

Figure 26-1: Selecting the Web Services application to deploy

This brings you to the pane shown in Figure 26-2. Select the server to deploy to and accept the default application name, as shown. Then click the Configure and Deploy button.

Now WebLogic Server reads the Web Services application and deploys its components. While it's doing this, it shows a status pane similar to that seen in Figure 26-3. Again, this is very similar to the deployment of JARs and WARs that we saw in earlier chapters. When it finishes, the Deployed status should be True, as shown in Figure 26-3.

At this point, your Web Services application is deployed and ready to test. It takes a lot longer to explain this in writing than it does to just do it in person.

Look carefully at Figure 26-3. In the nodes on the left, under Deployments ➪ Applications ➪ RequestNoLocalEJB, you'll see that there is a JAR and WAR with the same name showing up as deployed children of the EAR. Remember earlier in the chapter when we specified the name of the JAR, WAR, and EAR files in the `build.xml` file; this is how they show up in WebLogic.

In fact, when deployed in WebLogic Server, the EJB also shows up in the Deployments ➪ EJBs node. If you click on it to view its configuration, it will look just like the configuration options for any other EJB, minus the Staging parameter (see Figure 26-4).

Figure 26-2: Selecting the deployment options

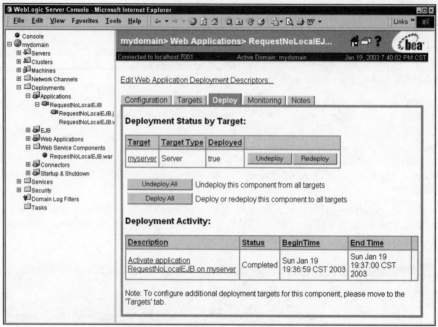

Figure 26-3: The deployment status pane

Figure 26-4: The EJB component of a Web Services application

On the other hand, when the WAR is deployed in WebLogic Server, the WAR shows up in the Deployments ⇨ Web Service Components node, not the Deployments ⇨ Web Applications node. WebLogic Server recognizes it as a special type of Web application, and we'll see why a little later on. Nonetheless, if you click it, you'll see that it has the same configuration options as any other Web application, minus the Staging parameter (very similar to what you see in Figure 26-4).

Test the new Web service

Now it's time to test our Web service. Recall the URI options in the `build.xml` file for the `servicegen` task that we created. We'll need that information to determine which URL to enter into the browser to view our Web service in action. For the example shown in Listing 26-1 running on a local server using the default port number, our URL ends up being `http://localhost:7001/web_services/RequestService`. When we enter that, we get the Web page shown in Figure 26-5. This Web page is part of the packaged WAR that was deployed in our EAR. For now, we'll concentrate on the `requestResearch` link near the top that allows us to test our Web service. Note that if we had more than one Web service operation, they would all show up as separate links here. When we click the `requestResearch` link, the Web page shown in Figure 26-6 appears.

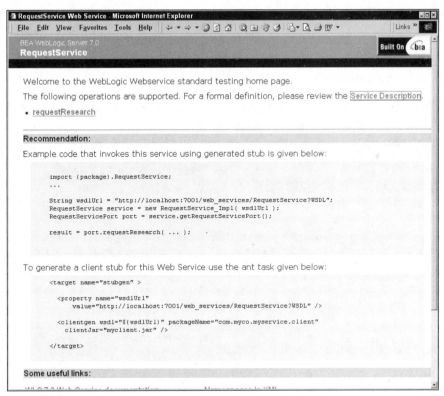

Figure 26-5: The home page for our Web service

Figure 26-6: Here it is—our Web service ready for action

This is the Web page for the operation of the Web service we're interested in—namely, the public interface of the EJB that we repackaged as a Web service. It lists names and types of all available parameters as well as an entry field for entering values for the parameters. If we go ahead and type **BEA** in the text box and click the Invoke button, the Web application will parse the parameters and operation name and invoke our Web service on the server. The Web service then acts on the parameters (in our example, the EJB at the core of the Web service will process the **BEA** that was entered for the first parameter) and returns a value to the Web application, which then parses it into HTML and displays it back to the browser. The result is shown in Figure 26-7.

At the top of the resultant Web page you can see that the Return Value is "Zeetrade recommends you buy BEA." (Recall from Chapter 15 that the RequestResearch session EJB can return one of a number of strings, so your result might not be exactly the same.)

So there's the result we've been looking for. In four short steps (build EJB, run `servicegen`, deploy EAR, test Web service), we miraculously turned a simple EJB into a complete Web service!

Your next question is: How? Now we'll start digging into what we've done and uncover what's really going on. On the one hand, it's great that WebLogic Server can do all this for you, but it's important to understand how it all works if you're serious about Web Services. First, let's finish explaining the rest of the Web page shown in Figure 26-7 and then we'll work on deconstructing the Web service EAR that we created. There's a lot of XML involved, so if you need a crash course in XML, check out the following sidebar.

If you look at Figure 26-7, you'll see two highlighted blocks of XML under the headings `Request Sent to the Server` and `Response from the Server`. The Request shows the actual XML that the Web application generated after you typed in **BEA** in Figure 26-6 and clicked Invoke. The Response shows the XML that the Web service generated and sent back to the Web application. This Response was then parsed by the Web application and displayed as the Return Value at the top of Figure 26-7. Remember, Web Services are simply a way of achieving universal communication by passing XML documents back and forth between systems.

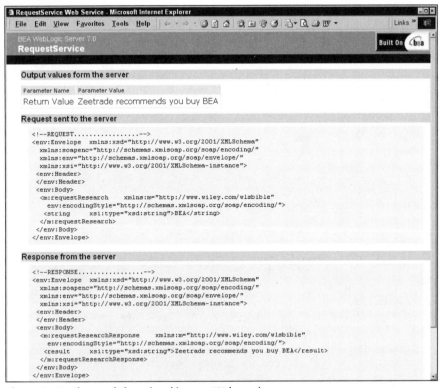

```
RequestService Web Service - Microsoft Internet Explorer

File   Edit   View   Favorites   Tools   Help         Links »

BEA WebLogic Server 7.0                                          Built On  bea
RequestService

Output values form the server

Parameter Name   Parameter Value
Return Value   Zeetrade recommends you buy BEA

Request sent to the server

<!--REQUEST...............-->
<env:Envelope  xmlns:xsd="http://www.w3.org/2001/XMLSchema"
   xmlns:soapenc="http://schemas.xmlsoap.org/soap/encoding/"
   xmlns:env="http://schemas.xmlsoap.org/soap/envelope/"
   xmlns:xsi="http://www.w3.org/2001/XMLSchema-instance">
 <env:Header>
 </env:Header>
 <env:Body>
  <m:requestResearch     xmlns:m="http://www.wiley.com/wlsbible"
     env:encodingStyle="http://schemas.xmlsoap.org/soap/encoding/">
    <string     xsi:type="xsd:string">BEA</string>
  </m:requestResearch>
 </env:Body>
</env:Envelope>

Response from the server

<!--RESPONSE...............-->
<env:Envelope  xmlns:xsd="http://www.w3.org/2001/XMLSchema"
   xmlns:soapenc="http://schemas.xmlsoap.org/soap/encoding/"
   xmlns:env="http://schemas.xmlsoap.org/soap/envelope/"
   xmlns:xsi="http://www.w3.org/2001/XMLSchema-instance">
 <env:Header>
 </env:Header>
 <env:Body>
  <m:requestResearchResponse     xmlns:m="http://www.wiley.com/wlsbible"
     env:encodingStyle="http://schemas.xmlsoap.org/soap/encoding/">
    <result     xsi:type="xsd:string">Zeetrade recommends you buy BEA</result>
  </m:requestResearchResponse>
 </env:Body>
</env:Envelope>
```

Figure 26-7: The result from invoking our Web service

The SOAP Request

Looking at the big picture, the Request shown in Figure 26-7 shows the main `env:Envelope` element that contains `env:Header` and `env:Body` subelements. *Envelopes* are the way you send and receive SOAP requests and responses, and they always contain a header and body, even if empty. As you can see, the header is empty in this example. Header elements can be used to help direct the request to the right server or service and might be used in the future for security, encryption, and other unforeseen uses. The concept of a header is that it keeps information about the message separate from the message itself, much as an HTML header keeps metadata separate from the body of an HTML page.

The body is where the action is. In our Web service, shown in Figure 26-7, the body contains an `m:RequestResearch` element, which is the name of our Web service's operation. This is the name of our EJB's public method, which the `servicegen` Ant task grabbed via introspection of our EJB. The `m:` namespace qualifier is defined by the `targetNamespace` attribute in the `build.xml` file we defined earlier. By using a namespace this way, we guarantee that our Web service's method names are unique within any XML documents they may be buried in.

An XML Primer

Using a J2EE server such as WebLogic Server pretty much assumes that you can read and write XML. You can get away with using an XML editor, though, so you might not know some of the precise nomenclature and features of XML used in Web Services. So here's a brief rundown of some of the pertinent features. The following descriptions are based on the following (incomplete) XML snippet:

```
<env:Envelope  xmlns:xsd="http://www.w3.org/2001/XMLSchema"
xmlns:env="http://schemas.xmlsoap.org/soap/envelope/"
  xmlns:xsi="http://www.w3.org/2001/XMLSchema-instance">
<env:Body>
  <m:requestResearch    xmlns:m="http://www.wiley.com/wlsbible"
    env:encodingStyle="http://schemas.xmlsoap.org/soap/encoding/">
   <string     xsi:type="xsd:string">BEA</string>
  </m:requestResearch>
 </env:Body>
</env:Envelope>
```

There's a lot more to XML than the brief definition given here, but here are some pertinent features:

✦ **Elements:** Like HTML, XML can contain elements with opening and closing pairs, such as `env:Envelope` and `/env:Envelope`, and `env:Body` and `/env:Body` in the preceding example. Between these pairs can be nothing, values, and/or nested subelements.

✦ **Attributes:** Elements can optionally have one or more attributes. These attributes are in the form `<name>="<value>"` and are separated by spaces. For example, the `env:Body` element has no attributes, whereas the `m:requestResearch` element has `xmlns:m` and `env:encodingStyle` attributes.

✦ **Namespaces:** This concept allows for conflict resolution. Say, for example, that you have a Web service that requires a `Body` element. But, oops, there's already a `Body` element in the SOAP XML! The way to get around this is by using *namespaces*, which are abbreviations or symbols that come before element and attribute names. In the previous example, the `Body` element is preceded by the `env:` namespace qualifier to produce `env:Body`. So if we need our own `Body` element, we would precede it with our own namespace qualifier, say `lou:`, to produce `lou:Body`.

So then how do we know that `lou:` is for my namespace, whereas `env:` is for SOAP's namespace? If you look carefully, you'll see `xmlns:` definitions spread throughout the example XML. These take the form of `xmlns:<symbol>="<URI>"` where `<symbol>` consists of the letters that will symbolize the namespace and URI is unique specification for the namespace. Note that the URI doesn't have to — and often doesn't — refer to a Web page, it's just a unique string that represents the namespace. Typically, you would use your company's Web address, or a unique variation thereof. In that manner, `env:` is defined above as `xmlns:env="http://schemas.xmlsoap.org/soap/envelope/"` whereas my `lou:` namespace might be defined as `xmlns:lou="www.mirandacorp.com/Lou/"`.

With that brief introduction under your belt, you should have no problem understanding the basic structure of the complex XML that Web Services require.

The `string` subelement of the `m:RequestResearch` element is the name of the first (and only) parameter of our EJB's RequestResearch method, and it has a type of `xsd:string` and a value of `BEA`. The parameter name and type were detected by introspection of our EJB again by the `servicegen` Ant task. The value of `BEA` came from our entry on the Web page shown in Figure 26-6.

The SOAP Response

As with the SOAP Request, the SOAP Response in Figure 26-7 has an `env:Envelope` element with `env:Header` and `env:Body` elements. Just as with the Request, the Response's header is empty and the meat is in the body.

The body typically contains either a return value or a SOAP-FAULT element, which is returned if there is a problem handling the request (bad parameter type, operation not found, and so on). WebLogic Server also allows you to generate a SOAP-FAULT by throwing a `javax.xml.rpc.soap.SOAPFaultException`; see the documentation for details. But in our simple case, we return a single string that is seen in the `m:RequestResearchResponse` element, which contains a `result` subelement with an attribute for its type of `xsd:string` and a value of `Zeetrade recommends you buy BEA`. The return type is derived by introspection of the EJB's methods by the `servicegen` Ant task, and the return value is generated by calling the EJB's method.

Now that we've seen how the Web application and the Web service interact with each other via XML, take a look at the next section to see the EAR file that was generated via the `servicegen` Ant task and learn how it was constructed.

Deconstructing the Web service EAR

At this point, we built and deployed the Web service EAR, but its internals have been a black box up until this point. We know that it has a Web application component because we already went to a Web page to enter a parameter and run our Web service. We also know that it contains an EJB because our original `RequestNoLocalEJB.jar` is the core of the Web service that returns advice on buying securities. And we know that we used an Ant `build.xml` file to generate it using WebLogic Service's `servicegen` task. But what exactly is it composed of, and what does that tell us about building and extending this simple Web Services example?

There are two ways to see what's inside the EAR. If you have an unzipping tool or are handy with Java's classes for jarring and unjarring files, you can use them to extract the files from the EAR. Another way to do it is to remember (from the description of the `build.xml` file that we created earlier) that if we leave off the file extension for the `destEar` and `warName` attributes in the servicegen `build.xml` file, an exploded directory will be created instead of EAR and WAR files. So we went ahead and removed the file extensions (.ear and .war, respectively) and the results of the build are the exploded directories and files shown in Figure 26-8.

Note The EAR can optionally include a client JAR file, in addition to the EJB JAR and WAR files. This client JAR is not shown in Figure 26-8, but its contents and information on generating it are described at the end of this section.

Figure 26-8: The exploded directories and files contained in the enterprise application that comprises our Web service

The exploded directory structure shows the typical contents of an enterprise application structure, with an embedded EJB jar and an embedded Web application. In the enterprise application's META-INF directory, we find the expected application.xml file; its contents are shown in Listing 26-2.

Listing 26-2: **application.xml**

```
<!DOCTYPE application PUBLIC '-//Sun Microsystems, Inc.//DTD J2EE
Application 1.2//EN'
'http://java.sun.com/j2ee/dtds/application_1_2.dtd'>
<application>
<display-name></display-name>
  <module>
    <web>
      <web-uri>RequestNoLocalEJBwar</web-uri>
      <context-root>web_services</context-root>
    </web>
  </module>
  <module>
    <ejb>RequestNoLocalEJB.jar</ejb>
  </module>
</application>
```

The contents show that this enterprise application is built from a Web application and an EJB. You can see that there's a web element inside the first module element, and it contains the web-uri that is the name of the Web application, as well as a context-root that we specified in the build.xml for the servicegen Ant task. The second module element contains the EJB reference for our original RequestService EJB that we made into a Web service. Now let's investigate that Web application further.

The autogenerated Web application

Surprisingly, there are no HTML pages or JSPs inside the Web application, as shown in Figure 26-8. This gives you a hint about portability: WebLogic Server 7.0 itself is providing some of the built-in functionality for displaying the Web pages for our Web service. So even though our Web service is fully compatible with SOAP in terms of being able to work with any other Web service, our Web service EAR can be *deployed* only on WebLogic Server 7.0.

As shown in the figure, the Web application's WEB-INF directory contains two XML files: web.xml and web-services.xml.

web.xml

The web.xml file is a standard J2EE Web application descriptor. Its contents are shown in Listing 26-3.

Listing 26-3: **web.xml**

```
<!DOCTYPE web-app PUBLIC "-//Sun Microsystems, Inc.//DTD Web
Application 2.3//EN" "http://java.sun.com/dtd/web-app_2_3.dtd">
<web-app>
</web-app>
```

Judging by the fact that there are no HTML pages or JSPs in the Web application, it probably shouldn't be too surprising that what we have here is basically an empty web.xml file. That should be a broad hint that there must be something special in the web-services.xml file.

web-services.xml

This file is not a standard J2EE descriptor, but rather a WebLogic Server-specific descriptor. Its contents are shown in Listing 26-4.

Listing 26-4: **web-services.xml**

```
<web-services>
  <web-service protocol="http" name="RequestService"
uri="/RequestService" targetNamespace="http://www.wiley.com/wlsbible"
style="rpc">

    <components>
      <stateless-ejb name="ejbcomp0">
        <ejb-link path="RequestNoLocalEJB.jar#RequestResearch">
        </ejb-link>
      </stateless-ejb>
    </components>
```

Continued

Listing 26-4 *(continued)*

```
    <operations>
      <operation method="requestResearch(java.lang.String)"
component="ejbcomp0" name="requestResearch">
        <params>
          <param location="body" class-name="java.lang.String"
style="in" name="string" xmlns:xsd="http://www.w3.org/2001/XMLSchema"
type="xsd:string">
          </param>
          <return-param location="body" class-name="java.lang.String"
name="result" xmlns:xsd="http://www.w3.org/2001/XMLSchema"
type="xsd:string">
          </return-param>
        </params>
      </operation>
    </operations>

  </web-service>
</web-services>
```

This file is composed of `web-service` elements, each of which has `component` and `operations` subelements. Its purpose is to describe a service in terms of the components (EJBs, Java classes, or JMS destinations) that make up the functionality of the service; and the names, parameters, and return values of the operations that make up that component.

Because we have only one service, made up of only one component that has only one method (operation), our `web-service.xml` file is quite simple. If we look at each element and its attributes, this is what we find. For a full description of the `web-service.xml` file, see the following URL:

`http://edocs.bea.com/wls/docs70/webserv/wsp.html#1001373`

The `web-service` element in our Web service has the following attributes:

✦ **protocol:** The protocol that this service supports. For WebLogic Server 7.0, this can be HTTP or HTTPS.

✦ **name:** The name of the Web service. This was defined in our `build.xml` file for the `servicegen` Ant task.

✦ **uri:** The terminal segment of the URL for getting to our Web service. This, too, was defined in the `build.xml` file.

✦ **targetNamespace:** The namespace used for defining our service in WSDL files and SOAP messages. This was defined as an attribute in our `build.xml` file.

✦ **style:** The type of Web service, either `rpc` or `document`. Choosing `rpc` makes it act like a remote procedure call, in that you can have multiple parameters to your method of any type. Using `document` style means your operations can take only a single parameter, which is an XML document itself. See the following URL for more information:

`http://edocs.bea.com/wls/docs70/webserv/design.html#1038901`

The `components` element has a subelement named `stateless-ejb`. This in turn has a `name` attribute; this name is used in the `operation` element (see following) to map an operation (method) to a component (EJB). This name is made up by the `servicegen` Ant task; there's no way to specify it. This is okay because it's used only internally.

Our simple Web service has only a single operation, so the `operations` element contains one `operation` subelement with the following attributes:

✦ **method:** The name and signature of the method. In our case, it has a single parameter of type String.

✦ **component:** The component that this method is derived from. Here, it's actually a method on our EJB and this name reflects that.

✦ **name:** The name we gave to our Web service operation, originally specified in our `build.xml` file.

The `operation` element has a `params` subelement, which in turn is composed of a `param` element for each parameter and a `return-param` element for the return value. In our listing, we see that the `param` element has the following attributes:

✦ **location:** This can be body, header, or attachment; it specifies where in the SOAP message this parameter is sent, although it's typically the body. See the following URL for more information:

`http://edocs.bea.com/wls/docs70/webserv/wsp.html#1066343`

✦ **class-name:** The Java class name of the parameter that's being sent.

✦ **style:** The parameter's dynamics: it can be `in`, `out`, or `in-out`. Typically, it's `in`, which means the parameter is sent to the Web service and its value is not changed during execution of the method (or if it is changed, it isn't returned). Specifying `out` means that no data gets sent to the Web service for this parameter, but a value is returned. Specifying `in-out` means that a parameter is sent to the Web service and potentially changed value is returned by it. If you specify `out` or `in-out`, special rules apply. See the following URL for more information:

`http://edocs.bea.com/wls/docs70/webserv/wsp.html#1066343`

✦ **name:** The name of the parameter. Note that this doesn't match the name of the parameter in the original method in the EJB. By default, `servicegen` will just name this after the parameter's type, hence "string" in our example. You can, however, change it to whatever name you want if you create your Web service manually, rather than through `servicegen`.

✦ **xmlns:xsd:** The namespace for the XML schema that defines the type.

✦ **type:** The XML schema type for this parameter.

The `return-param` element has all the same attributes as the `param` element, except `style` because a return value is always an `out` style as you would expect.

Original EJB

The EAR contains the original EJB in addition to the Web application. This is what provides the functionality for our Web service.

Client JAR

The EAR optionally contains a client JAR, which isn't used on the server, but instead provides a simple interface for stubs on the client side. This allows you to create a simple Java client that doesn't have to know anything about WebLogic Server, WSDL, SOAP, or Web Services. Your simple Java client will just call on the classes and interfaces in the client JAR, which acts as a proxy. So it's the client JAR that actually talks to the Web service. This lets you create a simple Java client that uses a Java interface to talk (indirectly) to the Web service.

In our `build.xml` shown in Listing 26-1, we specified that a client JAR should be included in our EAR by specifying a `client` subelement within the `service` element. You can also generate this client JAR independently of the EAR by using the `clientgen` Ant task. An example of using `clientgen` is shown at the end of Listing 26-1 in the `build.client` target.

Deconstructing the client JAR

When we explode the client JAR, we see that there are four `.java` files (and their compiled `.class` counterparts), one XML file, and a WSDL file. Let's go over the contents of these files.

XML File

The `RequestService.xml` is the simplest of the files included in the client JAR, and essentially consists of just one line:

```
<type-mapping />
```

This file is used for mapping custom Java classes to input and output parameters and return values. For example, if you have a `Customer` class, there would be mapping information here that would map fields in your customer class to XML if you specified a `Customer` as an input parameter to a method. Because we used only simple Java types (`java.lang.String`), no mapping was required. This file is generated automatically by `servicegen` when the `generateTypes` attribute is set to True (refer to Figure 26-1).

Java classes and interfaces

The function of the client JAR is to make it easy for your own Java client classes to talk to your Web service without having to know anything about Web Services. It is the classes and interfaces in the client JAR that make this proxying possible. The implementations of these classes use custom WebLogic Server APIs and thus are not portable, but those APIs are based on Sun's JAX-RPC, which you can find more information about at the following URL:

```
http://java.sun.com/webservices/docs/ea1/tutorial/doc/JAXRPC.html
```

Here, we'll cover just the generated classes and their interfaces. How to write your own Java client that uses these client JAR classes and interfaces will be discussed in the next section.

✦ **RequestService.java:** This interface represents methods to get your Web service's port. A port is a WSDL concept that we'll explain shortly, but suffice it to say that it is a mapping to your Web service's operations.

✦ **RequestService_Impl.java:** This class is the concrete implementation of the `RequestService.java` interface. Later, we'll show how to instantiate this class and call its `getRequestServicePort` method to get access to our Web service.

✦ **RequestServicePort.java:** This interface represents methods to actually call your Web service.

✦ **RequestServicePort_Stub.java:** This class is the concrete implementation of the RequestServicePort.java interface. Its `requestResearch` method is the way we actually call our Web service.

These classes are the foundation for calling a Web service seamlessly from Java code. After we explain the WSDL file's contents, you'll have all the pieces we need to write your own Java client to access a Web service.

WSDL file

The WSDL (Web Services Description Language) file in our client JAR is named after our Web service, namely `RequestService.wsdl`. WSDL files are XML files that describe Web Services: They list and match up the data types, operations, parameters, return types, and Web Service addresses. If you know the address of any Web Service, you access its WSDL by appending a "?WSDL" to its address. For example, a Web Service at

```
http://localhost:7001/web_services/RequestService
```

will display its WSDL file if you request

```
http://localhost:7001/web_services/RequestService?WSDL
```

Before we open up our WSDL file, however, a word of warning: WSDL gets complex and ugly very quickly. Rather than dump out a text listing of the WSDL file here and have you running for the exits, we'll display it in a kinder, gentler way. In fact, we'll give you a tip that you can reuse over and over again: Download the BEA XML Editor from its Web site and load the WSDL in that. The editor is available at BEA's Dev2Dev developer site at the following URL:

```
http://dev2dev.bea.com/resourcelibrary/utilitiestools/xml.jsp?highlight=
utilitiestools
```

Because the WSDL file is relatively large, even for this very simple Web service, we took a series of screen captures from the BEA XML Editor GUI and displayed them in a chain of figures. Figure 26-9 shows the big picture view with only the two highest-level XML elements opened up.

Note   In the BEA XML Editor's tree view, element nodes show up as semitransparent rounded squares, whereas attribute nodes show up as triangles.

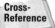

Cross-Reference   See the sidebar "An XML Primer" earlier in this chapter for a discussion of elements, attributes, and namespaces.

In Figure 26-9, the high-level picture emerges of an XML declaration along with a `definitions` element. This `definitions` element contains all the details about our Web service. Notice that there are namespace attributes along with five subelements at the bottom.

Figure 26-9: The big picture of RequestService.wsdl, with only the highest-level nodes shown expanded

In Figure 26-10, the namespace attributes of the `definitions` node are shown expanded, displaying the values associated with those attributes. The first and last namespaces are associated specifically with our Web service, whereas the rest are part of various SOAP standards. So, as we go through the rest of this WSDL file, any time you see an element or attribute with a namespace attached to it, this is where you come to find out where that namespace is derived.

At the bottom of Figure 26-10 are five subelements that comprise the four types of elements needed to define a Web service fully: message, portType, binding, and service. What these four types of elements do is to define the input and output (return value) parameters, map those parameters (and return values) to operations, map the operations to services, and map the services to a URL. The following sections briefly describe each of these elements.

message

The two message elements are shown fully expanded at the top of Figure 26-11. You may be wondering why there are two message elements for a single operation. Good question! There is actually one message element for each parameter type and one message element for the return type. Because we have one String parameter and a String return value, two message elements are required. These map directly to the EJB method in our `RequestNoLocalEJB.jar` file. Each consists of a name attribute (`requestResearch` for the input parameter, `requestResearchResponse` for the return value) and a part element. The part element has three attributes: a part namespace definition, a name, and a type. The type should match the types in the EJB method and the names are generated automatically by the `servicegen` Ant task. Follow the logic and it will start to make sense: The input parameter's message element has a name of `requestResearch` and a part subelement with a name of string and a type of `partns:string`, whereas the return value's message element has a name of `requestResearch Response` and a part subelement with a name of `result` and a type of `partns:string`.

Figure 26-10: The namespace attributes shown expanded, listing their values

portType

The bottom half of Figure 26-11 shows the `portType` definition fully exploded. A `portType` basically maps parameters and return values to a method name. Notice that the `portType` has a `name` attribute of `RequestServicePort` and an `operation` subelement. This `operation` is further composed of `input` and `output` subelements. Both `input` and `output` have a single attribute, `message`. And here's where it all fits together: The `input`'s message has a value of `tns:requestResearch`, whereas the `output`'s message has a value of `tns:requestResearchResponse`. Well, we just defined two messages with those names in the top half of Figure 26-11, so you see how `message`s (parameters and return values) are tied to `operation`s (methods).

binding

Okay, we have our parameters mapped to our methods, so aren't we done yet? Not yet. Remember, Web Services are flexible. We can use different transport protocols, such as HTTP or HTTPS. We can perform Web Service calls as RPC style or document style. All these variations have to be incorporated in the definition of our Web service operations. The binding section, shown in Figure 26-12, brings this all together. For each Web Service operation we want to define, we have to bind a `portType` to a SOAP style (rpc or document, for example) and a transport mechanism (HTTP or HTTPS, for example). This is done in the binding element's `type` attribute (here defined as the `tns:RequestServicePort` that we defined in Figure 26-11) and its `soap:binding` subelement which has its `style` (rpc) and `transport` mechanism (`http://schemas.xmlsoap.org/soap/http`).

The `binding`'s `operation` subelement has a name, `requestResearch`, which is the name of the `portType`'s `operation` subelement defined in Figure 26-11. It also has `soap:operation` and `input` and `output` subelements that further define its mechanisms.

service

So far, we defined parameters and return types, mapped them to operations, and defined the Web service operation's style and transport mechanism, so what's left? Well all that information is great, but how do you actually call the Web service? Where is it located?

Figure 26-11: The two message and one portType elements of the WSDL file

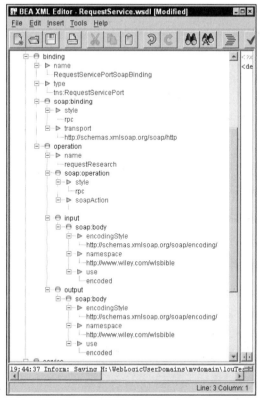

Figure 26-12: The WSDL binding element, fully exploded

That's where the `service` element comes in. It maps the `portType` and `binding` to a physical server address; in this case, `http://localhost:7001/web_services/RequestService`. You need this address to call the Web service.

This may seem awfully complex, but remember the purpose of a WSDL document: It allows a human or machine to read it and logically determine what services are available, at what location, with what operation names, composed of what kind of parameters and return values. As you can see, complex it may be, but it is also very powerful.

Writing a client to access the client JAR

Now that we know what's going on behind the scenes, let's try using our client JAR. The idea is that it should be simple. Even though we know what's going on with the WSDL and SOAP envelope and body, using the client JAR should insulate us from all that. Creating a client that uses the client JAR is simple. Our Web service even gave us a big hint: if you refer to Figure 26-5, you'll see the middle section that gives a rough idea of how to call into the client JAR from your Java client.

Unfortunately, it's only a rough hint, and there are some dependencies and things that need fleshing out. First, look at Listing 26-5 for how we wrote a simple client by using Figure 26-5 as a starting point. This instantiates a `RequestService_Impl` class with our WSDL definition and uses it to get a reference to the `RequestServicePort` interface. The `RequestService Port` interface corresponds to the port binding in the WSDL file and allows us to call the `requestResearch` operation with the "BEA" parameter as input. We then display the return value to standard output.

Listing 26-5: **BibleClient.java**

```
import com.wiley.wlsbible.requestservice.client.RequestService;
import com.wiley.wlsbible.requestservice.client.RequestService_Impl;
import com.wiley.wlsbible.requestservice.client.RequestServicePort;


public class BibleClient {

  public static void main (String[] args) {
    String result;
    String wsdlUrl =
"http://localhost:7001/web_services/RequestService?WSDL";

    try {
      System.out.println ("****\n Instantiating service proxy ...");
      RequestService service = new RequestService_Impl( wsdlUrl );
      System.out.println (" Instantiating port stub ...");
      RequestServicePort port = service.getRequestServicePort();

      System.out.println (" Calling web service with parameter of 'BEA'
...");
      result = port.requestResearch("BEA");
      System.out.println (" Web service return value:\n " + result +
"\n****\n");
    } catch (java.io.IOException ioe) {
      ioe.printStackTrace();
    }
  }
}
```

If you try to compile `BibleClient.java` as is, you'll get an error because you need to include a Web Services JAR in your classpath for both compiling and running the sample client. This file is named `webserviceclient.jar`, and it's in the `\lib` directory in your WebLogic Server directory (for example, `D:\bea\weblogic700\server\lib\webservice client.jar`). And don't forget to include the client JAR itself in your classpath.

After compiling and running the client, you should see output something like this:

```
****
  Instantiating service proxy ...
  Instantiating port stub ...
  Calling web service with parameter of 'BEA' ...
  Web service return value:
  Zeetrade recommends you buy BEA
****
```

Not counting the lines of code that print to standard output, it took us only three lines of pure Java code to call our Web service. And we didn't have to know anything about WSDL or SOAP. Pretty impressive, eh?

Creating a Web Service Manually

If we just spent a whole chapter explaining the easy way to create Web Services, you can imagine how difficult it can get doing it the hard way. But many times, you'll need that power, so WebLogic Server gives you a lot of options for using the full SOAP specification manually.

There are a variety of reasons why you might want to create a Web Service manually:

✦ For more control over the SOAP envelope or encoding.

✦ You might need custom data types (although this can be at least partially automated).

✦ To use messaging with JMS.

✦ You might want to use document encoding rather than RPC.

✦ To use simple manipulation of SOAP messages via handlers.

We discuss each of these reasons further in the next section.

We should also note that Web Services have changed dramatically from WebLogic 6.1 to 7.0. You can deploy services written for 6.1 on 7.0, but you need to do some regeneration first. And keep in mind that this is a short-term solution at best; the entire 6.1 Web Services functionality has been deprecated. See the WebLogic Server 7.0 documentation at the following URL for more information:

```
http://e-docs.bea.com/wls/docs70/webserv/migrate.html#1001373
```

Customizing WebLogic Web services

WebLogic Server 7.0 gives you a great amount of flexibility for putting your Web Services together. An overview is located at the following URL:

```
http://e-docs.bea.com/wls/docs70/webserv/overview.html
```

Following is a list of the major areas of available customization, along with links to more documentation at BEA's Web site.

✦ **Custom data types:** You can completely customize the mapping of parameters and return values to your own custom classes. You can even map elements in SOAP headers to your input parameters. For more information, see

```
http://e-docs.bea.com/wls/docs70/webserv/design.html#1061698
```

✦ **Java, EJB, JMS:** The Web service we created in our example was driven on the back end by an EJB. You can also have it driven by a simple Java class or by JMS destinations. For more information, see

```
http://e-docs.bea.com/wls/docs70/webserv/design.html#1053745
```

✦ **Message handlers:** Actually, you don't even need a back end driven by any code. You can insert message handlers into the Web service that processes the incoming SOAP message *and* processes the outgoing SOAP message. This can include viewing, changing, inserting, and deleting elements and attributes. These handlers can be in addition to, or instead of, any back-end handling. For more information, see

```
http://e-docs.bea.com/wls/docs70/webserv/design.html#1053805
```

✦ **Synchronous vs. asynchronous Web Services:** Our sample Web Service was synchronous: The client called a Web service method and the client waited for a response. You can also create asynchronous Web Services that return void immediately, and go off and do their processing while the client continues. For more information, see

```
http://e-docs.bea.com/wls/docs70/webserv/design.html#1052549
```

✦ **Document vs. RPC:** The sample Web service was RPC (remote procedure call)-based: we could create as many parameters as we needed, and SOAP encoding was used to define the parameters and return values in the SOAP message. Alternatively, you can have a document-based Web service in which the input parameter is an XML document. For more information, see

```
http://e-docs.bea.com/wls/docs70/webserv/design.html#1038901
```

WebLogic Ant tasks for Web services

In addition to the `servicegen` and `clientgen` tasks we already discussed, WebLogic Server provides a number of other Ant tasks to help you generate and deploy your Web Services, as described in the following list. For general information, see the following URL:

```
http://e-docs.bea.com/wls/docs70/webserv/anttasks.html
```

Cross-Reference   Ant tasks are described in more detail in Appendix B.

✦ **servicegen:** Allows the automated generation of a complete Web service. For more information, see

```
http://e-docs.bea.com/wls/docs70/webserv/assemble.html#1052288
```

✦ **clientgen:** Generates a client JAR that allows you to call a Web service from a Java client without having to know anything about Web Services. For more information, see

```
http://e-docs.bea.com/wls/docs70/webserv/assemble.html#1060527
```

✦ **source2wsdd:** Generates a Web Services deployment descriptor (web-services.xml) from a Java back-end class. For more information, see

http://e-docs.bea.com/wls/docs70/webserv/assemble.html#1056639

✦ **autotype:** Create items needed for when you have your own custom classes as parameters and/or return types. For more information, see

http://e-docs.bea.com/wls/docs70/webserv/assemble.html#1069205

✦ **wspackage:** After you generate (automatically or manually) all the components for a Web service, use this task to package them into an EAR file. For more information, see

http://e-docs.bea.com/wls/docs70/webserv/assemble.html#1069398

✦ **wsdl2Service:** This is useful if you've already defined a WSDL file, and now you want to go ahead and start coding it. Using a WSDL file as input, it generates a skeleton Java class that implements a service defined in the WSDL file that you specify. It also generates a web-service.xml file. For more information, see

http://e-docs.bea.com/wls/docs70/webserv/anttasks.html#1080773

✦ **wsgen:** *This is only for getting a WebLogic Server 6.1 service to run on WebLogic Server 7.0; do not use this for new Web Services.*

These Ant tasks can save you an enormous amount of time, even if you are creating your Web Services manually.

Summary

Web Services are simple in theory but excruciatingly detailed in practice. In this chapter, we saw how to create a service in four short steps by using an Ant task to convert an EJB into a full-fledged Web Service. Along the way, we described how a SOAP message is defined by a SOAP envelope that contains a header and a body and how WSDL documents are used to define a Web service in XML.

In addition to testing a Web client for our Web Service, we demonstrated how to create a Java client using the autogenerated client JAR from our Web service. Finally, we pointed you to further resources for creating Web Services manually, so that you can customize them infinitely to meet your company's business needs.

✦   ✦   ✦

Web Services with WebLogic Workshop

Web Services can sometimes seem like Pandora's box — it looks all neat and orderly and logical from the outside, but open it up and all sorts of ugly things pop out.

As with all great ideas, the concept of Web Services started out simply, but complexity was added as new features and functionality were needed. Because Web Services are the glue that holds everything together, they need to know about everything else to be useful.

As is common with software development, whenever a complex programming technology comes along, the need for a simple way to deal with that technology comes along with it. Enter WebLogic Workshop, a tool that comes with WebLogic Server 7.0 and allows you to assemble complex Web Services that can interoperate with other operating systems and languages with a few mouse clicks.

As wonderfully simple as Workshop is, it has sufficient depth to it that a single chapter cannot hope to explain it comprehensively. It can easily fill a book — in fact, it has: look for *BEA WebLogic Workshop: Building the Next Generation Web Services Visually* by Sean Christofferson, Srinivas Jayanthi, Wira Pradjinata, and Steven Traut (Wiley Technology Publishing, 2002).

In this chapter, we show you how you can use Workshop to create Web Services with a minimum of hassle, as well as how to test those services using Workshop.

What Is Workshop?

Workshop is a powerful IDE that simplifies the creation of Web Services applications by allowing an entry-level Java programmer to bind components together using a simple GUI. Figure 27-1 shows Workshop loaded with a Web Service that is being designed.

What you can't see in Figure 27-1 is just how much complexity is hidden by the Workshop GUI. Behind that pretty face lies a truckload of XML. XML documents are used extensively in Web Services, everywhere from sending and receiving messages to defining Web Service capabilities. One of the great things about Workshop is that you can let it take care of all the nitty-gritty details, or you can peek under the hood and tweak the XML yourself.

In this chapter we'll define a Web Service in WebLogic Workshop without tweaking any XML. We show you how to look at the underlying XML, but we'll keep it simple so you understand how easy Workshop can be.

Cross-Reference

If you really want to get into the gory details of the XML used in Web Services, we describe it in more detail in Chapter 26.

Figure 27-1: The Workshop IDE with a Web Service loaded for editing

Problems it solves

Workshop makes it easier for developers to create Web Services solutions. Think of it as a tool for creating services, much as JBuilder is a tool for creating Java code or Macromedia Dreamweaver is a tool for creating Web pages.

Detailed knowledge of Web Services and J2EE not required

Traditionally, creating Web Services in Java has taken two skill sets: Understanding XML, HTTP, and SOAP on the one hand and understanding the full breadth of J2EE on the other hand. SOAP knowledge is needed for the interface to the Web Services, and J2EE knowledge is needed for the interface to the code that actually does the work.

Developer productivity

Wouldn't it be nice to have a tool that simplifies SOAP and also simplifies the interfaces to the J2EE objects (EJBs and other Web Services)? Workshop does just that by providing a convenient GUI that obviates the need to know SOAP internals and makes it relatively easy to connect to other objects.

Architecture — How it works

Workshop is a sophisticated IDE that has a surprisingly simple and intuitivegraphical interface for creating Web Services. It also includes a debugger and automatically generates a simple client application that allows you to test your Web Service without creating a client yourself.

The way it works is simple. Follow these steps:

1. Configure Workshop to work with one of your WebLogic Server domains (or you can create a new one).

2. Create a new Workshop project, which is just a J2EE enterprise application directory structure in your chosen WebLogic domain.

3. Design your Web Service in the GUI. You specify input parameters and return values for the public Web Service interface, and you can hook your Web Service up internally to EJBs, JMS topics and queues, and other Web Services. You're totally insulated from the complexities of WSDL and XML, although Workshop gives you the power to edit them manually if you want.

4. As you design your Web Service, Workshop creates `.jws` files in the background, which are just normal Java source files with special Javadoc-style comments.

5. Add custom Java code functionality to the generated `.jws` files. Enter breakpoints in your code, if desired.

6. Click the Start and Debug icon in the toolbar. Workshop automatically parses the `.jws` files and then creates, compiles, and deploys servlets and EJBs to your WebLogic Server domain. It also brings up a browser window with a Web interface so you can test your Web Services. Think of it as you would JSPs — you create a Web Service (much as you create a JSP file); then a compiler takes the JWS file and converts it to Java code for servlets and EJBs (much as the JSP compiler converts JSPs into Java code for servlets).

Your Web Service is a middleman. You define the inputs and outputs to your Web Service clients on the left, and you define the components that your Web Service uses (databases, EJBs, JMS, and other Web Services) on the right.

JWS — An emerging standard?

In the preceding steps, you'll notice an emphasis on the JWS files. These are just normal Java source files with special comments in the code. JWS stands for Java Web Service, and it's a Java commenting convention that BEA has submitted as a standard. See the Java Community Process' JSR 181 at the following URL:

```
http://www.jcp.org/en/jsr/detail?id=181
```

JWS comments are an extension of Javadoc-style comments. Workshop has defined 25 tags that it adds to source code automatically as you work in the GUI. You can enter these tags yourself in the source code, but it's usually easier to let Workshop do the work for you. After the tags have been added, when you go to run your Web Service, a JWS compiler will process the JWS files and generate the "real" Web Service — a group of components including EJBs and servlets. Examples of JWS tags include `@jws:wsdl`, which specifies a WSDL file to use as a service, and `@jws:sql`, which specifies a SQL string and associated parameters.

For more information on JWS tags, refer to "Javadoc Tag Reference" in the Workshop Help system.

Automation

Workshop is not just a pretty face on Web Services; it also automates many steps in the process of creating Web Services. You can let Workshop take care of the mechanics of what gets done, and you can just concentrate on your business processes.

Autogenerate an entire enterprise application

One of Workshop's coolest features is that it generates complete Web Services for you. To do this manually, you'd need to code your own servlet and session EJBs or Java classes, as discussed in Chapter 26.

Automating XML/WSDL creating and parsing

By using a GUI interface, Workshop totally automates the creation of the XML documents, including the complex WSDL documents. It also seamlessly handles the parsing of the XML into Java classes, and vice versa. It also gives you the flexibility to manually intervene and do the mapping yourself, or even to write JavaScript functions to aid in the mapping.

InteroperabilityOne of the big concerns with a tool like this is its compatibility: Will it integrate with other Web Services tools, products, and APIs? The good news is that Workshop includes a control that enables it to work with any conforming WSDL Web Service.

Workshop can use Web Services created with other implementations of the SOAP specification. This list details where to get more information on compatibility with other popular Web Services implementations:

✦ **WebLogic 6.1 Web Services:** Workshop-generated Web Services are compatible with 6.1 services to the extent that you need to modify its out-of-date schema. See the Workshop Help topic "How Do I: Create a Service Control from a WSDL File Generated by WebLogic Server 6.1?"

✦ **Apache:** Workshop services are generally compatible with Apache SOAP, but there are some potential gotchas. Look up "How Do I: Use an Apache SOAP Web Service?" in the Workshop Help system.

✦ **.Net:** Workshop can use .Net Web Services as a service. For more information, look up the topic "How Do I: Use a .NET Web Service?" in the Workshop Help files.

For more information, see the Workshop Help system, in the "How do I . . . ?" topics.

Installing and Configuring Workshop

Before using Workshop, you need to make sure it's installed and configured properly. This will help prevent the most common errors when trying to create, run, or debug your Web Service. This section explains the process of configuring Workshop to work with a WebLogic Server domain.

Installing Workshop

Workshop is installed when you install in WebLogic Server 7.0. Note that it requires (and installs) the Sun JDK 1.4.

Creating a new Workshop domain

Use the Domain Configuration Wizard to create a new, empty WebLogic Workshop domain.

Cross-Reference
Chapter 4 explains how to use the Domain Configuration Wizard. There is more discussion of this wizard in the discussion of clusters in Chapter 24. At the beginning of the wizard, select the option to create a new Workshop domain.

Note
You can also create a new WebLogic Server domain to use or you can use an existing WebLogic Server domain. However, you must Workshop-enable it. See the Workshop Help topic "How Do I: WebLogic Workshop-Enable an Existing WebLogic Server Domain?"

Starting Workshop

WebLogic installation creates a Workshop submenu in the Windows Start menu. Click the Start button and choose Programs ➪ BEA WebLogic Platform 7.0 ➪ WebLogic Workshop ➪ WebLogic Workshop. Alternatively, you can go to the <WL_HOME> directory and navigate to the workshop directory. Then run Workshop.exe (Windows) or Workshop.sh (Unix). Note that in this directory, workshop.properties contains the properties that we configure in the next section.

Configuring Workshop

After we start Workshop, we need to configure it to see our new or existing domain that we want to use. In Workshop, setting preferences is done by selecting Tools ➪ Preferences. There are four tabs on this window: Display, Editor, Colors, and Path. All four tabs are explained in the following sections.

Display preferences

Like any IDE, you can configure display preferences. Figure 27-2 shows the Editor tab. Here is what shows up:

✦ **Window Font Size:** The font size for all non-editor windows. You must restart Workshop for this value to take effect.

✦ **Source View Font:** The typeface and size of the font to use for displaying code in the Source View.

✦ **Structure Pane Sorting:** The display order of the Structure pane (the Structure pane is described in the section "Using Workshop" later in this chapter).

✦ **Design View Sorting:** The display order of Design View (Design View is described in the section "Using Workshop" later in this chapter).

✦ **Project Tree:** In the Project Tree (the Project Tree is described in the section "Using Workshop" later in this chapter) you can hide (WebLogic) system directories or not.

Figure 27-2: Display preferences

Editor preferences

Figure 27-3 shows the Editor tab. It has these options:

✦ **Source View Options:** Selections for the way source code is displayed.

✦ **Indentation:** Options for automatically formatting your code as you enter it.

✦ **Code Completion:** With this option turned on, Workshop will automatically insert method names and types as you type them in.

Figure 27-3: Editor preferences

Colors preferences

Figure 27-4 shows the Colors tab. It lists each element type in a code source window. Click the color to bring up a color selection dialog box to change the color of all elements of that type.

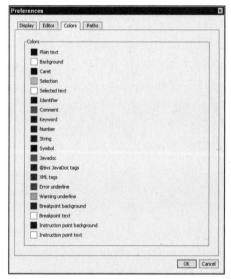

Figure 27-4: Colors preferences

Click OK to save your changes. As mentioned earlier, these configuration options are saved in the Workshop.properties file in the Workshop directory.

Setting the active domain and server: Paths preferences

Of the Workshop preferences, the most important thing to change is the path (domain) information. This enables Workshop to create your projects in the correct directory and to start and stop the correct WebLogic server at the appropriate times.

Workshop can connect to any WebLogic Server 7.0 domain that has been appropriately prepared, as we described earlier. Figure 27-5 shows the Paths tab. It has the following entries:

✦ **Name:** The DNS name of the server to connect to. For development purposes on your own machine, this is almost always localhost.

✦ **Port:** Enter the server's TCP/IP port number. This is the plaintext port configured for that server. It's typically 7001, unless you change your server's configuration in the WebLogic console.

✦ **Domain:** A drop-down list of available domains in the Config Directory (see next bullet). Select the Config Directory first and then choose the domain.

✦ **Config Directory:** Also known as the WebLogic User Domain Directory (see Chapter 4), this is the base directory for all the domains on a machine. Note that although WebLogic doesn't enforce that you have all domains underneath the Config (or User Domain) directory, now you see why it's a good idea to do it that way. It makes selecting a domain as simple as picking from a list. You can click the Browse button to open a file selection dialog box.

✦ **Browser Path:** The path to your default Web browser. Workshop uses this value to launch a browser for testing your Web Service. You can click the Browse button to open a file selection dialog box.

Figure 27-5: Paths preferences, in which you tell Workshop how to connect to WebLogic Server 7.0

Using Workshop

Now that you've configured Workshop, you're ready to start using it. Before we start creating a new Web Service, it's worth spending just a moment to go over the GUI interface. If you've used other modern IDEs, such as those from Borland, IBM, or Microsoft, you'll feel right at home using Workshop. Even if you haven't used those tools, you'll find it's easy to get up to speed quickly because all the tools you need are a click away.

Figure 27-6 shows an empty IDE window, whereas Figure 27-1 showed one with a sample Web Service loaded. The Workshop IDE is a Java application that requires JDK 1.4 or higher. Like most modern IDEs, you can right-click with your mouse just about anywhere to bring up a context-sensitive menu of options.

Project   Design   Source
  Tree   View   View   Properties Description
  pane   tab   tab   Project name   pane   pane

Structure pane   Project View pane   Tasks pane

Figure 27-6: Workshop IDE immediately after creating a new, blank project

The IDE is split up into the following regions:

✦ **Menu and Toolbar:** At the top of the IDE window is the menu with all the available commands (many of these commands are duplicated in the toolbar). It has options for opening, saving, and creating projects; cut, copy, paste, and undo; code indenting and searching; and building, running, and debugging your Web Services.

✦ **Status Bar:** At the bottom of the window is the status bar. It displays status information, allows you to start and stop the associated WebLogic Server instance, and displays editor-insertion point and key lock information.

✦ **Project Tree:** In the upper-left corner of the IDE window is the Project Tree. It is just a physical directory and file listing of what's in your domain's server's applications directory for this project. Each Web Service (which can have multiple methods) ends up in its own .jws file, and you can have multiple JWS files in a project. You can also create Java, HTML, JavaScript, and text files here.

✦ **Structure pane:** This is a logical representation of all the methods and objects available in the current document that is open in the DesignView/Source View. Workshop automatically generates some of these objects when you create a new Web Service, so there are some there that you do not create. For example, the context object (an instance of the weblogic.jws.control.JwsContext class) is available in all Web Services classes.

✦ **View pane:** Here is where you will do most of your work in Workshop. While you can
have multiple Web Services in a single project, this pane shows only one Web Service at
a time — the one currently selected in the Project Tree. The View pane is a window into
your Web Service that can be viewed two different ways: as a graphical representation
(Design View), or as a source code representation (Source View).

- *Design View* — Design View is the meat of what Workshop provides for you. Here
  is where you can graphically design and create your Web Services. We'll go
  through this in a lot more detail shortly, but basically you create public Web
  Service access methods on the left, and use public and private resources (such
  as databases, EJBs, JMS queues and topics, and other Web Services) on the right
  to create your Web Service. Design View shows only one Web Service at a time.
  Double-click a JWS file in the Project Tree to display its Web Service here.

- *Source View* — The Source View is the alter ego of the Design View, as shown in
  Figure 27-7 (only the Design View is visible in Figure 27-6). Instead of seeing your
  Web Service class graphically (as shown in Figures 27-1 and 27-6), Source View is
  the autogenerated code that Workshop creates along with any custom code that
  you write. This is the source of the JWS file for your Web Service, and includes
  the methods you defined, along with the services (databases, EJBs, and so on)
  and their objects.

  You can not only view code here, but you can edit code here, too; Workshop will
  not overwrite your changes. It is also two-way designing/coding. Any changes
  you make here will be reflected in the Design View.

  There are two drop-down lists at the top of the Source View. The one on the left
  shows a list of all objects in the JWS file (much like the top level of the Structure
  pane). The list on the right shows the available methods for the selected object,
  as well as the location of its definition.

Figure 27-7: Source View, showing the
drop-down lists, the source code, and the
build Output window

Note   If you have started a build or performed a file search, there will be an additional Output window that shows the result of the build or search.

✦ **Properties Inspector:** The Properties Inspector displays all the available properties for an object in the Design View. Note that clicking an item in the Structure pane will automatically select it in the Design View and display its properties in the Properties Inspector. As you click different objects, the Properties Inspector changes to show you the appropriate properties.

✦ **Description pane:** For the selected item in Design View, the Description pane shows its type (class), name, and a description of the object's purpose.

✦ **Tasks pane:** If available, this contains a list of possible tasks for the currently selected item in Design View. The task can have a hyperlink, and clicking the hyperlink starts the task.

Creating a Web Service

Workshop works with *projects*, so we need to create a new project (a project is composed of one or more Web Services). Each Web Service has one or more methods to communicate with clients and zero or more controls to do its work. Theoretically, a Web Service doesn't need any controls — you could code all its functionality in custom Java code — but in order to leverage other components such as databases and EJBs, you'll almost always have one or more controls in your Web Service.

The following sections show you how to create a new project as well as how to add new operations and controls.

Creating a new project

To create a new project, follow these steps:

1. Select File ↦ New Project from the menu. The New Project dialog box appears. Enter the name of your Web Service into the Project name field and click OK. This creates a subdirectory in your configured domain's applications directory. (Your configured domain is the domain you specified in Figure 27-2.)

Note   This project name is also used in the URL for your Web Service.

2. Immediately after clicking OK, a new dialog box pops up, as shown in Figure 27-8. You can add any of the listed file types. Enter the information as shown in the figure and click OK. Your Web Service has been created.

Figure 27-8: Entering details for
a new Web Service

3. Double-click `BibleHelloWorld.JWS` in the Project Tree, and you'll see a blank slate that should look like Figure 27-6. If you now go to the file system in Windows Explorer, you'll see that the layout in the Project Tree in Figure 27-6 looks just like the file system shown in Figure 27-9.

Figure 27-9: The file system layout for your
new project in your chosen domain

Notice the properties for your Web Service in the Properties pane. You can click each heading or element in the Properties pane and an appropriate description will show up in the Description pane.

Note   Because of the complexity of Workshop, we can only cover so much detail in one chapter. Our goal is to provide you with a solid foundation for exploring Workshop further. For this reason, the properties are described in fairly general terms. Use Workshop's Help menu to see more information.

The properties for a Web Service are the following:

- **target-namespace:** The namespace used for generated WSDL files.

- **conversation-lifetime:** The combination of `max-age` and `max-idle-time` determines how long WebLogic will wait before considering a conversation is dead.

- **protocols:** Select the protocols through which your Web Service must interact with clients.

- **wsdl:** If you're creating a service from scratch, you don't need to specify this property. If you're creating a service to interact with a predefined WSDL file, enter the filename here.

- **schema:** The filename of a schema so that you can use user-defined types in your Web Service.

4. You can add and edit other types of text files. Choose File ➪ New and you'll see a submenu of the types of files to add. Each of the options brings up the same dialog, which is shown in Figure 27-8. The file types you can add are:

- **Java:** This is just your average generic Java source file.

- **JavaScript:** JavaScript files have file extensions of `jsx`. Functions within `jsx` files can be created to do custom XML ⇔ ⇔ Java mapping, and these functions can be called from XML maps. Workshop provides a template whenever you create a file of this type.

- **Text:** If you specify Text, you can enter any file extension (such as `xml`, `html`, `cmd`, or `sh`). Again, these files are created in your Web Services applications directory, as shown in Figure 27-9.

Note Files other than Web Services files do not have a Design View, so no properties are available.

Adding operations

At the top left of the Design View is a drop-down list for adding operations. The two kinds of operations you can add are *methods* and *callbacks*. Methods are synchronous methods, such as a typical method call in Java. That is, the client code makes a method call and then waits for an answer from your Web Service; when your Web Service is finished with its work, it sends a return value back to the (waiting) client. Callbacks are asynchronous, such as JMS messages. You post a message back to a client with (presumably) an answer or result of some sort.

Callbacks typically are part of a *conversation*. A conversation is a series of methods and callbacks between a client and your Web Service. The conversation keeps track of which client it's dealing with, much as session state in a Web application keeps track of which user session it's dealing with. You keep track of session state by adding member variables, which we discuss in the "Adding member variables" section a bit later in this chapter.

A synchronous method might be something such as `isPartInStock("A4")`, to which your Web Service would return a boolean, either `true` (it is in stock) or `false` (it isn't). Because answering the question is just a matter of a quick database search, there's no reason to keep a conversation going.

On the other hand, an asynchronous conversation would be more along the lines of an online order. For example, the customer would call a method such as orderPart("A6"), which would be the first of several steps in the conversation. Because this is asynchronous, the client would then continue what it was doing (maybe harvesting orders from an internal database). Next, as part of this conversation, your Web Service might send a callback to the client, such as orderReceived("Order-34567"), to notify the client that the order has been acknowledged and given an order number. Then, after the order is shipped, another callback could be sent to the client, along the lines of orderShipped("Order-34567"), to tell the client that the order in fact shipped. This would be the endpoint in the conversation, and the Web Service and the client would end the conversation there and then do whatever cleanup they needed to do.

Adding a method

To add a method, click the Add Operation drop-down list and select Add Method. Then type in the name of the method. If you want to add or change the parameters or return type, right-click the method name in Design View and select Edit Maps and Interface from the context menu that appears.

After selecting this menu item, you may get a message box asking you to start your WebLogic server; click OK to start the server and domain you specified earlier. Now you'll see a dialog box with a progress bar. When it's done, a dialog box will appear, as shown in Figures 27-10 and 27-11. This dialog box shows the relevant portion of the XML used to call this Web Service from a client, as well as the Java signature for the method. If you click the Return XML tab, it shows the return value in XML.

You can edit the parameters and return type in the sample Java method signature window at the bottom of the dialog box. In that case, the XML mapping is still Default, which means Workshop will automatically change the XML as you edit the Java method signature. In Figure 27-12, we have changed the return type and added some parameters to the Java method signature and watched as WebLogic updated the XML automatically. Figure 27-13 shows the Return XML tab for this same method.

Figure 27-10: XML map for our simple method

Figure 27-11: Return XML tab of the XML map

Figure 27-12: XML map for our enhanced method

Figure 27-13: Return XML tab of the XML map for our enhanced method

Customizing the XML map

As we've just shown, modifying the Java method signature will cause Workshop to automatically modify the XML mapping for you. But you can also make changes directly to the XML. In that case, the mapping type goes from Default to Custom in the dialog box. This means it's completely up to you to make sure you map it correctly. It also means you can map it any way you want in case you need to map it to a particular client without changing your Web Services code.

If a static mapping is not powerful enough, you can use JavaScript in the .jsx files we showed you how to create earlier. Click the Help button in this dialog box for more details.

Viewing the generated JWS file

Now that we've customized the XML map, let's take a look at what Workshop generates in terms of Java files. Back in the Design View, click the name of your method or callback (or right-click and choose Go To Code In .jws). You'll be brought to the Source View and the generated code for your method, as shown in Figure 27-14.

Figure 27-14: Generated source code in the JWS file

Note the @jws:operation in the comment. This is Workshop's Java Web Service (JWS) tag language based on Javadoc standards. These tags tell Workshop's JWS compiler what code to generate, much as JSP tags tell the JSP compiler what code to generate for a servlet. See the Workshop Help for a list of all JWS tags and their meanings.

We'll go over Properties and Tasks for operations in the next section.

Adding a callback

A callback, like a method, is an operation, but it goes in the opposite direction. That is, the callback is the Web Service sending a message to the client. Usually, this is part of a conversation, as we discussed earlier.

Let's create a method and callbacks that correspond to our simple example: the orderPart method, and orderReceived and orderShipped callbacks. We do this by clicking the Add Operation drop-down list and selecting Add Method or Add Callback, as appropriate; then change the name as described. Don't worry about the XML maps for this simple example.

Properties

Click on the orderPart method in the Design View. In the Properties pane, you'll see the conversation section. Change its phase to Start. This tells Workshop that it's part of a conversation, and in fact begins the conversation.

Tasks

Click on the orderReceived callback and then look in the Tasks pane. You'll see a link labeled Change the conversational phase of this method. Click the link and the phase drop-down list will pop down; change its conversation phase to Continue. Repeat for the orderShipped callback and change its conversation phase to Finished. Notice that the arrows on the methods and callbacks that are part of a conversation have the letters S, C, and F in a colored circle, which stand for start, continue, and finish.

In between calls to orderPart() and orderShipped, Workshop will keep track of the conversation ID in calls to and from this particular client. The conversation ID is what makes the conversation unique among all clients.

Adding controls

Controls encapsulate the meat of a Web Service. Although you certainly could hard-code all the functionality of a Web Service directly in the JWS file, it is like coding an entire J2EE application inside a servlet. It's possible, but it's nonsensical.

What you really want to do is leverage existing code and databases and partition the work. To that end, you can use Workshop controls to automate the interface between your Web Service and the other functionality available to you. The functionality that can be encapsulated in a control is other Web Services, databases, EJBs, timers, and JMS queues and topics.

You configure controls on the right side of the Design View. Click on the Add Control drop-down list to add one of these controls. You can have more than one control in a Web Service.

Control definitions, which are like class definitions, are stored in .ctrl files. You then name instances of these controls and use them in your Web Services.

Service controls

Service controls encapsulate other Web Services. Let's say we want to create a new Web Service, and we want it to reuse the functionality that we already created for our BibleHelloWorld service.

To do that, we first need to create a .ctrl file out of our BibleHelloWorld service. In the Project Tree pane, right-click the BibleHelloWorld service and select Generate CTRL from JWS. This creates a control file that we can use in another Web Service. So create a new Web Service (File ➪ New ➪ New Web Service), name it BiblePartChecker, and click OK. The BiblePartChecker Web Service now shows up in the Design View.

Add a method on the left side of the Design View and name it isPartInStock. Add a service control on the right side of the Design View. Fill out the dialog box, as shown in Figure 27-15. You'll need to click the Browse button to find the .ctrl file for the BibleHelloWorld service. Click Create to create the control.

Figure 27-15: Defining a Web Service in a control

Your Workshop window should now look like Figure 27-16. In the Design View, a new control appears that—magically—contains all the same methods as our BibleHelloWorld Web Service. The Structure pane also shows the variable name (bibleHelloService) and all its Java methods.

Figure 27-16: The Web Service control added to an existing Web Service

Okay, now that we have a method on the left that's callable by the client and a control on the right that we can use—how do we connect them together? Click the isPartInStock method in the Design View to bring you to its code in the Source View (see Figure 27-17).

Figure 27-17: The autogenerated code for our method

Change the code so it returns boolean and takes a parameter of int for quantity and long for partID. Now we want it to return the value returned from our service control's getData method. Because our service control has a variable name of bibleHelloService, start typing in the body of our method:

```
return bibleHelloService.getD
```

After typing the period, a list of methods on that Web Service should appear, as shown in Figure 27-18. As soon as you type **getD**, it should automatically select the getData method; at this point, just press Enter and it will fill in the rest of the method name.

Figure 27-18: Filling in the code and using autocompletion

Add the quantity and partID parameters, and it should look like Figure 27-19.

Figure 27-19: The completed method, calling our other Web Service

Click on the Design View tab, and notice that the method signature has changed. The signature in the Structure pane also automatically updates, as shown in Figure 27-20.

Figure 27-20: Design View and Structure pane autoupdated after changing the code manually in the Source View

On the right side of the Design View, click the `bibleHelloService` control and notice its properties. Then, click on each method and callback and notice how the properties change. Also, notice that the properties match the properties we set on the original `BibleHello World` Web Service. The Design View even shows the same icons in the colored circles that we defined for conversation state. Workshop saves you a lot of time.

Timer controls

Timer controls are used for asynchronous Web Service methods. Let's say that order processing might take a couple of days or weeks if it's back-ordered. And maybe the customer wants to know that we're still aware about its order. We can create a timer that will fire once a day or once a week to send e-mail to the customer with the order status. The timer will use a call-back method to allow us to send the e-mail. The timer knows about the conversation, so when the conversation ends, no events will be fired.

Timers are somewhat different from other controls in Workshop. Creating a timer just instantiates a `weblogic.jws.control.TimerControl` class rather than creating a new class for each timer.

In the Design View, click Add Control and then click Add Timer Control. A dialog box pops up; fill it out as shown in Figure 27-21. This will allow us to send e-mail at every timer event.

The Design View now looks like Figure 27-22. Clicking on the `onTimeout` callback method takes us to the JWS file where we can add our custom code to send e-mail to the client. The timer calls this callback method whenever an event fires, either the first event or a repeating event.

Figure 27-21: Adding a timer control

Figure 27-22: Design View after adding a timer control

Database controls

You can access a database and issue SQL calls, including inserts, updates, deletes, and queries using a Workshop database control. Because a database control is an instantiation of a custom class, you can reuse that control in different Web Services.

In the Design View, click Add Control and then Add Database Control. Fill out the dialog box, as shown in Figure 27-23. Just as with other controls, you give it a variable name in Step 1. In Step 2, specify a new control name. In Step 3, we specify the JDBC data source that we want to connect to. This must be preconfigured in your WebLogic Server instance. We used the Domain Configuration Wizard to create a blank WebLogic Server instance for Workshop (see the beginning of this chapter), which provides us with a sample database connection that we selected using the Browse button in Figure 27-23.

Figure 27-23: Configuring a database control

After your control has been created, right-click it in Design View and choose Add Method from the context menu that appears. The new method appears.

You can now edit the Java method signature and its SQL in one of three ways:

✦ Right-click the method in Design View and select Edit SQL and Interface.

✦ Click Go To SQL in the method's Property pane.

✦ Click Edit the SQL Statement in the method's Task pane.

When you do this, the dialog box shown in Figure 27-24 displays. Modify the SQL statement to do what you want and edit the Java method to match the SQL. You can rename the method to anything that makes sense. Any input parameters to the method can be translated into SQL parameters by surrounding them with brackets, as shown for the {partID} in the SQL statement and the corresponding partID in the Java method. Here, we return a single value because we're querying for a single column via a primary key, but you can return a single value, a single row, or multiple rows. Click the Help button for details on how to return multiple values.

Figure 27-24: Editing the SQL and Java method signature

You could continue adding methods as we just described; a database control can have any number of methods that perform any SQL command. Of course, it probably makes sense to keep your queries in one database control; and it makes sense to keep inserts, deletes, and updates in one or more additional controls.

EJB controls

Using EJBs is easy with Workshop. Just as you must preconfigure a JDBC data source to use a database control, you must preconfigure and deploy an EJB before using it in Workshop. Then copy the EJB's client JAR into your Web Service project's `WEB-INF/lib` directory, so it's in the project's classpath. In our example, we copied the stateless session EJB from Chapter 15 into our project, as shown in Figure 27-25. You might also need to restart the server and reopen your Workshop project for it to find the newly configured EJB.

Figure 27-25: The Project Tree pane showing the Request.EJB in WEB-INF\lib

In the Design View, click Add Control and then click Add EJB Control. Fill it out as shown in Figure 27-26. As with other controls, fill in the variable name and the control name. In Step 3, click the Browse buttons to pick the JNDI name and Home and Remote interfaces from a list of all configured EJBs.

Note   No matter what we tried, we could not get the Browse button for the JNDI name to show us any configured EJBs. It kept telling us that there were no JNDI names assigned to EJBs in our server instance. We had to go to the WebLogic Server console, identify the JNDI name we deployed our EJB under, and type that in manually in the EJB Control dialog box.

Figure 27-26: Configuring an EJB control

After we clicked Create to create the EJB control, the Design View appeared, as shown in Figure 27-27. Note that Workshop automatically queried the EJB for its remote methods and added them to the control.

Figure 27-27: An EJB control with its methods automatically populated

Workshop takes care of many issues in dealing with EJBs, such as creation and instance tracking, but there are additional issues such as security. These issues go far beyond the scope of this chapter. Look up EJB controls in the Workshop Help system for information on dealing with these issues. There is also a book on WebLogic Workshop published by Wiley (see the introduction to this chapter for the full title) that covers these issues.

JMS control

Setting up a JMS queue or topic is easy with Workshop. In the Design View, choose Create Control ➪ Create JMS Control. Fill out the dialog box shown in Figure 27-28. As with database and EJB controls, you must preconfigure your resources in WebLogic Server before trying to use them in Workshop. For JMS controls, this means setting up your queue or topic and its JNDI names and connection factories.

Figure 27-28: Configuring a JMS control

Click Create to create the control. As shown in Figure 27-29, the Design View now shows the control along with a method you can call to send messages — `sendTextMessage` — as well as a callback method in our JWS file — `receiveTextMessage` — that gets called when a new message appears on the queue. You can create new methods and callbacks, as well as change the XML mapping for the messages. Look these topics up in the Workshop Help system for more information.

Figure 27-29: Design View showing a new JMS queue control with send and receive methods

Adding member variables

Member variables can keep track of information in a Web Service over the course of a conversation. For example, we might want to keep track of a customer ID between the time we receive an order (the start of the conversation, via a method) and the time we ship the product and e-mail the customer (at the end of the conversation, via a callback).

At the bottom of the Design View, you can right-click on the Member Variables text and select Add Member Variable from the popup menu. The New Member Variable dialog box appears. For this example, type **customerID** into the Variable name field, select String as the type, and click OK. The variable now appears at the bottom of the Design View.

Right-click the variable name in the Design View and select Go To Code in `.jws`. This brings us to the definition of the variable in the source code. Go ahead and enter a new variable in the Source View, such as `public long partID;` and click on the Design View tab. Notice that it shows up at the bottom of the variables list and in the Structure pane, as shown in Figure 27-30.

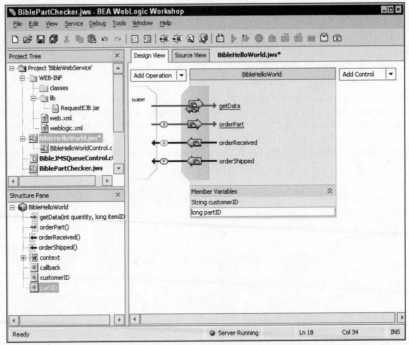

Figure 27-30: Variables added in the Source View show up in Design View and the Structure pane

Note that member variables must be serializable in order to maintain session state.

Testing and Debugging

Workshop provides a lot of power for generating code and connecting to other services, but it doesn't stop there. While it's generating your code, it's also generating a test client. Workshop also includes a built-in debugger.

Running and stepping through code

To prepare for debugging your Web Service, you need to do some setup on the server side. This includes getting WebLogic Server up and running, and telling Workshop where to add breakpoints. We discuss these topics in the following sections.

Starting the Server for debugging

To debug your Web Service, it has to be running. If your WebLogic Server 7.0 server isn't running, start it by right-clicking the server status icon at the bottom of the Workshop status bar and selecting Start WebLogic Server.

Adding breakpoints

You can enter breakpoints at any appropriate place in the JWS file — either the automatic generated code or code that you add yourself. For example, we opened the `BibleHelloWorld` Web Service and clicked the `getData` method in the Design View; this brought us to the Source View. We right-clicked the `return` statement and chose Toggle Breakpoint from the pop-up menu.

Note   Alternatively, you can press F9 or click the Toggle Breakpoint button on the toolbar.

The line with the breakpoint changes color, and a dot appears to the left of the line number if you have line numbering turned on in your preferences. Now when the code execution reaches the breakpoint, the debugger will pause the Web Service and let you add a watch, inspect values, and step in and over code.

Tip   Hover your mouse over the toolbar buttons to see what they do.

To start your Web Service and view the Workshop-generated client, click the Start and Debug toolbar button.

Running the client

After you click the Start and Debug toolbar button, your preferred browser should come up with a sample Web application. This is the client that Workshop automatically generates, as shown in Figure 27-31.

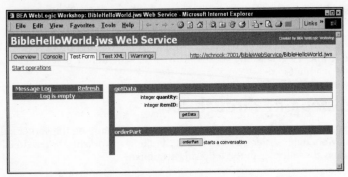

Figure 27-31: Workshop's autogenerated test client

The browser lists your Web Service's name at the top. Below that is a row of tabs: Test Form, Test XML, Overview, Console, and Warnings. By default, the Web page comes up with the Test Form tab selected. To the right of the tabs is the URL, which includes your host name, port number, Web Service project name, and Web Service name. Each tab has a different function, so let's go through them now.

Test form

This tab is split up into three general areas, as shown in Figure 27-41. At the top is a list of actions. Start Operations will take you to the home pane, in which you can send requests. Below the actions are two columns. On the left is the Message Log, which shows a list of all actions that have been performed in the current testing/debugging session. On the right is a list of all available SOAP methods and entry fields in which you can enter parameters. Note that for a group of methods that participate in a conversation, only the method(s) that are appropriate for the current state of the conversation are shown.

Because our methods are sitting right in front of us, screaming out for us to test them, let's go ahead and do just that. Enter appropriate values for the quantity and itemID (such as 5 and 1234) and click getData.

You won't see a response in the client right away. Let's not forget about the breakpoint that we just added. Click Workshop to bring it to the foreground, and you should see the Source View with the breakpoint highlighted; a current code execution arrow to its left; and a Debug window with Locals, Watch, and Call Stack. This is shown in Figure 27-32. The things you can do here are pretty typical as with any debugger, so click Continue on the toolbar to continue with our Web Service.

Take a look at the client browser window again, shown in Figure 27-33. Now the Message Log has an entry: getData. Follow the colored highlight to the right and you'll see the Service Request. This lists the request time, the method name, and the parameter values. Below that is the Service Response. This lists the response time, the method name, and the return value. You'll see that it returned false.

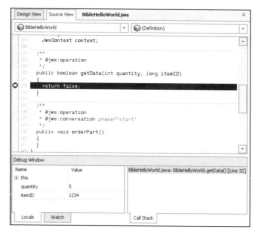

Figure 27-32: The Source and Debug windows in Workshop

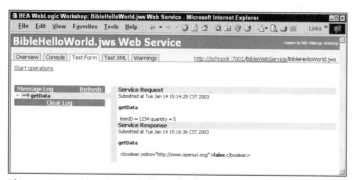

Figure 27-33: The client window after returning from a Web Service

At the top of the Test Form tabbed window, click the Start Operations link. We'll try the same Web Service, but this time we'll enter an invalid value such as **Hello** for the partID. After clicking getData, we won't hit our breakpoint because as our Web Service parses the XML (using the XML map we defined earlier), it encountered an error and returned that error before actually calling our custom code. This error is shown in Figure 27-34.

Okay, that was easy enough, but what if we want to dig deeper and get down-and-dirty with the XML?

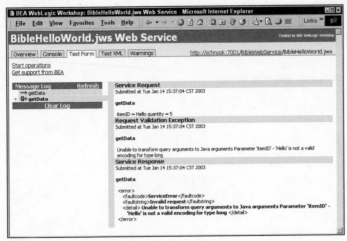

Figure 27-34: A SOAP faultcode returned for a bad parameter

Test XML

In addition to the polite interface shown on the Test Form tab, Workshop enables you to get to some of the raw XML on the Test XML tab. Click this tab and you'll see what's shown in Figure 27-35. Here, you can modify the XML and the client will send exactly what you edit. To reproduce what we entered in the polite view (the Test Form tab), replace Value_quantity with 5 and Value_itemID with 1234. After clicking getData, you'll get the exact same results you got before. But now you can modify more than just the parameters — you have free control over all the XML.

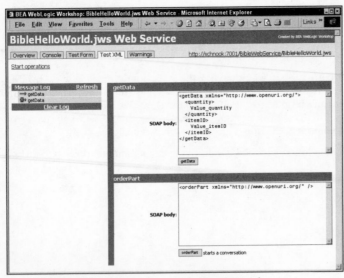

Figure 27-35: The raw XML data on the Test XML tab

Overview

Next, click on the Overview tab to see the big picture. This is shown in Figure 27-36.

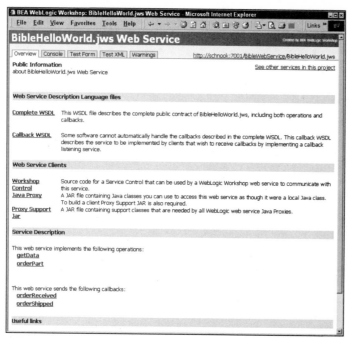

Figure 27-36: The Overview tab shows links to WSDL, client jars, and standards documentation

The Web Services Description Language Files section has two links. Clicking on either of the WSDL links will show you the appropriate WSDL file for this Web Service. Figure 27-37 shows just a small part of the full WSDL.

The Web Service Clients section has links that will provide .jar files with the appropriate files. Clicking these links will cause WebLogic Server to generate the .jar files automatically and let your browser download them. The links perform the following actions:

✦ The Workshop Control link will generate a CTRL file that you can use in Workshop to link other services to this service. However, it's probably easier to generate that right in Workshop by right-clicking the JWS file in the Project Tree and copying it to your new project if necessary.

✦ The Java Proxy link will generate a client .jar. You can create your own client that calls into the generated client .jar, and your code won't have to know that the generated client is really a proxy for the Web Service. But wait — you can't use this until you click the next link.

✦ The Proxy Support Jar link will generate a generic .jar that you must use with all your Web Service–specific Java Proxy .jars.

Figure 27-37: Part of the full WSDL for this Web Service

The Service Description section has links to all the methods and callbacks that this service offers. Clicking the links will bring you back to the Test Form tab for that service.

The Useful Links section has links to other sites that contain more information on SOAP and Web-Service related specifications.

Console

The Console tab is shown in Figure 27-38. Here, you can see and modify some settings for your Web Service. It tells you what technology (EJBs and so on) is used to create this service. Clicking the name of the technology brings up the WebLogic Server Console and shows you the monitoring page for the objects that are deployed using that technology (such as EJBs).

You can also change the Log settings for this service, and clear the Persistence settings or redeploy the EJBs.

Warnings

Click the Warnings tab to show Figure 27-39. This shows a list of warnings that Workshop has provided. In our case, it's telling us that we need to use our own custom URI for our namespace, rather than the default one.

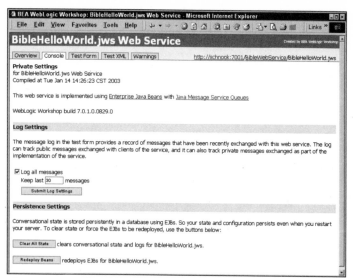

Figure 27-38: The Console tab has configuration settings for your running Web Service

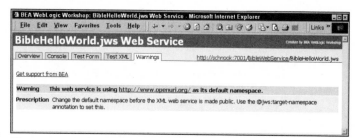

Figure 27-39: The Warnings tab alerts you to problems you may encounter in production

That's a valid concern for a production system, and that brings us to our next major topic.

Packaging and Deploying

As you develop your Web Services in Workshop, it's using WebLogic Server 7.0 in development mode. This means WebLogic Server automatically creates temporary directories and deploys the Web Services projects from there. Our project, for example, is compiled into EJB .jars and shows up in WebLogic Server temporary directories, as shown in Figure 27-40.

Figure 27-40: A Windows Explorer view of our domain's directory structure

Although this is fine for development, you want to package and deploy your Web Service to a WebLogic Server running in production mode. When WebLogic Server runs in production mode, you can't give it an exploded directory structure—it must be packaged as an Enterprise Application .ear file.

Use the `JwsCompile` command-line tool to compile and package a finished Web Service that you want to deploy to a production server. This command can take command-line arguments for all its options, or you can specify them in a configuration file. Keep in mind that the server name and port number get hard-coded in the final .ear file by this compiler. See the Workshop documentation for more information on `JwsCompile`.

After you've used JwsCompile to generate the ear file, you need to deploy the ear to a production server. Use the `weblogic.Deployer` tool (described in Appendix B) or the WebLogic Server Console to deploy the .ear file.

Summary

WebLogic Workshop is a powerful tool that works in synchrony with WebLogic Server 7.0 to make designing and building Web Services almost effortless. In this chapter, we showed you how to set up Workshop to work with a new or existing WebLogic Server domain. We covered using the GUI to create methods and callbacks that enable you to communicate with clients. We discussed controls and how to communicate with databases, EJBs, JMS queues and topics, and other Web Services. Finally, we went over running, testing, debugging, and deploying Web Services.

There's a lot more to investigate that we couldn't cover in this one chapter. But you should have a good idea of where to get started and how to get the information you need.

✦   ✦   ✦

Working with WebLogic and the J2EE Connector Architecture

This chapter provides a brief introduction into the world of the J2EE Connector Architecture (JCA) and API. The purpose of the JCA is to make enterprise application integration (EAI) achievable through a common interface to enterprise information systems (EISs).

EISs are common corporate back-end systems such as ERP systems, legacy databases, and mainframe transactional systems. It used to be that Java developers had to write custom code to talk to each of these systems. Now, with JCA, you plug in a JCA connector that knows how to talk to your back-end system and your code just talks to the connector via a standard JCA interface.

Think of JCA the way you think of JDBC — you don't write two sets of code to talk to Oracle or SQL Server, you just write to the JDBC API. Likewise, there's no need for ERP-specific code — you write to the JCA API and the connector takes care of the translation.

BEA has added some additional features for its JCA implementation in WebLogic Server 7.0, such as Additional Classloading Support, Secure Password Credential Storage, Flexible Connection Leak Detection, and Security Policy Processing of an ra.xml Specification. You can find more information at the following location:

```
http://edocs.bea.com/wls/docs70/jconnector/overview.
html#1235454
```

Introducing the J2EE Connector Architecture

In many companies and from experience in telecommunications, there are many third-party applications that must be used that are added to a system. An example of such a system is an OSS (Operational Support Systems). An OSS is a telecommunications system that can interface with other telecommunications systems and ordering systems to provide a customer with the ability to subscribe to a telecommunication service. These third-party components are needed to provide business objects that are necessary to complete the system.

An example of a third-party component is the Oracle ERP. It can process an Order Entry, the ERP notion of an ordering process, from end to end using out-of-the-box functionality. The business logic is proprietary to Oracle, and the effort of building a system to implement and order ERP would take more time and effort than any mid-size company could afford. Tables and fields that provide the end-to-end ordering in the Oracle ERP system are proprietary to Oracle and cannot be discussed without Oracle's consent. Other pieces of an OSS could be a NightFire solution for communicating to other telecommunication companies through a proprietary communication network.

NightFire and companies like it have put forth a large effort to understand the interfaces between telecommunication companies, and reproducing some of their efforts requires a lot of money and time. In many of these cases, it's better to buy some of these products than to have a company produce them. Many companies that use these products don't necessarily need to produce each and every one. This allows the organization using the products to concentrate on their core products and services.

Third-party products are needed to connect the organization's enterprise systems. The organization's enterprise system may not be standardized with the third-party applications. Connecting them so that they work together may require significant effort and the negotiation of various standards and technologies between many APIs. Some of these systems exist on multiple platforms. Some situations require that ports be made across COM (Component Object Model) and CORBA (Common Object Request Broker Architecture) for various systems to communicate to each other. Sometimes, multiple hops and software have to be invented to read a single entry across a proprietary system. Without a single standard that can work across multiple machines and with multiple enterprise applications, building the entire OSS becomes a difficult exercise in matching APIs to other APIs and messaging data that can work across multiple domains and work in the same manner.

Countless millions have been used in such efforts, and many see XML as a relief to move their data internally through their systems. To parse a single data element multiple times to move that data item from one end of the room to the other is time-consuming. It's even worse when it becomes so open that anyone that looks at the XML stream can read it in text form and gain access to data elements throughout the enterprise system. Selling a secure enterprise system is difficult when most of the data that is transmitted in the system is in human-readable form. Some of the benefits of the Connector API include Connection Management, Security Management, and Transaction Management. These topics are discussed in detail in later sections. But these management systems are the heart of the Connector API, and they are necessary infrastructure building blocks for providing a robust system.

Understanding the J2EE Connector Architecture

With many different products and specializations with e-commerce and back-end systems on the market, it has become imperative to find ways to have disparate systems communicate with each other effectively. An example of such a system is a J2EE-compliant system such as WebLogic that uses EJBs and a non-J2EE-compliant system such as Siebel that has proprietary information for order processing. Both of these systems use data, even somewhat differently, but to one system there is data known as an order, and to the other system there is also data known as an order. The two systems must somehow map what one system refers to as an order to what the other system refers to as an order. Accomplishing this task requires a common framework in which both systems can communicate (thus, the term *connector*) and in which they can map one form of data to the other. This is the motivation behind the Connector API: to provide the framework and architecture to connect different third-party systems to each other.

In the next few sections, we'll explain some of the key concepts required for understanding the Connector API, and delve into how a resource adapter talks to other components in the system via the concepts of the server contract and the Common Client Interface.

Key concepts

The Connector API version 1.0 was built to accommodate the mapping of data between various EAI and EIS systems. It has system contracts on the way data must be mapped between systems. For any data manipulation, it must maintain transactional integrity to ensure that rollbacks and commits can be supported. Security must ensure that the data does not get manipulated during movement and is protected from eavesdropping. Resources must be managed to ensure that the movement of data can be accomplished without running out of resources before the task has been accomplished. The following sections examine the key concepts in detail to see how they fit together.

EAI and EIS

Many pieces make up the Connector API version 1.0. The emphasis of the Connector API is to provide a generic framework that is not specific to the Enterprise Information System (EIS), the application server, and the application component. Without the Connector API, it would be difficult to decouple the different APIs. Even if they were decoupled, there would be no other specification that is vendor-neutral that would avoid a rewrite every time a new component is added from a different company.

The EIS makes up the data information on the back end that is being accessed for processing information and business logic across an organization's enterprise (see Figure 28-1). In a pure J2EE architecture, this is the piece that normally contains the legacy system or proprietary data system. One of the systems that also make up the EIS is the Enterprise Application Integration (EAI) system. The connector architecture could be considered a type of EAI. The purpose of an EAI is to integrate multiple third-party applications and sometimes just multiple types of business logic into a centralized enterprise form of connectivity.

The purpose of an EAI system is to be able to process XML systems for B2B and back-end systems of different integrators for business logic. One of these systems could consist of Oracle's ERP (Enterprise Resource Planning) to plan a system across an enterprise to provide end-to-end processing of an order, billing, and product catalog system. A typical EAI system comes from systems such as Tuxedo, Vitria's BusinessWare, and TibCo. A lot of these systems provide asynchronous transactions for publishing and subscribing messages that are separated from the application servers.

Figure 28-1: An EAI architecture with a separate application server

The problem with this type of architecture is that it separates the EAI from the application servers. For some EAI systems, the Java Server Page (JSP) would have to be translated into XML (Extensible Markup Language), stored on a message queue similar to JMS (Java Message Service), and then translated again into the EIS system. Because there are multiple translations and parsing, this type of system could have a slow reaction. Another issue: If an EIS system is decoupled from the application server's security management, transaction management, and connection management, it would have to implement its own services of these management systems, as well as synchronize with the application server's form of these managers to work across an enterprise and to coordinate the application's components. If an EJB needs to perform a commit on the client side, for example, the EAI system needs to synchronize that commit to the appropriate EIS system with the EAI's transaction management and the application server's transaction management to ensure the resource's transactional integrity. Managing multiple systems in this architecture can get complicated very easily. To simplify these types of issues, it's better to use the EAI as an application server or an application server as an EAI to avoid the issues between communicating between the different managers.

The Connector API is a mechanism to turn the application server into an EAI system. This makes the application server solely responsible for the security management, transaction management, and connection management. It also transforms the EAI system from a separate server and vendor into an extension of the application server.

Resource adapter

You must add several parts to the application server to implement the Connector API. Figure 28-2 shows how the application component, such as an EJB, will communicate to the resource adapter through a Common Client Interface (CCI). The purpose of the CCI is to provide a generic connector implementation independent of the application server. This connection is not aware of the security management, the transaction management, or the connection management. The CCI needs only some information of executing functions to a specific EIS system with data and getting data back. The resource adapter is responsible for managing the connection, which is aptly called a `ManagedConnection`. The application server has to interface into the resource adapter to provide the security management, the transaction management, and the connection management. The common interface for the interaction between the application server and the resource adapter is called the Service Provider Interface (SPI). The SPI interfaces between the providers; or in this case, the application server and the resource adapter.

The interaction between the application server and the resource adapters provides the security management, transaction management, and connection management (see Figure 28-3). The `ConnectionFactory` will interact with the `ConnectionManager` of the application server. The interaction and workings of the security management, transaction management, and connection management internal to the application server is application server-specific and not defined in the connector specification. What is defined is the interaction between the resource adapter and the application server. Some of the information for operation of the resource adapter will be defined in the resource adapter's deployment descriptor. Some of the things defined are the EIS system to interact with; the security authentication type; and the transaction demarcation type, such as XA and local transaction. The application server will get these instances of the transaction, `ManagedConnectionFactory`, and security instance from the resource connector. The application server will be listening for information from the `ManagedConnection` through the `ConnectionEventListener` that is created as part of the application server. The purpose of the `ManagedConnectionFactory` is to create an instance of a `ManagedConnection` that the application component will use to access the EIS, but will be managed by the managers of the application server based on the information provided in the deployment descriptor.

Figure 28-2: Resource adapter interfaces to the client, WebLogic Server, and the Enterprise Information Systems

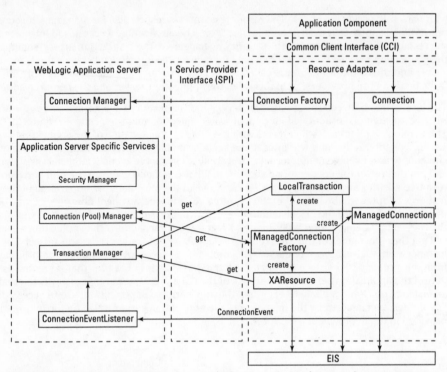

Figure 28-3: Common interfaces for connection, security, and transaction management

System contracts

So far, we've discussed some of the components that make up the Connector API. The heart of the matter is mapping data from one system to another and negotiating the interface between the two systems. The negotiation, or *handshaking*, in-between systems combined with the negotiation of data and the integrity of that data is commonly known as the *system contracts*. This includes the management of the transactions and connections involved with the movement of the data between systems.

Connection Management contract

One of the features of the Connector API is the support of Connection Management. Connection Management enables you to pool connections for reuse without the delay of allocating and deallocating the instance for each connection. It does this by providing a connection factory. Connection Management is a consistent application-programming model for acquiring connections for both managed and nonmanaged applications. It provides a generic mechanism for providing different quality of service (QoS) for transactions, security, error logging, and many more enhancements into the same connector. The connection pool can be application server-specific. In the WebLogic Server, a maximum and minimum number of connections are prepopulated.

A resource adapter provides interfaces for both connections and connection factories. Examples of JDBC-based interfaces for database connectivity are `javax.sql.DataSource` and `java.sql.Connection`. The connection and connection factory are defined for the CCI with the interfaces `javax.resources.cci.ConnectionFactory` and `javax.resources.cci.Connection`.

The application component, such as an EJB or servlet, first gets the connection by getting a lookup of a connection factory in JNDI of a `javax.resource.cci.ConnectionFactory`. Then the connection factory instance calls the `ConnectionManager` to request a `Connection` from the application server by using the `allocateConnection` function. The `Connection Manager` provides the QoS based on the application server. No specification exists for how the application server implements these services. The `ConnectionManager` will call the Connection Pool Manager internal to the application server. The application's Connection Pool Manager will call the `ManagedConnectionFactory` to get a `ManagedConnection`. A `ManagedConnection` is a `Connection` that is managed as a transaction through a `ConnectionEventListener` in the application server. Each `ConnectionEventListener` is registered with the `ManagedConnection`, enabling it to receive events. Depending on the type of transaction, it will call the `LocalTransaction` interfaces or the `XAResource` interface, or even possibly none of them for no transaction handling. The resource adapter calls the `XAResource` or `LocalTransaction`. The Transaction Manager of the application server will get the `LocalTransaction` or `XAResource` class that the `ManagedConnectionFactory` created. Whenever a `ManagedConnection` is created, the security management of the application server sends a JAAS `Subject` as part of the method invocation.

To simplify the preceding process, it's easier to say that the application server will use its Pool Manager, which is part of the Connection Manager, to interface to the `Managed ConnectionFactory`, which will create the `ManagedConnection`. The `ManagedConnection` is created or found in a pool that will have an associated transaction. This transaction is either XA, local, or none, depending on how it was defined. The Transaction Manager of the application server gets these transaction interfaces of the `ManagedConnection` to handle the transactions internally so that it can perform commits and rollbacks based on the other `ManagedConnections` and resources. The `ConnectionEventListener` is also associated with the `ManagedConnection` so that it can provide feedback to the application server if manual rollbacks and commits are performed from the EIS. These events that are sent to the `ConnectionEventListener` are defined in the `ConnectionEvent` class. The `Connection Manager` is the interface that is implemented by the application server for the resource adapter to get the original `Connection` that starts this process.

Transaction Management contract

The purpose of the Transaction Management is to, well, manage a transaction.

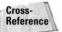

For information on the basics of transactions, see Chapter 6.

XA interface

The XA (X/Open Architecture) interface is a bidirectional interface between a Transaction Manager and Resource Managers. The X/Open group, which is now called the Open Group, can be found at `www.opengroup.org`.

The XA interface supports global transactions; that is, transactions that can happen across multiple EIS systems.

X/Open is a standards organization whose goal is to standardize several interfaces between components in a distributed transaction processing framework. The X/Open consortium was initially formed to promote the Open Systems Computing paradigm and application portability. X/Open specified the most popular Distributed Transaction Processing Model (DTP) in 1991. It defines the three basic modules:

✦ **Application Program (AP):** The application component, which uses the libraries provided by TM and RM to interact with them.

✦ **Transaction Manager (TM):** Responsible for transaction coordination and control of execution of transaction.

✦ **Resource Manager (RM):** Responsible for managing the access to the shared resources, such as files and databases.

Interaction exists between the AP and the TM, commonly known as TX; examples include begin, commit, rollback, and info:

✦ begin: Starts a transaction

✦ commit: Commits a transaction

✦ rollback: Aborts a transaction

✦ info: Gets the status of a transaction

The interface that defines the interaction between the TM and the RM is commonly known as XA. The Transaction Manager and the Resource Manager modules have to implement the interface bidirectionally to allow the Transaction Manager to interact with any Resource Manager.

✦ start: Starts a transaction

✦ prepare: Prepares a transaction in a 2PC

✦ end: Ends the association of the transaction

✦ commit: Commits the transaction

✦ reg: Registers the transaction with a TM

XA allows a transaction to be managed by a TM external to the resource adapter and EIS. A resource adapter defines the type of transaction support by specifying the transaction-support element in the ra.xml file. A resource adapter can support only one type. When an application component demarcates an EIS connection request as part of a transaction, the application server is responsible for enlisting the XA resource with the Transaction Manager. When the application component closes the connection, the application server de-lists the XA resource from the TM and cleans up the EIS connection after the transaction is complete. Part of the XA interface is to implement a two-phase commit protocol to ensure that there is synchronization between shared resources to ensure that they do not write at the same time.

Two-phase commit protocol

The steps of the two-phase commit protocol involve an interaction between an application, a Transaction Manager, and a Resource Manager, which in this case is part of the Data Transaction Manager in the following order:

Phase One:

The Transaction Manager issues the command to each Resource Manager to prepare to commit.

If all Resource Managers reply that they can commit, processing proceeds to Phase Two.

If any of the Resource Managers reply that they cannot commit, the Transaction Manager contacts all the Resource Managers to force an abort, and instructs them to discard all updates when waiting for that transaction.

If any of the Resource Managers cannot be contacted, those Resource Managers that could not be contacted could not be told to abort. The abort command is then stored in the Transaction Manager log awaiting the restart of the Resource Managers to be recontacted. After the Resource Managers are up and running again, the abort is forced.

Phase Two:

If all Resource Managers confirm that they can commit, the commit message is broadcast to each of the Resource Managers by the Transaction Manager.

If all Resource Managers are still active, they commit the updates.

If any of the Resource Managers fail to respond, it could be for two reasons: Either there was a communication failure or the Resource Manager failed. The Resource Manager is termed to be "in doubt" about the outcome. It will keep locks on the data until notification is received. After the line is up and running, the Transaction Manager will commit the transaction.

If the Resource Manager fails and then restarts, the Resource Manager must reconstruct the committed state of the resources that it manages. If it does fail, all the enlisted transactions are aborted, except those that prepared or committed prior to the failure. When the Resource Manager restarts, it asks the Transaction Manager about the outcome of the "in doubt" transactions in which it enlisted. The Transaction Manager then tells the Resource Manager the outcome of each "in-doubt" transaction, and the Resource Manager commits or aborts accordingly.

Local transaction

A local transaction is associated with a single physical connection and can be shared by multiple EJB components. To share a physical connection in the local transaction scope, the container assumes the connection to be shareable unless it has been marked unshareable in the `<res-sharing-scope>` tag of the deployment descriptor. The local transaction support allows an application server to manage resources that are only local to the resource adapter. They cannot manage the EIS resources and cannot participate in a two-phase commit protocol (2PC). When the support is defined for the local transaction, and the component requests an EIS connection, the application server starts a local transaction based on the current transaction context. When the application component closes that connection, the application server does a commit on the local transaction and also cleans up the EIS connection after the transaction has completed.

The transaction process starts by first getting a connection handle that is returned by calling `ManagedConnection.getConnection`, which in turn calls `LocalTransaction.begin`. The EJB gets a connection handle and performs a unit of work on EIS Resource Manager.

For local transactions, the application server implements the `javax.spi.LocalTransaction` to define the transaction contract between the application server and the resource adapter.

The resource adapter supports the local transaction with the `javax.resource.cci.Local Transaction`, as defined in the CCI. The application server implements the local transaction with the `javax.resource.spi.ConnectionEventListener` interface.

The function used in the `ConnectionEventListener` for starting the local transaction is `localTransactionStarted` using the `ManagedConnection` instance. Notifying that the connection was committed in the `ManagedConnection` is done by using the `localTransaction Committed`. Notifying that a local transaction is rolled back in the `ManagedConnection` is done by using the `localTransactionRolledBack` method.

To support the local transaction, the application server must support the `Connection EventListener` interface. This enables the application server to achieve local transaction cleanup and transaction serial interleaving. A resource adapter is required to send local transaction events through the `ConnectionEventListener` interface when an application starts a local transaction. The `ManagedConnection` registers this listener instance by using `ManagedConnection.addConnectionEventListener`.

If neither XA nor local transaction is set in the `ra.xml`, it means that a resource adapter does not support XA or local transactions. That means that if an application component needs to use that resource adapter, the application component must not involve any connections to the EIS, represented by the resource adapter, in a transaction. But if an application component needs to involve EIS connections in a transaction, the application component must interact with a resource adapter that supports XA or local transactions.

Security Management contract

The `PasswordCredential` class is a holder for the username and password. The `Generic Credential` interface is used for accessing the security credential of a resource principal. A `GenericCredential` interface can be used to wrap Kerberos credentials. Some EISs can support the GSS-API that is defined in `rfc2078.txt`. You can find all `rfcs` at `www.ietf.org`. The security over the communications between the application server and the EIS can be done with SSL. The username and password can be passed into the properties of the JNDI context during the `getConnection` method invocation. This is termed component-managed sign-on, which occurs when the authorization is specific in the deployment descriptor of the EJB or servlet.

For EIS sign-on, a basic password containing a username and password, or a Kerberos version 5 authentication mechanism can be used from the resource adapter to the EIS system. The authentication is specified in the `<authentication-mechanism-type>` tag of the deployment descriptor of the resource adapter. Authorization to an EIS resource can be applied at the application server, at the EIS, or neither.

Communication between the application server and the EIS is subject to threats, such as a man-in-the-middle attack, loss of data, data modification, and rerouting. The Connector API allows EIS sign-on by propagating the security context, consisting of a JAAS `Subject` with `Principal` and `Credentials` from the application server to the resource adapter in the `createManagedConnection` method. A `Subject` represents a person or a group. It can contain multiple passwords and keys. A `Subject` can have multiple `Principals` and `Credentials`. `Principals` are passed through the `Subject` during the `getConnection`.

The application server uses the `createManagedConnection` when it requests a resource adapter to create a new connection. It can pass in the `Subject` by using either the component or container-managed sign-on. In the container-managed sign-on, the application server is responsible for filling the `Subject`. Adding credentials can be done through the `Subject` class.

The Connector API does not define a standard format and requirements for security mechanism for specific credentials, but it does offer a `GenericCredential` interface to wrap `Credentials` as a Java and Kerberos wrapper. This allows the resource adapter to get the information about the `Credential`, as well as EIS sign-on. The only other mechanism for the Connector API is the GSS-API, the Generic Security Service Application Programming Interface. A `Subject` class can contain one to many `PasswordCredentials`, one to many `GenericCredentials`, or one to many `Principals` for sign-on. If the application server invokes the `createManagedConnection` with one or more `PasswordCredentials` in the `Subject`, the resource adapter will use this information to sign on to the EIS. The `Password Credentials` are set in the private credential set. The resource adapter extracts the username and password and uses this information for EIS sign-on.

The application server can invoke the `createManagedConnection` with one or more `GenericCredentials` passed in the `Subject`. The resource adapter will use this information as private or public keys (these could contain Kerberos keys). This method could also be used to process EIS sign-on. The resource adapter will extract these `Credentials`, and if Kerberos is selected as the authentication mechanism type, it will get this information out of the private `Credential` as Kerberos-based keys.

Another option is where the application server does not provide any security information by passing a null `Subject`. Then the component is responsible for the security in a component sign-on. This security can be placed in a `ConnectionRequestInfo` for component information; however, the application server cannot read this information because the `Connection RequestInfo` is a data structure for the resource adapter to pass information for its own data in the connection request. If the resource adapter does not find information in the `ConnectionRequestInfo`, it will use default security configuration.

Common Client Interface

The Common Client Interface (CCI) defines a standard client API for an application component, and EAI, to create and manage connections to heterogeneous EISs. The purpose of the CCI is to provide a generic framework that is independent of a particular EIS or EAI system.

Note   The CCI is a recommended client API, but it is not required. An alternative API can be used for client interaction, such as the JDBC API.

Not only is the CCI a generic API, but data can also drive various aspects of the EAI system. A metadata repository (see Figure 28-4) can be used to drive the CCI. An example is when a connector can decide to go to either an EIS system or ERP system, depending on the order type and format. The transaction can have a type value of batch or single to route the direction of the transaction. You don't want to hard-code this information because it can limit the capabilities of upgrading the system. This also limits adding more systems in the transaction routing when adding more transactions. To avoid hard-coded transactions, a connection can contain metadata specific to itself. It can look up in a routing table and have a new connection to route to that is based on that connection. One of the new connections leads to a legacy system, and one leads to the ERP system based on the type of order. Metadata has other purposes besides routing to EIS systems; another is to route messages that contain log information into a log file.

Figure 28-4: Metadata driving the CCI

The use of metadata allows EJBs, Java servlets, and other systems to get record results of data from an EIS system. Just as a JDBC connection can retrieve a ResultSet from a database, a CCI connection can retrieve a set of data from an EIS system such as ERP. Other records (see Figure 28-5) are IndexedRecords and MappedRecords. The ResultSet uses the SQL ResultSet interface, the IndexedRecord implements the java.util.list interface, and the MappedRecord implements the java.util.map interface.

The package that makes up the CCI is found under javax.resource.cci. The classes can be divided into interfaces to handle connections, interactions, and metadata, plus structures to handle records. The RecordFactory creates the generic MappedRecord and IndexedRecord on demand.

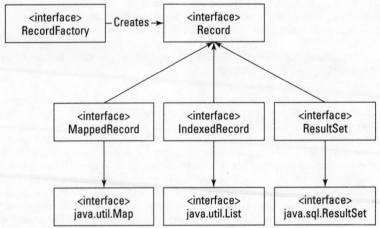

Figure 28-5: Types of Record sets

Connection interface

The connection interface consists of `Connection`, the `ConnectionFactory`, the `Connection Spec`, and `LocalTransaction`. The purpose of the `javax.resource.cci.Connection Factory` is to provide an interface for getting a connection to an EIS instance. The component will first get an instance from a JNDI namespace to look up a `ConnectionFactory` instance and then use this instance to establish a connection. The `getConnection` method from the `ConnectionFactory` will then be used to get a connection to an EIS instance. The `get Connection` method may also take a `ConnectionSpec` class that contains resource adapter-specific properties such as component sign-on. Some of the parameters that are defined in the `ConnectionSpec` are username and password. This `ConnectionFactory` interface also provides a method to get the `RecordFactory`.

Another class of the connection interface is the `javax.resource.cci.Connection`, which represents an application-level connection handle. This is used by the application component to access an EIS instance. A `ManagedConnection` through the `ManagedFactory` later represents the physical connection. The `ManagedConnection` is simply the connection that is managed through the application server for transaction integrity. The `Connection` can create an `Interaction` instance associated with the current `Connection` instance. This `Interaction` instance is for enabling the component to access the EIS components and data. An instance of the `getResultInfo` can also be used to get the `ResultSet` information for data access from the EIS instance. Metadata can also be retrieved in the `Connection` to provide instance-specific data for itself. If one is available, a local transaction can be retrieved for managing transactions locally, meaning that the resource is local to the managing agent and non-global to the enterprise.

Just as a `Connection` in the JDBC interface, auto-commit can be set in the CCI connection. This means that there is an implicit commit called on the transactions, which is `AutoCommit`. By default, it is set to `false`, which means not to implicitly commit.

Interaction interface

The `Interaction` interface is used for moving data between the application component and the EIS instance. The `Interaction` is created by the `Connection` instance. The core of the `Interaction` interface is the `javax.resource.cci.Interaction` interface, the `javax. resource.cci.InteractionSpec` instance, and the data structures used to interact with the EIS instance. The main interface for the EIS instance is the `javax.resource.cci. Record`. Some of the interfaces that extended from the record are `MappedRecord`, `IndexedRecord`, and `ResultSet`. These records are passed through the `Interaction` by using the `Interaction` execute method. The `InteractionSpec` is also passed through these methods. The `InteractionSpec` holds properties for driving an `Interaction` instance to an EIS instance. They are properties for the underlying EIS.

The properties for the `InteractionSpec` consist of two parts: the standard properties and the `ResultSet` properties. The standard properties define interaction with the EIS instance. There are two parts of the standard properties: a `FunctionName` and an `InteractionVerb`. The `FunctionName` represents the name of the EIS function, such as a business object function. The `InteractionVerb` represents the mode of interaction with the EIS instance. There are three possible `InteractionVerb`s: SYNC_SEND, SYNC_SEND_RECEIVE, and SYNC_RECEIVE. SYNC_SEND specifies to only send data to the EIS instance. SYNC_SEND_RECEIVE specifies to send a record to the EIS instance and receive information in the form of a record or `Result Set`. SYNC_RECEIVE can be used to specify to receive a record from a messaging system like a message queue. The `ResultSet` properties give information about the `ResultSet` record, which consist of `FetchSize`, `FetchDirection`, `MaxFieldSize`, `ResultSetType`, and `ResultSetConcurrency`. They define the size and types of the `ResultSet` for the direction.

Metadata interface

There are two main interfaces for the `Metadata` interface: the `ConnectionMetaData` interface and the `ResourceAdapterMetaData` interface. The purpose of the `ConnectionMetaData` interface, `javax.resource.cci.ConnectionMetaData`, is to give information about the EIS instance that is accessed through the `Connection` instance. The `ConnectionMetaData` interface is retrieved through the `getMetaData` method. Some of the information that can be reviewed by the `Metadata` interface is the product name and version of the EIS. The `ConnectionMetaData` interface is required to be implemented for the `Connection`.

The purpose of the `ResourceAdapterMetaData` interface is to contain information about the resource adapter implementation, not the EIS information. Because there is no EIS information, a connection does not have to be established to the EIS. Some of the functions of the `ResourceAdapterMetaData` interface are the version, name, vendor name, and connector specification number of the adapter.

The record

A *record* is a data structure used as input and output to the EIS function. There are two types of records: generic and custom. A tool that uses the metadata information from a repository at development time for information develops the custom record. The generic record is used at runtime from metadata information to build the type of record. This metadata is EIS-specific.

Most ERP and EAI systems have their own descriptive information for records. A typical record could be an order record that gets sent to an ERP system for when an order is placed from a Web site. This metadata information may not even be Java-specific; it could be based on an older EIS system such as CICS. But if the EIS uses vendor-specific information, the adapter must be able to understand this metadata if it is passing records to and from an EIS system. So, the metadata information must be available and understandable to the adapter vendor.

Connections may have to add a layer of translation to make the connectors record more generic. For example, if a system is passing order information to either a CICS or an ERP system, an order record needs to be built that accommodates both systems, but not particularly to any one system, so it can be used in both cases. This leads to the case of a component-view contract, which implies that the interface to the EIS from the application component is dependent on the component, not the EIS-specific information. To support this, a `Record Factory` must be in place to provide a record that would be dependent on the EIS-specific data. The `RecordFactory` does a lookup based on the specific EIS and specific component and returns a record that maps to both parties. The component creates the custom record for the EIS-specific record.

Some of these records may become very complex because of the different technologies used. A situation could arise in which an EJB has a connection to a CORBA object that has a connection to an older TCP stream object. The benefit of the connector interface is that it allows separate layers to focus on different aspects of the technology. In a scenario such as the one mentioned, an architect can work on the mapping of the records with the three different technical groups and focus on the data for the record and `RecordFactory`. Then the EJB and CORBA group can focus on the connectors through the ORB and EJB interfaces through their respective application servers, and the socket developers could establish an EIS interface for integrating into the legacy system. Without the Connector API, there would be no common interfaces for this type of communication between systems.

XML is another alternative, but the support of the services, such as transaction management and security, would have to be built independently of the transaction management and security extensions of the application servers for connectors. Using this methodology also allows individuals, such as an architect, to focus on the data independently of the transport. This mapping can take some time and effort on its own because it is not just a mapping of data, but of data types. The EJB uses the Java types, CORBA has its own types defined in the Interface Definition Language, and the sockets could be defined in the C language. So, if the first field is an integer for the type of message, it needs to match the same type across all three technologies. This is commonly known as *type mapping*.

Because more complexity may be involved in the `Record` interface, the `Record` interface can be extended into an `IndexedRecord`, `MapRecord`, and `ResultSet`. The `MapRecord` is taken from the Java utilities interface for a map, which provides a key/value pair for storing data. Doing a lookup on a key returns the value. The `IndexedRecord` is taken from the Java utilities for a list that is a linked list implementation for dynamically providing an ordered and indexed set of data that is traversed through one at a time. The last is the `ResultSet`, which is taken from the SQL interface of a `ResultSet` that is normally returned in a database query. A lookup of the data is normally done by doing another lookup on the `ResultSet`, such as a `getString` function, used to return an entry in the column from the resulting set that still contains table information. Using these types of records together can produce a very complicated and robust set of organizing data that can be permutated into more types of records. Because the `ResultSet` is based on a return from a query, it is not generated from a `RecordFactory`. But the `RecordFactory` does support getting a generic `MappedRecord` and `IndexedRecord` with the `createMappedRecord` and `createIndexedRecord` functions. Sometimes, it might not be adequate to work just with a recordset, but a stream of bytes such as a file structure. For this reason, there is also a `Streamable` interface for the purpose of working with a stream of bytes from Java I/O.

As mentioned earlier in the chapter, the `Interaction` interface transports these records into and from the EIS instance (see Figure 28-6). The `Interaction` interface is retrieved from the `Connection`. Before the record is passed through the `Interaction`, it must be retrieved from a `RecordFactory`, such as a generic `MappedRecord` and `IndexedRecord`. Otherwise, a custom record can be passed through the execute method.

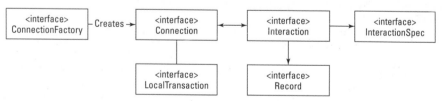

Figure 28-6: Common component interface

Using the J2EE Connector Architecture in WebLogic

So far, we discussed how most application servers can support the Connector API. The WebLogic Server has specific things that it can support out of the Connector API. Like all other application servers, it uses the ra.xml deployment descriptor, but the WebLogic Server extends some of these entries. To specify the minimum and maximum size of the connection pool, for example, it has an extra deployment descriptor called the weblogic-ra.xml. If the weblogic-ra.xml is not defined when running the .rar file, a default one will be created from the WebLogic application server. The .rar file is the resource adapter archive that is a compressed file used to load classes and any other files that may be required to run the resource adapter. The weblogic-ra.xml file must be deployed in the /META-INF/ subdirectory just as the ra.xml must be contained there. If a default weblogic-ra.xml file is automatically generated, the tags for <connection-factory-name> and the <jndi-name> need to be modified to point at the correct instance of the ConnectionFactory.

The WebLogic application server uses container-managed sign-on to sign on to the EIS. The WebLogic Server calls this the security principal map, in which the security principal is mapped from the weblogic-ra.xml entries. In the deployment descriptor of the weblogic-ra.xml, the element security-principal-map defines a relationship of the initiating-principal to the resource-principal. These entries are all optional entries in the WebLogic connector's deployment descriptor. The resource-principal defines the username and password, and the associated initiating-principal defines the caller's principal that initiated the process. A wildcard of * can be used in the initiating-principal to specify a resource-principal for all initiating-principals not defined explicitly. Because plaintext is not desirable for a password, BEA offers a password converter utility for setting a password to a ciphertext. The password converter tool is executed with the Java weblogic.Connector.ConnecterXML Encrypt command. The entry for the principal can look like the following:

```
<security-principal-map>
        <map-entry>
                <initiating-principal>*</initiating-principal>
                <resource-principal>
                <resource-username>rich</resource-username>
                <resource-password>password</resource-password>
            </resource-principal>
        </map-entry>
</security-principal-map>
```

For transaction support, the ra.xml still defines an XA transaction, local transaction, or neither. The error logging is handled through the weblogic-ra.xml file by the <logging-enabled> tag being set to true or false. The <log-filename> tag is used to give the filename to save the log. The logging tags work with the features of the ManagedConnection Factory set and getLogWriter functions. Another top-level XML tag for the WebLogic definition is the <jndi-name> tag that defines the name to bind the ConnectionFactory into the JNDI namespace. The WebLogic application components use this descriptor to find the ConnectionFactory.

By using the weblogic-ra.xml, there is also the possibility of generating multiple resource adapters inherited from a single deployed resource adapter. The new links to the single instance can have different pool information. All or none of the <pool-params> must be defined in the derived instances of the resource adapter, which helps with reusing the same resource adapter with only slight modifications to some of the attributes. The tag specified for this action is the `<ra-link-ref>`.

The next set of attributes in the deployment descriptor is for managing the WebLogic Server's connection pool. Depending on how they are set, they can maximize the connection resources while minimizing the creation time for each connection. The `<initial-capacity>` is the number of `ManagedConnections` that will be initialized at the startup of the WebLogic Server. This avoids creating all the connections at runtime by initializing them ahead of time. But creating too many may cause too much memory usage, so a threshold is needed for a limit of the number of connections. The `<max-capacity>` tag is used to limit the number of connections running at a given instance. If new connections need to be created because there are none in the reuse pool, there is the option to create a set of connections at a time, instead of one at a time. This is done with the `<capacity-increment>` tag. At given intervals, when connection resources are not being utilized, it might be desirable to free the resources used by the connectors if it seems that the resource adapter is no longer using them. The shrink properties are used to specify how long before an inactive connector should get taken out of the pool. This will reduce the size of the connection pool.

```
<pool-params>
    <initial-capacity>0</initial-capacity>
    <max-capacity>1</max-capacity>
    <capacity-increment>1</capacity-increment>
    <shrinking-enabled>false</shrinking-enabled>
    <shrink-period-minutes>200</shrink-period-minutes>
</pool-params>
```

Using the WebLogic Admin Console, you can monitor the connection pools. We discuss this in the next section.

Configuration

Before viewing the connection pool of the connector, a connector component has to be added into the WebLogic Server environment through the Admin Console of the WebLogic Server. To configure a connector, perform the following steps:

1. In the domain tree on the left, click the Connectors node under Deployments. The right pane will appear, as shown in Figure 28-7.

2. Click on the Configure a new Connector Component link. The right pane will appear, as shown in Figure 28-8.

3. Follow the instructions on the page: If your `*.rar` resource adapter file is not in the domain directory, click the `upload through your browser link` to get it there and then click the `[select]` link to the left of the resource adapter filename. In our case, we clicked the link next to `Bible_Connector.rar` shown at the bottom of the window.

4. Now, the pane changes to allow us to select the server(s) and cluster(s) to deploy on and to give it a name. Fill it out as shown in Figure 28-9 and then click the Configure And Deploy button.

5. The deployment pane should appear, along with a spinning arrow in the top right of the pane. This is WebLogic Server, telling us that it's in the process of deploying our connector. When the page refreshes, it should look something like Figure 28-10, which shows a successful deployment.

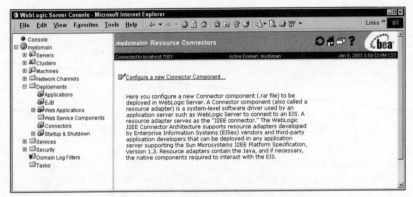

Figure 28-7: Configuring a new connector component

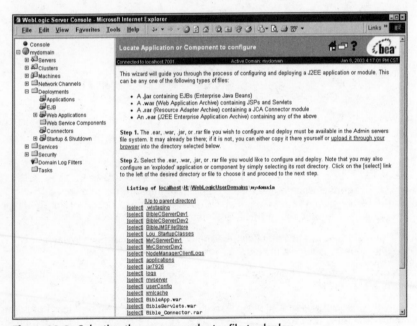

Figure 28-8: Selecting the resource adaptor file to deploy

Figure 28-9: Configuring the connector's deployment options

Figure 28-10: Viewing the deployment process and status

You can click the Configuration tab to fine-tune the deployment. The pane will appear as shown in Figure 28-11.

The following attributes are displayed in the WebLogic Console:

✦ **Name:** The name we associated with the connector component.

✦ **Path:** The path from which the RAR was loaded.

✦ **Deployment Order:** The order, relative to all other deployed applications, in which to deploy this component. The lower the number, the earlier it will be deployed relative to other applications.

✦ **Staging Mode:** The way the connector will be staged. This value will override the server's value. See Chapter 23 (specifically, the section on Servers ➪ Configuration ➪ Deployment) for a description of the Staging Mode.

You can select the Monitoring tab and then click the Monitor All Connector Connection Pool Runtimes link. You can view many attributes of the connection pool, such as Connections Rejected Total Count, and Number Detected Idle (see Figure 28-12).

Figure 28-11: Viewing and changing the connector's configuration.

Figure 28-12: Monitoring connectors

Development

Developing a connector is just like developing any other Java application in WebLogic 7.0. The `weblogic.jar` file that is included with the WebLogic 7.0 application server includes the Connector API files needed for development. Ensure that this file is in the classpath when developing with WebLogic 7.0. Logging routines are provided to help in the development process.

Logging

According to the J2EE Connector Specification, version 1.0, the application server must support the `getLogWriter` and `set` methods of the `ManagedConnectionFactory` to provide error logging and tracing for the resource adapter. The WebLogic Server supports this by its deployment descriptor: the `weblogic-ra.xml`. There are two fields that are of importance to the deployment descriptor for this support: logging-enabled and log-filename. The logging-enabled field defines whether logging is turned on or off. The log-filename field defines the filename for where the log will be captured.Deployment

The `Connection` is a J2EE component, and like most J2EE components, it requires a deployment descriptor. The deployment descriptor is needed to load the Resource Adapter Module (RAM). The RAM contains the required files, such as the native files, images, Java files, and any other files for deploying the resource adapter. The deployment descriptor is a contract on how to deploy the RAM into the resource adapter for the connectors. Using a deployment descriptor and a RAM allows the resource adapter to be deployed as a standalone unit into an application server or with other J2EE modules, such as the EJB deployment. This implies that there is a generic deployment of a resource adapter for multiple application components that can be loaded separately, and the resource adapter that is deployed with specific application components as a package deployment.

The RAM must be packaged by using the Java utility JAR, Java Archive, to RAR file type, Resource Adapter Archive. This RAM must contain the deployment descriptor in the RAR file; like most deployment descriptors, it must be under the `/META-INF/` directory to become `/META-INF/ra.xml`. The utilities and program files that are programmed in Java to support and execute the resource adapter must further be distributed in the RAR file as separate JAR files. These are normally stored in the root subdirectory and can be separated into multiple JAR files based on their functionality. The RAR may contain an `ra.jar` and `cci.jar` in the base directory for the Common Client Components, and the resource adapter utilities for implementing the RAM. Other files that may typically be distributed in the RAR file are native library files for support of the EIS and image files for the graphical user interface of the application component. Any platform-specific files must be included in the RAR.

The deployer is a piece that is responsible for deploying the elements of the RAR. It will ensure that the JAR files are loaded in the environment of the resource adapter. If it is a standalone RAM, it must be deployed so that the required application components have access to the resource adapter. The deployment descriptor defines to the deployer how it will load the resource adapter. It uses the information as metadata for declaring how to deploy. The deployment descriptor is configured in a XML file. The DTD (Document Type Definition) that defines the `ra.xml` file is `connector_1_0.dtd`. A DTD is needed to define the values that are acceptable for the `ra.xml`. But this information can be extended beyond the general information for more specific information that is meaningful for the specific application server that starts the deployer. The WebLogic 7.0 application server extends this functionality by adding an additional deployment descriptor that is specific to the application server called `weblogic-ra.xml`; the corresponding DTD is the `weblogic700-ra.dtd`. The deployer can also be configured through the WebLogic Console.

The elements defined in the `ra.xml` are very important for the operation of the resource adapter. Some of the first fields that should be mentioned are the vendor name, the version number, any licensing information, and the connector specification number. This is data to ensure that the correct resource adapter is being deployed. The next field that should be mentioned is the authentication mechanism. Defining the authentication-mechanism type to `BasicPassword` implies that the `javax.resource.spi.security.PasswordCredential` is being used. Setting the authentication-mechanism type to Kerbv5 implies that Kerberos version 5 is being used with Kerberos certificates and the `javax.resource.spi.security.GenericCredential` has been implemented in the resource adapter. So depending on the setting, authentication-mechanism type defines which authentication protocols will be implemented and the corresponding credential.

The `config`-property defines the properties for the `ManagedConnectionFactory` to use to connect to the EIS. These fields include port numbers, connection URLs, server names, usernames, and passwords to establish connections to the `ManagedConnectionFactory`. The `ManagedConnectionFactory` is normally implemented as a JavaBean. This also means that it uses `getter` and `setter` methods for passing of data. When configuring the `ra.xml`, a property has three pieces: `config-property-name` to define the property name that is being set, such as the `ServerName`; the `config-property-type` that defines the Java type being set like a `String`; and the `config-property-value`, which contains the data being set such as `MyServer`. Following this convention, the server's name that is to be connected on the EIS is called `MyServer`.

```
<config-property>
    <config-property-name>ServerName</config-property-name>
    <config-property-type>java.lang.String</config-property-type>
    <config-property-value>MyServer</config-property-value>
    <config-property-description>This is the name of the EIS
Server</config-property-description>
</config-property>
```

Most of the connector specifies the different interfaces that can be used to build the resource adapter and CCI components. One thing to note is that the `ra.xml` can redefine some of these interfaces. One such instance is the `Connection` interface that can be changed by defining it in `<connection-interface>`. This tag defines the `Connection` interface that the resource adapter will use. Another interface that can be defined is the `ConnectionFactory` interface.

Interfaces are not the only coding pieces that can be defined in the `ra.xml`, implementation classed for the `Connection`, `ManagedConnectionFactory`, and `ConnectionFactory` are also defined in the `<connection-impl-class>`, `<managedconnectionfactory-impl>`, and `<connectionfactory-impl-class>`. Other pieces that are specified in the `ra.xml` are the icons for the resource adapter and EIS type for the resource adapter for connection.

To create a RAR file, first compile the Java class files and put them in a staging directory. A *staging directory* is a directory containing only the files that will be put into the RAR file. You may want to create multiple JAR files for some of these Java resources; an example is a `CCI.jar` for the CCI-specific files and a `RA.jar` for resource adapter-specific files. Create a `META-INF` subdirectory that the XML files will be stored in. Create the `ra.xml` and `weblogic-ra.xml` files. Ensure that the proper class implementations are defined for the `ManagedConnectionFactory`, `ConnectionFactory`, and `Connection` in the `ra.xml` file. Create a JAR file that contains these files. The following is an example:

```
jar cvf myRA.rar *
```

Deploy the RAR into the WebLogic Server by using the Admin Console. If the resource adapter is not a standalone resource adapter, meaning that it has associated EJB clients to be deployed with, the EJB files need to be deployed in an EAR (Enterprise Archive) file and need to be JARed into the RAR as well with its deployment information. To add other files into the RAR file, simply copy them to the staging directory and add them to the RAR by using the JAR command:

```
jar xf myRA.rar *
```

One thing to consider when working with WebLogic Server is that only serializable `ConnectionFactory` implementations are supported.

Not everything has to be handled from the Admin Console. You can also view the deployed connection components, undeploy connection components, and deploy more connection components from the command prompt by using the `java weblogic.Deployer` command.

Summary

One thing that can't be emphasized enough is the need for the Connector API. Without using the Connector API, it becomes difficult to provide a standard solution for interfacing to EIS systems. Most organizations use third-party, non-J2EE components to some degree. But developing proprietary solutions without a common architecture can be very time-consuming and less reusable.

As time evolves and maintenance needs increase, standards provide a common ground for both developers and architects to communicate how to develop a common J2EE component. Using a standard, such as the connector specification, provides out-of-the-box documentation that has the benefit of being proven in other development initiatives. An important aspect to this discussion is the need for EAI to be integrated into the application server. The Connector API enables the application server to become an EAI solution. The need for using the same management systems of security, transaction, and connection services is very important unless an organization wants to spend a great deal of time and effort in getting into the way management systems manage each other.

A lot of work still needs to be offered in the study of connectors, and it should be evident that application servers could offer more tools for the building and deployment of connectors. A need also exists for multiple sets of connectors for different EIS systems so that organizations can plug their J2EE components into EISs from out-of-the-box components. From the specification and the motivation to try to standardize J2EE components into legacy systems, the Connector API is advantageous for moving data in-between disparate systems and contributes significantly to the evolution of enterprise components and connecting them across a wide range of distributed architectures. Without the connector specification, there would be a lot missing in architecture for the capability to provide interfaces into legacy systems and other third-party systems.

✦ ✦ ✦

Upgrading to WebLogic Server 7.0 from Earlier Versions

APPENDIX

✦   ✦   ✦   ✦

In This Chapter

Upgrading
WebLogic Server

Upgrading WebLogic
applications

Deprecated APIs
and features

✦   ✦   ✦   ✦

Like all successful software products, WebLogic Server has evolved and improved with age. WebLogic Server's evolution is unique, however, because it is closely tied to the evolution of the J2EE specification. In fact, one of WebLogic Server's greatest strengths is its robust and timely adherence to the specification because it permits WebLogic developers to take advantage of new J2EE features almost as soon as they hit the street.

The downside of BEA's zeal to keep WebLogic Server up to the current J2EE specification is that upgrading to a new version of WebLogic Server is a two-part process that can sometimes be quite involved. First, you must upgrade your server instances themselves, a process that usually entails conversion of license files and properties files. Then you must upgrade your applications, which is usually more complicated because you have to update them to match the new features both in WebLogic Server and in the J2EE specification. In this chapter, we give you some pointers and checklists on how to accomplish these tasks.

Upgrading WebLogic Server

A number of tasks are required in the process of upgrading your WebLogic server installation to WebLogic 7.0. BEA has provided a clear and simple upgrade path that involves only two steps:

1. Upgrading the WebLogic license file

2. Converting the `weblogic.properties` file

Of course, these simple points have a good bit of work behind them. But if you plan your server upgrade carefully, it should be an orderly and simple process.

Note   We highly recommend that you create a backup of your domain(s) before upgrading your server or applications.

The real work comes later when you upgrade your *applications* to function with WebLogic 7.0!

Upgrading the WebLogic license file

Upgrading your license file for use with WebLogic Server 7.0 is a two-step process. (If you're upgrading from a license prior to WebLogic Server 4.0, it's a three-step process because you must complete a preliminary step first. See the sidebar "Pre-WebLogic 4.0 installations.") First you must convert your old license to the new format, and then you must merge the new license with the pre-existing license file installed along with WebLogic Server. These steps are described in the following sections.

Converting a license to the Version 7.0 format

To upgrade your existing WebLogic license file to the `license_wls70.bea` file, you must visit a special BEA Web site and follow the instructions given there. The URL for the site is

```
http://websupport.beasys.com/custsupp/
```

You need to have a BEA WebSupport account to be able to submit this form, and you will be prompted for the name and password for that account. After you've been authenticated, select the link appropriate for the version number of your existing license; you can update as many as 10 license files at a time. The new license files will be mailed to you at the e-mail account you specify. Turnaround time can be anywhere from 10 minutes to a day or more (so they say — it's always been rather quick in our experience). In any case, you should plan for a delay and be pleasantly surprised when it arrives early.

Pre-WebLogic 4.0 installations

If you are currently running a version older than WebLogic 4.0, you must upgrade your license file from the `WebLogicLicense.class` file to a `WebLogicLicense.xml` file before proceeding.

For this upgrade, you must use the license converter utility provided with WebLogic 7.0. The `WebLogicLicense.class` file should be located on your classpath, in the `WL_HOME` directory, or in the directory in which you execute the `licenseConverter` utility.

From a command line, run the `setenv` script provided by WebLogic (`.cmd` or `.sh`, depending on your platform) to properly set up your environment; then type

```
$ java utils.licenseConverter -w c:\bea
```

In this example, `c:\bea` is the directory in which you want the new `WebLogicLicense.xml` file to be written.

You now need to convert the newly generated `WebLogicLicense.xml` file to a `license_wls70.bea` file. See the section "Converting a License to the Version 7.0 Format."

Merging your new license

Place the converted license files you received from BEA in the BEA home directory (on Windows, this is often `c:\bea`).

You can accomplish the license merging with a simple command-line application provided by BEA. First, ensure that your environment is set up by using the WebLogic `setenv` script. Then, if you are running on Windows, go to the BEA home directory and execute the following command:

```
UpdateLicense.cmd license_update_file
```

If you are running on Unix or Linux, execute this command instead:

```
sh UpdateLicense.sh license_update_file
```

Converting the weblogic.properties file

In versions of WebLogic prior to 6.0, server and application properties were stored in a `weblogic.properties` file. With the support of J2EE applications in WebLogic 6.*x* and 7.0, application configuration settings are stored separately from the server properties. They are now stored in XML deployment descriptor files associated with each J2EE application.

WebLogic provides a utility that parses existing `weblogic.properties` files and generates the appropriate XML files for each of your applications.

Using this converter utility creates a new WebLogic 7.0 domain and places the XML file for each of your applications in the new domain directory.

To use the converter, open the WebLogic Console home Web page (or from any page in the Console, click the Home icon in the upper right) and click the Convert weblogic.properties link under Helpful Tools on the main page. This takes you to the properties conversion page, as shown in Figure A-1.

Figure A-1: Selecting the directory containing the weblogic.properties to convert

You will be asked to browse to the original installation directory, so be sure that you have network access to that original server installation.

Note   If you have multiple servers running under your WebLogic home directory, you need to convert those servers separately.

After you have navigated to the proper directory, click the orange pentagon next to the installation directory. You will be asked to choose the server and cluster properties you want to convert. It is helpful at this point to have a text editor open so that you can view the contents of the `weblogic.properties` file; the selections on this screen do not always make sense out of context (see Figure A-2).

Figure A-2: The properties file conversion page in WebLogic Console

The table at the following Web page shows which values in the `weblogic.properties` file match which elements in your newly created `config.xml`, and how they map to the Console GUI:

    http://edocs.bea.com/wls/docs70/upgrade/MappingTable.html

It may be worth your while to browse the newly converted properties to ensure that the transfer occurred properly.

Upgrading file system dependencies

The directory structure of WebLogic Server has changed significantly in version 7.0. Keep this in mind as you edit any scripts or command files that reference environment variables, relative and absolute paths, or filenames. Not only is the server directory structure different, but typically now the domains are kept in a separate User Domains directory, rather than under WebLogic Server 6.x's Config directory.

The WebLogic Server 6.1 directory structure looked something like this:

```
C:\bea
        \wlserver61
                \bin
                \lib
                \config
                        \mydomain
                        \myOtherDomain
                        \myThirdDomain
```

where `C:\bea` is the BEA Home directory, `C:\bea\wlserver61` is the WebLogic Home directory, and `C:\bea\wlserver61\config` contains your custom domains.

WebLogic Server 6.1's single directory tree is split into two trees in WebLogic Server 7.0 — one for the WebLogic Server program and one for your custom domains:

```
C:\bea
        \weblogic700
                \server
                        \bin
                        \lib
    D:\UserDomains
            \mydomain
            \myOtherDomain
            \myThirdDomain
```

where `C:\bea` is still the BEA Home directory, but now `C:\bea\weblogic700\server` is the WebLogic Server Home directory and `D:\UserDomains` contains your custom domains.

Because of the directory structure changes we just described, make sure your command files, shell scripts, and Ant build files take into account the following:

✦ `bea.home`, typically `c:\bea`, may be different if you specified a new BEA Home when you installed WebLogic Server 7.0. However, your BEA Home directory doesn't generally change when you install new or updated BEA products.

✦ `WL_HOME`, typically `c:\bea\weblogic700`, must point to WebLogic Server 7.0's Home Directory.

✦ `CLASSPATH` should include WebLogic Server 7.0's `weblogic.jar`.

✦ `PATH` should include WebLogic Server 7.0's `bin` directory.

Upgrading security

WebLogic Server 7.0 has a completely revised and upgraded security architecture. If you are upgrading from a previous version of WebLogic Server, it can run in Compatibility Mode, which allows you to use your existing security. However, it is highly recommended that you upgrade as soon as possible to the new security architecture. For more information on WebLogic's security, see Part VI.

For more information on upgrading security from WebLogic Server 6.x to 7.0, see BEA's documentation at the following URL:

`http://edocs.bea.com/wls/docs70/upgrade/upgrade6xto70.html#1041313`

Upgrading WebLogic Applications

Now that you have migrated your servers to WebLogic 7.0, you can migrate your applications into J2EE application formats that match the current version of the specification.

Migrating J2EE Web applications

The most commonly migrated applications are Web applications (possibly packaged into .war files).

Two files describe Web applications under WebLogic 7.0: the web.xml and weblogic.xml deployment descriptors. For more information on these files and on packaging and deploying Web applications on WebLogic in general, see Chapter 18.

BEA's documentation shows the mappings between name/value pairs in the weblogic.properties file and XML elements and attributes in the web.xml and weblogic.xml files, respectively. You can find this documentation at the following URL:

```
http://edocs.bea.com/wls/docs70/upgrade/MappingTable.html
```

Skeletons of these files should have been created by the migration utility mentioned earlier and placed in your new domain directory. You should update these deployment descriptors by using the tools described in Chapter 18 to take full advantage of the configurations made available by WebLogic and the Servlet 2.3 Web application specification.

Note   Sessions created by versions of WebLogic Server previous to version 6.0 are not recognized in WebLogic 6.0 and later because the session cookie format has changed.

Following is a list of some items to consider when upgrading to the Servlet 2.3 Web Application format:

✦ If you have hard-coded URLs in your servlets or HTML, you may need to change them to reflect the new Web application path:

```
http://myweblogic:7001/webappname/your_files_are_here.
```

✦ If you have used relative URLs throughout your files, these changes should not be necessary.

✦ Objects stored in the session should be serializable if the application is going to run under WebLogic clustering. Also, dynamic classloading of your Web applications could cause ClassCastExceptions if nonserializable objects are stored in the session.

✦ Access Control Lists for your files are now security constraints defined in the web.xml file.

✦ Server-side includes (.shtml) are no longer supported. You need to convert to JSP files to get this functionality.

Migrating EJB applications

WebLogic 7.0 supports both the Enterprise JavaBeans 1.1 and 2.0 specifications, so EJBs that you developed for WebLogic 5.1 should be easy to deploy on WebLogic 7.0. It is important to note that the XML deployment descriptor parser for 7.0 is a bit more strict than the one included in 5.1, so you might have to include a few new entries in the deployment descriptor of your 1.1 EJB. The server will tell you which ones you have to add at deployment time.

Unlike WebLogic 5.1, you no longer have to run the `ejbc` compiler on the EJB prior to deployment. If `ejbc` has not been run on a bean at deploy time, WebLogic 7.0 will do it automatically for you.

 Note   Some developers think that it's good practice to run `ejbc` anyway — to expose possible problems with EJBs before they are deployed.

Only two features have been removed from EJB applications in WebLogic 7.0. The finder expressions used in the EJB 1.1 specification are no longer supported in 7.0. Also, the `weblogic.deploy` utility for deploying EJB to a running server is no longer supported.

Cross-Reference   See Chapters 14–17 for more information on how to deploy EJBs.

Migrating EJBs from 1.1 to 2.0

If you want to upgrade existing EJB 1.1 beans to 2.0, WebLogic conveniently provides an upgrade utility called DDConverter to help you convert your deployment descriptors to the 2.0 specification.

You feed the DDConverter utility your 1.1 EJB JAR file that contains your bean classes and your deployment descriptors; DDConverter outputs a JAR file containing the converted deployment descriptors.

Here's a sample command line:

```
$ java weblogic.ejb20.utils.DDConverter -d .\tmp myEJB.jar
```

You should specify an output directory that is different from the current directory (using the required `-d` flag) because the output will be a file of the same name as the input.

After running the utility, you should repackage the original EJB classes with the new deployment descriptors (don't include classes generated by the WebLogic 5.1 `ejbc` compiler).

For session beans, this is all you should have to do to upgrade from 1.1 to 2.0. For CMP entity beans, however, there are several additional steps.

In EJB 2.0 CMP beans, all getter and setter methods for bean properties are abstract, and the container takes care of creating the concrete implementation class. So, if you had the following `setXXX` and `getXX` methods in your 1.1 CMP bean:

```
private String name;
public String getName() {
```

```
  return name;
}
public void setName(String newName) {
  name = newName;
}
```

you would change this to the following:

```
public abstract String getName();
public abstract void setName(String newName);
```

Any finder methods you have declared that have return values of `java.util.Enumeration` should be updated to return `java.util.Collection` because CMP 2.0 can no longer return enumerations.

Migrating to Enterprise Applications

Something to note is the advent of the Enterprise Application Java application structure, which allows you to package many Java applications into a single deployable unit with a defined structure. This can support any number of Web applications, EJBs, and supporting files and classes bundled together in a single `.ear` file (packaged using the `.jar` format).

Cross-Reference   For more information on Enterprise Applications, see Chapter 18.

Deprecated APIs and Features

In the course of upgrading WebLogic Server to 7.0, BEA deprecated some APIs and features. Deprecation is a normal part of a product's lifecycle. Just as Sun occasionally deprecates Java APIs, so does BEA deprecate WebLogic Server features and APIs. Deprecation simply means that, while an API or feature is supported in the current version, it is being publicly marked for removal in a future version, potentially the very next version. This often occurs when a proprietary solution is overtaken by an addition to the J2EE specification, or when a new solution to a problem emerges that is not compatible with a previous solution.

Caution   A deprecated feature or API is a warning. When a WebLogic Server feature or API is deprecated, it's BEA's way of telling you it's time to move on. It's in your best interest to migrate to the new feature or API as soon as possible.

The deprecated features and APIs in this list all have equivalent new features and APIs that you can use instead:

+ **WebLogic Time Services:** Replaced by the JMX Timer Service.

+ **WebLogic Workspaces:** See the "Data Caching Design Pattern" topic in Progamming with WebLogic JNDI (`http://e-docs.bea.com/wls/docs70/jndi/jndi.html`) for alternatives to workspaces for temporary storage.

+ **Zero Administration Client (ZAC):** Replaced by JavaWebStart (`http://java.sun.com/products/javawebstart/`).

✦ **WebLogic Enterprise Connectivity (WLEC):** Tuxedo CORBA applications using WLEC should migrate to WebLogic Tuxedo Connector (`http://edocs.bea.com/wls/docs70/wtc.html`). To reiterate this point, BEA removed the WLEC examples, too.

✦ `weblogic.deploy`: Replaced by `weblogic.Deployer`. See Appendix B for more information on this new tool.

✦ `weblogic.management.tools.WebAppComponentRefreshTool` and `weblogic.refresh`: Both are replaced by `weblogic.Deployer` as described in the previous bullet item.

✦ `ApplicationMBean` **operations:** The `deploy`, `undeploy`, and `load` operations of the `ApplicationMBean` have been deprecated. Instead, use `weblogic.management.runtime.DeployerRuntimeMBean`.

✦ `ApplicationMBean` **attributes:** The `LastModified`, `LoadError`, and `isDeployed` attributes have been deprecated. These attributes are not available with the new two-phase deployment protocol.

Where to Find More Information

BEA provides a manual to assist with the migration process. For more information about how to upgrade servers and applications, go to `http://edocs.bea.com/wls/docs70/upgrade/index.html`.

✦   ✦   ✦

WebLogic Server Tools and Utilities

✦   ✦   ✦   ✦

In This Appendix

Using the command line

Using command-line tools

Introducing Ant

Using the Java GUI tools

✦   ✦   ✦   ✦

It's easy to get excited by all the technology that WebLogic Server 7.0 represents: Web applications, EJBs, JMS, and Web Services. We want it all *now*. It's easy to get so excited, in fact, that we can miss seeing the forest for the trees And, of course, it doesn't hurt that we have extreme time pressures to get the project done yesterday.

But step back and take a breath.

You might think you're most productive by jumping into, say, Chapter 26 on Web Services and getting into coding right away. However, there are a number of tools and utilities that can save you and your project an enormous amount of time, regardless of which technology you're starting out with (not to mention saving you from the boredom of hand-coding files that can be generated automatically or the frustration of not having your code compile because of some silly CLASSPATH error).

In this appendix, we'll take you through the process of setting up your WebLogic Server 7.0 environment so that things go smoothly. We'll cover how to use the following:

✦ The command line to build code and run tools

✦ The command-line tools to administer your server, deploy applications, and create deployment descriptors

✦ Jakarta's Ant, an open source build tool that's used in the examples in this book as well as in WebLogic's sample applications

✦ WebLogic's Ant extensions that help you automate new tasks

✦ The Java-based GUI tools to create and edit XML documents and deployment descriptors

You'll find that you'll be much more productive when you familiarize yourself with the many time-saving tools that BEA provides for WebLogic Server development and deployment.

A list of all available WebLogic Server tools is at the following URL:

```
http://e-docs.bea.com/wls/docs70/toolstable/
ToolsTable.html
```

Using the Command Line

The command line is your best friend, so get to know it. In Windows 2000, you might think it's as simple as clicking the Start button and choosing Programs ➪ Accessories ➪ Command Prompt, but that's just the beginning of the story.

Even before getting into server-side Java, you learned that there are some important parameters that must be set up in any Java programming environment, including the PATH and CLASSPATH environment variables. Even if you have these set up for generic Java development (or even for J2EE development using Sun's J2EE SDK), you still need to specifically configure the WebLogic Server setup.

For example, if you open up a command-line window in Windows 2000 and type the set command, you'll get an output something like that shown in Listing B-1.

Listing B-1: Results of the Windows set Command

```
ALLUSERSPROFILE=G:\Documents and Settings\All Users
APPDATA=G:\Documents and Settings\lou\Application Data
CLASSPATH=d:\p\OraHome1\jdbc\lib\classes111.zip;
CommonProgramFiles=G:\Program Files\Common Files
COMPUTERNAME=NOOK
ComSpec=G:\WINNT\system32\cmd.exe
HOMEDRIVE=G:
HOMEPATH=\
JAVA_HOME=d:\p\bea\jdk131_03
LOGONSERVER=\\NOOK
NUMBER_OF_PROCESSORS=1
OS=Windows_NT
Os2LibPath=G:\WINNT\system32\os2\dll;
Path=d:\p\Oracle\Ora81\bin;d:\p\Oracle\Ora81\Apache\Perl\5.00503\bin\mswin32-
x86;d:\p\Oracle\Ora81\Apache\jdk\jre\bin;G:\WINNT\system32;G:\WINNT;G:\WINNT\Sys
tem32\Wbem;C:\DMI\BIN
PATHEXT=.COM;.EXE;.BAT;.CMD;.VBS;.VBE;.JS;.JSE;.WSF;.WSH
PROCESSOR_ARCHITECTURE=x86
PROCESSOR_IDENTIFIER=x86 Family 6 Model 8 Stepping 3, GenuineIntel
PROCESSOR_LEVEL=6
PROCESSOR_REVISION=0803
ProgramFiles=G:\Program Files
PROMPT=$P$G
SystemDrive=G:
SystemRoot=G:\WINNT
TEMP=h:\temp
TMP=H:\Temp
USERDOMAIN=NOOK
USERNAME=lou
USERPROFILE=G:\Documents and Settings\lou
WIN32DMIPATH=C:\DMI\
windir=G:\WINNT
WV_GATEWAY_CFG=d:\p\Oracle\Ora81\Apache\modplsql\cfg\wdbsvr.app
```

We've highlighted three of the most important environment variables in Listing B-1: CLASS-PATH, PATH, and JAVA_HOME. You may be thinking, "Okay, these are set, so we're ready to rock and roll." Unfortunately, you need a reality check because it won't work. You need to fine-tune your environment, and we're about to show you how.

Understanding environment variables

There are a number of things to consider in setting up your environment. In the following sections, we'll discuss the theory of why environment variables need to be set a certain way and show you a very easy way that WebLogic can help you set them correctly.

JAVA_HOME and your JVM

First, *running* WebLogic Server requires only that a compatible version of a Java SDK be installed. WebLogic comes with Java 1.3.1, but you can use any Java SDK that is listed for your supported configuration at the following URL:

    http://e-docs.bea.com/wls/certifications/certifications/overview.html

Note   If your JVM does not support the -hotspot command-line argument, you must remove it from the startWLS.cmd file.

However, *developing* for WebLogic server requires a J2EE development environment in addition to the Java runtime SDK. If you don't use any WebLogic-specific APIs, you can use a Sun J2EE SDK, but it's easier to just go ahead and use the WebLogic-provided JDK and JAR files. In that case, your JAVA_HOME should be pointing to the Java runtime 1.3.1 that WebLogic Server installed, and your CLASSPATH needs to be set up as described in the next section. The WebLogic Server installer puts the JDK in your BEA home directory, C:\bea\jdk131 for example.

CLASSPATH

If you've ever run into a ClassNotFound exception during Java development, you probably are all too familiar with the horrors of setting up a correct CLASSPATH. As you can see in Listing B-1, that machine is set up to use Oracle thin driver because that's in the CLASSPATH. But notice that there's nary a mention of WebLogic Server JARs, and thus the CLASSPATH won't work as-is for WebLogic Server development.

At a minimum, there are two very important JARs that WebLogic Server provides: weblogic.jar and weblogic_sp.jar. The former contains all the classes implementing the J2EE APIs as well as custom WebLogic Server APIs. The latter contains a cumulative set of patches for WebLogic.

Note   It is extremely important that weblogic_sp.jar appears in your CLASSPATH before weblogic.jar so the JVM finds (and loads) the updated classes before it finds the old ones.

In addition to the WebLogic and service pack JARs, you need the tools.jar from the JDK, which can usually be found in the \lib subdirectory of the JDK directory. You might also need JARs for your database if you're using Type 4 JDBC drivers, such as the ones shown in Listing B-1.

PATH

You need WebLogic Server's \bin subdirectory in your PATH environment variable, which needs to be first in the PATH so that WebLogic's utilities are called rather than any other utilities with the same name getting called (this ensures, for example, that you're using the version of Ant that comes with WebLogic).

And as with any Java development, you need to have the JDK's \bin subdirectory in your PATH so that you can get at the java runtime command, the javac compiler, and other JDK utilities.

WL_HOME

Finally, you need to have the WL_HOME environment variable set so that various WebLogic scripts and commands can find the WebLogic Server home directory. Notice that WL_HOME isn't even shown in Listing B-1. That's actually a good thing, because it means WebLogic Server is a well-behaved program that doesn't mess with your system environment. However, the downside is that you need to manually add it to the environment settings when you developer for or run WebLogic Server. We'll show you how to do that in the next section.

Changing your environment variables

There are several ways to change your environment variables, both temporary and permanent. We'll just cover the ways you can do it in Windows. Unix/Linux geeks would be mortified if anyone accused them of not knowing how to set them!

Use the System Properties GUI tool

To change the environment values permanently, you can use the System Properties control panel applet in Windows 2000. To open the applet, click the Start button and choose Settings ⇨ Control Panel, double-click the System icon, select the Advanced tab, and click the Environment Variables... button.

Caution   Changing your environment variables permanently has system-wide repercussions, and it is not recommended.

We do not recommend that you do change your environment variables permanently, however. This change is permanent and global, and may affect other Java applications running on your system. For example, you may be running JBuilder on JDK 1.4, WebLogic on JDK 1.3.1, and Together Control Center on JDK 1.3.0. If you change JAVA_HOME or PATH globally, these Java applications may no longer work correctly. It's much better to leave your system-wide environment variables alone and change them only on a per-application basis, as described in the next section.

Using WebLogic's command file (setEnv.cmd)

Okay, here's the easy solution you've been waiting for. WebLogic has a very simple command file that does all the work in changing your environment variables temporarily for you.

Inside the domain directory for each domain that you create, there is a setEnv.cmd command file that sets up your environment variables for the command window in which you run it. All this file does is call the setWLSEnv.cmd file in the WebLogic Server \bin directory. The contents of the setEnv.cmd file are shown in Listing B-2.

Listing B-2: **setWLSEnv.cmd**

```
@rem *********************************************************************
@rem This script is used to set up your environment for development with
@rem WebLogic Server. It sets the following variables:
@rem
@rem WL_HOME     - The root directory of your WebLogic installation
@rem JAVA_HOME   - Location of the version of Java used to start WebLogic
@rem               Server. This variable must point to the root directory of a
@rem               JDK installation and will be set for you by the installer.
@rem               See the WebLogic platform support page
@rem               (http://e-docs.bea.com/wls/platforms/index.html) for an up-to-
date list of
@rem               supported JVMs on Windows NT.
@rem PATH        - Adds the JDK and WebLogic directories to the system path.
@rem CLASSPATH   - Adds the JDK and WebLogic jars to the classpath.
@rem
@rem Other variables that setWLSEnv takes are:
@rem
@rem PRE_CLASSPATH  - Path style variable to be added to the beginning of the
@rem                  CLASSPATH
@rem POST_CLASSPATH - Path style variable to be added to the end of the
@rem                  CLASSPATH
@rem PRE_PATH       - Path style variable to be added to the beginning of the
@rem                  PATH
@rem POST_PATH      - Path style variable to be added to the end of the PATH
@rem
@rem When setting these variables below, please use short file names(8.3).
@rem To display short (MS-DOS) filenames, use "dir /x". File names with
@rem spaces will break this script.
@rem
@rem jDriver for Oracle users: This script assumes that native libraries
@rem required for jDriver for Oracle have been installed in the proper
@rem location and that your system PATH variable has been set appropriately.
@rem
@rem For additional information, refer to the WebLogic Server Administration
@rem Guide (http://e-docs.bea.com/wls/docs70/adminguide/startstop.html).
@rem *********************************************************************
@echo off

@rem Set user-defined variables.
set WL_HOME=D:\p\bea\weblogic700
set JAVA_HOME=D:\p\bea\jdk131_03

@rem Check that the WebLogic classes are where we expect them to be
@if exist "%WL_HOME%\server\lib\weblogic.jar" goto checkJava
@echo.
@echo The WebLogic Server wasn't found in directory %WL_HOME%\server.
@echo Please edit the setWLSEnv.cmd script so that the WL_HOME
@echo variable points to the WebLogic installation directory.
```

Continued

Listing B-2 *(continued)*

```
@echo Your environment has not been set.
@goto finish

@rem Check that java is where we expect it to be
:checkJava
@if exist "%JAVA_HOME%\bin\java.exe" goto setWLSEnv
@echo.
@echo The JDK wasn't found in directory %JAVA_HOME%.
@echo Please edit the setWLSEnv.cmd script so that the JAVA_HOME
@echo variable points to the location of your JDK.
@echo Your environment has not been set.
@goto finish

:setWLSEnv
set
CLASSPATH=%JAVA_HOME%\lib\tools.jar;%WL_HOME%\server\lib\weblogic_sp.jar;%WL_HOM
E%\server\lib\weblogic.jar;%CLASSPATH%

set PATH=%WL_HOME%\server\bin;%JAVA_HOME%\bin;%PATH%

@rem Import extended environment

if exist extEnv.cmd call extEnv.cmd
if not "%EXT_PRE_CLASSPATH%" == "" set CLASSPATH=%EXT_PRE_CLASSPATH%;%CLASSPATH%
if not "%EXT_POST_CLASSPATH%" == "" set
CLASSPATH=%CLASSPATH%;%EXT_POST_CLASSPATH%
if not "%EXT_PRE_PATH%" == "" set PATH=%EXT_PRE_PATH%;%PATH%
if not "%EXT_POST_PATH%" == "" set PATH=%PATH%;%EXT_POST_PATH%

@rem Get PRE and POST environment
if not "%PRE_CLASSPATH%" == "" set CLASSPATH=%PRE_CLASSPATH%;%CLASSPATH%
if not "%POST_CLASSPATH%" == "" set CLASSPATH=%CLASSPATH%;%POST_CLASSPATH%
if not "%PRE_PATH%" == "" set PATH=%PRE_PATH%;%PATH%
if not "%POST_PATH%" == "" set PATH=%PATH%;%POST_PATH%

@echo.
@echo CLASSPATH=%CLASSPATH%
@echo.
@echo PATH=%PATH%
@echo.
@echo Your environment has been set.

:finish
```

Notice that the file sets the four environment variables that we just discussed: WL_HOME, JAVA_HOME, PATH, and CLASSPATH. Okay, so what do you do if you need to add something to the CLASSPATH?

Your first impulse may be to immediately modify setWLSEnv.cmd directly. *Don't do this!* You'll notice the file has pre- and post-PATH as well as CLASSPATH settings. Notice also that they are not defined in setWLSEnv.cmd, so it expects them to be defined somewhere else (hint, hint). Recall that setEnv.cmd calls setWLSEnv.cmd, so you can just define these PATH additions in setEnv.cmd. Because setEnv.cmd is specific to each domain, you can have different CLASSPATHs for different domains. If you edited setWLSEnv.cmd instead, the same PATH values would have to work for all domains. As you and your company get more sophisticated with your use of WebLogic Server, you'll find that keeping changes specific to each domain is much smarter than making global changes to WebLogic Server directory files, and it also makes it easier to upgrade to new versions.

So what's the difference between the pre- and post-PATH and CLASSPATH variables? The PRE_PATH and PRE_CLASSPATH variables will get added to the beginning of the PATH and CLASSPATH, respectively. The POST_PATH and POST_CLASSPATH variables get added on the end. Most additions to the PATH and CLASSPATH settings should go in the post settings. That's because you generally want WebLogic items first in the PATH and CLASSPATH. However, if there is a specific instance when you need to override the version of some API or utility that comes with WebLogic, you will want to put those items at the beginning of the PATH and CLASSPATH, and thus in the pre settings.

Caution
Overriding a utility or API by putting a newer version at the beginning of the CLASSPATH can wreak havoc on an otherwise stable instance of WebLogic. Make sure that WebLogic doesn't depend on a specific version of an API before trying to override it.

Cross-Reference
Sometimes, you don't need to override an API here. For example, if you need a different version of an XML parser, you can configure it through the WebLogic Server Console. See Chapter 23 for more information.

Using Command-Line Tools

BEA provides a number of command-line tools for WebLogic Server 7.0. In this section, we'll discuss these tools based on their functional role.

Note
Remember: Before running any of these tools, you must make sure that you've run setEnv.cmd in the command-line window in the domain directory.

EJB code generation

There is a fantastic tool for automating the drudgery of creating Enterprise JavaBeans called ejbgen. ejbgen generates the home and remote interfaces, as well as skeleton deployment descriptors, from an EJB implementation class. All you need to do is add JavaDoc comments in a specific format, and the ejbgen tool will parse those comments and generate the other files automatically. The result is that you no longer need to manually keep your implementation class in synch with your home and remote interfaces, which can be a huge time-saver.

These JavaDoc comment tags can be class-level tags or method-level tags. The tags can tell the tool how to do the following:

✦ Create session, message-driven, and entity beans, including CMP and BMP

✦ Establish relationships between EJBs

✦ Set up environment entries, finder methods (entity beans), and JNDI names

✦ Generate the `ejb-jar.xml`, `weblogic-ejb-jar.xml`, and `weblog-cmp-rdbms-jar.xml` deployment descriptors

There are also numerous command-line options for things such as adding suffixes to your remote and home interface names. More information on how to use `ejbgen` can be found at the following URL:

    http://e-docs.bea.com/wls/docs70/ejb/EJB_utilities.html#1079050

J2EE deployment descriptor generation

Instead of creating deployment descriptors by hand, you can autogenerate them. WebLogic provides two tools for this purpose: one for Web applications, and one for EJBs. More information on these tools is available at the following URL:

    http://e-docs.bea.com/wls/docs70/programming/packaging.html#1067820

Web applications

The command-line tool for creating Web app deployment descriptors is `weblogic.marathon.ddinit.WebInit`. All you need to do is pass it the name of the base directory (or WAR file) that contains the Web application. As an example, we ran this tool on the JSP directory for the examples from Chapter 12. (First, we made backup copies of the `web.xml` and `weblogic.xml` files in the `WEB-INF` subdirectory because those will get overwritten.) You can see how it was run and what the output was in Listing B-3. It generated new `web.xml`, `weblogic.xml`, and `taglib.tld` files. These files are not exactly the same as the ones we created earlier, and they will need some tweaking. But it's a great start.

Listing B-3: Input and Output of the WebInit Command

```
H:\src\WLSBible>java weblogic.marathon.ddinit.WebInit jsp
[ModuleInit]: Searching for class files
[ModuleInit]: 6 classes found
[ModuleInit]: found servlet class: 'com.wiley.wlsbible.jsp.AccountServlet'
[ModuleInit]: found JSP tag class: 'com.wiley.wlsbible.jsp.tags.LineClass'
[ModuleInit]: found JSP tag class: 'com.wiley.wlsbible.jsp.tags.SelectOption'
[ModuleInit]: Discovered module type for H:\src\WLSBible\jsp
[ModuleInit]: Found Web components. Initializing descriptors
[ModuleInit]: Writing descriptors
filters=0 servlets=1 tags=2
```

EJBs

The command-line tool for creating EJB deployment descriptors is `weblogic.marathon.ddinit.EJBInit`. It works in much the same way as for the Web application descriptor generator discussed in the previous section.

J2EE deployment descriptor updating

The DDConverter command-line tool converts older EJB deployment descriptors to those that will run in WebLogic Server 7.0. This means converting both J2EE standard 1.0 and 1.1 descriptors to 1.1 or 2.0 descriptors (ejb-jar.xml), as well as converting proprietary WebLogic Server 4.5 and higher deployment descriptors to 7.0 (weblogic-ejb-jar.xml and weblogic-cmp-rdbms-jar.xml).

For more information on using this tool, including options, see the following URL:

    http://e-docs.bea.com/wls/docs70/ejb/EJB_utilities.html#1025194

Deploying applications

BEA includes the weblogic.Deployer command-line utility for making deployment easy from the command line. This means you can incorporate these commands into command scripts or Ant tasks (we describe Ant in the section "Introducing Ant" later in the chapter). The Deployer utility can deploy and un-deploy applications on a single server or a group of servers and can also deploy all or part of an application resource.

**Cross-
Reference**
You can also deploy applications by using the WebLogic Console, as explained in Chapters 15, 16, and 17 (EJBs), 11 (Web Applications), 26 (Web Services), 28 (JCA), and 8 (Startup and Shutdown classes), or by using WebLogic Builder (see the "WebLogic Builder" section later in this chapter).

The commands that Deployer supports are listed in Table B-1.

Table B-1: Deployer Commands

Command	Purpose
activate	Deploys or redeploys the application on the specified server(s).
deactivate	Suspends the application on the specified server(s).
unprepare	Suspends and unloads the classes for the applications on the specified server(s).
remove	Undeploys and deletes all associated files for the application on the specified server(s).
cancel	Cancels a pending request if it hasn't already completed.
list	Lists all pending requests.

Note that Deployer replaces the weblogic.deploy utility that came with earlier versions of WebLogic Server. For more information on Deployer, including its many options, see the following URL:

    http://e-docs.bea.com/wls/docs70/programming/deploying.html#1124819

Database tools

BEA provides a few tools for database information, but the tools are documented incorrectly (as of service pack 1) at the following URL:

    http://e-docs.bea.com/wls/docs70/toolstable/ToolsTable.html/#998738

The correct way to call the `dbping` utility is by entering `java utils.dbping` at a command line. The utility will then display help text describing the options you can use to call the utility.

The correct way to call the `Schema` utility is `java utils.Schema` at a command line. Again, entering the command will display a help screen listing the correct command-line parameters.

Administration tools

`CheckConfig.exe` is a Windows-only executable that will display a huge list of configured settings for your environment. Just enter `checkconfig` at the Windows 2000 command prompt.

Introducing Ant

Ant is your best friend; get to know Ant! It's used everywhere in Java, from WebLogic and JBuilder to open source projects that you can use with WebLogic Server such as Log4J, Jakarta Commons Logging, and Struts. We also use it in all the example source code for this book.

Ant is simply a Java-based build tool that replaces `make` and tools similar to it. Instead of parsing obscure makefiles, Ant uses XML-based build files. Ant is not a traditional scripting language in that it doesn't have `for` loops or fancy comparators; instead, it has a simple dependency hierarchy that makes it easy to control how code gets built. Ant can do many things from Java compilation; to copying or FTPing files; to checking code in and out of version control systems; to building JARs, WARs, and EARs. It's also customizable in that you can add your own functionality by creating new Java classes that extend Ant.

WebLogic Server 7.0 comes with Ant 1.4. This is not the most recent version, however. Ant is currently at 1.5.1, and is available at `http://ant.apache.org/`. If you want to use Ant 1.4's HTML documentation, you can download a binary or source distribution at the following URL:

    http://jakarta.apache.org/builds/jakarta-ant/release/v1.4/

Ant comes bundled with most Java IDEs, so you may be able to run Ant targets without leaving your GUI environment. Keep in mind that the version of Ant bundled with other Java IDEs may not be the same version of Ant that comes with WebLogic Server.

Tip Consider editing your Ant build files with BEA's XML editor to make your life easier. It generates well-formed XML and provides both a GUI and text interface to edit the XML.

Note Again, you must run `setEnv.cmd` (or `setEnv.sh` for Unix) before you can use Ant at the command line. To verify that you are running the correct version (1.4), enter `ant -version` at the command-line prompt.

The Ant libraries that come with WebLogic are located in the in `<WL_HOME>\server\lib\ant` subdirectory.

Getting started with Ant

Ant is easy to understand after you learn the three core elements in its XML build files: properties, tasks, and targets. *Properties* are similar to Java constants: You define them once at the beginning of the build file and then use their values later on for comparisons or parameters. A task is like an API; a *task* is basically a predefined unit of functionality, such as copying a file or building a JAR. Tasks can take parameters, such as the name of the file to copy and its destination. A *target* is similar to a method: It's a name for a grouped set of functions. Targets typically include several related tasks.

A simple Ant build file

Let's take a look at the prototypical "Hello, World" sample and how it would look in Ant. Listing B-4 shows an Ant build file, which is typically named `build.xml`.

Listing B-4: **An Ant build.xml File for Hello, World**

```
<project name="AntExample" default="hello">

  <property name="username" value="Stranger"/>

  <target name="hello">
    <echo message="Hello, World!"/>
  </target>

  <target name="goodbye">
    <echo message="Goodbye, ${username}."/>
  </target>

</project>
```

Notice that the root element is `project`. Ant won't recognize a file—no matter what its name is—unless it has a root element named `project`. Within that root element are one `property` element and two `target` elements, each of which contains one `echo` element. As we've discussed, Ant build files are composed of elements that define properties, tasks, and targets. Properties are defined using the `property` element, targets use the `target` element, and tasks use any of a number of element names such as `echo` and many others. (Targets, tasks, and properties are discussed in more detail later in this chapter, in the sections "Targets," "Tasks," and "Properties," respectively.) Let's take a look at how each of these elements is composed and what it does:

✦ **The `project` root element:** The `project` element in this example has two attributes: `name` and `default`. `name` is any arbitrary name you want to give to this project. It's for your use only, however, because Ant doesn't use this attribute. The other attribute, `default`, tells Ant which target to run if you don't specify one on the command line. The value it contains must be a target listed somewhere in this build file. In this case, it's telling Ant to run the `hello` target.

✦ **The** `property` **element:** Next is the `property` element, with `name` and `value` attributes. This element allows you to define properties with a single value and reuse them throughout the build file. Using the syntax of `${<name>}` enables you to substitute the value of a property for its name, as we'll see shortly.

✦ **The** `target` **elements:** There are two targets in this example: one named `hello` and one named `goodbye`. The name of a target is important because you can reference it in multiple places. You can specify a target name on the command line, in the `default` attribute of the project, when calling a target from a different build file or when creating dependencies between targets. Because this project's `default` attribute is set to `hello`, the `hello` target is called by default.

✦ **Tasks:** Each target in Listing B-4 has only one task, `echo`, but each target can have as many tasks as needed. Like most tasks, `echo` has one or more attributes that you can specify. In our case, to keep it simple, we specify a single attribute that is the string that will be echoed to standard out. In the `hello` target, we specify a literal string. Notice in the `goodbye` target, though, we specify a property embedded within a literal string. As we mentioned earlier, a property name embedded within brackets and a dollar sign gets expanded to the value of that property.

Running Ant

To see our `build.xml` file from Listing B-4 in action, let's have Ant parse and run through this build script. Open a command-line window and make sure you've run the `setEnv.cmd` (or the `setEnv.sh` Unix script). Then go to the directory in which the `build.xml` file from Listing B-4 is located. Then just enter `ant` and press Enter.

If you don't specify any parameters, Ant will look for a file named `build.xml` in the current directory. (You can name your build file anything you want, but you need to use the `-build-file` command-line parameter to specify the name if it's anything other than `build.xml`.) Ant then opens this file and looks for an attribute named `default` in the project element. If found, Ant will run that target and ignore all other targets. When Ant finds and runs a target, it runs each task within that target in the order specified. So in our case, it runs the `echo` task within the `hello` target. The output should look like the following:

```
Buildfile: build.xml

hello:
     [echo] Hello, World!

BUILD SUCCESSFUL

Total time: 1 second
```

As you can see, first Ant displays (in the following order):

✦ The name of the build file it is parsing

✦ Each target it is running

✦ The name of each task within that target (including any output)

✦ Whether the build was successful or failed

✦ The total running time in seconds

Since the `hello` target was called (by default), "hello:" shows up in the output, followed by a listing of all tasks within `hello`. The only task we defined in `hello` is the `echo` task, so "[echo]" shows up in the output, followed by the results of calling it, which is "Hello, World!"

Now that we've shown Ant running the default target, what if we want to specify which target to run? In that case, you just enter it on the command line. If we entered `ant hello` on the command line, the output would be identical to that shown previously because we are explicitly specifying the same target (`hello`) that was chosen by default the first time.

If we want to run the goodbye task, we enter `ant goodbye` on the command line. The output will appear as follows:

```
Buildfile: build.xml

goodbye:
        [echo] Goodbye, Stranger.

BUILD SUCCESSFUL

Total time: 1 second
```

This is identical to the first example, except we see `goodbye:` in the output, which means the `goodbye` target was run. And we see that the output is `Goodbye, Stranger` because Ant combined the literal string "Goodbye," with the value of the `username` property that we defined earlier in the script to be "Stranger."

As you can see from the very simple example, Ant is flexible and works with easily human readable XML build files. But there's much more than what we've described so far.

Other command-line options

There are other command-line options you can use with Ant. Some of the more common ones include the following:

✦ `-version`: Displays the version of Ant that you're running

✦ `-verbose`: Displays a lot of debugging information as Ant parses and runs the build file

✦ `-projecthelp`: Shows any comments you've added to targets with the `description` attribute

✦ `-help`: Dumps out a list of all command-line options, including some not described here

Getting more sophisticated with Ant

So far, we've discussed only the most basic functionality of Ant. The following sections go into a little more detail so that you can create robust build files using Ant, making reproducible builds easy and effective.

Note

Ant is quite sophisticated, and we can still cover only a portion of its total functionality. The Ant JavaDoc pages have a list of all the features of Ant. For even more information on Ant, see *Jakarta Pitfalls: Time-Saving Solutions for Struts, Ant, JUnit, and Cactus* by Bill Dudney and Jonathan Lehr (Wiley Technology Publishing).

Properties

In Listing B-4, you saw a very simple example of defining a property. As you might expect, Ant can do much more than this. You can define properties in a number of ways:

✦ **The property task:** As we saw in Listing B-4, you can define properties using the Ant task called `property`; it takes `name` and `value` attributes that define the property.

✦ **A properties file:** As you might have guessed, properties can be defined in a Java properties file, a text file in the format `<name>=<value>` with each property on a separate line. You specify the name of this file in your build file by using the property task again, but this time with an attribute `file=<filename>`, which is either a relative or an absolute path to the properties file. Ant will read in this file and create a property corresponding to each entry in the file.

✦ **The command line:** You can specify property names and values on the command line using the syntax `-D<name>=<value>` as in `-Dusername=Lou` and you can repeat this as many times on the command line as you have properties to define.

✦ **System environment variables:** You can specify an attribute of `environment` for the property task and Ant will create a new property for each system environment variable, with the prefix you specified. For example, the following line, combined with a system environment such as Listing B-1, would create properties with the following names: `env.COMPUTERNAME`, `env.ComSpec`, `env.HOMEDRIVE`, `env.PROMPT`, `env.SystemDrive`, `env.TEMP`, and so on.

```
<property environment=env/>
```

✦ **Java system properties:** With no effort on your part, Ant automatically generates properties for each Java system property, such as `java.version`, `java.home`, `os.version`, `user.name`, `user.home`, and so on.

✦ **Ant built-in properties:** Again, without any action on your part, Ant defines the following built-in properties: `ant.java.version` (the version number of the JVM that was detected), `ant.version` (the version of Ant that's running), `basedir` (the absolute path of the base directory of the project; this is the current directory unless a different directory was specified in the project's `basedir` attribute), `ant.file` (the absolute path of the build file), and `ant.project.name` (the name of the project specified in the project element's `name` attribute).

With all of these ways of defining properties, and using pre-existing ones, Ant provides a very flexible way of customizing your build.

Targets

Targets are the logic behind your build file. They determine what gets executed, in what order, and with which dependencies. Targets are entry points into your build file: You can specify a target on the command line, and that target will be executed.

Dependencies and conditionals

Targets can (and usually do) have dependencies. A *dependency* means that the target won't get executed until its dependent(s) are executed. If a dependent has already been executed, it won't be executed again, and the dependent itself may have dependencies that will get executed before it does.

Dependencies are specified in a `depends` attribute on the target element. If you need more than one dependency, you can specify multiple dependencies separated by commas. For example, a typical build sequence would have a target named `buildEar` that would have a dependency on targets named `buildWar` and `buildJar`, whereas `buildJar` would have a dependency on `compile`, which would have a dependency on `clean`, which would have a dependency on `init`. An outline of a build file with this structure is shown in Listing B-5.

Note

Ant has some generally agreed-upon standards, but they're not requirements. First, property names are divided internally by periods rather than capitalization, as in `build.dir` instead of `buildDir`. Secondly, most targets have a dependency on a target named `init`, in which you use the `tstamp` task (see task definitions following).

Listing B-5: **Outline of a Typical Build File**

```
<project name="BibleBuild" default="buildEar">

  <target name="init">
    <tstamp/>
  </target>

  <target name="clean", depends="init">
    <!-- tasks go here, such as the delete task -->
  </target>

  <target name="compile", depends="clean">
    <!-- tasks go here, such as the javac task
         and maybe a copy task to copy the results
    -->
  </target>

  <target name="buildWar", depends="init">
    <!-- tasks go here, such as the war task -->
  </target>

  <target name="buildJar", depends="compile">
    <!-- tasks go here, such as the jar task -->
  </target>

  <target name="buildEar" depends="buildJar,buildWar">
    <!-- tasks go here, such as the ear task to create
         the EAR and the ftp task to put it somewhere
    -->
  </target>

</project>
```

You could add `compile`, `clean`, and `init` to the list of dependencies that `buildEar` has, but that would serve no purpose. Because `buildEar` already depends on `buildJar`, `buildJar` won't execute until its dependencies are met, and so on, you get the same effect with just the dependencies shown in Listing B-5. It also makes it a lot easier to update because adding a new target dependency can be done at a lower level. For example, if you want to add a target named `checkout` that happens before `compile`, just make sure that `compile`'s target is changed to `depends="init,checkout"` and then any target that depends on `compile` will share `compile`'s dependencies indirectly.

Newcomers to Ant often ask whether there's the equivalent of `if/then` statements and are often disappointed to find out that there isn't. Remember, Ant isn't a scripting language. You can usually get around a situation like this, though, by using two more attributes for a target: `if` and `unless`. These both affect the execution of a target based on whether a property is defined or not.

Note `if` and `unless` work based on the *presence* of a property, not the property's *value*. So don't think you can execute a target if a property is true or not execute if it's false. If you try that, you'll be confused because it will run whether the property is true or false. It won't run, however, if that property name has not been defined anywhere. So think about the logic of defining properties in terms of "yes it's defined" or "no it's not defined" rather than a property being set to true, false, or any other value. See the `condition` task definition, as follows.

Setting `if` to a property name means that the associated target will get executed only if that property was defined. Let's say you have a target named `integration` that FTPs the EAR file to a directory on an integration server. You don't want this to happen on every build — just the ones that the buildmaster builds. If you define some properties in an external property file, you can add an `integrate=x` property name-value pair to the buildmaster's property file, but not the developers'. Then you can add an if attribute, like this:

```
<target name="integration" if="integrate">
  <!-- tasks here -->
</target>
```

Because `integrate` is defined in the buildmaster's property file only, the `integration` target will get executed only on the buildmaster's machine. (Of course, this isn't a particularly secure way of handling the special case of FTPing files; all a developer has to do is add an `integrate` property to his or her properties file and she or he will magically become buildmaster! But you get the idea.)

`unless` works just the same as `if`, except that the target will always get executed unless the property is defined. So, really it's the opposite of `if`.

Calling other targets

Rather than having a dependency on another target, sometimes you need to explicitly call another target. Remember that dependencies always execute before the dependent target gets executed. Sometimes, you need to execute another target while in the middle of a target, rather than at the beginning.

Ant lets you call other targets both within the currently executing build file and in external files. In both cases, you can pass properties directly to the target you're calling, although in the former case they're called *parameters*; in the latter case, they are called *properties*. So if you want to call a target named `deploy` in the same build file and you want to pass it a domain name, use the `antcall` task like this:

```
<antcall target="deploy">
  <param name="domain" value="mydomain"/>
</antcall>
```

If, on the other hand, the deploy target is in another build file named `bible.xml`, you need to use the `ant` task like this:

```
<ant antfile="bible.xml" target="deploy">
  <property name="domain" value="mydomain"/>
</ant>
```

This gives you great flexibility in the way you set up your project. Sometimes it makes sense to organize your project into separate build files, and these mechanisms give you a simple way to call them.

Paths, Wildcards, and Sets

Before we get into Ant's tasks, it's worth going over some advanced features that can really come in handy.

Many Ant tasks take filenames, directories, and paths as source and destination values. It gets tedious and error-prone to enter these names one by one. So Ant provides a variety of ways to specify these values en masse. It has the concept of "nested elements" which simply means that files and directories can be specified in groups of nested elements, rather than just as element attributes, which is very limiting.

A number of Ant tasks support `PATH`- and `CLASSPATH`-like structures. These tasks include compiling, building JARs, copying and moving files, and others. Let's use the `javac` task as an example because you'll be using it quite a bit. First, here's about the most basic usage you'd want to use:

```
<target name="compile">
  <javac srcdir="source"
    destdir="classes"
  />
</target
```

That's fine, but what if you want to use multiple directories or explicitly include only Java source files? Ant will automatically ignore non-Java files during compilation, but if you turn on verbose output at the command line, Ant will dump out tons of useless messages about non-Java files that it found and is ignoring. Wildcards would allow you to specify that only Java files should be included in the source directory. You can use wildcards just as you would at a Windows or Unix command line, but Ant has an additional trick, too:

✦ **?** means match exactly one character

✦ ***** means match zero or more characters

✦ ****** means match zero or more directories

So `read??.txt` would match `readMe.txt` and `readme.txt`, but not `readme2.txt` (too many characters); `source/*.java` would match all Java files in the `source` directory, and `source/**/*.java` would match all Java files in the `source` directory and all subdirectories.

Continued

Continued

Your requirements for paths and classpaths can get pretty complicated very quickly, so the `javac` task, as well as other tasks, allows you to specify `src` and `classpath` elements with as many `path` and `fileset` subelements as you need. You can combine these with wildcards and path & classpath `id`s to create complex but reusable paths like this:

```
<path id="ejb.path">
  <fileset dir="ejbs"/>
    <include name="*.java"/>
    <exclude name="**/test/**"/>
  </fileset>
</path>

<path id="loggingJars" >
  <pathelement location="log4j.jar" />
  <pathelement location="commons-logging-1.0.1.jar" />
</path>

<classpath id="extendedClasspath">
  <path refid="loggingJars"/>
  <pathelement path="${classpath}"/>
</classpath>

<target name="compileEjbs">
  <javac>
    <src refid="ejb.path"/>
    <fileset>
      <include name="ejb/**"/>
      <exclude name="**/test/**"/>
    </fileset>
    <classpath refid="extendedClasspath"/>
  </javac>
</target>
```

In addition to these filesets, paths, and classpaths, Ant supports patternsets and filtersets to group items together. In the Ant Javadoc help system, there are links to more discussion on these topics at the top of the Core Tasks help frame. You may not need these for simple build scripts, but as your projects get more sophisticated, you'll appreciate the flexibility and reusability they provide.

Tasks

Just as Java has the based Java 2 API and extensions to it, Ant has what it calls core tasks and optional tasks. You can even write your own tasks or use tasks created by others; we show you how to do that a little later on.

Core tasks

Core tasks are built into the system and are always available to Ant. If you have Ant installed, you can be guaranteed that all core tasks will be available. The Ant Javadoc help has a list of all Ant core tasks, but Table B-2 lists some of the most commonly used ones for WebLogic Server development.

Table B-2: Commonly Used Core Tasks

Core task	Purpose
javac	The mother of all tasks for a build system, this task compiles your Java code.
java	Executes a Java class or JAR.
exec	Executes an operating system dependent executable. Of course, this breaks the cross-platform universality of Ant, so use only under the most dire circumstances!
ear, jar, war, zip, unjar, unwar, unzip	Create and extract EARs, JARs, WARs, and ZIP files.
javadoc	Runs the Javadoc compiler on your source.
condition	Sets a property if a certain condition is true. Remember that the if attribute of the target element would cause the execution of that target only if a property were defined; this is a good way to do it. You can do string comparisons on properties or test for certain operating systems, for example.
fail	Causes termination of the build with an optional message.
mail	Sends SMTP e-mail.
copy	Copies files and directories, optionally overwriting the destination and/or changing tokens within the file(s).
delete	Deletes files and directories.
move	Moves and renames files and directories.
replace	Replaces tokens within a file.

There are a number of other core tasks. Consult the Ant Javadoc help for information on the other tasks as well as more details about the tasks mentioned in this section.

Optional tasks

Tasks that Ant considers "optional" are ones that are not installed by default. They are in a separate Java archive named jakarta-ant-1.4-optional.jar. If you download and install Ant yourself, this file will not be included; it's a separate download. However, BEA includes this with WebLogic Server, so you'll always have access to these optional tasks. Some of the more useful ones for WebLogic development are listed in Table B-3.

Table B-3: Optional Tasks

Task	Purpose
ejbjar, wlrun, wlstop	Tasks to create EJBs and start and stop WebLogic Server.
junit, junitreport	Runs the open source Junit testing tool and generates consolidated reports.
propertyfile	Allows inserts and edits (as opposed to reads) of a property file.
script	Allows embedding scripting languages such as JavaScript.
ftp, telnet	An FTP and Telnet client.

In addition to these optional tasks, there are tasks for using Rational ClearCase, StarTeam, and PVCS, as well as other proprietary tools. Some of these have dependencies on other classes. See the Javadoc help for more information.

Extending Ant for WebLogic Server

One of the best things about Ant is that it's extensible, much like the XML it's based on. You can create your very own Ant tasks in Java, and it becomes an extension of the API. You can use these extensions and share them with other people. In fact, WebLogic Server comes with some extensions that BEA wrote. We'll show you briefly how to use these extensions shortly. Writing these extensions is beyond the scope of this book, but it's not difficult and is explained in the Ant documentation.

After you have the JAR file that contains the new task(s), you must make sure that JAR is in your CLASSPATH. After that's done, you can add those tasks to your Ant targets. There are two ways to do this: on a temporary basis and a permanent basis.

Temporarily adding an Ant task

Adding a new Ant task temporarily involves adding a definition of it to each and every build.xml file that uses it. If you don't plan on using a task very often, this is a very reasonable thing to do.

We'll use one of the BEA-provided Web Service Ant tasks as an example. Because these tasks are already in the CLASSPATH defined in setEnv.cmd or setEnv.sh, there's no need to add them manually to the CLASSPATH. However, there's still the issue of adding the definition to every build.xml file.

WebLogic comes with a ClientGenTask custom Ant task that can be used to generate a Web Service client. We want to use this task in our Ant build file, so we define a new task for it in a taskdef element with two attributes: name and classname. The value of name is used as the new task name; this becomes the name of a new element that you use when you want to run the task. classname is the fully qualified package and class name of the task class that WebLogic provided. In this example, clientgen is defined as a new task, and it exists somewhere in the CLASSPATH with the name weblogic.ant.taskdefs.webservices.clientgen.ClientGenTask:

```
<taskdef name="clientgen"
classname="weblogic.ant.taskdefs.webservices.clientgen.ClientGenTask"/>
```

Now, when we want to use our new task later on in the same `build.xml` file, we reference it something like this:

```
<target name="main">
  <clientgen wsdl="http://example.com/myapp/myservice.wsdl"
    packageName="myapp.myservice.client"
    clientJar="c:/myapps/myService_client.jar"
  />
</target>
```

Note that the new element must be named `clientgen` because that's the name we specified in the `taskdef`. You can use any name you want, as long as it doesn't conflict with other Ant tasks and it's a valid XML element name.

The Web Services Ant extensions were discussed in Chapter 26.

Permanently adding a task

Adding the `taskdef` to every `build.xml` file that uses it is fine in many cases. But if you find yourself using a new task over and over again, you might want to consider making the change more permanent.

You do this by adding the `name` and `classname` values (as shown previously) to the `default.properties` file that's located in the `org.apache.tools.ant.taskdefs` package. Because this package is located in the `ant.jar` file, you'll have to unjar and rejar it after you're finished. After you do this, Ant treats it like any other task, and you can simply use it in any `build.xml` file without having to create a `taskdef` first.

Using the Java GUI Tools

In addition to the command-line tools we've discussed in this chapter, WebLogic also comes with a few GUI tools. In the following sections we describe how to use these GUI tools.

WebLogic Builder

Another tool in your arsenal is a GUI tool that can make creating, editing, and packaging J2EE deployment descriptors almost effortless. WebLogic Builder can work with deployment descriptors for Web applications, EJBs, and enterprise applications. It creates and updates both standard J2EE descriptors as well as WebLogic Server 7.0 specific ones.

You start WebLogic Builder by running the `startWLBuilder.cmd` command in the `bin` subdirectory of your WebLogic Server 7.0 installation directory. Or, in Windows, you can click the Start button and choose Programs ➪ BEA WebLogic Platform 7.0 ➪ WebLogic Server 7.0 ➪ WebLogic Builder. A Java Swing application will appear.

You can create deployment descriptors from scratch by selecting File ➪ Open and then navigating to the base directory of the application.

Note   You need some J2EE components (JSPs, class files, and so on) for Builder to read in order to create deployment descriptors; it won't create a blank set of descriptors for you.

If you already have an existing Web application, enterprise application, or EJBs, you can use File ⇨ Open to open the application and edit the descriptors. Builder will find the descriptors in the applications, whether they are in exploded directories or in WAR/EAR/JAR files. If your application is in exploded format, Builder can even build an archive (JAR/WAR/EAR) for you by selecting File ⇨ Archive.

Once you open a set of descriptors, you get a Swing interface to edit them with, as shown in Figure B-1. On the left is a tree view of all the applicable XML elements. Click on one, and the right pane fills with controls you can use to modify the settings.

Figure B-1: WebLogic Builder with a Web application loaded

You can edit essentially the same deployment descriptor information that you can through the WebLogic Server Console.

Cross-Reference In Chapter 18, we covered using the console to edit a Web application deployment descriptor. Compare Figure 18-7 with Figure B-1 to see how editing the same information looks in two different interfaces: the Web interface of the console and the Swing interface of Builder.

In addition to modifying existing settings, you can add new ones. For example, if there is a Web application open, you can click the Servlets node on the left and then the Add button on the right. A tabbed dialog box will then appear with all the attributes you can set for a servlet, shown in Figure B-2.

As easy as GUI tools make editing this information, some people just want to get down-and-dirty with raw XML. In Builder, you can view raw XML by choosing View ⇨ XML Source. In this dialog box, shown in Figure B-3, you can search through, select, and copy the raw XML, but you cannot edit it.

Caution In fact, Builder is somewhat dumb in that it cannot detect changes in underlying files (archives, classes, JSPs, or even the deployment descriptors themselves) and will happily overwrite any manual changes you may have made to these descriptors while it's running. In other words, do not edit deployment descriptors through a text editor or any other program while Builder has them open.

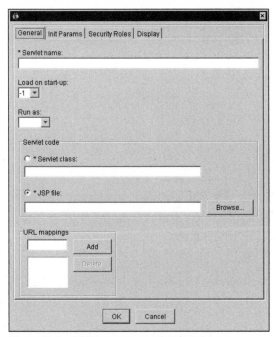

Figure B-2: Adding a new servlet descriptor

Figure B-3: Viewing the raw XML

In addition to all these editing tools, Builder allows you to deploy your newly created or updated application. To do so, choose Tools ➪ Deploy Module to deploy the application to a running WebLogic Server 7.0 instance. You'll be prompted for the server's information.

For more information on WebLogic Builder, see the following URL:

```
http://e-docs.bea.com/wls/docs70/wlbuilder/index.html
```

Other GUI tools

BEA provides other, simpler GUI tools to make your life as a developer easier. This includes a tool to package server files and a tool to edit XML, as described in the following sections.

AppletArchiver

AppletArchiver is a tool that will run an applet in its own window and then determine which files from the server need to be incorporated into a JAR or CAB file and automatically package them for you. Enter the following: `java utils.applet.archiver.AppletArchiver` at any command prompt.

BEA XML Editor

The BEA XML Editor is a free download from the Dev-2-Dev site (`http://dev2dev.bea.com/`).

Cross-Reference   See Chapter 26 for a description of using the BEA XML Editor.

Summary

In this appendix, we've shown you how to get the best use out of your development time for WebLogic Server.

First and foremost, we expounded on how important it is to remember that you need to set up your system environment before doing any Java development or using any command-line tools. Then we showed you a number of command-line tools that can make your life easier by automating the generation of EJBs and J2EE deployment descriptors, and discussed the Deployer tool that automates application deployment when you've made the move from development on a single workstation to testing and production environments.

We then moved onto Ant, which is both a general-purpose build tool as well as an extensible one. We showed you how to use Ant's `build.xml` files and how to configure a build file to use WebLogic's custom Ant tasks.

Finally, we covered the GUI tools that BEA provides. WebLogic Builder makes it easy to edit deployment descriptors, whereas the BEA XML Editor is a general-purpose XML editing tool.

The tools discussed in this chapter are like a Swiss Army knife in your pocket: They are small and often overlooked, but they pack a big punch.

✦   ✦   ✦

Index

Arguments parameter, 667
ASPs (Active Server Pages), 331
`<assembly-descriptor>` element of `ejb-jar.xml`, 429
asterisk (*)
   as Ant utility wildcard, 891
   for JSP scripting comments, 354
asynchronous components, 580
asynchronous conversations (Workshop), 820
asynchronous JMS messages. *See* receiving JMS
      messages
asynchronous Web Services, 804
`AsyncQueueReceiver` class, 218–221
`AsyncTopicSubscriber` class, 222–224
ATM machine
   as MVC example, 35–36
   as transaction example, 116
atomic transactions, defined, 116
Audit Provider Class parameter, 654
auditing
   defined, 608
   described, 590–592
   overview, 608
   security providers for, 621, 761
   security realm requirements, 621
authentication
   by applications, 11
   Authentication Provider, 619, 621
   basic, 307–308
   for `BibleServlets` Web application, 312–314
   certificates and certificate authorities, 592–593
   client certificates for, 309
   by Console, 307
   credentials, 592
   decoupling from authorization, 596–597
   DefaultAuthenticator, 761–762
   DefaultIdentityAsserter, 761–763
   defined, 306, 592
   described, 590
   form-based, 308–309, 312–314
   JAAS `LoginModule` for, 621, 637–639
   for JavaMail sessions, 258–259
   mutual, 592
   one-way, 592
   principal, 592
   secure protocols, 593–594
   security realm requirements, 619–620
   subject, 592
   terminology, 592
   user, 11
   of users by JNDI, 146–147
   for Web applications, 306–309

Authentication Provider
   default, 761–763
   iPlanet LDAP, 766–769
   SSPI, 619, 621
   third-party, 766
`<auth-filter>` element of `weblogic.xml`, 547
`AUTHORITATIVE` property for JDNI contexts, 138
authorization
   ACL, 11, 595–597
   by applications, 11
   Authorization Provider, 620–621
   DAC model, 595
   decoupling from authentication, 596–597
   DefaultAuthorizer, 763–764
   defined, 306, 595
   described, 590–591
   enterprise principals, 602
   JAAS, 601–602
   JNDI, 599–600
   LDAP, 597–599
   MAC model, 595
   overlap with other security layers, 603
   overview, 591
   privileges, 595
   roles, 595
   security realm requirements, 620
   user, 11
Authorization Flags for JAAS `LoginContext`, 636
Auto Deployed Enabled parameter, 654
Auto Kill If Failed parameter, 666
Auto Restart parameter, 666
Auto Update Interval parameter, 654
`AUTO_ACKNOWLEDGE` non-transacted acknowledge
      mode, 206
`autoFlush` attribute of page directive (JSPs), 349
`<automatic-key-generation>` element of
      `weblogic-cmp-rdbms-jar.xml`, 510–511
automation by Workshop, 810
Auto-refresh every parameter, 647
`autotype` task (Ant utility), 805
availability, clustering and, 11, 709
Average Commit Time parameter, 682

B

back doors (security), 612–613
backing stores (JMS)
   file, 197–198
   JDBC, 198–199
Backup Copies parameter, 658
backup (high-availability) pools, 94
Backup Hour parameter, 658

BodyTagSupport.getPreviousOut().write() method, tag library lifecycle and, 387
Borland JBuilder utility, 80, 517–518
brainstorming for Web application design, 310–311
Bridge page of Console Servers node Services tab, 690–691
brokerage, online. *See* JOB (J2EE Online Brokerage) example
BrowseQueue class, 231–232
browsers. *See* Web browsers
browsing JMS messages in a queue, 230–232
brute-force attack, 606–607
buffer attribute of page directive (JSPs), 349
/builder directory, 77
Builder tool, 432, 895–898
build.xml file. *See* Ant utility (Apache)
bulk mail, JavaMail for, 263–264
business logic for message-driven EJBs, 523
business methods
    Course CMP entity EJB, 500
    Department CMP entity EJB, 495–496
    Student BMP entity EJB, 480
business objects, session facades for accessing, 42–43
business processes, modeling with session EJBs, 438–439

C

CA (Certificate Authorities), 593
Cache Enabled parameter, 658, 767
Cache Size parameter, 658, 767
cache tag, 415
Cache TTL parameter, 658, 767
Caching Realm parameter, 654
caching stateful and entity EJBs, 577–578
CallableStatement objects, 90
CallbackHandler (JAAS)
    callback types, 640
    instance for LoginContext, 635
    populating callbacks, 640–641
callbacks
    adding to Web Services with Workshop, 822–823
    conversations, 819–820
    properties, 823
    tasks, 823
Capacity Increment parameter, 100
<cascade-delete> element of ejb-jar.xml, 505
CCI (Common Client Interface)
    connection interface, 853
    defined, 851
    for EJB communication with resource adapter, 844–845
    Interaction interface, 853–854
    Metadata interface, 854

overview, 851–852
    package, 852
    records, 854–855
CD-ROM, JAAS authorization for, 501–502
Cert Authentication parameter, 669
Certificate Authorities (CA), 593
Certificate Cache Size parameter, 669
certificates, authentication using, 309, 592–593
CGI (Common Gateway Interface), 331
Channel Overrides parameter, 670, 674
charset-params element of weblogic.xml, 547
CheapLoadtester.java class, 563–566
CheckConfig.exe administration tool (Windows), 884
Checkpoint Interval Seconds parameter, 650
checkResearchData() method of RequestDataManager.java implementation class, 449
Christofferson, Sean (*BEA WebLogic Workshop*), 807
ciphers, 606–607
class attribute of useBean tag (JSPs), 372
class diagrams
    JOB example, 51, 53
    overview, 53
Class Path parameter, 667
classes. *See also specific classes by name*
    helper classes, 39
    JAAS, 633
    locations for third-party and utility classes, 558–560
    tag library convenience classes, 389–393
    tag library supporting classes, 393–395
    WebLogic shutdown, 55
    WebLogic startup, 55, 165–167
classloaders
    defined, 558
    knowledge required, 16
    root, 559
    using, 557–558
CLASSPATH environment variable (Windows), 876–877
classpaths
    Ant utility, 891–892
    knowledge required, 16
    setting for command-line use, 877
clearBody() method of BodyContent class, 394
client application components, 38
client applications, 45
Client Cert Proxy Enabled parameter, 664
Client Certificate Enforced parameter, 669
Client Certificate Requested But Not Enforced parameter, 669
client certificates for authentication, 309
Client ID parameter, 195

Continued

Continued

<ejb-class> element of ejb-jar.xml, 429
ejbCreate() methods
  Course CMP entity EJB, 500
  Department CMP entity EJB, 495
  message-driven EJBs, 522
  RequestResearch.java implementation class, 446
  Student BMP entity EJB, 479
ejbgen EJB code generation command-line tool, 881–882
EJBGen utility, 432
EJBInit command, 882
<ejb-jar> element of ejb-jar.xml, 429
ejb-jar.xml deployment descriptor
  for AnalyzePortfolio stateful session EJB, 466–467
  for CMP entity EJBs, 502–508
  container-managed transaction attributes, 433–434
  elements, 429, 490–491, 503–505
  generating with ejbgen, 881–882
  for message-driven EJBs, 524–525, 537
  overview, 428
  for PrescriptionBean.java message-driven
    EJB, 537
  for Revenue EJB, 428–430
  for stateless session EJBs, 451–452
  for Student BMP entity EJB, 490–491
ejbLoad() method of Student BMP entity EJB, 480
<ejb-local-ref> element of web.xml, 547
<ejb-name> element
  ejb-jar.xml, 429
  weblogic-cmp-rdbms-jar.xml, 510
ejbPassivate() method
  RequestResearch.java implementation class, 446
  session EJBs, 442, 445
  Student BMP entity EJB, 477, 480
ejbPostCreate() methods
  Course CMP entity EJB, 500
  Department CMP entity EJB, 495
  Student BMP entity EJB, 480
<ejb-ql> element of ejb-jar.xml, 504
<ejb-ref> element of web.xml, 547
<ejb-relation> element of ejb-jar.xml, 505
<ejb-relation-name> element of ejb-jar.xml, 505
<ejb-relationship-role> element of
    ejb-jar.xml, 505
<ejb-relationship-role-name> element of
    ejb-jar.xml, 505
ejbRemove() method
  message-driven EJBs, 522
  session EJBs, 445
  Student BMP entity EJB, 480
EJBs (Enterprise JavaBeans). See also entity EJBs;
    message-driven EJBs; session EJBs
  architecture, 419–420
  bean-managed transactions, 434

calling from RMI servers, 185–189
CCI for communication with resource adapter,
    844–845
client-access models, 422–423
clustering, 742
code generation command-line tool, 881–882
compiler, 556, 581
components, 38, 423–430
container-managed transactions, 433–434
converting to Web Services, 781–791
defined, 419
deployment descriptor generation, 881–882
EJB-to-JSP integration tool, 416
enterprise application modules, 557
JAR files, 458
JavaBeans versus, 421
lifecycle management, 433
migrating applications to WebLogic Server 7.0, 871
migrating EJBs from 1.1 to 2.0, 871–872
packaging, 556
performance tuning, 577–578, 580
replica-aware stubs, 742
security policy for, 628–629
specifications, 430
types, 420–422
utility for generating deployment descriptors, 542
version 1.1 versus 2.0, 423, 430–432, 871–872
WebLogic EJB container services, 432–435
WebLogic Server utilities, 432
Workshop controls, 829–830
ejbStore() method of Student BMP entity EJB, 480
EJB-to-JSP integration tool, 416
elements
  Ant build.xml files, 885–886
  ejb-jar.xml deployment descriptor, 429, 490–491,
    503–505
  weblogic-cmp-rdbms-jar.xml deployment
    descriptor, 510–512
  weblogic-ejb-jar.xml deployment descriptor,
    453, 508–509
  weblogic.xml deployment descriptor, 547
  web-services.xml deployment descriptor,
    794–795
  web.xml deployment descriptor, 546–547
  WSDL file, 798–801
  XML, 790
Embedded LDAP page of Console domain node
    Security tab, 657–658
Embedded LDAP tab of Console Security node, 774
Enable Certificate Authentication parameter, 701
Enable COM parameter, 673, 676
Enable Default JMS Connection Factories parameter,
    690

Continued

Continued

Continued